MAGILL'S
LITERARY ANNUAL
1999

MAGILL'S
LITERARY ANNUAL
1999

*Essay-Reviews of 200 Outstanding Books
Published in the United States during 1998*

With an Annotated Categories List

Volume One
A-M

Edited by
JOHN D. WILSON

SALEM PRESS
Pasadena, California   Hackensack, New Jersey

LIBRARY OF CONGRESS CATALOG CARD NO. 77-99209

ISBN 0-89356-299-8

FIRST PRINTING

PRINTED IN THE UNITED STATES OF AMERICA

PUBLISHER'S NOTE

Magill's Literary Annual, 1999, is the forty-sixth publication in a series that began in 1954. The philosophy behind the annual has been to evaluate critically each year two hundred major examples of serious literature published during the previous year. Our continuous effort is to provide coverage for works that are likely to be of particular interest to the general reader, that reflect the publishing trends of a given year, and that will stand up to the test of time. By filtering the thousands of books published each year down to two hundred notable titles, the editors have here provided for the busy librarian an excellent reader's advisory tool. Individual critical articles for the first twenty-two years were collected and published in the twelve-volume *Survey of Contemporary Literature* in 1977.

For the reader new to the Magill reference format, the following brief explanation should serve to facilitate the research and review process. The two hundred works represented in this year's annual are drawn from the following categories: fiction; poetry; literary criticism, literary history, and literary theory; essays; literary biography; autobiography, memoirs, diaries, and letters; biography; history; current affairs; nature; language; science, history of science, and technology; economics; ethics and law; fine arts; philosophy and religion; psychology; sociology; travel; and women's issues. The articles are arranged alphabetically by book title in the two-volume set; a complete list of the titles included can be found at the beginning of volume 1. Following the list of titles are the titles arranged by category in an annotated listing. This list provides the reader with the title, author, page number, and a brief description of the particular work. The names of all contributing reviewers for the literary annual are listed alphabetically in the front of the book as well as at the end of their reviews. At the end of volume 2, there are four cumulative indexes covering works from the Annuals of 1977 to 1999: an index of Biographical Works by Subject, the Category Index, the Title Index, and the Author Index. The index of biographical works is arranged by subject rather than by author or title. Thus, readers will be able to locate easily a review of any biographical work published in the Magill annuals since 1977 (including memoirs, diaries, and letters—as well as biographies and autobiographies) by looking up the name of the person. Following the Category Index and the Title Index is the Author Index. Beneath each author's name appear the titles of all of his or her works reviewed in the Magill annuals since 1977. Next to each title, in parentheses, is the year of the annual in which the review appeared, followed by the page number. In all four indexes, titles that appeared in *Magill's History Annual*, 1983, and *Magill's Literary Annual, History and Biography*, 1984 and 1985, are indicated parenthetically by an "H" followed by the year of the annual in which the review appeared.

Each article begins with a block of top matter that indicates the title, author, publisher, and price of the work. When possible, the year of the author's birth is also provided. The top matter also includes the number of pages of the book, the type of work, and, when appropriate, the time period and locale represented in the text. Next, there is a capsule description of the work. When pertinent, a list of principal characters or principal personages introduces the review.

The articles themselves are approximately two thousand words in length. They are original essay-reviews that analyze and present the focus, intent, and relative success of the author, as well as the makeup and point of view of the work under discussion. To assist the reader further, the articles are supplemented by a list of additional reviews for further study in a bibliographic format.

Our special thanks go to the editor, John Wilson, for his expert and insightful contributions, as well as to all the outstanding writers who lend their time and knowledge to this project every year.

LIST OF TITLES

TITLES BY CATEGORY

ANNOTATED

TITLES BY CATEGORY

FICTION

page

TITLES BY CATEGORY

TITLES BY CATEGORY

TITLES BY CATEGORY

TITLES BY CATEGORY

TITLES BY CATEGORY

page

TITLES BY CATEGORY

page

SCIENCE
HISTORY OF SCIENCE
TECHNOLOGY

CONTRIBUTING REVIEWERS FOR 1999 ANNUAL

Michael Adams
*City University of New York
Graduate School*

Thomas P. Adler
Purdue University

Andrew J. Angyal
Elon College

Stanley Archer
Texas A & M University

Edwin T. Arnold
Appalachian State University

Karen L. Arnold
Montpelier Cultural Arts Center

Bryan Aubrey
Independent Scholar

Barbara Bair
Duke University

Dean Baldwin
*Penn State Erie-The Behrend
College*

Carl L. Bankston III
*University of Southwestern
Louisiana*

Dan Barnett
*California State University,
Chico*

Alvin K. Benson
Brigham Young University

Milton Berman
University of Rochester

Pegge Bochynski
Independent Scholar

Steve D. Boilard
Independent Scholar

Harold Branam
Savannah State University

Gerhard Brand
*California State University, Los
Angeles - Emeritus*

Peter Brier
*California State University, Los
Angeles*

Wesley Britton
*Harrisburg Area Community
College*

Keith H. Brower
Salisbury State University

David Buehrer
Valdosta State University

Jeffery L. Buller
Georgia Southern University

Thomas J. Campbell
Pacific Lutheran University

Edmund J. Campion
University of Tennessee

Thomas Cassidy
South Carolina State University

Dolores L. Christie
Ursuline College

Richard Hauer Costa
Texas A&M University

Mary Virginia Davis
Independent Scholar

Frank Day
Clemson University

Bill Delaney
Independent Scholar

Francine Dempsey
College of Saint Rose

M. Casey Diana
*University of Illinois at
Urbana-Champaign*

Jackie R. Donath
*California State University,
Sacramento*

Robert P. Ellis
Independent Scholar

Thomas L. Erskine
Salisbury State University

Rebecca Hendrick
Flannagan
Francis Marion University

Roy C. Flannagan
Francis Marion University

Robert J. Forman
St. John's University

Raymond Frey
Centenary College

Ann D. Garbett
Averett College

Leslie E. Gerber
Appalachian State University

Karen K. Gould
Independent Scholar

Lewis L. Gould
University of Texas at Austin

Hans G. Graetzer
*South Dakota State
University-Emeritus*

Jay Halio
University of Delaware

Diane Andrews Henningfeld
Adrian College

Anne B. Howells
Occidental College

Theodore C. Humphrey
*California State Polytechnic
University, Pomona*

Philip K. Jason
United States Naval Academy

Cynthia Lee Katona
Ohlone College

Steven G. Kellman
*University of Texas at San
Antonio*

Grove Koger
Boise Public Library

James B. Lane
Indiana University Northwest

Eugene Larson
Pierce College

Leon Lewis
Appalachian State University

Thomas T. Lewis
Mount Senario College

Douglas Long
Independent Scholar

Janet Lorenz
Independent Scholar

R. C. Lutz
University of the Pacific

David W. Madden
*California State University,
Sacramento*

Lois A. Marchino
University of Texas at El Paso

Chogallah Maroufi
*California State University, Los
Angeles*

Patricia Masserman
Microsoft Press

Charles E. May
*California State University,
Long Beach*

Laurence W. Mazzeno
Alvernia College

Janet McCann
Texas A&M University

Joanne McCarthy
Independent Scholar

Mark McCloskey
Patten College

Philip McDermott
Independent Scholar

Robert A. Morace
Daemen College

Daniel P. Murphy
Hanover College

John M. Muste
Ohio State University

Robert Niemi
St. Michael's College

Lisa Paddock
Independent Scholar

Robert J. Paradowski
*Rochester Institute of
Technology*

David B. Parsell
Furman University

David Peck
*California State University,
Long Beach*

Cliff Prewencki
Independent Scholar

Maureen J. Puffer-
Rothenberg
Valdosta State University

R. Kent Rasmussen
Independent Scholar

Rosemary M. Canfield
Reisman
Charleston Southern University

Bernard F. Rodgers, Jr.
Simon's Rock College of Bard

Stephen F. Rohde
Rohde & Victoroff

Carl Rollyson
Baruch College, CUNY

Joseph Rosenblum
*University of North Carolina,
Greensboro*

Robert Ross
University of Texas at Austin

John K. Roth
Claremont McKenna College

Kelly Rothenberg
Independent Scholar

Marc Rothenberg
Smithsonian Institution

Irene Struthers Rush
Independent Scholar

J. Edmund Rush
Write Away Now

R. Baird Shuman
*University of Illinois at
Urbana-Champaign-Emeritus*

Anne W. Sienkewicz
Independent Scholar

Thomas J. Sienkewicz
Monmouth College

Charles L. P. Silet
Iowa State University

Marjorie Smelstor
*University of Wisconsin - Eau
Claire*

Roger Smith
Independent Scholar

A. J. Sobczak
Independent Scholar

George Soule
Carleton College

Gerald H. Strauss
Bloomsburg University

Jack E. Trotter
Francis Marion University

William L. Urban
Monmouth College

Bruce Wiebe
Independent Scholar

John Wilson
Independent Scholar

James A. Winders
Appalachian State University

Michael Witkoski
Independent Scholar

Laura Weiss Zlogar
*University of Wisconsin-River
Falls*

MAGILL'S
LITERARY ANNUAL
1999

ABOUT A BOY

Author: Nick Hornby (1958-   )
Published: Riverhead Books (New York). 307 pp. $22.95
Type of work: Novel
Time: 1993-1994
Locale: London

A comic novel about a London bachelor who lies about having a child in order to meet single mothers and ends up befriending a twelve-year-old boy

> *Principal characters:*
> WILL FREEMAN, a bachelor without a career
> MARCUS BREWER, a maladjusted twelve-year-old boy
> FIONA BREWER, Marcus's mother, a single working mother who
>   attempts suicide
> ELLIE MCCRAE, Marcus's rebellious teenage friend

Nick Hornby began his career as a novelist promisingly with *High Fidelity* (1995), a witty, cogent depiction of a thirty-five-year-old man's inability to keep a girlfriend. A kind of *Underground Man* for the London hipster scene, Rob clings to his music store for a fragile sense of identity even as he stalks his previous girlfriend and recounts in gory detail his disastrous former romances. Hornby's prose combines a precise understanding of contemporary male rituals with an encyclopedic knowledge of popular culture. Immersed in a world of video recorders, compact disc players, and television shows, Hornby's characters prefer constructing top-ten lists to dealing with the emotional wreckage of their lives, and within that discrepancy lies the charm of the novel.

In his second novel, *About a Boy* (1998), Hornby turns from his earlier first-person narrative to a more ambitious, limited, third-person point of view that mostly shifts from Will Freeman's perspective (another bachelor in his thirties) to that of twelve-year-old Marcus Brewer and back again. While the first novel kept its focus on one man's desperate attempts to grow up, this one moves logically into the more sobering world of parenting in 1990's London, a bleak societal landscape littered with divorces, working mothers, neglected children, and delinquent dads. Scorning family life and its responsibilities, Freeman hits upon the idea of inventing a child and a missing spouse to help seduce single mothers. For a time his plan works, but Freeman gets gradually entangled in his lies. For example, he buys a child seat for his car and then has to sprinkle cookie crumbs over it to lend his car a family look. Soon enough, others start to catch on to his ploy, and Will finds himself unwillingly drawn into the lives of actual children and their unwed mothers.

Will's character closely resembles that of Rob in *High Fidelity*. They are about the same age, with the same ambivalent opinions toward commitment and parenthood, but while Rob runs a record store, Will is financially independent thanks to a steady supply of royalties from a Christmas song his father wrote in the 1930's. Lacking the ambition to pursue a career, Will passively lets popular culture supply the shape and substance of his days. In half-hour periods, Will turns from television shows to books to movies to club-rock bands to keep himself amused. He is ironic distance incarnate, preferring music that fakes emotion to anything more genuine. In his perpetual distraction he could remain the most poignantly time-wasting of all the characters in the book, but Hornby means to bring him into the therapeutic fold of outside friends. In this respect Will shows up the limits of total immersion in popular culture. He talks of having his time neatly arranged until he dies, but in the meantime he is not really alive. Marcus shows up in part to jolt Freeman from his solipsistic spectatorship.

While Freeman succeeds as a character, Hornby has more difficulty conveying the consciousness of Marcus Brewer, perhaps because here he takes on more pathos than he can easily integrate into the comic flow of the novel and because he has a harder time articulating the viewpoint of a child. Marcus arrives as a slightly out-of-focus bundle of adolescent problems. His single working mother suffers from depression and tries to kill herself with pills, the first of several suicide attempts in the novel. After Marcus moves with his mother to a big new London school, older kids beat him because he does not know how to look or act under his mother's idealistic hippie care. His hair is a frizzy mess, his clothes reveal that he has no sense of fashion, and he is completely cut off from the music scene, a state devoid of grace in a Hornby novel. All Marcus has going for him is a sharp wit and a strange ability to bring people together to provide a supportive substitute for a family.

Working through Marcus's problems is considerably less entertaining than a comic novel might presuppose. Too often, Will's conversations with Marcus resemble therapeutic dialogue in which he works through his fear of his mother's suicide attempt. Later, when Marcus starts to acquire a reputation as a comic, Hornby has his other characters chuckle at his jokes, thus providing his novel with an awkward laugh track. By having his characters laugh, Hornby seems complacent with his comic abilities, while the reader revolts against his self-congratulatory tone. In its effort to have its characters get somewhere and achieve something, Hornby's comedy is reduced to a means to an end instead of being an end unto itself. Considering how thinly sketched everyone is, such a shift in focus puts too much pressure on the slim plot. In a story in which the characters spend much of their time passively absorbed in popular culture, the narrative thread gets pretty thin indeed.

There are several ways in which the narrative machinery underlying *About a Boy* starts to show. For example, given that Hornby uses popular culture trivia to establish characterization, Marcus's lack of movie or television knowledge makes him something of cipher. Without that great pool of reference, Marcus's voice has to create itself out of the quotidian reality of his life, and so he repeatedly thinks of *Home Alone* movies as a weak correlative to his neglect, and he analyzes the tone of recent conversations with adults. Later he gains more of a sense of identity as he learns things from Will, but until then his struggling voice slows the pace of the novel.

In addition, Hornby's style, reminiscent of American minimalists such as Raymond Carver, tends to include precious little description and action. Instead, he tends to betray his teaching experience by emphasizing analysis, commentary, and exposition.

The results are often repetitive and static, with a strong leaning toward the therapeutic, leading one to wonder if Hornby had market pressure to complete this novel much more quickly than the last one. Sometimes Hornby summarizes a scene before dramatizing it, thus ruining any suspense in the process. For example, Marcus gives away that he fought with his school's headmistress before it happens in the narrative. At other times characters reflect on their conversations with an almost Jamesian attention to nuance. While Rob's increasing desperation kept *High Fidelity* moving along with high comic momentum, *About a Boy* depends on Marcus's slow maturation for its narrative drive, and the shifts in point of view overlap in such a way as to further slow the story line.

Moreover, when unable to bring his characters together naturally, Hornby tends to force connections between them. Kurt Cobain, singer of the band Nirvana, hovers like a grunge divinity over the whole novel. He makes his appearance as an ironic celebrity Christ on Ellie McCrae's sweatshirt, and his suicide attempts and final successful suicide provide milestones and echoes for the quandaries of the characters. As a structural component for the novel, Cobain provides correspondences, but Hornby never makes any kind of direct correlation between Nirvana's output and the disenchanted fictional world of the novel. If anything, Nirvana's rage and angst make *About a Boy* look pallid; watered-down punk prose turns rage into nonconventional family bonding. When Will considers Cobain's connection to Marcus, he finds that Marcus brings local people together much as Cobain brought together millions of fans with his art. Such connections beg the question as to why Cobain is included at all, except perhaps to lend a little celebrity glow to Hornby's novel.

Marcus discovers the limitations of celebrity hero worship when his punk female friend, Ellie, burgles a record store display to set the image of Kurt Cobain free on the day of his suicide. Protesting the exploitation of Cobain's death, she takes his life-size cardboard cut-out and sits with it on the side of the road until the police arrive. All of the principal characters descend into the police station for one last scene, and one senses Hornby straining to weave his plot strands together. Characters chuckle over Ellie's gesture, but it is her only way to respond to a crisis that remains locked away behind the newspaper print, the television screen, and the compact disc player. Her impotence is emblematic of Hornby's aesthetic.

In *About a Boy* Hornby searches for an effective fictional means to negotiate the media jungle. Complete ignorance of popular culture plainly has its risks, as does total immersion. As long as characters like Will Freeman remain locked in a solipsistic relationship with the media, they can humorously comment on spectator culture. Once Hornby leaves that culture, however, his prose tends to flatten out, and his lack of description can suggest a corresponding lack of depth.

As part of Britain's recent renaissance in the arts, Nick Hornby's *About a Boy* joins a wide array of readily exportable cultural products. Popular books by young authors such as *Trainspotting* (1996) and *The Diary of Bridget Jones* (1998) have earned appreciative international audiences, but one could also include the punk-inflected fashion designs of John Galliano, the music of the Spice Girls, and movies such as

Four Weddings and a Funeral (1994) as other manifestations of a surge in all things British. People describe London as the most vibrantly creative city in Europe at present; thus, Nick Hornby's humor is uniquely situated to take advantage of this trend.

Following on the critical and financial success of *High Fidelity*, *About a Boy* merits attention as the product of an up-and-coming author competing with the popular cultural interests of youthful readers. Hornby considers the trendy themes of unconventional parenting after the break-up of the nuclear family, the dictates of fashion in society, the travails of the working mother, the effects of clinical depression, and the womblike effect of total immersion in popular culture. In many ways British fiction has less and less difficulty appealing to American audiences, because increasingly British and Americans both see the same movies and watch the same television shows. When not shooting for humor, Hornby increasingly examines the pros and cons of growing up in the media's constant presence. While other authors might resist the increasing hegemony of the media, Hornby negotiates with it instead and uses it as the cultural backdrop for his characters.

Roy C. Flannagan

Sources for Further Study

Booklist. XCIV, April, 1998, p. 1304.
The Economist. CCCXLVII, May 16, 1998, p. S13.
Los Angeles Times Book Review. May 24, 1998, p. 2.
New Statesman. CXXVII, May 8, 1998, p. 48.
New York. XXXI, May 4, 1998, p. 128.
The New York Times Book Review. CIII, June 28, 1998, p. 13.
Newsweek. CXXXI, May 11, 1998, p. 84.
Publishers Weekly. CCXLV, March 16, 1998, p. 53.
The Times Literary Supplement. April 10, 1998, p. 24.
The Wall Street Journal. May 8, 1998, p. W10.

THE ACCIDENTAL ASIAN
Notes of a Native Speaker

Author: Eric Liu (1969-   )
Published: Random House (New York). 206 pages. $23.00
Type of work: Essays
Time: 1914-1997
Locale: The East Coast of the United States, mainland China, and Taiwan

Reflecting on his family's emigration from China to America, Eric Liu tries to come to terms with his own identity as an American-born, second-generation Asian American

> *Principal personages:*
> ERIC LIU, the author, American-born son to two Chinese immigrant
>   parents, Yale University graduate, and former speechwriter for
>   President Bill Clinton
> CHAO "BABA" LIU, Eric's father, a successful mathematician who stayed
>   in America after graduating from college
> JULIA LIU, the author's loving mother
> CARROLL HAYMON, the author's Caucasian wife
> MIN-YU "PO-PO" TU, the mother of Julia Liu
> TRINH DUONG, a Chinese-Vietnamese immigrant, executive director of
>   Chinese Staff and Workers Association in New York City
> AVA AND CORDELL HAYMON, the parents of Carroll Haymon
> ANDREA LIU, the author's sister

Despite the fact that its subject matter of assimilation and identity relates to the concerns of many people, Eric Liu's *The Accidental Asian* is at its heart a deeply personal book. Perhaps fittingly for an author who, in closing, expresses his desire that race may one day become an irrelevant category for all members of American society, the focus of Liu's interrelated essays is never very far from the personal experience of their narrator.

A goal-driven, well-assimilated, successful young second-generation Chinese American, Eric Liu nevertheless questions the degree to which his personality, and his young life's decisions, are also shaped by his family's heritage and his reaction to society's perception of himself. Thus, at the core of *The Accidental Asian* emerges the conflict between the claims of the individual for autonomy and self-actualization and the haunting perception that a person's identity may also be influenced by cultural legacy and societal categorization. The fascinating tension of Liu's work thus arises from the author's consistent juxtaposition of his persistent claim for a freely shaped individual identity and his uneasy reflections on the true meaning of his historical and biological legacy. Thus, moving beyond the personal and cultural-specific, *The Accidental Asian* asks questions of far wider relevancy.

Eric Liu begins his intellectual journey to the core of his self with a beautifully written examination of his relationship to his father, the late Chao Liu. Born to a pilot in Chiang Kai-shek's Chinese Nationalist air force in Nanjing in 1936, Chao was just a boy when his family fled to Taiwan shortly before the Communist takeover of mainland China in 1949. Moving farther away from his birthplace, Chao comes to the United States to study in Illinois. There he falls in love and marries Eric's mother Julia, another student from Taiwan.

As so often throughout *The Accidental Asian*, Liu's personal experience strikes a common chord. When Eric glances at an old photograph from his father's college days in 1962, his father's pose and style uncannily remind him of that of a young American student at Yale in a picture he has seen elsewhere. The striking difference is that the Yale daguerreotype picture was taken sometime in the 1890's. Thus, the idea that newcomers to American culture take with themselves older, already outdated pictures of style, fashion, and societal rules and attitudes of the new host country is brought home on a deeply personal yet also somewhat common level. Many new immigrants seem to remind America of its own cultural past.

It is to the author's credit that he offers these insights in a very quiet manner, leaving readers to arrive at conclusions themselves. Throughout his essays, Eric Liu asks more questions than he answers directly. This tendency is reinforced in his reflections on the fact that while his father had a fulfilling career with a blue-chip American company and led a socially integrated life, he nevertheless decided to hide his kidney disease from all Caucasian colleagues and friends. The family literally hid the home dialysis machine in the parents' bedroom closet, and his father's ailment was never disclosed. For Liu, this poses the question of how far his father's assimilation into American culture really went, considering how freely many native-born Americans tend to discuss their medical problems.

Almost inevitably, *The Accidental Asian* turns to three central elements often associated with cultural and racial identity: physiology, language, and food. Here, Eric Liu thoughtfully reflects on his Chinese body, which visually sets him apart from Caucasian Americans. He recoils when his features make him an immediate recruiting prospect for an Asian American college club. When he joins the Marine Officer Candidate School instead, Liu remarks that he "derived satisfaction from being . . . the only Chinese face" there, defying racial stereotypes. Yet with typical honesty, Liu questions his motivations for his acts. Was he really following his personal instincts, or was he merely out to disprove common assumptions?

When discussing language, Liu laments that his command of Chinese is minimal. He struggles with Chinese poetry and worries that he cannot even read a Chinese menu. Again, he wonders what price he may have paid for becoming so assimilated that his English surpasses that of many of his friends with American parents. Yet while he may not have mastered a menu in Cantonese, Eric tells of his triumph in eventually mastering the art of Chinese cooking. For him, the moment of reclaiming this part of his heritage comes when he frees himself from the written menu his parents made up for him. When he finally cooks instinctively, adding spices and other ingredients naturally and out of a true understanding of what his food should taste like, as his Chinese-born mother does, Eric feels that he has fully reconnected to a tradition nearly lost to him.

However, Eric's quest to define his identity as a young man straddling two cultures does not always come easily. Beneath his apparently surefooted steps in the world of traditional American culture, nagging questions as to the reality of his claim that he has an all-American self remain half-buried. Once he enters the arena of politicized college and public discourse, Liu finds himself confronted by challenges to his racial loyalties. Neither Chinese nor European American, Liu grapples with the political issue of being identified as Asian American.

The question of divided loyalties hits home when Liu is asked to critique on television a controversial *National Review* cover that depicts President Clinton "in yellowface" to draw attention to the "Asian money" scandal surrounding the 1996 national elections. While Liu had hoped to be able to subscribe to "the gospel of The Individual, of the 'unencumbered self' who has transcended such trivialities as race," he finds himself passionately objecting to the cover. While an Asian American employee of the magazine defends the cover page, another Asian American television studio employee shakes Liu's hand after the show in an obvious gesture of sympathy and approval. The incident, *The Accidental Asian* relates, leaves the author more confused than ever.

Thus, while he vehemently deconstructs the myth of a genuine Asian American identity by pointing to the individual Asian cultures from Japan to the Philippines, which in their very diversity oppose such a reductionist categorization, Liu comes to acknowledge that the term has its attraction for people of Asian descent living in America. Yet he can never bring himself to adopt a one-dimensional view of himself, and he challenges the reader to come to terms with the emergence of a new, but genuine, construction of the self that falls in between previously existing categories. He asks his readers, "Whatever it is that I am becoming, is it any less authentic for being an amalgam?"

Eric Liu's quest for the forces that shaped his self is taken another generation back as he reminisces about his maternal grandmother, Min-yu "Po-Po" Tu. After coming to America, she quickly settled in New York City's Chinatown, a place she refused to leave until her death. When Eric visits his grandmother, the food, the customs, even her caregiver are Chinese. Yet among "the accessories of her everyday life" is a plastic *Star Trek* mug he gave her in 1979, which she uses in the bathroom to hold her toothbrush.

For the author of *The Accidental Asian*, this detail of Po-Po's life in the new country is as telling as when he, his parents, and his sister Andrea once ran into Po-Po while on a shopping trip to Chinatown. Eric and Andrea already feel somewhat alien in the place. In a Chinese bookstore, brother and sister suddenly feel illiterate; Eric cannot even follow the text accompanying the illustrations of a Chinese children's book. Meeting Po-Po, the Lius leave quickly, feeling almost like transgressors. "The realization that her daily routine was our tourist's jaunt" deeply unsettles the second-and third-generation Chinese American family. People such as Trinh Duong, a Vietnamese refugee of Chinese descent who runs the Chinese Staff and Workers Association in New York City, may have a stronger claim to Po-Po's Chinese heritage than the well-assimilated Lius.

Only two of the seven essays collected in *The Accidental Asian* shift their focus somewhat from Eric Liu's personal to his more generally historical and contemporary political reflections. "Fear of a Yellow Planet" addresses the issue of white Americans' relations with Asian immigrants throughout the history of the United States and places Liu's struggle between self and biological heritage in a wider political context. In "New Jews," the author wonders aloud whether Asian Americans will become as integrated into mainstream American culture as it appears so many Jewish people have. Yet, while discussing interesting topics, these two broader essays lack the same immediacy of Liu's more personally connected musings.

In the end, the biggest challenge *The Accidental Asian* takes on is Eric's marriage to a white woman, Carroll Haymon. Half-jokingly, the author muses about whether it was fate that led them to find each other, since Carroll studied Chinese at home as a six-year-old girl in Louisiana. However, when they met, "what little of the language Carroll knew then, she soon forgot."

Even as Ava and Cordell Haymon, Carroll's parents, welcome Eric and his mother Julia to their home, the son cannot shake off the notion that his mixed marriage will further dilute his original heritage. As with all of his life's decisions, Eric feels that the very fact that his parents let him decide for himself has added more gravity to his choices. While he once overheard his father expressing the wish that his son marry a Chinese woman, his parents do not openly suggest this to him. After the death of Chao Liu, Julia betrays no sign of displeasure as she accepts Carroll into her son's life.

For all the apparent ease of his mixed marriage, Eric Liu keeps exploring the innermost recesses of his psyche to extract his exact motivations for having selected Carroll as his wife and partner. While insisting that he chose Carroll for personal reasons, at the back of his mind he hauntingly questions his deepest reasons for not marrying a Chinese or Chinese American woman. In the end, Liu leaves this question aside as one of the great mysteries of his life.

For readers interested in issues of identity and the conflict between heritage and self, *The Accidental Asian* offers much stimulating food for thought. Throughout the book, the voice of its author remains gentle but questioning. It is the tone of a young man who has dared to confront the most challenging dilemma of his existence. Throughout the pages of his book, Eric Liu probes what forces made him who he has become and how he will shape his future—and, ultimately, that of his and Carroll's children. *The Accidental Asian* represents a wonderful journey to the core of the author's soul and raises questions of great importance. That the author concludes with an open ending and no clear-cut answers may further endear sympathetic readers to his fine work.

R. C. Lutz

Sources for Further Study

Booklist. XCIV, May 15, 1998, p. 1571.
Far Eastern Economic Review. CLXI, August 6, 1998, p. 57.
Kirkus Reviews. LXVI, April 1, 1998, p. 471.
Library Journal. CXXIII, May 1, 1998, p. 124.
Los Angeles Times. July 9, 1998, p. E5.
National Review. L, August 3, 1998, p. 50.
The New York Times Book Review. CIII, May 24, 1998, p. 19.
Newsweek. CXXXI, June 22, 1998, p. 68.
Publishers Weekly. CCXLV, April 6, 1998, p. 67.
Time. CLI, June 22, 1998, p. 76.
The Washington Post Book World. XXVIII, July 19, 1998, p. 8.

THE ACCIDENTAL THEORIST
Essays on the Dismal Science

Author: Paul R. Krugman (1953-   )
Published: W. W. Norton (New York). 204 pp. $25.00
Type of work: Economics

A compelling, coherent set of sharp, witty essays on the major economic issues of the late 1990's, including unemployment, downsizing, globalization, economic growth, and financial speculation

Paul Krugman is the Ford International Professor of Economics at the Massachusetts Institute of Technology (MIT). In 1991 he received the John Bates Clark Medal, awarded by the American Economic Association every two years to the best American economist under the age of forty. Among Krugman's most recognized books are *The Age of Diminished Expectations* (1990), *Peddling Prosperity* (1994), and *Pop Internationalism* (1997). He writes a regular monthly column, "The Dismal Science," for the online magazine *Slate* and frequently writes articles for *Fortune, The Washington Monthly, Foreign Affairs,* and *The New York Times.*

Krugman has made it a personal crusade to promote sound economic thinking. Since the late 1980's he has been pointing out the fallacies of many ideological, fashionable economic ideas, such as the logic of supply-side economics and the evils of globalization. *The Accidental Theorist* is a collection of twenty-seven of Krugman's best essays written between the fall of 1995 and the summer of 1997. Although three of the essays are new, more than half were previously published in the online magazine *Slate,* while many of the others were published in conventional print media, such as *The New York Times* and *USA Today.* Krugman's essays combine his clever wit and clear analysis, applying and illustrating basic economic principles with simple examples and models. In some cases, however, the reader is still left wanting for more practical information about what can be done to resolve some of the exposed economic problems.

In *The Accidental Theorist* Krugman's overall goal is to point out that the fundamental concepts of economic theory are actually very simple and that they can be understood by the common public. However, as Krugman explains, the application of these concepts to particular issues, such as the effects of the money supply on economic growth or of technological progress on employment, requires careful, clear thinking, which most economists attempt to back up with specialized jargon and mathematical formulas. Although economic jargon and math sometimes make economic concepts clearer and simpler, in many cases the concepts would be more easily understood if they were stated in plain English. According to Krugman, many economists purposely obscure meaning by using sophisticated mathematical equations and language, which constitutes a form of "technical showboating." In fact, Krugman candidly states that many influential economists have misrepresented and even invented facts in order to gloss over gaps in their logic, thereby blatantly leading their audiences astray. He is tired of such nonsense. In the essays in *The Accidental Theorist* Krugman uses clear English interspersed with understandable examples to communicate to the general public simple truths about economic issues.

The essays in *The Accidental Theorist* are broken up into six major parts: jobs, right-wing wrongs, globalization, delusions of economic growth, financial speculation, and topics beyond the market, including environmental policies, traffic congestion, and medical care. Throughout the book, Krugman introduces thought experiments that help make economic theory more accessible to understanding, pointing out that real economics can be made meaningful only if one is willing to play with simple models in hypothetical settings. Some of Krugman's essays start with current issues, such as the crisis set off by the monetary policy of Thailand or corporate downsizing, while others expose seemingly plausible ideas as being false, such as blaming America's economic problems on the internationalization of commerce when they are really due to a failure to resolve domestic policy.

By examining pundits from across the political spectrum, Krugman enlightens the reader about the workings of our national economy. Trying not to take political sides, either left or right, Krugman points out some of the pitfalls of the "supply-siders" of the Reagan-Bush era and those of the "strategic traders" of the Clinton administration. However, it is very apparent that Krugman is more a supporter of the ideas of the left, spending one whole part of the book emphasizing the wrongs of right wingers and then repeating these issues again in a number of other essays later in the book.

In the first essay, titled "The Accidental Theorist," Krugman uses a change in hot dog technology in a "hot dog/hot dog bun" world to illustrate that the effects of productivity growth in a particular market do not necessarily dictate what happens to the economy as a whole. Indeed, growth in one sector of the economy may lead to job gains in another. Krugman uses this example to point out some serious fallacies in William B. Greider's book *One World, Ready or Not: The Manic Logic of Global Capitalism* (1997). Greider, posing as a practical man communicating with the common sense of the common man, tries to demonstrate that global supply is outrunning global demand. Instead of accomplishing his goal, however, he spins a 473-page yarn that can be characterized as picking the wrong facts to support his thesis. Krugman classifies Greider as an "accidental theorist," one who reaches conclusions that are based on invalid implicit assumptions.

The last essay in part 1 responds to some ridiculous ideas supported primarily by French Socialist Prime Minister Lionel Jospin. For example, Jospin and other Socialists in France propose that the solution to their country's chronic unemployment is to shorten work hours and increase government welfare. Krugman deflates the French balloon by pointing out that this fallacy never has worked and never will, as all reputable economists would agree.

Attacking supply-side economics in part 2, Krugman illustrates that tax cuts in all economic situations is not a good idea, but like a virus, the idea continues to rise again. Krugman argues that the government typically serves the public's will; consequently, taxes are necessary to provide essential services. The third essay in part 2 focuses on some nonsensical economic ideas espoused by Richard Armey, former Republican House majority leader. Krugman attacks Armey's portrayal of the United States as a nation of equitable income distribution by pointing out that America's income distribution has become more and more unequal since the mid-1970's. According to Krugman, the rich keep getting richer and the poor poorer. Overall, the theme of part 2 is that prominent people, particularly politicians, often use false assumptions to prove foolish, unintelligent things about economic issues.

In part 3, Krugman takes on the problem of globalization. He argues that international trade and investment have grown faster than the world economy as a whole. Hence, globalization has made national economics more interdependent, but, according to Krugman, the extent and importance have been greatly exaggerated. He claims that globalization has imposed no important constraints on America's economic and social policies, the shaping of which remain in American hands. In addition to generating greater world interdependence, globalization, Krugman points out, has benefited the poor people of the Third World by providing more jobs, even though wages are low. Writing of international trade, Krugman suggests that China's trade surplus should not be a concern, since it really reveals China's weakness rather than its strength. Many readers will question Krugman's claim that the distributional consequences of international trade are small by arguing that he may be neglecting the disturbing reality that increased economic openness in the world has occurred at the same time that inequality has mushroomed. Many economic models in economic books and journals indicate that free trade is only optimal given some very restrictive assumptions.

Similar to his doubts about the effect of globalization on America's economy, Krugman has similar doubts about technological change, as discussed in the first essay in part 4. The growth in technology has not translated into corresponding changes in the fundamentals of living. As Krugman points out, part of the solution lies in teaching students the essential fundamentals of reading, writing, and arithmetic prior to turning students loose with laptop computers. In addition, part 4 includes essays on business cycle fluctuations and long-term growth in which Krugman again uses simple models to reveal how real world economics works versus the economic theories in textbooks. Such textbook models often lead to unexpected or unintended, but correct, conclusions. Krugman concludes that the business cycle, consisting of fluctuating output and unemployment, is not dead, because new economic problems keep arising that are not correctly addressed. Krugman then argues that as society faces old economic problems in new economic environments, it is necessary to make new applications of old, correct economic principles.

Because of rigged markets, overinflated currencies, and the vast sums of money made and lost in the 1990's, Krugman uses part 5 of *The Accidental Theorist* to label and then analyze the 1990's as the great age of financial speculation. Currency crises involving the British pound in 1992, the Mexican peso in 1994-1995, and the Thai baht in 1997 suggest to many economists that old economic rules and conventional economic theory no longer apply, but Krugman concludes that such monetary declines are the normal result of currency rates that are not credible. Economists agree that in order to be credible, currencies should be indifferent to the exchange rate.

In part 6 Krugman explores some applications of economics to issues beyond the market. Discussing environmental politics, he supports a pollution tax that would help limit the emission of greenhouse gases. Writing of the link between pollution and traffic congestion, Krugman makes a very interesting proposal. What if the government imposed fees for the use of road space during rush hour traffic? Since road space is a scarce resource, should it not have limits imposed on it? Krugman also explores a variety of questions about medical technology. How much medical care should money buy? Should state-of-the art medical care in America be provided only for those who can pay for it, or should a medical welfare state be established?

Since the book covers many important technical topics with great clarity, the reader's desire to better understand economic principles and to decipher the economic rhetoric of politicians is encouraged and reinforced. However, this strength also reveals a weakness of the book. Although it clarifies many important economic issues and forces the reader to question many illogical economic conclusions, *The Accidental Theorist* does not generate an overall better understanding of economic fundamentals. As Carl Sagan so effectively conveyed the fundamental principles of astronomy to the general public, Krugman would like to do the same with economics, but he fails to do so in *The Accidental Theorist*. Krugman must not only make the general public more aware of broad economic issues and problems but also suggest and explain practical solutions that might help resolve more of them. Nevertheless, the book is basically solid and not boring. What Krugman has to say is clear, intelligent, important, and engaging.

When economic theory, coupled with a variety of implicit assumptions, is applied to real-world problems, the results often sound very plausible, but, as Krugman emphasizes in *The Accidental Theorist*, the conclusions can be very wrong and lead to ridiculous, sometimes very dangerous, economic policy. Krugman's ability to create simple models, or parables, that relate to the common person clarifies, enriches, and freshens old economic concepts in the setting of current economic issues. Krugman does a masterful job of illustrating that correct lessons in good economics do not have to be difficult. In fact, they can be very intriguing. He uses his models to expose many of the ill-conceived ideas of prominent economists as inexcusable ignorance, as he unravels and simplifies some long-held and lofty ideas of economics at a level that can be understood by the general public. For example, he makes some important contributions to the understanding of national economics by pointing out that common beliefs about the impact of production efficiency on labor demand are wrong, that the trade deficits with Japan and China are really unimportant, and that nations do not go bankrupt and out of business.

In teaching good economic lessons, Krugman reveals economic fallacies of both political sides, the right and the left. Although he realizes the necessity for government programs to serve the public's needs, he is likewise very skeptical about government intervention and the pitfalls of government-supplied "free lunches" versus a free market. Overall, *The Accidental Theorist* helps lay readers see beyond accepted economic pundits and slogans that too often pass for economic wisdom and, in so doing, provides a much better understanding of the workings of the national economy.

Alvin K. Benson

Sources for Further Study

Booklist. XCIV, May 15, 1998, p. 1571.
Boston Magazine. XC, August, 1998, p. 208.
Business Economics. XXXIII, October, 1998, p. 76.
Foreign Affairs. LXXVII, July, 1998, p. 124.
Library Journal. CXXIII, June 15, 1998, p. 89.
Publishers Weekly. CCXLV, March 23, 1998, p. 86.
The Washington Post Book World. XXVIII, June 14, 1998, p. 13.

AESTHETICS, METHOD, AND EPISTEMOLOGY
Essential Works of Foucault, 1954-1984, Volume II

Author: Michel Foucault (1926-1984)
Translated from the French by Robert Hurley and others
Edited, with an introduction, by James D. Faubion
Published: The New Press (New York). 486 pp. $30.00
Type of work: Essays

The second in a planned three-volume series in English translation of Michel Foucault's essays and interviews selected from the definitive four-volume Dits et écrits

With this second large volume in the New Press Foucault series under Paul Rabinow's general editorship, the selection of Michel Foucault's occasional pieces grows more imposing, if less so than Gallimard's four-volume definitive French collection *Dits et écrits*, edited by Daniel Defert and François Ewald. James D. Faubion, an anthropology professor at Rice University, is editor of this volume, which groups the French author's essays and interviews into two main sections: "Aesthetics" and "Method and Epistemology." Some of Foucault's most celebrated and frequently cited essays appear here, such as "What Is an Author?" "This Is Not a Pipe," "Nietzsche, Freud, Marx," and "Nietzsche, Genealogy, History." The sequence of essays and interviews follow the publishing history of Foucault's major works yet in many ways constitutes a separate corpus altogether, almost an "alternative" Foucault in some ways.

Volumes such as *Aesthetics, Method, and Epistemology* may give the appearance of existing merely to accommodate the dedicated reader of Foucault, one who desires as complete a collection of the author's work as possible. However, especially in the case of the interviews Foucault generously granted throughout his life, such an anthology may provide a good starting point for readers just beginning to contemplate his work and its place in twentieth century French thought. In interviews Foucault often clarified positions or made more direct professions of his methodological and political intent. He was also more inclined to address the question of his relationship to Marxism, psychoanalysis, or poststructuralism, subjects he liked to obscure in his major works. More often than not, he punctuated his remarks with a cathartic laughter difficult for some readers of his books to imagine.

Compared to the often austere tone of Foucault's major books, such as *Les Mots et les choses: Une archéologie des sciences humaines* (1966; *The Order of Things: An Archaeology of the Human Sciences*, 1970) or *Surveiller et punir: Naissance de la prison* (1975; *Discipline and Punish: Birth of the Prison*, 1979), Foucault's interviews appear more relaxed, especially in later years as he dispensed with the quasistructuralist jargon that infiltrated his discourse in the early 1960's. His fascination with the theoretical ferment in the human sciences at the beginning of his career can be seen in his treatment of Friedrich Hölderlin, the poet who is the subject of the first essay in the volume, "The Father's 'No.'" This essay was a review of a book on Hölderlin by French psychoanalyst Jean Laplanche, and Foucault at that time appeared to regard the German Romantic poet as a kind of structuralist *avant la lettre* who reduced human beings to meaningless "signs." A famous 1966 French cartoon depicted Foucault as part of a structuralist quartet that included Claude Lévi-Strauss, Roland Barthes, and Jacques Lacan. He always resented the association and repeatedly explained to interviewers in detail the reasons why he should not be considered a structuralist.

By the time (1972) of Foucault's scathing reply ("My Body, This Paper, This Fire," included in this volume) to Jacques Derrida's deconstructionist critique of his reading strategies, he had begun to exhibit much greater distance from theories of textuality. As some of the last items included in the section on method and epistemology show, Foucault's theory of discourse was never divorced from historical events, the world never reduced merely to a "text." Foucault's celebrated antihumanism, expressed in his wary examination of the forces at work in modern civilization that served to produce men and women as "subjects," nevertheless remained with him.

Reading or rereading these early and late essays on aesthetics, students of Foucault cannot help but be affected by the detailed and often disturbing biographical treatment accorded the author by Didier Eribon, James Miller, and David Macey. Foucault's aesthetic preferences appear to be part and parcel of his fascination with what he called "limit experiences," those that push body and mind alike to the threshold of what can be endured or imagined. Hence Foucault's admiration for the texts of "transgressive" writers in the modern French tradition: The Marquis de Sade, Raymond Roussel, Antonin Artaud, Maurice Blanchot, Georges Bataille, and Pierre Klossowski.

When, in the 1963 essay that Foucault wrote for the influential journal *Tel quel*, "Language to Infinity," one reads his digression on the story "The Secret Miracle" by Jorge Luis Borges, one is reminded simultaneously of the French philosopher's life and his death. In the Borges tale, a writer to be executed by a firing squad is granted an extra year—in his mind only—to reconsider and revise some of his writings. His execution actually takes place very soon after the sentence is rendered, but in his mind it is as if he has had the additional time to contemplate and revise his literary legacy. Dying of acquired immunodeficiency syndrome (AIDS), Foucault finished *L'usage des plaisirs* (1984; *The Use of Pleasure: Volume 2 of the History of Sexuality*, 1985) and *Le Souci de Soi* (1984; *The Care of the Self: Volume 3 of the History of Sexuality*, 1986) during his last few months and received the published books in his hospital bed one week before he died. Also, most hauntingly, he had spoken during his inaugural lecture at the Collège de France in 1970, citing Samuel Beckett, of his desire to disappear behind his writings, to make his exit as quietly and unobtrusively as possible.

Foucault did not set out to become a historian, but rather a philosopher. It was through his early philosophical investigations of questions of madness and mental illness that he encountered the kinds of problems and questions that led him into historical research. Historians especially will find the essays in the second part of the present volume profound and provocative on questions of historical methodology. His formulations on the pitfalls of researching the past are often startlingly original, partly because of his desire to dissociate himself from prevailing orthodoxies and certainly from what he thought of as an inherently Hegelo-Marxian insistence on linear schemes. Very much a man of his time, Foucault was motivated always to ask how far back one must search in order to discover different structures or modes of systems of thought or discourse. In the eyes of many interpreters, especially readers of the essay "Nietzsche, Genealogy, History," Foucault found his alternative to dialectical schemes in Friedrich Nietzsche's philosophy of history. For that reason, it is instructive to see how frequently in these late interviews Foucault is at pains to distance himself from Nietzsche. Sometimes, self-deprecatingly, this can take the form of denying that he had ever studied Nietzsche's writings in much detail.

The lectures and interviews included in *Aesthetics, Method, and Epistemology* provide vivid moments in which Foucault clarifies or memorably characterizes the import of some of his major books, as in the interview with Raymond Bellour called "The Order of Things," in which he neatly contrasts the thrust of the book that bears that title in English with his preceding book on madness. Foucault's own assessments of his works' significance are enormously valuable, as when he explores the contrast between his historical investigation of spaces and earlier European preoccupation with chronological development.

It is particularly interesting to observe in these selections how frequently Foucault, especially in interviews, can be seen rehearsing ideas he will later refine elaborately in his most important books and essays. The interview "On the Archaeology of the Sciences" is a fine example, one in which he considers some highly nuanced aspects of discourse and discursive fields that he was to refine elaborately in his *L'ordre du discours* (1970; *The Order of Discourse*, 1973). Readers of the previous volume of *Essential Works* were able to trace similar kinds of evolution through the course outlines included.

At times what the reader of Faubion's edited volume comes away with is a sense of the breathtakingly beautiful manner in which Foucault typically expressed himself, and for many readers, their first attraction to Foucault was purely at the level of style. Apparent enough to readers of French, this can be conveyed in carefully translated English, and one benefit of this volume and the one that preceded it is the care with which already capable translations have been improved upon, even if only slightly. Robert Hurley, who did most of the first versions of these translations, has proven himself over the years to be unusually attentive to the subtleties of Foucault's prose, especially in the books on sexuality.

Unfortunately for readers who may begin their consideration of Foucault with *Aesthetics, Method, and Epistemology*, the editor's introduction is far less helpful and less well-written than the one Paul Rabinow supplied for volume 1. Faubion seems to have succumbed to the temptation to dazzle with intellectual pyrotechnics of his own, even to outdo the occasional knottiness of Foucault's prose. At times his introduction is lost in minutiae and intricate etymological digressions. At others, he channels his energies into juxtaposing Foucault with myriad other Western thinkers, whether or not this is a valuable means of preparing readers for the selections that lie ahead. This is one of those introductions that might more profitably be read only after completing the rest of the book.

A larger problem for the three-volume series is the omission of some of the additional versions and commentaries the French edition contains. For example, English-language commentators on Foucault have relied heavily on his essay "What Is An Author?" for the way it seems to fundamentally challenge traditional forms and procedures of literary study. However, Foucault produced two different versions of this text, and no two exegetes necessarily use the same one. The first version, longer and more subtly argued, was given as a lecture in Paris in 1969, while the second, more forcefully stated, was given as a lecture in Buffalo, New York, in 1970. The earlier version appeared in Donald F. Bouchard's edited volume *Language, Counter-Memory, Practice: Selected Essays and Interviews* (1977), while Josué V. Harari's *Textual Strategies: Perspectives in Post-Structuralist Criticism* contains the second version, or so others have argued. Faubion presents his version as the English translation of the Paris lecture but acknowledges Harari's translation as the one he has slightly modified. Confusion continues on this score. How much better it would be if the reader in English could see both versions in succession, in order to judge the significance of their differences. *Dits et écrits* supplies both and also includes the audience responses to the 1969 lecture. It is unfortunate that the harsh economic realities of American book production deprives readers of the relatively greater riches that their French counterparts, at 215 francs per volume (about $37.00), enjoy.

What may be the finest achievement of this second volume in the series is to bring together writings and transcribed interviews both on aesthetics and methodological questions of research. No small part of Foucault's greatness as a thinker was in his transcendence of disciplinary boundaries. One senses that he was equally at home in many different domains within what the French commonly call the "human sciences" and that what moved him more than anything was the prospect of writing: writing without fixed boundaries or limits and always looking forward to the way an author is transformed by what he writes.

James A. Winders

Sources for Further Study

Artforum. XXXVII, December, 1998, p. 27.
Library Journal. CXXIII, February 1, 1998, p. 88.

AFRICA
A Biography of the Continent

Author: John Reader (1937-   )
Published: Alfred A. Knopf (New York). Illustrated. 801 pp. $25.00
First published: 1997, in Great Britain
Type of work: History
Time: Antiquity to the present
Locale: Africa

A sweeping, multidisciplinary, and analytical history of the entire continent of Africa by a photojournalist whose long experience in Africa has given him sympathetic and fresh insights into the continent

Although *Africa: A Biography of the Continent* is, at its core, a history of Africa, readers need go no further than its title to sense it is something a bit more than a mere history. Otherwise, why does author John Reader call it "A *Biography* of the Continent"? Human beings, as we have been trained to think, have "biographies," while places have "histories." Fortunately, Reader's preface is quick to define his terms:

> As a "biography" of the continent, this book presents Africa as a dynamic and exceptionally fecund entity, where the evolution of humanity is merely one of many developmental trajectories that are uniquely evident there.

In balder language, *Africa* weaves human history into what is known about Africa's geology, geography, and biological history. As the *Literary Review* has described it, the book constitutes "geography, history, anthropology, and ecology on a grand scale." Although its eight sections follow a broadly chronological arrangement, the book makes no attempt to chronicle every major epoch in every region of Africa. Instead, it examines broad ecological questions, narrowing its focus to particular times and places as they prove useful to illustrating Reader's points.

For a long book on an immense subject, *Africa* is written with exceptional passion and energy. Most of its fifty-five chapters can be read as individual essays arguing convincing theses. It is in presenting these theses that *Africa* is at its best. Reader makes his points by examining all relevant aspects of each issue in whatever detail is necessary, while citing the most up-to-date and compelling evidence and carefully explaining his reasoning. When Reader deals with particularly controversial issues, such as the Atlantic slave trade, he generally presents all sides and is anything but dogmatic. He is satisfied to present his case, move on, and let readers draw their own conclusions. And why not? His arguments are typically too persuasive to reject out of hand, and it is nearly impossible to find flaws in the evidence that he musters. For a photojournalist with apparently little scholarly training, he meets a high standard of scholarship.

In the study of human history, it has become a commonplace to observe that Africa is at once both the oldest and the youngest continent. It is the "oldest" because it was home to the earliest human beings; it is the "youngest" because all but a handful of its fifty-plus nations came into being in the late twentieth century. Until the 1960's—the period in which the most new nations became independent—Africa's history was a little-understood and rarely taught subject, even within the continent. The 1960's launched such an explosion in scholarly research and writing on Africa that perhaps 80 percent of the nearly one thousand titles Reader lists in his bibliography have been published since then. With the flood of historical works about Africa written over the past four decades, it is only natural to ask what a book such as Reader's can contribute to our understanding of Africa. The answer lies in his original, holistic approach to understanding why Africa has developed as it has, and how and why it differs from the rest of the world.

Several themes pervade this book. The most refreshing of these is that because all humankind originated in Africa, we are all, in a sense, Africans. For this reason, differences among peoples in different parts of the world can best be explained by looking at their unique environments, not at racial differences among the peoples themselves. Reader's discussion of African agriculture, for example, alludes to Africa's European invaders as "return migrants" and attributes the radically different ideas about farming that European tried to introduce to Africa to the vastly different environmental conditions they knew in Europe.

A second theme, closely related to the first, is the crucial importance of environment in human history. Reader has much to say about Africa's geology, climate, flora and fauna, and unique health problems. Indeed, his book might fairly be described as an ecological history of Africa. And what a challenging ecology African peoples have always faced! Among the special problems with which Africans have had to cope are poor soils, meager and erratic rainfall, stifling heat, and debilitating diseases such as malaria, sleeping sickness, and bilharzia. Similar problems have beset other peoples throughout the world, but Africa's problems have often been of a much larger scale. In Africa, drought and desertification, for example, have often threatened entire nations. Some diseases have sapped the energy of large segments of communities. Acquired immunodeficiency syndrome (AIDS) has hit Africa harder than any other part of the world; in some countries, more than a quarter of the population is estimated to carry the disease.

Virtually everywhere throughout the world, animal pests have damaged and stolen human-grown crops, but only Africans have had to compete with crop-destroying pests as voracious, powerful, and numerous as elephants. When epidemics have afflicted domestic animals, they have occasionally occurred on a colossal scale. During the 1890's, for example, when Europeans were aggressively seizing African territories, perhaps 95 percent of the cattle in the continent were killed by a viral disease known as rinderpest. In many areas of tropical Africa, tsetse flies made cattle-keeping impossible, and in some areas another parasitic disease made it impossible to keep horses.

Reader's examination of ecological issues goes a long way toward explaining basic questions about African history that more narrowly focused professional historians have not always answered satisfactorily. One such question is why Africa was so little urbanized before the twentieth century. Aside from ocean ports in North and East Africa, few population centers of any size arose in Africa. Moreover, many large centers that did arise—such as the Great Zimbabwe complex—did not endure. Reader has much to say on the subject of urbanization. To bring large numbers of people close together in urban communities made them more vulnerable to epidemics and placed great strains on already fragile ecologies.

Any discussion of urbanization is closely tied to another of *Africa*'s pervasive themes: demographics. Large parts of Africa offer harsh environments for human populations for reasons already mentioned: difficult agricultural conditions and disease. Reader comments repeatedly on what he calls the "underpopulation" of the continent—which even now is home to fewer people than the Asian nation of India, which has a tenth Africa's area. Without significant advances in agricultural technology, water supplies, fertilizers, and disease control, many parts of Africa simply have not been able to sustain large numbers of people. Reader sees the effects of these constraints throughout African history. For example, he attributes the collapse of West Africa's medieval Ghana Empire (not related to modern Ghana) to "ecology, not conquest . . . The herds were too big, there were too many people." Human populations could not grow significantly until they left Africa for less harsh environments—which is precisely why the descendants of Africans living in Europe and Asia became so numerous. Reader also sees South Africa's changing demographics as the primary driving force in the former white regime's abandonment of apartheid. Since the apartheid system had been predicated on an assumption the ratio of white to black South Africans would be much higher than it actually was by the 1990's, demographic realities made its collapse "inevitable."

Much of the passion that Reader brings to this book doubtless comes from his affection for Africa, in which he has lived most of his adult life. As an expatriate British journalist tied to no one African country or region, he brings an impartiality to his writing uninfected by patriotism or political orientation, and he has no obvious axes to grind. *Africa* exhibits his genuine admiration for African peoples and cultures. While he is no apologist for the crimes and excesses of Africa's many authoritarian regimes, he tends to view their misdeeds with a nonjudgmental detachment, as well as a desire to find rational explanations for their behavior.

Although Reader devotes an entire chapter to refuting what he calls the myth of an idyllic "Merrie Africa," he several times calls attention to Africa's comparatively peaceful pre-nineteenth century history. Indeed, in a discussion of political organization, he suggests that the "most distinctively African contribution to human history has been precisely the civilized art of living fairly peaceably together *not* in states." While acknowledging that for most Africans "life was arduous and unpredictable" and "slavery was commonplace," he seems inclined to attribute much of the conflict and violence with which modern Africa has become associated to the effects of outside influences. The most pernicious of these influences he identifies as European colonialism, which blanketed most of the continent from the end of the nineteenth century into the 1960's.

In addition to the violence generated by Europe's invasion of Africa and the vigorous resistances that Africans mounted, Reader blames colonialism for sowing the seeds of ethnic conflict that have been particularly destructive in some independent African nations by inventing the concept of "tribalism." He calls particular attention to the Belgian administration of Rwanda and Burundi, colonies that Belgium reluctantly took on after Germany's defeat in World War I. Both countries have become notorious for their alternating massacres of their own Tutsi and Hutu peoples. To the outside world, these genocidal conflicts appear to be "ethnic" in nature. However, the very real distinctions now felt between "Tutsi" and "Hutu" in each country are at least partly postcolonial legacies of the Belgian policy of classifying residents of each country as one or the other and forcing them to carry "ethnic" identity cards.

A constant feature of Reader's book that is both valuable and charming is its frequent, detailed asides on apparently peripheral subjects, which he demonstrates are more important than one might expect. He is rarely content merely to assert a point, such as the fact that the prevalence of tsetse flies in Africa's tropical regions has long deterred human development. He prefers to explain exactly how and why, delving into details about tsetse reproduction, their life cycles, and the nature of the disease they carry. Likewise, instead of merely asserting that the flooding of West Africa's great Niger River contributes less to agriculture than that of the Nile River, he explains how silting works, what sedimentary materials each river carries, and precisely what nutrients each river contributes to local agriculture. Reader offers similarly fascinating discussions of lactose intolerance among Africans, the impact of ironworking on forestation, elephant reproduction, diamond mining, and many other subjects.

Regardless of how much readers are interested in Africa, they are likely to find much of the information that Reader explains fascinating for its own sake—such as his discreet description of how human agents must assist camels to perform sexually to ensure they reproduce. Almost every detail that Reader mentions supports the broader points he is making. Only rarely does he slip in a trivial detail that is too much fun to pass up—such as the fact that Belgium's King Leopold II had his copies of *The Times* ironed before being delivered to him.

One of Reader's most remarkable feats in *Africa* is maintaining a balanced viewpoint. Although he builds strong cases for dismissing past beliefs about outside contributions to African cultures and for placing Africa squarely in the center of world history, he never leans toward the "Afrocentrist" tendency to exaggerate African virtues while diminishing the contributions of other parts of the world. The reason for this should be clear: The central message of *Africa: A Biography of the Continent* is that because all the world's peoples are as one, whatever individual peoples achieve is primarily a function of their environments.

R. Kent Rasmussen

Sources for Further Study

Booklist. XCIV, April 15, 1998, p. 1415.

The Economist. CCCXL, February 14, 1998, p. R7.

History Today. XLVIII, March, 1998, p. 53.

Los Angeles Times Book Review. July 19, 1998, p. 3.

National Review. L, June 22, 1998, p. 57.

New Statesman. CXXVII, February 13, 1998, p. 47.

The New York Review of Books. XLV, December 17, 1998, p. 64.

The New York Times Book Review. CIII, June 21, 1998, p. 14.

Publishers Weekly. CCXLV, February 16, 1998, p. 192.

The Washington Post Book World. XXVIII, May 17, 1998, p. 1.

ALEXANDER SOLZHENITSYN
A Century in His Life

Author: D. M. Thomas (1935-   )
Published: St. Martin's Press (New York). 583 pp. $29.95
Type of work: Biography
Time: 1918-1997
Locale: The Soviet Union and Vermont

Thomas presents a personal portrait of the greatest dissident writer of the Soviet Union, providing insights into Solzhenitsyn's struggle with Joseph Stalin and his successors and his relationship with the two women who provided strong support for his efforts to expose the evils of the Communist regime

Principal personages:
ALEXANDER SOLZHENITSYN, Soviet novelist, essayist, and poet
NATALYA RESHETOVSKAYA, Solzhenitsyn's first wife
NATALYA SVETLOVA, Solzhenitsyn's second wife

One might wonder why any Western writer would attempt a biography of Alexander Solzhenitsyn less than twenty years after the publication of Michael Scammell's exhaustive study of the novelist, which appeared in 1984. It is certainly fair to speculate, too, about why someone who has spent most of his career as a novelist, poet, and translator would be willing to take on such a daunting task. D. M. Thomas, author of a half-dozen volumes of poetry and a dozen novels, including the ambitious five-volume *Russian Nights Quintet* series, claims that the decision to take on this project was motivated principally by his love for Russian literature, which he sees as a seamless web of interconnected writings stretching back as far as the beginning of the nineteenth century, when the first dissident writer, Alexander Pushkin, became the darling of literary circles in Russia. As Thomas admits in the prologue to his work, "to write a life of Solzhenitsyn is inevitably to write about a century—or perhaps two." To learn about Solzhenitsyn's struggles against Communism is to see in microcosm the struggles of an entire nation against an ideology that stifled individual freedoms and brutally eliminated all who opposed the grand scheme concocted by Vladimir Ilich Lenin and his most zealous followers.

Despite Thomas's unstinting praise for his subject, this is a book that Solzhenitsyn did not want to see in print. Unhappy that Thomas was planning to rely on the memoirs of his first wife, Solzhenitsyn not only refused to grant Thomas an interview, but he even attempted to stop publication, going so far as to withdraw permission for the publisher, St. Martin's Press, to bring out a planned collection of his own writings. In the face of these objections, Thomas provides in *Alexander Solzhenitsyn: A Century in His Life* a story based largely on secondary sources. At times Thomas is openly fanciful in his speculations, relying on his talents as a novelist to create scene and dialogue. More frequently, however, to flesh out the narrative he relies on Solzhenitsyn's numerous autobiographical writings and the memoirs of those who know him. The records upon which he has been able to draw are voluminous, and his commitment to the project is infused with a belief that Solzhenitsyn "helped to bring down the greatest tyranny the world has seen" and that "no other writer of the twentieth century has had such an influence on history." Consequently, he writes about Solzhenitsyn with a certain degree of reverence and a keen interest in explaining the complexities of character that drove the writer to challenge Soviet authorities at the risk of imprisonment or even death.

The details of Solzhenitsyn's life are given primacy of place in Thomas's narrative. Readers not familiar with the outlines of the writer's life receive a solid overview of his boyhood in the provinces of the Soviet Union, his wartime service, his arrest and internment in a series of forced-labor camps, and his decades-long struggle to chronicle the evils and hypocrisies of Communist rulers whose habitual lies about progress covered up the oppression and deprivation suffered by millions. Thomas does an excellent job presenting the gradual shift in Solzhenitsyn's ideology from committed Communist to conservative reactionary. One sees the writer gradually abandoning his belief in Lenin and adopting a philosophy that celebrates the tenets of organized religion, including the practices of the Russian Orthodox church. The Solzhenitsyn seen at the end of this tale is one very different from the young writer inspired by Lenin's writings.

Solzhenitsyn is also very different from the idealized portrait that so many outside the U.S.S.R. had constructed of him from the works which had been published in Europe and America before he left the Soviet Union in 1974. For years a darling of Western liberal intellectuals and politicians while he toiled under the constraints of totalitarian rulers, Solzhenitsyn proved, once he arrived in the West, to be no toady of the liberal ideology. His harsh condemnation of Western democracy, which he says has produced nations of individuals more concerned about trivial pleasures than about genuine human happiness, caused him to lose favor with many who had been vocal supporters while he was still behind the Iron Curtain. What became apparent during his years in exile was his revulsion at the aims of the Enlightenment; in his view, the spirit of rationalism has led not only to the evils of Communism in the East, but also to the state of moral laissez-faire in the West that has been equally destructive to the human spirit.

Fans of Solzhenitsyn who have read novels such as *One Day in the Life of Ivan Denisovich* (1962) or *The First Circle* (1968), his accounts of forced-labor camps in *The Gulag Archipelago* (1973-1975), his autobiography *The Oak and the Calf* (1975), or his tributes to those who assisted his efforts in *Invisible Allies* (1995) will not be surprised at the descriptions of censorship, harassment, and torture he faced from the time he was arrested for anti-Soviet behavior during World War II until his expulsion from the Soviet Union.

The focus of Thomas's biography is on Solzhenitsyn's personal relationships, principally those with his two wives. The portrait of Natalya Reshetovskaya, who married the young Solzhenitsyn shortly before he was sent to the front in World War II, is especially well done. She emerges from Thomas's text as a character equally complex as her more famous husband. Perhaps because he relies so heavily on her memoirs, Thomas finds her a long-suffering helpmate who was treated shabbily by a husband more committed to his writing than to being a good marriage partner. She is not without faults, however, and Thomas is willing to bring out her tendencies to overdramatize her own plight as the rejected woman. Similarly, he attempts to be evenhanded in his portrayal of Natalya Svetlova, whom Solzhenitsyn met in 1968 and married in 1973. The much younger woman fulfilled the writer's desire for a wife who would cater to his unusual demands, while remaining a strong figure who could deal with outsiders forcefully, keeping them at arm's length from Solzhenitsyn so he would remain free from distractions.

While he clearly admires Solzhenitsyn as a writer, Thomas is willing to take his subject to task over personal failings. Certainly his portrait of Solzhenitsyn's relationships with women is hardly flattering. Although not a philanderer, Solzhenitsyn seemed to view marriage not as a union of equals but rather as a way for him to obtain dedicated help for his ongoing literary endeavors. From both of his wives—and from nearly a half-dozen other women whose assistance he sought during the decades when he was preparing multiple copies of his works for secret distribution—he demanded unquestioning loyalty and a willingness to take on tasks which he felt distracted him from his mission. These included household chores and a host of other everyday functions, such as answering the telephone.

In Thomas's view, Solzhenitsyn did not deal much better with men. The extent of his loyalty toward friends can be seen in his interactions with Alexander Tvardovsky, the editor who placed his reputation and job on the line to publish *One Day in the Life of Ivan Denisovich* in the U.S.S.R.'s premier literary journal *Novy Mir* in 1962. Initially much enamored with Tvardovsky's courage, over the next two decades Solzhenitsyn cooled about the extent to which he was indebted to the editor, finally belittling his assistance in rather dismissive language in *The Oak and the Calf* and *Invisible Allies*. Thomas is quick to point out the shift and to fault Solzhenitsyn for his change of heart. In similar fashion, he criticizes Solzhenitsyn for abandoning other old friends who stood by him in tough times, noting that for Solzhenitsyn only complete loyalty to his own brand of anti-Soviet ideology merited praise and reciprocal display of solid friendship.

Thomas is distanced enough from his subject to admit that as Solzhenitsyn grew older he gradually became more obsessed with documenting the evils of the Soviet state than with creating works of literary merit. By the time he began compiling the epic he would call *The Red Wheel*, Solzhenitsyn's mania for including every detail about Soviet atrocities had begun to distract from his ability to tell a story that readers would find aesthetically satisfying. In effect, Thomas acknowledges that the novelist had moved from being an interpreter of human suffering to a mere chronicler of information about the repressive Soviet regime.

In some ways, the problems surrounding the appearance of Thomas's work, evidenced by Solzhenitsyn's efforts to stymie publication, make this biography particularly noteworthy. The controversy has been further inflamed by the widely divergent opinions expressed in initial reviews. Noted critic George Steiner and others have taken Thomas to task for his propensity to apply Freudian analysis to Solzhenitsyn's character and to resort to novelistic techniques when direct evidence is lacking. On the other hand, a number of reviewers have been exceedingly high in their praise, including British critic A. N. Wilson, who claims that this is the definitive biography of the Soviet writer.

Whether Solzhenitsyn deserves the status Thomas affords him as the most important writer of the century may remain open to debate. Nevertheless, there is no question that his works were of great influence in exposing the evils of the totalitarian state under Stalin and his successors. In a number of his novels, most notably *One Day in the Life of Ivan Denisovich, Cancer Ward* (1968), and *August 1914* (1971, rev. 1983), Solzhenitsyn used the materials of history and personal experience to create novels of lasting merit, novels that explore the foibles of humanity and the resilience of the human spirit in the face of great adversity. Hence, any responsible study of his life is valuable as a document offering insight into one of the greatest creative minds of modern times.

What is especially valuable about Thomas's work is that he is able to look back retrospectively on Solzhenitsyn's career at a time when the Soviet Union, the evil empire against which he struggled for five decades, has disappeared. In *Alexander Solzhenitsyn: A Century in His Life*, Thomas is able to place Solzhenitsyn's personal struggles within the larger context of the internal campaign waged by a number of dissidents to topple the Communist government, which was built on a series of lies and a willful distortion of political and social realities. Because what Solzhenitsyn would characterize as the victory over Communism has been achieved, the measure of his accomplishments both as a novelist and a propagandist for change can be adequately measured. Thomas's biography is an important first step in that direction.

Laurence W. Mazzeno

Sources for Further Study

Booklist. XCIV, December 15, 1997, p. 666.
The Christian Century. CXV, June 17, 1998, p. 613.
Contemporary Review. CCLXXIII, August, 1998, p. 105.
The Economist. CCCXLVI, February 14, 1998, p. R14.
Library Journal. CXXIII, January, 1998, p. 101.
Maclean's. CXI, March 16, 1998, p. 60.
New Statesman. CXXVII, March 13, 1998, p. 52.
The New York Review of Books. XLV, December 3, 1998, p. 36.
The New York Times. CXLVII, March 13, 1998, p. 40.
The New York Times Book Review. CIII, March 1, 1998, p. 9.
Newsweek. CXXXI, February 16, 1998, p. 69.
Publishers Weekly. CCXLIV, December 1, 1997, p. 37.
The Washington Post Book World. XXVIII, March 1, 1998, p. 4.

ALL OF US
The Collected Poems

Author: Raymond Carver (1938-1988)
Edited by William L. Stull; introduction by Tess Gallagher
Published: Alfred A. Knopf (New York). 386 pp. $27.50
Type of work: Poetry

The poems of well-known fiction writer Raymond Carver show his trademark narrative techniques applied to a different genre

Raymond Carver is one of the twentieth century's most popular storytellers; fiction anthologies and literature textbooks nearly always feature samples of his work. "Where I'm Calling From" and "What We Talk About When We Talk About Love" have become as familiar to students as William Faulkner's "Barn Burning" and often more popular with them. Carver's stories use compressed, elliptical dialogue to telegraph intense emotions in psychologically persuasive, sympathetic characters. To read Carver's fiction is to feel powerfully in touch with the surface and depths of twentieth century life.

Carver's fiction was recognized immediately and received numerous awards during his life; he was nominated for the National Book Award for *Will You Please Be Quiet, Please* (1976), and for the Pulitzer Prize for the collection *What We Talk About When We Talk About Love* (1981). In 1988 he was inducted into the American Academy of Arts and Letters. Carver died in 1988 of cancer; his fiction has continued to gain recognition since his death. His combination of the casual and the violent, all presented in the precise idiom of the time and place, has won for him a permanent place in literature.

Carver is less well known as a poet, but he was publishing poetry as well as fiction over his writing years. However, his books of poetry were less well known and less widely and favorably reviewed. William L. Stull has collected them into a substantial volume, which in addition to the poems includes a preface; an introduction by his second wife, poet Tess Gallagher; and a number of appendices. The appendices include uncollected poems, Gallagher's introduction to *A New Path to the Waterfall* (1989), small-press sources of Carver's major books, a note on "In a Marine Light," bibliographical and textual notes, a life chronology, and a list of posthumous publications. These are followed by an index of titles and an index of first lines, providing almost one hundred pages of apparatus. Moreover, several sections are introduced by translations of foreign works, which highlight Carver's pet preoccupations and themes. The amount of supplementary materials underscores that this is a serious enterprise and perhaps suggests that Carver is as serious a poet as he is a fiction writer. Is this so?

Much of the poetry in *All of Us* was written relatively late in Carver's career. Although his first short books were poetry collections, the bulk of his poetry was published from 1985 on, and fewer than one hundred pages into this collection the reader finds himself in the company of a forty-five-year-old poet who has only five years left to live. From the beginning the poems are reminiscent and elegiac. Some of the work appeared posthumously in the collection *A New Path to the Waterfall*. Carver seems to have given up fiction in favor of poetry toward the end of his life, a choice some of his fans regret. However, his last work provides moving reflections on his coming death from cancer. These impressions could only have been presented as poems; the distancing structure of the short story would not have allowed such personal directness. Some of his earlier poems are on themes similar to Allen Ginsberg's and capture the essence of the 1960's. However, Carver never wrote high-energy, celebratory poems, even at his most optimistic. These are snows-of-yesteryear poems, sometimes wrenching, sometimes merely melancholy.

Generally, *All of Us* is a book that will spark arguments. It provides hundreds of brief narratives that can be seen as inconclusive short stories or as finished poems. Carver's life was tumultuous, involving divorce, two bankruptcies, alcoholism, and recovery; the peaks and valleys of his life form the basis for his fiction and poetry. In the short stories, the characters' looks, gestures, and laconic comments speak volumes. The longer speeches that characters may make as a last, desperate effort at communication or their soliloquies that follow their most painful epiphanies often lyrically present some impossible human dilemma without sentimentality.

The best of the poems create miniature stories or vignettes that reveal a bit of character and smile wryly at the ironies of contemporary life. Others attempt to do so, but without the support of a sustained narrative structure they fail to achieve the evocation of emotion Carver's spare, precise writing almost always accomplishes in fiction. Carver's poetry does not in general have the compactness of most contemporary poetry or of his fiction, and its meaning is much closer to the surface; when it does succeed, it does so as narrative. When it fails, it fails as narrative.

For example, readers who love the Carver short story "Where I'm Calling From" may not be very moved by the poem "The Phone Booth," in which there is so much less presented that the ironies of the little drama may seem too obvious. In "The Phone Booth," the speaker sees a couple in a phone booth weeping together, having just received some kind of terrible news. Then they separate, "she goes to lean against the fender/ of their sedan. And listens/ to him talk about arrangements." The speaker is waiting to use the booth and, witnessing this, he explains, "I don't have a phone at home, either." When his turn comes, the couple are back in their own car, but they, still sitting in the car talking, hear his bad news: "Before I can say two words, the phone/ begins to shout, 'I told you it's over! Finished! You can go/ to hell as far as I'm concerned!'" The weeping couple are for a moment startled out of their grief: ". . . their tears stilled/ for a moment in the face of this distraction." Then, after a brief pause, the couple and the speaker drive off:

> We
> don't go anywhere for a while.
> And then we go.

Despite the nice ending, the poem seems a sketch for a story. The reader may be interested in the ironies of contemporary life but not caught up by the characters. (The reader wonders if they could really hear that in the car. They have the windows rolled up.)

There is gold in the book, too. Some of the most intriguing poems celebrate Carver's imagined alter ego, Anton Chekhov, in whose life and works Carver saw parallels to his own. Like Chekhov's, Carver's family was poor. Like Chekhov's, his economic circumstances during childhood were painful, embarrassing, and unpredictable, and he created marvelous characters from the downtrodden, characters not quite able to understand or express their pain. Chekhov's stories were a major inspiration to him, and he reinvented the American short story in a Chekhovian vein. Chekhov is the subject of numerous poems and stories, many of which compare his world to Carver's. Other writers besides Chekhov are drawn into the poems, their characters and life events figuring in Carver's own life, and these more layered poems are among the most satisfying. "Kafka's Watch," a poem that claims to be "from a letter," catches the feeling of boredom and tedium that the German writer experienced in his job:

> I devour the time outside the office like a wild beast.
> Someday I hope to sit in a chair in another
> country, looking out the window at fields of sugarcane
> or Muhammadan cemeteries.
> I don't complain about the work so much as about
> the sluggishness of swampy time.

The speaker claims that one ends by ascribing "all that's happening/ to your watch alone." That it is Kafka's boredom both distances it and brings it closer.

The last poems are direct and moving; they provide the details of Carver's life with Tess Gallagher, his beloved companion and fellow writer whom he married when he knew he was going to die of recurrent cancer. They show him going through the stages of grief and arriving at an acceptance so translucent it could be confused with joy. These are poems of love and death, in which love finally outweighs death; the speaker, aware of his increasing limitation, expresses gratitude for his last years with his beloved and calls again on his spiritual father, Chekhov, whose work and life he continues to read as a gloss on his own. "Night Dampness," which is based on Chekhov's "Across Siberia," reads:

> I am sick and tired of the river, the stars
> that strew the sky, this heavy funereal silence.
> To while away the time, I talk to my coachman, who
> looks like an old man. . . . He tells me that this dark, forbidding river
> abounds in sterlet, white salmon, eel-pout, pike, but there is no one
> to catch the fish and no tackle to catch it with.

The last poems are heavily laced with Chekhov and others, and some present ordinary perceptions from a new perspective, that of the man about to die, intensely aware of his coming death and of every particular of his present life seen from that angle. Incidents become parables; nothing is allowed to pass without notice. In "For the Record" a story is recounted of "dozen of mares and stallions" that were "driven into a courtyard of the Vatican/ so the Pope Alexander VI and his daughter,/ Lucretia Borgia, could watch from a balcony/ 'with pleasure and much laughter'/ the equine coupling going on below." After this they watched Lucretia's brother shoot down ten unarmed criminals. "Remember this the next time you see/ the name *Borgia*, or the word *Renaissance*." The speaker decides to shelve the account, not knowing what to do with it exactly, and instead to go out for a walk, where he will

> . . . hope maybe
> to see those two herons sift down the cliffside
> as they did for us earlier in the season
> so we felt alone and freshly
> put here, not herded, not
> driven.

The last poem of the book, "Late Fragment," says directly what is more obliquely stated in some of the other poems:

> And did you get what
> you wanted from this life, even so?
> I did.
> And what did you want?
> To call myself beloved, to feel myself
> beloved on the earth.

All of Us: The Collected Poems will continue to enchant Carver fans; it is a verse account of his life. It provides unusual and striking insights into his experience. The poems are not poet's poems but are accessible to readers of fiction and biography who may not have much interest in contemporary poetry. Moreover, some of the characteristics that made Carver one of the foremost fiction writers of the second half of the twentieth century are visible in the poems. The earlier cozy, reminiscent hippie style poems, bringing back days of booze and disordered living arrangements and casting them in a melancholy glow, will appeal to other 1960's nostalgia buffs. This is highly personal poetry but without the embarrassment that mars so much confessional poetry. Carver's last poems show how he courageously confronted death and poignantly celebrated his final days with his fellow writer, lover, and, finally, wife.

Janet McCann

Sources for Further Study

Booklist. XCV, September 1, 1998, p. 58.
The Economist. CCCXLVIII, August 15, 1998, p. 72.
Library Journal. CXXIII, September 15, 1998, p. 83.
The New York Times Book Review. CIII, November 8, 1998, p. 22.
Publishers Weekly. CCXLV, July 27, 1998, p. 71.
San Francisco Chronicle. October 4, 1998, p. REV4.

THE ALL-TRUE TRAVELS AND ADVENTURES
OF LIDIE NEWTON

Author: Jane Smiley (1949-   )
Published: Alfred A. Knopf (New York). 452 pp. $26.00
Type of work: Novel
Time: The mid-1850's
Locale: Illinois, the Kansas Territory, and Missouri

Newlywed Lidie Newton experiences a turbulent year in the violent Kansas Territory during the decade before the American Civil War

Principal characters:
> LYDIA (LIDIE) HARKNESS NEWTON, the narrator and central character, who marries an abolitionist and accompanies him to Lawrence, Kansas, a center of antislavery activity
> THOMAS NEWTON, Lidie's husband, a native of Massachusetts, who migrates to the Kansas Territory to take part in the agitation to permit Kansas to enter the Union as a slave-free state
> FRANK BRERETON, Lidie's nephew, a clever rascal
> CHARLES BISKET, Thomas Newton's partner in a hauling business
> LOUISA BISKET, Charles's wife and Lidie's best friend in Lawrence
> RICHARD DAY, a Missouri slaveholder and farmer, who provides shelter for Lidie
> HELEN DAY, Richard's daughter, who befriends Lidie
> LORNA, a slave in Day's house
> DAVID R. GRAVES, an itinerant merchant who appears at several crucial points in Lidie's life

Jane Smiley is among the most versatile of modern novelists. Her early novels focused on relationships within families; one of them had the structure of a mystery novel. The works for which she has received high praise have been more varied as to subject matter. *The Greenlanders* (1988) is a mythic study of ancient Vikings. *A Thousand Acres* (1991) uses the plot of William Shakespeare's *King Lear* to investigate a contemporary midwestern farm family. *Moo* (1995) is a long and hilarious satire of life at a huge midwestern university. *The All-True Travels and Adventures of Lidie Newton* is unlike any of its predecessors, an episodic, realistic historical novel about the controversy over slavery in the years before the Civil War. This is new territory for Smiley, but she clearly feels at home in it.

Lidie Harkness is the youngest of six daughters of an unsuccessful businessman in Quincy, Illinois. At the age of twenty she is tall, strong, and plain (another character calls her ugly), and her married sisters despair of her ever finding a husband who would relieve them of the sisterly obligation to provide her with a home and enough housework to keep her occupied. Lidie is adept at avoiding work and prefers to spend her time reading or partaking of such exercises as riding horseback astride or swimming across the Mississippi River, an adventure in which she is abetted by her scapegrace nephew Frank, an amazingly mature twelve-year-old.

Her life changes drastically when Thomas Newton visits a friend in Quincy on his way to settling in the Kansas Territory. After a brief courtship, promoted by one sister, Lidie marries the quiet man who is several years older than she. He has worked in his father's sail-making factory in a suburb of Boston and spent several years at sea. Now he is headed for Lawrence, a "free state" town in Kansas, where he plans to homestead and to work with those opposed to allowing slavery in Kansas when it achieves statehood. He is sponsored by the Massachusetts Emigrant Aid Society. As part of his luggage he has a box containing twelve Sharps rifles, to be used by the abolitionists in the increasingly violent struggle with the proslavery faction. Thomas is a thoughtful man and he would prefer to see the dispute settled by nonviolent means, but he feels the antislavery faction must defend itself. His illicit cargo goes undetected as they make their way down the Mississippi to St. Louis and then up the Missouri to the brawling frontier town of Kansas City. The last stage of the journey to Lawrence takes place in the wagon of an itinerant teamster named David R. Graves, who is to turn up at crucial points in Lidie's life on the frontier. It is Graves who informs Lidie and Thomas that the slavery controversy is known as the goose question; to be "sound on the goose" is to be proslavery.

A claim has been staked in Newton's name, and the new friends the newlyweds make provide shelter for them in town and help Thomas to construct a rough cabin on his land. The early days of the couple's Kansas experience are relatively benign, as they adapt to each other and to a land that has its attractions but is far from the Eden of the advertisements. However, violence is never very far away as Missourians cross into the Kansas Territory with impunity to vote in Kansas elections and to harass the antislavery settlers. The violence does not all originate with one side. John Brown, whose later raid on the armory at Harpers Ferry, Virginia, was an attempt to provoke a revolution that would end slavery in the United States, was at the time of the novel active in this area in raids on slaveholders, and he is referred to as "Old Brown." His bloody raid on Osawatomie is one of the historical events alluded to in the novel.

Disillusionment sets in quickly for Lidie. The broiling Kansas summer is no help to the Newtons' efforts to adapt to their new surroundings. As the year turns toward winter, they are forced by the cold to move to town and to occupy a room in the small house of their friends Charles and Louisa Bisket. Thomas supports them by going into the hauling business with Charles Bisket. Lidie's nephew Frank turns up carrying a letter to Lidie from his mother, pleading with her to look after him, but Frank quickly proves to be thoroughly capable of looking after himself. He becomes a successful trader and a familiar sight around Lawrence, a cigar stub perpetually in the corner of his mouth. He soon falls in with a group of teen-age boys rumored to be active in raiding proslavery settlers.

The first half of the novel comes to a sudden end. With the coming of spring the Newtons plant a crop and begin the move back to their land and cabin. On one of their trips from town they are stopped by three armed Missourians, two men and a boy. When Thomas Newton asks what they want, he is shot twice and mortally wounded. To add to Lidie's grief, her beloved horse is also shot and killed. In her rage she can think only of vengeance and determines to go into Missouri to find and kill the men who killed Thomas. She leaves her friends in Lawrence, rides again in the wagon of David R. Graves, and heads for St. Louis and then up the Missouri to the newer, more primitive community of Kansas City.

Since she is large for a woman, with large hands and a plain face, she manages to disguise herself as a boy and use what remains of her money to frequent saloons searching for clues to the identity of the men who killed Thomas. Before long she hears about some men who have been in one of the taverns, boasting of having killed an abolitionist, and she learns their names. She then goes on a trek though Missouri, heading for Independence, walking most of the way to avoid curious inhabitants.

Lidie eventually collapses from exhaustion and hunger on the lawn of the plantation of Richard Day, called Day's End, where she is discovered by Lorna, a slave woman, and Helen, Day's young daughter. Lorna is not fooled by the disguise, in part because she finds that Lidie has had a miscarriage. Lidie has evidently been unaware of her condition, since she has never mentioned it before. The two women care for Lidie until Richard Day returns from a trip. Day, like his daughter and their slave, accepts Lidie's story that she is a poor widow looking for relatives. Over the course of a few days, while Lidie receives tender care from Helen and Lorna, Day falls in love with her and asks her to marry him.

In the meantime, Lidie learns that the men she has been seeking in the hope of avenging Thomas are acquaintances of Richard Day and sometimes visit Day's End. When they arrive with a group of other men she takes the pistol she has kept hidden in her meager luggage and prepares to kill them during dinner, accepting the certainty that she will be killed by the other men present. When she meets the men, however, she realizes that she cannot be certain of their identities, and she keeps the pistol hidden. Her reluctance is due in part to the kindness she has received from Richard and his daughter, convincing her that defenders of slavery may not always be vicious and hateful.

To avoid the necessity of responding to Richard Day's proposal, Lidie decides to leave secretly. Lorna, however, has recognized her in the meantime, having been hidden near Quincy after an earlier abortive attempt to escape slavery and having seen Lidie and Frank at the time. She threatens to expose Lidie unless Lidie agrees to take her along, masquerading as Lidie's slave.

The two women make their way to Kansas City, planning to take passage on a boat that will enable them to get to St. Louis and then up the Mississippi to free territory. They board a boat but are seen and recognized by the ubiquitous David R. Graves. Taken prisoner, Lidie is jailed and Lorna is returned to Day's End, from where she is sold down the river to harsher masters in Louisiana. Lidie is released when Richard Day improbably pays her fine. She returns to Quincy, and at the end of the novel makes a trip to Massachusetts to visit Thomas's family. While there she delivers a speech to a meeting of abolitionists about her experiences; it is not a success.

Some reviewers have not been kind to *The All-True Travels and Adventures of Lidie Newton*, largely because Smiley had earlier attacked Mark Twain's *Adventures of*

Huckleberry Finn (1884), which, she argued, provided an unrealistic picture of slavery and implicitly apologized for slavery in its portrayal of the relationship between Huck and the slave Jim. Smiley's novel has been seen as a generally misguided attempt to present a more accurate portrayal of the reality of slavery. The final section, dealing with the journey of Lidie and Lorna and ending with Lorna's capture and punishment, is clearly meant as a corrective to the final part of Twain's novel. At the same time there are other minor resemblances between the two works, including the attempt on the part of the central character to masquerade as a person of the opposite sex.

The weakest part of Smiley's novel is the final section, dealing with Lidie's attempt to assist a slave to reach freedom. The final section of *Adventures of Huckleberry Finn* has frequently been cited as the least believable and most foolish part of Mark Twain's novel, and it is ironic that the last section of *The All-True Travels and Adventures of Lidie Newton* should be the weak part of her book. The contradictory elements of the personality of Richard Day do not help.

There are other problems of less magnitude with Smiley's novel, including a flat prose style that fails to reflect the quirkiness and individuality of Lidie's personality; the absence of any mention of the sexual side of her marriage to Thomas Newton or of any suggestion that she even knows what sex is or what pregnancy entails, making her miscarriage a total surprise; and the disappearance of Frank Brereton from the novel after Thomas is killed, except for a brief mention at the end. Nevertheless, the novel is powerful in its evocation of the dangerous quality of life on the frontier and in the development of the singular personality of its central figure. If it is not Smiley's finest work, it is still a genuine achievement.

John M. Muste

Sources for Further Study

Booklist. XCIV, February 15, 1998, p. 949.
Christian Science Monitor. April 30, 1998, p. B2.
Library Journal. CXXIII, April 1, 1998, p. 125.
Los Angeles Times Book Review. April 5, 1998, p. 4.
Mademoiselle. CIV, May, 1998, p. 166.
The New York Times Book Review. CIII, April 5, 1998, p. 10.
The New Yorker. LXXIV, April 6, 1998, p. 104.
Publishers Weekly. CCXLV, February 2, 1998, p. 80.
Time. CLI, March 2, 1998, p. 77.
The Times Literary Supplement. September 25, 1998, p. 22.
The Washington Post Book World. XXVIII, April 12, 1998, p. 5.
Women's Review of Books. XV, July, 1998, p. 28.

ALWAYS IN PURSUIT
Fresh American Perspectives, 1995-1997

Author: Stanley Crouch (1945-   )
Published: Pantheon Books (New York). 321 pp. $25.
Type of work: Essays

A thoughtful essayist who made his reputation as a jazz writer surveys the American scene, particularly those aspects that have to do with race and African American life

For years the *New York Daily News*, which publishes a regular column by Stanley Crouch in which many of the essays included in *Always in Pursuit* first appeared, published a sports column by the crusty, cranky sportswriter Dick Young titled "Young Ideas." The title was something of a joke: Although Young had indeed been on the cutting edge of sports journalism at one time in his career, by the time he became a *Daily News* columnist, he had already calcified into a cranky version of himself, and the misnomer that attempted to hide this fact inevitably called attention to the emptiness of his bombast. In adding the subtitle, *Fresh American Perspectives*, to his new collection of essays, *Always in Pursuit*, Stanley Crouch risks making a similar mockery of himself if the reader does not happen to find his perspectives fresh. In fact, some of them do live up to the billing of "fresh" but, occasionally, only because they express ideas that have been around long enough that there are no longer many people expressing them. Yet whether or not his perspectives are "fresh," they are definitely his own, and he will certainly argue them with anyone willing to listen.

At his core Crouch seems to be an old-fashioned Great Society Democrat—old-fashioned in that he represents a point of view that predates the time when this point of view became the center and members of the party stood either to the right or left. For him the Great Society goals of equal opportunity, fair employment, and equal access to quality education for African Americans and whites alike are worthy goals still to be pursued, and if he is not exactly thrilled with the way that either affirmative action or welfare has been implemented, he knows quite well that there is much racial inequity still to be addressed. He is old-fashioned in that he rejects out of hand anything that smacks of cultural relativism and believes that there are indeed a core set of cultural values that are worth implementing, most of which in fact spring from Western tradition. He is old-fashioned in that, at a time when it is more common to express a belief in democracy than to believe in democracy, his understanding of American culture springs from a deep belief in American democracy.

Stanley Crouch made his reputation as a writer about jazz, and jazz and blues tempos are the key to his writing. For example, because he knows that the newspaper column is not a form that holds up well in book form, to inject some new life into his essays he loosely sews together a number of recycled columns to, as he says, "create something akin to a musical set presented by a jazz band." This is not a bad idea, as it turns out, and it makes the familiarity of the Tupac Shakur, Susan Smith, and Texaco race-discrimination cases about which he writes seem like the familiarity of old standards. The question the reader as listener is concerned with is, What is he going to do with this?

Stanley Crouch takes his intellectual bearings from Ralph Ellison and Albert Murray (perhaps the most influential of jazz writers), and he shares with these mentors a passion for Duke Ellington, whom he recognizes as the most complete of jazz artists. This is territory Murray covered in *The Hero and the Blues*, but Crouch replaces Murray's essentially academic tone with a more popular one. Crouch is more a jazz lover than a jazz gourmand, and he can assume his hero's canonicity in a way that Murray could not twenty years earlier; his task in writing about Ellington is more like that of an English teacher who tries to explain why William Faulkner is still fresh, not so much that of an academic critic who tries to show why Faulkner is great.

What Crouch adds to Murray's extensive writings on Duke Ellington is an appreciation of Ellington as a businessman, an essential characteristic of Ellington's unequaled fifty-year success in a field, popular music, in which most acts fizzle and burn out before their third recording. If this appreciation for Ellington's success is an important contribution to the discourse on Ellington, Crouch's general respect for success as success at times gets him into trouble. For example, he writes a paean to the late secretary of commerce Ron Brown that amounts to saying that because Brown was successful, he should be respected. Perhaps in some circles, but it should also be pointed out that if Ron Brown became an image of political craftsmanship, he also became an image of the political opportunist who finds ways to cozy up to big money.

Similarly, Crouch's rehashing of the O. J. Simpson trial proves to be fresh only in the author's willingness to judge the principals mainly on the basis of their success. Johnnie Cochran gets a thumbs up for winning the trial; Christopher Darden gets a thumbs down for losing it. Simpson emerges as a mixture: thumbs up for being O. J. Simpson, thumbs down for being illiterate and insipid. It may not be Crouch's fault that this material has been so thoroughly raked over that it is hard to find anything new worth saying, but it is his responsibility for putting what did not need saying between the covers of a book.

Perhaps the centerpiece of the book is his extended critical essay on Albert Murray. Although *Train Whistle Guitar* (1974) is one of the great African American novels and among the best American works to appear in the 1970's, it has not received the attention it deserves, in part because Murray, unlike other novelists, has never particularly focused his writing talents on fiction, instead spreading his efforts among autobiography, criticism, and fiction. He has not developed a "brand name" as a writer. Crouch's essay is clearly an attempt to address the critical neglect that Murray has suffered, and it is a thoughtful, sensitive essay. Among his nonfictional writings, Murray's *Stomping the Blues* (1970), *The Hero and the Blues* (1973), and *The Omni-Americans* (1970) all emerge as great efforts—insightful, essential commentaries on African American (Crouch would say "Negro") life and culture. Yet what about Murray's other writings? Murray's 1971 book of travels through the South, *South to a Very Old Place*, is a fascinating return to the South after most of the great civil rights battles, but it is not a great book in his estimation. The decade Murray spent collaborating with Count

Basie on Basie's 1985 autobiography, *Good Morning Blues*, was largely wasted effort. Similarly, although Crouch recognizes *Train Whistle Guitar* as the masterpiece it is, he also recognizes that its sequels, *The Spyglass Tree* (1991) and *The Seven-League Boots* (1995), interesting works of art though they are, do not test their hero, Scooter, nearly enough to let the character emerge as a figure about whom readers can care deeply. Such a warts-and-all appreciation of Murray's accomplishments as a writer is necessary for allowing his work to find the audience it deserves.

Anyone who is interested in reading Crouch's in-a-nutshell opinions on World War II, slavery in contemporary Africa, and the American involvement in Haiti will find them expressed in a collection of recycled columns titled "Foreign Intrigue." The book, however, would have profited from their removal. One can understand a working writer's attempt to collect two paychecks from one piece of writing, but it is hard to understand why a reader would want to support this. It is not that Crouch's opinions are unworthy or that his topics are unimportant. Quite the contrary. The subjects about which he writes and what he has to say are so important that it is unconscionable for him to leave it in a fragmented, half-defined form. Tearing off nine pithy, well-constructed paragraphs about the shamefully overlooked issue of slavery in contemporary Africa may be good work for a *Daily News* columnist who wants to bring this issue to light, but reprinting that column in essentially the same form is lazy for a writer of books. If he really cares about his topics, why not use the opinions and ideas expressed in the shorter columns as the starting place for a more complete meditation on these issues? Presenting them again in their present form gives the impression that Crouch is not so much a man who cares deeply about the world as one who cares deeply about the sound of his own opinions. The ability to be pugnacious and go several rounds with all comers is a great asset for any columnist, and this Crouch has. The less flashy ability to stop being pugnacious while in no way compromising the integrity of one's beliefs is more valuable, however, and Crouch's not inconsiderable ability to consider a problem at great length is the one around which he needs to build his books.

The great strength of Crouch's book is that he clearly relishes his self-appointed role as critic at large of the American scene. How else to account for his extended appreciation of John Ford, which compares the great film director to Louis Armstrong and Duke Ellington and makes the comparison work? Being in love with the sound of one's own opinions is not the worst sin a writer can commit, and in Crouch it can be downright charming, especially when he warns the reader that he is working on "a doozy of a conclusion" for the book's end. Indeed, it is a doozy of a conclusion, in part because it articulates in clear terms his understanding of the unconscionable manipulations of the concept of race by so many, from the abolitionists of the nineteenth century to Pat Buchanan and Louis Farrakhan. For Crouch, a believer in the American cultural melting pot, the obsolete concept of "race" will have to be abandoned, but it is going to take time. "VICTORY IS ASSURED," he promises the reader in his introduction, but it will take a willing spirit of jazz-blues improvisation to find this future victory. If it is unlikely that any reader will not find something to object to in what Crouch has to say, no reader should miss the importance of this hopeful, patient vision.

Stanley Crouch's *Always in Pursuit* reminds readers of the diversity of opinion among African American writers. Although his ideas will not seem as fresh to people who have followed his career through *Notes of a Hanging Judge* (1990) and *The All-American Skin Game* (1995), as in those earlier works Crouch brings to the discussion of the American scene (particularly issues of race consciousness) opinions that are not easily typified as "left" or "right" and which are presented in an amiably confrontational manner that is sure to provoke thought.

Thomas Cassidy

Sources for Further Study

Booklist. XCIV, December 1, 1997, p. 586.
Emerge. IX, April, 1998, p. 68.
Kirkus Reviews. LXV, December 1, 1997, p. 1749.
The New York Times Book Review. CIII, February 8, 1998, p. 12.
Publishers Weekly. CCXLIV, November 24, 1997, p. 58.
The Village Voice. March 17, 1998, p. 124.
The Virginia Quarterly Review. LXXIV, Summer, 1998, p. 426.

AMAZING GRACE
A Vocabulary of Faith

Author: Kathleen Norris (1947-   )
Published: Riverhead Books (New York). 384 pp. $24.95
Type of work: Religion; autobiography; essays
Time: The 1990's
Locale: The United States

A compilation of short essays on the special vocabulary used in religion (salvation, grace, evangelism), showing how these words gradually have become meaningful to the author in her quest for a mature faith in God

Kathleen Norris has written three books about her personal journey of faith. *Dakota: A Spiritual Geography* (1992) described her move from New York City to a small town in South Dakota, where she began to rediscover her religious roots by attending her grandmother's church.

While trying to deal with a personal crisis, Norris went on a retreat to a Benedictine monastery in Minnesota. After several periods of residency there, she described the experience of living in a community of monks and nuns in *The Cloister Walk* (1996, paperback edition 1997). This book received highly favorable reviews from literary critics and was on *The New York Times* best-seller list for four months.

Amazing Grace: A Vocabulary of Faith is Norris's third book in this series. It contains some eighty short essays, meditations, anecdotes, and historical vignettes. She believes that words such as "salvation," "grace," "evangelism," and "Trinity" can be stumbling blocks for people when they attend a church service. She wants to share her personal insights into the sometimes forbidding vocabulary of religion.

Several essays in *Amazing Grace* are entitled "Conversion," describing various stages in Norris's growing sense of belonging within a church community. Conversion for her is not a single event but a lifelong journey. A similar theme is found in the book by former president Jimmy Carter *Living Faith* (1996). Both Carter and Norris are frank in admitting to times of doubt and uncertainty in their religious quest. They do not claim to have all the answers, so the reader can identify with them as struggling human beings.

One of the essays in *Amazing Grace* is entitled "Bible." Before looking at what Norris says about it, readers might think through for themselves what is likely to be discussed in such an article. Could it be on evolution versus creationism? Would it tell about the discovery of the Dead Sea Scrolls? Is it about a literal versus symbolic interpretation of biblical miracles? Norris bypasses such intellectual matters. Instead she relates a conversation with an elderly man who had been given a leather-bound Bible by his grandfather as a wedding present. The Bible was put on a shelf, unread for many years. Eventually the man developed cancer, started reading the Bible, and was amazed to find that his grandfather had placed a twenty-dollar bill at the beginning of every book from Genesis to Revelation, totaling more than thirteen hundred dollars.

The impact of Norris's anecdote is a reminder that people too seldom take time for Bible reading and meditation.

For some Christians the concept of Trinity (Father, Son, and Holy Spirit) can be a stumbling block. How can there be "one God in three persons"? Norris provides a helpful, picturesque metaphor from the early days of the church, "an image of the Trinity as a plant, with the Father as a deep root, the Son as the shoot that breaks forth into the world, the Spirit as that which spreads beauty and fragrance." Such a poetic interpretation of the Trinity is more significant to Norris than an intellectual explanation.

In the essay "Creeds," Norris reveals her mental reservations about this aspect of communal worship. She says, "In working my way back to church, I found that even when the hymns, scripture texts, and sermons served to welcome me, the Creed that we recited each week often seemed a barrier, reminding me that I was still struggling with the feeling that I did not belong. . . . [The creeds] can seem like a grocery list of beliefs that one has to comprehend and assent to fully before one dare show one's face in church." Eventually she resolves this difficulty by viewing the creeds as a form of speaking in tongues, in which the literal meaning of the words is less important than their devotional content.

What images does a Pentecostal church bring to mind for the reader? Enthusiastic singing, uplifted arms, "Amen" responses during the sermon, personal testimonies. Norris is saddened by sectarian differences that have created an unfortunate schism between Pentecostals and the mainstream Protestant churches. The latter tend to view Pentecostals as anti-intellectual in theology and overemotional in worship, while many Pentecostals are conservative Christians who have low regard for their more liberal brethren. Norris reminds her readers of the original meaning of Pentecost, as described in the Book of Acts, when tongues of fire came down from heaven and people began to speak in many languages. She has a vision that Christian unity can be restored when people recognize the great variety of gifts that are all a part of ministry. Someone may have a special talent for preaching, for teaching, for healing the sick, for showing compassion, for writing, or for music. The significance of Pentecost for Norris is "each of us speaking in the language we know, and being understood."

In her essay "Prayer," Norris rejects the style of praying for a specific outcome, such as a miracle cure for an illness or success in a business venture. From a friend who is confined to a wheelchair, she has learned that "prayer is not asking for what you think you want but asking to be changed in ways you can't imagine." When a prayer is answered, it is never answered in the way that one expected. Prayer is "a dialog with God," asking for spiritual direction and God's mercy.

Norris has found that "Evangelism" can be a scary word, even to longtime, loyal church members. It carries an unfortunate image of someone haranguing people on a street corner quoting from the Bible, trying to win souls for the Lord. Norris gives examples of evangelistic language that can alienate a listener: "Are you washed in the blood of the Lamb?" "Are you saved?" "Do you know the Lord?" As a published author on the subject of religion, Norris sometimes is asked to speak at pastors' conferences or to preach in church. One Sunday morning her sermon topic was evangelism: How can people witness to their faith? Speaking from personal experience, she expressed her gratitude to the local congregation for not pressuring her to join the church until she was ready. She was thankful for the people who had made her feel welcome. They showed their Christian evangelism in actions rather than words, leading her to make a decision to become a part of this community of faith. At the conclusion of the church service Norris had a delightful conversation with a young woman who was attempting to find her way back to the church. By sharing some of the steps in her own journey of faith, she was able to help the woman to see the way ahead more clearly. Afterward, Norris was amazed at herself for having fulfilled the role of "evangelist."

In the chapter "Faith," Norris starts out from her personal experience. She says,

Faith is still a surprise to me, as I lived without it for so long. Now I believe that it was merely dormant in the years I was not conscious of its presence. And I have become better at trusting that it is there, even when I can't feel it, or when God seems absent from the world. No small part of my religious conversion has been coming to know that faith is best thought of as a verb, not a "thing" that you either have or you don't.

Norris recognizes that things can happen to shake one's faith in God. She tells about a woman in a Nazi concentration camp who lost her faith, but only for a while. Eventually the woman realized that God was with her even during the time of suffering. Norris describes faith poetically as a fluid that ebbs and flows, "sometimes strongly evident and at other times barely discernible."

As a necessary step in developing a mature faith, Norris had to evaluate the religious heritage received from her family. Her father's parents both were "born again" Christians who had accepted Jesus at a revival meeting when they stepped forward during the altar call. The grandmother believed that a Christian is someone who can name the date and time when they were "saved." The grandfather became a pastor who "never lost his revivalist fervor." On her mother's side, the grandfather was a small-town doctor who is described as a religious man but not a churchgoer. The maternal grandmother was the primary influence for Norris's Christian growth. For sixty years this woman had been married to one man, lived in the same house, attended the same church. Hers was not a dramatic conversion experience but a lifetime commitment to being a good neighbor. Norris greatly admired the "quiet piety" of her grandmother as well as her intimate familiarity with the Bible.

The essay entitled "Belief, Doubt, and Sacred Ambiguity" contains some ideas that may be difficult for readers to accept. Norris describes a discussion between a seminary student and a priest. The student asks what he can do if he is unable to believe some parts of the creed, such as the Virgin Birth. The priest answers him: "'You just say it. . . . You just keep saying it. . . . Eventually it may come to you. For some, it takes longer than for others. . . .'" After this discussion was published in a religious magazine, one letter to the editor compared the priest's advice to saying "the earth is flat" over and over again. Other respondents said that such mindless repetition implies people should not think for themselves. Norris responds with her personal testimony:

> I feel blessed to know from experience that it is in the act of worship, the act of saying and repeating
> the vocabulary of faith, that one can come to claim it as "ours." It is in acts of repetition that seem
> senseless to the rational mind that belief comes, doubts are put to rest, religious conversion takes
> hold, and one feels at home in a community of faith.

Norris describes the long secular period of her life in college and in New York with self-critical frankness: "For years I had drifted through life, more or less aimlessly, with little in the way of religious moorings, little sense of connection or commitment to other people." After her grandmother died, she decided to move into the now vacant house, leaving New York for a town of sixteen hundred people. It was there that she rediscovered the importance of belonging to a Christian community. In *Amazing Grace* she shares her journey of faith with other seekers.

Norris is a person with an inquiring mind. She writes with originality and imagination, leading the reader along unexpected paths. The first two books about her journey of faith established Norris as a writer who is open to a diversity of religious experiences. In *Amazing Grace* she takes the jargon of religion and explains how it gradually has become meaningful to her.

For some twenty years Norris lived a secular lifestyle as a writer and poet, with no need or desire to be connected with the church. Now she has returned to her religious heritage, but with a newfound, mature understanding. Her special ministry seems to be to help people who are trying to find their way back to a closer relationship with God. Her story will be of particular interest to seminary students, pastors, and adult Sunday school classes and can help to stimulate an open discussion of sensitive topics among people with diverse religious backgrounds. Her theological reflections will appeal to many readers because they are based not on abstract, theological arguments but on genuine experiences of religious insight in everyday living.

Hans G. Graetzer

Sources for Further Study

America. CLXXIX, August 1, 1998, p. 24.
Booklist. XCIV, February 1, 1998, p. 875.
Chicago Tribune. XIV, July 5, 1998, p. 2.
The Christian Century. CXV, June 3, 1998, p. 584.
Elle. March, 1998, p. 152.
The New York Times Book Review. CIII, April 5, 1998, p. 19.
Publishers Weekly. CCXLV, February 9, 1998, p. 92.
San Francisco Chronicle. March 29, 1998, p. REV5.
The Times Literary Supplement. August 14, 1998, p. 32.
Women's Review of Books. XVI, October, 1998, p. 17.

THE AMERICAN WAY OF DEATH REVISITED

Author: Jessica Mitford (1917-1996)
Published: Alfred A. Knopf (New York). 296 pp. $25.00
Type of work: Current affairs

The funeral industry's expensive orchestration of the death of the American citizen was first critiqued by Jessica Mitford in 1963; this updated version extends the battle to engage the newer forms of industry practice that, in the author's opinion, exploit and victimize the public

Since Jessica Mitford took on the funeral industry more than thirty-five years ago in her ground-excavating exposé *The American Way of Death*, the trappings surrounding dying in America have changed very little. The cost, however, padded by industry-initiated advancements, has increased dramatically. *The American Way of Death Revisited* reopens the casket of Mitford's concerns about the practices of the inevitable industry, especially its promotion of costly additions to the ceremonies of death and what the author sees as less-than-ethical marketing techniques. The exposed body, ill-preserved, lets out a mighty stench. The jacket cover of the current edition promises a "brilliant piece of satirical writing." Despite this claim, the interior product is good but does not quite reach the level of brilliance.

Mitford first exposed the travesties of the "American way of death" in 1963. The earlier book—perhaps the first to tackle such a difficult topic so inclusively—enjoyed sufficient popularity that it was republished about fifteen years later. In the 1998 edition Mitford remembers, with not a little glee, that publishers originally shied away from her work as unsalable. Who would pay to read about the funeral industry? The current revision not only updates the statistical material of the original but also adds chapters on developments in the industry since the first book was published. Mitford documents the increase in the cost of cremations and other peripheral services and the advancement of consumer protection laws to aid those faced with the unpleasant task of providing for the dead. Americans can prepay their funerals and live to regret the investment ("Pay Now—Die Poorer"). In arranging a funeral, those for whom death occurs in the late twentieth century have little choice but to deal with large multinational funeral conglomerates rather than cede the bodies and final rituals of their loved ones to a local and likely well-known family friend ("A Global Village of the Dead"). Although the consolidation of multiple small companies into a few giants is not unique to the funeral industry—one could cite the health care conglomerates and the increasingly fat book behemoths—the impact on vulnerable mourners seems more problematic. As an old African proverb states: When elephants fight, the grass suffers. In this case, those who must deal with the final disposition of loved ones have little choice but to deal with the elephants. The fight for the field is over. And the cost of the grass upon which the elephants now rest becomes dearer all the time.

In Mitford's view the funeral industry is concerned with monetary gain rather than the alleviation of grief. In the late twentieth century it was not uncommon for a family to pay as much as $8,000 or $9,000 for a funeral. Often these prices are for full-package funerals that include add-ons that the family neither wants nor needs. The "tour guides" of the industry, the funeral directors, lead their parties through the foreign world of ever-increasing functions to the souvenir shop of the dead. Since you will never pass this way again, it is imperative that you go in style.

As Mitford notes, "Gradually, almost imperceptibly, over the years the funeral men have constructed their own grotesque cloud-cuckoo-land where the trappings of Gracious Living are transformed, as in a nightmare, into the trappings of Gracious Dying." Dying in America has taken on all the expensive accessories of living in consumer America: high-quality "housing" in the form of caskets, fine fabrics to drape the deceased, the best cosmetology to bring a blush of life to the cheeks. American culture's denial of death reaches its summit, its finest hour, in the marvelous production of the funeral and its accompaniments, which exquisitely perpetuate the myth that dying can capture and preserve (might we say "embalm"?) the best of living. Mitford's documentation of these developments is as humorous as it is horrific. Making use of what she calls "keeping up with Joneses to the end," Americans can go out in style with hostess gowns or negligees, Fit-a-Fut Oxfords (for feet afflicted with rigor mortis) or comfy slippers (lest the trip to the afterworld be hard on the feet). Glamour extends to the beautification of the body itself, injected and painted, arranged and delivered to the decorated stage of the macabre for its final performance—looking better, perhaps, than it did in life.

Services from embalming, which Mitford documents as unnecessary and not required by law (as some funeral directors wrongly tell clients), to element-proof coffins, which do little for the deceased, proliferate to pump up the costs of burial. Whether any or all of these extras are necessary or even desirable is the subject of Mitford's exploration. By embalming all we do is protect the grieving from the diseases that the dead do not have; by sealing the loved one hermetically we guarantee that only the finest anaerobic bacteria will dine on the remains. Playing on the sensitivity of people at such a time, casket makers reserve the most unattractive of presentations for the caskets of lowest cost. The uglification of the notorious plain pine box has itself taken on an art form. To bury or even to burn mom or dad in such a hideous container is meant to imply that the relatives do not care about the dead. The family could, of course, choose the "Expressions" casket, which allows the mourners to write a final message to the deceased on the lid of his or her final home. Mitford pulls no punches in her indictment of such practices and possibilities. She wields a fistful of humor, however, poking fun at the seriousness of the subject. While the most exploitative examples of such practices have, since the original book was written, been officially proscribed by law, many of them still go on.

It was more than six times as expensive to die in 1998 (average cost: $4,700) as in 1961 (average cost: $750). Are Americans dying better at the close of the millennium than at midcentury? Mitford supports with evidence her conclusion that they are not. She describes not only the rising costs of traditional funerals but also some legally and ethically dubious practices connected with prepayments. Those who sell funerals are sometimes little better than the bait-and-switch con artists at the local used-car lot.

One's "free" grave may wash away long before it can be used or it may become an expensive one as the years progress.

Mitford is not easy on the industry as she caricatures its selling techniques. Although one of her better and funny holdovers from the first edition, the chapter that documents sales techniques does little to praise those who deal in death. In her discussion of the sales approaches suggested to funeral directors, there is a delightful comment about the funeral as a onetime purchase, unless there occurs the "rare but rewarding" instance of disinterments.

Mitford's practical aim is to offer alternatives in the form of low-cost funeral societies to bereaved families. How important and threatening these alternatives are to the established funeral industry is demonstrated in their characterizations of such groups as "the burial beatniks of contemporary America." Mitford herself, asked to speak on occasion to those within the industry, was not appreciated for her critique.

A comparison of the funeral practices of America with those of England is interesting. It is clear that not all modern societies are bound by the paraphernalia of the United States. English funerals generally offer limited viewing of bodies to family members, deemphasize expensive caskets and floral arrangements, and do not charge for embalming. The lucrative practices of America, however, are—like a kind of reverse migration of the European rat—beginning to float east to infect the first world.

Those faced with providing for the newly dead will find useful the index and a "Directory of Not-for-Profit Funeral and Memorial Services." The latter lists such groups by state, with full address and phone number. For those who wish to avoid the costly and coercive practices documented in the text, this is an invaluable resource. One assumes that Mitford herself, who died before the book was complete, had the last chuckle of triumph over the tyranny of the death industry. Perhaps her final "research" was more personal than public.

Overall, *The American Way of Death Revisited* holds the reader's interest and provides substantial information to make the author's point. Sometimes, however, one suspects that since the 1960's things may have improved in the industry more than Mitford is willing to concede and that she may be simply grinding an old ax. It is not always clear, for example, which chapters are totally new, which chapters have minor and perhaps only statistical revisions, and which have been imported in exactly the form in which they were written for the previous version. Quotations from articles in the 1950's and 1960's tend to make the reader a bit uneasy about whether the proper homework has been done to update the new edition. For the most part, however, Mitford balances her sharp critique with sufficient humor so that the reader is, in the end, won over to her perspective.

Mitford's newest offering should provide an excellent source for those facing the grim realities and decisions about the ceremonies surrounding death. Evidenced by the popularity of her earlier work and the urgent if macabre reality that the baby boom will provide an ever-increasing number of sales opportunities for the funeral industry, this book should attain the popularity and sales of its predecessor. The author has not only provided facts and figures to expose the problematic practices surrounding death, but she has also offered some suggestions for practical, dignified, and low-cost alternatives to what has continued to be the rule in the American way of death. This book may give its readers, as Mitford suggests, "the wit and gumption" to shop around until they find the sensible and reasonable funeral they wish. Since the original version of the book, laws aimed at consumer protection have been put into effect. It will be interesting to see what impact this new book has on both the effectiveness and the enhancement of these laws. Although Mitford herself did not live to see the publication of this revised work, it is likely that the work itself will have a long and productive life.

Dolores L. Christie

Sources for Further Study

The Atlantic. CCLXXXII, September, 1998, p. 24.
Business Week. September 21, 1998, p. 18B.
The Lancet. CCCLII, November 21, 1998, p. 1713.
Library Journal. CXXIII, July, 1998, p. 117.
Los Angeles Times Book Review. August 2, 1998, p. 6.
The New York Review of Books. XLV, September 24, 1998, p. 20.
The New York Times Book Review. CIII, October 4, 1998, p. 22.
Publishers Weekly. CCXLV, May 18, 1998, p. 58.
The Washington Post Book World. XXVIII, August 2, 1998, p. 3.

ANTARCTICA

Author: Kim Stanley Robinson (1952-   )
Published: Bantam Books (New York). 511 pp. $24.95
Type of work: Novel
Time: The twenty-first century
Locale: Antarctica

A futuristic story of environmental conflict and physical survival set in the bleak but beautiful Antarctica of the twenty-first century

> *Principal characters:*
> X, or EXTRA LARGE, a general handyman at McMurdo Station
> VALERIE KENNING, a mountaineer and guide in Antarctica
> WADE NORTON, the chief adviser to U.S. Senator Phil Chase
> MR. SMITH, a lawyer and environmental radical
> TA SHU, a Chinese geomancer, practitioner of feng shui, and tourist
> DR. GEOFFREY MICHELSON, a geologist and veteran of Antarctica
> JACK MICHAELS, Valerie's most egotistical tourist
> CARLOS, a Chilean scientist and energy prospector
> MAI-LIS, a "feral," head of an environmental commune
> ROBERT FALCON SCOTT, an English arctic explorer
> ERNEST HENRY SHACKLETON, a British polar explorer
> ROALD AMUNDSEN, a Norwegian polar explorer

Kim Stanley Robinson is one of America's premier science-fiction novelists. His trilogy on the establishment of human habitation on the planet Mars and its successful colonization won the genre's highest accolades. *Red Mars* received the Nebula Award and *Green Mars* and *Blue Mars* were each awarded the Hugo as best novel of the year. Robinson's science fiction forte is in hard science rather than fantasy. His Mars trilogy as well as *Antarctica* are all set in the near future, and the scientific theories and technologies he uses are well within the parameters of what is at least highly probable. This gives to all of his recent novels a verisimilitude that allows the reader to enter into his stories and their plots without an unrealistic or excessive suspension of belief. Robinson does not write fantasy.

Antarctica is not dissimilar to his Mars saga, except that the story is located on earth rather than in outer space. However, the earth's southernmost hemisphere is environmentally closer to that of Mars than many locales on the home planet. Robinson refers to it as the "Ice Planet." Temperatures are generally bitterly cold, winds frequently exceed those in more moderate locations, and human life is not native, arriving only something more than a century ago with the first polar explorers. The physical and psychological challenges of Antarctica are nearly as formidable as those the human species will meet if and when it first journeys to Mars. Nevertheless, by the twenty-first century Antarctica has become a locus of increasing activity for its uniqueness, for the challenges it presents to the explorer and adventurer, for the possibilities for scientific research, even for economic development. Individuals, governments, and private organizations have been drawn to its rugged landscape. In his work Robinson explores the diversity, challenges, and opportunities presented by Antarctica.

A major theme of *Antarctica* is broadly differentiating among those who are drawn to the Ice Planet for intellectual and scientific reasons, for aesthetic or emotional reasons, and for economic, political, or even military reasons. Should the continent be preserved essentially as it is, with minimal impact and intrusion, or is it someplace to be used—and possibly used up—like so much of the rest of the earth? Robinson's various characters carry on this debate over the future of Antarctica throughout the novel.

X, or Extra Large, is a 6-foot, 10-inch young American college graduate who came south searching for meaning and adventure but who has become something of a low-level gopher in the company which has the contract to administer McMurdo Station. Valerie Kenning, X's former girlfriend, is a guide for the new breed of ecotourist who wants to experience the ultimate challenge, but under professional leadership. Wade Norton, the chief adviser to a liberal California senator whose penchant is for foreign travel and who frequently calls Norton from different parts of the globe, is in Antarctica in order to assess the long-pending renewal of the Antarctic Treaty System. One of Val's tourists is Ta Shu, a Chinese geomancer and practitioner of feng shui, who broadcasts his commentaries back to his homeland via a video camera and who is the only character who speaks in the first person. Mai Lis is a "feral" who has dropped out in Antarctica and heads a commune of like-minded individuals. There are scientists, biologists, and geologists; some are involved in the ongoing quest for scientific breakthroughs, such as the geologist Geoffrey Michelson and his companions, while others are there in order to assess the resources for possible use. Representing radical political environmentalists, or ecoterrorists, is Mr. Smith. The individual characters are frequently archetypal rather than complex individuals, and each plays a supporting or subordinate role to the major character, which is Antarctica itself.

There are several other human characters who play a role in *Antarctica*, almost like the chorus in a Greek drama. These characters are not fictional but historical and long dead. The polar explorers of the early twentieth century are a presence throughout the novel, particularly Robert Falcon Scott, who died in seeking the South Pole, Ernest Shackleton, who survived one of the most harrowing of all Antarctic journeys, and the conqueror of the pole, the Norwegian explorer Roald Amundsen. Robinson's fictional characters discuss these almost mythic figures from the past, sometimes even following the same trails or paths they first blazed decades before. At other times Robinson inserts a short chapter or section about the early explorers, frequently narrated by Ta Shu, who states on one occasion that "All stories are still alive." From the historical past the explorers seem to silently comment on the endeavors, physical and intellectual, of their twenty-first century Antarctic descendants. It is an effective literary technique.

Other than the generalized and continuing relationship that each of the characters has with a challenging environment, the most dramatic event of the novel is an attempt by an unidentified group of ecoterrorists to dramatize their cause by sabotaging—or "ecotaging"—much of the communications technology and many of Antarctica's out-back camps and facilities and by kidnapping the various inhabitants. All of Robinson's major characters are desperately caught up in this major crisis, which creates several life-threatening situations. X has resigned from his unrewarding position at McMurdo and has gone to work for a energy resource group associated with a number of countries from the southern hemisphere. Here Wade joins them just in time to be cut off and isolated from the outside world. Val has been leading a small group over the very difficult route that Roald Amundsen followed in 1911. To follow exactly in the footsteps of earlier polar adventures has become popular in the small but thriving ecotourist business. One of her tourists, Jack Michaels, insufferable in his egotism, is injured, and with no communication possible—the communications satellites have malfunctioned due to ecotage—she is forced to lead her party well over sixty grueling miles through snow and ice to an outpost that has been destroyed and where she meets X and Wade's party. Because of Michaels's broken collarbone and a shortage of supplies, they dare not simply wait for rescue and attempt to regain McMurdo on their own. Their jerry-rigged hovercraft breaks down and a raging storm comes up, but they are saved by several "ferals," members of a survivalist community that, according to treaty, has no right to be in Antarctica. Val, X, Wade, and the others are brought to the commune, which is headed by an Antarctic nomad originally from Lapland named Mai-lis. The ecoterrorists, part of the approximately one thousand "ferals" living in Antarctica, are apprehended by Mai-lis's group and forced to leave the continent, a punishment possibly worse than death to those most committed.

There is, however, a resolution. It has been claimed that politics is the art of compromise, and if so Robinson writes political novels. As in the Mars trilogy, Robinson assembles many competing voices or factions to engage in dialogue, debate, and confer in seeking satisfactory solutions to the issues raised. Not every faction is entirely satisfied, but a consensus of sorts is reached. Even Mr. Smith, who speaks for the ecoterrorists, comes to accept the decisions about the pending renewal of the Antarctic Treaty: National sovereignty will play no part in Antarctica, the "ferals" will be allowed to stay, the goal for all should be zero-impact lifestyles on the continent, and only peaceable interaction will be allowed. The last clause of the consensus statement holds that what is true in Antarctica must be true everywhere else on the planet.

Robinson's science fiction novels, including *Antarctica*, are eminently readable. His plots are involving, and if his characters are at times somewhat predictable and two-dimensional, they are substantial enough to carry his story. However, he is not writing the old-fashioned space opera. *Antarctica*, like his three Mars novels, are primarily philosophical inquiries into what should be acceptable in the immediate future. Does humanity have the right to radically and fundamentally transform the environment—either in outer space or on Earth—into something more accessible to human beings? As one of Robinson's characters said, it is at least partially a question of capitalism versus science. Is the world ruled largely by scientists, businessmen, or politicians? Or perhaps it involves the untouched natural environment versus human involvement. These philosophical issues infused the three Mars volumes, and in *Antarctica* Robinson does the same for earth's own Ice Planet.

Through the experiences and words of his characters, not least through the musings of Ta Shu, who responds to the landscape through meditation, Robinson explores the impact of the present on the near future. In this novel, as in his previous Mars saga, Robinson comes across as something of an environmental moderate. The land/planet must not be raped and denuded, but humanity will inevitably have some impact. Nevertheless, granting the nature and needs of humanity, that impact must be as minimal as possible. Mai-lis contrasts the ecological "prags" (pragmatists) with the "fundies" (fundamentalists), placing herself in the former camp. Robinson's novels are more "prag" than "fundie." That position will neither satisfy the most radical of the environmentalists nor the profits-at-all-costs school.

The true hero of *Antarctica* is Antarctica and not just in the philosophical sense. Robinson's descriptions of the Ice Planet's physical environment are superb, and the reader can only marvel at the willingness of human beings to pit themselves against what to most would be an impossible landscape. As in his Mars trilogy, Robinson has a wonderful ability to create a landscape in words, and it is his word pictures that stay with the reader long after the complications of the plot, if not the issues, have slipped away. *Antarctica* succeeds on two levels. First, like the best of futuristic or science fiction literature, it leads one to come to grips with the issues humanity will be facing in the future. Second, if the characters are less than memorable, his word paintings of that formidable but beautiful land must inevitably engender in the reader an aesthetic or emotional response. As Ta Shu expresses it, "Blue sky; white snow. That is all language can say of this place; all else is footnotes, and the human stories."

Readers of Kim Stanley Robinson's *Blue Mars* (1996), the last volume in his Mars trilogy, looked forward in anticipation to his next novel. Most will be pleased with *Antarctica*, although there will be some enthusiasts who will still yearn for something more extraterrestrial, if not more esoteric. Unfortunately, Robinson is perceived as a writer of science fiction, and few authors have been able to transcend that genre and be taken seriously as mainstream writers. A similar complaint was voiced by Raymond Chandler, who noted how difficult it was for even a fine writer of detective novels to receive wider recognition. In one of America's leading book reviews, *Antarctica* was reviewed by a nongenre reviewer only in the science fiction column rather than in the main body of the publication. The year 1998 saw the publication of a new biography of Ernest Shackleton, and continuing discussion of such environmental challenges as the greenhouse effect, atmospheric warming, El Niño, and La Niña will undoubtedly fuel interest in the future of Earth's Ice Planet. One would hope that because of these concerns *Antarctica*'s audience will include more than science-fiction buffs.

Eugene Larson

Sources for Further Study

Booklist. XCIV, April 15, 1998, p. 1357.
Library Journal. CXXIII, July, 1998, p. 141.
New Scientist. November 14, 1998, p. 52.
The New York Times Book Review. CIII, July 12, 1998, p. 26.
Publishers Weekly. CCXLV, June 22, 1998, p. 72.
Starlog. October, 1998, p. 10.
The Village Voice. July 14, 1998, p. 124.
The Washington Post. August 20, 1998, p. B8.

THE ANTELOPE WIFE

Author: Louise Erdrich (1954-   )
Published: HarperCollins (New York). 240 pp. $24.00
Type of work: Novel
Time: 1862 to the late twentieth century
Locale: Largely Minnesota

Relinquishing her usual North Dakota setting, Louise Erdrich offers a blend of history and myth that impacts the troubled lives of three new Native American families across five generations

> *Principal characters:*
> BLUE PRAIRIE WOMAN, an Ojibwa woman living at the time of the
>   Dakota uprising
> SCRANTON ROY, a U.S. Cavalry soldier
> MATILDA ROY, the infant daughter of Blue Prairie Woman, rescued and
>   adopted by Scranton Roy
> AUGUSTUS ROY, Scranton's grandson
> ZOSIE SHOWANO ROY AND MARY SHOWANO, the seemingly
>   interchangeable twin granddaughters of Blue Prairie Woman
> ROZINA (ROZIN) ROY WHITEHEART BEADS, Zosie's surviving twin
>   daughter
> RICHARD WHITEHEART BEADS, a corrupt tribal politician, Rozina's
>   husband
> CALLY AND DEANNA WHITEHEART BEADS, twin daughters of Rozina
>   and Richard
> FRANK SHOWANO, the gentle Minneapolis baker in love with Rozina
> KLAUS SHOWANO, Frank's alcoholic brother and Richard Whiteheart
>   Beads' former business partner
> SWEETHEART CALICO, Klaus's mysterious, mute antelope wife of the title

In her seventh novel, Louise Erdrich uses as a historical backdrop the 1862 uprising of the Dakota (Eastern Sioux) people at a time when starvation stalked the reservation. However, her characters actually belong to the Ojibwa tribe, also known as the Chippewa. A young U.S. Cavalry private, Scranton Roy, is sent with his company to quell the Dakota rebellion but mistakenly stumbles into a neutral Ojibwa village and attacks the inhabitants instead. Sickened by guilt, he captures an Indian dog that is fleeing with an infant strapped to its back, names the baby Matilda and rears her as his own, nursing her with his own miraculous milk in a touch of Magical Realism. In this way the white Roy family begins its intricate relationship with the two Ojibwa families of Showano and Whiteheart Beads.

The child's grieving mother, Blue Prairie Woman, marries a man named Showano and bears him twin daughters, the first of four generations of twins. Not much is known about the first pair, but the second set, also named Zosie and Mary, figure prominently in the action as the two mothers of Rozina Whiteheart Beads and the grandmothers of Rozina's twin daughters, Cally and Deanna. Slowly Zosie, Mary, and Rozina reveal themselves as beaders-creators, while Cally eventually becomes an observer and chronicler of their story, a wise woman and "namer" in the way of her grandmothers.

Just as quilt-making provides the underlying framework for *Alias Grace* (1996), Margaret Atwood's novel of nineteenth century Canada, the traditional Ojibwa craft of beading serves here as both a literal and figurative underpinning. *The Antelope Wife* opens with a near mythic passage describing two archetypal beaders at work: "Ever since the beginning these twins are sewing. One sews with light and one with dark. . . . They sew with a single sinew thread, in, out, fast and furious, each trying to set one more bead into the pattern than her sister, each trying to upset the balance of the world." These cosmic twins embody the positive and the negative, the good and the bad, the whole of experience. Yet the reader remains largely unaware of their skillful, steady work as they sew "us all into a pattern, into life beneath their hands. We are the beads on the waxed string, pricked up by their sharp needles."

It is Cally Whiteheart Beads who notes that family stories also repeat their patterns from generation to generation: "Once the pattern is set we go on replicating it. . . . the vines and leaves of infidelities . . . a suicidal tendency, a fatal wish. . . . From way back our destinies form. I'm trying to see the old patterns in myself and the people I love." These patterns become more evident as the novel swells with accounts of lost daughters, lost mothers, lost wives, even lost dogs.

The number three seems to be significant: Blue Prairie Woman is identified by three different names and is the mother of three daughters. Disastrous love triangles occur: Rozina, who is married to tribal businessman Richard Whiteheart Beads, falls in love with Frank Showano, a baker. That triangle echoes the *ménage à trois* formed years before by twins Zosie and Mary Showano and Augustus Roy, the grandson of Scranton Roy. In love, Augustus once traded the precious red whiteheart beads for Zosie in marriage but soon found himself equally attracted to her sister. Each of these triangles results in death.

At least four of the male characters—Augustus Roy, Richard Whiteheart Beads, Frank Showano, and his unhappy brother Klaus—are smitten with dark, beautiful women. Klaus, an urban Indian besotted with the wild, speechless antelope woman he meets at a Montana powwow, binds her to him with strips of sweetheart calico. (She is given the name of this flowered cloth.) Even Scranton Roy quotes his mother's poem: *Come to me, thou dark inviolate.*

Food always plays an important role in the rituals of love, death, and holiday feasts. Klaus feeds Ojibwa love tea to his beloved before he carries her off to Minneapolis. Master baker Frank Showano longs to duplicate the delicate flavor of the *Blitzkuchen*, a cake baked by a German refugee in order to save his life, but he searches in vain for the missing ingredient. A conversation at the family's Christmas dinner reveals to Cally the terrible secret which her twin grandmothers share.

Yet it is hunger that forms the crucial element for these people throughout their lives. In the beginning the physical hunger of the Dakota triggered the events that now link these families together. The Ojibwa know hunger too, personified in their folklore as a terrifying cannibal known as the windigo, a hunger spirit that can also turn humans into cannibals. A being of ice, it is especially feared in winter. On the second night after Richard Whiteheart Beads kills himself, his former wife, Rozina, who has been obsessed with the funeral food, dreams of a strange windigo man: "He does not speak, but as he stands there he slowly unzips his body. It opens like a fearful suit. Inside, he is smooth as a cave of river ice. She can see, faintly, from within his rib cavity, faint glows of phosphorescence. Death has hollowed and scoured him out inside. . . ."

The windigo is used as a tale to frighten children, as a joke that is not entirely funny, and as the embodiment of real starvation. Before her baby Matilda was born, Blue Prairie Woman was known as the girl So Hungry, because she could never be satisfied. Such hunger led others to fear that she might be possessed by a windigo.

Another, more ghastly windigo story is hidden within the history of Augustus Roy and the Showano twins Zosie and Mary, who share him. When they try to trick him in the dark by each pretending to be the other, Augustus desperately bites Zosie's ear to identify her. Then he is suddenly gone. Rumors suggest that the sisters may have eaten him, but no proof is ever discovered.

There is also the symbolic hunger of the milkless infant Matilda Roy, of her mother Blue Prairie Woman with no babe to suckle, and of those starving children who cannot resist eating their mother's cherished red beads because they look like berries, even though they are made of glass.

Other Ojibwa legends tell of deer and antelope people, creatures that can change from one form to another, treading a thin line between the human and animal worlds. Matilda Roy, last seen running naked with an antelope herd, may even be an ancestor of Sweetheart Calico. Klaus Showano, attempting to explain his fascination with his antelope wife, warns, "If you see one you are lost forever. . . . Some men follow them and do not return. Even if you do return, you will never be right in the head."

Grandma Zosie has told Cally that the young Blue Prairie Woman, then called So Hungry, was once cooking food in the woods and was joined by a deer who loved her. "Of course, too bad that he's a deer," Zosie adds in a practical tone. She informs Cally and her sister Deanna that they and their mother Rozina are part deer. The children have already seen Rozina walking with Frank Showano, who appears to them with a deer's head on his shoulders. Such a fusion of everyday reality and the truth of dream and legend is accepted without hesitation by all the characters in accordance with their traditional Native American worldview.

Welcome flashes of humor also occur, particularly in the wisecracking monologues of the Indian dog Almost Soup, a four-legged stand-up comic. He has slyly avoided the hazard of becoming "puppy soup" by charming young Cally, who adopts him as a pet. Advised by his mother always to look a bit disreputable in order to save himself, Almost Soup offers his own wisdom to young pups: "Stay cute, but stay elusive." He spices up otherwise emotional proceedings by telling dirty dog stories. Another blackly comic scene occurs at the disastrous wedding of Rozina and Frank Showano when Richard Whiteheart Beads, the bride's first husband, threatens to jump off a cliff, escapes from the emergency room to menace the wedding party, and is ultimately felled by a blow to the head with a frozen turkey.

Erdrich is at her finest when she writes about Native American culture and consciousness, in which dreams may serve as a source of power or a blinding revelation and legends offer an alternate perception of the world. In this novel she returns to the richer poetic voice heard first in *Love Medicine* (1984) and *Tracks* (1988), moving away from the more commercial style of later work such as *Tales of Burning Love* (1996). *The Antelope Wife* may be read for entertainment, but it offers much more: the echoes of myth and history, a gradual emergence of the design shaped by the legendary beaders. One minor flaw is the inclusion of chapter titles in Ojibwa that remain untranslated; in such cases, the context is of little help.

In *Love Medicine*, Erdrich was one of the first authors to write successfully from within the worldview and mythology of Native Americans. Her short story chapters were told by multiple narrators in a style that strongly influenced subsequent novelists such as Amy Tan (*The Joy Luck Club*, 1989). The *Antelope Wife* continues this tradition and has generally been well received. Although the book was actually written before the 1997 suicide of Erdrich's estranged husband, author Michael Dorris, several reviewers have noted that Richard Whiteheart Beads's self-destructive behavior (his attempt at carbon monoxide poisoning that inadvertently results in the death of his daughter Deanna and his final gunshot to the head) seems to foreshadow Dorris' impending death. However, the novel's true accomplishment lies in Erdrich's return to the lyricism of her earlier work, her exploration of a broader historical and geographical area, and the introduction of a vital new group of characters. Her poetic skill and perceptive insights remain undimmed. This book is equal in power and technique to her best.

Joanne McCarthy

Sources for Further Study

Booklist. XCIV, March 1, 1998, p. 1044.
Library Journal. CXXIII, March 15, 1998, p. 92.
Los Angeles Times Book Review. May 17, 1998, p. 9.
The Magazine of Fantasy and Science Fiction. XCV, September, 1998, p. 48.
The New York Times Book Review. CIII, April 12, 1998, p. 6.
Newsweek. CXXXI, March 23, 1998, p. 69.
Publishers Weekly. CCXLV, February 9, 1998, p. 72.
The Wall Street Journal. March 20, 1998, p. W7.
The Washington Post Book World. XXVIII, May 17, 1998, p. 11.

ANTON CHEKHOV
A Life

Author: Donald Rayfield (1942-   )
Published: Henry Holt (New York). 674 pp. $35.00
First published: 1997, in Great Britain
Type of work: Literary biography
Time: 1860-1904
Locale: Imperial Russia, especially St. Petersburg, Taganrog, and Moscow and its environs

A detailed biography of Anton Chekhov including material about his relationship with various members of his family and his antecedents, his literary friendships, and the literary environment of prerevolutionary Russia

Donald Rayfield is a professor of Russian literature at Queen Mary and Westfield College, University of London. Among his previous books on Chekhov are *Chekhov: The Evolution of His Art* (1975), *The Cherry Orchard: Catastrophe and Comedy* (1994), *The Chekhov Omnibus: Selected Stories* (1994), and *Chekhov's Uncle Vanya and the Wood Demon* (1995).

In the preface to his two-volume short-story collection, W. Somerset Maugham compares Chekhov, as a writer of short fiction, with Guy de Maupassant. According to Maugham, Maupassant wrote stories of action, complete in themselves and of a limited length; Chekhov, on the other hand, wrote stories of atmosphere, of mood, less reliant on plot and story than character, providing anecdotal fiction stripped of its trimmings and often insignificant and inane. Chekhov's literary legacy is in his handling of the details of his fiction, which he does with a consummate touch, and in his insistence that nothing should be included in the story that does not have an organic relationship to the whole. Moreover, Chekhov's fiction is usually narrated from an ironic perspective, one devoid of moral judgment. Because his writing had such distinctive characteristics, he not only became one of the masters of the nineteenth century short story but also exerted considerable influence over twentieth century fiction and drama.

Anton Pavlovich Chekhov was born in Taganrog in the Crimea just north of the Black Sea. Chekhov's paternal great-grandfather, Mikhail, was a serf all of his life on the estate of Count Chertkov in the province of Voronezh, south of Moscow, where the Chekhovs can be traced back to the sixteenth century. Egor, his grandfather, energetic and successful, purchased his freedom in 1841 so that the author's father, Pavel, grew up in a modestly well-to-do family. Anton's mother's family came from a similar background in the Tambov province but went bankrupt, forcing his mother, Evgenia, to move to Taganrog. Pavel and Evgenia were married on November 29, 1854, and they had seven children, of whom Anton was the third son.

The young Chekhov grew up and was educated in Taganrog, where he received a fairly good schooling in the classics. His family life, however, was disrupted by frequent bouts of poverty because of his father's financial reverses as a businessman. After Pavel left Taganrog for Moscow to avoid his creditors, Anton assumed responsibility for the family's maintenance, a responsibility he would shoulder for the rest of his life. In the fall of 1879 Anton entered the medical school of Moscow University, where he was reunited with his family. In June, 1884, he was qualified as a general practitioner, and he practiced medicine in various capacities until his advanced tuberculosis and the increasing demands of his literary art forced his retirement during the years immediately preceding his death in 1904. The family's constant financial pressures kept him tied to both his practice and to his desk, which undoubtedly worsened his health and helped bring on his early death at the age of forty-four.

While still a medical student Anton began to write short sketches and humorous stories in order to support not only himself but also his wayward family. After he fruitlessly tried to break into various Moscow weekly journals with his journalism, his first acceptance came on January 13, 1880, when *The Dragonfly* published a satiric sketch of his, "A Don Landowner's Letter to a Learned Neighbor," based on his father's and grandfather's ignorant and menacing pomposity. For the next few years Anton was to write hundreds of short, often parodistic, short pieces—for the most part published under pseudonyms—for various Russian periodicals. As he became more successful, the income from his writing supported his family, and his growing fame as a writer provided the basis upon which he would later build his literary career as both a master of the short story and drama.

Even though Chekhov's early career as a writer was marred by frequent literary rejections and by the grinding poverty in which he lived with his family, his life was not one of unremitting gloom. He participated in Moscow student life, enjoyed outings with his brother Alexander, also a writer at this time, and his brother Kolia, an artist who frequently contributed to the same magazines as Anton. Anton also had numerous affairs, a habit he retained until late in his life, when he finally married the actress Olga Knipper. Although to a lesser extent than later, Anton's health also affected his early life, and he had infrequent bouts of inactivity brought on by his lingering fight against tuberculosis, a disease that affected several members of his immediate family and many of his friends, several of whom succumbed to it as the years went by.

In 1886 Chekhov met Aleksei Suvorin, publisher of the St. Petersburg-based *New Times*, who not only offered the writer financial stability by publishing his works, both in periodical form and also as books, but also served as his literary mentor. Suvorin, unlike the rather retiring Chekhov, was a considerable figure in Russian publishing at this time, and he introduced the young author to the larger world of letters. Although their relationship was occasionally tempestuous (they eventually severed their association), Suvorin and Chekhov initially prospered together. With Suvorin's support and encouragement Anton began to write longer and more complex stories and even an infrequent novella or short novel. Suvorin was also instrumental in Chekhov's career as a writer of plays, the literary accomplishment for which he is probably best known in the West.

As they had done in Taganrog when Anton was a child, the Chekhovs moved frequently both within Moscow and in the St. Petersburg-Moscow-Black Sea area of Russia. Chekhov's life was peripatetic, and he rarely settled in one place for very long, a lifestyle that ended only after he built a house in Yalta in 1899, married, and finally more or less settled down to a stable domestic life. Wherever he lived, however, he often visited friends, family, or literary acquaintances, both in Russia and abroad. During his various travels Anton kept writing, and from his pen flowed a considerable outpouring of fiction and eventually drama. He began his career as a dramatist in much the same way as he had begun as an author of short fiction—by writing short, often comic or satiric, one-act dramatic pieces. And as he had done with his early sketches, the success of his farces, monologues, and comic pieces finally encouraged him to chance longer, more fully developed plays.

Initially these plays, such as the *Wood Demon* and *Ivanov*, were unwieldy and long, largely unproducible or at least unacceptable for the theater of the times. However, Chekhov's mastery of the form grew, and when he became associated with the Moscow Arts Theater company, which had just become famous, he wrote such masterpieces as *The Seagull, Three Sisters, Uncle Vanya*, and *The Cherry Orchard*—works that assured him a place as one of the founders of modern drama and one of the world's great playwrights.

Chekhov's later life was marred by his declining strength and diminished literary productivity. The tuberculosis that had so long plagued his life slowly wore him down, and in the last few years he lived as a semi-invalid. He died on July 10, 1904, at a spa in Badenweiler, Germany, where he had gone for his health.

Anton Chekhov has been well served by his biographers. Several comprehensive biographies have appeared in English or in English translation in the last half of the twentieth century. David Magarshack's *Chekhov: A Life* (1952), Ernest Simmons' *Chekhov: A Biography* (1962), and Daniel Gilles's *Observer without Illusions* (1967) have been followed by a number of more recent studies, such as *A New Life of Anton Chekhov* (1976), written by Ronald Hingley, the editor of the Oxford edition of Chekhov's works, which was an update of his original, shorter work on Chekhov's life, *Chekhov: A Biographical and Critical Study* (1950). Hingley's biography is lengthy, scholarly, and informed by the author's encyclopedic knowledge of Chekhov's writings. The arrangement of Hingley's biography—by date, location, and descriptive title, such as "Yalta: The Years of 'Three Sisters' 1900-1"—is echoed in the organization of Rayfield's work.

The French writer/scholar Henri Troyat published a more idiosyncratic study of Chekhov in 1984 (English translation published in 1986) as part of his ongoing series of biographies of famous Russian authors, including Nikolai Gogol, Leo Tolstoy, Alexander Pushkin, and Fyodor Dostoevski. Troyat's *Chekhov* provides a highly readable account of the author's life but does not make as much use of his broad knowledge of Russian literature as the reader would have expected. Finally, the British short story writer and critic V. S. Pritchett published his *Chekhov: A Spirit Set Free* in 1988. This short and highly literary look at Chekhov's life is distinguished by Pritchett's remarkable style and his own intimate understanding of the short fiction form. It provides some excellent analyses of individual stories.

All of the more recent studies of Chekhov, especially those by Troyat and Hingley, used published versions of the correspondence Chekhov meticulously saved and catalogued during his lifetime and which was so lovingly maintained after his death by his sister, Masha, who gave her life to managing the archive and to keeping the Yalta home as a temple to her brother. This remarkable archive, consisting of thousands of letters both to and from Chekhov and of other correspondence by various family members and friends, contains a vast amount of materials about Anton and his family. It is this more intimate material which provides the basis for Donald Rayfield's *Anton Chekhov: A Life*, which concentrates on Chekhov's family life and his relationships with his friends and lovers. Rayfield quotes much more extensively than have Chekhov's previous biographers from the letters, allowing the authors of those letters to speak for themselves. It is a revealing experience to read firsthand the frustrations of Chekhov's mistresses, the anger and pleading of his family, and the sorrow and pain of the author. These sources furnish the accumulated detail of Chekhov's daily life, often rendered with remarkable literary skill by his friends, family, and literary/business acquaintances, and distinguish Rayfield's study of the master dramatist and short story writer from previous Chekhov biographies.

In the preface to *Chekhov: A Life* Rayfield describes all biography as "fiction," but fiction which must accord to the documented facts. Probably the most important difference between Rayfield's life of Chekhov and previous biographies is the enormous amount of documentation at Rayfield's command. Also in the preface he notes that most of the other biographies mine the same field of sources, namely Chekhov's published letters, reminiscences about his life, and literary studies of his writings. Besides these standard sources Rayfield has gleaned material from a number of archives, including the Manuscripts Department of the Russian State Library, the Russian State Archives for Literature and Art, the theatrical museum archives in St. Petersburg and Moscow, and the Chekhov museums in Taganrog, Melikhovo, and Sumy. By including this archival material, Rayfield's biography greatly expands the documentary information available about Chekhov's life, especially in the West and in English. For this extraordinarily significant act of scholarly discovery, Donald Rayfield's *Chekhov: A Life* deserves the enthusiastic reception it has received.

Charles L. P. Silet

Sources for Further Study

American Theatre. XV, October, 1998, p. 86.
Booklist. XCIV, March 1, 1998, p. 1086.
Choice. XXXVI, October, 1998, p. 324.
Library Journal. CXXIII, February 1, 1998, p. 86.
The New Republic. CCXVIII, March 2, 1998, p. 27.
The New York Review of Books. XLIV, November 6, 1997, p. 61.
The New York Times Book Review. CIII, March 15, 1998, p. 12.
The Times Literary Supplement. July 18, 1997, p. 4.
The Wall Street Journal. March 9, 1998, p. A16.
The Wilson Quarterly. XXII, Autumn, 1998, p. 95.

APPALACHIA

Author: Charles Wright (1935-   )
Published: Farrar, Straus & Giroux (New York). 67 pp. $20.00
Type of work: Poetry

In a distinctly postmodern American style, Wright uses language and landscape to explore time, death, and possibilities of the spiritual

Charles Wright's *Appalachia* completes a poetic trilogy that began with *Chicka-mauga* (1995) and continued with *Black Zodiac* (1997), which won the 1998 Pulitzer Prize in poetry. The trilogy, actually Wright's third, can be viewed as the culmination of his career, a career marked by numerous other awards. *Appalachia* shows again why Wright is generally considered one of America's leading contemporary poets, although not all reviewers have cared for his characteristic style and themes. The important point is that enthusiastic reviewers (the majority) and those less enthusiastic have recognized and reacted to the same thing—Wright's distinctive voice, which is both of his time and not of his time.

In some ways, Wright's style is the epitome of laid-back postmodernism. His poems tend to be loose collages of images, allusions, and ideas. Since he often repeats the same themes and strategy from poem to poem—look at a landscape and think of time, death, and maybe God—the images, allusions, and ideas seem almost interchangeable. The different poems give the impression of being variations of the same work in progress. This impression of loose, repetitious form is emphasized by free-verse lines that usually carry across the page, that sometimes break down to the next level, and that are grouped in short segments of the poem. Wright also offends linguistic purists by jauntily mixing levels of discourse, juxtaposing popular culture and expressions with serious intellectual fare, as illustrated by some of his titles: "Autumn's Sidereal, November's a Ball and Chain," "Giorgio Morandi and the Talking Eternity Blues," and "After Rereading Robert Graves, I Go Outside to Get My Head Together." As these titles also illustrate, Wright does not scruple to use a cliché, even outdated ones: "God is the fire my feet are held to," "keep on keeping on," "[h]ow few and how far between," and "hubba-hubba."

Naturally, a few reviewers have found Wright's style prosy, but his rich mix of images, allusions, ideas, and levels of discourse gives his work tension and density not found in prose. Yet his style remains flexible enough to move with ease and suddenness from the mundane to the spiritual. He can also suddenly turn on an image: "Sunlight suffused like a chest pain across the tree limbs"; "As leaves fall from the trees, the body falls from the soul"; ". . . my body snug in my life/ As a gun in its carrying case"; and "Eternity puddles up." Finally, in his style Wright has succeeded in capturing the American vernacular. Such a smart-alecky mixing of levels of discourse is quintessentially American, and it fits right in with Wright's title: In Appalachia, such linguistic freedom is favored as a sign of independence, verbal agility, and perspective. While Wright is not from Appalachia (he was born in western

Tennessee), he has lived in close enough proximity to pick up on the practice, which at any rate is common throughout American society.

His style, then, makes Wright an American spokesperson for his time. What is most impressive about Wright, however, is that even with this laid-back style, in the midst of a time when the media have trivialized thought, he has held onto a sense of the timeless, the spiritual. He can go from his backyard to the big issues in a moment, somewhat like a contemporary Plato explaining the eternal forms or Immanuel Kant discussing the *noumena*. In Wright's thinking, there is "the secret landscape behind the landscape we look at here," and "[t]he body inside the body is the body I want to come to. . . ." As Wright acknowledges, "[t]he dregs of the absolute are slow sift in my blood. . . ." Some of the inspiration for Wright's thinking can be seen in his allusions and in a page of notes at the end, where, along with references to Bob Dylan and Mac Wiseman, he lists such sources as Simone Weil, Martin Buber, and Thomas Merton.

Wright's thinking is not dogmatic but inquiring, a search: He reflects the modern dilemma of facing time and death in an age of religious disbelief. Wright cannot seem to decide whether or not God is dead. He says it is so several times, but in other places he speaks as if God exists. Time and death, however, remain certainties, as evidenced in the succession of months and seasons described in *Appalachia*. Against time, one can shore up very little:

> It's all so pitiful, really, the little photographs
> Around the room of places I've been,
> And me in them, the half-read books, the fetishes, this
> Tiny arithmetic against the dark undazzle.

Death would seem to be even worse, a total dissolution of self.

Yet in the very mystery of death there is hope. No one knows what lies on "the other side," as Wright calls it. Much of *Appalachia* is an exploration of possibilities of "the other side" that is posited on the existence of a realm beyond the material. In the ages of religion, this realm was clearly mapped; in the modern world, however, it can only be intuited or known indirectly through language and material evidence. The saints and mystics whom Wright studies rely on the first method, intuition, but their method is too rigorous for Wright: "Only perfection is sufficient, Simone Weil says./ Whew. . . / Not even mercy or consolation can qualify." Instead, as a poet Wright relies first on language, especially a set of analogies, and then on the material world that supplies the analogies: "What mask is the mask behind the mask/ The language wears and the landscape wears, I ask myself." Throughout *Appalachia*, Wright carries on a running debate with the mystics about which method is most effective.

For mystics, the spiritual realm is beyond the reach of language. Conceding that language consists of "[s]ad word wands, desperate alphabet," Wright sums up his and the mystics' positions as follows:

> Still, there's been no alternative
> Since language fell from the sky,
> Though mystics have always said that communication is languageless.

> And maybe they're right.—
>   the soul speaks and the soul receives.
> Small room for rebuttal there . . .

In turn, Wright finds the mystics' spiritual trance unappealing:

> Some dead end—no one to tell it to,
>   nothing to say it with.
> That being the case, I'd like to point out this quince bush,
> Quiescent and incommunicado in winter shutdown.
> I'd like you to notice its long nails
> And skeletal underglow.

As these lines indicate, the dormant quince bush provides a small example of the analogy on which Wright rests his case.

Wright develops his case at length in *Appalachia*, especially in two series of poems entitled "The Appalachian Book of the Dead" and "Opus Posthumous." There are six poems altogether entitled "The Appalachian Book of the Dead," which is an obvious allusion to the Egyptian *Book of the Dead*, a collection of ancient writings centered around the theme of immortality, of new life rising out of death like the lotus plant warmed by the breath of Ra. The analogy still applies in the succession of months and seasons described in *Appalachia* and seems to be confirmed by the "Opus Posthumous" poems that end each section of the book. The analogy is also suggested constantly in imagery. "April eats from my fingers"; people are "hardy perennials" with "knotty egos like bulbs"; ". . . the gates of the arborvitae/ The gates of mercy look O look they feed from my mouth"; "All forms of landscape are autobiographical."

In several poems, Wright spends quality time lying on his back contemplating the heavenly bodies, but for the most part he finds the source of his analogy closer to home, in the landscape. The Blue Ridge, which stretches up and down the Appalachians like a spine, rises impressively just west of Charlottesville, where Wright lives and teaches at the University of Virginia. It is this landscape that most often inspires Wright's work, though he also finds inspiration in the Apennines, which form the backbone of Italy. The misty Blue Ridge also is a link to the ancient Chinese poets to whom Wright alludes; they too anchored their work in spectacular mountain landscapes and focused on the spiritual. Traditionally, mountains have been thought of as closer to the divine: God met Moses halfway on Mt. Sinai, the Greek gods lived on Mt. Olympus, and West Virginia is almost heaven. Wright's continuing search for this realm makes him a poet to be read and valued.

Harold Branam

Sources for Further Study

Booklist. XCV, November 1, 1998, p. 466.
The Chronicle of Higher Education. XLV, September 18, 1998, p. B10.
Kirkus Reviews. November 15, 1998.
Library Journal. CXXIII, October 1, 1998, p. 94.
Publishers Weekly. CCXLV, September 28, 1998, p. 95.

ARK BABY

Author: Liz Jensen (1959-   )
Published: The Overlook Press (Woodstock, New York). 1998. 344 pp. $23.95
Type of work: Novel
Time: 1844-2006
Locale: England

Victorian angst, religious and Darwinian, meets postmillennium fears in the twenty-first century via cross-species reproduction

Principal characters:
  TOBIAS PHELPS, the natural son of THE FROZEN LADY and THE
    GENTLEMAN MONKEY; adopted son of Parson and Mrs. Edward
    Phelps
  DR. IVANHOE SCRAPIE, taxidermist to Queen Victoria
  CHARLOTTE SCRAPIE, also known as THE LAUDANUM EMPRESS,
    Scrapie's wife
  VIOLET SCRAPIE, author of *The Fleshless Cook* and wife of Tobias Phelps

Tobias Phelps is a foundling, deposited as a very new baby on the altar in a church under the care of Parson Phelps in the village of Thunder Spit on the Northumbrian coast of England. Parson Phelps, mistaking the baby boy for a piglet at first, accepts him as a gift from God to himself and his wife, childless after many years. Tobias is an extraordinarily hairy infant, and he has suffered a serious wound to his coccyx, but the warm-hearted and grateful Phelpses take him to their bosoms and rear the foundling as their own. For five years he does not speak, but upon his fifth birthday, moved by the extraordinary vision of the cake baked for him by Mrs. Phelps, he utters his first words: "What a delicious-looking cake. . . . Please, dear Mother, would you kindly be so good as to cut me a slice?" From these and other hints it is soon clear that the author is an unusual talent, for this first novel, covering 152 years, weaves together in a fanciful fashion a host of themes as disparate as British veterinary practices, the voyage of the *Beagle*, religious reaction to Charles Darwin's *On the Origin of Species* (1859), the questions of cross-species reproduction, human fertility in the postmodern world, vegetarianism, and love.

Tobias, ever the outsider, the other, in the tiny village of Thunder Spit is a foundling, a redhead who "smells different," whose feet are oddly shaped with their great toes nearly perpendicular to the foot. He finds in the sea his constant companion, a huge toybox ever spewing forth new miracles for his delight. His father, the good Parson Phelps, calls the treasures Tobias brings home to him "God's doodlings." Phelps believes that "molluscs and other sea-creatures were drawn from the margins of the Lord's great sketchbook, in which the masterpiece was man." Thus, Jensen sets the scene for her whimsical treatment of many of the great cultural themes of both the nineteenth and twentieth centuries: the natural world and its multitude of species, their origins, the great debate between creationism and evolution, the consequences of this debate for humanity struggling to make sense of life, Victorian (and postmodern?)

ideas of man's hegemony. She also asks some profound questions when sketching a vision of mid-nineteenth century British life as vividly as Dickens, all the while alluding to a host of nineteenth century writers. Chapters are set in the same locale 150 years later, as the descendants of the nineteenth century villagers wrestle with their own questions about the meaning of life. The parsonage and church are long since redundant and have been turned into private dwellings, and even the configuration of Thunder Spit itself has changed by the filling in of the estuary.

A crisis faces these twenty-first century Thunder Spitters and, indeed, all England. For mysterious reasons, no British female has been fertile since the turn of the millennium. The British, this proud race, once the rulers of the world, now appear to be descending into extinction. Thus, while secularism, televised sports, pub life, the world of commerce, courtship, and copulation all proceed apace in 2006, with various fads and interminable discussions about causes and consequences, humanity—the British form at any rate—apparently has reached an evolutionary dead end. Jensen asks what if? What if the fate of the species rests in genetic material of a copulation that occurred in an Ark sent to collect samples of as many species as possible so that they could be killed, mounted with their genitals removed, covered with Victorian pantaloons, and exhibited as an example of humanity's supremacy, the Victorian rage for Crystal Palace exhibitions perhaps being the key here? Weaving together various strands, the novel offers a surprising answer.

Jensen's style is lively, marvelously eclectic, full of sly allusions to many of the standard nineteenth century authors. She provides such delightful forays into magical realism as the funeral of the Laudanum Empress, described by the empress herself to Abbie Ball, her descendant, 150 years later. Accidentally poisoned by Violet, Charlotte Scrapie, the Laudanum Empress,

> had long been concerned with a ceremony of the more gloomy variety, involving not white lace, but black. The happy hours she had spent preparing for this day! Earth to earth, ashes to ashes, dust to dust! Ding-dong, loud and long and tragic may the bells toll! A time to live, a time to die, a time to love, a time to hate, a time to bawl your eyes out and blow long and hard into a big black hanky!
>
> "It was a marvelous funeral," bragged the Laudanum Empress to Abbie Ball, a hundred and fifty years later. "Far be it from me to boast, but it was certainly one of the most moving occasions I have ever attended."

It is also the occasion for Violet's turning vegetarian out of guilt (misplaced we learn later) over having poisoned "my own mother." Violet Scrapie, from her earliest childhood, had been a creature of ample proportions. Growing up in the Scrapie kitchen presided over by the Belgian, Cabillaud, she had from the beginning eaten everything, a great deal of everything, centering on meat of every kind, participating in the research for Monsieur Cabillaud's magnum opus, *Cuisine Zoologique: une philosophie de la viande*. As a result she had grown to a "monstrous size," yet she was gifted with a pretty face. Encased in mourning garb, she rushes forth a week after the funeral from Cabillaud's kitchen, her real home since the age of two, swearing that she will have nothing more to do with the "wretched book." In Oxford Street she encounters a placard bearing the words "Meat is Murder." It is attached to a man, Henry Salt, organizer of the Vegetarian Society, a meeting of which she attends, followed by a visit to a brilliantly sketched Victorian butcher shop.

"Too much blood," she wails and becomes a vegetarian, but not just any vegetarian. The same energy and focus that impelled her work on Cabillaud's cookbook now informs her conversion to vegetarianism, her coming of age. In an exuberant scene, Violet and her soon-to-be former mentor, come to a parting of the ways in a "sudden, bitter exchange" that

> proved to be but the *hors d'oeuvre* to a whole menu of conflict, whose main course was the marinated and long-simmered substance of Violet's grief, accompanied by an ethical dispute on animal rights featuring *mille-feuille* and crushed garlic and coriander, leading into a rich, repercussive meringue and sherry trifle of a debate on personal morality, an argument with scalloped icing and raspberries, a confrontation of furiously clashing flavours, multiple toxins, and flagrant disjunctions of taste.

Jensen's nineteenth century scenes are sharply observed, cinematic in their sweep, and capture—often wittily, always graphically—the flavor and feel of the time and place. Tobias arrives in Hunchburgh to attend a seminary, tipped out from his train

> on to thronged streets . . . the centre of the city was bustling; a million chattering voices filled the air; the cries of the stall-holders, the shrieking laughter of women, the plaintive whimpers of beggar children thrusting out grubby palms for halfpennies. . . . I saw a man with a painted face, juggling apples, and spotted a young urchin, a pickpocket, jostling the crowd who watched.

Arriving at the seminary, he meets the abbot and hears immediately from him that the Church is

> a dying profession. I fear the Church is headed for extinction. And Darwinism hasn't helped. All this stuff about being descended from monkeys and apes has turned people away. In a hundred years' time, this seminary will be gone, and your little church in Thunder Spit will be but an empty shell.

As it turns out, it becomes the home of Abbie Ball, the great, great granddaughter of Tobias Phelps and Violet Scrapie, the mother of Blanche and Rose. Such are the twists of Jensen's plot.

This novel argues that we are the products of our genetic inheritance, often in quite unexpected ways, and alludes to the work of such famous nineteenth century scientists as Gregor Mendel, Charles Darwin, Sir Charles Lyell, and Jean-Baptiste Lamarck, and especially to P. Henry Gosse's *Omphalos: An Attempt to Untie the Geological Knot* (1857). *Ark Baby* asks what might happen if, say, six or seven generations back in one's lineage, beyond the limits of what most people know with any assurance, couplings and other events occurred that, if known, would explain one's own "unique" behavioral and physical characteristics. The novelist, Jensen says, explores these matters wittily, going far beyond the dry lines of a genealogical chart into the cultural hearts, stomachs, and generative organs of one's ancestors. Or one's own umbilical cord, pickled in a jar, such as Tobias believes has come into his possession. In the seminary Tobias had become used to grappling with such fundamental questions as to whether or not Adam possessed a navel. "Not: What does one do with an anonymous umbilical cord, when it is presented to you in a jar, as your sole heritage?" Tobias meditates on the mystery surrounding his own origin, his mother, his father, his very identity.

If the sins of the fathers are indeed visited upon the children—as the Greeks, among others, asserted—then too are the solutions and salvations of the present generation's problems, even, perhaps, the threat of extinction. Mysterious, its causes unknown, such a threat hangs over the United Kingdom in the new millennium. Darwin had read Thomas Malthus's *Essay on the Principle of Population* (1838) before developing his own theories; Jensen weaves them together in ways that subtly involve other branches of science, such as mathematics, to lead the reader to her surprising conclusion. Since Einstein, mathematicians have discovered how difficult it is to understand and explain the four-dimensional universe and develop theories and models involving additional dimensions to explain the nature and consequences of the fourth dimension. Novelists, of course, are not restricted to such formulas and theories, but may make subtle and powerful uses of them.

Ark Baby moves freely between two time periods separated by 150 years over the same landscape, in the same community. The ectoplasmic presence that transcends the "normal" boundaries of time and space, first with the use of the mind-altering drug laudanum (an opium derivative) and later by becoming the family ghost—one rendered inexplicably substantial and vocal—is the Laudanum Empress, Charlotte Scrapie. While not the central figure of the novel in either of its two time periods (the 1840's and 1850's and 2005-2006), she is nevertheless a significant presence in both, a compelling metaphor to explain the nature of cultural and biological inheritance. She is a marvelous invention.

However, she is not the only "transgenerational" device that Jensen creates and manipulates to enact her theme that humans are the products of cultural as well as biological DNA. "Buck de Savile," as Bobby Sullivan renames himself when he escapes London (and possible prosecution) for a new "locum," a new life in a new locality. Buck/Bobby is thus two men, which is certainly helpful as he falls into a sexual relationship with the twin daughters of Norman and Abbie Ball, Rose and Blanche, a union the consequences of which become surprisingly significant for the fate of the British race. As he has re-created himself, so must the race re-create itself or face extinction. The young women's work on their five-generational genealogy chart reveals, as they say, "So we're incredibly interbred." "Practically a species in your own right, then," Buck says. So they are. So their offspring are. However, as Buck views the first babies seen since the millennium, he sees that the

> new *Homo Britannicus* did not take the form of four little Buck de Saviles, spiritual grand-children of Elvis Presley, as I might have wished. Nor, as one might have expected, did it take the form of four miniature Roseblanches. . . . "Two miniature Violets, and two miniature Tobiases . . . with more than a hint of towel-holder" as the Laudanum Empress observes. "This is the future. . . . Do your best to deserve it."

Theodore C. Humphrey

Sources for Further Study

Kirkus Reviews. LXVI, March 1, 1998, p. 287.
Library Journal. CXXIII, April 15, 1998, p. 113.
The New York Times Book Review. CIII, May 24, 1998, p. 14.
Publishers Weekly. CCXLV, March 2, 1998, p. 61.

AT THE WATER'S EDGE
Macroevolution and the Transformation of Life

Author: Carl Zimmer (1966-   )
Published: The Free Press (New York). Illustrated. 290 pp. $25.00
Type of work: Archaeology, history of science, nature, and science

A summary of research and theories of the evolution of land-based animals from creatures in the sea and of the evolution of some animals, such as whales and dolphins, from ancestors who returned from the land to the water

Carl Zimmer is a senior editor at *Discover* magazine and a winner of numerous awards for science journalism. In this, his first book, Zimmer attempts one of the most valuable and challenging goals of science journalism: the presentation of current scientific findings and thinking to general readers. His subject is macroevolution, the development of new species with fundamental variations in physical features, such as fins or arms and legs, over long periods of time. Macroevolution is distinguished from microevolution, the small changes from one generation to the next produced by natural selection. Some of the biggest macroevolutionary transformations have been the emergence of air-breathing, land-traveling tetrapods (four-limbed animals) from gilled water animals and the later return of some descendants of these tetrapods to the water.

Zimmer begins his exploration of the cutting edge of scientific research on shifting life forms at the water's edge with the story of his own brief return to the sea. While diving along the coast of the Grand Bahama Island to watch how scientists study dolphins, the author was struck by the differences and similarities among a yellowtail snapper, the dolphins, and himself. Life underwater and life on ground surrounded by atmosphere pose radically different challenges. Still, humans, fish, and cetaceans (mammals such as whales and dolphins) are all vertebrates; they all have backbones. This is evidence of kinship. Moreover, even though humans and dolphins are clearly more closely akin to each other than either are to fish, both dolphins and fish are creatures of a watery world utterly foreign to humans.

To answer the question of how these distant relatives took on their current forms, Zimmer looks briefly at the development of biology as a historical science under the influence of Charles Darwin. He describes the attempts of Richard Owen, an influential nineteenth century biologist and opponent of Darwin, to account for creatures that could not easily be classified as fish, reptiles, or mammals. These included the platypus and the *Lepidosiren*, an apparent fish with lungs. Owen, believing that the different forms of life were variations on archetypes created by God, wanted to maintain boundaries between different classes of animals.

Scientists in the decades following Owen have found that life has crossed boundaries and classifications, and they have begun piecing together this macroevolutionary puzzle. On the basis of extensive research and interviews with contemporary scientists, Zimmer gives us an image of the puzzle's emerging solution. He presents the reader with two of the earliest tetrapods yet discovered, *Ichthyostega* and *Acanthostega*.

Ichthyostega was discovered in the 1930's in Greenland by the Swedish paleontologist Gunnar Save-Soderbergh. It had a tail that resembled that of a fish but characteristics in its limbs of a tetrapod. *Acanthostega* was discovered by more recent scientists, most of whom Zimmer has interviewed, but it is even older than *Ichthyostega*. *Acanthostega* had limbs that would have allowed it to move around on the floors of swamps but were not strong enough to allow it to move around on dry land—clear evidence of an intermediate stage between water-dwelling and land-dwelling animals.

Zimmer pulls together the most recent evidence from a variety of scientific fields to suggest how the evolution from fish to tetrapod took place over the course of ten million years. According to physiologists, lungs may have developed before the movement out of the water in order to enable marine animals to take in oxygen from the air and increase endurance in pursuing prey. The famous claim of late nineteenth and early twentieth century scientist Ernst Haeckel that "ontogeny recapitulates phylogeny" or that the growth of individual embryos repeats the history of species, has been found to be false as a strict rule. Modern embryologists, however, have found enough similarities between growing embryos and evolving species to suggest that embryology can sometimes indicate how evolutionary changes took place. Supported by evidence from paleontology, embryology suggests how hands gradually emerged from fins.

After describing the apparent process of the movement from sea to land, Zimmer turns to look at those who made the return journey. He investigates how certain land mammals became cetaceans. About fifty million years ago, wolf-like mammals began making the macroevolutionary movement back across the water's edge. One of the first pieces of evidence about this movement turned up in the nineteenth century when the early American paleontologist Dr. Richard Harlan obtained a skeleton of a massive animal that had been found in Louisiana. Believing it was a reptile, Harlan named it *Basilosaurus*, or "King of the Reptiles." Richard Owen entered the story of evolution once again, however, and demonstrated that *Basilosaurus* was actually a sea-going mammal.

Discoveries of recent years have provided clues to the ancestors and descendants of *Basilosaurus*. During the 1970's the paleontologist Philip Gingerich discovered fossils of a coyote-sized, land-dwelling predator. These fifty-million-year-old fossils were the remains of *Pakicetus*, the oldest known whale. One of Gingerich's students, Hans Thewissen, later discovered fossils of a creature known as *Ambulocetus*, a 49-million-year-old mammal with a head like a crocodile and squat limbs on either side of its body. These discoveries were followed by those of *Rhodocetus*, an animal with a flexible backbone from 46 million years ago that is similar in appearance to a modern dolphin, and of the 40-million-year-old *Dorudon*, a mammal with a skeleton fully adapted to life under water but with teeth like those of land predators. From these ancestors came the two suborders of contemporary cetaceans: mysticetes, the baleen whales that have curtains of horny fronds attached to their upper jaws instead of teeth, and odontocetes, the toothed whales such as dolphins, porpoises, sperm whales, and killer whales.

Zimmer draws on the work of molecular biologists to look at how closely modern cetaceans are related to other mammals. Cladistics, a method of classifying animals into branching groups by genetic similarities, suggests that whales are actually descended from hoofed mammals and are most closely related to hippopotamuses and somewhat more distantly related to cattle, giraffes, and pigs. He is careful to point out the debates and speculations about where the cetaceans should be placed among mammals.

The book's discussion of the mystery of echolocation is particularly interesting. Echolocation is the ability, shared by bats and odontocetes, to locate surrounding objects by making sounds and listening to the echoes of these sounds bouncing off of objects. Dolphins, porpoises, and other odontocetes band together in packs for hunting and use their echolocation to find and pursue their prey. Echolocation is made possible by a piece of fatty tissue, known as a "melon," located in the skull. The purpose of the melon is to shift the direction of sound waves, in order to send signals out along different paths. Although the melon is now used for echolocation, many scientists believe that it originally evolved for a totally different purpose: as a nose plug for diving deep under water. This form of perception is apparently a comparatively recent adaptation: *Dorudon* could not echolocate. It may also be a reversible adaptation. Some researchers maintain that both odontocetes and mysticetes, the baleen whales that do not have echolocation ability, evolved from a common ancestor that could echolocate. As the mysticetes began to specialize in a form of grazing by moving through the waters trapping fish in the baleen hanging from their upper jaws, they lost the need to echolocate.

The two central concepts of macroevolution, as Zimmer describes it, are exaptation and correlated progression. The term "exaptation" was invented in 1982 by the scientists Stephen Jay Gould and Elizabeth Vrba to replace "preadaptation," a word that had made it seem as if the evolutionary process were somehow predicting future developments. Exaptation is an evolutionary change produced by adapting to one environmental challenge that happens to prepare a species for another, unrelated environmental challenge. Thus, the development of air-breathing lungs to give fish more stamina in pursuing prey was a form of exaptation. Lungs later made it possible for some animals to adapt to life out of the water. If the melon of the toothed whales came into existence as a nose plug and later came to play a part in echolocation, this was another instance of exaptation. Correlated progression, a term coined by the scientist Keith Thomson, refers to the influence of evolving body parts on one another, so that a change in one area of the body brings about changes in others.

Many of the developments Zimmer describes are complex and may often require close attention from readers who have little scientific background. Zimmer manages to simplify many of the twists and turns in the scientific evidence with his clear writing. His narrative benefits from the assistance of illustrations by Carl Buell. An evolutionary chronology and a glossary in the back of the book will also help most nonscientific readers.

Zimmer's experience as a journalist gives him an understanding of how to present scientific information as a readable and enjoyable story. Although the anecdotes meant to give color to the work occasionally seem to be digressions from the main points, overall Zimmer does an excellent job introducing his readers to some of the latest trends in evolutionary biology. His descriptions of the scientists at work enable him to give a picture of science as an ongoing, human enterprise. He deserves to be placed alongside Stephen Jay Gould and Richard Dawkins as one of the best of contemporary popular writers on evolutionary biology.

Although evolution is well established as a scientific explanation of life, it continues to be challenged by many people, often on religious grounds. Zimmer's book makes some of the newest evidence in favor of the evolutionary view available to a wide audience and therefore makes an important contribution to a major modern debate. It also appears at a time when there seems to be rising public interest in the issue of evolution, as demonstrated by a spate of best-selling books concerned with evolutionary approaches such as Edward O. Wilson's *Consilience: The Unity of Knowledge* (1998) and Steven Pinker's *How the Mind Works* (1997).

The need to unify scientific studies, to pull ideas in different scientific disciplines together, is a principal theme in much of the new literature on evolution, particularly in Edward O. Wilson's work. Zimmer's demonstration of how paleontology, embryology, genetics, molecular biology, and other disciplines have assisted one another in reconstructing the evolution of species is an example of the work of scientific unification.

One of Zimmer's contributions to the literature on evolutionary biology is the attention he draws to macroevolution. Microevolution, the process of generation-to-generation changes brought about by natural selection, is widely taught in schools and fairly familiar to the educated public. Macroevolution, the process by which entirely new species come into existence, is much less known. Since most of *At the Water's Edge* is based on discoveries made in the last quarter of the twentieth century, it not only serves as an introduction to a relatively unfamiliar area of science but also communicates the area's newest ideas and findings.

Favorably reviewed in major publications such as the *New York Times Book Review*, Carl Zimmer's first book was widely regarded as one of the best works of popular scientific writing of 1998.

Carl L. Bankston III

Sources for Further Study

Audubon. C, May, 1998, p. 110.
The Atlantic Monthly. CCLXXXI, May, 1998, p. 130.
Booklist. XCIV, March 1, 1998, p. 1078.
Choice. XXXV, July, 1998, p. 1879.
Library Journal. CXXIII, February 1, 1998, p. 108.

Kirkus Reviews. LXVI, February 1, 1998, p. 188.
Natural History. CVII, May, 1998, p. 13.
Nature. CCCXCV, October 8, 1998, p. 558.
New Scientist. CLX, November 7, 1998, p. 59.
The New York Times Book Review. CIII, May 3, 1998, p. 22.
Publishers Weekly. CCXLV, February 9, 1998, p. 83.

AUTOBIOGRAPHY OF RED
A Novel in Verse

Author: Anne Carson (1950-   )
Published: Alfred E. Knopf (New York). 149 pp. $23.00
Type of work: Poetry

A modern epic that draws on classical themes in creating a rich tapestry of allusion and nonmetrical poetry

In the brief period between the publication of *Plainwater: Essays and Poetry* (1995) and the milestone book *Glass, Irony, and God*, with its centerpiece "The Glass Essay" (1995), Anne Carson reached an uncommon level of critical appreciation. With this reputation in tow, each succeeding new work will be held up to high expectations, with comparisons to other writers (such as Ann Lauterbach, Medbh McGuckian, and Henri Michaux) as well as backward glances to her own earlier efforts. This position forces artists to push the boundaries of past glories; to move up from such a precarious perch, creative minds must use the themes and techniques that built their reputations while expanding their scope and substance.

If such comparisons within a fairly young canon cannot be avoided, it is helpful to trace the steps that led up to a new artistic contribution to that canon. Throughout *Plainwater* and *Glass, Irony, and God*, Carson's themes and techniques merged her classical scholarship and innovative experiments with structure. This far-reaching fusion gave her the distinctive voice of individuality steeped in academia and deeply fought personal soul seeking. Poems such as "The Glass Essay" reached and challenged readers on a variety of levels, because Carson successfully interwove three elements: personal reflections on identity, references to literary influences, and visions of the nature of poetry. Her use of visuals in "The Glass Essay" clearly prefigured similar techniques in *Autobiography of Red*, in which much of her style is based on line structure and layout for the eye while using colors, light, and dark juxtapositions as her scaffolding for images and metaphors.

This complexity has made her work as interesting to the poetic technician as to the reader, and such virtuosity has led to high praise in critical commentaries. But Carson's sometimes top-heavy gamesmanship and use of obscure, esoteric allusions have proved distracting and defeating, notably when she is not writing from her personal experience. These faults will trouble some readers of *Autobiography of Red*, as they troubled readers of Carson's previous four books.

This fifth exercise in the avant-garde is challenging, inviting comparisons with two of her cited mentors, Homer and Gertrude Stein. From Homer, Carson takes a mythos of personalities and reworks ancient narratives into a postmodern parable. From Stein, she derives a playful wordplay, a deceptively simple tone that helps make her complexity readable.

Carson is far more than a synthesizer of influences. More important, she is a synthesizer of techniques, perhaps the most interesting creator of new images in the modern poetic scene, and a pioneer in the usage of white space on the printed page.

Autobiography of Red is not an autobiography of her protagonist, Geryon, the mythological winged monster who lives in a red world of red shadows tending red cattle trapped "in a bad apple." Nor is she retelling the story of Geryon as originally spun by Greek poet Stesichorus, whose epic had the red monster killed by Herakles in the fulfillment of one of his mythological labors. Rather, Geryon lives in a modern world, is molested as a child, and is betrayed in a love affair with Herakles. Layered onto this plot diversion, echoing "The Glass Essay," the narrative is partially about the writing of Geryon's autobiography of artistic discovery. At its deepest level, the book is about the search for understandable meaning in a world of words, words so complex and ambiguous that Geryon must find expression and focus without them. Geryon's search for this discovery, as in all epics, forces him to move from childhood to mature uncertainty, from one confusion to another. This trope parallels the search for identity in "The Glass Essay"; again, it is a masterful weaving of major ideas appropriate to Carson's newly expanded novel-length scope.

At the beginning of the poetic fragments and sequences, Carson poses a long series of either/or riddles that open up into a tapestry of interrelated images. Part of Geryon's quest is to find the meanings of words, as he first hopes to nail awareness into facts, times, and information. However, this hope leads to skepticism. Meanings for Geryon are blurred when the babysitter appropriates words that belong to the mother and when the insane write in political candidates on ballots. Resolutions are beyond words, as when death is the state "where one cannot speak" and reality "is a sound to be tuned in to." When Geryon turns to photography, he "relinquished speech," not answering questions while seeking to focus his lens. In the "IV Tuesday" passage, the missing side of a phone conversation is indicated by a series of ellipses, leaving the reader to fill in the omitted thoughts:

> Maria? It's me can you talk? What did he say?
> . . .
> Just like that?
> . . .
> Bastard
> . . .
> That's not freedom it's indifference
> . . .
> Some kind of attic
> . . .
> I'd throw the bum out

Again employing visual metaphors, Carson has Geryon grow from childhood to college student to worker. He learns the coldness of words. When he works with government documents in a basement, he is instructed to "turn off the lights when not in use." He learns that social expectations are reflected in his words, as when his mother wants to know if his school compositions have happy endings. This image merges with his realizations when he turns from words to photographs, and his mother reminds him to use the lens cap when not in use. To become an artist, to learn "How does distance look?" Geryon first focuses his lens on lips looking for "intelligent words" from his mother's throat. However, his images become visually oriented—a nonworking mind is a "defective light projector," but he is in the dark without "his reading light." He makes a project of finding the sounds of colors and discovers that postcards combine words with pictures. With this synthesis Geryon comes to awareness, with poetic images such as "dancing is meaning placed on motion." "The Glass Essay" is evoked for its use of paintings of nudes that demonstrate different states of female consciousness. As in "The Glass Essay," the imagery is reinforced with word spacing and line length, alternating expansions and contractions of lines to indicate the opening and narrowing of awareness.

This set of images is juxtaposed by repeated references to smoke, ash, lava, and volcanoes, leading to another wide variety of possible interpretations. Linking this set of motifs with her main themes, Carson writes that "the words floated by like ash," and the world of technology is seen through buses exhaling smoke. Most characters smoke cigarettes, and the scientific, geological passages on volcanoes give way to sexual allusions and surreal photographs of a circus freak called "The Lava Man." Carson's climactic moment occurs when Geryon makes a pilgrimage to the Andes and a volcano. Atop the volcano, Geryon's dormant wings open under the eye of the camera and over the eye of the volcano, resulting in final self-realization. The autobiography proper closes with Geryon, Herakles, and Ancash, "neighbors of fire," immortalized as they stand by a "volcano in a wall."

This interplay makes *Autobiography of Red* the sort of text teachers are keen on explicating in the classroom. However, Carson's use of nonmetrical prose and lines are more poetic for the eye than the ear and will continue to annoy readers who want easy definitions of genres with which to label their artists. Like William Vollmann, Carson's mirror opposite in his attention to meter in prose rather than traditional line structure, Carson is as interesting for her style as for her substance. Still, it is easy to argue that her classicism tends to make this work more appropriate for readers knowledgeable about classical allusions and literary context that are beyond most readers' backgrounds. Many readers without graduate degrees in literature may find the work difficult to grasp, particularly if they attempt to integrate the introductory material and appendices into their understanding of the main text.

Furthermore, top heavy insertions of scientific data both slow the pace and seem metrically out of place, and her whimsical footnotes and appendices on the legend of Stesichorus's blinding by Helen of Troy are of little help in illuminating her story. Her bogus "Interview" with Stesichorus provides clues to her intentions, discussing "concealment drama" that both hides information with an aesthetic will toward blindness while the playwright sees for all humanity. In this section, in which the playwright seems to speak with Carson's own voice, the updated Greek writer indicates that the artist is responsible for humanity's visibility. The artist, Carson says, is unable to blink, wishing to forget the disagreeable past. Geography and character are linked without explanation, and the final riddle claims no distinction between a guinea pig and a volcano. Such enigmas erode any interpretations of the work readers may have arrived at by the end of the main text, forcing them to rethink their reactions to the book. This new level of complexity is stimulating but perhaps dissatisfying for readers seeking tangible aphorisms to hang meaning on.

In the main, Carson is not as remote as Ezra Pound in his use of world culture, but nonacademic readers may be unhappily distracted by her esoteric allusions. However, the many layers and poetic explorations of *Autobiography of Red* should appeal to a wide range of readers. Like "The Glass Essay," Carson's new work will be examined from several perspectives and will likely remain of literary interest for some time to come.

Wesley Britton

Sources for Further Study

Booklist. XCIV, April, 1998, p. 1294.
Library Journal. CXXIII, May 15, 1998, p. 88.
Los Angeles Times. May 8, 1998, p. E4.
The Nation. CCLXVI, June 1, 1998, p. 32.
The New Republic. CCXVIII, May 18, 1998, p. 37.
The New York Review of Books. XLV, November 9, 1998, p. 57.
The New York Times Book Review. CIII, May 3, 1998, p. 23.
Poetry. CLXXIII, December, 1998, p. 181.
Publishers Weekly. CCXLV, March 30, 1998, p. 70.
Review of Contemporary Fiction. XVIII, Fall, 1998, p. 233.

BADGE OF COURAGE
The Life of Stephen Crane

Author: Linda H. Davis (1953-   )
Published: Houghton Mifflin (New York). 430 pp. $35.00
Type of work: Literary biography
Time: 1871-1900
Locale: New York, New Jersey, Mexico, Florida, England, Greece, Cuba, and Germany

A portrait of the writer as a perpetual adolescent, a man careless with his life and health but always in full command of his charm, and enigmatic to the last

Principal personages:
STEPHEN CRANE, a novelist, journalist, and celebrity
THE REVEREND JONATHAN TOWNLEY CRANE, his father
MARY HELEN PECK CRANE, his mother
AGNES CRANE, his beloved sister, who died young
EDMUND,
TOWNLEY, and
WILLIAM CRANE, three of Stephen's brothers
FREDERIC LAWRENCE and
CORWIN KNAPP LINSON, Crane's friends in bohemian days
NELLIE CROUSE and
LILY BRANDON MUNROE, women whom Crane wooed in vain
AMY LESLIE, a *Chicago Daily News* drama critic, Crane's lover
CORA TAYLOR, a Florida madam, Crane's "wife"
HAMLIN GARLAND and
WILLIAM DEAN HOWELLS, prominent American writers who
    championed Crane
JOSEPH CONRAD, a Polish-born English novelist, Crane's closest literary
    friend
RICHARD HARDING DAVIS, a famous war correspondent, Crane's rival
JAMES B. PINKER and
PAUL REVERE REYNOLDS, Crane's long-suffering agents
THEODORE ROOSEVELT, the future president, a New York City police
    commissioner and Crane's enemy

In her preface to *Badge of Courage: The Life of Stephen Crane*, Linda Davis attributes her interest in Crane to *The Monster* (1898), a novella about a black man who is horribly disfigured by fire while saving his employer's son. This "evoked" the death of the biographer's own father in similar circumstances, a slightly uncanny coincidence that left her determined to learn more about Stephen Crane. Unfortunately, her book never really illuminates the more obscure corners of Crane's genius. Like the many people who knew Crane, Davis has been seduced by his charm, which served all of his life as a shield for his mystery.

Davis begins the first chapter in 1890, with an incident from Crane's nineteenth year during a brief stint as a student at Lafayette College in Easton, Pennsylvania. There a group of sophomores, out for a night of hazing, broke in on the new student—to find him quaking with fear behind a gun. Apparently, this is how Crane saw himself, but he masked his fear with the many roles he played: rebellious preacher's child, reporter, writer, cowboy, war correspondent, lover. Although he usually found a receptive audience, he remained isolated.

The Monster, for example, concerns an only child, based loosely on Crane, who was in fact the youngest child of a family of nine. Yet the isolated hero is such a common feature in Crane's fiction that a biographer should deal with these entangled issues of isolation and fear. Davis leaves that work to the reader, unfortunately, but she does provide substantial intriguing material to help in the process.

Though he would later affect a Western drawl and be most at ease among society's marginal elements, Crane was born into a middle-class family proud of its heritage, education, and faith. His father was a popular Methodist minister and his mother an ardent prohibitionist. Though his mother was strictly religious and distant, his father was highly regarded for both his personal integrity and his sense of humor.

It is never possible to explain genius, but Crane, like many writers, remained fixated on the unresolved issues of his childhood, in his case the death of his father when the boy was eight. In his fiction, death replaces the father as the force against which the hero must measure himself in the act of rebellion. The inevitability of death so overwhelms every other fact that it stripped Crane of all illusion about religious and social conventions, which, in his view, blind people to the realities of existence.

He credited his father with the kind of moral probity and personal integrity that he felt most people lacked. His mother's piety, on the other hand, almost ensured rebellion. Still, that by itself cannot explain Crane's complete disillusionment with religion. Nor was it the usual rebellion of the preacher's child, although there was always something adolescent in his desire to shock. Crane, however, saved himself and his writing from fatuous self-indulgence by the power of a most remarkable clearsightedness.

Still, the fact remains that he never grew up. This may have been partly the result of his being the baby of the family; in addition, his health was never good. Davis believes that Crane had the tuberculosis that killed him from the time he was a child, but there is no proof that he had the disease until near the end of his life. Davis bases her guess on Crane's famous disregard for safety and his repeated prediction of an early death for himself, but these could just as easily derive from the sickly child's need to overcompensate, a drive that made him a standout catcher in college.

There is also more than a small element of adolescent bravado about Crane that accounts for his lifelong restlessness. He was always on the move, away from things as much as toward them. He wanted to live in the moment, a loud, action-packed moment. This suited his taste for war, but until he actually saw military action, he had to settle for adventures of a different kind. He always loved the outdoor life and spent his summers as a very young man camping out in Sullivan County, New York, listening to the local stories that he used in his first published fiction.

He went to college, first Lafayette and then Syracuse University in New York, but did not stay long. In Syracuse, he got a job through his older brother Townley as a stringer for the *New York Tribune*. Covering the police beat, he became drawn into the social life of petty criminals. He then moved to New York City and quickly established himself in bohemian circles.

To gather the material for his first novel, *Maggie: A Girl of the Streets* (1893), Crane exposed himself to the more authentic poverty of the truly wretched. Though his health may never have fully recovered, he made his derelict life appear as much a lark as his summer camping trips. Yet though he seemed most at ease in bars and brothels, this did not keep him from pursuing unattainable middle-class women. In this way, he had his cake and ate it too, maintaining romantic illusions that in no way infringed on his actual behavior. He felt about the poor the same way that he later did about the common soldier, that somehow their experience was more honest and real than his own. This led to a romanticization of poverty and war, offset to a great extent, fortunately, by his genius for observation. For this reason, Hamlin Garland and William Dean Howells, major literary realists of the period, hailed *Maggie* when few noticed it.

In style, Crane, often considered the first modern American writer, was predominantly a realist, but with an emphasis on interior psychological states. This combination made his next book *The Red Badge of Courage* (serialized 1894; published 1895) an international sensation. Crane, who had never seen battle, would later say he learned all he needed to know from football, but the truth is more likely the other way round: that his view of war colored every other activity, from a child's snowball fight to the struggle for existence in the slums of New York. It is significant that his war stories are not so much about the clash of armies as about the psychological plight of a single soldier who has to prove himself.

Though he wrote many other novels, including *George's Mother* (1896), *The Third Violet* (1896), and *Active Service* (1899), not to mention countless stories, he was known as the author of *The Red Badge of Courage*. Despite his resentment of the book, he used fame to his advantage, especially in getting work. The Bacheller-Johnson Newspaper Syndicate, which serialized the novel, sent him out west. He wrote little journalism of note on the trip, but he would later use his experiences in some of his best stories, including "The Bride Comes to Yellow Sky" (1897) and "The Blue Hotel" (1898). He also visited Mexico, playing the cowboy and outracing a gang of drunken desperadoes.

He was back in New York by May, 1895, and he had a productive, if not profitable, year writing. The city, though, became less hospitable after he made enemies in the police department, run at the time by Theodore Roosevelt. When Crane in September, 1896, testified on behalf of a prostitute harassed by the police, officers threatened him and fabricated rumors about his drug use and lifestyle. This made great copy, as did his first book of poetry, *The Black Riders and Other Lines* (1895). Though very influential, with its striking imagery and lack of traditional structures, his poetry was easy to lampoon. Thus Crane, both lionized and mocked, found himself plagued by unwelcome fame and notoriety for the rest of his life. In this, too, he was modern, more famous for who he was than for what he did.

He left New York and headed for Cuba, where Americans were aiding the rebels fighting Spain. This was still technically illegal, so he had to wait in Jacksonville,

Florida, until he could be "smuggled" into Cuba. In Florida, he met Cora Taylor, who ran a bordello called the Hotel de Dream. When he finally sailed for Cuba on January 1, 1897, the boat sank, an incident he turned into his greatest story, "The Open Boat" (1897).

Just as important, Cora rushed to his side, cementing their relationship. Together they went to London, where Crane found himself far more admired than in his own country. Having adopted England as his future home, he sailed for Greece to cover its war with Turkey and get his first taste of battle, which he thought remarkably like his fictional account. He returned to London as a literary lion, but trouble loomed. Reviews of his new books were poor and sales minimal. He churned out articles and stories, sending them off to his agents, whom he badgered for advances, even before the stories were sold.

At the same time, he tried to live the life of a country gentlemen, complete with an estate where he welcomed such friends as Joseph Conrad. He wrote some of his best stories at this time, including *The Monster*, but he became increasingly desperate for money.

Crane was particularly relieved when the start of the Spanish-American War in 1898 gave him an excuse to run away from his troubles, at least temporarily. He got himself hired by the English journal *Blackwood's*, but he never took his duties seriously. By the end of his Cuban adventures, he had worked for several different newspapers and alienated them all. He used them, basically, to see the war, where, for the most part, he played it cool under fire—in fact, he seemed to invite enemy fire. He left only when he was so sick with malarial fever that he was sent to a New York sanitarium, where he was diagnosed with tuberculosis.

Keeping his sickness secret, Crane went to cover the conquest of Puerto Rico before sneaking back into Cuba, where he lost himself in the dives of Havana. Cora, desperate for money and afraid Crane had left her, got the British counsel to help bring her husband home. Crane spent his last year writing and entertaining friends while fending off creditors and borrowing money where he could. Though he never married Cora, people thought him devoted to her, but more as a son than lover; while Cora, like a mother, provided the life he wanted, with dogs, horses, and visitors.

He wrote constantly, but he never had a chance to work himself out of debt. His health was deteriorating, too. For Cora's sake, he agreed to visit a resort at Badenweiler in Germany's Black Forest, but he died there on June 5, a week after his arrival.

It is hard to decide whether Crane squandered his talents or was supremely lucky in making the most of what talent he had. This is the kind of question with which Davis never really deals, nor does the book leave the reader with the desire to run out and read Crane. Yet Davis has written a lively account of a writer who will remain his own greatest character, the template for the hero and antihero of the century he would not live to enter, intoxicated by youth, vigor, and an oddly innocent notion of his own guilt.

Philip McDermott

Sources for Further Study

American Scholar. LXVII, Autumn, 1998, p. 146.
The Atlantic. CCLXXXI, September 1, 1998, p. 137.
Booklist. XCIV, July, 1998, p. 1850
Library Journal. CXXIII, July, 1998, p. 89.
The New York Times. CXLVII, August 18, 1998, p. B6.
The New York Times Book Review. CIII, August 23, 1998, p. 9.
The New Yorker. LXXIV, September 7, 1998, p. 85.
Publishers Weekly. CCXLV, May 11, 1998, p. 56.
The Wall Street Journal. August 6, 1998, p. A13.

BAG OF BONES

Author: Stephen King
Published: Charles Scribner's Sons (New York). 529 pp. $28.00
Type of work: Novel
Time: Primarily the mid-to-late 1990's
Locale: Derry, Maine, and Sarah Laughs, Maine

A novelist comes to terms with both his wife's death and his own writer's block as he becomes involved in a young woman's fight to retain custody of her daughter

> *Principal characters:*
> MIKE NOONAN, a recently widowed gothic romance novelist
> JO NOONAN, Mike's deceased wife
> MATTIE DEVORE, a young widow with whom Mike falls in love
> KYRA DEVORE, Mattie's daughter
> MAX DEVORE, Mattie's tyrannical father-in-law
> SARAH TIDWELL, a blues singer from the 1900's

Stephen King's highly publicized split with his longtime publisher Viking and the reputed selling price he placed on *Bag of Bones* have placed more expectations upon him than usual. *Bag of Bones* easily lives up to these expectations, but is it his best novel ever? Probably not, but it is definitely the best work he has released in the past ten years and fits comfortably as one of his best to date. It is also his most mature work short of the unfinished novel-for-television *Golden Years* (1991). It represents a new direction for King; for both King and his fans, this is a good thing.

King promotes *Bag of Bones* as a "haunted love story," which proves to be a fitting description. The novel opens with narrator Mike Noonan recounting the death of his wife, Jo, who collapses outside the Rite Aid pharmacy of a brain aneurysm. Because they are both relatively young—Mike is close to his fortieth birthday as the novel opens—Jo's death is especially devastating. An even more devastating blow comes when Mike learns that Jo was pregnant and had not told him. Because Mike has a medical condition that makes it difficult for him to father a child, Jo's death causes him to question whether the unborn child is really his or whether his wife had been having an affair.

As Mike slowly adjusts to life without Jo, he is forced to make another adjustment. Mike is a successful writer of gothic romance fiction, often describing himself as a male equivalent of writer V. C. Andrews, but after Jo's death he discovers that he is unable to write even a simple sentence. The writer's block is so severe that Mike feels as if he is choking to death, at one point almost literally suffocating himself as he tries to bring himself to turn on his word processor. In an attempt to regain his muse and put Jo's death behind him, Mike returns to Sarah Laughs, the vacation cabin he and Jo purchased soon after he became successful. Sarah Laughs (also referred to as "TR-90" or the "TR") was named after Sarah Tidwell, a southern blues singer who had passed through the TR with her son and her fellow accompanists, the Red Tops, at the beginning of the 1900's. As Mike quickly learns, Sarah Laughs is haunted by ghosts, and Sarah Tidwell's is but one of many.

Mike soon meets TR residents Mattie Devore, her daughter Kyra, and Mattie's father-in-law, Max Devore, a withered old man of incalculable wealth who is used to getting anything he wants. Mike rescues Kyra from walking down the middle of Route 68 and quickly becomes friends with both Kyra and Mattie. Mattie is the widow of Lance Devore, Max Devore's stuttering son. Lance had nothing to do with his father after learning that his father had tried to bribe Mattie into not marrying him. After Lance's death from a freak accident, Max returns to Mattie's life in an attempt to get acquainted with his granddaughter, Kyra. The truth is, however, that Max wants to gain custody of Kyra and take her away to California and will do whatever it takes to accomplish this. To help Mattie fight off Max's army of high-priced lawyers, Mike uses his own considerable resources to retain a lawyer for Mattie named John Storrow, a young New York lawyer unafraid to take on someone of Max Devore's social stature.

As Mike gets drawn into Mattie's custody battle, he also gets drawn into the ghosts that haunt the TR-90 community. Ghosts have long been symbolic manifestations of the subconscious demons that everyone carries inside, and for Mike they are no different. He is a widower who has lost his soul mate and feels the guilt of all the things that should have been done differently, as well as the guilt of falling in love with Mattie and a child that he and Jo had never been able to have together. Kyra's name is a further reminder of his pain; Mike and Jo had planned to name their daughter Kia, which is what he initially mistakes Kyra's name to be.

The other ghosts that haunt the novel soon begin to manifest themselves. As Mike sleeps at night in Sarah Laughs, he comes to realize that there are at least three separate spirits haunting his cabin. One, he is sure, is Jo, and one he comes to figure out is Sarah Tidwell. The third only manifests itself as a crying child, and Mike cannot determine if it is Kyra or some other child. Mike and Kyra share a special psychic connection reminiscent of King's earlier novel *The Shining* (1977). Mike and Kyra are able to share dreams and even appear to have the same ghosts haunting their homes, ghosts who communicate by rearranging magnetic letters on each of their refrigerator doors. At one point, Mike and Kyra share a dream where they are both at a turn-of-the-century fair where Sarah Tidwell is playing. Another time, Mike talks to Mattie on the phone and knows exactly what she is wearing and what she and Kyra are doing, and he suspects that she shares the same connection with him. The fact that these unusual occurrences are taken in stride seems to suggest that King is focusing more on the human emotions than the supernatural events that take place.

What King has set up are contrasting dynamics of love, both honest and corrupt. The love between Mike and Jo, Mattie and Lance, and eventually Mike and Mattie are all genuine, in contrast to Max Devore and his obsession to gain custody of Kyra. Even pure love, however, comes under a shadow of suspicion. Mike learns that Jo had been sneaking away to the TR without telling him, further reinforcing his suspicions of her having had an affair. As Mike becomes further embroiled in the custody battle with Max Devore, his search to determine the truth about Jo's affair finally leads him to a set of journals Jo was keeping, notes from a research project that was her real reason for sneaking away to the TR.

Jo's notes explain how everyone related to the people who murdered Sarah Tidwell and her son have paid for this sin by losing a child of their own. All of these children's names bear a striking resemblance to Kito, the name of Sarah's murdered son. Sarah is exacting her revenge by murdering the children of those who murdered her own child. Mike, related to one of the people who murdered Sarah and Kito, has been drawn into this circle of retribution from the beginning, and the death of his unborn daughter, Kia, was not the accident it seemed to be. Mike also realizes that Kyra, the last descendant of this tragedy, is to be the final sacrifice used to put Sarah Tidwell to rest. Mike's return to the TR, it seems, has been a carefully orchestrated tragedy. Everything is tied to Sarah's purposes, even Mike's writer's block. Mike's writing abilities return while he is at Sarah Laughs, but by the end of the novel he realizes it was simply to lead him to the information he needed to put Sarah's spirit to rest. Sarah's ghost may have destroyed his wife and child, but Jo's ghost gives him the means to save Kyra.

Bag of Bones makes references to classic literature, most notably Herman Melville's *Bartleby the Scrivener* (1853) and Daphne du Maurier's *Rebecca* (1938). Mike often compares his early dreams of Sarah Laughs to the famous line from *Rebecca*, "Last night I dreamt I went to Manderley again," and he later dreams that he hears Sarah Tidwell singing of Manderley. King's novel also bears resemblance to another modern supernatural novel, Peter Straub's *Ghost Story* (1979). *Ghost Story* is also a novel of men haunted by a guilty past who each begin to suffer retribution for their sins. King is well aware of this *Ghost Story*; he considers it one of the top ten best modern horror novels in his classic study of the genre, *Danse Macabre* (1981). Unfortunately, as fine as King's writing is in *Bag of Bones*, it does not compare to Straub's mastery of atmosphere and surreal sense of terror.

The usual King trademarks that fans have come to expect are present in *Bag of Bones*. King, perhaps more than any other author since William Faulkner and his fictional Yoknapatawpha County, creates a sense of literary history within his novels that ties them all together. King references several of his other novels, most notably *The Dark Half* (1989), *Needful Things* (1991), and *Insomnia* (1994). For longtime fans, this serves both to update King's readers as to what their favorite characters are currently doing and to unify King's body of work. King's ironic sense of humor is also evident. When Mike's literary agent tells him of all the other best-selling novelists who have novels coming out in the fall of 1998, the most notable name missing from the list is that of Stephen King himself.

Bag of Bones shares much in common with the southern novel and its themes. Guilt is a predominant theme of many southern works, especially those of Faulkner, Edgar Allan Poe, and Tennessee Williams. Racism, not a theme usually associated with northern writers, has been successfully transplanted by King via the traveling Sarah Tidwell. By the end of the novel the evils of the community have become so entrenched in the soil (another similarity to Faulkner's fiction) that they begin to affect Mike himself, and he has to fight the urge to kill Kyra himself. Only by reburying the past—in this case, by literally reburying Sarah Tidwell's body—can things finally be put to rest. Mike dissolves Sarah's body with lye and her spirit finally leaves the TR. Jo's spirit also leaves, and all is quiet once more at Sarah Laughs.

Of the three most important best-selling modern horror writers—Anne Rice, Clive Barker, and King—King is the only one who continually tries to reinvent himself out of the mold into which his novels have placed him. In the 1990's, he not only tried feminist fiction with his novels *Gerald's Game* (1992), *Dolores Claiborne* (1993), and *Rose Madder* (1995), but he also singlehandedly revived the chapterbook novel format with *The Green Mile* (1996) simply because he wanted to see if he could write fiction "on the spot," or without the safety net of being able to go back and fix mistakes later. King's attempts at reinventing himself have not always been met with warm critical reception, but he cannot be faulted for trying. He has always publicly emphasized story over structure, often comparing his novels to fast food instead of gourmet meals, which is why his novels are often regarded by critics as not worthy of any serious consideration. This is too bad, because the point most critics miss is that King writes to entertain. *Bag of Bones* will be seen as King's triumphant return to the traditional horror novel his fans expect from him, but, most important, it proves that he is still one of fiction's premiere storytellers.

Kelly Rothenberg

Sources for Further Study

Booklist. XCIV, September 1, 1998, p. 6.
Library Journal. CXXIII, July, 1998, p. 137.
Los Angeles Times Book Review. September 27, 1998, p. 3.
National Review. L, September 1, 1998, p. 46.
The New York Times Book Review. CIII, September 27, 1998, p. 9.
Newsweek. CXXXII, September 21, 1998, p. 94.
Publishers Weekly. CCXLV, June 22, 1998, p. 81.
Time. CLII, October 12, 1998, p. 116.
The Wall Street Journal. September 25, 1998, p. W6.
The Washington Post Book World. XXVIII, November 1, 1998, p. 5.

A BEAUTIFUL MIND

Author: Sylvia Nasar
Published: Simon & Schuster (New York). Illustrated. 459 pp. $25.00
Type of work: Biography
Time: 1928-1994
Locale: West Virginia; Princeton, New Jersey; Santa Monica, California; Massachusetts; Paris

The brilliant mathematician John Nash was awarded the Nobel Prize in Economics in 1994, after three difficult decades of struggling with paranoid schizophrenia

> *Principal personages:*
> JOHN NASH, the brilliant but prickly mathematician whose work on
>   game theory eventually earned him a Nobel Prize
> ELEANOR STIER, mother of Nash's first son, John David Stier
> ALICIA LARDE NASH, Nash's wife, who watched over him during his
>   sickness even after their divorce
> JOHN CHARLES NASH, Nash's second son, who also became a
>   mathematician and, like his father, developed paranoid schizophrenia

John Forbes Nash, Jr., was born on June 13, 1928, in Bluefield, West Virginia. His father, John Nash, Sr., was an electrical engineer who left Texas to work for the Appalachian Power Company in Bluefield, where he met Margaret Virginia Martin, whom he married in 1924. Nothing in the birth or upbringing of John Nash, Jr., offers any clue to his later illness. John and Virginia Nash were educated and loving parents to both him and his sister, Martha, born in 1930. John was a healthy, handsome child but quiet and introverted. His mother taught him to read by the age of four and apparently watched closely over his progress at school, where he was a difficult pupil given to constant talking and indifference to rules.

A significant event in Nash's life came at the age of thirteen or fourteen when he read E. T. Bell's book of biographical sketches, *Men of Mathematics*. Bell gave vivid accounts of the mathematical problems that inspired his subjects when they were young, and his essay on Pierre de Fermat and number theory especially appealed to the youthful Nash. His precociousness and his mean practical jokes set Nash apart from other high school students in Bluefield, but he excelled in his studies and took courses at Bluefield College along with his high-school work, doing so well that he was accepted at the Carnegie Institute of Technology and won a full scholarship, one of ten Westinghouse awards given nationally.

Nash's three years at Carnegie were difficult socially, for his awkwardness and attraction to other boys elicited the ridicule of his fellow students, but the talented teachers in the mathematics department nurtured his brilliance so well that in 1948 he was accepted in the graduate programs at Harvard, Princeton, Chicago, and Michigan. During his first year at Princeton, Nash became absorbed in board games, especially the difficult games "Go" and "Kriegsspiel," and soon devised his own topological game known as "John" or "Nash." (Nash's game was apparently an independent invention of one already invented by a Dane, Piet Hein, and sold by Parker Brothers as Hex.) Nash's matriculation at Princeton coincided happily with the beginning of John von Neumann's tenure at the Princeton Institute for Advanced Studies. Von Neumann was acknowledged as the most brilliant of living mathematicians, and his presence around Princeton was a great boost to creative thinking. In 1944, with Oskar Morgenstern, he had published *The Theory of Games and Economic Behavior*, the seminal text in game theory which was built around zero-sum, two-person games in which one contestant's gain was an opponent's equivalent loss.

Nash first became interested in bargaining problems when he took a course in international trade at Carnegie. Thus, Nash was already prepared to tackle these puzzles when he encountered game theory at Princeton, and in his second term there he wrote "The Bargaining Problem" to demonstrate how in economic exchanges an equilibrium point can be reached if all players are playing their best strategies. Nasar says, "He proved that for a certain very broad class of games of any number of players, at least one equilibrium exists—so long as one allows mixed strategies." Nobody at the time realized the significance of the so-called "Nash equilibrium" for later work in economics, social science, and biology.

In 1950 Nash spent the first of several summers working in Santa Monica, California, at RAND (for "research and development"), an Air Force think tank interested at the time in game theory. Back at Princeton in the fall, Nash clinched his credentials as a pure mathematician with a paper on "Real Algebraic Manifolds" and accepted an instructorship at MIT for 1951. As a new instructor—at twenty-three the youngest in the department—Nash quickly became known for his superciliousness but also for his genius. The MIT years were punctuated by summers at RAND, where Nash's attraction to other men led to his dismissal in August, 1954, when he was caught in a police sting in a men's room in Palisades Park.

Two years earlier, however, Nash had met a young nurse, Eleanor Stier, and on June 19, 1953, they were the parents of a son, John David Stier. Nash's behavior toward Eleanor Stier did him no credit. The social gulf between them led Nash to keep Eleanor a secret from his friends, and his refusal to marry her or support her and their son forced her to put the child in foster care. Twelve years later, after a period of hospitalization for schizophrenia, Nash resumed seeing Eleanor and John, who had had a miserable childhood in a succession of foster homes. Nash promised to pay for John's college education. Their closeness dwindled after a few months, but in 1993 John Stier—now an Amherst graduate working as a registered nurse—spent several days with Nash and even accompanied him on a trip to Berlin. Nasar comments that Nash meant well, "But, as in so many other relationships in his life, Nash's intentions weren't always matched by the emotional means to carry them out satisfactorily."

After the birth of John Stier in 1953 and Nash's dismissal from RAND the following summer, Nash must have been in a low mood when he returned to MIT in the fall of 1954. His fortunes picked up when he became close to one of his former students, Alicia Larde, twenty-one years old, a smart and beautiful MIT physics major born in San Salvador to a prosperous family that moved to the United States in 1944. The courtship went slowly after their first acquaintance in the MIT music library, but by early 1956 they had become intimate. One night that spring, as they lay in bed at Nash's apartment, the doorbell rang and Eleanor Stier strode in. Alicia was stunned by Eleanor's revelations but calmed down quickly when she decided Eleanor was no threat to her. Given these developments, Nash was probably relieved to win a Sloan Fellowship, a three-year research grant that allowed him to return to Princeton for a year at the Institute for Advanced Study.

Before taking up his grant at Princeton in the fall of 1956, Nash spent a month in Seattle at a summer institute conducted by the University of Washington and enjoyed a close relationship with Amasa Forrester, who had been a first-year graduate student at Princeton during Nash's final year there. However, the most important event that summer was the discovery by Nash's parents that he had a girlfriend and a son in Boston, whom he had no intention of claiming or supporting. When Nash's mother called him to inform him of her knowledge, she insisted that he return to Boston immediately and marry Eleanor. By this time Eleanor had engaged a lawyer and was demanding child support. Worried that the lawyer would report his situation to the university, Nash agreed to pay.

Nash loved New York City, and he decided to live in an apartment on Bleecker Street during his year at the Institute for Advanced Studies. His father, who had been ill all year, died suddenly in September, and this blow only intensified his difficulties with his mother over Eleanor Stier and their son. Moreover, he may well have felt that the discovery that summer of his secret life helped bring on his father's death at the age of sixty-four. These worries must have been on Nash's mind when he began thinking about marrying Alicia. Something of Nash's sensibility appears in his remark to a friend that he thought Alicia would make a good wife because she watched so much television—that is, she would not be any great nuisance to him. At any rate, Alicia moved to New York and spent Thanksgiving with Nash and his family in Roanoke, Virginia, where his sister lived. Everyone got along fine, but Virginia Nash found the beautiful young physicist not the domestic type she had always foreseen as a daughter-in-law. In February, 1957, Nash and Alicia Larde were married in St. John's Episcopal Church in Washington, D.C., and they went to live in an apartment on New York's Upper East Side.

At the Institute for Advanced Studies Nash worked on two major problems, one involving elliptic partial differential equations and the other an attempt to revise quantum theory. The first resulted in a paper published in 1958 that some mathematicians consider his best work, but his struggle with quantum mechanics wore him out. Nash later said that it was work on quantum mechanics—an effort he called "possibly overreaching and psychologically destabilizing"—that led to his collapse into schizophrenia.

After a trip to Europe in the summer of 1958, the Nashes returned to Cambridge and discovered that Alicia was pregnant. That winter Nash's behavior started alarming people, especially the incoherent lectures that he gave at Columbia and Yale and a letter rejecting an appointment at the University of Chicago with the excuse that he was going to become the Emperor of Antarctica. His condition became so bad that in

April, 1959, Alicia had him committed to McLean Hospital in Cambridge for two months. His son, John Charles Nash, was born a week before his release, by which time Alicia had moved in with an old friend from her student days, Emma Duchane. After holding what he named a "Mad Hatter's Tea" for the MIT mathematics department, Nash resigned from the university and with a reluctant Alicia sailed for Europe in July on the *Queen Mary*, leaving the infant—known only as Baby Epsilon—with Alicia's mother.

The 1960's were difficult for all the Nashes. Nash was in and out of hospitals several times, and Alicia divorced him in 1963. By 1970 Nash was pitiable in his loneliness and Alicia took him in to live with her in Princeton. Nash gradually returned to normality by 1990, probably in great part because of Alicia's care and the fact that he had refused the powerful medications urged on him in various hospitals. He believes that he willed himself back to health by monitoring his impulses in much the way one would control one's diet. A big triumph came in 1990 when he was elected a Fellow in the Econometrics Society, although only after a battle.

The fight over Nash's election to the Econometrics Society was a mere prelude to the big row that his nomination for a Nobel Prize occasioned, a story that Nasar tells very well. The campaign to win a Nobel Prize for Nash began in 1984, when Ariel Rubenstein of Hebrew University put Nash at the top of his ten-page report on potential candidates who worked in game theory. After several false starts, the prize committee decided in 1993 to make an award for game theory in 1994, fifty years after the publication of von Neumann and Morgenstern's famous book. Nash immediately became a leading candidate, but he encountered powerful opposition on the committee before finally triumphing with two co-winners, Reinhard Selten and John Harsanyi.

The ceremony went off smoothly, with Nash giving a short speech in which he hoped that the prize might improve his credit rating enough that he could get a credit card. Nash conducted himself very well during his visit to Sweden and later gave a talk at Uppsala on "the possibility that the universe isn't expanding." He returned to Princeton to resume life with Alicia—not remarried but comfortable. He was, however, disappointed by the failure of his son John Charles Nash to recover from his own illness.

Frank Day

Sources for Further Study

The Economist. CCCXLVIII, September 12, 1998, p. S11.
Library Journal. CXXIII, May 15, 1998, p. 94.
The New England Journal of Medicine. CCCXXXIX, July 16, 1998, p. 205.
New Scientist. CLIX, September 5, 1998, p. 48.
The New York Review of Books. XLV, April 23, 1998, p. 17.
The New York Times Book Review. CIII, June 14, 1998, p. 5.

Publishers Weekly. CCXLV, May 11, 1998, p. 58.
The Sciences. XXXVIII, September, 1998, p. 35.
Technology Review. CI, July, 1998, p. 84.
The Washington Post Book World. XXVIII, August 2, 1998, p. 1.

BECH AT BAY
A Quasi-Novel

Author: John Updike (1932-   )
Published: Alfred A. Knopf (New York). 241 pp. $23.00
Type of work: Novel
Time: 1986-1999
Locale: Czechoslovakia, New York City, Los Angeles, and Sweden

> *Updike's third installment in his Bech series has his novelist alter ego battling old age and creeping cultural irrelevance*

Principal characters:
HENRY BECH, a semi-famous, unprolific American novelist
ISAIAH THORNBUSH, a competing New York writer and friend of Bech
EDNA, the directress of The Forty, an honorary organization supporting the arts
MORRIS OHRBACH, a Hollywood agent
RACHEL TEAGARTEN, a young computer whiz who bears Bech's child, Golda
ORLANDO COHEN, a prominent literary critic

A master stylist, poet, short-story writer, novelist, and critic, John Updike has come to dominate the American literary scene since his first novel *The Poorhouse Fair* (1959). More than two dozen critical books have been written about his works, not to mention the many articles and essays published about him yearly. Specializing in sex, religion, and middle-class American mores, Updike has written nearly a book a year in an easy profligacy reminiscent of Joyce Carol Oates. His strong, painterly descriptive ability was developed in part from his artistic training at the Ruskin School of Fine Art at Oxford. A frequent writer for *The New Yorker*, Updike has influenced writers such as Ann Beattie, Anne Tyler, and Nicholson Baker, who wrote a booklength discussion of that influence entitled *U and I* (1991). While his popularity as a writer peaked in the 1980's, his more recent works such as *In the Beauty of the Lilies* (1996) and *Toward the End of Time* (1997) have depended more on research for inspiration and have earned more mixed reviews. Because of the sheer volume and range of his oeuvre, however, Updike is one of the few remaining examples of a "man of letters," adept at all aspects of the literary game. His many collections of critical essays provide a rare overview of world fiction from a nontheoretical bias.

Given his achievement, it makes sense that Updike chose a doppleganger fictional creation, Henry Bech, to convey his views on literary celebrity. First appearing in a loosely arranged collection of short stories entitled *Bech: A Book* (1970), Bech is in many ways Updike's alter ego. His writer's block ironically contrasts with Updike's extreme profligacy. His Jewish alienation differs from Updike's Christian leanings, but mostly his wry underdog perspective supplies a perfect vehicle for Updike to express his thoughts on the literary fame game in America. Readers call in the middle of the night to ask Bech about a book written decades before. Publishers ask him to sign copies of his books until he can no longer write his name. When Bech finds himself with writer's block (which is most of the time), he goes on junkets around the Third World, Europe, or in Communist countries—a traveling theme that all three Bech books share. When Bech stays in America, he reluctantly participates in television interviews, readings on college campuses, and book signings. Throughout the short stories, one rarely glimpses Bech writing. Instead, he drifts on the vagaries of his celebrity, a creature well-suited for our fascination with authors at the expense of their works, and the results are often both funny and poignant.

In an interview, Updike once described how he never wanted "to let a good thing go unflogged," and so after *Rabbit, Run* (1960), Rabbit Angstrom appeared repeatedly for a total of four novels until his death in *Rabbit at Rest* (1990). In the same fashion, Bech, who began as a "vehicle" for Updike's "impressions," then inspired a second collection of stories *Bech Is Back* (1975), a book more substantial than its predecessor in its organization, characterization, and plot development. Having invented his "quasi-novel" form in *Bech: A Book*, Updike bound together the second book with a three-pronged collection of epiphanies or "Illuminations" at the beginning, all having to do with writing, and concluded the volume with a lengthy story concerning Bech's failing attempts to marry into a family and fit into suburbia. In between these more sustained pieces, Updike included the usual travelogues, this time to Scotland, Israel, Australia, and Canada.

In *Bech at Bay* (1998), Bech has grown noticeably older (in his sixties and seventies) for most of these stories, and their themes tend to center around questions of potency and the power of language. With his writing largely finished and his love life on the wane, Bech looks around for something to do. In his metafictional way, he feels like a character no longer needed by his author, in danger of being erased. As his physical powers fade, Bech begins to lash out against enemies, real or imagined. He fathers a child in his seventies, begins surreptitiously killing critics who had panned his work, and presides over a literary foundation on the edge of dissolution. Through all this, he keeps coming back to the same questions—where does the writer belong? How much does language matter? The fact that the artist's foundation gets sold out to pave the way for a Donald Trump-like real-estate development implies an increasingly radical disjuncture between the arts and the corporate wheeling and dealing that surrounds it. Bech seems to preside over a dying culture, and yet Updike refuses to let the darker implications of his vision get in the way of these determinedly upbeat stories. The reader has to look in the margins to get beyond Updike's instinct to please. *Bech at Bay* incongruously blends apocalyptic forebodings with a stubbornly cheerful aesthetic.

To gauge this change in Bech's position, one can compare the first story of the collection "Bech Czechs It" (1986) with the rest of the collection, mostly set in the late 1990's. In this story, upon arriving in Prague for one of his usual junkets, Bech visits Franz Kafka's grave. This occasion prompts much meditation on the layers of bureaucracy still oppressing whatever attempts the Czechoslovakians make to express themselves. At one point, a gypsy woman hands him a *samizdat*, an illegally typed and bound book, and Bech wonders over its "unexpected" beauty. Within the context of Russian spies, bugs, and constant surveillance, the printed word attains a grace reminiscent of the first books printed by ancient monks. While Czech authors go to jail for writing poetry, Bech finds that there is "nothing that he had ever written that he would not eagerly recant." Because of this tension between Czech heroism and American rights that Bech takes for granted, this story has a complexity and moral weight missing from the later, more parodic works in the collection.

Later stories tend to cast around for narrative drive. In "Bech Pleads Guilty," a story set back in the 1970's, high-level Hollywood agent Orlando Cohen sues Bech for libelously calling him an "arch-gouger" of his clients, thus obliging Bech to travel to Los Angeles for a protracted court appearance. Updike uses the occasion to reflect on Los Angeles, the differences between the East and West coasts, and O. J. Simpson-style courtroom dynamics. Faced with the very litigious Cohen in person, Bech begins to feel a perverse guilt, even though he eventually wins the case. Again, Updike explores the value and power of words, how they can set in motion an entire if somewhat futile legal proceeding. Rich as it is in description, the story has precious little human drama, all of it flattened by Los Angeles's blank freeway-ridden cityscape. Bech thinks of Cohen's resemblance to his father, of the Promised Land, of his ability to lie under oath, but not much happens. It reads like a promising idea that lost its narrative drive in midstream.

Ever the aesthete, Bech's itch for pleasure takes odder forms as he ages. His romantic dalliances strain credulity as he enters his seventies (or perhaps his romances seem more perfunctory with repetition). In his seventy-fourth year, Bech finds a twenty-six-year-old girlfriend named Robin. She becomes his sidekick for his Batmanlike capers in Gotham, and she wants to bear his child, serenely oblivious to the fifty-year-gap between them. Bech begins humorously enough by shoving into a crowd in a subway station to kill off a book critic, but then he begins sending out poisoned letters until another dies, then works in cahoots with his computer-savvy girlfriend to send subliminal e-mail messages to another critic until he jumps off his penthouse apartment balcony. By the time he dons a cape and slippered shoes to begin breaking into the apartment of another critic, one wonders at the weightlessness of these bloodless and largely characterless killings. Who is the bad guy here? Critics? As much as Updike inoculates his prose with critical barbs that anticipate and parody the critical treatment of this book, one cannot help wondering what is grounding this fantasy. Are readers meant to abhor Bech's new impotent lashings out, his attempts to prop up his vanity by striking back against all the negative reviews he has ever received, or are they supposed to laugh at the postmodern mockery of film noir conventions? After each slaying, Bech and Robin enjoy reading the obituary section of *The New York Times* over breakfast. If Updike means all this as a joke, it wears thin pretty quickly, in part because the villains are so thinly sketched. These remain victimless crimes. The fantastic noirish city backdrop and Bech and Robin's gumshoe talk might have had some resonance with a real opponent, but since Bech has never seriously been harmed by criticism, much like his maker has not, his killings seem like action for the sake of action, an irrelevant and idle writer's fantasy ballooned up to a unwieldy story.

In the end, Bech wins the Nobel Prize much as he won a place in a pantheon of noted authors at the end of *Bech: A Book*. Across the country, critics are outraged that this "passe exponent of fancy penmanship" would win the award, and Bech finds himself at a loss deciding on how to justify his work during his acceptance speech. He travels to Stockholm with his girlfriend and eight-month-old baby, Golda, and agonizes about what to say. He wonders about the obscenity of "aesthetic bliss" in a "world of suffering." He even considers recounting the sufferings of the Jews in Europe and America, but Updike is never as successful depicting Bech's Jewish identity as he is in depicting his authorial consciousness. Ultimately, his aesthetic resists any grand political summation. Asserting the primacy of the quotidian detail, he decides not to "generalize away the miracle, the quizzical quiddity, of the specific." So, instead of really giving the speech, he allows his baby daughter to say "Hi!" to the august audience, in the end asserting rebirth over bitter old age.

Probably the last installment in a three-part series, *Bech at Bay* records John Updike's impressions of the writer's place in *fin de siècle* America. In a cultural milieu dominated by machines, computers, television, movies, and sampled popular music, Bech finds himself besieged by corporate takeovers, lawsuits, talk-show hosts, critics, and award institutions. Updike experiments with parodying film noir conventions and has Bech lash back at his critics by killing them. Ultimately, the plot matters less in this quasi-novel than Bech's wry observations. Determined to remain optimistic in the face of the writer's old age and increasing obsolescence, Bech carves out his Updikean aesthetic, seeking order, peace, and the tranquillity of art in the face of critics, the media, old age, and other forces that keep him at bay. As he says: "My life has been spent attending to my inner weather and my immediate vicinity."

Roy C. Flannagan

Sources for Further Study

The Atlantic. CCLXXXI, November 1, 1998, p. 137.
Booklist. XCIV, August, 1998, p. 1925.
The Christian Century. CXV, October 21, 1998, p. 977.
Library Journal. CXXIII, September 1, 1998, p. 219.
Los Angeles Times Book Review. September 27, 1998, p. 11.
New York. XXXI, October 19, 1998, p. 73.
The New York Times Book Review. CIII, October 25, 1998, p. 7.
Publishers Weekly. CCXLV, July 20, 1998, p. 204.
Time. CLI, November 9, 1998, p. 114.
The Washington Post Book World. XXVIII, October 18, 1998, p. 3.

BEYOND BELIEF
Islamic Excursions Among the Converted Peoples

Author: V. S. Naipaul (1932-   )
Published: Random House (New York). 408 pp. $27.95
Type of work: Current affairs, religion, and travel
Time: July, 1995, to May, 1997
Locale: Indonesia, Iran, Pakistan, and Malaysia

V. S. Naipaul revisits Indonesia, Iran, Malaysia, and Pakistan, which he toured in 1979, to investigate Islamic culture and politics

In 1979, V. S. Naipaul traveled through Iran, Pakistan, Indonesia, and Malaysia. The itinerary had a theme: He wanted to find out how Islam was faring in countries whose citizens descended from non-Arab converts. The book he wrote afterward, *Among the Believers: An Islamic Journey* (1981), is a disturbing album of profiles, interviews, history, personal drama, and analysis, which together portray Islam among converts as culturally confused, turbulent, wholly authoritarian and legalistic, and politically stultifying. Yet the religion is also precious to the faithful, for whom it gives life identify and purpose, defines community, and instills moral certainty.

Beyond Belief: Islamic Excursions Among the Converted Peoples returns readers to the four countries seventeen years later—five months of travel during 1995. It was a moderately stable time for the countries, prosperous for Indonesia and Malaysia, shortly before the Asian economic crisis began. Of the people whom Naipaul revisits, many are materially and politically better off than they had been. Yet like the first book, the tone is grim, although relieved occasionally by situational humor or lovely scenic descriptions, as the reader finds Naipaul questioning those around him, thrusting himself into dangerous company, considering local history and culture, sizing up personalities, noting both the absurd and the noble, and, always, portraying the individual as a cobbled-together chimera of incidental personal experience, half-understood values, taboos, and malleable desire. Readers are fortunate to have in Naipaul an acute observer who is also a master prose stylist, but the book is sobering.

In the preface, Naipaul warns that *Beyond Belief* is not so much a travel book as *Among the Believers* was. The emphasis is on storytelling, not opinion; his authorial role as commentator is muted. He is relentless in getting people to talk about themselves and records their stories at length. The ordering of material naturally follows Naipaul's trips through each country, but beyond that, readers may find the connection among stories, anecdotes, and historical summaries a little obscure. Often the stories appear to be emblematic, capturing some essential effect of Islam or of a nation's culture, and it is left to the reader to decide exactly which effect. Occasionally, particularly in the book's last section, "Malaysian Postscript," the sequence of stories seems to have as little continuity as a jumble of photographs—although sharply focused, dramatic photographs.

While his presence in the narrative is reserved, Naipaul nevertheless is part of the book's story. He is almost confessional at times, remarking upon parallels between what he observes in his host countries and his own experiences growing up in Trinidad. Those experiences make him particularly sensitive to the dilemmas posed by cultural mixing. His parents were Indian Hindus who settled in the British Caribbean. He was educated at Oxford University. As a novelist, he, like Joseph Conrad, has written about cultural conflicts among European and Third World countries. This background gives him a particular ability to remain disinterested. At one point, Naipaul, summarizing the credo of a Pakistani journalist, appears to describe himself: Valuable writing is more than a facility with words, he says. It comes from a "moral wholeness" in the writer, which finds lodging only in an independent intellect. Naipaul has it.

The soul of the book lies in the people Naipaul profiles. They are diverse, and the diversity is what first brings depth to a subject few Western readers know much about, life in Islam. To give readers perspective, Naipaul compares their 1995 lives with those in 1979. One of the most arresting characters of *Among Believers* is Imaduddin, an engineer turned religious advocate whose "mental training" seminars are designed to prepare young Indonesians to be effective exponents of Islam. In the first book, he is much persecuted by the government but full of energy and boundlessly devout. The energy and faith reappear in the second book, but he has become successful, the protégé of the country's president and director of an organization for Islamic intellectuals. As Naipaul tries to hold him still long enough for an interview, Imaduddin begins to sound more and more like a modern politician and even a little menacing. In contrast, one of the scariest people in the first book has had the opposite fate. In 1979, Ayatollah Khalkhalli of Iran was at the height of his powers as Ayatollah Khomeini's "hanging judge." He sent hundreds of political enemies of Iran's Islamic revolution to the firing squads, and he giggled with glee at his power as Naipaul tried to question him. In 1995, he has been cast aside by Iran's leaders, a pitiful, paranoid shut-in in the holy city of Qom. Naipaul's interview is a scene of dark irony. Khalkhalli petulantly evades all questions, suspicious that Naipaul has been sent to discredit him further.

Linus, an Indonesian, is one of the most attractive personalities in the book. A poet, he planned in 1979 to celebrate village life in his poetry and to make a living as a writer. By 1995 he has done so, bringing out an epic poem that sold well and made him famous, but his life is almost tragic. The village culture he so loves is disintegrating around him as Indonesia's booming economy draws people away from farming and fills the land with dwellings for acculturated workers commuting to the city; moreover, Islamic fundamentalists threaten him for praising customs and Hindu rites that predate Islam in Indonesia.

Some glimpses of daily life in the book are chillingly familiar despite the locale. For example, in Iran, Naipaul talks with veterans of the Iran-Iraq war, an eight-year conflict that haunts the country. Veterans speak with disillusionment reminiscent of American reaction to the Vietnam War. Meanwhile, despite the strict Islamic code of conduct in Iran, the youth range from rich-kid slackers to Nazi skinheads with little interest in the generation that fought the revolution and war.

A central theme of the book gradually clarifies the seemingly random cultural oddities Naipaul encounters. Islam in converted countries, he argues, grows in a "spiritual vacancy." The vacancy plagues peoples who, for the sake of Islam, turned away from their ethnic or national history. History for them is a kind of neurosis, Naipaul remarks. It is a disturbing perception, and readers may well wonder if it is overstated. It is true, in any case, that converted Muslims look to Mecca and the Koran's tales of Mohammed for meaning, and they adjust their own history to make them seem more Arabic or pretend that their history has no meaning. The conservative tendency of converted Muslims is to subtract all cultural features except those of the Koran and apocryphal tales about Mohammed and his heirs. Among the most conservative and intense Muslims in the four countries, the simmering rage for purity frequently erupts in violence. This is the principal trait of fundamentalists, a term Naipaul himself uses, although it appears they regard Islam not so much as fundamental as singular, in that to them there is not, or should not be, anything else in the world.

So it is a bitter pill to fundamentalists that the West, with its un-Islamic ways, thrives—all the more bitter because the material wealth and technology of the West exert great attraction on many intellectuals with whom Naipaul speaks. Repugnance at Western morality aside, many Muslims view non-Muslim culture as a resource to exploit. The richest and brightest attend Western universities, especially those in the United States and Great Britain, studying practical subjects such as engineering and business. Like Imaduddin, they bring the knowledge back to their homelands and adapt it to local and Islamic institutions. Again like Imaduddin, Naipaul complains, they seem utterly oblivious of the kindness and help shown to them by their host professors and perversely keen on condemning the host country's culture as evil. Furthermore, activists, when in trouble at home, use America or England as an asylum, a kind of free zone in the deadly game of tag with their rivals in Islamic politics. As for the poor and powerless, non-Islamic countries are also a resource in that they provide jobs. Pakistan, for example, finds jobs abroad for so many workers who send money home to relatives that it has turned into a remittance economy. For these reasons, Naipaul judges Islam to be parasitic.

Islam flourishes because there is a need for it. The point is obvious, but, as Naipaul shows, the underlying attraction of Islam arises from the helplessness people in postcolonial Third World countries feel toward the more powerful, confusing culture of the West. Islam, he says, has replaced communism as the consoler of the poor, a telling insight. Islam is a set of ideas the West does not dominate, it is exclusive to the faithful and fosters moral superiority, and it encourages some degree of solidarity among the ethnic groups and nations in the Islamic world. The stern power of Islam, often so perplexing to Western readers, becomes clear as Naipaul's sources affirm their attachment to the faith.

While he often warms to the people he meets, Naipaul appears to find Islam itself unsettling at best and repugnant in its conservative tendencies toward chauvinism and dogmatism. In his skillful narration, the transplanted Islam of all four countries seems ill-suited to modern government and economics, hypocritical to the non-Islamic world, repressive toward women, and so convinced of its own truth and righteousness as to be ominous.

Beyond Belief supplies a badly needed view of countries about which American readers are largely underinformed or misinformed. It reveals the strength of the faith but also the lack of political unity among the faithful. It portrays Iran, worn out and financially stressed, as increasingly interested in rapprochement with the United States, which may surprise readers. It hints at the roots of turmoil in Indonesia, the world's third-most-populous nation; although the book was written before rioting paralyzed the capital, Jakarta, and forced a change in leadership, signs of unrest and tension haunt Naipaul's sources. Most worrisome, Naipaul depicts Pakistan as volatile and reactionary, frightening qualities for a nation that possesses nuclear weapons.

From Naipaul's quilt of interviews, history, and first-person impression, readers should understand better how the faithful and not-so-faithful express Islam in their lives and how the conflicts within the countries are likely to set them at odds with the world. Considering that Iran, Malaysia, Pakistan, and Indonesia contain a twelfth of humanity, anyone interested in international affairs, if only for practical business purposes, is well advised to read about Naipaul's excursions.

Roger Smith

Sources for Further Study

Booklist. XCIV, May 15, 1998, p. 1567.
The Christian Century. CXV, September 9, 1998, p. 835.
The Economist. CCCXLVIII, September 12, 1998, p. S7.
Foreign Affairs. LXXVII, September, 1998, p. 162.
Library Journal. CXXIII, May 15, 1998, p. 91.
The New Republic. CCXIX, July 13, 1998, p. 27.
The New York Review of Books. XLV, July 16, 1998, p. 8.
The New York Times Book Review. CIII, June 7, 1998, p. 6.
Publishers Weekly. CCXLV, May 25, 1998, p. 82.
The Wall Street Journal. July 14, 1998, p. A16.

THE BIOTECH CENTURY
Harnessing the Gene and Remaking the World

Author: Jeremy Rifkin (1945-   )
Published: Jeremy P. Tarcher/Putnam (New York). 271 pp. $24.95
Type of work: Ethics and science

Rifkin identifies seven coincident social, economic, and technological forces that underlie the forthcoming biotechnical revolution

Since the mid-twentieth century, computer technology and the life sciences have developed side by side at breakneck speed. By the end of the century, they converged into an inconceivably omnipotent force with broad social, economic, and philosophical implications.

Humankind, often unwittingly, has been drawn into a biotechnical age that will likely define not only the first half of the twenty-first century but will also have a lasting impact on all subsequent centuries and human activities, much as the Industrial Revolution of the nineteenth century affected not only its own time but all subsequent history. Despite the problems and hazards brought about by the industrialization of the world, twentieth century humans would fare badly if they were magically catapulted into the preindustrial age. The conveniences the Industrial Revolution made available have created for the masses a life considerably easier than life before it. Humankind, nevertheless, has been forced to cope with the problems that went together with industrialization and urbanization.

Jeremy Rifkin, founder and president of the Foundation on Economic Trends in Washington, D.C., has discussed such problems in a number of his earlier books, most notably *Who Should Play God?* (1977) and *Entropy* (1989), both collaborations with Ted Howard, and in *Biosphere Politics: A Cultural Odyssey from the Middle Ages to the New Age* (1991), *Beyond Beef: The Rise and Fall of the Cattle Industry* (1992), and *Voting Green* (1992), a collaboration with Carol Grunewald. Many scientists consider Rifkin an alarmist whose views are too extreme to be credible.

When *Who Should Play God?* was published in 1977, its predictions of the creation of transgenic species, cloning of vertebrates, test-tube babies, the renting of surrogate wombs, the fabrication of human organs, and human gene surgery struck molecular scientists, politicians, scientific writers, and others concerned with biotechnology as unrealistic, as events surely that would not occur within the next century. Within twenty years, these predictions had all been realized.

Rifkin is not a lopsided environmentalist. He is quick to applaud much of what genetic research has accomplished, particularly genetic screening and genetic surgery that can, for example, detect and correct many genetic anomalies in fetuses. He acknowledges that agriculture, and by extension the whole human race, has benefited from biotechnology. His concern is that humankind does not yet realize what the long-term effects of biotechnical meddling may be.

Part of his thesis is that the paradigm of nature espoused by Francis Bacon in the late sixteenth century has been the compelling paradigm of science ever since. Bacon is considered the founder of modern science, but, as Rifkin points out, he "urged future generations to 'squeeze,' 'mould,' and 'shape' nature, in order to 'enlarge the bounds of human empire to the effecting of all things possible.'" Humans, for Bacon, were the center of all nature, a commonly held view during the Enlightenment. Scientists have accepted this philosophy as a guiding principle and have employed it, tacitly or overtly, to justify much of their activity. When science moves out of the laboratory and into the marketplace, the commercial possibilities of scientific advances are staggering. Rifkin questions, with seeming justification, the ethics of those whose interest in science is largely commercial.

In support of his skepticism, Rifkin notes that in 1974 eleven leading molecular biologists published an open letter to their fellow molecular biologists urging a moratorium on recombinant deoxyribonucleic acid (DNA) experiments that posed a considerable risk. The following year, when 140 biologists from around the world met to consider this proposal, most indicated in an informal poll that they wanted to get on with their work unimpeded by the safeguards the document proposed. On the third day of the conference, when several attorneys outlined the legal responsibilities of scientists who create biohazards, the scientists began to have second thoughts. Their reservations, however, were based on fears of legal liability rather than on concerns about the long-term effects of their scientific experiments. Clearly, the economic interests of most of those who attended the conference were far more persuasive than the scientific interests. The specter that Harold Green of George Washington University Law School presented of the possibility of multimillion-dollar lawsuits resulting from biohazardous experiments turned the tide. The biologists finally voted overwhelmingly in favor of a two-point safety program. In Rifkin's view, however, they did so for questionable reasons.

Rifkin addresses the matter of objectivity in the scientific community. Clearly, most scientists aim for objectivity in conducting experiments and in reporting their results. Rifkin warns, however, that despite their strenuous attempts to be unbiased, objective, and value free, what molecular biologists and other scientists see "ultimately depends upon what [they are] looking for. The search is always preconditioned by the biases of the researchers." Certainly the Baconian paradigm is firmly fixed in the minds of many eminent scientists, whose training has been strongly influenced by it. The conquest of nature is more important and justifiable in their eyes than are attempts to achieve the integrative, systemic approach to nature that ecological study promotes and pursues. Rifkin's fear is that molecular biologists are loosing forces that may eventually elude their control and that, taken to the extreme, could threaten all life on Earth, the great biosphere whose natural balance has already been severely compromised by the relentless inroads made upon it by industrial and scientific development.

The splitting of the atom and the unraveling of the DNA double helix, according to Rifkin, represent "the two premier scientific accomplishments of the twentieth century, the first a tour de force of physics, the second of biology." He cautions, however, that the splitting of the atom led to forces so difficult to control, so frightening that only two atom bombs have ever been used against human populations and that the growth of nuclear energy, once thought to offer the solution to the world's energy problems, is being severely reined in because of the hazards of disposing of nuclear wastes and because of the danger of nuclear meltdowns.

The biotechnical revolution may create situations even more resistant to controls than those the nuclear revolution has created. Biological warfare can effectively obliterate an enemy. A shift in air currents, however, may annihilate those on the offensive rather than those they seek to destroy, to say nothing of hundreds of thousands of innocent people caught in the crosswinds, whose environment might suddenly become fatally poisoned. If genetic testing and tampering can ascertain and alter the characteristics of fetuses, extreme population imbalances are predictable. What Chinese family, for example, would opt for a female offspring if genetic manipulation could guarantee a male? Would fetuses found to have irreparable genetic defects be permitted to grow to term? Would homosexual fetuses be routinely aborted or genetically altered to eliminate their sexual propensities?

Rifkin has organized his book around seven biotechnical and social forces that underlie the biotechnical revolution he foresees in the twenty-first century. First, he focuses on the ability of molecular biologists to create a new resource base through identifying, isolating, and recombining genes in animals, including humans. Second, a thriving and highly profitable enterprise has already arisen in patenting genes, cell lines, tissue from bioengineering, organs, organisms, and the procedures for altering them. Rifkin foresees further the growth of global industries focusing on artificial biotechnical products and processes which, already fast developing in agriculture and medicine, will spread to other fields and will have global economic implications. Next, the Human Genome Project, already under way, will, within a short time, map all of the human genome, making possible the control of characteristics in sperm and egg cells and in embryos that will result in the sort of eugenic civilization darkly predicted by George Orwell and Aldous Huxley in the mid-twentieth century.

These developments will coincide with a proliferation of scientific studies biased in favor of a Baconian-inspired biotechnology that the overall public will be brainwashed into accepting. Along with this, the increasing sophistication of computers will result in their ability to handle all the complex genetic information required for the effective implementation of genetic engineering. Finally, Rifkin predicts that Darwinian interpretations of evolution will be replaced by concepts that organisms are not permanent forms but are constantly changing. This argument will provide justification for the reorganization of the political, economic, and social lives of everyone living in the brave new world of the biotech century.

Rifkin's greatest concern is that the enormous economic profits to be reaped from biotechnology will completely blind the greedy to the long-term consequences of their actions. The world has no shortage of opportunists who will grab what they can for themselves, giving no thought to the welfare of generations yet unborn. Another fear, certainly, involves the possibility that political or religious fanatics will manufacture and use materials that could very well annihilate life on the planet. Such people are obsessed by the righteousness of their causes and can, in the name of that righteous-ness, justify in their own consciences any destructive act, even one that might lead to worldwide destruction.

A receptive, uncritical public may be the greatest danger to humankind as the biotech century proceeds. A generation born under certain circumstances soon adjusts to those circumstances, and regardless of how abnormal they are when measured by previous standards, they soon come to seem normal to those who have known little else throughout their lifetimes. Rifkin contends that consumers create markets as much as markets create consumers. A public that wants genetic screening or the cloning of humans will eventually have its way, and herein lies a considerable long-term danger to humankind.

One might question, for example, why the public or any major segment of it would support the cloning of human beings. Those who do not wish to marry but want to continue their family lines may find appealing the notion of being able to create a human essentially identical to themselves physically and, to an extent, mentally. Also, a clone in some future never-never land might be created for the sole purpose of providing spare parts for the original donor of the genetic material from which the clone has been created. The religious, ethical, and social implications of using clones for spare parts are chilling, but they must certainly be considered, because the very real possibility exists that this is a use to which clones might be put.

People who dismiss such speculation as something that cannot happen in the foreseeable future should reflect on the reaction to the prognostications of Rifkin and Ted Howard, his collaborator, in *Who Should Play God?* They might do well to remember that the notion of the Earth as heliocentric was considered heretical during the first millennium and half of the common era and that the thought of humans being able to fly was part of the science fiction of earlier times. What reasonable person in 1950 would have considered it possible to send a vehicle to the moon, place a human on that distant outpost, and return him or her safely to Earth? Humans are still sufficiently imbedded in the past to think quite frequently of the future as distant and virtually unrealizable. However, civilization is moving at a great speed. The future in biotechnical terms is tomorrow or, if one has been napping, may even be yesterday.

R. Baird Shuman

Sources for Further Study

Business Week. April 13, 1998, p. 14.
JAMA: Journal of the American Medical Association. CCLXXX, August 12, 1998, p. 575.
The Nation. CCLXVI, April 13, 1998, p. 11.
The National Catholic Reporter. April 24, 1998, p. 16.
Nature. CCCXCIII, May 7, 1998, p. 31.

The New York Review of Books. XLV, April 23, 1998, p. 14.
The New York Times Book Review. CIII, March 22, 1998, p. 34.
Publishers Weekly. CCXLV, February 16, 1998, p. 195.
The Progressive. LXII, May, 1998, p. 43.
Sierra. LXXXIII, September, 1998, p. 80.

BIRDS OF AMERICA

Author: Lorrie Moore (1957-   )
Published: Alfred A. Knopf (New York). 291 pp. $23.00
Type of work: Short fiction
Time: The 1990's
Locale: Chicago, New York, Wisconsin, Italy, and Ireland

Lorrie Moore seasons despair with humor in twelve sharply written stories about cancer, failed marriages, travel, and real estate

Principal characters:
RUTH, a woman who turns to shooting practice to keep crows off her property
"MOTHER," a writer whose baby turns out to have cancer of the kidney
SIDRA, an actress who moves to Chicago and dates a mechanic
ABBY, a woman who initiates a quest to kiss the Blarney Stone with her mother
OLENA, a librarian
AILEEN, a woman mourning the loss of her cat
QUILTY, a blind man who travels the United States with his gay lover, Mack
ADRIENNE, a woman attending an academic conference in Italy
BILL, a law professor dating one of his former students

With the critical and commercial success of *Birds of America* (1998), Lorrie Moore has established herself as one of the foremost writers of the 1990's. A professor of English at the University of Wisconsin at Madison and an occasional reviewer of fiction, Moore published her first collection of short stories, *Self-Help*, in 1983. Since then, she has produced another collection, *Like Life* (1988), and two novels, *Anagrams* (1986) and *Who Will Run the Frog Hospital?* (1994). While her earlier stories were known for their sardonic send ups of self-help manuals, her vision has darkened over time in narratives populated by increasingly isolated characters. She tends to gravitate to unsettling, uncomfortable topics and then find a kind of gallows humor in them. As in her earlier work, *Birds of America* concerns such topics as cancer and its effects on the people who suffer from it, their forced break from everydayness. Her stories tend to yoke together opposite extremes—a shy, bookish librarian with an anarchist community activist, a drifting Hollywood actress with a Chicago mechanic who has never seen her movies. Even though Moore's stories have lengthened and become more novelistic in their concern with place and identity, her humor remains her strongest asset. She writes of hilarity in the face of powerlessness, and absurdity that sometimes borders on hysteria; the more bleak the situation, the more she leaves the reader uncertain whether to laugh or feel concern. Moore's defiant, devil-may-care attitude helps make her characters' alienation, failure, and disfranchisement more bearable.

Moore achieves some of her best effects through style, a poetic attention to the sound of language, the odd turn of phrase, the disjointed rhythm of an unexpected extra clause. In "Community Life," the librarian Olena considers the atmosphere of a coffee shop: "there was in the air that kind of distortion that bent you a little; it caused your usual self to grow slippery, to wander off and shop, to get blurry, bleed, bevel with possibility." The alliteration begins just as the clauses shorten, creating a staccato rhythm that reinforces Olena's pleasant sense of disorientation with a new suitor. In other stories, characters resort to an exaggerated attention to the absurdities of language as a kind of defense against the real-life tensions around them. Feeling defensive about people's reactions to his much younger girlfriend, Bill, the law professor in "Beautiful Grade," makes puns, dwells on names, and considers the weakness of the political phrase "don't count on us." Within Bill's hyperliterary but fragile perspective, Moore riffs out ironic variations on his every thought: "He [Bill] believes in free speech. He believes in expensive speech. He doesn't believe in shouting 'Fire' in a crowded movie theatre, but he does believe in shouting 'Fie!' and has done it twice himself—both times at *Forrest Gump.*" Moore writes felicitous turns of phrase on every page. In another story, one finds a woman whose "brains had been sucked dry by too much yoga" just as "a vacuum cleaner can start to pull up the actual thread of a carpet."

As her style plays ironic variations on itself, Moore's plotlines often negotiate between interior and exterior worlds. Characters cocoon themselves from both the natural and cultural wilderness that surrounds them. Damage to property often serves as a metaphor for the threats to the body or the psyche, and increasingly one realizes that no one is safe. In "Four Calling Birds, Three French Hens," Aileen worries over the birds, squirrels, and possums that threaten her yard after her cat Bert dies. In "Real Estate," Ruth buys a house and discovers the encroachments of a menagerie of animals as well as a young teenager in her attic. If outside agents do not break into her body in the form of cancer, they break into her home in the form of squatters, animals, or prowlers. Eventually, she learns to fire a gun and kills a thief, thus underscoring the aggression underlying her effort to maintain some kind of autonomy. After shooting the man, she walks off by herself in despair. Moore's portrait of her hysteria is one of the most chillingly effective of the collection.

In her strongest story, "People Like That Are the Only People Here: Canonical Babbling in Peed Onk," Moore takes the grimmest scenario, a baby developing cancer of the kidney, and expands it into a controlled rage at cosmic injustice amid the niceties of modern medicine. Curiously, Moore uses this context to reflect on the inadequacies of writing, of trying to shape a narrative around such an absurd situation. The main character, a writer and teacher known impersonally as "Mother," resembles Moore herself. At one point, a doctor asks her to sign one of her earlier novels, clearly a reference to *Who Will Run the Frog Hospital?* The character's husband wants her to keep notes about their baby's operation to help raise money to pay for everything, but she balks at this "nightmare of narrative slop." Meanwhile, she resists the blandly sinister hospital procedures, the internal and external threats to her baby, and the nightmarishly cheerful compliance of other parents. As the tone jumps back and forth between existential dread, gallows humor, queasy clinical detail, and parental love, the story consistently leaves the reader off balance. The enormity of the illness keeps clashing with the innocence of the other boys in the ward, most of whom are balding from chemotherapy. While other parents acclimatize themselves with Kafkaesque resignation to perpetual self-sacrifice for their children, the Mother remains in open revolt throughout. At the close, she resolves that she "never wants to see any of these people again."

Moore is less effective in some of the shorter stories. When she has less time to develop her themes and characterizations, she falls back on more sketchy grotesques to speak for her. "Agnes of Iowa" ends with a homely couple sitting in a coffee shop in New York City. The husband makes a clown face, and Agnes tries to return it, making a "look of such monstrous emptiness and stupidity" with her newly dyed red hair that her husband laughs "like a dog." Since characters like these have worse problems than most people, Moore has to be careful about her mocking wit cutting off all readerly sympathy for them altogether. In "Charades," a Christmas family parlor game barely rises above the grotesque. Since everyone puts on an act, real identity gets buried under social personae. In the nearly plotless pathos of "Dance in America," another threatened child, Eugene, has cystic fibrosis, and another household suffers the impingements of nature when raccoons crawl into a chimney. The dance instructor narrator has recently broken up with her boyfriend, but at least they can all dance away the evening, and through that gesture defy the fates conspiring against them. This makes for a sad story, but the closure does not seem earned, the characters more stand-ins for modern maladies than fleshed-out people.

Yet these are quibbles in light of the stories' many strengths, their laugh-out-loud one-liners, summary analyses, and skillful use of point of view. In "Real Estate," Moore includes two pages of one word, repeating "Ha! Ha! Ha! Ha! Ha! Ha! Ha!" to establish the derangement of her jealous, morbidly fixated main character. Bill in "Beautiful Grade" cannot stop cracking jokes. If he did, he might expose his fears of age and of remaining a bachelor. Sometimes Moore will allow a character's cliches to speak for them, as with the mother in "Which Is More Than I Can Say About Some People." The mother's banal language serves to mask her fear of losing face in front of her daughter. Other writers occasionally hover over a story's landscape; in "What You Want to Do Fine," Moore negotiates with the shade of Vladimir Nabokov by cheerfully making the influence of *Lolita* overt. She names the older man Quilty, substitutes a gay male couple for Humbert Humbert and his nymphet, and adapts the American roadside trash culture of Nabokov's novel for a contemporary audience.

The stories often end with Joycean epiphanies undercutting whatever illusions a character has built up, and yet Moore carefully weighs the economies of their loss. At the end of "Agnes of Iowa," a character reflects, "Every arrangement in life carried with it the sadness, the sentimental shadow, of its not being something else, but only itself." Others contemplate escape of one sort or another. While the woman in "Missing" imagines herself escaping like a bird out the window from her boyfriend's infidelity, Ruth answers her in "Real Estate" by realizing that the body "possessed its own wishes and nostalgias. You could not just turn neatly into light and slip out the window." Occasionally, the stories end on a simple note of reconciliation. Given the extreme conditions these characters face, simple forgiveness becomes the best virtue on which to fall back.

With this third collection of short stories, Lorrie Moore displays a darkening, maturing dissection of the 1990's spiritual and physical maladies of middle-class Americans. A sort of female cross between Raymond Carver and Woody Allen, Moore writes of characters torn between the securities of suburbia and the enticements of the city, the dream of romance and the reality of a failed marriage, and underlying it all, the attempt to maintain normalcy amid growing unease and lack of control. She enjoys challenging the reader with light send-ups of extreme juxtapositions: children who have cancer; an actress dating a mechanic; and a blind man's perspective of a journey. Through all these combinations, the sick keeps cropping up amidst the semblance of health, just as the public increasingly bullies the private sphere. Moore keeps showing the boundaries crumbling, until only a defiant humor remains. If a woman must mourn her dead cat, she can at least add ice cream to her stages of bereavement. In "Agnes of Iowa," Agnes reflects on the humor that "seemed to embrace and alleviate the hard sadness of people having used one another and marred the earth the way they had." Moore's stories salvage a saving wit out of the same ingredients.

Roy C. Flannagan

Sources for Further Study

Booklist. XCIV, August, 1998, p. 1968.
Library Journal. CXXIII, September 1, 1998, p. 218.
New York. XXXI, September 14, 1998, p. 116.
The New York Review of Books. XLV, October 22, 1998, p. 15.
The New York Times Book Review. CIII, September 20, 1998, p. 6.
Ploughshares. XXIV, Fall, 1998, p. 224.
Publishers Weekly. CCXLV, July 20, 1998, p. 207.
The Times Literary Supplement. October 30, 1998, p. 27.
Vogue. CLXXXVIII, September, 1998, p. 430.
The Wall Street Journal. September 18, 1998, p. W8.

BIRTHDAY LETTERS

Author: Ted Hughes (1930-   )
Published: Farrar, Straus, & Giroux (New York). 197 pp. $20.00
Type of work: Poetry
Time: 1956-1963
Locale: England and America

After thirty-five years of near silence, Ted Hughes offers his version of his tumultuous marriage to Sylvia Plath

> *Principal personages:*
> TED HUGHES, an English poet who in 1984 became England's poet laureate
> SYLVIA PLATH, an American poet and Hughes's former wife

Sylvia Plath was a pretty, blond American girl with a seemingly placid exterior when Ted Hughes first met her at Pembroke College, Cambridge University, in the winter of 1956. Plath was also an aspiring poet who had won a scholarship. Hughes, too, was an aspiring poet. At first glance one might think it was this mutual interest that brought them together. Their biographies indicate that it was that—and something more. Hughes revisits their first encounter in the seventh of the eighty-eight poems that make up *Birthday Letters*:

> You meant to knock me out
> with your vivacity. I remember
> Little from the rest of that evening.
> I slid away with my girl-friend. Nothing
> Except her hissing rage in a doorway
> And my stupefied interrogation
> Of your blue headscarf from my pocket
> And the swelling ring-moat of tooth-marks
> That was to brand my face for the next month.
> The me beneath it for good.

Plath had, apparently, shocked him by biting his cheek—hard. As the poem "St. Botolph's" indicates, this violent gesture was a portent of things to come.

The two married in the summer of 1956. They spent the next three years shuttling back and forth between England and the United States, where Plath taught for a year at her alma mater, Smith College. They returned to England in 1960, settling into a seemingly perfect existence. The two poets—both handsome, ambitious individuals—divided their time between London, where they became known in literary circles, and a country house in Devon. Besides beginning their writing careers, they had two children together, a daughter, Frieda, in 1960, and a son, Nicholas, in 1962.

Then, for reasons still in dispute and perhaps finally inexplicable, Hughes began seeing another woman, Assia Wevill. Separated from Hughes, Plath spent a bitterly cold winter alone in Devon with the children before returning to London to face an equally cold winter. It was during this period that she began writing the shatteringly personal poetry that would appear after her death. On the morning of February 11, 1963, after leaving milk out for the children, she turned on the gas.

It was not Plath's first foray into suicide. In 1953, she suffered a nervous breakdown and attempted to kill herself, an experience she would later fictionalize in her novel, *The Bell Jar* (1963). Looking back on his life with Plath in *Birthday Letters*, Hughes indicates that the first attempt (there were almost certainly others) made the last one inevitable—just as it made the breakup of their marriage inescapable:

> We walked south across London to Fetter Lane
> And your hotel. Opposite the entrance
> On a bombsite becoming a building site
> We clutched each other giddily
> For safety and went in a barrel together
> Over some Niagara. Falling
> In the roar of soul your scar told me—
> Like its secret name or its password—
> How you had tried to kill yourself. And I heard
> Without ceasing for a moment to kiss you
> As if a sober star had whispered it
> Above the revolving, rumbling city: stay clear.

One might say that Hughes has read too much Greek tragedy were it not for the fact that Plath herself was filled with a sense of tragic inevitability. Left alone with two small children, she saw herself repeating her mother's experience. Her father, Otto Plath, was a German immigrant who became a professor of biology. He was also an autocrat who, after he developed diabetes, refused treatment because he believed that he was dying of cancer. For several years he demanded—and got—his family's complete attention. Then, when his daughter was eight years old, Otto Plath died, leaving his wife penniless with two young children to support. The loss seemed not to have affected the young Plath very much, but then came the suicide attempts and a recognition of her deep attachment to and hatred for her father. Toward the end, when she was writing furiously—turning out almost one ferocious poem a day—Plath identified Hughes with her father and damned them both as oppressors. In "Daddy," composed in October, 1962, she wrote:

> I was ten when they buried you.
> At twenty I tried to die
> And get back, back, back to you.
> I thought even the bones would do.
>
> But they pulled me out of the sack,
> And they stuck me together with glue.
> And then I knew what to do.
> I made a model of you,
> A man in black with a Meinkampf look
>
> And a love of the rack and the screw.
> And I said I do, I do.

It comes as little surprise, then, that after Plath's death Hughes had little to say publicly about the whole nasty business. That did not mean, however, that he did not try to influence the public debate about her life and work. Plath died without leaving a will, with the ironic result that it was Hughes who inherited control over her literary estate. One of his first acts was to destroy her last journal, because, he said, he did not want their children to read it. That act may have been somewhat understandable, but when he continued to censor her life by bowdlerizing some of her poems and suppressing others and obstructing literary critics as well as biographers, the voices of his antagonists and accusers grew deafening. Hughes remained aloof, using his formidable sister Olwyn as a go-between; she was charged with defending Plath's honor and—not incidentally—his own. It is hardly an accident that Olwyn helped shape the first full Plath biography, Anne Stevenson's *Bitter Fame* (1989), or that the portrait of Hughes that emerges from it presents *him* as something of a martyr.

It is largely as a martyr—or perhaps just a helpless, innocent bystander—that Hughes presents himself in *Birthday Letters*. His wife, the lovely girl with the "long, perfect, American legs," turns out to be fatally flawed, doomed by her obsession with her dead father. With Hughes, we watch her struggling with her poetry, struggling with her sanity, struggling to stay alive. In something approximating chronological order, the eighty-eight poems trace key episodes in their lives together, as the seeds of her instability blossom into hysterical despair. Hughes can do nothing but doggedly attend her as the drama of her life plays itself out. According to *Birthday Letters*, Plath's true antagonist was not an uncaring husband but an oppressive father.

Once, in one of the volume's few really powerful poems, "Epiphany," Hughes half admits fault, and it is telling that he does so in the context of describing an animal— nature having always been his forte. Once, in London, he encountered a young fellow carrying a fox cub inside his jacket. The fellow offers to sell the little fox to him for a pound, but Hughes rejects the offer, thinking of how it might inconvenience his wife and new baby. But then he wonders

> Is what tests a marriage and proves it a marriage—
> I would not have failed the test. Would you have failed it?
> But I failed. Our marriage had failed.

Mostly, however, *Birthday Letters* seems meant to answer his critics, to justify his reasons for leaving Plath. From the outset, he indicates, it was Plath and her destiny that controlled events. Hughes claims in "Visit" that when the two met in 1956 he was already unwittingly "being auditioned/ For the male lead in your drama." And indeed, throughout the traumas that follow—the illnesses, the pregnancies, the breakdowns— Hughes portrays himself as acting the part of the nurse, the dogsbody, the able but hamstrung assistant. In "Suttee," he declares that he was midwife to the "deity" resurrected after her first suicide attempt. When Assia Wevill enters the picture, in "Dreamers," she does so as an agent of Fate, joining the cast of a fable as just another one of the "inert ingredients/ For its experiment." It was all, Hughes would have it, preordained:

The dreamer in her
Had fallen in love with me and she did not know it.
That moment the dreamer in me
Fell in love with her, and I knew it.

One cannot help but wonder how Plath would have responded to such representations. *Birthday Letters*, however, is a one-sided conversation, with all but two of its poems addressed to a "you" that does not answer. Clearly Hughes believes that Plath—through her poetry and her journals—has already had her say about what went wrong in the marriage. However, it is probably her version that will remain longest in readers' minds. Whereas the poetry in *Ariel* is harsh, original, and memorable, *Birthday Letters* is filled with uninspired, mostly narrative verse that suits Hughes's sense of himself as a passive participant but does little to make his case. He surely has one—few believe that his relationship with Plath was filled with casual bliss—but these lukewarm recollections of long ago and far away cannot begin to compete with the hellish vision conveyed by poems like "Daddy."

The appearance of *Birthday Letters* made headlines in both America and England. The publication of few books of poetry has commanded so much public attention in the twentieth century. Although the poet in question is England's highly respected poet laureate, the media has paid attention to *Birthday Letters* not because of its craft but because of the scandalous events that occasioned it. Some of these events date from more than three decades ago, while others—such as Hughes's seeming attempts to quash certain aspects of Plath's biography—are more recent. After the many years during which he maintained an Olympian silence on the subject of his relationship with Plath, Hughes's version of events was met with breathless expectation.

Unfortunately, his attempts to explain himself fall rather flat. Perhaps it was inevitable that *Birthday Letters* would be filled with self-justification, but few could have expected it to be so uninspired, so uninvolved. The last poem in the collection, "Red," describes Plath's obsession with the color of blood, an obsession born of her fear of death. Blue, says Hughes, was better for her. If only Plath had had a little more of his coolness, she might have survived—or at least been able to hang on to him:

But electrified, a guardian, thoughtful.

In the pit of red
You hid from the bone-clinic whiteness.

But the jewel you lost was blue.

Perhaps it is not fair to read so much biography into what is, after all, poetry. Yet Hughes clearly expects—even invites—readers to do so. In the end, however, the verse fails to measure up to the life, and we are left with a feeling of gratitude that Plath was not able to temper her wrath.

Lisa Paddock

Sources for Further Study

America. CLXXVIII, March 21, 1998, p. 33.
The American Poetry Review. XXVII, September, 1998, p. 11.
Commentary. CV, May, 1998, p. 74.
Los Angeles Times Book Review. March 15, 1998, p. 7.
The Nation. CCLXVI, April 20, 1998, p. 25.
The New York Review of Books. XLV, March, 1998, p. 7.
The New York Times Book Review. CIII, March 1, 1998, p. 4.
Newsweek. CXXXI, February 2, 1998, p. 58.
Poetry. CLXXII, June, 1998, p. 154.
Time. CLI, February 16, 1998, p. 101.

BLINDNESS

Author: José Saramago (1922-   )
Translated from the Portuguese by Giovanni Pontiero
Published: Harcourt Brace (New York). 294 pp. $22.00
Type of work: Novel
Time: Modern times
Locale: An unspecified city in an unspecified country

*When an epidemic of blindness spreads through a city, the first people stricken are isolated
in a hospital, and the society around them falls into chaos*

> *Principal characters:*
> THE DOCTOR'S WIFE
> THE DOCTOR
> THE GIRL WITH THE DARK GLASSES
> THE BOY WITH THE SQUINT
> THE FIRST BLIND MAN
> THE FIRST BLIND MAN'S WIFE
> THE THIEF
> THE OLD MAN WITH THE PATCH OVER ONE EYE

José Saramago's eerie story of an epidemic in a contemporary city begins with the scene of a man sitting in a car at a traffic light. The light turns green but the car does not move, even when the drivers in the cars behind it begin honking their horns. The man has suddenly gone blind; his world has turned to a milky whiteness.

A passerby drives the blind man home. Later, the blind man's wife returns and discovers her husband's condition. She takes him to an eye doctor by taxi because the passerby has stolen the blind man's car. Immediately upon arriving at the doctor's office, the blind man is ushered in to see the doctor ahead of the other patients, who include a girl with dark glasses suffering from conjunctivitis, a young boy with a squint accompanied by his mother, and an old man with an eye patch over a hollow socket and a cataract in the remaining eye. The doctor is mystified by the sudden complete loss of sight and by a blindness of whiteness instead of the usual darkness.

The man who had stolen the car is suddenly overcome by the same white blindness that had stricken his victim. The girl with the dark glasses goes blind while having sex for money in a hotel room. The doctor loses his sight at home in the company of his wife and calls the Ministry of Health to warn of a possible epidemic. Others are infected by the strange eye disease.

The government, concerned about an apparently spreading plague, begins rounding up the sufferers and quarantining them in an abandoned mental hospital. When the police arrive to take the doctor away, the doctor's wife jumps into the car and falsely proclaims that she has just gone blind in order to be allowed to go with her husband. Through the rest of the story, she will be the only central character with sight and ultimately the only person with sight, the only witness to the degradation of people in a sightless world. At the hospital, they meet the man who had gone blind in the car, the man's wife, the car thief, the girl who had lost her vision in the hotel, and the boy with the squint who has been taken away from his mother. These people continue to be nameless, as well as sightless, as if their social identities had been stripped away along with their eyesight.

More people enter the hospital as more are affected by the epidemic, and the government rounds them up in a futile effort to contain the spreading affliction. The hospital is guarded by armed soldiers who have orders to shoot anyone who comes too near the surrounding walls. The soldiers themselves keep going blind, however, and have to be replaced by others. Inside the hospital, conditions deteriorate because the sightless are unable to clean themselves or their surroundings adequately. When the frightened soldiers open fire on some of the internees, the others are slow to pick up the bodies, so that the place is infected with the dead as well as with excrement. This theme of uncleanliness runs throughout the novel, with pollution—both physical and moral—presented as a consequence of lack of vision.

The only blind internees who are able to organize themselves effectively are members of a gang headed by one man who has managed to smuggle a gun into the hospital. The gang takes control of the food brought in intermittently by the military. The gang members force the other internees to pay for food. First, the others have to surrender everything they have of value. Then the women in the various barracks of the hospital must submit to sex with the ruthless men in order to purchase food for their barracks. Without sight, the only social order possible is of the cruelest and most exploitative character.

The doctor's wife stabs the leader of the gang to death with a pair of scissors and another woman sets fire to the gang's barracks. The fire spreads to the entire hospital and the blind flee, hoping the soldiers will not open fire. The soldiers are all gone, however. The doctor's wife leads the small band, her husband, the girl with the dark glasses, the first blind man and his wife, the boy with the squint, and the old man with the patch over one eye, back to the city. Civilization has ended. Everyone has gone blind. People cannot find their way home, so they stay in whatever shelter they manage to locate. The grocery shelves are ransacked by sightless hands groping for food. Corpses lie in the streets, half devoured by dogs and other animals. People defecate everywhere.

The doctor's wife becomes the guide and caretaker for her little band, finding them food and leading them to her home. With this one person who can see, the group is able to retain something of its humanity. When it rains, they collect the water and bathe. A dog joins the group, licking the tears from the cheeks of the doctor's wife when she cries, and the dog becomes known as the dog of tears.

At the very end of the story the white blindness is lifted from the city. It is still unclear just what it was or even if the inhabitants of the city were ever really blind. The doctor and his wife hold an enigmatic conversation that is heavy with the symbolic significance of the loss of sight. "Why did we become blind," one of them asks. "I don't know, perhaps one day we shall find out. Do you want me to tell you what I think, Yes, do, I don't think we did go blind, I think we are blind, Blind but seeing, Blind people who can see, but do not see."

At one level, the novel presents a political allegory. Saramago joined the Portuguese Communist Party in 1969 and has long been concerned with issues of social justice and the misuse of political power. Vision is a metaphor for the ability to see things as they are, and the corruption and degradation of the people in Saramago's tale follow from their lack of vision. However, the vision lost by those in this story is not a narrowly ideological vision; Saramago never descends to mere political propaganda. Loss of sight is a metaphor for loss of consciousness, but consciousness of precisely what remains an elusive and mysterious matter. The blindness is much more profound than a failure to see some theory of political relations or social change.

The white blindness is an elusive symbol of a problem broader than political evil alone. The inability to see is usually thought of as darkness, but this blindness is an all-encompassing light. Saramago's symbols do not lend themselves to easy interpretation. The loss of vision, the imprisonment of the afflicted, the bodily and environmental filth tease the reader into pursuing evasive hints of meaning.

The epidemic of blindness begins an analysis of human social relations. The word "analysis" literally means "breaking down," and in this novel we can see the breakdown of social order. Saramago's writings are often described as parables, and *Blindness* does have much of the quality of a parable. Perhaps, however, it may be more accurately described as a thought experiment by means of fiction. All events follow from a single premise, the disappearance of sight. Fear of a mysterious threat provokes repression from a government. With the loss of clear understanding in the face of the mystery, people lose even the most basic control over their lives. Stripped down to its essentials, life becomes a Hobbesian struggle for survival. Still, even when thoroughly degraded, people retain the urge to reach out to one another and the capacity for feeling.

The philosophical perspective of the story may be characterized as pessimistic but not cynical. Even the doctor's wife, the most admirable character, owes many of her virtues to the inexplicable accident of keeping her sight. Even she, moreover, has to struggle through an uncleanliness that is moral as well as physical. None of the main characters completely lose their humanity, however. At the beginning of the story the car thief seems to have been initially motivated by the desire to help someone in need, only afterward deciding to steal the blind man's car. The young woman who had prostituted herself in the hotel becomes a surrogate mother for the boy with the squint. The loss is never complete, and there is always some hope.

The characters in the novel can be anyone. They have no names. Their country has no name. Their city has no name. The characters seem real, however, and Saramago manages to instill in his readers sympathy for these anonymous people. In this way the author makes the story as universal as a parable but simultaneously maintains the concreteness and immediacy of modern fiction.

The translator, Giovanni Pontiero, died before completing his revisions of the manuscript. Still, it conveys Saramago's strange style. He uses no quotation marks for conversation and separates the quotations of his characters only by commas. At times, this makes it difficult to identify just who is talking, but the difficulty seems to be intentional. It is as if the words in the novel are as anonymous as the characters; the words do not belong to their speakers but exist in the shifting from one speaker to another. The narrative shifts as well, moving from the consciousness of a character to objective reality and back again, as if to convey the interweaving of thought and the external world. Although some readers might find this style confusing at first, the writing is not difficult for those who enter its flow, and readers will quickly find themselves caught up in the momentum of events.

José Saramago has long been considered one of Portugal's greatest writers. His books have been translated into more than twenty languages and widely praised. After he was awarded the Nobel Prize for literature in 1998, critical and popular interest in his work became even greater. His ability to combine elements of fantasy with a sharp sense of bitter reality and sympathy for human suffering have drawn wide praise. Many have compared his writings to those of the influential Latin American "magic realists," although Saramago himself maintains that magic realism has not been an influence on his work. Others have found in Saramago's writings echoes of George Orwell's *1984*, Franz Kafka's *The Trial*, and Albert Camus' *The Plague*.

Blindness was well received. The British edition of 1997 was considered one of the best books of the year by many reviewers. The American edition of 1998 has also been praised by literary critics, such as novelist Andrew Miller in *The New York Times Book Review*. Written by a master, *Blindness* deserves its recognition as a masterpiece of modern fiction.

Carl L. Bankston III

Sources for Further Study

Booklist. XCIV, August, 1998, p. 1969.
Library Journal. CXXIII, August, 1998, p. 134.
Los Angeles Times Book Review. September 6, 1998, p. 2.
The New Republic. CCXVIII, November 30, 1998, p. 48.
New Statesman. CXXVII, October 16, 1998, p. 58.
The New York Times Book Review. CIII, October 4, 1998, p. 8.
Publishers Weekly. CCXLV, July 13, 1998, p. 62.
The Times Literary Supplement. December 19, 1997, p. 20.
The Village Voice. September 22, 1998, p. 150.
The Washington Post. October 9, 1998, p. D1.

BRAIN STORM

Author: Richard Dooling (1954-   )
Published: Random House (New York). 401 pp. $25.00
Type of work: Novel
Time: The early twenty-first century
Locale: St. Louis, Missouri

A witty satire about the American mania for better living through science, legislation, and litigation

Principal characters:
    JOE WATSON, a young lawyer
    SANDRA WATSON, his wife
    ARTHUR MAHONEY, a senior partner at a prestigious corporate law firm
    WHITTAKER J. STANG, a federal judge
    ELVIN BRAWLEY, a murder victim
    JAMES F. WHITLOW, a racist accused of murdering Brawley
    DR. RACHEL PALMQUIST, a forensic neuroscientist
    MYRNA SCHWEICK, a criminal lawyer
    FRANK DONAHUE, a U.S. attorney
    DIRT, a private investigator

One cannot tell from reading his latest novel, *Brain Storm*, whether Richard Dooling's clients in Omaha, Nebraska, are in good hands, but his readers certainly are. Having honed his narrative skills in two previous novels, *Critical Care* (1992) and *White Man's Grave* (1994), Dooling, a National Book Award finalist, wastes no time getting the reader's attention. "'The beheadings are almost identical,' said Joe Watson, placing his memo on the walnut expanse of Arthur Mahoney's worktable." Catchy, certainly, but what is that walnut worktable doing in this Raymond Chandlerish sentence? Perhaps it is there to indicate that things are not necessarily what they seem.

The beheadings mentioned here are from two computer games, CarnageMaster and Greek SlaughterHouse, and the aptly named Watson is no Philip Marlowe or Sherlock Holmes, but only a first-year associate at a prestigious St. Louis law firm. With 572 lawyers worldwide, the firm of Stern, Pale & Covin specializes in corporate law and has perfected the twin arts of "good lawyering" (that is, "ass-covering") and the computer-assisted multitasking that has made "interleaved billing" the latest and fastest means to profits for the firm and a partnership for the ambitious associate. Todd Boron "made partner by billing 3,500 hours a year, every year, for nine years, which averages out to 67.3 billable hours per week, every week, which comes out to 11.2 billable hours per day—if you assume he took Sundays off for spiritual upgrades—and 9.6 billable hours per day, every day—if you assume he didn't."

Watson may dismiss "Boron the moron" as "a legal robot," but his own status seems only marginally better. He is a legal geek specializing in computer-assisted research who (in the hyper-masculine world of corporate law) worries about his small office but takes pride in the size of his RAM (random access memory) and who keeps careful track of his own billable hours in a frantic effort to keep up with the monster mortgage payments on the suburban house his wife insisted they buy.

Feeling himself on trial at the office and at home (where he literally cannot afford to spend much time), Watson feels not just beleaguered but guilty. He should, for he is Catholic. His sense of guilt is compounded by his failure to heed his calling—not to the priesthood, but to criminal law. This is not to say that his sense of vocation was originally strong, let alone divinely inspired. As Watson confesses (adapting Prussian army officer Carl von Clausewitz on war and politics), law school was for him little more than a continuation of his undergraduate education by other means.

Something of a Saul on the road to the Damascus of junior partnership, Watson is struck down not by the light of God but by the court order of an irascible federal judge who does to Watson what is done to all lawyers recently admitted to the bar in that area: He assigns him a *pro bono* case.

Watson's case is hardly typical. It is a murder case to be tried in federal court, because the murder took place on a military base. In this case the U.S. attorney is seeking the death penalty "under the Hate Crime Motivation or Vulnerable Victim provisions of the new federal sentencing guidelines," ostensibly because the victim was both African American and deaf. In fact, the U.S. Attorney hopes to run for a seat in the U.S. Senate and knows that the case offers the opportunity for a great deal of free favorable publicity. Of course, *pro bono* cases are not good for a corporate law firm's bottom line and even worse for a firm's image when the case attracts so much media attention and the defendant is as unlikable and seemingly guilty as James F. Whitlow, an ignorant racist with a "Jesus hates niggers" tattoo and ties to a local militia.

Although he at first tries to help his young associate, senior partner Arthur Mahoney decides to cut the firm's losses by cutting Watson loose when he refuses to plead Whitlow out. In a way Watson wants this case, wants to practice real, criminal law, but in another way he does not, because he feels incompetent and, of course, guilty about feeling incompetent and about how his family will have to suffer as a result of his decision to defend a creature as loathsome as Whitlow.

Although cut off from the firm's resources and from his $100,000 a year salary, $10,000 semi-annual bonus, and family, Watson receives help from a number of interested parties. One is Judge Stang, "a cantankerous graduate of the Roy Bean school of jurisprudence," who has knowledge of and faith in Watson's abilities. The other is Myrna Schweick, the diminutive "punk rock [criminal] lawyer" for whom Watson worked briefly before his wife bullied him into the much more lucrative (if otherwise unrewarding) practice of corporate law. (Myrna's surname subtly links Dooling's satiric novel to Jaroslav Hašek's well-known anti-war satire, *The Good Soldier Schweik* [1920-1923]).

Watson's "passing infatuation with criminal law," as his wife puts it, is more than matched by his infatuation with the neuroscientist who is working as an unpaid consultant on the case. Dr. Rachel Palmquist is as beautiful as Myrna is grotesque—and just as cartoonish. Having had his first novel adapted for the screen, Dooling draws *Brain Storm*'s characters as cinematic caricatures. Rachel is the scientist as played by the likes of Demi Moore or Sharon Stone; Myrna is a Danny DeVito lawyer in drag;

Watson is Jim Carrey or Tom Hanks; and Judge Stang is Paul Newman in a reprise of his Roy Bean role.

Rachel, the neuroscientist as femme fatale, plays Beatrice to Watson's Dante, guiding him through the Brave New World of the Gage Institute's Psychon Project (an advanced mutant strain of the behaviorist PISCES project in Thomas Pynchon's 1973 meganovel, *Gravity's Rainbow*). Dismissing free will as folk psychology, "the goddess of brain science" thinks of people like Whitlow as malfunctioning machines to be tested and repaired. (Appropriately enough, one of Stern, Pale & Covin's clients is a company named "Abulia," a form of mental disorder in which volition is impaired or lost.) Rachel may be childless (she would react to children, she says, the way Superman does to kryptonite), but she is hardly sexless. She turns men into laboratory chimps, mere stimulus-response mechanisms. This is her idea of pillow talk as she masturbates a wired-up Watson:

> "Generalized muscular tension, perineal contractions, involuntary pelvic thrusting with a peri-odicity of zero-point-eight seconds, white-hot medial preoptic." She giggled. "The lateral hypo-thalamus brings accessory networks into play," she whispered. "Houston, we have bursts of impulses in the hypothalamic supraoptic and paraventricular nuclei, down the axon terminals. Heart rate climbing. Skin flushed. Vasodilation. Muscle spasms. Involuntary vocalizations . . . *Aaaand* . . . Boom! Massive discharge of oxytocin from the posterior pituitary gland."
> He turned his head, panted, and moaned.
> "Neuroscience," she said. And kissed him.

Watson may be a randy legal geek, but he is also old-fashioned enough to want more from Rachel than e- and voice-mail, neurosex, and a worldview that defines the human in purely mechanistic terms and the soul as nothing more than a vestigial organ. Still, it is Rachel who breaks the connection ("affair" seems too romantic a word given the purely pragmatic nature of her interest in him). It was a career move, a way of gaining access to a human research subject. Once Whitlow has been examined and surgically repaired, Rachel grows bored and moves on to other cases, indeed, to "other countries, where the governments are more receptive to genetic and medical solutions to these problems."

Corporate law and neuroscience are not Dooling's only targets. No one will be able to listen to, let alone be moved by, public officials righteously railing against this or that supposed outrage against society quite the same way after hearing the U.S. Attorney fulminate against hate crimes and all who would stand in the way of his prosecution of those charged with them (obstacles transformed into stepping stones to higher ratings in the polls and more votes on election day). Then there are the numerous interest groups that sign on to the case, each artfully crafted by Dooling as a reflection of its already distorted self, each so intent on its particular grievance as to miss anything beyond its narcissistic nose. The legal profession, technophiles, forensic consultants, neuroscience, politicians, the media, the militias, hate crimes, hate groups and hate literature (including that of *The Bell Curve* kind), and—of course—good old greed all take a beating, both for what they do to and collectively say about the state of the union in an age of too much legislation and litigation and too little common sense and personal responsibility.

Emblematic of the whole, even if it may appear as little more than a comic interlude, is the Saturday morning scene in which the pastoral peace of Watson's residential suburb is shattered by the arrival of the landscape trucks loaded with power mowers, blowers, edgers, and trimmers, as well as tankers filled with the chemicals "dedicated to maintaining the sort of lawns you find in perfect neighborhoods." This is the sort of neighborhood in which Mrs. Hodgkins would live if only her weed-infested neighbor, Watson, would cooperate, which he does not.

Meanwhile, Mrs. Hodgkins, still bald from chemotherapy, dedicates herself to finding those responsible for the fatal cancers of her husband, daughter, and three dogs. After much research, she "identified the culprit: electromagnetic fields from high-tension wires six blocks away." Needless to say, this avenging angel plans to sue the local utility company. What *Brain Storm* demonstrates so exhaustively and uproariously is that in this and other matters it is the cure—whether chemical, legal, or political—that is cancerously out of control and as toxic as the well-intentioned but nonetheless wrongheaded legislation passed to eradicate the social weeds.

As in his earlier novels (including *Blue Streak* [1996], his spirited defense of free speech in the face of sexual harassment and hate crimes laws), Dooling proves that he is immensely knowledgeable in a variety of areas. Moreover, he possesses a similarly impressive store of common sense. However, although the eminently sensible Dooling may be dismayed and bemused by the unreasonableness and even idiocy of much of modern American life, he is not outraged by it. Aberrations aside, he implies, law is good, Judge Stang is right, and technology does help.

Dooling's satirical gaze is wickedly funny but not withering, and his novel ends hopefully, happily, with everyone getting pretty much what he or she deserves. Its irony muted, Dooling's satire on the fate of privacy, free speech, personal responsibility, conscience, and consciousness in these overly determinist, litigious, politically correct times resolves itself into something of an apprentice novel of a slightly futuristic, wonderfully farcical kind. *Brain Storm* successfully demonstrates that the biggest threat in this age of blockbuster disaster movies, such as *Armageddon*, *Deep Impact*, and *Godzilla*, comes not from giant asteroids and gargantuan lizards but from a misguided quest for perfect solutions and a gross lack of common sense.

Robert A. Morace

Sources for Further Study

ABA Journal. LXXXIV, July, 1998, p. 88.
Booklist. XCIV, February 1, 1998, p. 902.
Kirkus Reviews. LXVI, January 1, 1998, p. 8.
Library Journal. CXXIII, January, 1998, p. 139.
The New York Times Book Review. CIII, April 19, 1998, p. 16.
Publishers Weekly. CCXLV, February 23, 1998, p. 51.

BRAINCHILDREN
Essays in Designing Minds

Author: Daniel C. Dennett (1942-   )
Published: The MIT Press (Cambridge, Mass.). 418 pp. $40.00; paperback $20.00
Type of work: Essays

A collection of essays originally published between 1984 and 1996 that reflect an interdisciplinary approach to the philosophy of mind, including explorations of artificial intelligence and animal behavior, to gain insight into the nature of human consciousness

Daniel Dennett is a leading contributor and researcher in the new approach to the philosophy of mind, which includes cognitive science, technology, artificial intelligence, consciousness, epistemology, and other areas of investigation. This controversial thinker is almost a cult figure in the new philosophy and the most interesting writer in this eclectic field.

Brainchildren, Dennett's representative, retrospective work, contains a selection of twenty-six essays published since *Brainstorms* (1980), his first essay collection. The essays in *Brainchildren,* originally published in specialized and relatively obscure journals and conference proceedings, deal mainly with Dennett's familiar areas of interest: artificial intelligence, philosophy of mind, animal behavior and cognition, and ethics. His approach is philosophical but with a scientific bent. In "Self-portrait," he characterizes himself as a philosopher with a long-standing interest in the nature of consciousness, personhood, and the self. A few selections, such as one dealing with the debate between Dennett and Fred Dretsky, are not easy to read. But with repeated reading, some attention, and a willingness to be occasionally baffled, the reader is rewarded with insight rarely attainable by the layperson. In general, however, Dennett guides the uninitiated reader by meticulous attention to definition, word choice, and use of metaphors.

Brainchildren is, in one sense, Dennett's way of defending his arguments in two earlier works—*Consciousness Explained* (1991) and *Darwin's Dangerous Idea* (1995)—which put him at the center of debate about the origin and nature of consciousness. Many pieces are critical responses to the published contributions of other philosophers, such as John Searle, Ray Jackson, Richard Rorty, Jerry Fodor, Richard Nagle, Roger Penrose, and Antonio Damasio.

The first ten essays in *Brainchildren* are about different facets of Dennett's views on philosophy of mind, consciousness, and intentionality. He attributes the mind's complexity to the fact that it is both biological and sociological. Hence the interdisciplinary nature of his study. In a broad sense Dennett conceives of philosophy of mind as a field of study that attempts to connect thoughts on diverse but related topics such as the existence of "qualia," multiple personality, artificial intelligence, and animal cognition.

Dennett argues that mind and consciousness are complex artifacts, deserving of multidisciplinary investigation. Mind, for example, is partly biological, partly social, and partly metaphysical. To get an accurate picture of the mind—to understand how it arose and how it works—requires a clear-headed metaphysical analysis within the context of scientific research from several fields. With this kind of approach, Dennett firmly established his place at center stage among the philosophers and scientists of the same camp after publication of *Darwin's Dangerous Idea* and *Consciousness Explained*.

In *Brainchildren*, Dennett deals with one of the most provocative notions in the philosophy of mind: qualia. Qualia are like sense data, such as a tomato's redness, which is a mental quality that appears to consciousness and is quite different from its scientific definition (e.g., as motions of molecules in the air). In two essays Dennett considers qualia as decorations of perceptions by invoking a new and improved version of his famous zombie examples. For Dennett's purposes, zombies are entities who lack consciousness but behave just like humans. His zombie metaphors are quite ingenious and useful in his analysis of consciousness.

In "Speaking for Our Selves," coauthored with English psychologist Nicholas Humphrey, Dennett presents a novel view of Multiple Personality Disorder (MPD), as a response to Julian Jayne's *The Origin of Consciousness in the Breakdown of the Bicameral Mind* (1976), which once made quite a stir in the psychological community. For Dennett, multiple personality is a useful way of exploring aspects of consciousness. Dennett and Humphrey evaluate the idea of selfhood and question mainstream notions of MPD. Is there a core or an actual personality in every person with MPD? Are all other "personalities" or "alters" added as "nonpersons" or "subhumans"? Or are they legitimate, viable personalities, worthy of even legal consideration? Dennett claims that "alters" in some sense are real selves but devoid of some basic elements needed to give them the status of "people." However, the question remains: If alters cannot be people, then what *can* they be? What ontological status do we ascribe to them?

In "Information, Technology, and the Virtues of Ignorance," Dennett argues that the mind is able to "frame" problems in order to deal with a universe of stimuli pouring in from all directions. When we are engaged in anything, as a matter of survival, we isolate the problem at hand, limit the context of engagement, and disregard the multitude of irrelevant possibilities. According to Dennett, animals, even single-celled organisms, do the same in order to get on with the business at hand. Humans and animals are habituated mentally and neurologically to isolate the "salient" data and to disregard the irrelevant.

This is also the way we communicate desires, beliefs, and expectations. We "isolate" the salient elements in a discourse and adopt a "stance" or mode of interpretation that presupposes the rationality of people. The way we understand one another and interpret the relations of things in the world is through pattern recognition and analogies.

Dennett continues the discussion by giving variations on the arguments he used earlier in *Consciousness Explained*. He continues to refute the conventional notions of consciousness in favor of his new reformulation based on a wealth of new discoveries in neuroscience, dazzling inventions by the artificial intelligence community, and new research in the psychology of humans and animals. As before, he continues to tackle the question of whether or not we can ascribe consciousness to sophisticated robots and animals.

Three of his essays contain rebuttals to critics of *Consciousness Explained*. In one, Dennett reiterates his arguments about his "Multiple Drafts" model of consciousness. In another he challenges opponents of his zombie arguments to come up with arguments of their own which do not beg the question. In "Real Consciousness," he defends his general disposition that there is no "unitary" consciousness (or even a unitary theory of cognition). The mind is a diversified toolbox for accomplishing many mental activities, e.g., perception, cognition, attention, and emotion. Dennett believes that in the midst of the clutter and chaos of mental activities and commotions (many "demons" in the mind), the diverse and disparate mental entities can function and coexist without disturbing the integrity of the "self."

Dennett is one of the rare philosophers who give artificial intelligence a prominent place in modern, mainstream philosophy. He uses artificial intelligence brilliantly as a metaphor to tackle such difficult problems as consciousness. In addition to offering original ideas about artificial intelligence, he expresses views about how and why it is important to philosophy and how philosophers ought to approach it.

He is keenly aware of the limitations and enormous potential of artificial intelligence. In "Can Machines Think?" he points out misconceptions and misuses by zealots of the Turing machine, named after the English mathematician Alan Mathison Turing (1912-1954), who constructed the earliest primitive digital computers. Turing's invention is an abstract, mathematical machine that provides the universally accepted theoretical basis for evaluating and constructing thinking machines.

In dealing with human consciousness as a unique and unparalleled phenomenon in nature, Dennett toys with the hypothetical possibility of robot consciousness. In this discussion he includes his experiences with the Massachusetts Institute of Technology's Cog project, which investigated issues such as the possibility of "artificial life."

Dennett also engages in a discussion of animal behavior (ethology). In "Do-It-Yourself Understanding" and "Self-Portrait," he shows that philosophizing about biology is an entirely different enterprise than that of physics, which has distinct borderlines and definitions. Dennett contends that nearly all biological concepts have blurred edges and somewhat inefficient definitions.

Dennett deals effectively with the notion of animal minds and the human ability to access them. His approach is almost as ingenious as that in Thomas Nagel's famous essay, "What It Is Like to Be a Bat" in his *Mortal Questions* (1979). In discussing the animal mind, Dennett enlivens his arguments with reports on animal cognition experiments. For example, rabbits do not transfer visual perceptions laterally. If they perceive an object with only the right eye, they are unable to recognize the same object later with only the left eye. In another study, he points out that snakes use three different sensory modalities to hunt and consume their prey: vision to hunt and strike, smell to find the prey in their coil, and touch to swallow the prey headfirst.

Aside from examining experiments by other scientists, in "Out of the Armchair and Into the Field" Dennett recounts his own experiences studying vervet monkeys in Kenya. The point of all these ethological studies is to see what they can offer to understanding the human mind and to investigating whether animals too have consciousness, beliefs, or even creativity and originality. Ultimately he wants to use his ethological investigations to answer questions about human intentionality and dispositions.

Dennett's answers are usually informed by and framed in an evolutionary context. In "Real Patterns," for example, he makes a connection between transformations of the structure of the mind influenced by the regularities of sensory interactions with the physical world and the formation of beliefs, opinions, and dispositions.

In the final essay, "Information, Technology, and the Virtues of Ignorance," Dennett contends that as a result of adaptive-evolutionary processes, humans have learned to concentrate on a few salient stimuli and to disregard massive numbers of others. He suggests that this natural selection of salience should also be applied to ethics, e.g., assessing moral obligations in our chaotic information age. He suggests that "willful ignorance" may be valuable in making decisions about particular ethical dilemmas. Some ethicists consider this view controversial, for it ignores many important problems in the world that require everyone's attention. However, Dennett's evolution-based morality is in line with some other moral theorists of the evolutionary persuasion, such as Allan Gibbard, author of *Wise Choices, Apt Feelings: A Theory of Normative Judgement* (1990), and Frans de Wall, author of *Good Natured: The Origins of Right and Wrong in Humans and Animals* (1996).

For many people the mind is, in a sense, a sacred domain to be protected against scientific encroachment. There is a fear of "evil scientists" who may engage in devious projects if they come to know the mind as well as they know physics or biology. This fear is irrational because, as Dennett explains, the full complexities of the mind and human consciousness may never be spelled out with the same degree of accuracy and comprehensiveness as the subjects of the hard sciences. Moreover, Dennett suggests that the best way to stay safe is to keep well informed through the "evil scientists'" writings about what mischief they intend.

Some critics also worry about Dennett's ascription of some kind of self-consciousness to robots and computers. However, such self-consciousness is different in kind and degree from that of humans. He contends that a machine, no matter how sophisticated, will never possess anything resembling human consciousness. This does not mean that people cannot ascribe some kind of crude self-consciousness to animals or even computers. For example, the computer does possess some kind of self-watching or self-monitoring program. However, Dennett not only doubts that there will ever be a self-conscious computer or robot but also sees no advantage in constructing any machine with a self-consciousness resembling that of humans.

Brainchildren reinforces Dennett's reputation as one of the foremost philosophers of mind, who has successfully brought together diverse fields of study, such as philosophy, ethology, artificial intelligence, and several others, into one fruitful and ingenious project for understanding the human mind and consciousness. His brilliant analogies, stories, and experiments have opened the way for alternative and eclectic approaches. His contributions to such fields as artificial intelligence and animal behavior are just as original as his study of the mind.

Brainchildren is a culminating work, bringing into focus many abstract ideas expressed in Dennett's previous books. It is also a book in which the author answers many of his most important critics. His contribution to the understanding of human consciousness is the outstanding aspect of his work. He has clearly exposed the inadequacies of traditional views and set the research agenda for a new, multidisciplinary theory of the human mind and consciousness.

Chogollah Maroufi

Sources for Further Study

Choice. XXXV, July, 1998, p. 1874.
Library Journal. CXXIII, March 15, 1998, p. 89.
Publishers Weekly. CCXLV, February 9, 1998, p. 88.
San Jose Mercury News. June 14, 1998, p. B2.
Science News. CLIII, May 16, 1998, p. 306.
Scientific American. CCLXXIX, July, 1998, p. 113.

BRECHT AND METHOD

Author: Fredric Jameson (1934-   )
Published: Verso (New York). 184 pp. $25.00
Type of work: Literary criticism

A major neo-Marxist literary theorist assesses the position of one of the twentieth century's central figures in dramatic literature as a modernist and postmodernist thinker

Many modern dramatists have some claim to being regarded as theorists by virtue of having contributed theatrical manifestos along with their plays. Among the more important of these are August Strindberg on naturalism and expressionism; Antonin Artaud on theater of cruelty; Tennessee Williams on a plastic theater; and Arthur Miller on modern tragedy. Yet probably none has been more pervasive on later dramaturgical practice than Bertolt Brecht's "Short Organum for the Theatre," in which he distinguishes between the dramatic form and the epic form of playwriting. The former refers to a theater that is linear in construction, one that embodies and incarnates events so as to involve and draw audiences into the action and thus promote their feeling, whereas the latter designates a theater that is more episodic in nature, one that narrates or relates events and characters from the outside and asks audiences to observe and confront what they see, thereby provoking thought. When Brecht—whom Fredric Jameson sees as influencing Walter Benjamin and, most decisively, Roland Barthes— broke onto the French theatrical scene in 1954 with performances of *Mother Courage and Her Children* (1949) and *The Caucasian Chalk Circle* (1954), he not only came to "crystallize" Marxism for a generation of postwar intellectuals but also introduced a mode of thinking that was itself a new kind of aesthetic. What Jameson, probably the most influential of the neo-Marxist literary theorists, provides in *Brecht and Method* is both a description and a cultural analysis of that theory and aesthetic.

Jameson touts Brecht as responding in his plays to several social and artistic impetuses: an interest in dramaturgical and theoretical innovation; a demand for a new kind of political literature; and a desire to provide voice to diverse groups that previously had been kept in a condition of subalternity. Yet for all of his radical innovation at the time, his works now might appear—in the wake of such theater artists as Samuel Beckett and Robert Wilson—"obsolescent," while his influence on contemporary thought seems submerged and not readily apparent. Jameson would argue, though, that Brecht is "everywhere" present today without his name necessarily being attached and without the public's generally being aware of it. Jameson's project is thus to reclaim, or rescue, the body of work for a postmodern age. Jameson himself, in his 1991 study *Postmodernism: Or, The Cultural Logic of Late Capitalism*, delineated three stages in the development of capitalism and then linked each one to a literary/theoretical/philosophical movement: market capitalism to realism; monopoly or imperialistic capitalism to modernism; and postindustrial or international capitalism to postmodernism. What he sets out to do with subtlety and ingenuity in *Brecht and*

Method is to recuperate Brecht for modernism and appropriate him for postmodernism.

Jameson defines the Brechtian dialectical method in terms of its style, its thought or doctrine, and its plot or narrative. Insisting that it should not be regarded as a philosophical system, Jameson sees it as a construction of "contradictions," breaking up elements so that they then can be subjected to analysis. Consequently, Brecht has often been viewed—though perhaps unjustly—as coldly intellectual, propagandistic, even off-putting when contrasted with more traditional dramaturgical practice that aims at achieving empathic identification between audience and characters. It is not difficult to see why Aristotelian models, built on catharsis that arises from perceiving universal dimensions that flatten out social distinctions and so unify the audience, would be antithetical to the Marxian analysis occurring in an epic theater whose intent is to divide audience members one from the other and thereby recast and replay the class struggle. Jameson, more systematically than might at first appear, discusses the stylistic techniques that mark Brecht's plays. Most of these exist in service of distantiation or estrangement—Brecht's famous V-effect—which forestalls or even defeats emotional response so that acts of intellection or rational analysis remain primary.

Jameson fruitfully likens Brecht's distantiation method in theater to Sergei Eisenstein's montage theory in film, in that for both of these modern artists, technique has meaning in and of itself and form is not only inseparable from, but also in service to, content. At various points in his text, Jameson considers Brecht's "non-formalist" storytelling, with its tendency to break down the narrative into brief episodes, themselves often introduced by printed (or spoken) lines. Jameson compares these to the chapter headings in eighteenth century novels and, in fact, employs similar headings before each of the twenty brief sections of his own text. Often, the episodes are preceded or interrupted by songs, and then perhaps followed by a moral or proverb, an abstract formulation that, if not actually juxtaposed in some way with the acted-out anecdote, reduces the narrative content to a "grammatical minimum." Whether the moral requires the audience members to reflect and arrive at their own judgment or offers them a judgment for their assent that has already been formulated, the challenge for them is to question rather than simply to reaffirm existing norms. Jameson even proposes that what is offered in Brecht's great final plays—*Mother Courage and Her Children*, *The Caucasian Chalk Circle*, and *The Good Person of Szechuan* (1943)—is just such an image of judgment being enacted.

The actors on Brecht's stage, rather than lose themselves in the characters as would be demanded by the great Russian director Konstantin Stanislavsky, or by practitioners of what has come to be known as American Method acting, are instead to remain somehow outside the characters, quoting lines as if in the third person, even speaking stage directions to the audience. Events are thus presented as though they were "historical," so that what had been seen as natural is now perceived as socially and culturally constructed, and the concept of self is deconstructed as radical absence or as only an imaginary presence. Just as the actors stand outside the characters and observe them, so, too, is the audience called upon to contemplate. Jameson finds a lesson about the theory of estrangement explicitly embodied in *The Three-Penny Opera* (1929), where an aesthetic of empathy literally wears itself out as the audience is forced to "interrogate" Macheath's great energy and glee over a corrupt society and thus become questioningly judgmental. Thus the Brechtian call to contemplation and consumption establishes itself finally as an activity, as praxis; the pleasure of the collective experience in the theater derives ultimately from its usefulness, since ideology can only be judged on the basis of its consequences.

Yet such didacticism has generally been regarded as taboo in modernist art, which is supposedly resistant to political content, and so this becomes the primary space where Jameson must recuperate Brecht for modernism. He does so in part by establishing that if ideas were foreign to certain modernist theoreticians of a decidedly imagist bent, such as T. E. Hulme, such was not the case for others such as T. S. Eliot, in whom Jameson detects "a didactic posture not without its analogies to that of Brecht himself." The great theme of modernist works, with all their irony and ambiguity and fragmentation, Jameson proposes, is the New, "the incomparable excitement of the breaking of a new dawn and the coming of a new time." Through an intricate argument—by far the most stunning in the book—Jameson reads *Galileo* as "autoreferential" to Brecht's own aesthetic theory. *Galileo* as a dramatic work with some basis in fact exists both in and out of history: As existing in history, it is nonallegorical in form and resistant to aestheticization; as existing out of history, it can be seen, however, as allegorical. If Galileo's pedagogical and scientific innovations are thought of as analogous to modernism's project or agenda, then by his submission to the Church's authority he commits the cardinal sin against the New. On the political level, as an allegory of the antinuclear movement, Galileo's recantation becomes at one with J. Robert Oppenheimer's acquiescence in the use of the bomb. Galileo's failure is seen as indicative of a "counter-revolutionary" movement, in the same way that doctrinaire Stalinism subverted Leninism, or in the way that Cold War strictures came to undercut the Western leftist movement of the 1930's. On the aesthetic level, Jameson reads Galileo's submission as prototypical of Brecht's own decision to compromise a stark minimalist notion of theater as proletarian tract with adumbrations of theatrical spectacle that make it more obviously pleasurable for audiences.

One of the ways in which Jameson sees Brecht as celebrating modernity is through the near apotheosis of the machine itself, particularly in the radio play *The Lindbergh Flight* (1929), about the marvelous—at least before he "rediscovered his own origins the wrong way in the Hitler period"—man in his flying machine who "astonishes the emptiness of Nature itself . . . like the world before the appearance of life"; who when he flew, was "[t]ruly an atheist" displacing "God himself" as center of a universe emergent "between the light and the twilight." The medium of radio becomes a part of the message: Here words and music, which are often juxtaposed in the stage plays to contradict and undercut one another, exist in a kind of symbiotic relationship. The radio is also an instrument of information technology, and thus a form of production. Yet such a mechanical production is not of the "regressive" aestheticizing type but rather expresses a futurist enthusiasm for the new technology. In this way, Jameson is able deftly to accomplish his appropriation of Brecht for postmodernism.

As a theorist himself, Jameson spends a good deal of time pondering the precise relationship between Brechtian theory and practice. While not itself a work of art, the theory exists as more than simply a guide to stage production; the text, in fact, must be seen as "provok[ing] the theory and giv[ing] it content, occasion" by somehow including all the commentaries on the text. Partly Brecht is new precisely because he theorized and foregrounded a process of thinking about texts that audiences can perceive abstractly: "[T]he final performance is also a pretext for all the theoretical inquiries that necessarily precede it in practice, and ought then to follow it in theory." Thus the theory contains his literary works inside itself and becomes the central object of study, which is what makes Brecht himself Brechtian. The notion of study is, of course, central to Brechtian theater as what an audience is called upon to do, as is suggested by the generic subcategory "learning plays," which are associated with classrooms. Teachers and sages become prominent figures in the plays, showing that pedagogy is privileged, since pedagogy is needed to teach the new and to effect change. In fact, teaching is often what is represented dramatically in the plays, which are designed to demonstrate how one teaches, as in the marvelous opening scene of *Galileo*.

What is primarily studied and taught in Brecht's plays—and this undoubtedly accounts for why Jameson finds him such a kindred spirit—has to do with the nature of business and capital, with production and consumption. Within *Brecht and Method*, Jameson provides a partial translation and explication of the *Me-ti*, or what he variously (and without any explanation for the precise difference) renders as "*The Book of Changes*," "*The Book of Shifting Ways*," "*The Book of Turning Ways*," and "*The Book of Twists and Turns*." Growing out of Brecht's Herr Keuner stories from the 1920's and 1930's, this work dating from the mid-1930's is a collection of political parables and commentaries on leftist politics of the period, using events and figures transposed to China in order to argue essentially for the necessity of a party composed of workers' organizations. He studies the issue of capitalism as well in the better known plays: in *St. Joan of the Stockyards* (1931), presenting in Mauler a full-dress psychological portrait of the capitalist as Brechtian tragic figure, or in *Mother Courage and Her Children* of a businesswoman who lives in terror of losing her capital (her wagon—one of the great symbols of the modern stage) as opposed to losing her money in the sacrifice of her children. In *The Caucasian Chalk Circle*, Jameson sees dramatized the conflict between the capitalist exploiters, who consume the fruits of production, and the oppressed peasants who produce them, culminating in the restoration of the ruling dynasty. In another of his brilliantly insightful analytical moments, Jameson reads Grusha's hesitation to take up the endangered child—"hideous is the temptation of goodness!"—as an epiphanic moment for the audience, since ordinarily the temptation would be to perpetuate evil rather than to do good. Jameson terms this a supreme example of estrangement, for it forces audiences to confront their own "temptation to some new kind of goodness, namely that of *praxis* itself."

The confluence between author and subject in *Brecht and Method*, between Marxist theorist and Marxist practitioner, creates a fairly rare opportunity for theorizing as praxis, for seldom do lifelong interests and expertise so carefully mesh. Yet this conversation between Jameson and Brecht probably cannot hope to have—except with advanced students of literature and theory—as wide a currency as several earlier studies of Brecht, such as those by Eric Bentley, for example. For as difficult as Brecht may be as both a dramatist and a thinker, Jameson is just that much more difficult as a theorist. Yet through the dense Jamesonian syntax, with its long, colon-laden sentences, breathtaking insights do manage to shine.

Thomas P. Adler

Source for Further Study

Choice. XXXVI, March, 1999, p. 1272

BRIDGET JONES'S DIARY
A Novel

Author: Helen Fielding
Published: Viking (New York). 271 pp. $22.95
Type of work: Novel
Time: The 1990's
Locale: London, England

A comic send-up of the novel of manners, updated by a narrator-diarist who is a thirty-something British "Singleton"—and worried about being so

> *Principal characters:*
> BRIDGET JONES, an unmarried, self-conscious, modern young British
> woman in her thirties who chronicles her quest for love and—barring
> that—self-improvement
> MARK DARCY, one of England's most prominent young lawyers
> DANIEL CLEAVER, Bridget's boss at the publishing firm where she first
> works
> PAM JONES, Bridget's mother, who, in the midst of a midlife crisis,
> becomes a presenter for the television show "Suddenly Single"

Bridget Jones begins the year—and her diary—with a set of resolutions dedicated to reducing her alcohol and tobacco intake, reducing her weight, and developing inner poise and a "functional relationship with responsible adult." This last resolution—as well as all the others, in fact—translates into finding a man. Bridget, now in her thirties, is alternately envious and contemptuous of those she refers to as the "Smug Marrieds," but she is obsessed by a question frequently put to her by her mother and her mother's friends: Why, at her age, is Bridget still single? Her anxious search for a mate has prompted many critics to label *Bridget Jones's Diary* a postfeminist work, but in fact it is prefeminist, in that it resembles nothing so much as early nineteenth century novels—in particular Jane Austen's *Pride and Prejudice* (1813).

Like Elizabeth Bennet, the heroine of Austen's novel, Bridget is plagued by a vulgar mother from whose clutches she is ultimately saved by a man named Darcy—who also, again as in Austen, saves her family from ruin by rescuing one of its members from the clutches of a bounder. Like Austen's heroine, Bridget is at first put off by her hero's externals—in this case, Mark Darcy's diamond patterned sweater and bumble-bee socks. In Austen's novel, the foolish heroine must first work her way through her prejudices about Darcy and another unsuitable suitor before finding true love. Fielding's Bridget Jones follows much the same course. (Lest we miss the similarities, Fielding has Bridget confess, after watching a television production of *Pride and Prejudice*, that Austen's Darcy and Elizabeth "are my chosen representatives in the field of shagging, or, rather, courtship.")

Another of Bridget's New Year's resolutions is to stop obsessing about her boss, Daniel Cleaver. Like her other resolutions, this one immediately falls victim to her insecurities. After putting up token resistance to what her feminist friend Sharon calls "fuckwittage"—that is, the inability of most men to commit themselves to a relationship—Bridget tumbles happily into bed with Daniel. Her happiness, like her occasional weight losses, lasts but a short while. Daniel does indeed engage in emotional manipulation, and when Bridget eventually discovers that he is involved with another woman—one he intends to marry—our heroine is doubly humiliated by the woman's appraisal of her: "Honey. . . . I thought you said she was *thin*." Only then does Bridget begin to lend credence to Mark Darcy's dire warnings about his rival's character.

Bridget is clearly a product of the information age. On the lighter side this means that she is a booster for the television game show *Blind Date* and takes as role models older—but still glamorous—women such as the film star Susan Sarandon and publishing luminary Tina Brown. One of her most cherished goals is to be able to emulate the late wife of the late critic Kenneth Tynan. Kathleen Tynan, according to a magazine article, had "inner poise," a quality she manifested by writing "immaculately dressed, sitting at a small table in the center of the room sipping a glass of chilled white wine." Bridget contrasts this impossibly composed image with her own inability to write a press release, as she lies "fully dressed and terrified under the duvet, chain-smoking, glugging cold *sake* out of a beaker and putting on makeup as a hysterical displacement activity." This kind of juxtaposition—Bridget's confessions of her attraction to society's glittering surface, followed by her darker commentary on its superficiality—is what makes Fielding's novel at once so amusing and so telling. Bridget may appraise herself and her foibles in comic terms, but she knows the score: "my reward, I know, will be to end up all alone, half-eaten by an Alsatian." Like Elizabeth Bennet, she has reason to be concerned about her marriageability.

In considering the alternative, Bridget need only look at her own mad mother. The loud, audacious Pam Jones, now a presenter for a vulgar television show called "Suddenly Single," has recently ditched Bridget's long-suffering father for a younger man, a Eurotrash swindler named Julio. Clothed in bright-hued polyester separates and spouting 1960's feminist slogans, Pam is a ghastly—if amusing—anachronism, one minute declaring her need for independence and the next breathlessly inquiring of a "Suddenly Single" interview subject, "Have you had suicidal thoughts?" But Pam's vagaries are at bottom not much different from her daughter's. A self-admitted child of *Cosmopolitan* culture, Bridget is capable of denouncing men one minute and declaring defeat the next, conceding—while immersed in such masochistic beautification rituals as leg waxing—to having been traumatized by supermodels. At times it seems that her range stretches only from *Women Who Love Too Much* to *Men Are From Mars, Women Are From Venus*—two possibly interchangeable self-help books of the 1990's.

In the end both Pam and Bridget are rescued from self-immolation by that archetypal white knight, Mark Darcy, who beguiles a fugitive Julio to return to England to face his creditors (thus saving Pam from probable prosecution for acting as his accomplice in defrauding time-share investors). Then Darcy beds (and presumably later weds) a grateful Bridget. The white knight figure is, of course, as old as literature itself, and although the Pam device seems to creak a bit, it does have its precedent, once again, in *Pride and Prejudice*, where Darcy's rescue of Elizabeth's sister from a cad helps speed the plot along to its foregone conclusion.

As many literary precursors as *Bridget Jones's Diary* has, it has still managed to stir up considerable controversy among those readers who have chosen to interpret it as social commentary—which of course it is. In a June 29, 1998, cover story written for *Time* magazine, Ginia Bellafante addressed the question "Is Feminism Dead?," employing Fielding's novel as exhibit A in support of her point that the radical feminism of the 1960's has given way to self-involved, self-destructive female personages such as Bridget Jones. The fact that *Bridget Jones's Diary* was a best seller first in England and then in the United States is cited as further evidence of Bellafante's thesis.

Bridget Jones and her diary are the imaginative creation of British journalist Helen Fielding, who says she invented them when she was asked to write an autobiographical newspaper column detailing her own inner woes. Loathe to publicly air details of her private life, Fielding instead thought up a creature who embodied every woman's insecurities—all of them. Fielding admits that she and Bridget share certain attributes: Not only is Fielding herself single, in her thirties, and living alone in west London, but she found her inspiration for Bridget in her own undergraduate diaries. From these she garnered the device of listing calories, cigarettes, and alcoholic drinks consumed, which she uses to introduce nearly every one of Bridget's diary entries. But while breathing life into her creation by lending her particularity, Fielding has also managed to make Bridget universal, so much so that "Bridget Jones" has made its way into the language as an adjective, as in "That's very Bridget Jones," indicating a peculiarly late twentieth century headlong rush from one chaotic situation to the next. Surely every woman who employs this phrase conjures up for herself the indelible image of Bridget—late again—rummaging through her dirty laundry only to find that all of her black tights are either shrunken, covered with shredded Kleenex lint, or twisted up into shapes resembling the Gordian knot.

The distance Fielding manages to keep between herself and Bridget—however slim—is the source of the book's humor. Not only is her heroine waist-deep in disorder, she is aware of her plight. The very fact that Fielding has written her novel in diary form, with all the self-consciousness such an exercise implies, is the first tip-off. Then there are passages such as this (concerning Bridget's draft of a response to Mark Darcy's party invitation): "Seem to remember from childhood am supposed to reply in same oblique style as if I am imaginary person employed by self to reply to invitations from imaginary people employed by friends to issue invitations." What Bridget comes up with is a polite, proper response, but not before trying out some archaic phrasings Elizabeth Bennet herself might have used. This is only one of the more explicit examples of Bridget's awareness of writing for an audience.

While some critics see Fielding's heroine as an archetypal victim of the evils perpetuated by the modern world she inhabits, the author views Bridget in rather different terms: "If Bridget is popular, it's because she lives in a state of nameless dread, thinking everyone knows how to live their life except her. What she doesn't realise is that lots of other people feel the same way." In short, Bridget's appeal is the same as that of her nineteenth century fictitious predecessor: She is both smarter than she seems and dumber than she should be, at once clear about her failings and purblind to her most glaring faults. It is such qualities that allow readers at once to identify with the protagonist and to feel superior to her. Few novelists' gambits are more engaging.

Yet, remarkably, many commentators have refused to see Bridget for what she is: a literary heroine for our time. Instead of acknowledging the distancing mechanisms in the novel and seeing the satire in *Bridget Jones's Diary*, they take the narrator at her word. Viewed from this perspective the book can be seen as sad social commentary, its exaggerations merely a statement about the state of modern womanhood writ large. It is all that—and more. If one declines to take up Fielding's invitation to laugh at Bridget—or, more accurately, to laugh with Bridget at herself—*Bridget Jones's Diary* can seem a paltry thing. The very fact that it has stirred up such controversy, however, argues for the opposite conclusion. If those decrying the book had merely dismissed it, rather than labeling it evidence of the end of modern feminism, it might never have become a best-seller. On the other hand, enough readers might have intuited its relevance to their lives without the media debate about the novel's merits to have made it successful. Whether it is pre- or postfeminist, *Bridget Jones's Diary* serves as a clear reminder of how important it is to retain a sense of humor. This is what sets Bridget apart—both for readers and for Mark Darcy, who sums up her appeal very neatly indeed: "Bridget, all the other girls I know are so lacquered over. I don't know anyone else who would fasten a bunny tail to their pants. . . ."

Lisa Paddock

Sources for Further Study

Business Week. July 13, 1998, p. 27.
Library Journal. CXXIII, May 15, 1998, p. 114.
Los Angeles Times Book Review. September 27, 1998, p. 10.
Ms. IX, July, 1998, p. 91.
The New Republic. CCXIX, September 7, 1998, p. 36.
The New York Times Book Review. CIII, May 31, 1998, p. 31.
The New Yorker. LXXIV, August 3, 1998, p. 70.
Newsweek. CXXXI, May 4, 1998, p. 82.
Publishers Weekly. CCXLV, April 20, 1998, p. 42.
The Washington Post Book World. XXVIII, July 5, 1998, p. 4.

CALAMITIES OF EXILE
Three Nonfiction Novellas

Author: Lawrence Weschler
Published: University of Chicago Press (Chicago). Illustrated. 199 pp. $25.00
Type of work: Biography
Time: c. 1916-1998
Locale: The United States, Iraq, England, Czechoslovakia, South Africa, France, and Spain

Three stories of politically active exiles from totalitarian regimes—an Iraqi, a Czecho-slovakian, and a South African—provide insight into the nature of both exile and totalitarianism

Principal personages:
KANAN MAKIYA, scholar and son of a prominent Iraqi architect
JAN KAVAN, head of a smuggling operation into communist Czechoslovakia
BREYTEN BREYTENBACH, leading author in the Afrikaans language

Exile was originally a form of punishment. The archetypal Babylonian exile was a punishment for Jewish uprisings. Among the ancient Greeks exile was a punishment for homicide (see, for example, *Oedipus Rex*). Among the ancient Romans, voluntary exile was an alternative to capital punishment. Around the eighteenth century, Europe began to exile its criminals to penal colonies in America, Australia, and Siberia. Throughout history, political exile has been a punishment for being on the wrong side.

In some ways, exile is a punishment worse than death: one lives on without the familiar surroundings that help define one's existence—places, culture, often one's language and family. In ancient Hebrew society, one was forced "beyond the pale" to live among howling beasts. In old Anglo-Saxon society, one became a wanderer racked by memories of the warm meadhall. For African captives who survived the Middle Passage, exile was part of the suffering associated with American slavery.

In the modern world exile remains a form of punishment, but the meaning of exile has vastly expanded. Most modern exiles are escapees from repressive regimes, as apparently were the Viennese grandparents of Lawrence Weschler, to whom he dedicates his book *Calamities of Exile*. The subject of his book is three such escapees, identified in his evocative section headings: "Oedipus in Samara: Kanan Makiya in and out of Iraq," "The Trials of Jan K.: Jan Kavan in and out of Czechoslovakia," and "A Horrible Face, But One's Own: Breyten Breytenbach in and out of South Africa."

The story of Kanan Makiya derives its title from the fact that his father, Mohamed Makiya, was Iraqi dictator Saddam Hussein's favorite architect. In 1989 Kanan Makiya, living in the United States, published his book *Republic of Fear: The Politics of Modern Iraq* under the pseudonym Samir al-Khalil. The pseudonym obviously shielded the author and kept open the possibility that he could return home, but it was also a necessary protection for his family still in Iraq. Yet at the same time that the book attacked Saddam Hussein and his regime it also attacked the author's prominent father for pandering to the regime. Maybe that was another reason for using the pseudonym.

Eventually the father also fled Iraq, the son revealed his pseudonym, and other details of their relationship with the Iraqi regime and each other came out. Their story introduces what Weschler, in the dedication to his grandparents, calls the "complicated" nature of exile. One of the themes running through *Calamities of Exile* is the complications that exile causes within families, as some members flee, others remain behind, and some even side with the oppressive regime. Another theme is the conflicted feelings of the exile. It seems that one can never quite free oneself from entanglements with the homeland, no matter how horrible it might be. Or maybe one does not want to.

In the case of Kanan Makiya's father, it was not merely that doing business with a dictator was profitable. It was also a matter of pride, as strange as that sounds. Steeped in Islamic history, especially as it centered around Iraq and Baghdad, Mohamed Makiya was motivated by intense nationalistic and cultural pride. Thus, he jumped at the chance Saddam Hussein gave him to rebuild Baghdad to its former glory. To him it was insignificant that his visions of architectural splendor coincided with those of a dictator. As he stated, "I'm an architect. . . . I love to create, and these were the greatest opportunities of my creative life. . . . I was in the position to be doing all of it for my country." His case illustrates how people's frame of reference remains tied to their cultural roots: One first seeks honor in one's own country. However, for Makiya as an architect and for the writer Breyten Breytenbach, the cultural ties were even more important as the prime source of their artistic inspiration and creativity.

"The Trials of Jan K.," the story of the Czech Jan Kavan, also contains a complicated father-son relationship, but the story is most significant for what it shows about the nature of totalitarianism. As the title suggests, Communist Czechoslovakia was truly Kafkaesque. The extensive reach of the Czech secret police, known as the StB, is omnipresent in the story. Maintaining the massive infrastructure of agents, informers, collaborators, recorders, and archivists must have eventually contributed to economic disaster. In the story half the population seems to be keeping tabs on the other, with secret agents doing double duty as neighbors and friends—or pretending to be neighbors and friends, just as people brought in for questioning sign confessions implicating others or pretend to become collaborators in order to go free.

It is not surprising that the secret police collected a dossier of hundreds of pages on Jan Kavan, who, from his base in London for some twenty years, ran the biggest smuggling operation in and out of Czechoslovakia, founded and ran a press agency steadily attacking the regime, and under assumed identities slipped in and out of Czechoslovakia several times. What is surprising is that after the Communist regime fell in 1989 and Jan Kavan returned to Czechoslovakia, he was officially charged with being a former secret police collaborator. Apparently his own success worked against him: How could anyone do all Kavan did without working hand in glove with the secret police? However, this bizarre thinking is consistent with the widespread belief in Czechoslovakia that the 1989 anti-Communist revolution had been staged by the secret police just so they could go on running the country. Such suspicions and second-guessing illustrate the mess that totalitarianism can leave. As a number of

Czech politicians and intellectuals in the story say, after decades of living in a Kafkaesque society, the Czechs were still in the process of trying to rediscover their moral bearings.

In the book's third section, "A Horrible Face, But One's Own," the themes developed in the previous two sections become intensified. Family relations are all over the political spectrum, the artist as a young man cannot abide exile, and the totalitarian reach becomes intimate. The story of these complications is illustrated by three paintings of Breyten Breytenbach, a visual artist as well as a writer. The first painting, titled "A Family Portrait," is actually Breytenbach's slightly surreal portrait of himself at three stages: a smirking boy, a smiling but scared young man (two hands cuffed together and his third hand reaching out to shake), and a scarred and subdued older man (left eye almost closed, the right hand a bird's head). The second painting shows an orange in four stages of being consumed. The third painting, created just after the artist's release from over seven years in South African prisons, is another self-portrait, this time of the artist as a battered-looking older man with eyes totally closed (consumed?).

In contrast to Jan Kavan, Breyten Breytenbach must have been the most inept spy ever. A South African artist and writer living on the Left Bank in Paris, he lacked any aptitude for espionage. Yet in his writings he repeatedly attacked South Africa's apartheid regime and its ruler, John Vorster, to whom he addressed the famous poem "Letter from Abroad to Butcher." Increasingly, Breytenbach felt that expressing political commitment in his writings was insufficient; he must also commit himself. Thus, he joined a branch of the African National Congress (ANC) in exile, which sponsored "his training in the techniques of conspiracy, smuggling, and subterfuge." Eventually Breytenbach allowed himself to be persuaded that he was the right man to slip back into South Africa, manifesto in hand, and organize underground opposition to the regime. However, even before Breytenbach caught the plane in Rome, the South African police were on to his assumed identity and his plans—perhaps tipped off by a member of his own group or a rival faction of the ANC. The South African police allowed him to enter the country, followed his movements for weeks to identify his contacts, and finally arrested him in the Jan Smuts Airport, where his attempt to exit the country unfortunately coincided with the arriving flight of John Vorster and an airport bristling with security officers. Breytenbach relates these and subsequent events in his *The True Confessions of an Albino Terrorist* (1983).

In *Calamities of Exile*, subsequent events reveal a personal, even intimate, side of totalitarian regimes. For example, Breytenbach's arrest and conviction definitely complicated relations between him and his family. His brother Cloete, a press photographer, had been traveling on the plane with Vorster; another brother, Jan, was a South African military hero, founding leader of an elite unit then storming through neighboring Angola. Yet Breytenbach's brothers, sister, and stressed parents stuck by him, even if some of them happened to be on different sides politically. Also sticking by Breytenbach was his Vietnamese wife in Paris, Yolande, who traveled back and forth for years and eventually won his early release from prison.

Much less savory were the relations Breytenbach developed with his captors. Of particular interest is the relationship with his lead interrogator, Kalfie (Little Calf) Broodryk, who played mind games with Breytenbach, got Breytenbach to dedicate a book of poems to him, and finally helped persuade Breytenbach to abase himself at his trial (to no avail). Droves of young ladies showed up at his trial to follow it with more than juridical interest. In prison, Breytenbach served the early part of his time on death row or in solitary confinement. When Yolande visited him, the guards eavesdropped on their conversations and later entertained Breytenbach with details of their "full body search" of her. One friendly young night guard, Pieter Groenewald, smuggled paper supplies to Breytenbach in prison and letters and artwork out, and the two passed the long nights together spinning wild plans for escape, sabotage, and other such exploits. Unfortunately, the young guard conveyed all these plans to his superiors, which resulted in further charges of terrorism against Breytenbach.

Of most interest is the love/hate attitude of the regime itself toward Breytenbach. As the foremost writer in Afrikaans, the language with which the regime identified, Breytenbach remained a cultural icon at the same time he was a nemesis. In exile, he collected literary awards from the country while attacking it. He made triumphal literary tours of the country immediately before and after his imprisonment. Throughout his imprisonment, his poems remained in literary anthologies used in schools. The regime's behavior toward him exposes inherent contradictions that perhaps foretold its downfall, as though it survived only by means of self-inflicted wounds.

Through its three narratives, *Calamities of Exile* provides a close-up personal view of the nature of exile and totalitarianism. Despite treating only three examples, the book is also a reminder of all the exiles among us, refugees from repressive political regimes around the world. These are only the political exiles. If the meaning of exile is extended metaphorically, then it seems that in the modern world exile has become almost a way of life. Few people stay where they were born (and perhaps grew up); if they do, their birthplaces are usually transformed around them. Mobility and change— across borders, cultures, languages—define modern existence. What this permanent exile means for the sense of self has not yet been worked out, but books such as *Calamities of Exile* can give readers an idea.

Harold Branam

Sources for Further Study

Booklist. XCIV, February 15, 1998, p. 956.
Boston Globe. June 7, 1998, p. C2.
Chicago Tribune. May 31, 1998, XIV, p. 9.
Kirkus Reviews. LXVI, March 15, 1998, p. 394.
Los Angeles Times Book Review. November 1, 1998, p. 5.
Mother Jones. XXIII, September, 1998, p. 82.

The New York Times Book Review. CIII, June 28, 1998, p. 18.
Publishers Weekly. CCXLV, March 9, 1998, p. 54.
The Spectator. CCLXXX, April 25, 1998, p. 38.
The Washington Monthly. XXX, July, 1998, p. 51.

CARNIVAL EVENING
New and Selected Poems, 1968-1998

Author: Linda Pastan (1932-   )
Published: W. W. Norton (New York). 301 pp. $27.50
Type of work: Poetry

A collection of poems by a great American autumnal poet, whose perspective is partly on the subject and partly on registering the sense of its being past or its constant passing

In this volume, Linda Pastan reaches back over her previous nine collections and adds a selection of her more recent work. It is a generous offering and a momentous achievement. With it, Pastan solidifies her place as the great autumnal poet. Her *Carnival Evening: New and Selected Poems 1968-1998* participates in and majestically caps the close of the last third of what has been an especially fertile century in American poetry.

Calling her poetry "autumnal" is not to suggest that there is a narrowness of range to her substantial body of work. Nor is the label meant to indicate anything about a season of life that Pastan is exploring in her seventh decade. Rather, hers is an autumnal sensibility; it has been so from the start, and why not? Autumn provides an enormous span for the imagination. It is, after all, in the more northerly climes, a full fourth of what one experiences in life. As a Marylander for many years (and that state's poet laureate from 1991 to 1994), Linda Pastan has reveled in bud and blossom but more profoundly felt the chill of fall and the fall of leaf. However, it is not the season itself that dominates Pastan's work (although it has an important place); rather, it is the autumnal mood. She is concerned with the way things (people, relationships, ambitions) change and fade and often decay.

Many of Pastan's poems are charged with an urgency about time's pressure; she persuades or reminds the reader that whoever he or she is, young or old, youth is past or passing. Green is going and gone. Thus, everything is to be grasped and valued in its fullness, its splendor, before one cannot taste and appraise, before it is no longer ripening or ripe. Pastan would agree with Wallace Stevens when he announces (in "Sunday Morning") that "Death is the mother of beauty," although Pastan's tropes are less overtly philosophical. If people had eternity, she suggests, they would not have to make choices: Everything, endlessly, would come their way. However, people do not have eternity; they must decide what to honor and hold onto.

Not surprising, then, is the nostalgic strand in Pastan's work, a strand that thickens in her later volumes. As she herself passes through the stations of life, she considers these stations carefully and remembers those dear to her whom she has now somehow replaced. She voices her roles as homemaker, wife, mother, grandmother, heir to Jewish-American traditions and sensibilities. She travels back to a Bronx childhood to find the wellsprings of the sophisticated woman and the accomplished artist. However, the perspective, by and large, is partly on the subject and partly on registering the sense of its being past or its constant passing. Memories glow in their very fading.

The poet pulls images and events back from their vanishing acts, but the reader feels the counterpull of autumn, brilliantly evoked, toward winter and desolation. (The poems that live most fully in the present are the ones about wifely intimacy and its occasional frustrations. Pastan's handling of these matters is never sensational or exhibitionist. She voices an earned wisdom of love's delights and dilemmas. Taken together and placed in a separate collection, these poems would generate greater power than they do in a more dispersed volume.)

Is Linda Pastan, then, an elegiac poet? Perhaps not. Although mournful at times, she is less given to mourning than to a complex mode of celebration. What she fears, or quietly decries, is that one's attentiveness can rarely do justice to the world's plenitude of expression. Her success is in helping to battle sloth, quietly chastening herself and her readers. Do you not feel how it is all fading? she seems to ask. Will you not at least prolong this autumn with me, this autumn that is everything because we have waited so long already? We have always been too young, too naïve, too selfish, too distracted—but it is not quite too late. And what we have left, although it is only almost enough, is—paradoxically—plenty. Enough to make you dizzy. Enough to make you miss death altogether. Or choose it naturally, without despair.

Linda Pastan, like John Keats in "Ode to a Nightingale," can sing the fantasy of a fullness that welcomes death. This mood is in the title poem of her collection *An Early Afterlife*, the poem with which she closes *Carnival Evening:* "Why don't we say goodbye right now/ in the fallacy of perfect health," the speaker asks, "before whatever is going to happen/ happens." The Keatsian yearning is posed in many earlier poems as well, including one called "In the Middle of Life":

> Tonight I understand
> for the first time
> how a woman might choose
> her own death
> as easily
> as if it were a dark plum
> she picked
> from a basket
> of bright peaches.
>
> It wouldn't be despair
> that moved her
> or hunger,
> but a kind of stillness.
> The evenings are full
> of closure: the pale flowers
> of the shamrock fold
> their fragile wings, everything
> promised has been given.

One aspect of the autumnal mood, then, is the comfortable acceptance of cessation at a moment of perfect ripeness. More characteristic, in Pastan's work, than fading into the fullness of late harvest is the underscoring of its fleetingness. How to hold on?

Poetry is the preservative, the fixative. Each Pastan poem is a spray of words and images drying before the colors further fade. Her poems and lines tend to be short, pared down, a domestic poet's lyrical version of home economics. She looks for value and gives it. Her poems have decorum, but she seems to wrestle with that decorum. One senses, over and over, that hidden riots are about to break out, that each shedding oak or elm might suddenly become a maypole. There is some conjuring, perhaps intentionally unfinished, toward chaos, dispersion, reckless gaiety. Yet Pastan's modest, precise, no-fat crafting keeps these forces in check. Is her vision more of "carnival" or more of "evening"? In the long run, her long career would seem to assert, the distinction thins.

Pastan, on occasion, reaches to traditional forms. Perhaps the challenge is unavoidable for an artist so careful about the weights and measures of her free verse lines. Collected in the present volume are sections of a sestina ("Shadows"), a pantoum ("Something about the Trees"), and a sonnet sequence. These poems are handled with such mastery and freshness that one wishes that Pastan would indulge this impulse more often. No doubt she returns her talent to these forms as the well-used knife must return to the whetstone. In the "The Imperfect Paradise" one can appreciate Pastan's formal mastery, noting that although a debate is formulated regarding the merits of spring and winter, the close resolves in autumn's special power:

SEASONAL

Which season is the loveliest of all?
Without a pause you smile and answer spring,
Thinking of Eden long before the fall.
I see green shrouds enclosing everything
And choose instead the chaos of the snow
Before God separated dark from light.
I hear the particles of matter blow
Through wintry landscapes on a wintry night.
You find the world a warm and charming place,
My Adam, you name everything in sight.
I find a garden of conspicuous waste—
The apple's flesh is cold and hard and white.
Still, at your touch my house warms to the eaves
As autumn torches all the fragile leaves.

Pastan's writing might also be defined by what is absent or rarely present in her poems. There is scant attention to the world of work or the world of politics. Popular entertainment and science are not concerns of her muse. She shuns what is merely topical or merely intellectual. Of course, references and responses to art and literature are frequent, although there is less name- and learning-dropping than one might expect from a poet who is obviously bookish. Surely Pastan is learned in the ways of her art, but she manages to make that art comfortably personal while free of cranky idiosyncrasies. Distancing quirks and overwrought puzzles are not her way. Her work has been given that frighteningly trivializing appellation "accessible." So it is, without being simple or simpleminded. Pastan is truly considerate of her readers. She cares about getting through and about getting it right. She succeeds.

The price that Linda Pastan has paid for her special talent and dedication is the price of faint praise. She has garnered her share of awards and distinctions, but who can name them? So many critics and fellow writers admire her work, but how often is she quoted? Perhaps she has suffered, too, from the lack of a public persona. She is not a newsmaker; if she aspires to celebrity status, it has not found her. Attention to her work has not received the boost that often comes to the poet of controversy and partisan declamation. Rarely topical and always modest in her management of the "I" who voices her lines, Pastan does not leave readers with the ragged, bleeding edge of self-display that invites, too easily, either sympathy or the delights of shock. She is a finisher, a polisher, a closer. She has been in the poetry game for the long haul, and *Carnival Evening* casts a long shadow. It is certainly deserving of its National Book Award nomination—and much more.

Philip K. Jason

Sources for Further Study

Booklist. XCIV, April, 1998, p. 1295.
Boston Globe. June 10, 1998, p. D3.
Library Journal. CXXIII, April 15, 1998, p. 84.
Publishers Weekly. CCXLV, March 30, 1998, p. 77.
The Washington Post Book World. XXVIII, April 5, 1998, p. 2.

CAVEDWELLER

Author: Dorothy Allison (1951-   )
Published: E. P. Dutton (New York). 352 pp. $23.95
Type of work: Novel
Time: The 1980's
Locale: California and Cayro, Georgia

A novel about death, family, love, women's friendships, craziness, growing up, and the origins of the blues

> *Principal characters:*
> DELIA BYRD, a mother determined to recover the daughters she
>   abandoned ten years earlier when she fled her battering husband and
>   joined a rock and roll band
> RANDALL PRITCHARD, an easygoing rock and roll singer who fathers
>   Delia's third daughter Cissy
> CISSY, the-ten-year old daughter of Delia and Randall, the cave dweller
>   of the title, whose growing-up story is a major thread in the novel
> CLINT WINDSOR, Delia's abusive first husband
> ROSEMARY DEPAU, Delia's good female friend from her band years
> DEDE WINDSOR, the daughter who most takes after Delia
> AMANDA WINDSOR, Delia's religious daughter

Dorothy Allison, the author of *Bastard out of Carolina* (1992), the acclaimed best-seller and finalist for the National Book Award, has written another novel exploring the nature of family and friendship, love and loss. *Bastard out of Carolina* was an unremittingly dark southern gothic exploration of child abuse that changed the face of the literary molester forever from Vladimir Nabokov's urbane, sexually arrested man/child Humbert Humbert to the cruel and ignorant persona of Allison's thwarted Daddy Glen. *Cavedweller*, on the other hand, turns the reader's compassion to more common but often equally destructive lapses in judgment, passionate excesses, and plain stupidity with which unthinking and confused adults often burden young and innocent lives. A great deal of the difference in tone between the two novels has to do with the narrative voice. While *Bastard out of Carolina* is presented through the eyes of its young protagonist, whose confusion, hurt, and rage make a direct appeal to the reader's sympathies, even though the story is told with an almost preternatural objectivity, *Cavedweller* is told by a traditional omniscient narrator, who in a truly God-like way, seems equally empathetic to all the characters, even though the book ends up being primarily the story of young Cissy's coming of age.

Cavedweller opens with the line, "Death changes everything," which could in many ways be a coda for the entire novel as well. In the first chapter Cissy's father, Randall, has died in a motorcycle wreck, catapulting her mother Delia into action after ten years of booze and rock and roll. Sober and contrite, she journeys from Los Angeles to Cayro, Georgia, on a deeply felt and deeply flawed mission to regain her lost daughters and reunite Cissy with her true kin. Her passionate intensity and lack of common sense on the cross-country journey foreshadow things to come and clearly capture the plight of children whose lives are governed by fiercely loving, but often irresponsible, adults.

Delia's yearning for her hometown is, not surprisingly, unreciprocated; from the cook at the local diner to her Granddaddy Byrd, nobody in Cayro is glad to see her. Nobody thinks she has any right to reclaim the daughters she abandoned years earlier for a career singing blues with the itinerant band Mud Dog. This is an old-fashioned town with old-fashioned values, and Delia, like Hester Prynne in Nathaniel Hawthorne's *The Scarlet Letter* (1850), will have to repent patiently and publicly. She has a complete breakdown, leaving her daughter Cissy not only bereaved by her father's death but also alone and beleaguered in an inhospitable new town. Delia's previously abandoned daughters, Dede and Amanda, have been raised with much Christian discipline but little Christian charity by their Grandma Windsor and are no more disposed to comfort their newly arrived mother than the other flinty residents of Cayro. Redemption will come slowly, it seems, and mostly through the ministrations of female friends, the first of which is M. T., recently divorced and eager to resume her childhood friendship with the now slightly famous Delia.

It is clear even this early in the novel that in Delia, Allison is portraying the anatomy of a blues singer. The first few riffs have already been played: the death of a loved one, loss and abandonment, the false allure of the highway, shame and repentance, abuse and abnegation, booze and the kindness of strangers. These are the staples of the blues universe, and the women who sing these painful songs, who move audiences to tears and jubilation, earn the right to mesmerize by paying for their moments of glory with their own aborted private lives. While Delia has quit drinking and singing, she has only just begun to pay the real price, as she confronts her family and her past and fights to get her daughters back.

Delia begins to replace impetuosity with patience, passion with guile. When she realizes that Grandma Windsor will never give her daughters back to her, she makes a Mephistophelean deal with her abusive ex-husband: Delia will take care of the cancer-ridden Clint Windsor until he dies if he will give her custody of the girls. Cissy, now almost twelve years old, must deal not only with her worn-out mother but also with her new ersatz family: her mother's dying ex-husband and the two wary, disgruntled teenagers—her half-sisters—who are no more pleased to be there than she is. Cissy's plight becomes ever more depressing, with no end in sight. The situation would be almost untenable if it were not for the appearance of Rosemary Depau, Delia's best friend from her roadie days. This gorgeous black amazon from Los Angeles introduces another kind of angst into deeply southern Cayro but brings much needed help to Delia and her girls. As Delia explains to Dede, laying bare one of the important themes of the novel: "Someday you will have a friend like that, a woman you can trust with your life. . . . No woman is safe who doesn't have one. Any woman who does, well, she an't never on her lonesome." The reader can almost hear the mournful strains of a steel guitar behind those heartfelt lines.

Clint Windsor's death marks the middle of the novel and the transition of the reader's interest from Delia, whose hard work and quiet resignation begin to look like redemption, to Cissy, who has just discovered caving; to Dede, whose interests run to cars and boys; and to Amanda, whose equally religious beau marries her and gives her children of her own to fret about. In an interesting conversation between Cissy and Dede, they exchange stories about their worst memories. While the reader flinches in expectation of the egregious horrors of Allison's *Bastard out of Carolina*, a more mundane story of everyday ugliness unfolds. Dede's worst memories are of her father, Clint, and his neglectful, drunken ways. Cissy immediately tells about the dramatic fights between Delia and Randall. They would yell and break things, curse and scream, but never actually hit each other. Do such parents damage their children? As surely as if they had hit them with a belt.

Dede is afraid to love Nolan, presented as an almost angelic man in a world of careless, frustrated, hateful, alienated men, because she has formulated the idea that love between a man and woman ruins everything. Cissy only feels safe in the deep recesses of Paula's lost cave, which she shares with her two spelunking buddies Jean and Mim, who, she discovers much later than the reader, are lesbians. Like Aunt Raylene in *Bastard out of Carolina*, Jean and Mim present one way out of the seemingly endless cycle of anguish and hurt created by the man-woman thing, a solution Allison knows firsthand through her own relationship to Alix, her real-life lover of ten years. Cissy has her caves the way her mother has music, her sister Dede has cars, and her sister Amanda has religion, but while caving provides Cissy with considerable solace, even she knows it is not the basis of a life. Three more chords of the blues have been struck by Delia's daughters: deep alienation, the pain of not being able to love fully, and spiritual longing.

Delia's daughters all carry both the good and the bad of Delia in them, so it is not surprising to find that the end of the book is the telling of each of their great trials and greater humanity. Dede, who is most like her mother, has to shoot her besotted Nolan before she can let herself trust him enough to love him. Amanda's gallstone surgery leads to a total emotional collapse, complete with bouts of drinking and obsessive compulsive behavior, but perhaps cures her of her self-righteous religiosity. Cissy and her friends confront death in the cave, a most aggressively broadcast plot element, and come out with much more curiosity about and appreciation for life and sunlight. Even Delia has some insight into the things she has done to her daughters and the path she has traveled and is ready to write some new songs with her old pal Rosemary. Unfortunately, the melancholy blues refrain that rang out with such touching authenticity throughout the book has been inexplicably and too abruptly replaced by a Hollywood soundtrack.

Bastard out of Carolina was a near-perfect novel, and it is tempting to compare *Cavedweller* to it disparagingly because its incidents are sometimes contrived, its cave metaphor a bit tired and overworked. Its language sometimes falls short when it reaches for transcendence, its evocation of the music of the times is often thin, and its finish smacks of pandering to the public's taste for happy endings. Nonetheless, *Cavedweller* is a lot like Delia—it only fails a little because it tries to achieve so much. Unlike so many modern novels—constipated, minimalist explorations of brand names and minutia—*Cavedweller* tries to come to terms with age-old verities: good and bad, love and hate, judgment and forgiveness, mothers and daughters, men and women, life and death. It is important to remember that a .300 batting average is considered excellent when you are playing in the big leagues.

Not since William Faulkner and Flannery O'Connor has southern "poor white trash" had such a powerful voice in American literature as Dorothy Allison. Her lucid, hard-hitting prose, her remarkable powers of observation, her honesty, her courage in the face of taboo subjects have allowed her to carve out a literary turf that has lain barren since the political correctness wars of the 1990's. *Cavedweller* is an excellent example of the kind of mainstream novel currently being written by unabashedly feminist authors, a novel that will take its place comfortably in the literary canon of the future based on its literary quality alone.

Cynthia Lee Katona

Sources for Further Study

Artforum. XXXVI, March, 1998, p. S30.
Booklist. XCIV, February 1, 1998, p. 876.
Library Journal. CXXIII, March 1, 1998, p. 125.
Los Angeles Times Book Review. March 15, 1998, p. 8.
The Nation. CCLXVI, March 30, 1998, p. 25.
The New York Times Book Review. CIII, March 15, 1998, p. 19.
Newsweek. CXXXI, March 30, 1998, p. 66.
Publishers Weekly. CCXLV, January 19, 1998, p. 369.
Time. CLI, April 13, 1998, p. 221.
The Washington Post Book World. XXVIII, April 5, 1998, p. 1.

THE CHAN'S GREAT CONTINENT
China in Western Minds

Author: Jonathan D. Spence (1936-   )
Published: W. W. Norton (New York). 279 pp. $27.50
Type of work: History
Time: 1200's-1900's
Locale: China and the West

A study of how the West has perceived and interpreted China and the Chinese people from the late Middle Ages down to the late twentieth century

Jonathan D. Spence is the Sterling Professor of History at Yale University and the author of a number of major works on Chinese history, including the highly praised best-seller *The Search for Modern China.* Spence's previous studies have largely explored the history of China and the Chinese or, occasionally, the tale of western residents in China, such as in *The Memory Palace of Matteo Ricci.* In *The Chan's Great Continent* Spence discusses the impact that China—or perhaps even more, the idea of China—had on the West over the centuries, from the era of the Venetian traveler and storyteller Marco Polo to that of Richard M. Nixon, who used the phrase "Polo II" in planning for his meeting with Mao Zedong in the 1970's. The West's contacts with China, which reflected one perceived reality or another, were frequently fantasy creations that had little to do with the actual China and invariably said as much about the West as they did about China.

Originally delivered as the William Clyde DeVane lectures at Yale University in 1996, Spence's elucidation of the western reaction to Chinese civilization was presented for a general audience rather than for experts in Chinese history, although the author notes that his remarks and now writings are scholarly enough to satisfy academic specialists. Nevertheless, the hallmark of Spence's work has always been its accessibility, not least in that he is a fine writer and can tell a fascinating tale. Spence notes that modifications were made in bringing his oral lectures to written form, particularly in the inclusion of lengthy quotations to more fully illustrate his themes, an obvious advantage to the reader.

The Chan's Great Continent takes its title from Marco Polo's story of his long sojourn in China with his father and uncle in the late thirteenth century. Polo was not the first westerner to write about contact with the Chinese. That honor belonged to William of Rubruck, a Franciscan friar, who, although he got to China itself, was sent in 1253 to request Khan Mongke's support in the struggle between the Christian West and Islam. Polo's great significance is that he related his service under Kublai Kahn, China's Mongol ruler, to Rusticello of Pisa, who put Polo's tale into an existing popular format that may or may not have reflected precisely what Polo had said. When published in 1485, shortly after the invention of the printing press, one diligent reader was Christopher Columbus, who was intent on achieving his own Chinese experience. There are difficulties in Polo's written account, as he does not mention either tea, calligraphy, or foot binding, for example, although these lapses could well have been due to Rusticello rather than Polo himself. But in the broader sense, Polo anticipated later commentators, whether they actually experienced China in person or not, by using comparisons with China as a means to comment on aspects of western civilization.

Many of Spence's westerners will be familiar but others less so. One of the latter is Galeote Pereira, a Portuguese who visited China in the mid-sixteenth century. He noted the severity of punishment, a theme discussed by many western writers, but he praised the government-supported hospitals and rest homes and the system of Chinese justice. Gaspar da Cruz, a Dominican friar, read Pereira's account and was the first westerner to comment on the foot binding of women, the language, and tea. A Jesuit priest, Matteo Ricci, arrived in China in 1583 and remained there until his death in 1610. Spence has devoted a full monograph to Ricco elsewhere but notes here that Ricco's account of China was highly favorable: He praised China as a well-ordered, unified country, unlike sixteenth century Europe, which was caught up in religious wars. Ricco also admired Confucius but noted that so-called ancestor worship was one of the barriers to the possible Christianization of China.

The seventeenth and eighteenth centuries saw a different perception of China, this time through the reports of western diplomats such as the Scottish doctor John Bell, who accompanied a Russian delegation to China in 1714. An exacting observer, Bell commented on the Great Wall, the Emperor Kangxi, and how ordinary Chinese lived. He generally interpreted China in a positive light, unlike British commander George Anson, who arrived in 1743 and whose attitude reflected a new-found British hubris. To Anson the Chinese were duplicitous and dishonest. His account was read by Lord George Macartney, who arrived in China in 1787 as George III's representative. Macartney found the Chinese hard working but was much put out by the demand that he "kowtow," or ritually bow, to the emperor—he was only willing to go down on one knee. By the end of his trip his dislike for China had become uppermost; he described China as "an old crazy first rate man-of-war" doomed under its puppet leaders to be soon "dashed to pieces on the shore."

Fascination with China also led to a cult of "Chinoiserie." This had less to do with political, economic, or social systems and more to do with an idealized interest in Chinese-style wallpaper, willow-pattern plates, furniture, pavilions, pagodas, and gardens. Even productions of Shakespeare were set in China. Daniel Defoe commented favorably about those "ancient, wise, polite, and most ingenious people," but later, in *Robinson Crusoe*, he has Crusoe condemning China's failures in commerce, architecture, cities and ports, navies and armies, and religion. Spence claims that Defoe, like Anson and Macartney, was reflecting his own British values rather than an objective assessment of China. However, Oliver Goldsmith, in a series of "Chinese Letters," even defends Chinese luxury as contributing to stability and wisdom and finds the British overbearing and condescending. There was a different China for every taste and attitude.

Western philosophers also wrote about China but from a distance. None were ever in China. Gottfried Wilhelm Leibniz compared China and the West and found the former inferior in logic, metaphysics, mathematics, and military science but ahead of the West in civil life, ethics, and practical philosophy. The Frenchman Baron Montesquieu, in *The Spirit of the Laws*, however, condemned the Chinese government as an absolute despotism, arguing that civil peace in China only existed because of force. Voltaire found more to praise in China but claimed that in comparison to the West, where progress was the rule, China was a stagnating civilization.

In the nineteenth century many westerners, a number of them Protestant missionaries and many of them women, journeyed to China, some spending years there and many commenting in books and letters about their experiences—sometimes positive, other times negative. Drawn by California's Gold Rush and railroad construction, Chinese began emigrating to the United States in the mid-nineteenth century. Mark Twain, Brett Harte, and Jack London commented on the Chinese emigration, and not always in complimentary fashion. However, in spite of negative stereotypes, they were also sympathetic to the Chinese or perhaps outraged at their fellow Americans' frequent bigotry, using Chinese characters to comment on western civilization's shortcomings. London's "The Chinago" told the story of Ah Spong Hi's unjust conviction and execution at the hands of western justice, but the story was rejected numerous times before finally being accepted for publication. On the other hand, the infamous literary figure Fu-Manchu, whose creator Sax Rohmer (Arthur S. Ward) had him planning to create a worldwide "Yellow Empire," quickly became the stock Chinese villain in books and films. At that time Chinese villains were more popular than Chinese victims.

Westerners were often influenced by China's exotic reputation. Several French authors, including Gustave Flaubert in his *Sentimental Education*, Pierre Loti in *The Last Days of Peking* and other works, the dramatist Paul Claudel, and especially Victor Segalen in his poetry and his novel *Rene Leys*, portray a seductive and sensual China, which both drew and repelled western sensibilities. Americans also used various Chinas. D. W. Griffith's 1915 movie *Broken Promises* is the story of interracial love and violence set in London, and Ezra Pound's fascination with China abounds in his poetry, from *Cathay* (1915) to his monumental Cantos. Eugene O'Neill's play, *Marco Millions* (1927) interprets Marco Polo as a stereotypical western materialist. China, real and imagined, was a useful foil to comment on western culture.

Pearl Buck's novel *The Good Earth*, which sold over a million copies after its publication in 1931 and which also became a successful movie, was one of the most popular attempts to portray China to the West. Instead of a China of urban fleshpots, silk and opium, and dastardly villains, Buck told the story of a Chinese peasant caught up in the eternal struggle for survival. The book's popularity was due not only to Buck's compelling story but also because in the Great Depression of the 1930's even the West was struggling economically. However, the idea of the Chinese as "the other" also continued. John Steinbeck, in "Johnny Bear," told the story of a doomed love affair in rural America between a Chinese field hand and Miss Amy, a respectable white woman. This tale was related by the village idiot, which meant that their story was not really told at all.

The twentieth century saw Chinese exoticism often replaced by Chinese politics, particularly Communist politics, to which many westerners were attracted as a consequence of the failure of Western civilization in the trenches of World War I and the failure of capitalism in the Great Depression. Andre Malraux's *Man's Fate* (1933) tells the story of the purge of Shanghai's Communists by Chiang Kai-shek in 1927, and Bertolt Brecht's play *The Measures Taken* (1930) features a revolutionary uprising in Mukden. Edgar Snow's *Red Star Over China* (1937) gave one of the most admiring and sympathetic interpretations of Chinese Communists and their leader, Mao Zedong. Times change, however, and the Cold War brought new interpretations of Chinese Communism. Spence discusses at some length Karl Wittfogel, a German Communist who came to interpret Chinese Communism under Mao as the latest example of oriental despotism, which went back to the days of Emperor Qin Shihuanghi, one of the most ruthless emperors in China's long history. In the twentieth century an earlier agrarian despotism had been replaced by a more comprehensive despotism, both socially and intellectually. Wittfogel's interpretation was accepted by President Richard M. Nixon and his Secretary of State, Henry Kissinger, in the 1970's. Kissinger drew an explicit comparison between Mao and past despotic emperors.

In the final chapter of his book, Spence examines three short stories by Franz Kafka, Jorge Luis Borges, and Italo Calvino, all of whom use themes and images of China in exploring the human condition. Calvino has Polo and Kublai Khan huddled over their maps, speculating on cities past, present, and future, real and fictional, anticipating their own futures and their realities. Spence concludes with the comment, "The secret lies in the ear, the ear that hears both what it wants and what it is expecting." For centuries, China in its various guises, past and future, real and imaginary, admirable and deplorable, has captivated the West.

Jonathan Spence is undoubtedly the most widely known historian of China in the Western world. His various published works range from insightful monographs to topical surveys to a beautifully illustrated history of twentieth century China. Given his reputation, any of his books is sure to be widely reviewed and inevitably offered to the general reading public through several of the many book clubs. China continues to be a highly topical subject as it is apparently making its halting transition from Communism to something approximating capitalism and as it hopefully moves politically closer to western-style democracy. Every prognosticator sees China as the new superpower of the twenty-first century. Some are optimistic about this evolution of events, while others in the West see such a development with much foreboding. The future China presents various images to the West, and as in the past China induces in the West differing fears and hopes. In assisting the reader to see how westerners have perceived and created numerous Chinas in the past, Spence's book will hopefully help in assessing the coming Chinas with less fantasy and more objectivity.

Eugene Larson

Sources for Further Study

Booklist. XCV, September 15, 1998, p. 172.
Far Eastern Economic Review. CLXI, October 15, 1998, p. 57.
Los Angeles Times Book Review. November 29, 1998, p. 4.
The New York Review of Books. XLV, December 3, 1998, p. 21.
The New York Times Book Review. CIII, November 15, 1998, p. 19.
Publishers Weekly. CCXLV, August 3, 1998, p. 62.
The Wall Street Journal. September 4, 1998, p. W12.
The Washington Post Book World. XXVIII, August 30, 1998, p. 5.

CHARMING BILLY

Author: Alice McDermott (1953-   )
Published: Farrar, Straus & Giroux (New York). 280 pp. $22.00
Type of work: Novel
Time: 1983, with flashbacks to 1945.
Locale: Manhattan and its environs; Woodside, Bayside, Rosedale, and East Hampton, New
   York

*Forty-seven mourners gather to remember Billy Lynch following his funeral and, through
their reminiscences, resurrect the physically absent Billy as the protagonist of the novel*

> *Principal characters:*
> BILLY LYNCH, a charming Irish American
> MAEVE, Billy's long-suffering wife
> EVA KAVANAUGH, Billy's first love, whom he thinks is long dead
> DENNIS LYNCH, Billy's cousin and best friend
> DENNIS'S UNNAMED DAUGHTER, the novel's narrator
> HOLTZMAN, Dennis's stepfather, Billy's part-time employer
> SHEILA LYNCH HOLTZMAN, Dennis's mother, Holtzman's wife

Forty-seven friends and relations have gathered for the funeral and burial of Billy
Lynch, a charming Irish American with a drinking problem who, at age sixty, has
finally drunk himself to death. Set initially in the Bronx in a remote tavern with an
ambiance resembling that of an Irish pub, the novel's action takes place on the day of
Billy's funeral and on the two days following it. In reminiscing about him, those who
gather to mourn him take the reader back as far as World War II; in so doing, they
create a convincing persona who, despite his physical absence, is the novel's protagonist.

In this novel, her fourth, Alice McDermott deals with many of the topics she has
considered in the past: the power of sexual desire, the ironies of fate, memories of lost
worlds, the seemingly contradictory illusiveness and constancy of time, and the effects
of community on its inhabitants. In none of her previous novels has McDermott been
in quite such masterful control of her material as she is in *Charming Billy*, although
in *Weddings and Wakes* (1992), she moves in the direction of this novel, which won
the 1998 National Book Award in Fiction.

Billy Lynch represents a type of Irish American, a sentimental, often melancholy
fellow who worked in a routine job for Consolidated Edison. Liquor has been his
solace in a life that has known hardship, loss, and sorrow. The loss Billy has mourned
for three decades is that of Eva Kavanaugh, an Irish girl he met when she came to New
York to visit her sister, Mary.

Billy fell in love with Eva, and by the time she returned to Ireland to look after her
elderly parents, the two were engaged to be married. Eva promised to return to Billy,
who subsequently sent her five hundred dollars to pay the passage back to the United
States. Although he sent Eva two or three letters a week, as time went on, he heard
nothing from her.

Before long, Billy's cousin and closest friend, Dennis Lynch, received a call from Eva's sister, who needed to see him. When they met, she revealed to Dennis that Eva had married someone in Ireland and had spent the five hundred dollars Billy sent her to make a down payment on a petrol station outside Clonmel, where she lived. Not wanting to break Billy's heart, Dennis told his cousin that Eva had died of pneumonia in Ireland. When Billy suggested that he should visit her grave, Dennis discouraged him from doing so by saying that such a visit would only revive sad memories for Eva's parents. Instead, Billy wrote to them and told them to keep the five hundred dollars he had sent to help with Eva's final expenses. He continued to write to them every Christmas and in September, the month of her supposed death, but never received responses to his letters.

The shadow of Eva's death hung heavily over Billy for thirty years, until in 1975, when back in Ireland to take the pledge of abstinence, he met Eva and learned of Dennis's deception. Billy had married Maeve in the early 1950's. His marriage was clouded by his memories of Eva and by his undying devotion to her memory. The melancholy that these memories evoked gave Billy the excuse he needed for drowning his sorrows in liquor, which he had happily consumed in substantial quantities even before Eva entered his life. Billy was generally an affable rather than a belligerent drunk. He came by his alcoholism honestly through a host of alcoholic progenitors.

Billy's death was somewhat easier than much of his life had been, although, in his coffin, his face was bloated from his excessive drinking. When Dennis went to identify the corpse in the Veterans' Administration Hospital where Billy had been taken and where had died three hours after he fell in the street, its skin was so dark that Dennis said to the attendant, "But this is a colored man." After a bout of drinking, he collapsed on the pavement, suffering an internal hemorrhage that filled his stomach with blood and quickly rendered him unconscious.

McDermott unfolds her story through an unnamed, enigmatic narrator, Dennis Lynch's daughter, who flies in from Seattle for Billy's funeral. Readers learn little about the narrator except that she has a college education and has married Matt West, son of a man who had rented the Long Island cottage of Dennis's mother when he walked out on his wife and three sons many years earlier.

Dennis always believed that if the cottage his mother inherited from her second husband had not been available, West would not have deserted his family. He assuaged his conscience, however, by telling himself that when he sold his house in Rosedale and retired to the cottage, West would return to his wife, which is exactly the way it worked out

The shadowy narrator, which McDermott has employed in some of her earlier novels, serves a purpose that an omniscient narrator could not serve. In subtle ways, McDermott traces the course three generations of Irish Americans have followed in an almost archetypal way: They progress from New York, the first generation laboring at menial jobs in order to survive, to Long Island, the second generation moving to the suburbs when they take jobs like Dennis's desk job with Con Edison, then to some distant place—in this case Seattle, where the members of the third generation, the first to be college educated, migrate and make a new life.

McDermott does not specifically mention the changes that have taken place in the old Irish American neighborhoods, but she reveals these changes in nuanced ways: Indian neighbors bring a casserole of chicken and rice to Maeve after Billy's funeral but do not come in to sit with the family. Maeve casually mentions other neighbors who are not Irish American, suggesting only that they are good neighbors. It is McDermott's ability to present such details with the restraint and subtlety she does that makes her characters come to life in ways that fully engage readers.

Marriage is a major theme in *Charming Billy*. In the novel, marriage is usually a matter of accommodation rather than the fulfillment of youthful passion. Had Billy married Eva, passion would have been a strong underpinning in the marriage. With Eva's supposed death, Billy has little stomach for romance. When Maeve comes into Holtzman's shoe store with her father and spies Billy, who works part time in the store, she becomes the aggressor. She comes back to the store on Saturdays when she knows Billy will be working. She goes so far as to throw one of her father's shoes in an incinerator to give them an excuse for going to Holtzman's again.

It takes Billy three years to decide that marriage to Maeve is reasonable. In many ways, she is the perfect mate for him. She is plain, a devout Roman Catholic of limited passion who had once considered entering a convent. She has always been dutiful to her father, who, like Billy, is an alcoholic. Her marriage to Billy is comfortable for both of them, although it is not marked by the kind of passion Billy's marriage to Eva would have involved. Although Billy loves children, he and Maeve remain childless.

Similarly, Dennis marries his wife, Claire, essentially by default when his romance with Eva's sister Mary ends. In this marriage, Dennis learns to love his wife, his romantic feelings for her increasing when she falls victim to a terminal illness. Finally, long after his wife's death, Dennis retires to the house on Long Island that he has inherited from his mother, invites Maeve to visit him there, and ultimately marries her, a marriage of accommodation for both of them rather than one dictated by passion.

Dennis's mother, Sheila, is among the most interesting characters in the book. Orphaned at twelve, she is reared by dutiful but reluctant relatives. She goes to school and works part time in a bakery, the owner of which molests her. Largely to escape, she quits school and takes a job in the mail room of a large company. She is attracted by a bon vivant, Daniel Lynch, unmarried and in his forties, whom she marries when she is eighteen and by whom she has two children, including Dennis.

After Daniel dies, Sheila meets Holtzman, whose chief qualifications for marriage are that he is economically stable and owns two houses, including a modest summer place on Long Island. She marries Holtzman and seemingly gets along well with him, but their marriage is again one of accommodation. Holtzman is a kindly person who employs Billy and Dennis upon their discharge from service in World War II; he hires them to fix the cottage he has bought. It is there that the two meet Eva and Mary, who are nannies for a wealthy couple with seven children.

After Eva returns to Ireland wearing Billy's diamond on her finger, Billy needs money to pay for her return passage to the United States. Holtzman somewhat reluctantly hires Billy and gives him a five-hundred-dollar advance on his salary—the equivalent of ten months earnings—so that Eva can return. Eva misuses Billy's money, but Billy continues his Thursday-night, all-day-Saturday employment in Holtzman's shoe store until Holtzman retires years later.

Deception is a controlling theme in the novel. There is the obvious deception regarding Eva's alleged death; there are also the uncountable deceptions that are a part of any alcoholic's addiction. Yet underlying a great deal of the book are deeper deceptions, ones that relate to religious faith.

In writing about Billy's not returning to the Long Island cottage that he loved during the time he thought Eva was dead and about his not taking Maeve to that cottage even after the myth of Eva's death is exploded, McDermott writes of Maeve, "There was, for instance, her capacity to believe. There was as well her capacity to be deceived, since you can't have one without the other, each one side of the other."

This sentiment takes on greater significance when it is viewed in the light of an earlier passage regarding Dennis's feelings after Claire's death: "He could not convince himself then, he said, in those days and months after her death, that heaven was any more than a well-intentioned deception meant to ease our own sense of foolishness, to ease pain. . . . [H]e could no longer see death as anything other than the void that met a used-up body, a spent mind." The book is peppered with these kinds of religious doubts, which are juxtaposed to the blind faith of an unquestioning Roman Catholic such as Maeve.

Charming Billy is a model of nuance and control. In this novel, McDermott has raised restraint to new level. Rather than pummel her readers with facts about her characters, the author, through the use of her stealthy narrator, plants seeds that germinate in reader's minds.

R. Baird Shuman

Sources for Further Study

America. CLXXVIII, May 9, 1998, p. 23.
The Antioch Review. LVI, Fall, 1998, p. 494.
Booklist. XCIV, December 15, 1997, p. 683.
Commonweal. CXXV, March 27, 1998, p. 10.
Library Journal. CXXII, November 1, 1997, p. 116.
Los Angeles Times Book Review. January 1, 1998, p. 10.
The Nation. CCLXVII, November 23, 1998, p. 27.
The New York Times Book Review. CIII, January 11, 1998, p. 8.
Publishers Weekly. CCXLIV, October 6, 1997, p. 73.
Time. CLI, January 12, 1998, p. 92.

CHECHNYA
Tombstone of Russian Power

Author: Anatol Lieven (1960-   )
Photographs by Heidi Bradner
Published: Yale University Press (New Haven, Connecticut). Illustrated. 436 pp. $35.00
Type of work: History
Time: 1990-1997
Locale: Chechnya

> *Anatol Lieven sees Russia's humiliation in Chechnya as evidence of the complete collapse of state power in Russia and the corruption that is widespread among the Russian elites*

> *Principal personages:*
> GENERAL DZHOKHAR DUDAYEV, president of the Chechen Republic until his death in April, 1996
> GENERAL ASLAN MASKHADOV, Dudayev's successor as Chechen president

Anatol Lieven is a British journalist with a broad knowledge of Russia who has authored a previous study of the Baltic revolution. In *Chechnya* Lieven has written a penetrating study in three parts of Russia's misadventures in the Republic of Chechnya. Part 1, "The War," includes Lieven's "A Personal Memoir of Grozny and the Chechen War," an account of the background to the war (1991-1994) and of the war itself, which lasted from December, 1994, to August, 1996. Part 2 conducts a postmortem of the "The Russian Defeat," analyzing the collapse of state power in Russia and focusing on the social, cultural, and military roots of the Russian defeat. Part 3, "The Chechen Victory," devotes three chapters to the Chechens' cultural and religious traditions and Chechnya's long, contentious relationship with Russia.

Lieven traveled to Chechnya several times both before and during the war, interviewing soldiers and civilians on all sides, recording his impressions of the battered landscape, and hunkering down during bombings. In his introductory memoir, the corruption that pervades the collapsed Soviet Union is well exemplified in Ruslan Labazanov, a Chechen hero because he allegedly murdered a Russian KGB officer. A former martial arts instructor and mafia boss, Labazanov was first a bodyguard in the entourage of General Dzhokhar Dudayev, president of the rebel Chechen government. In 1994 Labazanov switched to the Russian side and two years later was killed under mysterious circumstances. Something of Labazanov's style emerges in his mistress—a "strange steel orchid" with "vampirical white make-up"—who wore a black miniskirt and boots. She was further gotten up with an AK-47, a machine pistol, and a bandolier.

If Labazanov and his crowd represented the worst element flourishing in those disordered times, the talented Chechen rebel commander Shamil Basayev, though clearly a terrorist, proved a more personable host. Basayev had been a fireman in the Soviet army, a building worker, and a computer salesman in Russia. Lieven met Basayev several times between 1993 and 1997 and obviously respected his courage and intelligence. Basayev's outlaw tactics—taking civilian hostages, occupying a hospital by force—were fiercely criticized, but in all of his behavior he impresses Lieven as a true Chechen.

Lieven's long chapter on the origins of the Chechen war tells a tangled story of revolt, corruption, and the geopolitics of oil. Chechen discontent with Russian policies led to Moscow's appointment in 1989 of Doku Zavgayev as the first Chechen First Secretary of the autonomous republic. In 1989 Ruslan Khasbulatov, a supporter of Russian president Boris Yeltsin, was elected to the Soviet parliament from Chechnya and soon clashed with Zavgayev, who permitted the founding of the Chechen National Congress in 1990. The strong man of the Congress quickly proved to be Dzhokhar Dudayev, a general in the Soviet air force. Lieven sketches Dudayev's powerful friends, some of them shady characters, who raised money for Dudayev and helped advance his career.

Under Dudayev and his henchmen, the National Congress supporters took over the Supreme Soviet in Grozny on September 6, 1991, and Zavgayev resigned. On October 27 Dudayev held presidential and parliamentary elections, winning the presidency easily, and on November 2 the Chechen parliament declared complete independence. Yeltsin's military intervention failed—partly because of demoralization among the Russian soldiers—and by mid-1992 the Russian troops had been driven out of Chechnya.

Corruption and financial pressures led to disillusionment with Dudayev within a year of the Russian troop exodus. The Chechen government earned over $300 million dollars in oil profits between 1991 and 1994 but nobody could account for it. Moreover, the enormous oil deposits on the Azerbaijani shore of the Caspian Sea made control of the whole region of great concern to Turkey, Russia, and the United States. These compelling considerations, combined with Moscow's anger at four bus hijackings by Chechen bandits in the North Caucasus, prompted Russia to send troops into Chechnya on December 11, 1994.

Russia's poor planning for the war led to disastrously low morale among its troops and an embarrassing performance. Grozny was the scene of bitter fighting, with the Russians helpless in urban guerrilla combat against the determined Chechen volunteers. Under the talented general Aslan Maskhadov and Shamil Basayev, the Chechen forces fought superbly. Basayev's confinement of several hundred civilian hostages in a hospital in Russian-controlled Buddenovsk forced Yeltsin to agree to peace talks. Lieven believes that Russia's failure to pursue the doctrines of Carl von Clausewitz hobbled its campaign in Chechnya. Clausewitz taught the need for total mobilization in a war that sought the enemy's complete destruction, and given the Russians' military incompetence in Chechnya, anything less than an all-out effort was doomed.

Lieven describes Dudayev as arrogant and unreliable, and he thinks that Dudayev's death from a Russian rocket in April, 1994, enabled the later peace negotiations. Dudayev's successor, Vice-President Zelimkhan Yandarbiyev, proposed a truce, and the Russian security chief, General Alexander Lebed, negotiated an agreement with Maskhadov according to which the Russians withdrew from Chechnya and Chechnya's constitutional status was put on hold until 2001. In January, 1997, General

Maskhadov won the presidential election, and on May 12 Yeltsin named Maskhadov the president of the "Chechen Republic of Ichkeria," which embraced both Chechnya and Ingushetia.

Lieven finds in the Russia of the 1990's an analogy to the "cacique" (chief) system so common in Latin America. The liberal capitalist revolution in Russia has brought to power a corrupt elite that is selling off the nation's raw materials for its own enrichment without contributing anything to the national economy. This destructive "privatization," says Lieven, "is exactly what has always happened over the past two hundred years when a ruthless liberal capitalist ideology combines with a corrupt bureaucracy and a weak legal order, and is prepared to justify almost anything in the name of 'progress.'" The Italian Communist Antonio Gramsci used the term "passive revolution" to describe a radical redistribution of power among the elites without changes in economic structures or property relations. Lieven finds the term apt for the Russian revolution of the 1990's, in that the masses did not participate, but emphasizes that Russian property relations have been completely transformed. The result is a weak state—a liberal capitalist hegemony—combined with a weak society, and Lieven sees no hope for change; he even fears that Russia may become economically dependent.

Lieven devotes two chapters to the failure of what he calls "the Serbian," or "neo-Cossack option." This option has three parts:

> the move by major sections of the Communist ruling elite to radical nationalist positions in an effort to preserve their own power, with resulting attempts by state forces to whip up national fear and terror, especially among members of a given nationality living beyond the state borders; the mobilisation of local ethnic groups, above all from such diasporas, partly as a result of "manipulation" and partly on the basis of real historically based fears and hatreds and local fighting traditions; and the exploitation of the resulting conflicts by criminal gangs and warlords posing more or less sincerely as nationalist militias.

Speculating on the possible mobilization of the Cossacks, Lieven makes clear that whatever they once were as elite troops, they are today nothing of the sort. As for the Russian diaspora, it reveals little interest in nationalist causes, largely because of its failure to evolve a distinct identity of its own.

In part 3, an analysis of the Chechen victory, Lieven emphasizes the uniqueness of a victory won without the backing of an organized state or any formal military or political structures, and he attributes this victory to Chechen social norms and traditions, materially aided by Soviet weapons and military training. Russians and Chechnyans have a long history of war in the Caucasus, with their brutal long war in the mid-nineteenth century producing a Chechen national hero, Imam Shamil, who established stern rule based on the principles of Sufi Islam. Shamil's eventual defeat in 1859 was followed by decades of sporadic bloodshed, until Joseph Stalin deported half a million Chechens and Ingush to the Kazakh steppes, an exile that ended in 1957.

Lieven depicts the Chechens as a loose gathering of clans devoted to military egalitarianism, a hard and often cruel ethic. He traces Chechnya's modern identity to two sources: Russian conquest and the Sufi religion imposed by the non-Chechen

Shamil. In trying to conquer the Chechens, Russia unwittingly spurred them to develop institutions and means of resistance. Despite the importance of Islam to the Chechens, Lieven argues that Chechnya's struggle in the 1990's has been more nationalistic than religious, with religion serving mainly as "spiritual clothing for their national struggle."

Lieven's depiction of a thoroughly crippled Russia incapable of military success or social revolution undoubtedly will stimulate controversy. Although he rejects Francis Fukuyama's thesis in *The End of History and the Last Man* (1992) that the liberal capitalist model is fixed permanently, Lieven sees no possibility of change in Russia until a new age has swept the whole world. Lieven rejects several influential Western interpretations of Russia and its history. The Harvard historian Richard Pipes has argued that powerful continuities have shaped Russian history from the Middle Ages through the czars and the Soviet Union into the post-Soviet regime, but Lieven points to the changes in Russia over the last eighty years in refuting Pipes's thesis. A second interpretation sees Russia as "deeply, perennially and primordially imperialist, aggressive and expansionist," a view that Lieven derides as fatuous in its disregard for the expansionist policies of other nations over the centuries. His chapter on Russia's military incompetence, "A Fish Rots from the Head," stresses that Moscow is in no position to be aggressive, whatever its intentions.

Lieven describes the Russian people as exhausted by the betrayals of Communism and no longer able to believe in the unique mission for Russia envisioned by many nineteenth century prophets. Russian nationalism has always suffered from Russia's expansionist absorption of other ethnic groups, a process that separated Russian national identity from ethnicity, and Lieven asserts that the collapse of the Soviet Union can be explained by the failure of Russians to regard it as a Russian empire. For these reasons Lieven stresses that "ethnic Russian nationalism, carried to its logical conclusion, and hegemony over the other former Soviet republics are incompatible, even if Russia were to become much more powerful." Although he judges such a scenario as unlikely, Lieven warns against the possibility of an ethnic nationalism in Russia comparable to that under Kemal Atatürk in Turkey. Although some scholars have already seen the parallels between the dissolved Ottoman Empire and the defunct Soviet Union and proposed Atatürk's program as a positive model for Russia, Lieven fears that such a program would lead to ethnic bloodshed.

Lieven has written a superbly detailed and thoughtful study of Russia's problems as revealed in its debacle in Chechnya. His forthright conclusions will spark considerable polemic.

Frank Day

Sources for Further Study

Current History. XCVII, October, 1998, p. 347.
The Economist. CCCXLVII, June 13, 1998, p. S10.

Foreign Affairs. LXXVII, May, 1998, p. 147.
Library Journal. CXXIII, April 1, 1998, p. 112.
The New Leader. LXXXI, August 10, 1998, p. 14.
The New York Review of Books. XLV, September 24, 1998, p. 44.
The New York Times Book Review. CIII, June 21, 1998, p. 5.
Publishers Weekly. CCXLV, April 20, 1998, p. 53.
The Times Literary Supplement. June 5, 1998, p. 13.
The Washington Post Book World. XXVIII, June 21, 1998, p. 6.

THE CHILDREN

Author: David Halberstam (1934-   )
Published: Random House (New York). 783 pp. $29.95
Type of work: History
Time: 1954-1965
Locale: The United States

David Halberstam, who as a young reporter covered the Civil Rights movement, chronicles the lives of several young African American college students who changed history

> *Principal personages:*
> MARION BARRY, student at LeMoyne College, later to become mayor of Washington, D.C.
> JAMES BEVEL, student at American Baptist College
> GLORIA JOHNSON, student at Mount Holyoke and later Meharry College
> BERNARD LAFAYETTE, student at American Baptist College, later to become its president
> JAMES LAWSON, seminary student recruited by Martin Luther King, Jr., to lead the student protests
> JOHN LEWIS, president of the Student Nonviolent Coordinating Committee (SNCC); later a distinguished member of the U.S. Congress
> CURTIS MURPHY, student at Tennessee State University
> DIANE NASH, student at Fisk University; leader of the Nashville student sit-ins
> RODNEY POWELL, student at Meharry College

When one thinks back to the great heroes and heroines of the Civil Rights movement, figures such as Martin Luther King, Jr., and Rosa Parks immediately come to mind. Less well remembered are the thousands of young people—white and African American, from the South as well as the North—who served as the foot soldiers of the movement. Author David Halberstam dramatically recounts the courage and sacrifices of several participants in the sit-ins, Freedom Rides, and demonstrations that turned the tide against racial injustice in America.

After graduating from college in 1955, Halberstam began his career in journalism at a small-town Mississippi newspaper. He was fired after less than a year for publishing some freelance articles sympathetic to the emerging civil rights movement. His subsequent job at the *Nashville Tennesseean*, one of the state's most influential newspapers, placed him at the birthplace of the nonviolent student movement. Halberstam was one of the few journalists at the time who truly knew what was happening. Most national reporters were outsiders who did not really understand the South. For a time he was the only one to cover the activities of the students. But Halberstam dreamed of becoming a foreign correspondent, and had he not been sent by *The New York Times* to cover the Congo in 1961 and Vietnam in 1962 (for which he won a Pulitzer Prize), he most certainly would have gained fame as a civil rights reporter. Soon the Nashville students would come to understand just how important national media coverage would be to their cause.

The central focus of the early part of the story is the work of James Lawson. As a young Methodist missionary, Lawson had traveled to India and was strongly influenced by the teachings of Mohandas Gandhi. He returned to America convinced of the power of nonviolent protest as an instrument of social change. When Lawson was thirty-one years old, King recruited him to train college students in the Gandhian techniques of passive resistance. Lawson went to Nashville, Tennessee, in 1959 to offer a series of workshops to students from nearby colleges. Their first victory was the desegregation of Nashville's lunch counters, which helped to spread the civil rights struggle and to place the student leaders at the forefront. However, this also resulted in Lawson's expulsion from the Vanderbilt Divinity School for his "radical" beliefs.

The idea of direct social action against segregation was seen by many older members of the Civil Rights movement as a dangerous course to take. They preferred a more gradual approach, challenging discriminatory laws through the courts. The 1954 Supreme Court case of *Brown v. Board of Education* officially outlawed racial segregation, but most people believed that the actual implementation of desegregation orders would take some time, and many states had done little or nothing to comply. The older generation of African Americans had survived by grudgingly accepting the status quo and hoping that somehow the future would be better for their children. They believed that openly challenging segregation, especially in the Deep South, would bring violence and even death to those who dared to participate. Students coming into a southern city would be seen as "outside agitators," and those who lived there and were sympathetic to the movement risked the loss of their jobs, their homes, or even their lives. All of these threats were very real, as the primary weapons of the Ku Klux Klan were fear and violence. Perhaps the students were somewhat blinded by their youthful idealism, but all were well aware of the risks. They went on to prove their commitment to the cause time and again, displaying remarkable courage in spite of being repeatedly beaten and jailed.

The ultimate challenge to the totality of segregation in the South was the Freedom Rides. Segregation of interstate public transportation facilities was prohibited by federal law, but this was rarely, if ever, enforced. The Kennedy administration was anxious to avoid any sort of confrontation in the South for fear of alienating the South's strong Democratic base of support. The idea was to travel by bus through several southern states and attempt to use the segregated facilities at each stop. Arrests by the local police or threats of violence by local Klan groups would force the federal government to protect the students. The first Freedom Ride started in Virginia on May 4, 1961. When John Lewis stepped off the bus in Rock Hill, South Carolina, he was savagely beaten. During the next leg of the journey, from Atlanta, Georgia, to Anniston, Alabama, the bus was run off the road and set afire on the outskirts of the city with the Freedom Riders trapped inside. As they escaped with their lives, the students were beaten by an angry white mob that had been following close behind. The shocking violence in Alabama convinced many to think twice about volunteering and threatened to end the Freedom Rides. Yet it was the unflagging courage of the Nashville group that kept them going.

The Freedom Rides were effective in arousing the anger of Americans mainly because a new element had been added: the rapid rise of the media as a major force in American culture. Before the escalation of the Vietnam War in the mid-1960's, the students had made the civil rights struggle a major national news story. This was greatly amplified by the emerging prominence of network television news. No longer could a racist sheriff in a small southern city allow demonstrators to be abused and beaten without it being flashed across the networks and into homes all over America. In spite of media attention, however, cities in the Deep South were more determined than ever to preserve what they considered their way of life: segregation.

Halberstam's intimate portraits of the students remind us that these courageous young people were making a tremendous sacrifice. Not only did they face the real possibility of physical injury and in many cases even death, but many of the African American students who participated had also decided to postpone or terminate their college educations in order to join in this great crusade. For most African American families at that time a college degree offered a rare chance for their children to move into the middle class and escape the poverty and humiliation so long endured by the parents, many of whom had made great sacrifices to send their children to college. Most participants in the struggle would acquire a criminal arrest record as well, which would further damage their chances of a better future.

Halberstam paints vivid portraits of the participants: James Lawson, leader of the students and dedicated pacifist who was expelled from Vanderbilt Divinity School for his beliefs and later in life headed a church in Los Angeles; Diane Nash, the shy Fisk University coed who rose to become one of the most fearless and skilled leaders of the student movement; James Bevel, brilliant, creative, and uncontrollable, who lobbied for a March on Washington in 1963 and pushed King to take a stand against the Vietnam War long before it was fashionable for national leaders to do so; John Lewis, born on a farm in rural Alabama and admired for his simple honesty and unshakable courage, who was later elected to the U.S. Congress; Curtis Murphy, the brilliant engineering student who felt the calling to abandon his studies at Tennessee State and join in the movement; Rodney Powell, a young medical student who dedicated his life to engaging in community-service medicine among the poor and became one of the most distinguished public health doctors in America; Gloria Johnson, who married Powell and went on to become the first African American woman psychiatrist to be tenured at Harvard medical school; Bernard Lafayette, courageous organizer of African American voter registration drives in Selma, Alabama; and Marion Barry, a tragic figure who became mayor of Washington, D.C., only to become disgraced by allegations of corruption and drug abuse. Halberstam reminds us that these "children" were ordinary men and women who, swept along by the current of the Civil Rights movement and convinced by their bedrock Christian faith that they were indeed doing God's work, rose to become genuine leaders and heroes of their generation.

By the spring of 1964, the philosophy of nonviolence was challenged by a rising tide of African American militancy. Demonstrators were tired of being beaten and jailed, and the effectiveness of passive resistance was being seriously questioned. Many also began to realize that the fundamental focus of the movement had shifted as well: The crusade for equal public accommodations became a push for voting rights. Again, brave young people went South to register African Americans in districts where they were discouraged in every way possible from exercising one of their most fundamental rights as American citizens. As they did to gain passage of the landmark 1964 Civil Rights Act, the Student Nonviolent Coordinating Committee joined forces with the old-guard Southern Christian Leadership Conference led by King to lobby for passage of a voting rights bill. Moved by the determination of these two groups and the continuing violence in Southern cities against the protesters, President Lyndon B. Johnson signed the bill in 1965. Ironically, the assassination of Malcolm X, the rising star of the militant movement, and the Watts riots in Los Angeles that same year marked the end of the nonviolent crusade. Their task largely accomplished, the brave young soldiers of the early civil rights movement, who had sacrificed greatly and accomplished so much, went their separate ways.

Halberstam's narrative is dramatic and gripping. He is at his best when describing the students in the thick of battle; the portrait he paints gives readers the feeling that they are somehow there alongside the fighters. The last third of the book, however, which is devoted to updating the lives and whereabouts of Jim Lawson and the Nashville students, adds little to the overall power of the story and could have been much shorter. Although it is interesting to read about what had become of them in later life, Halberstam goes into far greater detail than necessary. The real strength of his narrative comes from the first two thirds of the book, ending with 1965. In addition, the chronology jumps around from chapter to chapter; characters are introduced and then suddenly reappear many pages later. For readers not familiar with the historical sequence of events, this could be a source of confusion.

In spite of these criticisms, this is an important and compelling story. Halberstam's journalistic skills create a "you are there" narrative that moves readers and powerfully reminds them of the incredible racism, hatred, and intolerance in the America of the 1950's and 1960's. The dramatic gains in civil rights can only be truly understood in the light of these brave young people who sacrificed their fortunes, futures, and—in many cases—their lives to build a better future for African Americans.

Raymond Frey

Sources for Further Study

Black Issues in Higher Education. XV, September 17, 1998, p. 39.
Choice. XXXV, July, 1998, p. 1912.
The Christian Century. CXV, July 15, 1998, p. 689.
The Economist. CCCXLVIII, July 11, 1998, p. S8.
Los Angeles Times Book Review. March 22, 1998, p. 6.

The Nation. CCLXVI, May 11, 1998, p. 30.
The New York Review of Books. XLV, June 25, 1998, p. 27.
The New York Times Book Review. CIII, March 15, 1998, p. 9.
Time. CLI, March 23, 1998, p. 86.
The Washington Post Book World. XXVIII, March 22, 1998, p. 1.

CHOPIN IN PARIS
The Life and Times of the Romantic Composer

Author: Tad Szulc (1926-   )
Published: Scribner's (New York). Illustrated. 444 pp. $30.00
Type of work: Biography
Time: 1831-1849
Locale: Paris and Nohant, France; Warsaw, Poland; Palma de Mallorca

Both a biography and a study of the relationship between a major composer of the Romantic period and his musical, literary, artistic, and cultural milieu

> *Principal personages:*
> FRYDERYK FRANCISZEK (FRÉDÉRIC FRANÇOIS) CHOPIN, the composer
>   and pianist
> MIKOLAJ CHOPIN, his father
> EUGÈNE DELACROIX, the painter
> JULIAN FONTANA, Chopin's lifelong associate and the posthumous
>   publisher of his works
> FERENC LISZT, the composer and pianist
> GEORGE SAND, pen name of Amandine Aurore Lucille Dupin, Baronne
>   Dudevant, author of *Indiana* (1832) and *Consuelo* (1842)

Tad Szulc's credentials as a biographer were well established with his highly successful *Pope John Paul II: The Biography* (1996). Two of Szulc's other works, *Fidel: A Critical Portrait* (1987) and *Then and Now: How the World Has Changed Since WWII* (1990), received the prestigious Overseas Press Club of America award for best book of the year on international affairs. Szulc's background as a biographer, journalist, linguist, and student of world politics serves him well in *Chopin in Paris*, a highly readable account of the composer's most productive period.

Chopin in Paris begins shortly after the establishment of the French July Monarchy (1830) and continues until the year of Chopin's death. Between these two events Szulc uncovers a wide range of information about nearly every aspect of early nineteenth century social and cultural life. Like many of the Romantics, Chopin produced works that were influenced by diverse trends in contemporary thought. He debated the superiority of Neoclassical and Romantic art with Eugène Delacroix. He loved the opera, being especially fond of the works of Vincenzo Bellini (1801-1835), whom he met in 1831. He learned about recent developments in literature and radical politics through his liaison with George Sand. Chopin's years in Paris also brought him into contact with many of the leading figures in nineteenth century music: Ferenc Liszt, Hector Berlioz, and Felix Mendelssohn were all close, though not always amicable, acquaintances. He heard Niccolò Paganini perform often and knew the sisters Maria Malibrán and Pauline Viardot, both stars of the operatic stage. Most of all, Chopin loved the poetry of his native Poland. The poet Adam Mickiewicz became a close friend of Chopin during Mickiewicz's own stay in Paris. Chopin set to music the works of Mickiewicz and those of the Polish author Stefan Witwicki.

Szulc's strength is his ability to move with ease among this motley cast of characters, explaining the role that each of them played in shaping the style of the great genius. Szulc is as comfortable discussing piano construction in the early nineteenth century (Sébastian Erard's perfection of the double escapement made it possible for Chopin to repeat notes at full volume far more quickly than could occur in the works of his predecessors), as he is addressing performance practice, social history, and political developments. Given least attention is Chopin's music itself. Szulc is not a musicologist and is content to allow earlier musical analyses of Chopin to stand unchallenged. The result is that *Chopin in Paris* is much more a biography and work of cultural history than it is a critique of Chopin's oeuvre. It brings to life the spirit of a fascinating city that left a major impact on the art of so many Romantic composers.

By all rights, Chopin should never have been in Paris at all. Traveling on a Russian passport he was forced to acquire due to the Russian occupation of Poland, Chopin was granted a visa to journey only *through* Paris. His real destination was officially recorded as London, and a stay in Paris was permitted only "in passage." Chopin would later joke that he remained on French soil "in passage" for the rest of his life. He arrived in Paris in September, 1831, and became a French citizen four years later. Although Chopin maintained strong ties to his native country—Chopin's father always wrote him in French from Warsaw and Chopin always responded in Polish from Paris—Szulc finds no evidence to support the claim that Chopin seriously considered returning to the land of his birth. Descended from a family that had long been of mixed Polish and French heritage, Chopin was at home in both worlds. He flourished in the bustling environment of Paris, although he had forged his soul in the mixed German and Slavic culture of his native Poland.

Szulc's image of Chopin differs in several ways from the fragile, tubercular genius depicted by previous biographers. To begin with, Szulc makes it clear that Chopin's illness never really interfered with the composer's demanding schedule. Even as his health began to fail, Chopin taught private lessons at least six hours each day. (For most of his life, Chopin earned more from teaching than he did from publishing compositions.) In the evenings Chopin would frequently attend the opera or fulfill other social commitments. He would finally begin writing music late at night, then catch a few hours sleep before the whole exhausting process would begin again.

Chopin's compositions were rarely, if ever, the result of a flash of inspiration. He would work on each piece as long as a decade, setting it aside so that he could begin new works and then return to it whenever he had a spare moment. Like Wolfgang Amadeus Mozart before him, Chopin had the ability to work productively despite family tragedies, personal setbacks, and the frequent chaos of his physical surroundings. Although he spoke of music as flowing from his soul, many of his liveliest and most optimistic works were composed during times of great sorrow.

Szulc argues that the rigors of Chopin's schedule probably cost him his one serious opportunity for marriage. Following a series of romantic encounters with Maria Wodzinska in Dresden and Marienbad in the mid-1830's, Chopin anxiously awaited an invitation to see her family in 1837. Chopin believed that if this were to occur, it would lead to a formal announcement of their engagement. Yet Maria's mother, Madame Wodzinska (who seems sincerely to have liked Chopin), had doubts about the young musician's health and future. She made him promise to do everything he could to improve his health for one year, avoiding late-night engagements as much as possible, before she would agree to discuss the marriage. As the year progressed, however, and Madame Wodzinska continued to receive word of Chopin's daunting schedule—including, Szulc suspects, rumors about his burgeoning relationship with George Sand—the possibility of the composer's marriage to Maria grew more remote. The letters Chopin received from the Wodzinskis became increasingly less frequent, and Maria herself began substituting the more formal closing "Adieu" for the hopes she had once expressed of seeing Chopin soon. The two never met again, and Maria later married someone else.

A major portion of *Chopin in Paris* details the composer's turbulent relationship with George Sand. Szulc refuses to speculate on the degree to which this was a sexual liaison. He presents Chopin as almost completely asexual. Chopin's first sexual experimentation seems to have left him with a venereal disease. After such an inauspicious beginning, Chopin's later attractions to women were more sentimental than physical. Sand, too, had an unusual sexual history. After the early death of her father and a disappointing marriage to Baron Casimir Dudevant, the young Aurore Dupin Dudevant sought male companionship through a lengthy series of affairs. She was particularly attracted to delicate, "consumptive" men, gradually coming to believe that it was the sexual union itself that destroyed or incapacitated them. Aurore tried repeatedly to balance her desire for physical intimacy with her ideal of a true Platonic relationship. In Chopin, Szulc suggests, Dudevant—who adopted the pen name George Sand from the saint's day on which the idea was first proposed and the surname of Jules Sandeau, her lover of the moment—found a perfect compromise: a companion of the heart who was well disposed to sentimental attachment but who seemed to disdain, even to fear, sexual intimacy.

The eight years that Sand spent with Chopin were the closest thing to a stable marriage that either of them would ever know. Yet neither had the type of disposition that made a permanent relationship possible. Sand regularly began a new relationship as soon as an old one was collapsing. (When Alfred de Musset fell ill after accompanying Sand to Venice, she promptly began an affair with the twenty-six-year-old doctor called to treat him.) For his part, Chopin suffered from mood swings that were intensified by declining health. Szulc speculates that Chopin may have suffered from manic depression, the illness now known as bipolar disorder. The Polish word *zal*—untranslatable by any single English word and having connotations that include "sadness, longing, nostalgia, regret, resignation, contrition, resentment, complaint, and even anger"—is used by Szulc to describe some of Chopin's most poignant works. It is an appropriate term for his life as well.

Chopin's illness, enervating him and destroying him from within, was a suitable image for Europe as it approached the middle of the nineteenth century. Szulc describes this period as a time of delicate beauty, of charm and grace that seemed all the more precious because it was short-lived. *Chopin in Paris* catalogues "the impressive gallery of famous consumptives" who distinguished the Romantic Age: "Schubert, Goethe, Balzac, Chateaubriand, and Paganini. And, of course, Violetta in Verdi's *La Traviata*, inspired by Dumas's *fils's La Dame aux camélias*, and Mimi in Puccini's *La Bohème* (based on Murger's *Scènes de la vie de bohème*)." "Consumption" became almost the emblem of the Romantic spirit. It symbolized the final, feverish burst of energy that arose at a time of severe inner weakness. The awareness that his life would be short made Chopin redouble his efforts. Ironically, that same exertion was probably a contributing factor to the rapid advance of his illness.

Unfortunately, *Chopin in Paris* is marred by poor editing. Szulc is repetitious as an author, and a more capable editor would have eliminated some of the book's unnecessary passages. For example, on page 135 Szulc says that "[the Marquis de] Custine did for Russia what Alexis de Tocqueville, another French aristocrat, did for the United States a few years earlier." On page 247 he repeats this observation, saying that "Custine did for Russia what his fellow French traveler, Tocqueville, did for the United States several years earlier with *Democracy in America*." Similarly, the reader is twice told that Chopin leapt from his chair when a passage of Muzio Clementi was played poorly by a student, shouting "What is that? Is it a dog that has just barked?" Twice Szulc mentions that more than 60 percent of Parisian women were "fully literate," although he never explains what "fully literate" means. Other observations are likewise made two, three, even four times. For example, after explaining how Chopin became acquainted with Mickiewicz's poetry and then befriended the poet himself (page 52), Szulc reintroduces Mickiewicz as "a close friend of Chopin" on page 171. These errors detract from what could have been an exceptional volume, giving the impression that a work which should have been a triumph of careful research was completed in haste.

Written just prior to the sesquicentennial of the composer's death, *Chopin in Paris* offers insight into both an important period in Chopin's life and the major influences on his musical style. Szulc avoids merely summarizing what is known about Chopin from earlier works. At the same time, he does not resort to being novel merely for its own sake. *Chopin in Paris* never attempts to psychoanalyze the composer nor does it present him, as others have done, as an oppressed victim of the Russian and French empires. It succeeds as all good biographies should by presenting its subject as a unique individual even while it traces the degree to which he benefited from his social and historical environment.

Not a biography intended for musicians or specialists, *Chopin in Paris* is nevertheless an excellent introduction to the composer for the general reader. It is particularly successful in capturing the "spirit of place" that was Paris in the early nineteenth century and in explaining the sometimes complicated historical events that occurred during the composer's lifetime.

Jeffrey L. Buller

Sources for Further Study

Booklist. XCIV, January 1, 1998, p. 742.
Kirkus Reviews. LXVI, March 1, 1998, p. 326.
Library Journal. CXXIII, February 15, 1998, p. 144.
Los Angeles Times Book Review. April 26, 1998, p. 10.
Music Educators Journal. LXXXV, July, 1998, p. 54.
The New Leader. LXXXI, April 6, 1998, p. 18.
The New York Times Book Review. CIII, April 5, 1998, p. 37.
Publishers Weekly. CCXLV, January 26, 1998, p. 74.

CITIES OF THE PLAIN

Author: Cormac McCarthy (1933-   )
Published: Alfred A. Knopf (New York). 293 pp. $24.00
Type of Work: Novel
Time: The early 1950's
Locale: The American Southwest

This novel completes Cormac McCarthy's "Border Trilogy" and unites the main characters from the first two books as companions for a last stand as cowboys in the rapidly modernizing Southwest

> *Principal characters:*
> JOHN GRADY COLE, expert cowboy who intends to marry a young
>   prostitute but dies after avenging her murder
> BILLY PARHAM, best friend of John Grady Cole and a fellow cowboy
>   who attempts to save Cole from the tragedy that engulfs him
> MAGDALENA, teenage prostitute with a terrible history of being
>   brutalized by men; she loves Cole and is murdered by Eduardo
> EDUARDO, coldhearted Mexican pimp and manager of The White Lake
>   house of prostitution in Juarez
> AN OLD MAN, teller of stories to John Grady Cole and regarded by other
>   characters as insane
> MAC, well-meaning ranch manager where Cole and Parham work

Cities of the Plain is the third novel in Cormac McCarthy's western "Border Trilogy." The first book, *All the Pretty Horses*, featured John Grady Cole, and the second, *The Crossing*, featured Billy Parham, two teenage boys involved in similar adventures. Both leave the American Southwest on horseback in the mid-twentieth century and ride deep into Mexico. They experience magnificent and terrible initiations into manhood. John Grady Cole, in *All the Pretty Horses*, falls in love with the daughter of a high-class hacienda owner, is banished to prison for this presumption, then wins a knife fight in prison by bleeding only slightly less than his attacker, who dies. Billy Parham, in *The Crossing*, returns a wolf to Mexico after trapping it live in America, only to see it tortured and killed by Mexican ranch hands. He and his brother wander in Mexico on horseback until the brother is killed. Like John Grady Cole at the end of *All the Pretty Horses*, Billy returns to America scarred but still very much the archetypal cowboy. Both are skilled in the outdoor masculine routines of training horses and roping cattle, and thanks to their Mexican sojourns both are essentially independent of modern America and the mass leveling of its institutions.

In *Cities of the Plain* Cormac McCarthy places these young men on ranches working at their cowboy trade. It is the mid-1950's, a few years after their spontaneous tours of Mexico. A looming purchase of ranchland by the U.S. Military threatens to end the cowboy way of life. Tragedy looms. John Grady Cole insists on marrying a teenage Mexican prostitute who also happens to be an epileptic. The ranch they live on—where the brotherhood of cowboys thrives partly because contact with women is minimal—is near the titular cities of the plain, the twin border towns of El Paso, Texas, and Juarez,

Mexico. In Juarez the need for women is satisfied by houses of prostitution. John Grady Cole's companions treat the prostitutes as a slightly higher form of cattle, preferring heft to beauty: "I'm goin to tell you right now cousin, when the mood comes on you for a fat woman they just wont nothin else satisfy."

Cole, unlike the others, surrenders his heart to a young woman working at The White Lake, a higher-class brothel. Billy Parham, nearing thirty years old and nine years older than Cole, dispenses wisdom to Cole on the latter's love life. Cole ignores it, which leads to the novel's tragic and bloody conclusion—a knife fight with Eduardo, manager of The White Lake. Parham is a form of El Paso—rugged, realistic and rational—and the younger Cole, blindly in love, is influenced psychically by Juarez. He is recognized by other cowboys as the most skilled, the most graceful horseman, the best that a cowboy can be—a natural. Yet his Juarez psyche weakens him. He is the id to his close friend Billy's commonsensical American ego.

Cole's inability to be sensible in love, to see where he is going, is the most dominant example of human passivity before fate exemplified by other characters and events in the novel. The grass no longer grows as it once did in Texas, and the country dries up. All large-scale intentions, such as a revolution fought in the streets by men wearing the very suits for battle they wore to their weddings, are imbued with directionless futility: "The executions against the mud walls sprayed with new blood over the dried black of the old and the fine powdered clay sifting down from the bullet holes in the wall after the men had fallen and the slow drift of riflesmoke and the corpses stacked in the streets or piled into the woodenwheeled carretas trundling over the cobbles or over the dirt roads to the nameless graves." This sentence embodies in its grammatical structure, beginning as an intentional statement with subject and verb, then lapsing into predicateless phrases, McCarthy's central irony: individual human desire swamped by history. "Fine powdered clay" sifts from bullet holes. History overwhelms and renders human passion pointless.

McCarthy's vision is double. First there is the light that shines from pastoral cowboys. When they speak to one another their conversation is regional and folksy. They make an interesting and attractive pattern. Their simplicity and freedom as cowboys in the outdoors is enviable. They are good at what they do. They care for each other and for their animals. This mythical American open spaces reality is shaky, however. Living, even for cowboys, is a half-paralyzed squirming in the omnipresence of history. This is the other, darker half of McCarthy's vision. The characters are engulfed in a blending of harsh, haunted geology and anthropological mystery: "He ate his lunch at noon in an outcropping of lava rock with a view across the floodplain to the north and to the west." McCarthy contrasts "lunch" with "lava rock" to suggest Cole's insignificance. Eating that lunch, he views "ancient pictographs among the rocks, engravings of animals and moons and men and lost hieroglyphics whose meaning no man would ever know." Amid volcano, floodplain, vast space—"north," "west"—mankind, McCarthy suggests, developed and hacked assertions and signs in stone. Mankind, of which folksy Parham and Cole are examples, is as incomprehensible as those rocks sheltering Cole from the wind. Rocks that shelter is another prime

McCarthy irony about human life on earth.

To live is to walk as a blindfolded target through a shooting gallery. McCarthy perpetually plays the theme of vulnerable people attacked by a viciousness in nature not of their doing. A decade before middle age. Billy already reflects: "When you're a kid you have these notions about how things are goin to be. . . . You get a little older and you pull back some on that. I think you wind up just tryin to minimize the pain." John Grady Cole will have no part of capitulating to self-protection, however. He lets his heart lead him into a preposterous, impossible love affair. He sells his horse to raise money, thinking he will buy Magdalena from Eduardo, with Billy as his agent. "She is whore to the bone. I know her," the pimp Eduardo tells Billy, refusing the deal and showing in human form that viciousness which mocks a young man's heartfelt intention.

Its theme of humanity vulnerable before a harsh cosmos will not make this book an American classic. It is McCarthy's writing and imagining of the moment-by-moment experience of the characters that establish all three books in the Border trilogy as great literature. This is authentic fiction, wherein the author's power of dreaming penetrates the reader's conscious world. The simplicity of the characters rides in the density of vision. Here is Magdalena, John Grady Cole's prostitute and wife-to-be waking up after suffering an epileptic seizure. She has been taken to a primitive hospital: "The ceiling of the room was of concrete and bore the impression of the boards used to form it, the concrete knots and nailheads and the fossil arc of the circlesaw's blade from some mountain sawmill. There was a single sooty bulb that burned there with a grudging orange light and a millermoth that patrolled it in random clockwise orbits." Nothing here is a throw-away line. McCarthy tries to produce a genuineness of the felt world. This is not Magdalena's eyesight, but McCarthy's. That concrete ceiling would be a concrete ceiling and nothing more in the hands of a typical novelist intent on pursuing a story line. For McCarthy it is an opportunity to inhabit and dream a room in Mexico. Matter is nothing to scoff at, and McCarthy won't scoff. Mention concrete and then look at it long enough, as a fictional dreamer, to make it real for the creator of the work and for the reader who attentively reads it.

Just as concrete and other common substances take on visionary power, so ordinary people are given words to speak of which they might not be capable in the real world. McCarthy is unashamed to assign power to what is ordinary, to let his eloquence inhabit everything he imagines. Even the pimp, Eduardo, becomes visionary. During a knife fight with John Grady Cole—Eduardo kills Magdalena when she attempts to join Cole in America—Eduardo offers a philosophical critique of American boys looking for excitement in Mexico, between passes of his stiletto across Cole's leg and stomach: "Your kind cannot bear that the world be ordinary. That it contain nothing save what stands before one. But the Mexican world is a world of adornment only and underneath it is very plain indeed. While your world—he passed the blade back and forth like a shuttle through a loom—your world totters upon an unspoken labyrinth of questions."

This novel will be accepted by those whose imaginations can tolerate a Mexican pimp making fairly astute points about American boys before receiving Cole's own blade beneath his jaw and into his head so that he dies unable to speak another word. It will be accepted by those whose imaginations can tolerate McCarthy's description of Cole's own death from loss of blood. Cole is now dust—victim of the inevitable pattern his single, well-meaning life cannot defy. In the epilogue to *Cities of the Plain* a traveler meeting the now old Billy Parham at the end of the novel says: "The world of our fathers resides within us. Ten thousand generations and more. A form without a history has no power to perpetuate itself. What has no past can have no future." Yet Cole's future was to die bloodily after receiving such an insult to his dream as to make him want only to kill and then die. A hint is given about the significance of Cole's fate by this same traveler: "Every man's death is a standing in for every other. And since death comes to all there is no way to abate the fear of it except to love that man who stands for us." Cole stood for Billy and others? Possibly. Yet here, as the traveler continues speaking, McCarthy unleashes an unsuspected theological assumption: John Grady Cole's death has already been lived through by someone else centuries ago: "He passed here long ago. That man who is all men and who stands in the dock for us until our own time come and we must stand for him. Do you love him, that man? Will you honor the path he has taken? Will you listen to his tale?" A sudden, tacked-on Christian vision of life as a vale of tears, something to be endured however long it takes? McCarthy evidently ends his novel endorsing vulnerability before the mechanism of destruction as something that must be practiced and accepted. His novel should help make enduring vulnerability sweeter for the many readers willing to imagine with him one more marvelously improbable passage.

Bruce Wiebe

Sources for Further Study

Los Angeles Times Book Review. May 24, 1998, p. 4.
The Nation. CCLXVI, July 6, 1998, p. 38.
The New York Review of Books. XLV, September 24, 1998, p. 26.
The New York Times Book Review. CIII, May 17, 1998, p. 16.
Newsweek. CXXXI, May 18, 1998, p. 75.
Publishers Weekly. CCXLV, April 6, 1998, p. 58.
Time. CLI, May 18, 1998, p. 95.
The Times Literary Supplement. June 19, 1998, p. 24.
The Wall Street Journal. May 8, 1998, p. W10.
The Washington Post Book World. XXVIII, May 24, 1998, p. 5.

CIVILITY
Manners, Morals, and the Etiquette of Democracy

Author: Stephen L. Carter (1954-   )
Published: Basic Books (New York). 338 pp. $25.00
Type of work: Current affairs and ethics

A serious investigation into the collapse of civility in America and what right-minded citizens might be able to do about it

Stephen L. Carter is the William Nelson Cromwell Professor of Law at Yale University. He is an author with a long history of concern for issues vital to the moral and ethical health of America and its beleaguered democracy. In *The Culture of Disbelief* Carter examined the trivialization of religious devotion by American law and politics. In *Integrity*, which is in many ways a useful precursor to *Civility*, Carter underscored the necessity of taking the time to deliberate about what is right and wrong. He exhorts people to have the courage to do the right thing, even when there are obvious costs; and he shows the importance of being able to articulate what has been done in the cause of justice and why it has been done. Only with this kind of integrity, firmly in place, will civility ever have any real meaning, and investing civility with meaning is the primary purpose of Carter's new book, *Civility*.

Civility, in Carter's view, is not synonymous with manners or etiquette, although it invariably involves these; it is a much deeper commitment to respect or even love fellow citizens in a way that will govern persons' actions toward them. Civility is not simply the acquisition of polished outward forms but a deeply moral belief that it is wrong to treat others as if they are objects or as if they do not matter. It is clear throughout *Civility* that Carter's own convictions about civility stem from his own profound Christianity, a Christianity as deep, abiding, fair-minded and magnanimous as the teachings of Christ himself. Consequently, his words ring out, not just to the choir, but to all persons of good will, no matter what their religious convictions or lack of them might be.

In the first section of his book, "The Collapse of the Three-Legged Stool," Carter reviews American history concerning civility, discusses the role of the 1960's in our current democratic dilemma, and puts forth the first few of the fifteen rules suggested throughout the rest of the book for the project of reconstructing civility in American life. The three legs of Carter's metaphorical stool are family, religion, and the common school. All three legs were relatively intact in the often eulogized 1950's. America was undefeated in war, had a much imitated Constitution, practiced an unofficial religion in its own nationalistic form of Protestant Christianity, was the world's greatest industrial power, enjoyed a low divorce rate, and had a system of public education that was the envy of the world. There were only three television stations in those halcyon days and all the programs were alike, because the myth was that all the viewers were alike as well—white, prosperous, middle class and content in their own version of a Levittown suburb.

A myth so militantly Pollyannaish was bound to give way to other realities eventually, but while it held sway, it also gave the nation a common ground on which to build upon the notions of civility handed down from the nineteenth century. Consensus, however, is often just the flip side of repression, so Carter is quick to point out that the same set of shared values that created the Comic Book Code also produced the anti-Communist House Committee on Un-American Activities. The repression of the 1950's ensured a backlash with which all of America is more than familiar: the 1960's.

Suddenly, all the fundamental verities came into question. The Civil Rights Act of 1964 gave official recognition to the fact that America was a country of more than one race. The Vietnam War proved that Americans of good will could differ about their sense of nationalistic duty and that American military invulnerability was highly questionable. The Free Speech movement empowered students in ways never before imagined, and the academy abdicated its authority in ways that still undermine its ability to educate America's youth. The Chicago Democratic Party convention in 1968, the Kent State massacre of 1970, the assassinations of President John F. Kennedy and Martin Luther King, Jr., the 1963 publication of Betty Friedan's *The Feminine Mystique*, the proliferation of television stations with different kinds of programming, and the explosion of the Apollo spacecraft with three American astronauts on board all shook America's faith in its cherished institutions and ushered in an era of postmortem relativism that redefined the terms of engagement.

Other people were no longer fellow travelers; they were strangers who might make one's way in life more difficult by making one rethink all the comfortable traditions of a collective past. The mistake of the 1960's was to conclude that because some of the old myths had cracks and because some of the old rules were demonstrably bad, all rules had to be abandoned. The problem for the student of civility is to figure out how to return to the basic goodness of a shared culture without squelching dissent or creating new monoliths of repression. Carter, who believes that civility is basically an ethic for relating to strangers, posits that we can achieve this lofty goal, one citizen at a time.

Carter's view of civility is simple but demanding. He believes that civility requires of persons that they sacrifice their own ease and convenience not just for those they happen to know but also for strangers as well. It instructs them to practice generosity, even when it has costs, and to trust, even when there is risk. It challenges people not only to avoid doing harm but also to actively seek to do good. It enjoins them to follow the norms of the community whenever such norms are not actually immoral. Finally, it encourages them to approach every human being with a sense of awe and gratitude. Clearly, everything in modern American society is antithetical to such ideas. The modern ethos is one of ego gratification, winning at all costs, public self-aggrandizement, and increasing isolation from family, friends, and neighbors. Without question, civility has its work cut out for it.

In the second section of Carter's book, "Incivility's Instruments," he closely examines the many forces that work so powerfully in American culture against the model of civility he proposes. Many of his demons are the usual suspects. The nastiness of our politics is one clear factor. While recognizing that American politics have always been blemished by personal attacks, Carter points out that never before in the history of democracy has a candidate's whole political mission been so obviously to sully the reputation of the other side. Slander breeds more slander, not intelligent dialogue on political issues. Incivility in America's politicians generates apathy in America's voters, which in turn endangers the country's entire political way of life. The stakes are very high. The television talk-show circuit exacerbates this tendency, and the incivility seen every day on programs such as *The McLaughlin Report* make one wonder if the old rules of forensic debate, such as respect for one's opponent, are being taught at all.

Carter is not in any way suggesting that everyone in the public or private sphere be nice to one another. In fact, he argues that civility assumes that we will disagree but that we can do so without being disagreeable. Civility asks us to listen to others in the understanding that they might be right and that we might be wrong. It also allows for criticism of others. In fact, it sometimes requires criticism, because when people love their neighbors, they do not want to see them continue in the error of their ways. All of this can be done without the name calling, invective, and ridicule that are so much a part of public discourse. It can also be done, Carter believes, without the intervention of legislation, except as a last resort—an interesting position for a professor of law.

The third section of Carter's book, "Civilizing the Twenty-first Century," is helpful in sorting through some of the available solutions. To begin with, any discussion of change must begin with children, shaping their ability to distinguish between instinct and desire, on one hand, and morally rigorous civility on the other. Who has the responsibility to teach about right and wrong, good and bad behavior? Carter argues that the locus of this important ethical activity is the family, with as little interference from the state as is consistent with the public good. Children need more "moral time" with parents, and they need to see their parents put civility into action every day. Parents who can disagree with each other in a loving and respectful way show children how to settle schoolyard disputes without resorting to guns. Parents who reason with their children raise children who are capable of reason.

However, parents modeling civility in their own homes must also be aware of powerful outside influences on their children's ethical development. This is difficult in a society in which parents are often seen as adversaries of their children's best interests by their neighbors, their schools, and their government. Parents who spank their children to teach them not to cross the street without looking may find themselves accused of child abuse by casual passersby and the courts. Carter believes that this is a clear case in which a truly civil society must exercise the trust that civility demands, assuming always that parents have their children's best interests at heart, even though there is a small risk that they do not. Families have a huge job to perform: They must battle the violent images that television beams incessantly into their homes; they must contend with the smut that the Internet is capable of disseminating indiscriminately to adults and children alike; and they must deal head on with the messages of political correctness being taught in the schools, which have made a whole generation of children so tolerant that they are incapable of discriminating, in any meaningful way, between good and bad behavior.

Carter tells the reader forcefully and lovingly where he got his courage to write this prayerful book: religion. Carter is quick to make the concession that religionists are just as capable of incivility as anyone else. Dogmatism, proselytizing, and a lack of active listening all make it easy to want to remove some religionists from the public debate. However, Carter sees religion's ability to dissent in moral ways from the prevailing winds of American culture as one of its great challenges and duties. His fear is not that religious views will become paramount in American politics but that secular market-based views are driving America's churches. Carter sees a need for a balance. He supports neither the church-state agenda of the political right, which would weaken the church's ability to advocate from the outside for the forces of civility in the wider society, nor the silent church agenda of the political left, which would deny the church's right to take an active part in enriching and civilizing American life. He accepts a church that is possibly at odds with society but a church dedicated to making society more civil. The barbarians are at the gates, and people must have the moral nerve, the sheer civility, Carter says, to invite them in for cream cheese and jelly sandwiches and to learn to live with them as neighbors.

Stephen L. Carter's *Civility* is a timely book that adds a sweetly reasoned voice to the heated debate over the decline of civility in contemporary America. While the political left frets about rights and entitlements and the sacrosanct nature of the individual and the political right builds prisons, pandering to Wall Street and trying to legislate good behavior, Carter quietly takes the problem out of their clearly inadequate hands and gives it back to the family and the citizens of this country. What is most impressive about Civility, what really distinguishes it from other books in this growing genre, is the true evenhandedness and civility with which Carter engages his opponents. A writer who practices what he preaches is one to whom others might well listen.

Cynthia Lee Katona

Sources for Further Study

The Christian Century. CXV, April 8, 1998, p. 366.
Insight on the News. XIV, June 22, 1998, p. 36.
National Catholic Reporter. November 6, 1998, p. 23.
The New Republic. CCXIX, October 5, 1998, p. 40.
The New York Times Book Review. CIII, May 10, 1998, p. 12.
Nieman Reports. LII, Fall, 1998, p. 61.
Publishers Weekly. CCXLV, March 16, 1998, p. 41.
The Village Voice. May 26, 1998, p. 141.
The Washington Monthly. XXX, May, 1998, p. 50.
The Washington Post Book World. XXVIII, May 24, 1998, p. 11.

CLEMENT GREENBERG
A Life

Author: Florence Rubenfeld
Published: Charles Scribner's Sons (New York). $21.00
Type of work: Biography
Time: 1909-1994
Locale: New York City

A meticulous, shrewd account of the life and work of an American critic who recognized very early that American abstract expressionists would dominate the art world after World War II and who came to occupy a position of power that impressed and alienated both artists and rival critics

Principal personages:
> LIONEL ABEL, a New York intellectual, one of Rubenfeld's principal sources
> HAROLD ROSENBERG, a New York intellectual and Greenberg's chief rival as a critic of modern art
> WILLIAM PHILLIPS, editor of *Partisan Review*, in which many of Greenberg's most important articles appeared
> ALFRED BARR, director of the Museum of Modern Art and one of Greenberg's adversaries
> JACKSON POLLOCK, an American abstract expressionist painter whom Greenberg touted as the best artist of his generation
> DAVID SMITH, a sculptor close to Greenberg
> WILLEM DE KOONING, an abstract expressionist painter and Pollock's chief rival
> T. S. ELIOT, a poet and critic and a major influence on Greenberg's criticism
> HELEN FRANKENTHALER, an abstract expressionist painter who became Greenberg's lover
> MARTIN GREENBERG, Clement's younger brother who worked with him at *Commentary*
> MORRIS LOUIS, a second-generation abstract expressionist championed by Greenberg

Florence Rubenfeld begins her impressive biography of Clement Greenberg with the story of how she approached this formidable critic in his declining years, seeking his cooperation for a biography that would certainly reveal not only his towering stature as an interpreter of modern art but his pugilistic personality that frightened and angered the New York intellectual and artistic community. When Rubenfeld met Greenberg, he had behind him five decades of participation in the heady, competitive atmosphere of Manhattan. He had made a name for himself in 1939, writing about "Avant-garde and Kitsch" in an essay that explored how high art became vulgarized in modern mass society.

Steeped in the writings of great modernists such as T. S. Eliot, Greenberg sought to keep the tradition of high or elite art sacrosanct—in other words, completely separate from developments in popular culture, which tended to debase the complexity and profundity of great or classical art. Greenberg knew that no such rigid distinctions could be enforced; rather, he argued for a constant vigilance among those concerned with upholding the standards of high art and for a school of criticism that sought in America (not in Paris, then the art capital of the world) new forms of art that continued the great Western tradition. In subsequent essays and appearances on public panels, in sessions with collectors and gallery owners, Greenberg campaigned for his notions of high art. While many embraced his standards and his tastes, others grew to dislike what they deemed his ruthless methods of promoting the art he liked.

Rubenfeld knew that she was approaching a critic who would be wary of a biographer. Indeed, Greenberg at first declined to cooperate with Rubenfeld. Yet when his friends asked him if they should talk to Rubenfeld, Greenberg did not try to dissuade them. Rather, he refrained from expressing enthusiasm for Rubenfeld's project. As she gathered material, the persistent biographer sought Greenberg out again. Gradually, he began commenting on her information—sometimes rebutting what her sources said, sometimes amplifying positions he felt she did not grasp completely. Although Greenberg was not an easy man to deal with, it is a tribute to both him and his biographer that they were able to carry on a sustained—if sometimes tense—dialogue. A courageous man, Greenberg evidently was not afraid of having his less flattering sides exposed. He feared misrepresentation of his person and his views, but he did not try to thwart Rubenfeld or cut off her sources of information.

Thus, Rubenfeld's beginning achieves what is so often missing from modern biographies: a sense of both the biographer and the subject. Perhaps because Ruben-feld approached Greenberg in a genuine spirit of inquiry, he became less combative. After all, he was used to controversy and to attack, not to disinterested biographical narrative. The tone of Rubenfeld's biography is sympathetic, but it never minimizes Greenberg's aggressive, even authoritarian, methods.

How did Clement Greenberg achieve his legendary status as the arbiter of art in postwar America? He combined an unusual number of talents. The son of Jewish immigrants, he learned early on to defend himself with his fists. Just under six feet tall, he was not a physically impressive man, but he was quick to strike out at an opponent. He got into several brawls with critics and artists. Indeed, his physical assaults on his opponents became part of his swaggering persona—as were his affairs with women such as Helen Frankenthaler, who became one of the greatest of the abstract expressionist painters.

Greenberg was not just tough and intimidating. He was tenacious. When he broke through to fame in New York's intellectual circles with "Avant-garde and Kitsch," he had already spent a good decade immersing himself in the artistic and intellectual currents of his time. He had graduated from Syracuse University and gravitated to the center of intellectual debate at the renowned *Partisan Review*. There he befriended editor William Phillips, who gave Greenberg the opportunity to hone his erudite and precise style. Unlike many New York intellectuals, Greenberg could combine his interest in literature and art and write about both impressively. Except for his rival, Harold Rosenberg, Greenberg had no peers, since most *Partisan Review* contributors confined themselves to commenting on politics, history, society, and literature. What Greenberg had was an "eye." Artists such as Jackson Pollock and David Smith welcomed Greenberg into their studios, where he commented not only on their completed works but on the creative process itself, often making suggestions about works in progress. Greenberg himself painted, and while his own work did not match the greatness of the painters he advised and criticized, his "eye" and his technical facility made him a credible witness to, not just a critic of, modern art.

Greenberg could anticipate developments in art much more quickly than his contemporaries. It took the art world ten years to catch up with his high opinion of abstract expressionism. Right after World War II, Greenberg was beginning to predict that the abstract expressionist painters would soon supplant their European counterparts in importance and that New York would become the world art capital. Greenberg did not mind remaining a minority of one for many years. Not only did art buyers not follow his lead but he was also opposed by Alfred Barr, the extraordinarily influential director of the Museum of Modern Art. Barr, like virtually all critics in the late 1940's, could not take artists such as Jackson Pollock and Willem de Kooning seriously. Pollock's so-called "drip paintings" seemed to be the antithesis of art. They had no structure, no line—in short, his work had none of the attributes traditionally attributed to great art. Yet Greenberg persisted, and by the 1950's the art world—critics, collectors, and museum directors—confirmed his earlier judgments. By the late 1950's abstract expressionist paintings that had never sold were now commanding the highest prices in galleries and auctions.

Rubenfeld clears up a number of misrepresentations about Greenberg's criticism. Because he was so high-handed and sure of himself, his opinions were often distorted and exaggerated. For example, Rubenfeld notes that Greenberg was a foe of representational art, but he did not uphold abstract art as the superior form. Rather, he argued that in the postwar period the finest art being created happened to be abstract expressionism. Greenberg never suggested that new forms of representational art could not once again prove to be great. Instead, he was arguing that the new art created in New York was simply the best then available.

Greenberg contributed, however, to the impression that he favored only abstract expressionism because he confined both his social and professional dealings to artists such as Pollock, de Kooning, Smith, and later Morris Louis—a Greenberg discovery from the second phase of abstract expressionism. Beginning in the late 1950's Greenberg began to tout a new generation of abstract painters such as Mark Rothko, who experimented with color. Those artists who submitted to Greenberg's strictures could indeed find him a tyrant; he blatantly told artists what was good and bad about their work. Greenberg thought he was merely being honest. He simply could not remain tactful when he thought that art was of inferior quality. Needless to say, he lost many friends who were offended by his candor.

Greenberg's natural inclination to be blunt and to satisfy his own feelings—artistic and sexual—was encouraged by therapists of the Henry Stack Sullivan school. They counseled Greenberg (beginning in the 1960's) to have an active, promiscuous sex life, to break off ties with his family, and to jettison relationships that inhibited him. The Sullivanians were reacting against what they deemed to be the tyranny of Freudian therapy and to the cloying and claustrophobic atmosphere of family life. Unfortunately, this type of therapy, as Rubenfeld shows, only encouraged Greenberg in behavior that must be called self-indulgent. On the evidence that Rubenfeld provides, there was no reason, for example, for Greenberg to reject his younger brother Martin, who became Clement's colleague at *Commentary* magazine. The older brother had always been domineering anyway—always as quick to give advice to family members as he was to artists. His problem had never been that he was put down by his own family.

Greenberg so alienated artists, critics, and intellectuals of his generation that they welcomed his rival, Harold Rosenberg, who popularized the term "action painting" to account for the free form, apparently spontaneous results of drip painting and other forms of abstract expressionism. As Rubenfeld and other critics of Rosenberg have noted, "action painting" was a catchy term, but it meant very little. It was simply not true that painters such as Jackson Pollock treated their canvases as "events," not completed works of art. Nevertheless, the need for a rival theory and a voice to check Greenberg's was so strong that Rosenberg's inferior work carried the day—for a period.

One of Rubenfeld's finest achievements is to put Greenberg's life and work into a pleasing, compact form. She does not slight the details of his sexual affairs, his harsh treatment of his only son, and his cruel baiting of younger critics who became part of his entourage, but she also gives clear, succinct explanations of Greenberg's key essays and the controversies they engendered. She quickly treats his physical and mental decline—days and days of drinking, beginning as early as 10:00 A.M.—but she does not minimize the damage it did to himself and others.

Rubenfeld's biography is an important contribution not only to the history of American art and art criticism, it is also a revealing look at the world of New York intellectuals, especially that group which clustered around the *Partisan Review*. Significantly, one of the last members of that New York generation, Alfred Kazin, who died just before Rubenfeld's biography was published, endorsed her approach, pointing out that she had captured both the competitiveness of the art world and its personalities and sketched a profound portrait of Greenberg, who, in Kazin's words, "really cared about art." In achieving such a sensitive balance between the subject and his times, Rubenfeld has produced a model biography.

Carl Rollyson

Sources for Further Study

Artforum. XXXVI, March, 1998, p. 13.
ARTnews. XCVII, May, 1998, p. 102.

Booklist. XCIV, March 15, 1998, p. 1194.
Commentary. CV, June, 1998, p. 57.
The Nation. CCLXVI, June 29, 1998, p. 33.
National Review. L, May 18, 1998, p. 56.
The New York Times Book Review. CIII, March 29, 1998, p. 8.
The New Yorker. LXXIV, March 16, 1998, p. 70.
Publishers Weekly. CCXLV, February 2, 1998, 73.
The Times Literary Supplement. May 22, 1998, p. 22.

CLONE
The Road to Dolly and the Path Ahead

Author: Gina Kolata (1948-   )
Published: William Morrow (New York). 288 pp. $23.00
Type of work: Ethics and science
Time: The 1990's
Locale: Roslin, Scotland; Geneva, Switzerland; Washington, D.C.

Science writer Gina Kolata recounts the 1996 cloning of Dolly the sheep in Scotland and the implications of the event for humankind

In the December, 1984, issue of *Science*, James McGrath and Davor Solter, well-recognized scientists, wrote, "The cloning of mammals, by simple nuclear transfer, is biologically impossible." On July 5, 1996, around 5:00 in the evening in the hamlet of Roslin, Scotland, a few miles south of Edinburgh, the birth of Dolly disproved this prognostication. Dolly, a sheep cloned by taking cells from the udder of a donor sheep, growing them in a petri dish, inserting them into a sheep's egg from which the nucleus had been extracted, and implanting them in a host sheep, was a living reality.

This feat was accomplished by embryologist Ian Wilmut, who worked for more than a decade on the research project that eventuated in Dolly. Bent over a microscope for long hours in a cubicle heated to the exact internal temperature of a sheep, Wilmut, sponsored by PPL Therapeutics, Limited, was hired to develop designer animals as a source of pharmaceuticals for human use. He sought ways to create genetic defects in animals that could be studied to find ways of dealing with comparable defects in humans. He sought means through genetic manipulation of causing animals to produce antibodies that, permeating their milk, could be used to attack diseases. The drugs resulting from these antibodies could be extracted and sold by PPL.

News of Dolly's birth was withheld from the public until February, 1997, because PPL had patents pending to protect Wilmut's revolutionary accomplishment. Those involved in the experiment at the Roslin Institute were sworn to secrecy until the patents were granted. By early 1997, however, these scientists had prepared a brief paper reporting on their research and its results, that was disarmingly titled, "Viable Offspring Derived from Fetal and Adult Mammalian Cells." They submitted it to the scientific weekly *Nature*, which scheduled it for publication in its February 27, 1997, issue.

As was customary, *Nature* informed the press of cogent articles in each forthcoming issue a week before the distribution of that issue. On February 20, when *Nature*'s report arrived in Kolata's e-mail box at *The New York Times*, she first learned of an event whose scientific and social impact is compared by some to splitting the atom or breaking the sound barrier.

Journalists receiving advanced information from *Nature* agree not to break any stories about articles scheduled to appear in the forthcoming issue until it has been distributed. If, however, a story breaks somewhere earlier, journalists are no longer bound by *Nature*'s mandate. Kolata recognized the importance and possible consequences of a story about cloning a mammal as complex as a sheep, realizing that if such a mammal can be cloned, human cloning is not far behind. She informed her editors of the anticipated impact of the *Nature* article and prepared a detailed piece for publication after the distribution of the February 27 issue of *Nature*. The story broke in Great Britain on February 22, thereby relieving Kolata of the restraint imposed by *Nature*. Her account made the first page of *The New York Times* second edition the following day. Kolata wrote another first-page story, this one considering the theological and ethical implications of cloning.

If the first shot fired at the Battle of Lexington was "the shot heard 'round the world," the birth of Dolly was the birth reported 'round the world. Embryologists and molecular biologists in the farthest reaches of the planet quickly learned of this monumental event and reacted to it, their voices joined by those of physicians, theologians, bioethicists, politicians, and entrepreneurs who saw in the announcement promise of making a quick buck. Ian Wilmut became an international celebrity overnight. The shock waves sent out by Dolly's birth reached well beyond Roslin and Dr. Wilmut. The Center for Bioethics at the University of Pennsylvania, for example, had typically received about five hundred Internet hits a month, but after Dolly was born it was fielding up to seventeen thousand a day.

In *Clone*, Gina Kolata writes with an admirable gusto about an event with far-reaching consequences, the details of which unfold like those in a well-crafted mystery story. Kolata was the first journalist to talk with Ian Wilmut after Dolly's birth. She also spoke with a broad spectrum of people from disciplines that would be directly affected by the cloning of a complex mammal—embryologists, molecular biologists, philosophers, theologians, bioethicists, and others who had a stake in this precedent-shattering event.

Obviously, the implications of Wilmut's success in cloning Dolly focused on the uses to which his new techniques in cloning would be put. Before Dolly, scientists had cloned cows and sheep from embryo cells, but Dolly was the first clone created from a cell of an adult sheep, in this case, a cell from a six-year-old sheep that, with the birth of Dolly, would have an identical twin six or seven years younger than herself. In order to accomplish his landmark feat, Wilmut removed many cells from the udder of the donor sheep, placing each in a petri dish filled with nutrients that permitted the cells to grow for five days. The nutrients were then reduced to five percent of what the cells required in order for them to continue growing, plunging them into a kind of suspended animation.

In this quiescent state, the cells lost their differentiation and reverted to the state of the undifferentiated genes they had originally been. The next step in the process was to harvest sheep ova, remove the nuclei and all the genetic material from them, and then embed in each egg one of the cultured cells. Placed in the ova of sheep, the cultured cells imprinted their genetic codes upon the ova, which stimulated the initial process of creating a lamb embryo. The egg was then placed in a host sheep that, in the case of Dolly, carried it to term. Of 277 adult cells Wilmut and his colleagues introduced into ova, thirteen resulted in pregnancy and just Dolly's resulted in a live birth.

If Dolly's birth seems unlikely to be replicated in humans, one has only to remember that when the Wright Brothers flew the first heavier-than-air vehicle at Kitty Hawk, North Carolina, in 1903, their contraption was airborne for 852 feet in the longest of its four flights during that crucial day in aviation history. Within fifteen years, airplanes were being used in World War I combat. Once the genie is loosed upon the world, whirlwind progress is predictable.

Kolata discusses the ethical implications of cloning. She considers questions of good and evil, reminding her readers of the possibility that creating our own identical twins "brings us back to the ancient sins of vanity and pride: the sins of Narcissus, who so loved himself, and of Prometheus, who, in stealing fire, sought the powers of God." She analyzes how the thought of cloning humans challenges important questions of self, identity, and long-cherished values.

As a scientific journalist, Kolata attempts always to remain neutral in her discussion, presenting possibilities related to every aspect of the issue. She comments on cases of infertility in which those previously condemned to childlessness would, through cloning, be able to experience parenthood. She also mentions the appeal of this process to gay and lesbian couples wishing to have children who share their genetic characteristics. A clone may, in the eyes of society, be the child of the person from whose cell that clone originates, but such an offspring is also an identical twin of the donor, although such a twin would, because of environmental factors, develop an individual personality. The person who carries a fertilized egg to term, Kolata reminds her readers, is not the parent of the offspring.

She cites the case of a sixty-year-old woman whose daughter was born without a uterus. An egg produced by the daughter's ovary was fertilized with her husband's sperm. The fertilized egg was then implanted in the uterus of the woman's mother, who ultimately gave birth to her daughter's child. In this case, there was no question about the parenthood of the child. The daughter and her husband were the parents, the grandmother merely the host who carried the fertilized egg to term.

Kolata cites Ruth Macklin, an ethicist at the Albert Einstein College of Medicine, who reminds skeptics that "if the cloned person was not created from the cell of another, he or she would not have been born. Is it really better never to have existed than to exist as a clone?" Macklin's question of whether the "psychological burdens of knowing that one was cloned would be of such magnitude that they would outweigh the benefits of life itself" raises concerns about whether ethics can legitimately be reconstructed to accommodate current situations.

Many who think about cloning produce images of the replication of entire entities, the specter of which elicits memories of Dr. Frankenstein's monster. Kolata reminds her readers that molecular biologists and embryologists are working strenuously toward cloning such tissue as bone marrow that might be used in transplants for people who need them. These scientists are also attempting to clone organs from the healthy cells of people who require organ transplants. Accomplishing such an end would eliminate the severe shortage of cadaver organs available for transplantation, while simultaneously eliminating the problem of rejection. People benefiting from such transplants would receive organs that are genetically identical to the organs needing replacement.

In a valuable historical chapter in *Clone* entitled "Three Cloned Mice," Kolata explores extensively the claims of the German researcher Karl Illmensee, who achieved a remarkable reputation as a geneticist, working first with fruit flies and later with mice. By genetic manipulation, mice with characteristics such as sensitivity to salt that causes hypertension could be produced for laboratories. The mouse possesses in its cells virtually all the genetic material found in human cells, but this material is arranged differently. Because mice reproduce quickly and have short life spans, they make ideal experimental animals. Millions of them are used in scientific laboratories every year.

Illmensee claimed in 1977 that while working with Peter Hoppe at the Jackson Laboratory in Bar Harbor, Maine, he had cloned three mice using early mouse embryos rather than the kinds of cells Wilmut used in his work. Illmensee's scientific reputation was such that few questioned his remarkable claim. When various other scientists attempted to replicate his experiment, however, they failed. Illmensee, unlike most scientists who make significant discoveries, generally refused to cooperate with other scientists who asked him to instruct them in his techniques. Considerable suspicion was cast upon his claims, and his work is now essentially discredited by the scientific community.

In *Cloning*, Gina Kolata presents with considerable intellectual vigor a well-balanced account of the cloning of Dolly. She has also presented an accurate account of cloning experiments in the past and a thorough discussion of the ethical, economic, and social implications of this phenomenon. Throughout the book, Kolata maintains a lively writing style that will appeal to readers.

R. Baird Shuman

Sources for Further Study

Booklist. XCIV, December 1, 1997, p. 596.
Business Week. February 2, 1998, p. 16.
Issues in Science and Technology. XIV, Spring, 1998, p. 90.
Library Journal. CXXII, November 15, 1997, p. 73.
Natural History. CVII, September, 1998, p. 11.
The New England Journal of Medicine. CCCXXXIX, July 9, 1998, p. 134.
New Scientist. CLVI, November 29, 1997, p. 52.
The New York Review of Books. XLV, April 23, 1998, p. 14.
The New York Times Book Review. CIII, December 28, 1997, p. 7.
Publishers Weekly. CCXLIV, November 3, 1997, p. 69.

CLOUDSPLITTER

Author: Russell Banks (1940-   )
Published: HarperCollins (New York). 758 pp. $27.50
Type of work: Novel
Time: 1832-c. 1900
Locale: New York, Kansas, Virginia, England, and Belgium

A fictional account of the life of the controversial abolitionist John Brown

> *Principal characters:*
> JOHN BROWN, the radical abolitionist hanged after the failed raid on
>   Harpers Ferry, Virginia, in 1859
> OWEN BROWN, third son of John Brown and the novel's narrator
> JOHN BROWN, JR. first son of John Brown
> FRED BROWN, second son of John Brown
> LYMAN EPPS, former slave and a close friend of John Brown
> SUSAN EPPS, wife of Lyman Epps
> GERRIT SMITH, prosperous New York abolitionist
> FREDERICK DOUGLASS, escaped slave who became one of the leading
>   lights of the abolitionist movement
> HARRIET TUBMAN, former slave and a leader of the Underground
>   Railroad
> SARAH PEABODY, niece of Sophia Hawthorne

Known primarily as a writer of contemporary working-class fiction, Russell Banks seems to have departed from his established metier by producing a prodigious work of historical fiction. Actually, Banks's change of subject and genre is more apparent than real. Along with an abiding interest in questions of social class, Banks has been equally fascinated by America's tortured racial politics. Thus, John Brown is a natural choice of topic. Beyond his iconic status as an enduring and still highly controversial bellwether of race relations, Brown attracted Banks's attention for more personal reasons. The fiery abolitionist once lived and is now buried close to Banks's home in Keene, New York, near Mount Marcy in the Adirondacks, which the Indians called "Cloudsplitter." Banks's focus on Brown also represents a continuation of his decades-long inquiry into troubled families ruled and riven by obsessional, violence-prone patriarchs, a theme manifest in numerous Banks short stories and several novels, particularly *Affliction* (1989).

Undoubtedly another reason that Banks chose to write about Brown is that Brown constitutes a figure of sufficient historical importance to power the proverbial "big book." Although a respected writer with an impressive track record, Banks has never quite achieved the literary status accorded to such contemporaries as Don DeLillo, Robert Stone, or Thomas Pynchon. Over six years in the making—and some quarter million words in length—*Cloudsplitter* is far and away Banks's most ambitious work; it gives every indication of being a calculated bid for the literary home run that would propel the author to the coveted first rank of "serious" writers.

In an important "Author's Note" that prefaces the novel, Banks emphatically and repeatedly warns readers that although his account of John Brown's life has some basis in historical fact, it "is a work of the imagination" and should "be read solely as a work of fiction, not as a version or interpretation of history." Such a disclaimer is, of course, meant to neutralize objections from historians to the book's deliberate factual inaccuracies, distortions, and wholesale fabrications. Still, a troubling question remains about the hybrid genre of fictionalized biography (or quasi-biographical fiction) exemplified by *Cloudsplitter:* Is such massive poetic license really warranted or even necessary, especially in the case of a life history that is more gripping and dramatic than most fiction? Banks's implicit answer is that his novel supplements, enhances, perhaps exceeds strictly factual accounts by giving us the *human*, familial side of a story that is usually encoded in the somewhat impersonal, externalized terms of a political narrative. More specifically, *Cloudsplitter* centers on the effects that John Brown's fanaticism had on the material and psychological health of his immediate family—an issue marginalized in most accounts.

In keeping with these unusually subjective aims, Banks tells his story through the voice and viewpoint of Owen Brown, John Brown's third son, who was at his side during all the crucial battles. A somewhat shadowy personage in the historical accounts, Owen Brown provided Banks with the perfect narrator, one whose relative anonymity allowed Banks unlimited leeway in developing his characters. Mediating his story through Owen Brown's subjectivity also allowed Banks a plausible way to rationalize the novel's historical inaccuracies as merely symptomatic of Owen's psychological projections and needs. Indeed, Banks goes out of his way to make Owen an eccentric, unreliable narrator who admits "the habit of lying to an exceeding degree." At the same time, the Conradian device of using Owen Brown as narrator lends the novel verisimilitude; however self-serving and deluded Owen's story might be, it is still the purported account of an eyewitness very close to the actual events. To get around the fact that Owen has been dead for a century, Banks has him writing at the turn of the century to Miss Katherine Mayo, research assistant to Oswald Garrison Villard, John Brown's 1910 biographer.

Cloudsplitter starts on a ponderous note, with Owen delivering a long and rather tortured apologia to Miss Mayo for offering his version of the events that led up to Harpers Ferry. The reader gathers that Owen Brown is an intelligent introvert who has led a virtually posthumous existence in the forty years since his father's execution, slowly going mad from loneliness, political alienation, and survivor's guilt. He claims to want to relate his "confession" as a means of spiritual catharsis and expiation so that he can die in peace. An equally important motive—one he shares with Banks—is to correct the received version of "an American history that at bottom is alien to [him]," a history that has caricatured John Brown as simply a religious fanatic or madman.

Owen's narrative proper begins in 1832 with the death of his mother (John Brown's first wife, Dianthe Lusk Brown), an event marked by Owen as the turning point in the life of the Brown family, when it went from being relatively "normal" to a family "like some ancient Hebrew tribe of wanderers and sufferers, burdened by the death of women and children and by our endless obligations to our father's restless, yet implacable, God." After a series of anecdotes illustrating John Brown's Old Testament probity and sternness as a father, Owen goes on to describe, in excruciating detail, his father's dealings in land speculation in Ohio in the 1830's, which culminate in financial ruin during the Panic of 1837. Owen's (that is, Banks's) portrait of John Brown as an incredibly inept businessman is historically accurate. Stubborn and self-righteous, rigid yet arbitrary, a sloppy accountant but honest to a fault, Brown worked like a fool but was always deep in debt. Bankruptcy in 1839 eventually drove Brown and his family east, to Springfield, Massachusetts, and then on to North Elba, in the Adirondack region of northeastern New York state.

Although a relatively minor phase to historians, the Browns' residence in North Elba from 1848 to 1855 is given considerable attention by Banks. Brown's move there is both pragmatic and political, an escape from his failures in the Midwest and an increase in his commitment to the antislavery cause. Learning that a wealthy abolitionist named Gerrit Smith has set aside land in the Adirondacks for former slaves to settle and farm, Brown rents a farm from Smith there. Once settled, Brown works hard at farming, herding, and his tannery business to support his large and ever-growing family. He also does everything he can to help "Timbuctu," the struggling black community nearby. His most passionate involvement, however, is with the Underground Railroad, which helps fugitive slaves escape to Canada. In an incident fabricated by Banks, Brown and his sons John and Owen get into an armed confrontation with a "slave catcher" named Billingsly. In the ensuing melee, the slave catcher and a jailer are wounded and Elden Fleete, Brown's black cohort, is shot dead—a harbinger of much bloodletting to come.

Shortly thereafter Brown takes Owen to England to help him dissolve his wool business by selling all his stock. (In reality, Brown went to England alone and *before* moving to North Elba.) Banks uses the long sea voyage as a stage setting for a fictional encounter between Owen and Sarah Peabody, niece of Sophia Peabody, the wife of Nathaniel Hawthorne. Unmarried, Sarah is pregnant and voyaging to Europe, presumably to dispose of her baby in some way or to live in social exile. The story she tells Owen of an extramarital affair that cannot be acknowledged in public by her married lover closely resembles *The Scarlet Letter* and tantalizingly suggests that Hawthorne is the father of her child. Owen is deeply affected by Sarah and her story, so much so that he comes upon a profound insight about his own life: Although she was "trapped by her pregnant female body, in fact my fate was not sealed, and I wasn't trapped. For I was, indeed, my mind. As were most men. And I could change it. I could simply change my mind, as she said." Shortly after her encounter with Owen, Sarah commits suicide by jumping into the ocean. Owen is devastated, but the insight he has gained from their meeting leads him to decide "for the first time, the only necessary time" that his "father's visions [are] worthy of [his] belief," a decision that transforms a young man with a confused and inchoate personality into a resolute warrior in his father's cause.

From that point on, Banks's otherwise glacial narrative begins to gain some momentum. In business terms, the trip to England is disastrous (as it was for Brown in real life). Forced to sell his wool at rock-bottom prices, John Brown is ruined all over again, a fate that is strangely liberating, because it forecloses any hope of wealth, thus freeing Brown to concentrate all his efforts on the fight against slavery. The trip to Europe has also involved a visit to Waterloo, site of Napoleon's final defeat. There, Brown regales Owen with his analysis of the battle. To Brown's way of thinking Napoleon lost because he failed to do the unexpected thing (i.e., immediately attack Wellington's forces, instead of waiting for the rain-soaked ground to dry), an analysis that says as much about Brown's tactical mind and temperament as it does about Napoleon's.

The return from Europe marks the beginning of the final, and most exciting, phase of Owen's/Banks's narrative. In love with Lyman Epps' wife, Susan, Owen Brown develops an intense, brooding rivalry with Lyman—until Lyman accidentally shoots himself in an incident for which Owen takes full moral responsibility. Shattered by Lyman's death, Owen joins his brothers, John and Fred, who have moved to Kansas, a territory on the verge of becoming a state and, therefore, a crucial battleground for Free-State forces contending with proslavers as to its status when it enters the Union. The sons are soon joined by their father and brothers Oliver, Jason, and Salmon, and the stage is set for Banks's chilling account of the Browns' bloody massacre of pro-slavers at Osawatomie, Kansas, an event that not only seals the fate of the family but of the entire nation, which will erupt in full-scale civil war a few years later.

After the Osawatomie massacre the Browns (minus John and Jason, who defect, and Fred, who is killed in battle) join with a variable number of cohorts to become a small guerrilla army conducting "swift, daring, terroristic raids against the Border Ruffians and their supporters." Although successful and highly publicized, these raids are not enough for John Brown, who has long dreamed of establishing an Appalachian "subterranean passway"—that is, a fortified corridor to bring slaves out of and northern invaders into the South. On October 16, 1859, against Frederick Douglass's advice, Brown conducts his (in)famous raid on the Federal Arsenal at Harpers Ferry, Virginia, which he hoped would instigate a slave revolt. Banks's narrative ends in the midst of the faltering raid, with Owen fleeing west, away from Harpers Ferry, and his father's terrible fate.

Although it is too long, too slow, and too self-consciously oracular to be very popular (or to qualify as a serious contender for the Great American Novel), Russell Banks's *Cloudsplitter* is an extremely impressive imaginative achievement. The question of John Brown's relative sanity is not necessarily resolved but, in Banks's hands, Brown is rendered fully human and, in many ways, admirable—no longer the wild-eyed lunatic of popular legend. Although too ponderous by half, Banks's novel matters because race matters, which is why John Brown's life and death continue to have a profound impact on the American psyche.

Robert Niemi

Sources for Further Study

The Economist. CCCXLVII, June 13, 1998, p. S15.
Los Angeles Times Book Review. March 8, 1998, p. 4.
The Nation. CCLVI, March 16, 1998, p. 27.
The New York Review of Books. XLV, April 9, 1998, p. 8.
The New York Times Book Review. CIII, February 22, 1998, p. 9.
The New Yorker. LXXIV, April 6, 1998, p. 1102.
Publishers Weekly. CCXLIV, December 1, 1997, p. 44.
Time. CLI, March 2, 1998, p. 76.
The Times Literary Supplement. May 22, 1998, p. 7.
The Wall Street Journal. March 16, 1998, p. A20.

THE COASTS OF BOHEMIA
A Czech History

Author: Derek Sayer
Translated from the Czech by Alena Sayer
Published: Princeton University Press (Princeton, New Jersey). Illustrated. 442 pp. $29.95.
Type of work: History
Time: 1520-1968
Locale: The Czech Republic

The cultural history of the Czech people as expressed in folklore, literature, and the arts reflects their central position in the most important modern controversies—religion, ethnicity, and the nation-state

> *Principal personages:*
> ALFONS MUCHA, a Secession-style artist
> FRANTIŠEK PALACKÝ, an historian and nationalist activist, "Father of the Nation"
> MILAN KUNDERA, a satirical novelist
> FRANZ KAFKA, a groundbreaking novelist
> LEOŠ JANÁČEK, a composer
> TOMÁŠ GARRIGUE MASARYK, the first president of Czechoslovakia

In every nation, there is a continuing debate about what is the essence of the culture. This is certainly true of the Czechs, who today can see themselves alternately or collectively as part of the West Slavic language group, of the Austro-Hungarian empire, or of the European Economic Community. The debate about what being Czech means is not an idle matter for idle intellectuals but one that concerns the heart and soul of a people with whom outsiders are familiar but whom they seldom know. Derek Sayer's *The Coasts of Bohemia* examines this ongoing debate in a thorough and compelling fashion.

The history of the Czechs is that of a people who allowed immigrants into their country and have repented of it ever since. The Czechs were immigrants themselves, coming west in that vast migration of Slavs that pushed Germans across the Elbe and out of Bohemia and Moravia. However, in the days when there were still vacant lands to be filled with farmers and towns begging for artisans and merchants, when rulers were accustomed to having a splendid variety of multicultural subjects, the kings of Bohemia invited Germans to take up poor lands in the mountains, open businesses in the towns, and become priests in the churches. They intermarried with powerful German dynasties; eventually one of these, the Luxemburgs, inherited the throne and made Bohemia into the most powerful and important state in the Holy Roman Empire.

It appeared that in the course of time the Czechs would be absorbed into the larger and culturally and technologically more advanced Germans or isolated into pockets of quaint rural poverty, as had happened to small Slavic and Baltic peoples elsewhere on the eastern frontier of the German-speaking world (or to the west on the Celtic fringe). Just before 1400, however, a religious revival that stressed preaching to the common people in Czech led to a massive confrontation with the dominant German minority. In the course of this confrontation—the Hussite wars—the inspired Czechs beat back seemingly overwhelming numbers of Germans and Hungarians and won for themselves religious liberty and a sense of Czech nationhood.

This triumph was negated in one day in 1620 at the Battle of White Mountain. Czech Protestantism was suppressed, and the Czech nobility was dispossessed of its lands. The Germans were in control, and they remained so until the nineteenth century. This was not altogether a loss, in that the Czech people became increasingly Western European and less Eastern European, but it was not an ideal method of national progress.

When the nationalist movement swept Europe in the post-Napoleonic period, it seemed that the Czechs would not be affected. The governing class, the educated classes, the mercantile class, and the Church were all composed of Germans or German-speaking Jews. It was said at one time that if the ceiling of a small meeting room were to collapse, all the members of the Czech national revival would be killed. This explains to a great degree Western ignorance of Czech history and culture (one of William Shakespeare's plays, for example, contains a reference to the "coasts of Bohemia"). The rest is the result of distance from the English-speaking world, the difficulty of learning Slavic languages, and politics. The cost of this ignorance was high: Neville Chamberlain dismissed Czechoslovakia in 1938 at Munich as "a faraway country" inhabited by quarreling peoples "of whom we know nothing."

Chamberlain was wrong, but he was not misinformed. At the turn of the century, when he was educated, the Western world knew the Czechs largely through the poster art of Alfons Mucha, who was living in Paris. When Mucha returned to his home to paint a cycle of patriotic canvases, he was forgotten by the Western public, scorned by contemporary artists, and discouraged by the German-speaking political elite. Czech was not yet a literary language. In fact, its peasant roots had only recently received the artificial grafts that allowed it to function as a means of educated discourse and elegant creativity. The first novels, the first Czech language histories, and the national theater bloomed at the same time that a national school system began to educate the entire Czech-speaking population. This, together with a population explosion at the end of the nineteenth century and the growth of commerce and industry, soon gave Czechs an absolute majority in all the cities and most of the towns of Bohemia and Moravia.

František Palacký made these newly literate masses aware of their legacy and potential. A Pan-Slavist, Palacký organized the Pan-Slavic Congress in 1848, which was disrupted by the revolution of that year. It is significant that Palacký was called "the father of the nation" (*Otec národa*) rather than "the father of the homeland" (*Otec vlasti*), because the latter emphasis on the kingdom of Bohemia would have included the many Germans who lived in the Czech lands. As he put it, "We were here before Austria, and we will also be here after it!"

The German speakers were naturally worried. They had forgotten neither the medieval Hussites nor the thoroughly reactionary opposition to the reforms of Holy

Roman emperor Joseph II. They understood that German fluency was necessary to professional and commercial success in the Austro-Hungarian empire. The suggestion that they should become primarily Czech speakers was unhesitatingly rejected. However, becoming bilingual was insufficient to meet the demands of the extreme nationalists and seemingly not worth the effort. Bedřich Smetana's *Prodaná nevěsta* (1866, *The Bartered Bride*) was internationally popular, but only in German translation. Leoš Janáček, although considered superior, was unknown. Antonín Dvořák was familiar largely because of his tone poems. In short, Czechness was folklore, nothing more and perhaps less.

For too many people, Czechs and Germans alike, Jaroslav Hašek's novel *Osudy dobrého vojáka Švejka za světové války* (1920-1923, *Good Soldier Švejk*) represented the true character of the Czech people. Švejk may have been a lovable character for a novel, but no serious person would want to hire him. Similarly, some of the invented past and the narratives of the historical past were attractive but not something that serious scholars could repeat. The birth of Czech nationalism, like that of many other nationalisms, was a combination of painful labor and unrealistic optimism. Suddenly, in 1918, there was a Czechoslovak state, a combination of peoples undreamt of before inside borders designed for a nightmare.

Czechs were not even a majority inside this new state. They constituted 49 percent of the population, while Germans constituted 23 percent (one-third the population of Bohemia). The Germans were followed by Slovaks, Hungarians, Ukrainians, Russians, Gypsies, and Jews. Some regions where minorities were in the absolute majority could have been given to neighboring states, but such a practical proposal ran up against practical problems. The ancient boundaries of empire remained, but they now enclosed the problems of a modern national state.

The effort to make Czech the national language soon infuriated both Germans and Czechs, as did the effort to rewrite history, replace historical monuments, and create a new national culture. The Sokal gymnastic society became a unifying movement, Prague became a respectable capital, and the arts and literature were encouraged. Under the leadership of the redoubtable and humane scholar Tomáš Garrigue Masaryk and his successor Edvard Beneš, Czechoslovakia remained a democratic island throughout the interwar period, a troubled time when neighboring states opted for dictatorships one after the other.

This was not an easy period for hyphenated citizens. Franz Kafka, for example, was legally classified as Jewish, not Czech, and he wrote in German. However, he spoke fluent Czech and realized that Jewishness and Germanness were becoming increasingly incompatible. He died of tuberculosis at a young age, but three of his sisters survived to perish in the Holocaust. There was more than a hint that the upper classes and the merchants had betrayed both the nation and the people by adopting German. Nationalist composers such as Janáček emphasized Czechness in the face of the German musical traditions emanating from Vienna.

The nation-building artistic elite began to die off rapidly in the 1930's, leaving behind a state with still unresolved questions. For example, were the Czechs a nation or a people? This question, almost unintelligible to someone from the English-speaking world, makes sense to those whose national anthem begins with the words: "Where is my home?" This timing was unfortunate, in that the divided nation which had to face the Nazi threat lacked the kind of leadership that had given the Hussites victory over far greater odds.

The horrible years of the Nazi occupation ended with the student uprising in Prague that the approaching Soviet and American armies guaranteed would be successful. The post-World War II Czechoslovak state was shorn of several minorities—Ukrainians and Russians joined unwillingly their Socialist Motherland, the Jews had been shipped to Auschwitz, and the Germans were expelled. After a brief interlude, the 1948 coup made Czechoslovakia a Soviet satellite. The Communist rewriting of Czech history took the now-traditional replacing of statues and approved books to a new level of national mythologizing. Easy associations could be made to the Hussite era (revolutionary and military songs, new street names), to the Sokol spectacles (now called the Spartakiáda), to realistic art (Mucha was forgotten), to the class struggle (Czech peasants against German nobles and bourgeoisie), and to Pan-Slavism (the Soviet big brother).

This totalitarianism intruded into the most trivial aspects of life and memory, reorganizing a little here and redefining there, but all the while cloaking itself in the most familiar emotional and intellectual garments. In the end it produced only soul-stifling acquiescence. The emphasis was on indoctrinating children. Adults were considered incapable of appreciating the socialist realism of the future workers' paradise.

Czech resistance to this and to Communist futurist fantasies took the form of literary surrealism, imaginative art, and avant-garde film. The adults fought back with adult material filled with hilariously absurd situations that usually involved sex. Milan Kundera was only the foremost of a galaxy of colorful writers whose irony and satire undermined the gray humorlessness of Soviet rule. Additional themes involved nostalgia, moral ambivalence, and emotional and physical exile. Stories about ordinary people living through pseudo-ordinary times sapped the moral authority of the Soviet regime. In 1968, the Velvet Revolution attempted to give Communism a human face in Czechoslovakia—an uncustomary form of political revolution that sought to keep the names and slogans of the last regime but change the reality. In 1989, the Czechs pulled the mask off entirely. Shortly thereafter, they allowed the Slovak caboose to detach itself. The Czechs were, at last, masters of their own fate.

Somewhere in museum-filled Prague there needs to be yet one more museum—a repository of outdated statues. The once-prized busts of Franz Joseph, Vladimir Ilich Lenin, Joseph Stalin, and Klement Gottwald, of literary heroes no longer read, artists no longer in favor, and local politicians long forgotten could be lessons to the nation that Bohemia is closer to the sea than might be realized.

The Coasts of Bohemia is not an easy book, no more possible to master in a single sitting than the complicated history of the Czech people. Yet the Czechs are like a promontory on the land mass of modern European history. In addition to the heights of the mountains that surround the Czech land and that trail off into the east as far as Romania, there are numerous shores upon which the interested reader can land. The price of this adventure must be paid in time, in perseverance, and in turning back pages to reread what has gone before.

William L. Urban

Sources for Further Study

Booklist. XCIV, April, 1998, p. 1302.
Choice. XXV, November, 1998, 579.
Foreign Affairs. LXXVII, September, 1998, p. 161.
Kirkus Reviews. LXVI, February 15, 1998, p. 253.
Library Journal. CXXIII, May 15, 1998, p. 98.
The New Republic. CCXIX, September 7, 1998, p. 28.
Publishers Weekly. CCXLV, January 26, 1998, p. 75.
The Washington Post Book World. XXVIII, October 11, 1998, p. 13.
Washington Times. May 31, 1998, p. B7.

COLD NEW WORLD
Growing Up in a Harder Country

Author: William Finnegan (1952-   )
Published: Random House (New York). 421 pp. $26.00
Type of work: Sociology
Time: The 1990's
Locale: The United States

The lives of teenagers from four geographic regions of the United States reveal a common sense of disenfranchisement from the American Dream

William Finnegan is a journalist who has been a staff writer for *The New Yorker* since 1987. He has been a reporter in war-torn regions of Africa and has written three books about his experiences: *A Complicated War: The Harrowing of Mozambique, Dateline Soweto: Travels with Black South African Reporters*, and *Crossing the Line: A Year in the Land of Apartheid.* In *Cold New World: Growing Up in a Harder Country*, Finnegan decides to tackle a different war, one of poverty and racism in America.

The book is divided into five sections, corresponding to the four different regions Finnegan has studied and the conclusions he has drawn. The book contains forty-three pages of notes, which provide rich historical detail and statistics, and a bibliography. Each of the four sections features a central person, who allowed Finnegan into his or her life, and is enriched by commentary from the person's family and friends and from community figures such as police, social workers, and local politicians. Finnegan reports compassionately and fairly on his subjects' lives, even though what he sees and hears sometimes makes him painfully aware of his own social prejudices and the advantages he had growing up. He describes himself as a liberal, and his ability to draw close to people so different from himself and elicit their opinions and histories is only possible from a liberal stance. Yet he decries "liberal consumerism," which, he claims, has replaced any meaningful culture in people's lives.

In each of the locations Finnegan visited—New Haven, Connecticut; San Augustine, Texas; the Yakima Valley of Washington State; and Lancaster, California— he found evidence of economic decline among members of his own generation, the parents of his teenaged subjects. Drugs played a central part in the local cultures of all four locations, but not all of Finnegan's subjects were involved with drugs. In fact, only one parent was an active drug user. However, the parents of these teens were unable to provide them with even the standard of living they had enjoyed while growing up. Physical violence, either as an inevitable part of the drug scene or the street fighting of rival gangs, figured strongly in all the subjects' lives. At times Finnegan finds himself shocked at the teens' acceptance of vicious physical attacks and their ability to engage in violence. He is also troubled by the entrenched racism and the social assumptions of local police agencies and the political elite, as revealed through his interviews with them.

In the first section, entitled "New Haven," we meet Terry Jackson, a sixteen-year-old occasional cocaine dealer whose attempts to renounce dealing and make a new start are constantly derailed. (Finnegan states in his introduction to the book that he has changed some of the names in this story, but apparently not in the others.) Although Terry has forbidden Finnegan from meeting any of his friends, the author does have contact with Terry's mother, Anjelica, herself a drug abuser, his younger brother, Buddy, and his grandparents, who live in the same town. Finnegan notes the disparity between the lives of Terry's grandparents, who own a modest home, and Terry's mother, who lives alternately on the streets or in some type of public housing. Finnegan relates the history of the town, New Haven, Connecticut, and clearly traces the downward economic slide that has produced the world in which Terry must live.

The "easy" and large amounts of money available through the drug trade tempt even Terry's mother, who receives gifts from Terry through this bounty. Although Finnegan attempts to maintain his journalistic distance, he is often moved to intercede for Terry with local authorities. Finnegan believes, probably correctly, that his presence as a white, middle-aged journalist often influenced the outcome of Terry's travails, including a charge of cocaine dealing in which Terry was picked up in a general sweep. In despair at Terry's public defense lawyers, Finnegan managed to arrange for a private lawyer to work *pro bono* on Terry's case, which resulted in a dismissal of the charges. Although Terry wasted most of the opportunities that came his way, eventually he moved from Connecticut and found work in another city. A local social worker, Lisa Sullivan, said tellingly: "These kids know that the whole society hates who they are. And they can't *help* who they are." The selfless, concerned community activists working with the kids seem to be fighting a losing battle against the bleak environment in which they all live.

Next Finnegan examined a community in Eastern Texas, San Augustine, that had been torn apart by a major drug bust. Operation White Tornado successfully rounded up dozens of suspects and resulted in hefty jail terms for many, African American and white. A surprisingly small amount of cocaine was netted in the bust, however, and residents disputed local law-enforcement officers' claims that 75 pounds of cocaine with a street value of $3 million moved through the area each week. Finnegan finds that almost everybody has a friend or relative who is in prison because of the bust. As in New Haven, local poverty makes the temptation and easy money of drug dealing irresistible to some. There is the added accusation that the former local sheriff failed to pursue suspected drug dealers and users, although lengthy investigations failed to turn up any evidence of this.

In this section of his book, Finnegan does not focus on one of the accused dealers or suspected drug abusers. He gets to know the life of Lanee Mitchell, a twenty-three-year-old black divorced mother who faces a long commute to the Tyson chicken plant each day and nostalgically dreams of the rural past of her ancestors. As Finnegan discovers, however, those old days were hardly better, as they were filled with terrorism and financial ruin brought about by jealous, racist whites. Indeed, Finnegan discovers that a current of racism still exists among the white citizens who control the town and among local law-enforcement officials. Again, Finnegan traces the history of the area, which he finds representative more of a southern way of life than a western one, and finds a region in economic decline that will never see better days. Aside from the "entrepreneurs" who went to jail for their involvement with drugs, only those who leave the area meet with any measure of success. Young African Americans have less opportunity than those of their parents' generation and continue to face discrimination and active resistance to their attempts to make a better life for themselves.

In the third section, Finnegan traveled to the Yakima Valley in central Washington State to examine the lives of teenaged Mexican Americans. Here we meet Juan Guerrero, who suffers from the strongest sense of loss and aimlessness. Juan is a gang member and street fighter who cannot relate to the union organizing efforts of his parents, Rosa and Rafael, who work picking grapes for a local winery. Juan rejects all aspects of his "Mexican" cultural heritage, from food and music to clothing styles. He refuses his parents' desire to send him to Mexico to live with relatives, where they hope he will stay out of trouble. It is clear that Juan's culture stems from the liberal consumerism that Finnegan discussed earlier.

The better life that Rosa and Rafael hoped to find in the United States eludes their troubled son. This is the shortest section of the book, perhaps because Juan does not seem to ever really open up to Finnegan, as did his other contacts. Juan drifts through his life without any real plans or aspirations, laying low at his parents' house when rival gang members are after him. He is attached only to the loyal friend who fights beside him; even his girlfriends are expendable. He is bright but does not care to apply himself to his studies. Finnegan encourages Juan to travel, offering him some money and places stay with friends along the way. Instead of inspiring Juan, however, this leads only to his celebration of rootlessness and detachment.

The final section explores the lives of white teenaged skinheads in the Antelope Valley, north of Los Angeles. Lancaster, California, is a suburban nightmare of unfinished developments and children left to roam unattended while their parents commute great distances and work long hours or abuse drugs in their own despair. Finnegan discovers a rabid racist climate in the Antelope Valley, which is filled with skinhead gangs who war with each other and carry out racist attacks on minorities. One skinhead group claims that it is "antiracist" and even has a half-African American member. This causes the neo-Nazi skinhead gang to constantly battle the antiracists.

Mindy Turner, Finnegan's contact in this case, is a seventeen-year-old girl who spent time in the neo-Nazi gang and now has renounced her racism and attempted to join the antiracists. Such abandonment of her first gang is resented, however, and she is attacked by a girl gang member and constantly threatened. She is devastated when one of the antiracists kills a neo-Nazi, who has crashed their party along with some of his fellow gang members. Mindy is also fond of corresponding with skinheads in prison, although she cannot articulate her reasons for doing so. Finnegan reports the widespread epidemic of methamphetamine use in the Antelope Valley, both by teenagers and their parents, which contributes to violence, especially child abuse. The booming growth in the area has outstripped the means to support it, and the downward trend is evident. People who relocated to escape the troubles of Los Angeles found themselves trapped when home prices fell. A general feeling of despair pervades the area.

Although Finnegan manages to avoid being present at most of the illegal happenings, he does attend a ska concert, the favorite music of the skinheads, and witnesses a melee between rival skinhead gangs. He is also intimidated by some of the neo-Nazi skinheads when he encounters them in public. He sees the roots of their anger and racism in their abandonment by their parents and society. Many of the skinheads claim that their movement is all about a certain kind of music and fashion, but their beliefs reveal strong political positions, usually arrived at without the benefit of historical research. Finnegan sees their anger and violence and tries to say that it is not their fault. He blames the hedonistic generation that preceded theirs (his own generation) for the teenagers' failures. The taxpayers turned their backs on young people when they voted to lower tax payments that once supported schools and universities.

William Finnegan's *Cold New World* is a powerful book that describes a trend in communities across the nation that should concern every American. Finnegan shows that America is moving inexorably toward a great separation of classes; the gulf between the haves and the have-nots is increasing and the social sympathies that once offered relief are in disfavor. The worst part of this is that these teenagers seem all too aware of their position and the constricting of opportunity. It is thus no wonder that they turn to the immediate pleasures of their lives, music, sex, and drugs, for consolation. Without a strong social culture and adult involvement in their lives, they find their identity with gangs. If only the economically powerful could read this book and find in it a reason to turn from capitalist greed back to a struggle for equality. But would they? Finnegan points his finger at government as well as individuals. He shows how the social programs of the past bought America a "golden age" of American prosperity. He is not sure that the globalization of corporations can be called to account but hopes that a renewed labor union movement might work.

Patricia Masserman

Sources for Further Study

Booklist. XCIV, May 15, 1998, p. 1570.
Business Week. June 1, 1998, p. 26.
Dissent. XLV, Summer, 1998, p. 104.
Library Journal. CXXIII, June 1, 1998, p. 137.
The New York Review of Books. XLV, July 16, 1998, p. 12.
The New York Times Book Review. CIII, June 14, 1998, p. 9.
Publishers Weekly. CCXLV, April 13, 1998, p. 63.
Time. CLI, May 25, 1998, p. 80.
The Village Voice. May 12, 1998, p. 135.
The Washington Post Book World. XXVIII, June 28, 1998, p. 7.

COMMANDING HEIGHTS
The Battle Between Government and the Marketplace
That Is Remaking the Modern World

Authors: Daniel Yergin and Joseph Stanislaw
Published: Simon & Schuster (New York). 457 pp. $26.00
Type of work: History, economics, and current affairs
Time: The 1980's and 1990's

A wide-ranging and inclusive discussion of the revival of the competitive market system at the end of the twentieth century

Daniel Yergin is president of the Cambridge Energy Research Associates, the vice chairman of Global Decisions Group, and a prominent consultant on the international scene. His *The Prize: The Epic Quest for Oil, Money, and Power* was the recipient of the Pulitzer Prize and was made into an eight-part Public Broadcasting System television series. He has also written about the Cold War in *Shattered Peace* and co-authored *Russia 2010*, on the future of noncommunist Russia, as well as *Energy Future* and *Global Insecurity*. His co-author, Joseph Stanislaw, is an adviser on international markets to both governments and businesses.

Like *The Prize*, *Commanding Heights* ranges across the world, includes many prominent personalities, and features numerous historical anecdotes. Both studies, while organized on a historical basis, speak to current events: history becoming the present. In *Commanding Heights*, the authors tell the story of the world's economies, particularly since the end of World War II, and argue the revolutionary importance of the change from government planning and governmental-political control of national economies to the revival of the competitive market system as the world's dominant economic engine.

Their story opens in Moscow's Izmailovo outdoor market in the early 1990's, where anything and everything was for sale, from czarist memorabilia to South Korean electronics. For Yergin and Stanislaw, this was symbolic of the beginning of a return to Russia of the market economy. Ironically, also available at the Izmailovo market as historical curiosities were pins bearing the face of Vladimir Ilich Lenin; the title, *Commanding Heights*, refers to a statement made by Lenin in 1922 at the time of the adoption of the Soviet Union's New Economic Policy, which allowed for limited private trade and agriculture and thus represented a step back from the anticipated communist utopia. Lenin was attacked by his Marxist colleagues for backtracking, but he argued that the state would still continue to control the "commanding heights," or the most important elements in the economy. In time, particularly after the Great Depression of the 1930's and World War II, the idea that the state or the government must hold the "commanding heights" of the nation's economy was widely accepted, and not only within the communist bloc. Great Britain and the other countries of Western Europe increasingly moved into what was called the "mixed economy," a combination of capitalism and socialism, and India and much of the Third World also nationalized key industries, communications systems, banks, and financial institutions, concomitantly expanding the welfare state. Where public ownership was less the resort, as in the United States, then heavy government regulation of the economy was the result. By the late 1980's, the Soviet system, with its state-controlled economic system, failed, and the Soviet Union imploded. An era had come to an end, not only the end of communism but also of government domination of national economies in general.

The authors pursue a historical survey of how so many individuals and governments had come to believe that the market system had failed. They find the explanation in the Communist Revolution, the Great Depression, and the challenges of World War II: laissez-faire capitalism no longed worked. Ideas have consequences, according to the authors, not least those of John Maynard Keynes, who contended that governments, through spending policies, deficit financing, and taxation, could successfully guide a nation's economy. The victory of Great Britain's Labour Party in 1945 was a notable sign of changed perceptions and approaches; on the opposite side of the world, when India achieved independence in 1947, Jawaharlal Nehru, the new prime minister, pushed Britain's former "jewel in the crown" into the socialist orbit. Yet it was not merely socialists and others on the left who became converts to government control. The otherwise conservative Charles de Gaulle of France claimed that the state "must hold the levers of command," and Britain's Conservative prime minister Harold Macmillan noted, "You [the voters] have never had it so good." In the United States, the Republican Richard Nixon supported full employment through government programs, wage and price controls, and a Cost of Living Council, commenting, perhaps ironically, "Now, I am a Keynesian."

By the 1980's, however, the economies of many of the world's nations were stagnating and even declining. Events were important. The oil embargoes hurt many national economies, and the increasing use of computer technology was reducing the isolation and independence of the individual nation state or ideological groupings such as the communist bloc. Yet the authors argue that ideas also played a crucial role in restoring the market as the alternative to government ownership, nationalization, socialism, or regulation. In this context, the sainted heirs of Adam Smith were Friedrich von Hayek, author of the 1944 book *The Road to Serfdom*, and Milton Friedman and the other free-market economists associated with the University of Chicago. In 1979, Britain's Conservative Party, led by Margaret Thatcher and her intellectual market guru Keith Joseph, defeated the Labour Party with the slogan, "Labour is not working." Thatcher and Joseph are among Yergin and Stanislaw's chief heroes. Not only did they break the consensus that had existed for several decades about the necessity of government domination of the economy, but they also did so against great odds in what appeared to be a quixotic quest. By the end of the 1990's, a market-oriented Britain led by Prime Minister Tony Blair, whose Labour Party had accepted the Thatcherite revolution and abandoned its long commitment to nationalization, was outperforming the economies of most of the countries of Western Europe, which were slower in moving into the competitive market system.

Southeast Asia's economic emergence receives much discussion, particularly in contrast to the economic failures in the communist world, Africa, and Latin America. However, as befits a study that comments on current trends and developments, the authors note that the so-called Asian miracle has recently become less miraculous, beginning with economic troubles in Japan that are ascribed to bureaucratic interference, an inflated property market, and lending policies based on political rather than market considerations. As Japan sneezed, the little tigers of Asia caught cold, bringing on the currency crash of 1997. In its aftermath, the authors contend, a new balance between the government and the marketplace will be necessary, with less political control and more market independence. Communist China is a special case, still ideologically socialist but in reality becoming increasingly capitalist—a condition justified by Deng Xiaoping as "socialism with Chinese characteristics." How the contradiction between China's economic freedoms and the lack of political liberty available under its authoritarian political system is resolved will perhaps be the key to the twenty-first century.

During their research, Yergin and Stanislaw interviewed more than eighty people, including such notables as Britain's Thatcher, Russia's Yegor Gaidar, Germany's Helmut Schmidt, Peru's Alberto Fujimori, and America's Friedman. While this brings a valuable personal dimension to the story, the result is that *Commanding Heights* is often told from the top down, from the perspective of economists and leading politicians. However, the authors also have an eye for the small but revealing incident. When formerly communist Poland adopted the market system, there was almost no market. The initial results were product shortages and a sudden rise in prices. Eggs were the key: If the price of eggs stabilized, the program would be a success. It did, and the market reformers breathed a sigh of relief.

According to the authors, Ronald Reagan's contribution to the market revolution was perhaps more symbolic than actual. The conservative Reagan had long campaigned against the powers of government, claiming that government was more the problem than the solution. Yet he was relatively illiterate when it came to economics, and Yergin and Stanislaw argue that Keynesian economic policies remained in force in the early years of the Reagan administration through the concept of supply-side economics. The result was a massive increase in the national debt, which was compounded by the military buildup that occurred during the 1980's. In the worldwide market revolution, Thatcher's significance would prove to be greater than Reagan's.

If the balance is shifting back toward Adam Smith's "invisible hand" and the primacy of the market, a process accompanied by privatization and deregulation, what will be the functions of government in the future of what is becoming a global economy? The authors argue that government's functions will be reduced, but still essential, particularly in education, the environment, and the security of citizens. Is the turn to markets permanent? While strongly in favor of the market revolution, the authors remark that there is nothing inevitable about the future. They offer several cautionary notes. Admitting that the market makes for greater disparities of income, they warn that the system must ensure fairness and opportunity, which in part are determined by the equitability of the legal system. Also, national identity and values must be accommodated in a world that includes more than forty thousand multinational firms. Environmental protection must be pursued, in both the first and the third worlds. The market must assist in finding solutions to the demographic changes taking place now and into the twenty-first century, especially the welfare challenges of an aging population. Above all, the market must be successful economically in what the authors call "delivering the goods"—and not merely to the few at the top.

Commanding Heights is ambitious and largely successful. Serviceably written, it provides the general reader with a satisfactory historical survey of today's most important revolution, the market revolution. Yergin and Stanislaw believe in the primacy of a market economy, and the book is written to support their thesis. At times, because they attempt so much—in essence, the book is a history of the world during the past fifty years—there is a repetitiveness in the restatement of their thesis and their findings. What they do not do is to provide a balanced or in-depth critique of the dangers, if any, implicit in the market revolution. They warn of certain challenges, which are momentous, but only briefly, and then suggest few solutions. Others are less confident; John Gray's recent *False Dawn: The Delusions of Global Capitalism*, for example, argues that the imposition of global capitalism will ultimately create disaster on the scale of Soviet communism. Yet, of course, that was not the story that Yergin and Stanislaw set out to tell. *Commanding Heights* is a valuable contribution from the pro-market perspective, with many of the strengths and a few of the weaknesses to be expected of a work that seeks to interpret the recent past as it transitions into the near future.

Eugene Larson

Sources for Further Study

Commentary. CV, April, 1998, p. 62.
Commonweal. CXXV, April 24, 1998, p. 26.
The Economist. CCCXLVII, April 18, 1998, p. S5.
Foreign Affairs. LXXVII, January, 1998, p. 135.
Fortune. CXXXVIII, August 3, 1998, p. 48.
The Nation. CCLXVII, July 6, 1998, p. 42.
The New York Review of Books. XLV, October 8, 1998, p. 32.
The New York Times Book Review. CIII, February 8, 1998, p. 7.
Publishers Weekly. CCXLV, January 26, 1998, p. 81.
Washington Monthly. XXX, March, 1998, p. 39.

CONFEDERATES IN THE ATTIC
Dispatches from the Unfinished Civil War

Author: Tony Horwitz (1958-   )
Published: Pantheon Books (New York). Illustrated. 406 pp. $27.50
Type of work: History, autobiography, and current affairs
Time: The 1990's
Locale: The Southern United States

An account of journalist Tony Horwitz's travels through the South as he examines the Southern memory of the Civil War and its effects on the culture and society of the region

> *Principal personages:*
> TONY HORWITZ, journalist
> ROBERT LEE HODGE, Civil War "hardcore" reenactor
> SHELBY FOOTE, historian and author
> MICHAEL WESTERMAN, murder victim
> ROBERT E. LEE, Southern general
> THOMAS J. "STONEWALL" JACKSON, Southern general

At the beginning of the last decade of the twentieth century, Tony Horwitz woke in his Virginia home to the sounds of the Civil War. This is the beginning point of Horwitz's engaging and revealing examination of the significance presently attached to the "War Against Northern Aggression" in the American South. Like V. S. Naipaul's *A Turn in the South* (1989) and Jonathan Raban's *Hunting Mister Heartbreak: A Discovery of America* (1992), *Confederates in the Attic* gives an outsider's view of this contradictory place called the South, a place of both geographical and mythological origins. Horwitz is the descendant of Russian Jews who came to America at the beginning of the century. He grew up in the industrial North, but, like his grandfather before him, Horwitz was fascinated by the Civil War and found himself drawn inexplicably to the Confederate side. He tells us that as a child he pored over Mathew Brady photographs, read aloud with his father from the ten-volume collection *The Photographic History of the Civil War* (1911), and even constructed a panoramic mural, his own "cyclorama," of Civil War battles on the walls of his attic. Growing up, he lost interest in the history, although he spent some time as a student activist in Mississippi. He later became a Pulitzer-prize winning journalist stationed in such places as Bosnia, Iraq, and Australia. Upon returning to America, he moved to the hills of northern Virginia, and there it is that "the Civil War crashed into my bedroom," waking him both literally and figuratively into a world of memory and loss.

It is easy to make fun of the South, in part because Southerners are so quick to do it themselves. Southern humor is, of course, often a form of self-protection, but it is usually insightful and honest as well. Southerners, both black and white, are masters of the put-on, of giving strangers what they perhaps unknowingly expect, of seeming to confirm broad, biased assumptions while slyly undercutting those assumptions with a look, a tone, or a verbal wink. For this reason, books on the South written by non-Southerners are sometimes uncertain in their own tone. It takes a while to learn the language. Such is the case with this book. When Horwitz, for example, visits a Confederate museum in Charleston, S. C., he writes, "Every item in the museum seemed to carry a similarly Gothic tale, told with the same blend of decorum and dirt that left me guessing whether [the curator, June Wells] meant to praise or skewer her subjects." This uncertainty, freely admitted as it is, is reassuring, for it indicates a reporter who is willing to let the story tell itself, not impose the narrative from outside. One of the growing charms of this book is the personage of Horwitz himself, a man who is openly conflicted and yet honestly sympathetic and understanding. As a Jew, he is offended by the anti-Semitism he sometimes encounters. As a liberal humanist, he is repulsed by the racism and bigotry that so often shows itself. And yet, ironically (as he clearly realizes), the one moment he gives in to angry frustration occurs near the end of the book in an argument with a black woman who is director of the Voting Rights Museum in Selma, Alabama. "But the South had changed on me," he writes, "or I'd changed on it. My passion for Civil War history and the kinship I felt for Southerners who shared it kept bumping into racism and right-wing politics. And here I was in Selma, after holding my temper with countless white supremacists, losing it with a black woman whose passion I'd initially admired." Such a moment, so contradictory and nevertheless so revealing of the complexities of the evolving South, makes Horwitz's journey all the more compelling. There are no easy answers.

Horwitz is first induced to undertake these travels of discovery through his meeting with Robert Lee Hodge, a "hardcore" Civil War reenactor (a word Hodge disdains). Hodge, whose portrait graces the cover of the book, is one of many quirky and yet quite real characters Horwitz meets. Unlike some works of this type, *Confederates in the Attic* avoids the impression that the author is condescending to the eccentricities of the "characters" he meets, although many of them are, indeed, eccentric. Rather, Horwitz seems thoroughly open to different points of view, respectful if not accepting, understanding that the reader is able to make individual judgments without the prodding of the narrator. Most of these people appear only once and are gone, but Hodge is the figure that holds the book together. A self-described fanatic on the war, Hodge waits tables during the week and freelances Civil War articles to support his chosen way of life as a Southern soldier, one for whom authenticity goes far beyond clothes and weapons, even to the portrayal of death itself. "As the Marlon Brando of battlefield bloating, he was often hired for Civil War movies," Horwitz writes (employing a sense of humor that serves him well throughout the book). Hodge introduces Horwitz to the art of battlefield reenactment, but, more important, he reveals the passion with which some of these people have invested themselves in a time and history lost to many. Horwitz travels with Hodge on an intensive "Civil Wargasm," a road trip that tries to cram as many miles and battlefields as possible into a short period of time. Pushing past the point of exhaustion (to compromise in any way is to "farb out"); going without bathing, change of clothes, and convenience food; sneaking onto national parks through the woods at night so that they might experience sleeping on the very ground soaked with soldier blood a century and a quarter earlier, Horwitz and Hodge achieve a kind of crazy sympathy and awareness that is nevertheless true.

"That's the epitome of the Gasm," Horwitz quotes Hodge. "So much stuff that you can't possibly take it all in, and you don't know what to do with it anyway. So you just let it wash over you."

Readers of this book will have a similar experience, for there is a lot to consider in Horwitz's journey. He begins in North Carolina, where he meets almost stereotypical followers of the Old South mythology—they salute the Confederate flag and hold quizzes on Confederate trivia—and then moves on to Charleston, South Carolina, where the war officially began with the firing on Fort Sumter. There he also encounters odd folk: "Idiosyncrasy was a point of pride in Charleston," he writes. By this point, readers might well think that Horwitz intends to follow the same path trod so successfully by John Berendt in *Midnight in the Garden of Good and Evil* (1994), substituting eccentric Charleston gentry for those of Savannah. What follows, however, is a surprise and a relief. In the next chapter, Horwitz travels to Guthrie, Kentucky, the childhood home of novelist and poet Robert Penn Warren. Horwitz is drawn there not because of Warren but because of a murder, the killing of a young local white, Michael Westerman, by a black teenager from the North who had been sent south to remove him from bad city influences. This section is deeply troubling on many fronts—racial, social, and ideological. Horwitz feels more out of place in this rural, Appalachian area than in any other region he visits during his exploration; he is afraid of these reclusive hill people, of whom Westerman was a part. He is more easily sympathetic with the young killer and the boy's mother, for they fit his preconception of the displaced and dismissed who seemed trapped by violence. By the end of his stay, Horwitz is baffled, admitting that there are no simple answers to such problems. "Dying for Dixie" gives the book a moral weight that keeps it grounded through the rest of Horwitz's travels.

Prejudice is ultimately the central focus of the book, as it has to be, and Horwitz's own biases are as forthrightly examined as are the more obvious ones the reader might expect to find. As a Northerner, the grandchild of a Russian immigrant, and a Jew, Horwitz nevertheless admits his romantic attachment to the "Lost Cause," even as an adult. He understands why some Southerners (not limited by social class) might find a sense of self-worth and identity in such a myth. He also recognizes, however, that much of the belief is a myth and that it has been used for despicable purposes. One of the recurring disputes he encounters is the displaying of the Confederate flag and the playing of "Dixie," a debate that tends to divide along racial lines. For one group this is a point of honor, for another, a reminder of systematized degradation. The book offers Horwitz the opportunity to talk through such problems, to reveal his own conflicting ideas, and thereby to encourage his readers to do the same. The author's meeting with historian-novelist Shelby Foote, whose three-volume *The Civil War: A Narrative* (1958, 1963, 1974) and whose appearance in Ken Burns's enormously popular documentary television series (1990) have made him the spokesman of popular choice on things pertaining to the war, illustrates the complexity of these debates. Foote, as thoughtful and reasonable a voice as one might hope to find, astonishes Horwitz with some of his conclusions. He offers a modified defense of the

Ku Klux Klan and admires its founder, Nathan Bedford Forrest. He also argues that the Confederate battle flag should be seen as a "combat standard, not a political symbol." "Slavery was the first great sin of this nation. . . . The second great sin was emancipation, or rather the way it was done," Foote says, condemning the abuses of Reconstruction. His conclusion that African Americans "are fulfilling every dire prophecy the Ku Klux Klan made. It's no longer safe to be on the streets in black neighborhoods. They are acting as if the utter lie about blacks being somewhere between ape and man were true" surprises Horwitz and, no doubt, the reader as well.

Ultimately, however, what Horwitz discovers is that, with the exception of small enclaves of reenactors, history buffs, and unreconstructed rebels, memory of the Civil War is either distorted beyond recognition or simply lost. As he points out, this momentous occurrence is no longer taught in high schools, or is done so with such brevity that the lesson becomes a mockery of the reality. He is also terribly disheartened by the prejudice he finds on both sides of the ideological fence. A group of black students suggests that he title his book "Rednecks of the South," "Crackers of the South," or simply "Bigots" or "Peckerwoods." The Civil War means nothing to them, since for them little seems to have changed. When Horwitz argues, "Blacks fought in the War and slavery ended because of it," one student responds, "No it didn't. . . . We just don't call it slavery anymore." As he leaves, Horwitz records that "it saddened me that I sometimes felt like an enemy on the premises, among both whites and blacks."

The book ends on such a rueful note. "But while my travels had brought me to some understanding of others' obsession, I still felt strangely unable to explain my own," Horwitz concludes. Nevertheless, his book should be read for the questions it asks rather than for the answers it cannot give. It is, in full, a fine example of social reporting and cultural analysis, a major contribution to the ongoing national debate on race, region, and culture.

Edwin T. Arnold

Sources for Further Study

Booklist. XCIV, February 1, 1998, p. 895.
The Economist. CCCXLVII, June 13, 1998, p. S15.
Historic Traveler. V, November, 1998, p. 64.
Library Journal. CXXIII, February 1, 1998, p. 99.
National Review. L, June 22, 1998, p. 61.
The New York Times Book Review. CIII, April 5, 1998, p. 7.
Newsweek. CXXXI, April 13, 1998, p. 77.
Publishers Weekly. CCXLV, January 5, 1998, p. 48.
The Wall Street Journal. April 2, 1998, p. A20.
The Wilson Quarterly. XXII, Spring, 1998, p. 108.

CONQUESTS AND CULTURES
An International History

Author: Thomas Sowell (1930-   )
Published: Basic Books (New York). 493 pp. $35.00
Type of work: History
Time: 200 B.C. to the present

Sowell posits that conquests can have positive as well as negative effects on cultures; he argues that often it is the cultural response of the conquered, not the attitude or intent of the conqueror, that determines whether the subject society prospers

There is nothing particularly new in Thomas Sowell's books except the willingness to state boldly facts and theories that run counter to conventional wisdom. Among his currently unfashionable ideas is the proposition that the histories of individual groups and states conform to general patterns of human behavior. *Conquests and Cultures* completes the trilogy begun in 1994 with *Race and Culture* and followed in 1996 by *Migrations and Culture.* The thesis of all three is that "racial, ethnic, and national groups have their own respective cultures, without which their economic and social histories cannot be understood." These cultures represent traits that can be useful or even necessary in one time or place and that tend to persist even when the conditions that produced them change. In some cases, this gives advantages to one group in competition with others; in other cases, it places a group at a tremendous disadvantage.

The theme Sowell elaborates in this volume is the impact of conquest upon subject peoples. Again, this is nothing particularly new—historians have long deplored the horrible process by which the Romans acquired their empire, then gone on to praise the long-term benefits of peace and good government that the *Pax Romana* brought to all their subjects. As one character in the 1979 film comedy *Monty Python's Life of Brian* asked, "apart from the sanitation, the medicine, education, wine, public order, irrigation, roads, a fresh water system, and public health, what have the Romans ever done for us?" Peace, of course. Modern nationalists, like ancient ones, say that this is not enough: better to live in independent anarchy and poverty than to be ruled by foreigners.

In one provocative passage after another, Sowell demonstrates that European colonialism had similar impacts wherever it appeared: short-term horrors in the beginning, followed by long-term benefits. Even more provocatively, he gives the colonialists the benefit of having some good intentions in acquiring their empires, especially the British desire to end the slave trade. It was certainly not money that motivated most colonialists, because colonies cost money, and the colonial powers gave independence to their conquered subjects quickly once World War II eliminated the surplus wealth that had allowed them the luxury of overseas empires.

Did the colonies bring in wealth? Not unless you fudge the facts, as did Lenin, by mixing in European investment in the United States with investment in backward regions. The evidence suggests that the colonies were the beneficiaries of European largess rather than sources of European prosperity. Sowell's arguments rest essentially on common sense rather than abstruse economic analysis. If the colonial states had been plundered of their wealth by the Europeans, then the post-colonial states should have been wealthier once they attained independence and the European states poorer. In fact, almost universally, the opposite occurred.

Sowell does not linger to discuss the theories of neo-colonialism, which he considers self-serving propaganda by leftists and nationalists. He blames the poverty of post-colonial states on the political, social, and economic policies adopted by the new rulers—policies they learned from European intellectuals and academics in their youth. In effect, the post-colonial world served as a gigantic social laboratory that revealed how destructive state control is, no matter how noble or idealistic the motivations are.

On the other hand, freedom by itself is no guarantee of prosperity. Freedom is only a condition that allows group characteristics to flourish or mutate. Sowell admires groups, especially minorities, that consciously make the adaptations to new circumstances that permit them first to survive, then to prosper. The Roman and British models demonstrate that economic and social freedom, but not political freedom or democracy, most assuredly are essential conditions for the potential to make successful adaptations.

Why are some groups more creatively successful than others? In a thoroughly old-fashioned manner, Sowell insists that the most important determining factor on culture has been geography. In his most brilliant chapter, Sowell demonstrates that Africa really never had a chance to create the kind of civilization that could defend itself against exploitation by Arabs and Europeans. First of all, there was a lack of navigable waterways that could facilitate trade. Second, disease made it impossible to have draft animals over much of the continent, so that goods could be transported only by human beings; this also meant that animals could not be used for farming and fertilizer. Third, the highly variable rainfall produced regions of flooding and regions of repeated droughts. Since urban life could not develop fully, much of Africa remained in rural poverty. The only easily transportable wealth was in slaves, which were sold by the dominant tribes in large numbers first to the Arab world, then to Europeans. The Arab trade was twice as large as the European, began earlier, and lasted until the European powers abolished it.

Sowell dwells on the antislavery movement in the West because it is central to his argument that conquest sometimes brings benefits to subject peoples. What economic benefits did an abolition of slavery bring to the West? If the Leninist argument were correct, the colonial powers should have extended slavery, not curtailed it; they should never have abandoned the colonies just as wages were rising at home. Sowell answers his own questions, saying that sometimes Western civilization does things because they are right, no matter what the consequences.

Why is such an argument so rare? "Moral intimidation" is one reason, responds Sowell. No one wants to be an "apologist" for Western civilization. Another is the belief that "society" is at fault for everything that goes wrong. Sowell snorts, why then is "society" not given credit when some group prospers? Sowell insists on going beyond the political posturing to look at the facts, and the facts do little credit to those who insist on the primacy of current theories about human behavior and the use of state power to modify that behavior.

Sowell resolutely believes in the ability of groups to modify their cultural characteristics. Again and again, he demonstrates that traits that worked well, say for the Indians in North America, are fatal if the group persists in maintaining them in a farming or industrial society. In such a context, there is simply no place for a culture that insists that men are hunters and warriors who cannot stoop to women's work as farmers and factory workers, that rejects education and the discipline of the workplace. Sowell demonstrates that given equal education, white, black, and Native American men earn essentially the same annual incomes; the income differences for the groups as a whole represent differences in education. Frustrating as it might be that some groups refuse to study science, to open small businesses, or to save money, Sowell notes that there is always some group, usually a minority, that is willing to step into the gaps.

The various responses to conquest are not racial phenomena. Russians fit the pattern perfectly. For centuries, Russian rulers have despaired about popular resistance to progress; in frustration, they turned to brute force in an effort to speed up the process of change. In the end, however, they always ended up allowing minorities (Jews, Germans, Armenians) to be the merchants, artisans, and middlemen. Medieval Polish and Czech rulers, unable to persuade their subjects to move out of farming, invited Germans and Jews to develop the mines, drain the swamps, and found the cities. What was the fate of the Slavic people for this long-term backwardness? To give their name to the very word "slave." What was the cause of this backwardness? Geography is a partial answer: The more isolated a region was by virtue of its mountains or vast plains, the more likely it was to be impoverished and to be raided by its neighbors for human merchandise.

The great empires provided the one essential ingredient for progress: peace. People who ceased to fear invasion and domestic turmoil could farm the lands that were once military borders, they could transport goods in safety, and they could give more time and energy to art, music, religion, and philosophy. In addition, great empires provided the means for people and ideas to move about, enriching each subject people to the fullest extent that the group allowed itself to evolve. This cross-fertilization meant that, for example, when the British fought the Iroquois, the British had the advantage of materials and traditions drawn from across the world, while the Indians had only their own culture upon which to draw. The conclusion was foreordained, the process being merely speeded up by the terrible impact of infectious disease.

Sowell has little patience with those who attribute every evil of conquest to evil motives. It was the gentle priest who went from the bedside of the ill to the baptism of children who spread disease, not the cynical conquistador whose ethos prized victory in battle and whose interests were in enslaving or taxing the defeated peoples, not in annihilating them. Nor has he sympathy for those who argue that minorities are by definition innocent victims. The facts are otherwise. No race, no ethnic group, and no religious body has a monopoly upon good and evil; in fact, Sowell argues, the West comes out pretty well in the game of comparative victimization.

He makes the point strongly that adverse judgments about groups cannot be waved aside as prejudice and stereotypes. Cultural characteristics do exist. Yet since they probably have little or nothing to do with genetics, racism is an overrated explanation. Rather, socially transmitted traits reflect the "cultural capital" that developed in particular circumstances and that persists despite the changes in the world. One can explain the origins of cultural capital from geography and history, but it is foolish to expect that ideological explanations will assist any group to escape the economic and social consequences of persisting in behaviors that are not appropriate to changing conditions. Instead, human capital has to be more intelligently invested and preserved. If education is the key to success, then a group has to see to it that its youth achieves education. Racism vanishes after a group achieves economic success, not before.

There are no "pure" races left, nor many pure cultures. Efforts by groups to maintain purity result only in isolation, which historically makes them vulnerable to conquest and today leads only to poverty. The hope for the future lies in those educated people on every continent who share in a common world culture. As the concepts of personal freedom that lie at the foundation of Western civilization spread across the world, the totalitarian ideologies of racism and social planning recede. The opportunities are now present. Yet Sowell reminds us that it has rarely been opportunities that have been lacking, but rather the willingness of people to take advantage of those opportunities.

William L. Urban

Sources for Further Study

Booklist. XCIV, April 15, 1998, p. 1401.
Forbes. CLXII, July 6, 1998, p. 52.
Foreign Affairs. LXXVII, July, 1998, p. 122.
Headway. X, September, 1998, p. 14.
Library Journal. CXXIII, May 1, 1998, p. 116.
National Review. L, June 1, 1998, p. 50.
The New Republic. CCXVIII, November 16, 1998, p. 36.
Publishers Weekly. CCXLV, April 6, 1998, p. 68.
Reason. XXX, December, 1998, p. 70.
The Wall Street Journal. May 19, 1998, p. A20.

CONSILIENCE
The Unity of Knowledge

Author: Edward O. Wilson (1929-   )
Published: Alfred A. Knopf (New York). 332 pp. $26.00
Type of work: Science

Wilson argues that all knowledge is ultimately unified and that the search for that unity should form the next great wave in intellectual endeavor; ultimately, such a search is not merely an academic exercise but may well determine whether humans as a species can make the wise choices necessary to their biological and ethical survival

Edward O. Wilson's latest book borrows its title and central term "consilience" from the nineteenth century writer William Whewell. He prefers this term over such alternatives as "coherence" because it is less ambiguous; by it, he means "the intrinsic unity of knowledge"—not merely in the natural sciences but in all branches of learning, from physics and chemistry to the social sciences and the humanities, including ethics and religion. At present, consilience is an assumption, a working hypothesis, that has proven itself in the natural sciences, "from quantum physics to the brain sciences and evolutionary biology," and that is beginning to make itself felt in the interdisciplinary study of the human brain being carried out by biologists and psychologists. Much of Wilson's book is devoted to arguing that this assumption is being proven true across more and more disciplines and hence should be pursued as a goal in areas currently considered vastly different from and perhaps even hostile to the natural sciences.

After defining his terms and setting his goal, Wilson begins his argument by surveying the goals and methods of the Enlightenment, that period in Western intellectual history beginning (according to Wilson) with Francis Bacon's insistence on inductive reasoning and ending symbolically with the death of the Marquis de Condorcet (1743-1794) in a filthy prison cell, victim of the Reign of Terror. The goals of the Enlightenment were to free men's minds from superstition and to pursue knowledge in all of its forms with objectivity and rigor. The methods that proved most successful were scientific reductionism (dividing the subject of inquiry into smaller and smaller constituent parts) and mathematical modeling. Sir Isaac Newton's studies in light and gravity are among the highest achievements of Enlightenment thinking. The Enlightenment ideal of scientific objectivity and the unity of all learning was overthrown by the Romantic Revolt and its emphasis on subjectivity and feeling, the mystical and ineffable. Jean-Jacques Rousseau, William Wordsworth, and Johann Wolfgang von Goethe engineered the split that still exists between the sciences and humanities, what C. P. Snow called, "the two cultures." Its most extreme manifestation is postmodernism, with its insistence upon knowledge as a mere "construct," having no objective validity or verifiability.

Much of Wilson's survey of the Enlightenment and its aftermath will be familiar to readers of Jacob Bronowski and James Burke—or to viewers of their respective television series. Few readers will object to Wilson's overview of the history of science or to his biologist's perspective on the evolution of the human brain and its improbable but real abilities to do science. But Wilson unabashedly asserts that science produces genuine knowledge (not merely momentarily accepted constructs), that its history is a story of progress (a very unfashionable word), and that its methods can lead to objective truth: "Criteria of objective truth might be attainable through empirical investigation. The key lies in clarifying the still poorly understood operations composing the mind and in improving the piecemeal approach science has taken to its material properties."

Wilson attempts to show how the quest for consilience through the understanding of the workings of the mind can shed light on dreams—the basis of both creative and insane thought. Rejecting Sigmund Freud, Wilson outlines the physiology of dreaming and attempts to show how an understanding of the brain's chemistry can shed light on this universal phenomenon. Key to his claims for consilience is the belief that if we understand the workings of the mind, we will have found the vital link between all forms of knowledge, for the mind is the seat of all we know and can know. Here, Wilson's argument becomes (for the layman at least) technical and hard to follow. His description of what is currently known about how the brain works is as clear as could be expected, but it is still not easy for the neophyte to digest. Most readers will have to take it on faith that Wilson's description is accurate. Perhaps the most interesting and revealing part of this discussion is Wilson's explication of the place of feeling in thought, his meditations on the self, and his argument for the existence of free will.

Another central step on the road to consilience is the place where Apollo meets Dionysus—at the intersection of reason and feeling, science and art. The polarization of these two impulses leads to the perpetual war of nature versus nurture, a conflict that Wilson resolves by arguing that the two are not opposites but complements. He calls this the "gene-culture coevolution," meaning that human evolution has helped to direct culture and that culture, in turn, has helped to direct evolution. This is a record that science has only begun to trace. The basic unit of genetically based culture Wilson calls a "meme." It is the central concept in linking science and the humanities. Since we cannot perform controlled experiments on humans, and because only a few genes that affect behavior have been identified, at the moment we must work within the limit of "*heritability*, the percentage of variation in the trait due to heredity," those traits that have been studied by comparing the behavior of separated pairs of identical twins and the genetic basis of diseases such as cystic fibrosis. Examples of the genetic basis of behavior include the universality of certain human reflexes and the language of facial expressions. Such epigenetic rules as have been discovered lend credence to the idea that culture has arisen from our genes and that for a full understanding of ourselves the humanities and sciences must cooperate.

Wilson expands on this link between biology and culture by summarizing ideas he advanced in *Genes, Mind, and Culture* (1981) and *Sociobiology* (1975). He argues for the existence of human nature and demonstrates another link between genetics and culture by referring to Edward Westermarck's pioneering studies in incest avoidance, an empirical investigation that directly contradicts Freud's notion of the Oedipus complex. Wilson admits, however, that as yet no direct link has been found between genes and incest avoidance; in his view, though, the evidence points to a coevolutionary link between genes and behavior. The study of human behavior has until recently been in the hands of the social sciences, which Wilson takes to task for their refusal to seek consilience with the natural sciences and one another, for their reliance on folk psychology, and for their lack of genuine theory. To correct these errors, Wilson recommends that the social sciences turn to epigenetic rules, those "innate operations in the sensory system and brain . . . that allow organisms to find rapid solutions to problems in the environment. They predispose individuals to view the world in a particular innate way and automatically to make certain choices as opposed to others."

In a similar manner, he attacks interpreters of the arts for not looking to biology and psychology for understandings of why humans create art and respond to it. He is particularly hard on postmodern theories such as deconstruction that deny the possibility of knowledge and that show no grasp of science (neurobiology in particular), psychology, or anthropology—all of which Wilson regards as crucial to understanding the origins and meaning of artistic creation. There is no reason, Wilson argues, why art and its interpretation cannot be made part of the overall chain of cause and effect that makes up genuine knowledge. From here it is a short step to an investigation of ethics and religion, where the traditional conflict is between transcendentalists, who locate the origins of morality outside humanity (in the dictates of a deity, for example), and empiricists, who regard moral ideas as purely human inventions. Wilson, of course, favors empiricism and speculates that moral imperatives may be traceable to material causes—that is, to human evolution. It is quite possible, he argues, that moral ideas such as patriotism and altruism may confer survival value. The link, at least, must be explored, as must the biological roots of the religious impulse.

In the final chapter, "To What End?" Wilson argues that understanding ourselves is the most important endeavor the social sciences and humanities can undertake, for what is at stake is not merely academic respectability but the survival of a species that threatens to destroy itself by despoiling its ecosystem.

Only a reviewer as broadly and deeply involved in the sciences and as well read as Wilson in every subject from anthropology to sociology could adequately evaluate Wilson's argument and his program. Moreover, his idea of consilience is one that can be tested only by years of attempting to achieve it. A beginning has already been made in the natural sciences, but pursuing it in the social sciences and humanities is probably a project for generations of scholars. If it is ever achieved, it will then seem obvious; only if we fail in repeated attempts will we be certain that it is impossible.

Moreover, there are clearly problems with Wilson's diagnoses and prescriptions. For one thing, it is doubtful whether science has achieved the level of consilience Wilson claims for it. Indeed, there are natural points of contact and overlapping areas of inquiry where cooperation between fields is both profitable and common. And, to be fair, results in one field that directly contradict results in another will always need to be explained or reconciled. Still, superspecialization in the sciences continues apace, even as attempts at consilience are creating areas of commonality.

Beyond this, Wilson's central claim—that developments in the science of the mind will lead to breakthroughs that will help to explain and give validity to research in the social sciences and humanities—must be regarded skeptically. Although Wilson cites some promising studies about the neurochemistry of the brain and its relevance to the "softer" disciplines, many experts will remain unconvinced. Can our responses to art, even presuming the validity of the archetypes Wilson relies upon, be explained as the result of cause and effect? The relation of genes to behavior is and will remain problematic and contentious—as Wilson himself acknowledges.

Having said all this, one must grant that Wilson has performed a unique service in this book. Bucking nearly all the present trends in academia and the media, he has dared to challenge every thinking person to reconsider the Enlightenment ideal. Unfortunately for Wilson, and perhaps for all of us, it seems unlikely that academia will take up Wilson's challenge. To embark on the project, social scientists and humanists would first have to admit that the assumptions and methods of their disciplines are deeply flawed. Second, they would have to embark on a systematic study of science, something only scattered humanists, social scientists, and psychologists have so far shown themselves willing to do. Meanwhile, the whole system of academic awards militates against research toward consilience. Tenure is achieved not by breaking new intellectual ground but by following well-trodden paths. Academic journals want research that follows accepted lines of inquiry and reinforces current theories and prejudices. Academic organization discourages cross-disciplinary research. The scholars best in a position to follow Wilson's lead are those well established in their careers or, like Wilson himself, retired from academia. Near the beginning of his book, Wilson says, "Every college student should be able to answer the following question: What is the relation between science and the humanities, and how is it important for human welfare? Every public intellectual and political leader should be able to answer that question as well." Colleges and universities could respond to Wilson's challenge by placing his question at the center of their curricula. They almost certainly will not. If consilience is to be achieved at all, it will probably come from scientists themselves, who have already seen its rewards in their own work and who can cross the divide between the two cultures far more easily than their colleagues in the humanities and social sciences can reach out to them. Nevertheless, one can hope that at colleges and universities all over the world, interdisciplinary discussion groups will form around *Consilience* and that scholars and teachers will seriously and systematically consider the validity and feasibility of Wilson's arguments and proposals. If something like this does not happen, it will be a genuine shame—for a book as well written, well argued, modestly presented, and clearly as important as Wilson's deserves a considered, rigorous response.

Dean Baldwin

Sources for Further Study

American Scientist. LXXXVI, May, 1998, p. 280.
Commonweal. CXXV, July 17, 1998, p. 23.
The New England Journal of Medicine. CCCXXXIX, July 16, 1998, p. 205.
New Scientist. CLIX, August 22, 1998, p. 42.
The New York Review of Books. XLV, April 23, 1998, p. 14.
The New York Times Book Review. CIII, April 26, 1998, p. 11.
Newsweek. CXXXI, June 22, 1998, p. 59.
Publishers Weekly. CCXLV, January 26, 1998, p. 76.
Scientific American. CCLXXVIII, June, 1998, p. 97.
Time. CLI, April 6, 1998, p. 75.

DAMASCUS GATE

Author: Robert Stone (1937-   )
Published: Houghton Mifflin (Boston). 500 pp. $26.00
Type of work: Novel
Time: The 1990's
Locale: Israel

A richly allusive novel of intrigue that suggests the inherent need for union and transcendence amid seemingly irreconcilable extremes

Principal characters:
CHRISTOPHER LUCAS, a journalist and author, the central character
PINCHAS OBERMANN, an Israeli psychiatrist, Lucas's literary collaborator
SONIA BARNES, a nightclub singer, Lucas's friend
ADAM DE KUFF, a Jewish mystic originally from a wealthy New Orleans family
RALPH (RAZIEL) MELKER, a jazz musician and student of Jewish mysticism
JANUSZ ZIMMER, a Polish journalist and soldier of fortune
NUALA RICE, an Irish nurse and political activist who works at the International Children's Federation
RASHID NAGUIB, a Palestinian doctor employed by the United Nations Relief and Welfare Agency (NNRWA); Rice's lover
THEODORE EARL ERICKSEN, an American evangelical fundamentalist minister employed by the House of the Galilean, a study group
LINDA ERICKSEN, his wife, also employed by that organization

Robert Stone's concern with the need to believe, to love, and to transcend ideologies recurs in all of his novels. *Damascus Gate*, however, treats this familiar theme in an epic format and with amazing élan. In the hands of a lesser writer, integrating such an enormous number of characters within a coherent plot would in itself be daunting. Stone imposes an even greater burden on himself by making the seemingly irreconcilable contradictions within his characters the very heart of his novel. Plot and purpose drive the narrative rather than display of process, the prevailing characteristic of postmodern fiction. Despite the rich allusiveness, the mythic, literary, and religious tropes, even the hidden humor, *Damascus Gate* combines the humanity of Salman Rushdie with intrigue equal to that of John Le Carré. Still, it remains at its essence a characteristic Stone novel.

Its hypothesis is clear from the outset. Jerusalem is a magnet for extremes and contradictions. Those most drawn to the city often have contradictory, extreme, and self-destructive elements within their own personalities and backgrounds. This makes Jerusalem a flash point for disaster and deliverance, hatred and love, treachery and devotion. Often, classifying a single event as good or evil depends merely upon perspective. This is not, however, mere relativism.

Christopher Lucas, the central character of the novel, acutely feels these contradictions within himself as he watches the ravings of a *majnoon*, a religious lunatic, in the shadow of Jerusalem's Damascus Gate. The *majnoon* joins together an enormous string of curses and obscenities until his final imprecation to heaven makes his obscene litany almost a prayer, a final act of faith that distills the sum of human pain. The clergy of the various denominations of the Anastasis, the church constructed on what is by legend the site of Jesus Christ's tomb, frantically shut the doors of their chapels to keep out the madman. A posse of Greek Orthodox clergy forcibly expel the madman into the waiting arms of Israeli police, even as the *majnoon* calls the Anastasis a den of thieves.

Ironically, this wild scene recalling Christ amid the moneychangers takes place on Easter Sunday; it occurs in variation later in the novel with Lucas as *majnoon*-Christ. On Easter in Jerusalem, human nature renews its perversity amid its annual celebration of transcendence. The new Christ is merely a *majnoon*, as indeed the founder of Christianity must have seemed to the religious establishment of the day.

Stone's aptly named hero perceives his own affinity to the madman. He is a journalist turned writer of books who has traveled as much as the saint of his first name. His writer's powers of observation and his sympathy with the pathetic state of humanity have made him a modern physician of souls, like St. Luke. He understands that the suffering of Christ stands in direct relation to his own pain and that of the human race.

Lucas's unusual family background has heightened his sensitivity to human suffer- ing even as it has exacerbated his personal dilemma. He is the illegitimate son of a devout but non-practicing Catholic mother who was a singer of classical art songs and a humanist Jewish father, a Columbia University professor whose visits Lucas barely remembers. Lucas attended Catholic schools, but he remembers principally that a boy surnamed English called him a "Jewish bastard." He is acutely aware that to Orthodox Jews he is not a Jew at all. As early as the incident with English, Lucas had realized that he was not in spirit one of the Catholic schoolboys. In short, Lucas feels that he is everything human, yet not part of any community of humanity. He wonders sadly with whom he will stand on Resurrection Day, an eternally lost soul.

Perhaps it is these musings that lead him to accept a writing project that Pinchas Obermann, an Israeli psychiatrist, suggests. Obermann treats many individuals suffer- ing from what he calls the Jerusalem Syndrome. He has given this label to a condition of extreme religious or political beliefs that has brought many to Jerusalem. The city, he believes, has become a manic gateway to extreme behavior that holds the promise of either ineffable bliss or Armageddon. Obermann's files, which Lucas uses in his research, become the means through which he meets the many complex characters of the novel. Their own communities would categorize each as normal, yet each has a fierce dedication to some religion, cause, or ideology; each, in a different way, is a *majnoon*.

Sonia Barnes is, without doubt, the most complex and fascinating of the novel's characters. Her exoticism bewitches Lucas immediately, and Barnes works similar magic on readers of the novel. Her mother was an ardent Jewish American communist, her father an African American jazz musician. Barnes herself feels drawn to Islam, primarily because its discipline imposes structure on her life and has allowed her to throw off her enslavement to drugs. She has her father's musical talent; she is a nightclub singer who performs a variety of songs. These range from a style of earthy reality that resembles that of Sarah Vaughan to the delicate lyricism of Spanish art songs that contemplate the light of heaven, eternal love, and escape from the tawdry world. Barnes dresses as a Muslim woman when she walks through Jerusalem's Arab quarter, yet she can resemble the French chanteuse Edith Piaf when she sings her soulful saloon songs. She has lived in Cuba, and she feels sincere commitment to Fidel Castro's social reforms; she calls her nightclub audience "comrades" in a kind of half-jest and self-parody. She has done social work among dying children in Africa. Because her mother was Jewish, the Orthodox community allows her to call herself a Jew, yet she is obviously much more than this.

Readers admire Barnes's generosity and spirit, and these qualities attract Lucas as well. Barnes is all the things Lucas is not but might like to be; though this attracts him to Barnes, it paradoxically inhibits their relationship. Barnes's own spiritual search brings her under the influence of Adam De Kuff, the heir to a New Orleans family fortune and another of Obermann's patients. De Kuff is a fragile, ascetic man passionately interested in all things spiritual. It is this that has brought him to Israel and that draws him to still another patient of Obermann, a drug addict, jazz musician, and student of the Kabbala named Ralph (Raziel) Melker. Melker is the son of Jewish American parents from the Midwest. His father, a congressman, has allowed Melker to emigrate to Israel and adopt a Jewish first name, presumably in the hope that the young man will reorder his life. It seems equally likely that Melker's father wishes to rid himself of an embarrassing political liability.

For reasons not entirely spiritual, Melker convinces De Kuff that the older man is the Messiah returned for the Last Judgment, and he uses arguments based on the Kabbala to prove it. The two travel about Israel like a latter-day Christ and St. Peter. De Kuff proves a charismatic speaker, half-convincing even Melker of his divine destiny. Like Christ and his followers, they incur the wrath of the religious and political authorities even as they draw the multitudes, among them Barnes. Partly because of her involvement with De Kuff, but also because of his Jerusalem Syndrome project, Lucas finds himself a reluctant adherent. All this plays out against the religious and political tensions of late twentieth century Israel, yet the outcome is an eerie mix of the contemporary, the mythic, and the biblical.

Lucas's ancillary involvement with Nuala Rice, a Dublin nurse who works for the International Children's Federation, provides a supporting subplot. Rice is a Palestinian sympathizer who does her work among the displaced in the camps of the Gaza Strip. She has fallen in love with an American-trained Palestinian doctor, Rashid Naguib, at work in Gaza for the United Nations Relief and Welfare Agency (UNRWA). Rice would like Lucas to write an exposé on the brutality of Israeli occupation forces in the Strip, but her motives are more complex than they first appear. Again the drug world intrudes, and the outcome for Rice and Naguib is both grisly and poignant.

Theodore Ericksen, an American fundamentalist minister, and his wife Linda Ericksen add a political dimension to the novel's plot. The Ericksens are administrators at the House of the Galilean, which has among its projects the reconstruction of Solomon's temple. Accomplishing this goal necessitates having to clear the various modern mosques that inconveniently stand on the site, and this leads to an unlikely conspiracy of Israelis (both secular and orthodox), Christian fundamentalists, Dooms-day cultists, archaeologists, and assorted terrorists. Lucas, who meets the Ericksens through Obermann, comes to see how the rumor of this conspiracy relates to his Jerusalem Syndrome project. He quickly finds himself involved in this additional web of intrigue.

This outline does little to describe the multidimensional quality of *Damascus Gate*. Characters of inexhaustible variety—Israeli soldiers and shopkeepers, Copts and gypsies, priests, ministers, and rabbis of every theological stripe, diplomats and soldiers of fortune—drive the narrative at a fast pace. The novel contains a primer on Kabbala as well as on Orphic mystery religion and the syncretic god Sabezios. Description of Gaza's squalor finds its counterpart in Mount Hebron's sublimity, and biblical or mythic echoes resonate in virtually every scene. Drugs make the Sea of Galilee appear to flow against its course, and people appear to walk on its waters or to part its waves. The fate of a musician resembles that of the mythic musician Orpheus. An ardent Israeli settler dies among the Gaza Palestinians like Pentheus at the hands of the maenads of Dionysus. Lovers die in a lonely mountain retreat like Benito Mussolini and his mistress Clara Petacci. What is more, the civil, political, and religious authorities of the novel could have added a chapter to the works of Niccolò Machiavelli.

Despite all this, Stone's novel remains an entertainment, and it is filled with subtle humor. At one point, Lucas finds himself trapped in a spinach field, and he suddenly seems like Cary Grant in an Alfred Hitchcock film. Even as Palestinians riot in Jerusalem's Arab quarter, Lucas spreads the rumor that Salman Rushdie has come to Israel, and this sends Muslim rioters in another direction toward the presumed location of the infidel. All the while, a European resident who lives in the Jewish quarter of the city solely because he hates Jews plays the music of Richard Wagner and Carl Orff at ear-splitting levels on his stereo because Israel prohibits its public performance.

Astonishingly, Stone unites all these elements into a coherent novel. The strange world he describes is one he knows firsthand. Raised by his mother, a woman with alcohol-abuse problems, Stone found himself in a series of Catholic boarding schools and ultimately dropped out of high school. Like the protagonist of his novel, Stone felt Catholic and yet not Catholic. Like many young men of the 1950's, he read Jack Kerouac's *On the Road* (1957), but unlike most he actually made the pilgrimage from New York to San Francisco and joined the Dharma community, which included Kerouac, Neal Cassady, Allen Ginsberg, and Gary Snyder. This accounts for Stone's ability to describe commune life and his knowledge of Sufi and Kabbalic mysticism and the drug culture.

Still, what one notices first about Stone's writing is its glorious humanity and generosity of spirit. His experience in the world has not made him cynical or arrogant, perhaps just regretful of what humanity could achieve were it able to transcend the differences it insists on emphasizing. In any event, Stone has accomplished in *Damascus Gate* exactly what one feels postmodern novelists would give anything to have managed: a coherent yet highly literate work of art that treats a question of timeless importance. It is a novel one cannot help but think that Rushdie himself would enjoy.

Robert J. Forman

Sources for Further Study

Commonweal. CXXV, June 5, 1998, p. 24.
Los Angeles Times Book Review. May 17, 1998, p. 2.
The Nation. CCLXVI, May 11, 1998, p. 50.
The New Republic. CCXVIII, May 25, 1998, p. 29.
The New York Times Book Review. CIII, April 26, 1998, p. 14.
The New Yorker. LXXIV, April 13, 1998, p. 74.
Publishers Weekly. CCXLV, February 16, 1998, p. 200.
Time. CLI, May 25, 1998, p. 82.
The Wall Street Journal. April 24, 1998, p. W4.
The Washington Post Book World. XXVIII, May 3, 1998, p. 1.

THE DEATH OF ADAM
Essays on Modern Thought

Author: Marilynne Robinson (1944-   )
Published: Houghton Mifflin (New York). 254 pp. $24.00
Type of work: Essays

A collection of essays on a variety of political, economic, environmental, religious, and social issues arguing the imperative need to reconceptualize and change both the individual and the collective understanding of culture

Marilynne Robinson, who received her Ph.D. in English from the University of Washington, is a professor of creative writing at the University of Iowa. This connection of the scholarly and the arts reveals itself in all of her writings. She is the author of the acclaimed novel *Housekeeping* (1981), widely acknowledged for its themes of impermanence and transcendence but particularly celebrated for its lyricism and sustained use of precise, distilled, poetic language. Her second book, *Mother Country* (1989), is an award-winning nonfiction work about nuclear pollution in Great Britain; it is a searing attack on the plutonium processing business and, by extension, an indictment of attitudes and practices related to nuclear power. Reviewers of that volume, too, repeatedly praised Robinson's mastery of language and her meticulously crafted prose. *The Death of Adam: Essays on Modern Thought* continues in this vein, showcasing her exceptional ability to write with a stunning elegance that also reveals a brilliant thinker with a passionate belief in the importance of her subject. The ten essays in this collection ultimately have as their theme nothing less than a vision of altering the way knowledge is apprehended, altering both the individual consciousness and the larger collective consciousness in order to save the world.

In the introduction to *The Death of Adam*, Robinson notes that these essays were written for various occasions and publications over the past few years and that they share in common a characteristic preoccupation with "the state of contemporary society." All of them, she accurately states, are "contrarian in method and spirit. They assert, in one way or another, that the prevailing view of things can be assumed to be wrong, and that its opposite, being its image or shadow, can also be assumed to be wrong." The essays demonstrate that there are different and more desirable modes of thought, and furthermore, that it is only by adopting and adapting to altered ways of conceptualizing the past and also the present "view of things" that humanity has much hope of survival.

The specific subject matter Robinson considers is ultimately of less significance than this overriding sense of impassioned urgency and the need for a will to change. In these ten essays, topics range from Darwinism to Calvinism to nineteenth century schoolbooks, with plenty of other titles such as "Facing Reality" and "Family." In several cases, there are topics that a reader may think it unnecessary even to consider—either one already knows enough about it or it is not relevant anyway. Robinson, though, is persuasive. These are present concerns. In fact, one of her main themes is that, all too often, both common wisdom and specialist wisdom contain misapprehensions of the past and lack a thoughtful examination of the present.

The first and longest essay in the collection, "Darwinism," provides a cogent example of Robinson's argument that primary sources are seldom read and that the context of the original works is often ill-understood. Contemporary culture assumes that it "knows" what the nineteenth century English naturalist Charles Darwin wrote and knows what attitude to have about it. Darwin's *Origin of Species* (1859) and *The Descent of Man* (1871), most people today would say (including those who write about Darwin), either show Darwin was a clear-headed scientist who essentially bypassed notions of God by proving the evolution of life forms or, its opposite, that Darwin was wrong about evolution and that creation theory should be included in biology text-books. The facts—the actual texts and the historical context—Robinson suggests, are much more convoluted. The same is true about the popular shorthand version of Darwinism as "the survival of the fittest."

The full title of Darwin's first book (seldom included in mention of it) is *On the Origin of Species by Means of Natural Selection, or the Preservation of Favoured Races in the Struggle for Life*. The title alone implies that "whatever is, is right," the product of raw struggle, and that there is a teleology, or reason, behind it all that favors the elimination of species that die in the struggle. In *The Descent of Man*, Darwin explicitly argues that

> . . . we build asylums for the imbecile, the maimed, and the sick; we institute poor laws; and our medical men exert their utmost skill to save the life of everyone to the last moment. There is reason to believe that vaccination has preserved thousands who from a weak constitution would formerly have succumbed to smallpox. Thus the weak members of civilized society propagate their kind. No one who has attended to the breeding of domestic animals will doubt that this must be highly injurious to the race of man.

This is "pure Malthus," Robinson writes. Darwin read *Essay on the Principle of Population* (1798), by English political economist Thomas Malthus, with its grim theory that if birth is not controlled, poverty and war serve as natural restrictions, and that alleviation of misery only results in greater misery. Darwin adds to this the idea that larger countries, having larger populations, have more competition to weed out undesirables and thus have a right—even duty—to conquer smaller, less "fit" countries. More to the point of Robinson's analysis, Darwinism grew out of "primitive economics" and was readily adopted by nineteenth century capitalists to support their notion of "progress," the notion of self-interest and unbridled competition in the marketplace, in what has become global economics. Robinson writes:

> The idea of progress implies a judgment of value. We are to believe the world will be better if people are forced into severe and continuous competition. If they work themselves weary making a part for a gadget assembled on the other side of the earth, in fear of the loss of their livelihoods, the world will be better for it. If economic forces recombine and shed these workers for cheaper ones, the world will be still better. In what sense, better? To ask is to refuse to accept the supposedly inevitable, to deny the all-overriding reality of self-interest and raw competition, which will certainly overwhelm us if we allow ourselves some sentimental dream of a humane collective life. This economics implies progress and has no progress to show.

For the biblical Adam of Genesis, whose name means "Earth," Robinson suggests that Darwinists have substituted the claim that human beings are but another link in the evolutionary chain, denying any biological basis for true social behaviors—all the arts and sciences and philanthropies that are possible only when people are sociable and collaborative and rely on the mental capacities of which human beings are capable. It is worth reflecting, Robinson writes to conclude the essay, "how much was destroyed, when modern thought declared the death of Adam."

Robinson's subtleties of thought and logic do not lend themselves to facile summary; her arguments need to be followed as written. In each of the essays, she develops her ideas through a cumulative process of showing the connections between attitudes and actions and between knowledge and responsibility. In "Puritans and Prigs," she traces the development of morality, which she defines ultimately as "a covenant with oneself which can only be imposed and enforced by oneself," noting that while individual ideas of rightness vary, everyone can distinguish instantly between a moral lapse and a difference of standards. "Prigs" and zealots, she suggests, want to believe they are different, and better, than other people; although they may claim to enlighten others, they are not open to other points of view and have no intention of building consensus and reforming society. In "Dietrich Bonhoeffer," she praises the German Lutheran pastor and theologian who repeatedly protested the Nazi treatment of Jews in the 1930's. He was imprisoned for his actions and was executed in April, 1945. Robinson sees Bonhoeffer's life and thought as one; that is, his actions were consistently guided by his belief in the rights of the individual, regardless of religion, and that persecution of others is never supportable. In "McGuffey and the Abolitionists," Robinson notes that most commentators on the McGuffey Readers, a series of American school textbooks that first appeared in the 1830's, regard the publications as a successful moneymaking scheme by William Holmes McGuffey and some of his friends and review the contents as sentimental statements of minor aspirations for the middle class, emphasizing thrift and work. What Robinson finds is that the contents more often emphasize kindness and generosity and the normalization of democratic attitudes and manners. Furthermore, the modest prices and widespread availability of the textbooks were part of the commitment of McGuffey and others to establish and strengthen public education, particularly in the Midwest and the South before, during, and after the Civil War. Although the textbooks do not deal specifically with slavery, McGuffey and his circle were abolitionists who supported nonviolence; the Readers are contemptuous of war and promote instead ideals of democracy.

Another characteristic of each essay in the collection is that its range is much greater than is suggested by the title. "Facing Reality" encompasses much more than contrasting the fictional and the factual. "Wilderness" does more than make a plea for environmentalism. "Psalm Eight" certainly includes much more than a discussion of one of the Old Testament psalms in the Bible. Here Robinson speaks of her own childhood and early love of reading; she writes that she has spent her life trying to see and understand the great mystery of existence, of time, not timelessness. She reflects:

> What is eternal must always be complete, if my understanding is correct. So it is possible to imagine that time was created in order that there might be narrative—event, sequence and causation, ignorance and error, retribution, atonement. A word, a phrase, a story falls on rich or stony ground and flourishes as it can, possibility in a sleeve of limitation. Certainly time is the occasion for our strangely mixed nature, in every moment differently compounded, so that often we surprise ourselves, and always scarcely know ourselves, and exist in relation to experience, if we attend to it and if its plainness does not disguise it from us, as if we were visited by revelation.

This is Robinson in full form, awakening her readers. *The Death of Adam: Essays in Modern Thought* is such a work throughout. It not only reflects geopolitical and historic concerns but also challenges readers to consider the meaning of life and how to live it. Like her two previous books, *Housekeeping* and *Mother Country*, this one should be well reviewed and well received, sometimes even by those who may not recognize they want or need to read it. The books that shape thought in meaningful ways are often not the quick best-sellers, the short-lived easily read romances that can be made into blockbuster movies. Often they are nonfiction works from thoughtful, informed, and impassioned minds, as is this one; but only rarely, as in *The Death of Adam*, is the use of language so striking and so much of part of the message itself.

Lois A. Marchino

Sources for Further Study

Booklist. XCV, September 1, 1998, p. 63.
Boston Globe. September 13, 1998, p. C2.
The Christian Century. CXV, November 18, 1998, p. 1101.
Library Journal. CXXIII, September 15, 1998, p. 86.
Publishers Weekly. CCXLV, July 27, 1998, p. 60.
San Francisco Chronicle. October 4, 1998, p. REV5.

THE DESTRUCTIVE ELEMENT
New and Selected Poems

Author: Turner Cassity (1929-   )
Published: Ohio University Press (Athens, Ohio). 246 pp. $29.95; paperback $15.95
Type of work: Poetry

Formalist poet Turner Cassity's most recent collection includes the best of his earlier work plus a powerful array of new poems

Turner Cassity's *The Destructive Element: New and Selected Poems* is a striking collection that will convince skeptical poetry readers of the range and adaptability of formalism. The new poems are followed by selections from Cassity's earlier books, in chronological order, and an epilogue poem that serves as an envoi. The poems run the gamut of formalist possibility from clear, witty, and brief epigrams to complex, allusion-laden meditative poems. The work clearly defines the trademark Cassity poem. The poet's distinctive mix of philosophical speculation, irony, nose-thumbing at the current pieties, and complex wordplay is a constant throughout the book.

Cassity's work is associated with the new formalist school of poetry and is often discussed with that of other formalist poets such as Dana Gioia, Timothy Steele, and Edgar Bowers. Cassity has been around long enough to have been directly influenced by the formalists of the 1950's, when the rhymed and metered poem dominated in *Poetry Magazine* and elsewhere. The earliest of the books from which selections have been made is dated 1966, but Cassity was constructing his signature ironic balances for some time before this. At one point he described himself as "the wildest of the students of the late Yvor Winters." There is some of Winters in this work, including carefully measured metrics and a sense of controlled distance, but irony has replaced much of the elegiac tone of Winters (though Cassity gets in some elegy as well). Some of Cassity's work has a blend of balanced epigrammatic irony; other poems are apparently more straightforward. It is hard to tell, sometimes, exactly where the poet's true sympathies lie, as the poems are layered with irony. It is perhaps this in-your-face irony that Cassity is thinking of as "wild."

The travels that compose much of this poet's life are the taking-off point for the poems. Cassity's years in Africa, where he was a civil servant, are reflected in the poems, as well as his time spent in the Caribbean in military service and later jaunts all over the globe. How history and place intersect is analyzed in meditative poems; these may, at first, appear to belong to the (to many readers) unwelcome category of "local color" travel poems but upon second reading prove to be more than scenes noted by the intellectual tourist eye. Rather, they are moralistic considerations on the conflict between beauty and practicality, and the many ironies that result from this conflict. Cassity also looks at the ironic contrast between a place in its natural state and after it has been changed by technology and use; perhaps this kind of reflection is what once led him to call his poems "colonial pastorals." What attitude the poet really holds toward the profit motive, toward using and spending as opposed to guarding and preserving, would be hard to fathom beneath the layers, and the poet would likely disclaim any position statement attributed to the work.

Whether the reader agrees with any putative politics, there is much to be derived from this poetry. A pleasure is that it is demanding and yet yielding—there is a good deal of background knowledge of places and events expected, but not required, of the reader. Most of the message comes through even if some of the names are unfamiliar. Another delight is the sound—these poems should be read aloud. For those who circle the new formalists warily, the poems are of an appropriate length for the reader who is disinclined to curl up with Edmund Spenser's *The Faerie Queene*; most of them are one or two pages in length. They may be enjoyed singly and in groups.

The forms themselves are varied and contain plentiful echoes. "Allegory with Lay Figures" clearly evokes T. S. Eliot:

> In dark blue suits intently go
> The brisk young men of Tokyo.
>
> They scorn the scooter, purchase cars,
> They meet their girls in coffee bars.

Poem and message are Eliot-like—the surprise is in the setting and in the realization that Eliot's world has not been replaced, just displaced.

Some Cassity poems use other kinds of couplets, often iambic pentameter, end-stopped, with overtones of Alexander Pope. He uses off-rhyme with casual expertise, setting up ironies that will be reinforced by the rhyme. "The Chinaberry Tree" begins:

> Its shape uncertain in the bloom that scrims it,
> Purple, and itself a haze of gnats,
> The tree that will be knowledge, or what seems it,
> Beckons in the rising heat and waits.

Eden's apple is equated with the inedible fruit of this tree, and the parallel becomes a comment on human nature:

> Soft blossoms harden in their unmeant Eden
> Toward the green, emetic berry: scent
> Nil, outline clear—late come-on for a want
> Too uninformative to seem forbidden.

Full of ironic twists and turnarounds on every level, from symbol to image to rhyme, this brief poem is wittily serpentine.

Indeed, Cassity's poetry is frequently fun. In the more playful of the poems, he may choose twisted Byronic rhymes or exact ones, or somewhere in between. The leap of rhythm provides high spirits even if the poem's theme is somewhere between those of humorist Richard Armour and the dark twinklings of Robert Frost. "Links" begins with a familiar setting, which promptly acquires symbolic shadows:

> My young grandfather, for the me of four,
> Blew smoke rings. I, these long years more,
>
> Without much gift, can, nonetheless,
> Redeem my breath from utter shapelessness.

Shadows or no, the effect of the poem tends to be to make the reader want to blow smoke rings—especially the poet-reader, who would like to breathe thin air into visible shapes and would like others to admire his or her skill.

Another direction Cassity's poetry takes is even more like Frost's work. Both Cassity and Frost talk in iambic measures about the parallels between nature's behavior and human activity, but Frost tends to see the impenetrable barrier between humans and nature more sympathetically. Cassity's world is a darker one, with negative forces—indeed, a destructive element—at work within and without. In "Acid Rain on Sherwood Forest," the speaker comments, "We have, as usual, let sentiment/ Define the natural." The poem concludes:

> Had Cain
> No weapons but his hands he would be Cain,
> And Abel dead of strangulation. Child
> Of nature, little boy of five or six,
> Why have you pulled the rubber suction cup
> From off your arrow and begun to sharpen it?

The layered irony often prevents conclusive interpretation. In this, Cassity's work is reminiscent of the poetry of Wallace Stevens, whose shifting personae and syntactical ambiguities leave the poems open to contradictory readings. The prominent Christian presence is a case in point: What is to be made of it? These poems are laced with Christian symbolism, appropriated with the same effrontery as are icons and holy things from a variety of other sources. In "Carpenters," the construction of the Cross makes part of a meditation on the subject of payment and work, and on the general subject of employment: "Forgiven, unforgiven, they who drive the nails/ Know what they do: they hammer." The biting conclusion once more reverses expectations:

> Judas who sops, their silver his accuser, errs
> To blame the unrewarded.
> They guard the branch he hangs from. Guilt occurs
> Where it can be afforded.

Throughout the work, biblical figures appear and vanish, illustrating Cassity's dark lessons. If the Christian vision they afford is not comforting, it is in accord with the doctrines of predestination and original sin.

One is always tempted to look for "development" in a book that covers decades of a poet's work. Social-protest poet Ai claimed that if she found she was writing the same kind of poem repeatedly, she would chuck the new work out. Cassity does not share this position. The waxing and waning of particular themes could be noted, but style remains constant and therefore recognizable and distinctive. Like Frost, Cassity has found something that works and continues to do it, finding new areas to subject to his approach. Only once does he stray from his appointed patterns, and even in this exception, the point of his digression is that it really is not a digression. "Laying It on the Line" uses puns and metrical play in a graceful—though still ironic—love poem, which asks "How does a heart of stone/ write a love poem?" and answers "In free verse, of course,/ to show how little rigid/ he really is." If to write such a poem is a "noble Roman/ equivalent of opening my veins," the conclusion finds its way back to the iambic rhythm: "But as you see, the beat keeps coming back."

In dealing with new formalism, the phrase "lapidary poems" always comes to mind, and some of the poets sought after a sparse, tightly constructed, epigrammatic style. While there is some of this in Cassity, a few poems are frankly humorous, some are deliberately ornamental, and others have a cultivated "off" quality—as though some element of Cassity is in concord with the postmodern avoidance of or disbelief in closure, even while the poems themselves may close with resounding couplets.

New formalism has proved to be an important strain of poetry at the end of the twentieth century, challenging postmodernism in its assumptions and style. Where postmodern poetry tends to abolish borders, appropriate work from other arts and artists, and make use of pastiche, formalists set up boundaries and follow defined traditions, revitalizing the old patterns with contemporary messages. Cassity will remain one of the foremost new formalists; his work both exemplifies and undercuts their position. Some of his work is memorable for its sheer sound and energy. His elusiveness is attractive; it is a challenge to peel away the levels of language, only to be told by the final poem that "He Whom Ye Seek" is not there (in a rhetorical act of appropriation with which some readers are not going to be happy). Cassity is, of course, there, and the game is to catch glimpses of him or even views he did not intend to disclose.

One minor flaw of the collection is that it contains no index of titles and first lines. This kind of poetry in particular seems to need such an index; it is easy to develop favorites and annoying to have to scan the table of contents or leaf through the book looking for them.

Janet McCann

Sources for Further Study

Kirkus Reviews. LXVI, March 1, 1998, p. 300.
The New York Review of Books. XLV, April 23, 1998, p. 34.
Publishers Weekly. CCXLV, February 23, 1998, p. 70.

DREAM CHILDREN

Author: A. N. Wilson (1950-   )
Published: W. W. Norton (New York). 218 pp. $23.95
Type of Work: Novel
Time: 1970's-1990's
Locale: London, New York, and Philadelphia

> *Several women are held together by their love of Oliver, an aging philosopher and pedophile, but his love and his plans to marry drive them to extremes*

Principal characters:
> OLIVER GOLD, a middle-aged philosopher and former college fellow
> JANET ROSE, owner of house at 12 Wagner Rise, Michal's mother
> MICHAL ROSE, Janet's daughter
> ROBERTA ("BOBS") O'HARA, Michal's twelve-year-old daughter, beloved by Oliver
> CATHERINE CUFFE, a beautiful red-haired Irish woman in her mid-thirties, once Oliver's student, now a philosopher and lover of Michal
> LOTTE, a large Austrian woman in her mid-thirties; once a nanny, now the housekeeper
> MARGOT REISZ, a neighbor, an old woman
> CAMILLA BAYNES, a thin, mousy American in her mid-thirties, engaged to Oliver
> ROSALIE BAYNES, her mother, a stylish and intelligent woman

In the middle of the 1970's, Oliver Gold found himself in an enviable position. He possessed a first-class university degree. He became a successful barrister, but when he wanted to return to academic life, his old college gave him a fellowship. Soon he turned philosopher. Although he was not a bloodless and analytic positivist, he maintained that moral laws were only useful assumptions made at a particular time in history. After he wrote a book that made him famous and fashionable, he was often asked to take part in intellectual discussions on the radio.

Then, in a radio discussion of child abuse, Oliver delivered a surprise. Consistent with his general views, he argued that a sexual taboo operated only when society generally agreed that a specific behavior was taboo. The Victorians had their prohibitions, long gone now. Only a few years ago, homosexuality was unlawful, but not anymore. In fact, the only taboo now left concerned the sexual feelings of children. Yet why should paedophilia be judged to be wicked? It was not so in many other cultures. How can one argue that children do not have free will in this matter? That children do not have sexual feelings? His career in broadcasting was finished. (Wilson may here draw on Margaret Drabble's 1989 novel *A Natural Curiosity*, in which a character expresses almost identical opinions on a television talk show.)

Before readers come upon these arguments in chapter 5, they may have suspected that something odd was afoot. Earlier Wilson novels have dealt with sexual taboos; brothers, sisters, and cousins commit incest in *The Sweets of Pimlico* (1977) and *A*

Bottle in the Smoke (1990). *Dream Children* opens with a prelude detailing an episode, purportedly being broadcast in the 1990's, of the American television real-life program *Court TV*. The episode shows a middle-aged woman charging, on the basis of her recently recovered repressed memory, that she had been molested as a child.

The main action of *Dream Children* is set in the mid-1980's. Oliver is living in a large house in the Muswell Hill district of North London, a house owned by Janet Rose, an aging widow of a marginal literary personality. Janet is not intelligent, but she is smart enough to know her only chance of getting respect is by retelling and even inventing stories about the literary parties she and her husband gave in the 1950's.

In Janet's house, 12 Wagner Rise, live several women. There is her disturbed divorced daughter, Michal, a social worker who spends her time with equally disturbed young people. There is Michal's own neglected daughter, whose real name is Roberta O'Hara but who is called "Bobs." There is Catherine Cuffe, a university lecturer in philosophy who is Michal's lesbian lover. There is Lotte, an ominous and buxom Austrian woman who had come as a nanny and remains as a housekeeper. There is also an assortment of animals that Bobs keeps and loves: a rabbit, a cock, a budgerigar, and a rat. At the emotional center of the household is Oliver, who had been introduced into the house by his former pupil Catherine some time after the child-abuse broadcast. His presence mysteriously seems to have calmed the emotional tensions of the volatile group. They love him. He is particularly valuable because he gives Bobs the parental care her mother is too busy to provide.

Oliver, though, is about to alter the chemistry of 12 Wagner Rise by marrying. To make matters worse, the woman he is to marry, Camilla, is an American. She seems to be rich and will probably want to lure him all the way to the United States. Each of the adult woman is distraught; only Bobs seems cheerful.

To this mix, chapter 5 adds not only the arguments about pedophilia but also strong evidence Oliver, a man now in his fifties, and Bobs, now about twelve, have been lovers for a long time. At this point, some readers may want to close their books.

They will be missing a remarkable story of the varieties of love and isolation told in a manner that is anything but prurient. Wilson masterfully distributes his sympathies among his finely realized characters. When Janet embroiders her memories, she inspires pity; her one moment of boozy confidence ends in humiliation. Catherine's sensual yearning for Michal is made graphic, as is her intense intellectual but sexless love for Oliver, her tutor and master. Camilla, a small, mousy woman and an improbable bride, is taciturn and unfathomable for much of the novel, but in the end she reveals her misery and her fierce tenacity. Her mother, Rosalie, is the only sane and conventionally decent person in the novel. She shows how attractive sanity and decency can be, and she touchingly yearns to understand and love her uncommunicative daughter.

At the novel's center are Bobs and Oliver. Even though Wilson does not take readers into Bobs's mind until the very end, she is a convincing mixture of ordinary girlish traits and a wisdom that is more than sexual. She is strong—stronger than any of her elders, and she knows her strength.

Oliver gets most of Wilson's attention. Many would think it impossible to give a sympathetic portrait of the inner life of a pedophile—but if it is possible, Wilson does it here. Oliver's sexual life unfolded in unfortunate ways, from intimacy with his stepmother, through a public-school homosexual liaison, to an unsuccessful attempt to have heterosexual intercourse. Then, like his heroes John Ruskin and Lewis Carroll, he comes to focus on young girls. They are not real girls, but imaginary ones, the "dream children" of the novel's title. When he meets Bobs, he feels that a miracle has happened. His dream child is incarnate, and he is filled not only with sexual desire but also with tender love for her. She reciprocates. He fills notebook after notebook with rapturous details of their love, a story he knows will someday rank with the classic accounts of William Hazlitt, Jean-Jacques Rousseau, and even Dante Alighieri. Only when Oliver reflects on the risks he runs (and that Bobs is about to enter puberty) does he decide to propose marriage to the unlikely Camilla.

Dream Children is a novel full of mysteries, and Wilson skillfully puzzles his readers about when events are taking place and what exactly has happened. Scattered references to such political leaders as Ronald Reagan and Margaret Thatcher locate the central events in the 1980's. Wilson carries the story through into the early and the late 1990's. Some questions about what is happening are answered in a page or two, but many persist longer. What is the point of the *Court TV* prelude? Is the woman's repressed memory accurate? Why does Lotte wield a knife? Why is Camilla so desperate to get married? Who is sabotaging Rosalie's bed and Oliver's car? What exactly do Oliver and Bobs do together? (Wilson skirts this issue, but by the end of the novel readers will have a fairly good idea.) More important to the story, who stole Oliver's notebooks? To whom may the thief have shown them? What should Oliver do if and when he is exposed? Should he kill himself? Should he kill Bobs too?

Most of these questions are answered, but two greater ones remain: What can readers make of the story? What does Wilson make of it? At the very end of the novel, an older Oliver appears, cheerfully squiring a new young girl, and readers imagine the worst. Oliver seems to end up happy even though he has left in his wake a number of disasters: madness, recrimination, false accusations, divorce, sexual malfunction, and suicide. What is a reader to make of Wilson's sympathetic treatment of this pedophile and the triumph he is accorded at the end of the novel?

Readers will differ in their answers. Some may be disgusted by Wilson's sympathy for Oliver or by his treating such a subject with a light touch. A better perspective comes from comparing *Dream Children* to an important work by another novelist, one whom Wilson knows well. Several years before this novel was published, Wilson was about to write the biography of one of the twentieth century's greatest novelists, Iris Murdoch. (He was subsequently fired from the job.) Although many readers will compare *Dream Children* to Vladimir Nabokov's 1955 *Lolita* (another novel about sex between an older man an a prepubescent girl), a more revealing comparison is to Murdoch's 1966 novel, *The Time of the Angels*. In it, an Anglican priest, accepting the assertion that God is dead, concludes that angels are now free from all constraint, that angels and human beings are free to perform all varieties of what once were thought to be evil and unspeakable acts. One of that priest's acts is to commit incest with his daughter.

In *Dream Children*, Wilson's usual sophisticated and satirical tone is far from the macabre atmosphere of Murdoch's novel, but his novel may best be read in its light. His central character has come to much the same conclusion as Murdoch's: Sexual taboos are a product of the age. Oliver lives his life according to his philosophic ideas; he differs from Murdoch's priest in that, in spite of everything, he thinks of himself as a good person. What feels right to Oliver must be right for him and must be right for his partner. Yet these are not necessarily the novel's judgments.

At first reading, it might seem that Wilson has written a trendy and shocking novel, like those of the young Ian McEwan. Yet *Dream Children* has a moral. Its ending should not be seen as ambiguous. Oliver is wrong; unreal dream children can cause real disasters to real people. Oliver's triumph closes the darkest of comedies.

Wilson's story is full of other dangerous dream children, imaginary constructs that give some satisfaction. Janet's memories have become fiction, but they hurt nobody. Yet if Lotte's imaginings do not quite lead to a death, Catherine's illusions do. Camilla's breakdown leads her to the vilest of dreams; when she tries to impose them on the real world, the result is much suffering. Only Bobs is left with no dream children, though readers may wonder how lucky she is to have escaped them.

Dream Children's apparently sympathetic focus on pedophilia makes it one of the year's most controversial novels, even though a thoughtful reading reveals that its sympathy does not imply moral approval. Its theme aside, *Dream Children* is a major novel written with a sure hand by a major British novelist—his best in several years. The novel's satire and wit will delight many readers; its wide-ranging sympathy will move many others. All readers should be appalled by how an apparently good man can come to Oliver's conclusions and then act upon them.

George Soule

Sources for Further Study

Booklist. XCIV, July, 1998, p. 1862.
Library Journal. CXXIII, July, 1998, p. 139.
New Leader. LXXXI, September 7, 1998, p. 13.
The New York Times Book Review. CIII, August 30, 1998, p. 17.
Publishers Weekly. CCXLV, June 8, 1998, p. 45.
The Spectator. CCLXXX, May 16, 1998, p. 36.
The Times Literary Supplement. May 15, 1998, p. 21.
The Wall Street Journal. August 12, 1998, p. A12.

THE DREAM PALACE OF THE ARAB WORLD
A Generation's Odyssey

Author: Fouad Ajami (1945-   )
Published: Pantheon Books (New York). 344 pp. $26.00
Type of work: Essays

Interweaving personal experience, literary criticism, and historical reflection, Fouad Ajami bemoans the failure of secular Arabic modernism to change Arabic societies

Principal personages:
> FOUAD AJAMI, the author, who chronicles his own life's journey from Lebanon to America
> BULAND HAIDARI, a poet from Iraq who dies in London
> KHALIL HAWI, a Lebanese poet and professor who commits suicide to protest Israel's incursion into Lebanon
> ANTON SAADAH, a Greek Orthodox nationalist executed by the Lebanese government
> ALI AHMAD "ADONIS" SAID, a prominent Syria-born writer, poet, and exile
> SADDAM HUSSEIN, the Iraqi dictator whose invasion of Kuwait leads fellow Arabs to invite American troops into their lands
> AYATOLLAH RUHOLLAH KHOMEINI, the leader of the Iranian revolution, who establishes a fundamentalist regime that is not copied by other Arab states
> GAMAL ABDEL NASSER, the Egyptian nationalist leader whose hopes are dashed by military defeats at the hands of Israel
> ANWAR AL-SADAT, Nasser's successor, whom Ajami portrays in a dark light
> NIZAR QABBANI, a Syrian poet whose life leads him to Lebanon and England

From the outset, a strong sense of nostalgia and melancholy permeates the pages of Fouad Ajami's perceptive work *The Dream Palace of the Arabs*. As Ajami points out, the funeral of exiled Iraqi poet Buland Haidari in London in the summer of 1996 is symptomatic of what Ajami perceives as the ailment of the contemporary Arab world. Having failed to transform their countries into secular, modern national states that could offer their citizens personal liberty, a flourishing culture, and a stable economy coupled with nationalist pride in strong, independent states, too many of the region's elite citizens have left their homes in exchange for an alienating future in Western society.

Immediately drawing in the reader to the lost world of his own past, Fouad Ajami evokes a haunting picture of his birthplace, "at the foot of a Crusader castle, the Beaufort, in a small village in the south of Lebanon," in 1945. His family of Shia Muslims had come to Lebanon from Persia, the contemporary Iran; indeed, the name Ajami means "the Persian" in Arabic.

When Ajami grew up in a secular Lebanon, his narrative tells, the Arabic world experienced a period of great optimism. Literary life flourished, and Arabic poetry saw a period of great activity and creative renaissance. Young Arabs of his generation looked to such leaders as Egypt's ruler Gamal Abdel Nasser, whose overthrow of the monarchy seemed like a new beginning for many. Yet within decades, this new start had failed, and political repression and a backsliding into theocratic, fundamentalist policies was evident.

Interweaving personal narrative, literary criticism, and an informed study of the recent history of Arabic lands from Algeria to the Persian Gulf, *The Dream Palace of the Arabs* chronicles in rich detail the tale of a dream that failed. From the vantage point of the late 1990's, Ajami tells of how high hopes have been dashed in the harsh political, economic, and military environment of the area. While Ajami's generation inherited the dream of a modernist revolution from the thinkers of the period between the world wars, their aspirations did not come to fruition. Throughout its narrative, *The Dream Palace of the Arabs* reveals how many of their hopes had been based on dreams and projections.

After shaking off their Turkish masters and freeing their countries from Ottoman rule after World War I, many Arabic nations in the Middle East became European colonies or protectorates. With the departure of the Europeans during the period of decolonialization after World War II, possibilities for the new nations seemed endless. Yet even as the Arabic world readied itself for a new era of freedom from foreign rule, Ajami reveals, there were signs that the new order would not be without its problems. It is no historical accident that so many of the poets and intellectuals featured in *The Dream Palace of the Arabs* were exiles from the countries where they had been born.

Buland Haidari, "Adonis" (the pen name of Ali Ahmed Said), and Nizar Qabbani had left the repressive regimes of Syria and Iraq for a first exile in then-liberal, cosmopolitan Lebanon. Yet even in Lebanon, there was death for those who sought to defy the old order of the clans and landowners. While dreaming of a radically new pan-Arabic society, Anton Saadah had been betrayed by a Syrian colonel to the authorities of the Lebanese government. Captured, the radical writer was sentenced to death and, "in the early hours of dawn, on the eighth day of August 1949 . . . was taken to a firing range by the sea, where he was shot." Even against this backdrop, Ajami asserts, intellectual life in Lebanon still flourished in the 1950's and 1960's. Poets such as Khalil Hawi had a rich following, and young people dreamed of a better future. Modernization and nationalism still appeared to be the path of the future for the Arab lands.

Ultimately, Ajami demonstrates in the first two chapters of his book, all these dreams were "a supreme delusion" and failed for two reasons. Moving at ease from lines of poetry to evocative descriptions of the landscape against which the events unfold, Ajami's narrative is unsparingly critical in its examination of dashed hopes.

First, the Arabic beneficiaries of the old order, the ancient elites of "the merchants" and landowners, refused to give in to new dreams. Second, as new leaders arose, from Nasser to the Ayatollah Khomeini, they turned out to have "promised more than they could deliver." As *The Dream Palace of the Arabs* turns to war, "the cruelest and most honest test" of dreams, Ajami asserts that "the enormity of the Arab defeat" in the Six

Day War of 1967, which was echoed twenty-four years later by Saddam's defeat in the Persian Gulf War, proved a merciless corrective for collective dreams.

"Arab nationalism had been a project of the intellectuals," Ajami writes. With the Arab forces in shambles after their attempt to extinguish the state of Israel in 1967, what remained of the illusion of political unity fragmented with "the defection of the Egyptian state from Arab politics" when Anwar al-Sadat made peace with Israel. Thus, Ajami asserts, "the continuity of a culture was shattered."

While a reader may take exception to Ajami's negative portrayal of Sadat, there is in his narrative nevertheless a genuine reflection of the bitterness of a generation. Intellectuals of Ajami's circle had seen their wildest political, national, social, and cultural dreams founder and come to naught in the heat of desert battles. Ajami's text again reflects the sadness of a people who lost everything they had held valuable and sacred after internecine warfare came to Lebanon after the outbreak of civil war there in 1975. Ajami's judgment on Khalil Hawi's suicide in 1982, when Israeli troops entered Lebanon in force, is relatively restrained; the author perceives Hawi's act as both anticlimactic and partially motivated by personal, rather than exclusively political, depression.

The Dream Palace of the Arabs judges the experience of the Gulf War to have been "a battle between a local predator and a foreign savior." Noticeable throughout Ajami's pages is the notion of a deep intellectual regret that Saddam's brutal inter-Arab aggression necessitated the appearance of the Americans to liberate Kuwait. Unable to free themselves from the evil in their midst, Arab people had to rely on the foreigners to create a solution.

Ajami's rich, sympathetic knowledge of Arab lands, literature, culture, and society provides the serious reader with wonderful insights into this part of the world. His technique of trying to access the soul of Arabia primarily through its fine literature, and his detailed description of landscape and culture, reveals a deep love for the world the author has left behind for America.

As Ajami's harsh criticism of Egypt as a "disappointment" reveals, the dreams of his generation have failed to become reality. Quite accurately, Ajami demonstrates how much the ideas of Arab modernism and nationalism were dreams, fictions, aspirations, and desires. The author and his friends did indeed seek a "dream palace" to supersede a harsh reality.

Yet Ajami, too, finds some hope among the ruins of failure. Accordingly, he balances his reckoning with Egypt's political and economic elite with a final assessment. For all of its misgivings and shortcomings, Ajami states, "Egypt's gift to other Arabs is the gift of its civility." In a place where the knife attack on Nobel Prize winner Naguib Mahfuz still caused widespread outrage and condemnation, there is still a place left for the dreamer. Egypt, Ajami feels, had not yet to exile its poets.

The final chapter of *The Dream Palace of the Arabs* is reserved to Ajami's critical reflection on the peace process between Israel and its Arab neighbors. With great insight, Ajami describes the fundamental unease with which Arab literary intellectuals responded to "the culture of peace," which seemed to spring from the Oslo Agreement of 1993. With an Israeli-Palestinian accord apparently in the making, a radical paradigm shift appeared to descend on the Arabic people of letters.

Ajami deftly chronicles the multiple battles among the intellectuals. There were those who embraced the prospect of peace and those who rejected it as "betrayal." Ajami himself arrives at a middle position. "There had been no intellectual or psychological preparation for peace," Ajami explains, remarking, "Men love the troubles they know." For genuine peace to become acceptable for the majority of Arabic intellectuals, Ajami states, there must be a shift away from a situation in which "little honor would be extended to pragmatists" and the "political culture of nationalism reserved its approval for those who led ruinous campaigns in pursuit of impossible quests." Ajami closes on a melancholy note. In his estimation, the gulf between Arabs and Israelis remains immense, and popular support for a peace that comes from a position of perceived weakness remains weak. To give up old principles may be hard for many, he suggests.

Overall, however, *The Dream Palace of the Arabs* takes its readers on a fascinating tour of the literature, exceptional poetry, culture, landscape, and society of the Arab lands. There is great melancholy for hopes that failed to materialize, dreams that went unrealized, and a past destroyed in part by unyielding extremism. The intellectuals whom Ajami presents to the reader come alive as sincere people who sought hard to find answers to better their societies and who dreamed of a better future. Their disappointments are part of the harsh realities of life in a strife-torn region, where military and economic reality remains the ultimate test for the viability of revolutionary aspirations.

R. C. Lutz

Sources for Further Study

Booklist. XCIV, January 1, 1998, p. 768.
Commentary. CV, March, 1998, p. 73.
The Economist. CCCXLVII, April 18, 1998, p. S4.
Foreign Affairs. LXXVII, March, 1998, p. 160.
Library Journal. CXXIII, February 15, 1998, p. 141.
Los Angeles Times Book Review. February 22, 1998, p. 10.
The New York Times Book Review. CIII, February 22, 1998, p. 8.
ORBIS. XCIV, Fall, 1998, p. 619.
Publishers Weekly. CCXLV, January 5, 1998, p. 50.
The Washington Post Book World. XXVIII, March 1, 1998, p. 1.

DREAMER

Author: Charles Johnson (1948-   )
Published: Charles Scribner's Sons (New York). 236 pp. $23.00
Type of work: Novel
Time: 1966-1968
Locale: Chicago and southern Illinois

A novelist with a philosophical bent looks back at Martin Luther King, Jr., and the Civil Rights movement from an interesting and unusual perspective

> *Principal characters:*
> MARTIN LUTHER KING, JR., a civil rights leader
> MATTHEW BISHOP, a young civil rights worker
> AMY GRIFFITH, a civil rights worker in whom Bishop takes a romantic
>   interest
> CHAYM SMITH, King's double

Charles Johnson was one of the late John Gardner's most successful writing students—Raymond Carver was the other—and in Johnson's fiction the influence shows. It shows most in Johnson's passion for ideas and in the way that, throughout his career, he has practiced what Gardner termed "moral fiction" and Johnson prefers to call "responsible fiction." Nowhere is Johnson's sense of responsibility to reader and society alike more evident or important than in *Dreamer*, his latest, as well as riskiest, novel.

Much of Johnson's story takes place in Chicago during the summer of 1966, the year Martin Luther King, Jr., made the risky decision to take the Civil Rights movement north. Johnson's narrative ploy is nearly as daring, though not unprecedented. Playing a variation on a tactic exploited so brilliantly by E. L. Doctorow, Robert Coover, Don DeLillo, Salman Rushdie, and others, he weaves together history and imagination, historical personages and fictional characters. One of *Dreamer*'s two most important imagined characters is the novel's semiautobiographical narrator, Matthew Bishop. "Cursed with a shy, Victorian presence," the frog-eyed, bespectacled, and bookish Bishop dropped out of college following the death of his mother the year before and joined the movement as a way to keep her already fading memory alive. Bishop, who reveres his mother (who, in turn, revered King), never knew his father, one of the novel's several literal and metaphorical deadbeat dads who are the polar opposites of King and the responsible novelist.

Part of Bishop's Southern Christian Leadership Council job involves "recording the Revolution, preserving its secrets for posterity—particularly what took place in the interstices." One of those interstitial events is the arrival of Chaym Smith at the "foul-smelling flat" rented for King in Chicago's "Slumdale." Unlike Saint Peter, who denied Christ three times, Bishop announces Smith's coming three times. "There's someone here to see you," he tells King. "I think you'd better take a look at him"—and well he should, for Smith is a dead ringer for the soon-to-be-dead King, his mirror image. Like all mirror images, however, Smith is a figure in reverse. Likened at one point to a photographic negative, Smith seems in many ways the negation of everything King represents. He is "the kind of Negro the Movement had for years kept away from the world's cameras, sullen, ill-kept, the very embodiment of the blues."

The startling, fantastic physical similarity between the two men serves to underscore the differences in the backgrounds of these two equally gifted individuals. One is beloved and encouraged by his family, the other orphaned, crippled, his formidable intelligence and good intentions gone at first awry then to waste, his Kinglike dreams turned into nightmarish reality. Yet even after so much bad luck and worse treatment, Smith still wants to be of use. Knowing of the threats made against King (indeed, having been attacked himself by those who mistook him for King), Smith offers to be his stand-in ("Greater love hath no man than this, that a man lay down his life for his friends," as the Bible puts it). As a civil war rages in Chicago and throughout the United States, Smith wants to play a part, but the war without is matched by the war within the enigmatic Smith, a man at once self-sacrificing and suicidal, reverential and resentful. If, as King wrote in *Chaos or Community* (1967), "A riot is at bottom the language of the unheard," then in Smith one finds just such a riot of conflicting voices and motives. Even the noble King vaguely fears the lowly, servile Smith to some extent: "You keep that man away from my wife, you hear?" However, King also wants to help Smith, to save him, and so he tells Bishop and another volunteer, Amy Griffith, to take Smith to a remote house that Griffith's grandmother owns in southern Illinois and teach him about the Civil Rights movement.

Once away from King, in the company of the two naïfs—Griffith and Bishop—Smith makes it clear that he has no interest in either the movement or salvation. Unwilling to be taught, this "remarkably talented mimic" wants only to learn about King so that, the reader suspects, he can undermine King in some unspecified manner in much the same way he seeks to undermine Bishop's faith in history (one more narrative lie), family (just so much kitsch), and nonviolence. Yet even as Smith plays Dionysus to King's Apollo, a Darth Vader easily seducing Bishop with the power of the dark side, he also teaches Bishop the ways of self-control he learned at a Buddhist temple in Japan.

Back in Chicago, this deeply divided figure, caught between spiritual yearning and murderous resentment, undergoes a conversion experience of sorts. Hearing King speak at a black church, Smith experiences the good in King firsthand, a good that for all his physical resemblance to King, Smith can recognize but never share (all this in language that clearly echoes Claggart's similar recognition concerning the essential goodness of the charismatic, though inarticulate, Billy in Herman Melville's *Billy Budd, Foretopman*). Yet even as he comes to understand so acutely his own powerlessness, his inability to be what King is, Smith also hears himself, his deepest, truest self, in King's voice. Afterward, playing King (in both senses: acting as and parodically playing at), he is shot by a black man who sees King as nothing more than a convenient and highly visible object for all his personal misfortunes and frustration. Smith survives, but the experience of hearing King (or hearing himself in King) and nearly dying in King's place, as King, effects a profound change, one that both alters and heals. It is a change that Bishop later literally sees in the notebooks and drawings he finds under Smith's bed: from the early works, "anguished and grotesque," to the more recent ones that "were simplicity itself," "delicate, lovingly detailed studies" revealing "the world's mystery and wonder." Bishop, however, is not the only one observing Smith. Two Federal Bureau of Investigation (FBI) agents arrive and make Smith an offer he cannot easily refuse: Either go to jail for earlier criminal acts or work for them in a way that, while not spelled out in the novel, is clear enough for any reader to imagine. The reader is also, and purposely, left to speculate as to Smith's fate once he leaves with the agents and disappears from the novel (and history), but only after handing Bishop the Commitment Form, now signed, that he had scoffed at before.

Mixed in with the first-person account in which Bishop bears witness, as it were, to Smith's part in the interstices outside the movement's official history are a number of highly reflective, italicized chapters that, although told in the third person, deal with King in a decidedly intimate, highly introspective manner. As a result, the picture of King that emerges from *Dreamer* is remarkably complex, managing to be at once reverent and human, a portrait of the civil rights leader as a man as divided in his own way as Smith was in his. The novel's King is the public man venerated by some, despised by others, a man "more tired, acclaimed, hated, gaoled, and hunted down than any other Negro in history," and the private individual tormented by the toll his work is taking on his family.

King is divided, or doubled, in another way. He is the latter-day Booker T. Washington espousing self-improvement during the movement's early years and the determined advocate of social justice and sweeping economic change during the later years. He is a man who becomes the leader of a group on the basis of the intelligence, articulateness, and solidly middle-class appearance, manners, and background that separate him from the vast majority of those he claims to represent, but "represent" in what way? In terms of what they are or what they can be? King stirred millions with his words. "I have a dream," he said, a dream of equality and assimilation for all African-Americans, indeed for all Americans. However, Johnson's King has another dream as well, the dream of escape from the ceaseless demands of public life, or, more generally, the demands of earthly life itself. Numerous times in the novel King returns, mentally and spiritually, to the Indian state of Kerala that he had visited some years earlier. Thus, it is not only Gandhi's theory of nonviolence, theory of satyagraha (truth force), and championing of the Harijans that King took from India, but something even deeper.

> In the region between waking and slumber, he [King] relived his trip to Kerala, feeling the heat, and watching the locals hang pots on coconut trees to collect their milk . . . , which became so intoxicating that crows sipping from the pots fell drunkenly to the ground and stumbled about cawing at the wrong time of day. For a few moments he dreamed of journeying there again for the rest he needed so badly, and to probe deeper into their concept of Maya—the world as itself a cradle-to-crypt dream, in which all men were caught and only the blessed allowed to awaken.

It is a dream toward which the novel moves even as it marches inexorably forward to Memphis. "It should have been a triumphant march, an exuberant overture, or trial run for the Poor People's Campaign" planned for later that year in Washington, D.C. Instead, the march intended to protest "the city's blatantly racist treatment of its black sanitation workers" became "the greatest mistake of his life." Johnson's writing is just as powerful here, sketching, in a single long paragraph, the shock of King's assassination and its aftermath, the "one hundred and twenty-five cities . . . erupting in flame"—as it is earlier, in a still longer paragraph describing the viciously racist mob that turned out to jeer at King on the day of the Marquette Park march two years before. Then, Johnson could add, "into this chaos stepped King"; now he could add only that "a prophet had fallen," with no one to take his place, least of all a young Jesse Jackson, about whom *Dreamer* is especially, if briefly, critical.

Against the violence that erupts following the assassination, the slow building of a viable black community in the Chicago suburb of Evanston that is described so lovingly and in such rich detail over so many pages early in the novel seems itself a lost dream by novel's end. Yet for all its gloom, *Dreamer* is a hopeful work, although at times a little too earnest for its own good. Johnson pushes his Cain-Chaym theme too insistently, though he deals more successfully and subtly with various civil wars tearing individuals, the black community, the Civil Rights movement, and the country apart. Although much of the overreaching language and intrusive philosophizing is intentional, reflecting the yearnings of Bishop's goodhearted but still sophomoric character, they jar nonetheless. Similarly, the wisdom of love that is the novel's message often seems too abstract or merely added on to be convincing. This is especially noticeable in the concluding coda, in which Bishop sums up the meaning of the life and death of King in language that, instead of lyrically soaring to transcendent heights, merely drifts before ending with a pompous whimper rather than a biblical bang, which, even if typical of a Bishop, seems altogether unworthy of a King.

Dreamer arrives, however, at an opportune moment. Important books by David Halberstam, Taylor Branch, and Gerald Posner, along with the death of James Earl Ray, the man found guilty of shooting King, have fueled renewed interest in the movement, King, and, of course, conspiracy theories. As Bishop says late in the novel, concerning the events surrounding the investigation into King's death, "the facts grew stranger with each new string I pulled." Enumerating these troubling facts but refusing to dwell on them, Bishop moves on to the possibility of an even bigger conspiracy, one in which everyone is included, "because we didn't listen when he was alive," because "The Way of agapic love, with its bottomless demands, had proven too hard for this nation. Hatred and competition were easier. Exalting the ethnic ego proved far less challenging than King's belief in the beloved community." If Johnson's language is not always up to the challenge, his head and heart surely are. He keeps his eye on King's vision, and he keeps King's eye, and Smith's too, on the reader. The cover portraits of King and Smith wrap around onto the dust jacket's inside flaps, leaving an eye on each to stare at Johnson's readers, reminding them not to fail a second time, reminding them of what once might have been and what yet may be.

Robert A. Morace

Sources for Further Study

Emerge. IX, June, 1998, p. 67.
Library Journal. CXXIII, April 1, 1998, p. 122.
Los Angeles Times Book Review. April 19, 1998, p. 5.
The Nation. CCLXVI, April 27, 1998, p. 27.
The New York Times Book Review. CIII, April 5, 1998, p. 14.
Publishers Weekly. CCXLV, February 23, 1998, p. 50.
The Times Literary Supplement. October 23, 1998, p. 23.
The Village Voice. May 19, 1998, p. 152.
The Washington Post Book World. XXVIII, April 12, 1998, p. 1.

AN EMPIRE WILDERNESS
Travels into America's Future

Author: Robert D. Kaplan (1952-   )
Published: Random House (New York). 393 pp. $27.50
Type of work: Current affairs, history, and travel
Time: 1996-1997
Locale: The western United States and Mexico

A commentary on the American West that finds cities evolving in ways that make traditional community values and government increasingly irrelevant to local economy and administration

A contributing editor for *Atlantic Monthly*, Robert D. Kaplan is an observer and analyst of modern conflicts. In such best-selling books as *Balkan Ghosts* (1993) and *The Ends of the Earth* (1996), he finds that societies are fragmenting along religious, class, or economic lines, that traditional national governments are becoming ineffectual or irrelevant, that police and military units are altering tactics to protect the wealthy from the growing armies of the poor, and that all such change is accelerating because of technology and the urbanization of the world's population.

In *An Empire Wilderness*, like a modern Alexis de Tocqueville, Kaplan, reared on the Eastern Seaboard, wanders through territory foreign to him—the West, the region that has always represented America's deepest hopes and sensibility because it was the frontier and therefore the land of opportunity. The physical frontier ceased to exist by the beginning of the twentieth century, but as Kaplan argues, the West still represents opportunity because, less burdened by traditions and richer in resources than the East, it is more open to change. Kaplan went hunting for trends and, not surprisingly, uncovered signs of not just change but also a transformation of the American political, economic, and racial landscape. Kaplan's critics charge that he has made a career out of worrying about social trends that seem untethered to traditional order. *An Empire Wilderness* is sure to encourage such criticism. While humor does sometimes enter the narrative, the evolutions of Western society that Kaplan discerns alarm him.

Whether readers should also feel alarmed is another matter. In his preface, he points out that the book is not a formal, comprehensive study. In fact, although Kaplan cites histories and formal studies by others, his mode of argument is not essentially objective. He recounts two trips that he took through the West and reports what he saw, what he heard Westerners say, and how these shaped his understanding. The book, then, is the "story of an idea as it emerged." Impressions steer the narrative.

Intimately intellectual, the book has considerable persuasive power. Kaplan is a penetrating observer; unafraid to make value judgments, he is yet sensitive to the subtleties of human interactions. Moreover, his style is supple and moving. He writes lovely scenic descriptions, knows how to let the character of his interviewees emerge from quotations and dialogue, and sometimes interjects analogies that are so unexpected and trenchant that the reader recognizes a powerful, independent intellect in him. Still, personal-point-of-view journalism is inherently selective; if it is to be convincing, it must show readers a large, diverse selection to avoid appearing biased or arbitrary. Here Kaplan shines. He interviewed a great variety of people (or overheard their conversations). During his main expedition, he traveled from St. Louis through Kansas, Nebraska, Wyoming, Montana, Idaho, Washington, and into British Columbia before stopping in Oregon. One side trip took him through Oklahoma, New Mexico, and Arizona and deep into Mexico; for a second side trip, he accompanied a busload of students from the military's Battle Command Training Program to the Civil War battlefields around Vicksburg, Mississippi. The narrative is studded with the remarks of military officers, real-estate developers, law-enforcement officials, academics (especially historians and social scientists), bureaucrats and statistics collectors, drug traffickers, atomic-bomb makers, journalists, writers, poets, politicians, homeless people, economic development promoters, and a cab driver—African Americans, Asian Americans, American Indians, whites, and Latinos. The reader witnesses the diversity of the West along with Kaplan.

The interviews, conversations, and eavesdropping form a mosaic that conveys the dominant theme: America is becoming homogenized, as is everywhere else in the world. Transportation, telecommunication, advertising, and computer technology expose people—wealthy and educated people, at least—to common ideas and modes of thought, thereby drawing them together culturally. As one place in the West becomes like every other place, there is a concomitant loss of local character, a "placelessness," and less community behavior.

Decentralization comes from this placelessness and from the growing chasm between the haves and the have-nots. The wealthy and the upper middle class move out of cities and into gated communities with their own security guards and shopping malls; they earn their living from the global economy and computer networking. As a result, multinational corporations often influence them more than their government, and there is a premium on having the educational or class background that qualifies one for this transnational information-age society. Meanwhile, the poor and the lower middle class are left behind in the inner cities, the infrastructure of which grows ever more dilapidated. Kaplan finds that public schools, especially in the slums, suffer particularly from neglect. Underfunded and overcrowded, they fail to prepare most students for the professional jobs needed in the global economy. The schools thus no longer help the poor rise out of poverty; they help keep the poor in place. Professional jobs in new high-tech industries and finance are filled instead by well-educated immigrants, especially from Asia and India.

Kaplan offers several examples of decentralized cities—decayed hubs surrounded by "posturban pods"—including St. Louis-East St. Louis, Omaha, and Tucson; to him, though, Los Angeles is the epitome. He finds it a vast sprawl of pods connected by highways taking people to jobs either downtown (which, he says, is deserted after working hours) or in other pods. The pods are segregated by economic class and race with little mutual intercourse.

A second major theme of the book is that Westerners are forming close ties across international borders. Economic and cultural interests draw them there. In the Southwest, Mexico is more important to the economy and culture than is, for example, New England. In fact, illegal drug trafficking accounts for so substantial a portion of the Southwestern economy, according to Kaplan's sources, that were the federal government's War on Drugs to succeed, the region would fall into a depression. The North American Free Trade Agreement (NAFTA) and the *maquiladora* factories, foreign-owned but employing northern Mexicans, also mesh international interests as Mexican workers buy American goods, often on shopping trips north of the border.

In the Pacific Northwest, Kaplan finds, cultural similarities between Vancouver, British Columbia, Seattle, Washington, and Portland, Oregon, in addition to the region's common agriculture, aquaculture, and high-tech economy, may produce more than business affiliations. He interviewed promoters of local and international planning committees who foresee a quasi-autonomous binational region—perhaps, eventually, even a new nation—called Cascadia, whose economic links will be to Pacific Rim nations. To future residents of a Southwestern-Northern Mexican quasi-state or to Cascadia, the federal government may become largely irrelevant to daily life. Indeed, Kaplan suggests that the functions of the federal government and its technologically sophisticated, professionalized military may shrink to a handful: principally, protection against terrorists, disaster relief, and arbitration in disputes between regions.

This Balkanization of the nation is the most unsettling possibility discussed in *An American Empire*. It is also the hardest to swallow. No economy can be entirely local, however wealthy and connected a region's populace, so how would local and regional economics work? How would resources be managed? Moreover, who would be in control of the national government? How could patents, copyright, and intellectual rights be decided, central issues in a technological culture? Who, or what, would hold the allegiance of the military? The future is inherently vague, and Kaplan cannot be expected to be clairvoyant, yet while his ideas fascinate, his vision of the future remains murky.

As the West goes, so goes the nation, Kaplan says. The entire country will become a loose affiliation of post-urban pods, like medieval city states, overseen by an imperial bureaucracy in Washington, D.C. The book's title, taken from Hart Crane's poem "The Bridge," reflects the basic idea: a postmodern empire, as if a recrudescence of the old European and Chinese systems in wilderness of American culture, displacing the great Enlightenment-inspired experiment of nationhood defined by representative democracy and equality under a shared law.

Several features of American character and at least one contribution from outside the nation are fostering the slow, subtle, mundane changes that will effect the transformation, according to Kaplan. First is apathy among voters. He cites statistics from the mid-1990's that suggest only about 5 percent of Americans involve themselves in politics, except by voting. When people do not actively control their own government, other entities, such as multinational companies, will do so, he argues. This apathy is more than political, however. Kaplan quotes Bertrand Russell's observation that modern life forces people to act against their instincts and thus is undirected and trivial. In a culture of diversion, people look for constant excitement to replace the lost feeling of belonging. This is hardly a new criticism of modern life. Kaplan might as well have quoted Henry David Thoreau's remark that Americans lead lives of "quiet desperation." On the other hand, Kaplan assures the reader, Americans will keep their well-known optimism in a stable future with ever greater wealth, and because of it may not comprehend the creeping changes in order to take advantage of them. Immigrants are likely to be the ones who profit. Kaplan interviewed several who have already done so. The influx of immigrants, well educated or not, who have more ties to a foreign culture than to America will hasten the changes, and make it even more likely that the America of 2050 will reflect the America of 1950 only in name.

Kaplan does find a few counterexamples to the trend toward posturban pods. He notes the lively commerce and socializing in the traditional downtowns of Missoula, Montana, and the Pacific Northwest cities. There, urban planners have intentionally tried to stop the sprawl by improving city-center public transportation and facilities. Although charmed by what he finds, Kaplan appears to regard this urban renewal as an attempt to hold onto an obsolescent past, self-defeating and sterile in the long run. Such New England-style, largely white enclaves may characterize Cascadia in the near future, but nowhere else.

Kaplan's vision of the future departs widely from the standard American view at the end of the twentieth century. That view expects a continually expanding gross national product, world leadership as the only superpower nation, and preservation of the mythic American values of individualism and free competition, if in a modified form to accommodate multiculturalism. To Kaplan, that America is already moribund. He occasionally compares the United States at the end of the twentieth century to Rome at the beginning of the fifth century; he suggests that the modern equivalent of the Visigoths are already taking over while citizens, self-absorbed and optimistic, hardly notice.

Kaplan's ideas have already impressed politicians—particularly U.S. president Bill Clinton—and journalists. That fact alone places the book among the year's most influential commentaries on contemporary life, but if *An Empire Wilderness* helps unsettle complacency about America's future and encourages readers to reappraise themselves as citizen, it will provide a signal service. Whether its vision of the future proves lucid and Kaplan's concluding observation that the nation's next era will be its most difficult and last is correct, only the future, a volatile arbiter, will decide.

Roger Smith

Sources for Further Study

Booklist. XCIV, August, 1998, p. 1956.
Commentary. CVI, November, 1998, p. 65.

Insight on the News. XIV, October 19, 1998, p. 36.
Los Angeles Times Book Review. October 4, 1998, p. 3.
The Nation. CCLXVI, November 16, 1998, p. 42.
National Review. L, December 7, 1998, p. 63.
The New York Times Book Review. CIII, September 6, 1998, p. 4.
Publishers Weekly. CCXLV, August 24, 1998, p. 39.
The Wall Street Journal. August 27, 1998, p. A12.
The Washington Post Book World. XXVIII, October 18, 1998, p. 4.

ENCOMPASSING NATURE: A SOURCEBOOK
Nature and Culture from Ancient Times to the Modern World

Author: Robert M. Torrance (1939-   )
Published: Counterpoint (Washington, D.C.). 1248 pages. $46.00
Type of work: Nature
Time: The ancient world through the eighteenth century
Locale: Worldwide

*A comprehensive anthology of writings about nature drawn from sources ranging from
ancient civilizations through the eighteenth century to the beginning of the Romantic Period*

Most anthologies of natural history writing begin with the Romantic Period, as if
nothing of consequence was thought or written about the natural world before then.
Recent scholarship in environmental history, however, has called that assumption into
question. Classicist and scholar Robert M. Torrance has assembled the first comprehensive anthology of natural history writing, ranging from the works of the ancient
world through those of Enlightenment Europe. The richness and diversity of Torrance's selections—many in original translations—should demonstrate that contemporary culture's alienation from nature is not shared by all the cultures of antiquity but
is a consequence of modern technology and of the particular cultural evolution of the
West.

As Torrance writes in his preface, *Encompassing Nature* had its genesis fifteen years
ago as an anthology of readings for a course at the University of California at Davis
entitled "Man and the Natural World." Torrance went on to help found the "Nature
and Culture" program at U.C.-Davis and to write *The Spiritual Quest* (1994). Afterward, he returned to his work of compiling a "wide-ranging sourcebook of materials"
about nature from the Western and non-Western worlds. Torrance's selections include
poetry and prose of every imaginable variety: creation myths, cosmologies, tribal
myths, children's stories, sacred scriptures, philosophical and scientific treatises.
Encompassing Nature is not a book to be read from cover to cover, but it is a rich
reference source to consult for its comprehensive collection of the environmental
wisdom of the premodern world. It is carefully edited, with extensive notes and
introductions to each selection.

As Torrance demonstrates through his selections, virtually every great culture of
antiquity enjoyed a sustaining relationship with nature. Sacred groves, streams,
springs, rocks, mountains, and gardens were all revered for religious, aesthetic, and
practical reasons. Without a mechanized technology, there was no drive to dominate,
control, or destroy the natural world. Nature was a force to be respected, the Sacred
Other, a seamless web of life in which humans found their place. The modern sickness
of separation from nature is not yet evident. Restraint, care, and usufruct were
universally practiced for practical and spiritual reasons. Throughout a wide range of
climates and habitats, humans survived without overwhelming other forms of life.
Ancient peoples understood the capacity of their lands to produce the basic needs of

life. Priests, shamans, or elders placated the local gods to ensure that the hunt and harvest would be sufficient to sustain the village. They knew the capacities of their local environment and took pleasure in the subtle changes of climate and season.

Creation myths and cosmologies bound ancient peoples to a greater sense of being. There was no sense of humans as a special creation, set apart from the rest of the living world, nor of the world itself as existing solely for human exploitation. On the contrary, an animistic sensibility generated an overall kinship and respect for life. Ancient civilizations provided time and leisure for arts, reflection, and contemplation, not the mindless, frenzied, destructive mechanical recreation of modern consumer culture. Poets, sages, mystics, hermits, and saints drew upon nature for inspiration. A reverence for nature has not been the recent discovery of the Romantics and their followers but has always been part of the human sensibility, especially for the ancient cultures that lived much closer to nature than modern artificial technology permits.

One of the chief pleasures of *Encompassing Nature* is discovering unknown treasures of nature writing in the non-Western cultures, especially those of the Orient. Torrance includes selections from ancient Indian culture—the Hymns of the *Vedas*, the teachings of Jainism, the *Bhagavad Gita*, and Sanskrit court poetry. His selections of Chinese and Japanese writing are particularly extensive, and there the reader may sample from a rich tradition of nature poetry and prose reaching back to the Chou Dynasty and the Yellow Emperor. Even when it becomes stylized, Chinese and Japanese nature poetry seems more precise and evocative than that of the Western pastoral tradition, with its silly and sentimental nymphs and satyrs, shepherds and shepherdesses. The iconographic focus on the precise image, with the use of empty space as contrast, evokes a spirituality and a sense of the sacred too often absent in the West. Chinese landscape painting and poetry evolved as closely related forms of aesthetic expression and, in turn, deeply influenced Japanese modes of expression. Perhaps the religious traditions of the East—Taoism, Shintoism, and especially Zen Buddhism—made nature more immediate and accessible to the Eastern sensibility. Indeed, nature poetry is a major genre, if not the primary focus and subject, of Oriental poetic reflection and contemplation. The exquisite poems of Li Po, Tu Fu, Han-shan, Muso Soseki, Matsuo Bashō, and others demonstrate that virtually all the categories of aesthetic contemplation of nature were invented in the East and only much later discovered and incorporated into Western verse.

There are new discoveries to be made in ancient Eastern prose as well. Kamo no Chomei's *An Account of My Hut*, a twelfth century Japanese *Walden*, expresses a Buddhist scholar's desire to escape from the strife-torn world of imperial politics in medieval Kyoto. Kenko's *Essays in Idleness*, a collection of 243 loosely connected personal reflections, expresses a Buddhist sense of the world's impermanence and the transitory beauty of nature.

Before the nineteenth century, there is little in the West to compare with the range and depth of Eastern nature writing. Many of the Western nature selections—whether literary, religious, or philosophical—share a tendency toward the abstraction and conceptualizing of nature. The pernicious effects of the Western separation of subject and object, of fact and value, of the sciences and the humanities, of the natural and the supernatural, are also evident in the selections. Perhaps Western dualism is implicated, or perhaps the Western philosophical habit of abstraction—the tendency to view nature rationally, analytically, quantitatively—encourages detachment from nature. Perhaps Westerners have insisted too much on their separateness, their exceptionality, their transcendence, rather than their commonality with the nonhuman world.

With some exceptions, the Western inability to be at home in the world seems evident in Torrance's selections. The honest and unsentimental portrait of country life in Hesiod's *Works and Days* contrasts with the Homeric deification of nature in the gods, the artificiality of the classical pastoral tradition, or the abstract musings of Greek philosophy. The religious appreciation of the world as God's creation in the *Psalms*, the *Song of Solomon*, and the *Book of Job* seems but a minor note compared with the dominant interpretation of *Genesis* as a warrant to conquer and subdue the natural world. As evident from the earliest European colonial charters, Western attitudes toward nature were too often based upon literalistic and fallacious interpretations of *Genesis* that were used to reinforce an instrumental ideology of extraction, the suppression of indigenous peoples, and the commodification of nature for the benefit of the crown. For the European mind, the concepts of wilderness and desert were burdened with negative cultural associations.

One has to go back to the beginnings of European vernacular literatures to find a direct appreciation of the natural world: in the Celtic poems of early Ireland, in Old English lyrics such as "The Seafarer," in the medieval English "Sir Gawain and the Green Knight," in medieval French and Spanish lyrics, in some secular Latin lyrics, and in early Italian verse. Many of these selections express a clear preference, however, for the garden or the humanized landscape rather than for wild nature. Mountains, for example, were rarely mentioned before Petrarch climbed Mt. Ventoux in the fourteenth century. Even amid the richness of Renaissance nature poetry, there is a distinct preference for stylized, imaginary, or pastoral landscapes rather than wild nature, for cultivated gardens rather than wilderness.

With the beginnings of the Renaissance, a new tradition of scientific writing grew—including the works of Nicolas Copernicus, Galileo, Johannes Kepler, Sir Isaac Newton, and William Harvey—that tried to comprehend the natural world as divine revelation expressed through natural laws. The shift from a geocentric to a heliocentric cosmos further displaced humans from nature. Philosophers such as Gottfried Leibniz, Baruch Spinoza, Blaise Pascal, Thomas Hobbes, John Locke, David Hume, and René Descartes turned to nature for evidence of regularity, harmony, and order: a deistic cosmos run according to natural law. Yet for the Enlightenment, a "state of nature" also came to imply a savagery against which the human society measured itself. Increasingly, however, nature became merely a context for the human intellect, an object of dissection and study rather than ethical or moral concern.

What seems missing from so much of premodern environmental writing is any real ecological insight—a dynamic sense of humans living within rather than apart from the natural world. What is needed is an understanding of culture as human ecology—a kind of comparative ecological anthropology that would permit humans to understand how cultures impact their land. What is the impact of the local environment on the human imagination? How does human habitation alter the environment? How does the culture reflect those environmental changes?

Where in classical literature, for example, are references to the impact of the massive deforestation of much of the Mediterranean world? The ecology of the Nile floods is reflected in Egyptian cosmology, but what about the more destructive periodic flooding of the Yellow River in China? What about the impact of cross-cultural exchanges of diseases and pathogens, especially between the Old World and the New, which decimated Native American populations? What about the record of the environmental impact of different cultural concepts of land ownership and use? For those interested in addressing these difficult questions, an anthology such as *Encompassing Nature* can help provide the sources and materials for a more comprehensive environmental history.

Encompassing Nature is a historically based, cross-cultural anthology of reading about both nature and culture, but given its history-of-ideas approach, its emphasis is more on human culture than on nature. One can observe the historical development of the Western tendency toward abstraction, already evident in the pre-Socratic philosophers, which has the effect of separating humans from nature. As David Abram argues in *The Spell of the Sensuous* (1997), the Western habit of mental abstraction obliterates the immediacy of the natural world and tends to favor ideas about the world rather than perceptions of the world itself. While indigenous humans could read the book of nature directly, we can now think about nature only in increasingly abstract and specialized ways, separated by disciplinary boundaries and technologies. As a cultural history of the idea of nature, *Encompassing Nature* is indeed a major intellectual achievement, but it is not a history of the ecology of culture, although it certainly provides the sources for such an approach.

After studying *Encompassing Nature*, a cultural ecologist might well ask how the tendency to think of nature abstractly took such firm hold in the West. Is it a consequence of a dualistic intellectual heritage? Is there a causal connection, as some have asserted, between ideas about nature and current environmental problems? What is the connection between the rise of capitalism, the commodification of nature, and environmental degradation? The task of analyzing and evaluating the selections in *Encompassing Nature* leads one to the work of cultural historians and human ecologists such as Paul Shepard and David Abram, who have tried to link the genesis of destructive attitudes toward nature to cultural constraints on the psychological development of the self that discourage direct knowledge of the more-than-human world.

Andrew J. Angyal

Sources for Further Study

Los Angeles Times Book Review. November 8, 1998, p. 3.
Publishers Weekly. CCXLIV, August 11, 1997, p. 33.
San Jose Mercury News. June 21, 1998, p. B8.
The Washington Post Book World. XXVIII, June 14, 1998, p. 2.

ENDURING LOVE

Author: Ian McEwan (1948-   )
Published: Doubleday (New York). 262 pp. $23.95
Type of work: Novel
Time: The late twentieth century
Locale: The English midlands

The measured life of a rational man is disrupted by the intrusion of a stranger who insists that they are totally and completely in love

Principal characters:
    JOE ROSE, a freelance technical writer
    CLARISSA MELLON, his wife, a university lecturer in literature
    JED PARRY, a young man infatuated with Rose

In a succession of novels set primarily in the United Kingdom during the last decades of the twentieth century, Ian McEwan has explored the disorder and fragmentation of a society in which his characters are grasping for some sort of value or direction to give their lives a semblance of meaning, or at least make them tolerable. As Michael Adams has astutely observed, all of McEwan's novels are, to some extent, a "meditation on alienation," his protagonists depicted in a struggle with political and psychological forces that seem to be expressions of the darker sides of human behavior. Inexplicable evil, random violence, casual cruelty, and pointless endeavors plague people who are essentially decent but often unsure of how to proceed in a world where chaos and stupidity seem to be in ascendance. Because of his insertion of scenes so grotesquely bizarre that they are unavoidably amusing, McEwan's books have tended to balance a dark vision of society with a comic stance that alleviates the grim circumstances they describe, and his main characters have often found some degree of surcease from their difficulties. Jeremy, the narrator of *Black Dogs* (1992), the novel preceding *Enduring Love*, states that there is "the possibility of love transforming and redeeming life." This is a position that McEwan supports but one which is not examined in much detail in his other work. In *Enduring Love*, he has not only examined and developed it in depth but has also gone further to consider how "the possibility of love" can be both life-enhancing and dangerously lethal, approaching a familiar subject and sentiment with such powers of invention that its ultimate power is renewed and revealed again.

Utilizing the kind of unusual situation that has become one of the distinctive elements of his writing, McEwan begins the novel with a devastating incident that completely unsettles the pleasant, comfortable, moderately fulfilling life of Joe Rose, a freelance writer specializing in explaining complex scientific phenomena in journals and on television programs. Rose is in his early forties, a "large, clumsy, balding fellow," as he describes himself, who is aptly and affectionately seen as "the world's most complicated simpleton" by his wife of seven years, Clarissa Mellon. Her work as a lecturer in literature at a mediocre university is moderately rewarding, and although they are childless because of a botched surgical procedure in Clarissa's youth, their relationship has an affirmative intimacy and mutual dependence that has enabled both of them to feel generally grateful and satisfied most of the time. On the way to a picnic in the lush English countryside of Chiltern Hills, they see a balloon with a small child moving out of control, and Joe joins several other bystanders in an attempt to anchor the carriage to the ground. A sudden wind shift pulls the balloon out of their grasp, and as the men are forced to relinquish their grip, one person holds onto the mooring rope. He is carried aloft and falls to his death. The horror of this is sufficient to leave Joe and Clarissa severely shaken—"I've never seen such a terrible thing as that falling man," Joe says—but what takes it beyond "mere tragedy" is that one of the other bystanders who ran to help, Jed Parry, has also experienced a kind of fall. He has become, in the instant of their meeting, totally and completely in love with Joe, in spite of Joe's utter displeasure with Jed's fervent protestation of affection.

Joe and Clarissa have established a kind of personal fortress to keep the harshness of life in England at the end of the twentieth century at a safe remove. Their life together is a place of retreat and restoration, providing protection against a world where illness, argument, petty aggravation, and pervasive ugliness are rampant. Most of their friends are separated or divorced, Clarissa's school is administered by uneducated oafs, Joe is troubled by his career decision to forsake pure science for reductive popularizing, and he is tormented by guilt since he feels that he and the others could have held onto the balloon's rope and saved the man whose heroic efforts were not only deadly but also unnecessary, as the balloon with the boy eventually landed safely. He and Clarissa regard the balloon tragedy as a trial and expect to help each other through the crisis.

This is one aspect of the "enduring love" that the title proposes. Jed's sudden declaration of ardor, however, compounds the equation and compels Joe to consider the most basic components of a structure he has previously enjoyed without much introspection. This, in itself, is not necessarily unpleasant because of his inclination for analytical reflection. Jed's wild devotion, though, cannot be contained by the methods of rational inquiry to which Joe is accustomed.

Jed is in his late twenties, affluent, idle, intelligent, and a religious zealot. Nothing that Joe does or says has any affect on "Jed Parry's love and pity." No matter how strenuously he tries to convince Jed that affection is neither returned nor in any way welcome, Jed finds a way to interpret everything as a secret signal or a type of lover's game. This is another version of enduring love—a frightening kind of fixation that would be overwhelming even if reciprocated and that is, in Joe's case, an introduction to the irrational that his entire life has worked to contain. For McEwan, it also represents one of the sources of the modern world's malaise. The forces of evil that are present in all his work are traced in *Enduring Love* to one of their originating points in the all-consuming selfishness of a person who is totally convinced that they are justified in their actions and that nothing anyone else does or says ultimately matters much. Jed claims to be guided by a vision of God, but he is actually a devilish monster of self-regard, oblivious to the claims and needs of others. His love is a form of narcissism, directed inward, and his expressions of devotion for Joe are actually designed to glorify his conception of himself.

Jed is a striking and frightening character but is not especially sympathetic—aside from his obvious pain and yearning—partly because his evangelical zeal makes it useless to try to alter his convictions and partly because the narrative consciousness of *Enduring Love* is located very specifically within Joe's perspective. McEwan has made Joe a convincing, trustworthy companion as well as an appealing, decent man so that it seems natural to assume and support his position. In addition to his care and concern for other people—as exemplified by his real interest in Clarissa's well-being beyond her capacity to cherish him—his ease and pleasure in the company of children, and his readiness to assist people in peril or pain, his mental processes are quite captivating to the degree that *Enduring Love* intermingles the theme of romantic love with issues more conventionally found in what has been called a "novel of ideas."

Joe is keenly aware of his own emotional and psychological responses to things as they occur and also relishes what he calls "the desired state, the high-walled infinite prison of directed thought." McEwan uses theories of evolutionary biology and particle physics to create metaphors for Joe's way of seeing, and the clarity with which the author handles theories of scientific inquiry parallels Joe's ability to present complex issues in contemporary science to the layman. As engaging as Joe's musing may be as an impressive act of mind, though, his life becomes really gripping when he finds that he must find new strategies for "fending off mad, wild, unpredictable forces."

By placing this relatively ordinary, reasonable man in a situation of tremendous stress, McEwan is able to introduce some scenes of spectacular action that unleash a surge of immense energy into the flow of the narrative. The balloon disaster is only the first of several such episodes, including an attempted assassination in a restaurant, a hilarious sojourn into a sinister posthippie commune to purchase a gun with which Joe hopes to defend himself, and a final confrontation with Jed, who has made Clarissa a hostage to his desires. Joe is somewhat out of his element in each case and illustrates some of the essential strengths of his character by acting with sense and resolution when no clear course is apparent. The fact that none of these confrontations has a really satisfactory outcome reinforces their plausibility while not lessening their impact, another example of the relish that McEwan has previously shown in his other work for graphic descriptions of excessive violence.

In *Enduring Love*, however, McEwan relies less on the spectacular incident than in any of his other books. The conclusion is an appropriate continuation of the changes that have occurred in Joe and Clarissa's lives and suggests that any confidence in stasis is illusionary, that the condition of existence in the modern world (and perhaps at any time in human history) is one of continuous alteration.

Joe's pattern of reflection on the circumstances of his life is linked to his (and McEwan's) consideration of the necessity for a coherent narrative to make sense of a shifting, elusive "reality." As Joe says, "What I liked here was how the power and attractions of narrative had clouded judgment," even as he recognizes that "by any standards of scientific inquiry, the story, however charming, was nonsense." The importance of a scientific method (as opposed to the fundamentalist beliefs of Jed) is emphasized throughout the novel, but it is juxtaposed with a growing acceptance of the importance of romantic intuition. No single, rigid stratagem is sufficient for dealing with the world, and the incompatibility of differing views of various events is made evident by the letters from Jed and from Clarissa that McEwan includes, by the results of police investigations, and by the placement of several appendices after the close of the narrative in which McEwan extensively notes the "scholarship" devoted to the psychic syndrome afflicting Jed. Whether the citations are as much the product of McEwan's imagination as Jed's letters (and the remainder of the novel), or whether they are actual studies of a particular pathology is left to the reader to determine by electronic research or some other means of confirmation, should this be required to satisfy someone's curiosity. More significantly, the amalgam of the imaginative and the determinable reinforces one of McEwan's central themes and leads toward his primary point that the enduring values of human affairs—especially the "possibility of love"—are what makes life bearable.

As critics such as Michael Adams have noted, McEwan has "long been considered one of the best of the English novelists born after World War II, but his first three novels and two collections of short stories have not brought him the recognition he deserved." *The Comfort of Strangers* was short-listed for the prestigious Booker Prize in 1981, and *The Child in Time* (1987) was the winner of the Whitbread Novel of the Year Award. *Black Dogs* was also short-listed for the Booker Prize and reached a wider audience both in Great Britain and the United States than his other work. *Enduring Love* has been promoted by his publishers as "the finest novel Ian McEwan has written in his remarkable career," and while this is a typical claim, initial response has been enthusiastic, as indicated by A. O. Scott's review, which describes the book as something like "*Fatal Attraction* with a screenplay by [Ludwig] Wittgenstein" and asserts, "It holds in place a varied architecture of philosophical speculation and closely rendered human situations. Plus a crazy stalker and some guns. What's not to love?"

Leon Lewis

Sources for Further Study

Artforum. XXXVI, March, 1998, p. S20.
Commonweal. CXXV, May 8, 1998, p. 24.
JAMA, The Journal of the American Medical Association. CCLXXIX, June 10, 1998, p. 1837.
Library Journal. CXXII, November 1, 1998, p. 116.
Los Angeles Times Book Review. January 25, 1998, p. 2.
Nature. CCCXCI, February 12, 1998, p. 654.
The New York Times Book Review. CIII, January 25, 1998, p. 7.
Publishers Weekly. CCXLIV, October 27, 1997, p. 50.
The Times Literary Supplement. September 12, 1997, p. 12.
The Washington Post. January 28, 1998, p. D2.

ERRATA
An Examined Life

Author: George Steiner (1929-   )
Published: Yale University Press (New Haven, Connecticut). 206 pp. $27.50
Type of work: Autobiography

One of the twentieth century's foremost interpreters of comparative literature reviews his life, interests, and beliefs

Approaching his seventieth year, George Steiner has written a compact, eloquent, impassioned, and deeply sad memoir that stresses his intellectual life while subordinating his personal life. As a self-proclaimed champion of canonical values in literary studies and as a mandarin defender of the European intellectual tradition, he regards himself as besieged and the arts and humanities as endangered into obsolescence. Above all, he broods darkly on the twentieth century being the most bestial period in recorded history: "Man has, on a pervasive scale, been diminished."

Steiner's accomplishments as a cultural scholar and critic are commanding. He has written sixteen books that span an astonishing arc from ancient Greek literature to chess, philosophy, philology, linguistics, aesthetics, religion, fiction, and poetry. Perhaps his most important studies have been *Tolstoy or Dostoevsky* (1959), *The Death of Tragedy* (1961), *In Bluebeard's Castle: Some Notes Towards the Redefinition of Culture* (1971), and *After Babel: Aspects of Language and Translation* (1975). In 1984 Oxford University Press published a selection of his essays in *George Steiner: A Reader*. In the introduction Steiner called the book "an interim statement." *Errata* is another interim report on the intellectual concerns of one of the twentieth century's most erudite humanists.

Steiner's parents were Austrian-Jewish, Zionist yet secular. Even though his father was a successful investment banker, he insisted that the family leave anti-Semitic Vienna, Austria, for Paris, France, as early as 1924. A man of formidable will and intellect, Steiner, Sr., had his son learn French and English at an early age and determined that George would be a teacher and scholar, at home not only with books but also in museums and concert halls. At the age of six the boy was introduced to *The Iliad* and *The Odyssey* in their original Greek, with the father daily examining the son on his understanding of the texts. In 1940 the family was fortunate enough to reach New York City. George was enrolled in a French Lycée in Manhattan, where he read Greek and Latin authors, Jean Racine and Paul Claudel, as well as William Shakespeare.

Shakespeare evokes a somewhat divided, though admiring, response from Steiner. In *The Death of Tragedy*, he separates Shakespearean drama from the genre of absolute tragedy as found in classical Greece and seventeenth century France. Rather, Shakespearean tragedy is pluralistic and tragicomic, with the mature Shakespeare refusing to compact the universe into a black hole; even *King Lear* (1605-1606), Steiner insists, has countercurrents of humane reconquest and hints of dawn. In *Errata* Steiner is sympathetic to the philosopher Ludwig Wittgenstein's critique that Shakespeare's art lacks an overtly ethical-metaphysical dimension as is available in, for example, Sophocles' *Antigone* (441 B.C.; English translation, 1729), Euripedes' *Bakchai* (405 B.C.; *The Bacchae*, 1781), and Jean Racine's *Bérénice* (1670; English translation, 1676). Shakespeare's characters have no coherent ethics, no mature philosophy, let alone any enacted evidence of a transcendent faith. Discussing the role of religion in the arts, Steiner finds it suffusing virtually all great works, Shakespeare's being the only "towering exception. There is in his plays a seeming absence of any ascertainable religious position." This is an overstatement. Modern writers often fail to take religious positions; witness Stendhal, Gustave Flaubert, Émile Zola, Henrik Ibsen, Anton Chekhov, August Strindberg, Thomas Mann, Ernest Hemingway, Alberto Moravia, and many more.

Steiner's procedure in *Errata* is to avoid personal revelations in any depth. Rather, he uses the bare bones of his activities to probe into his abiding passion for the life of the mind. Thus he devotes only a few paragraphs to his study for a B.A. at the University of Chicago. What fascinated him there were classes in Aristotelian-Thomist epistemology, social anthropology, poetics, and philosophy. In a later chapter on his teachers, he paints vivid vignettes of his most memorable Chicago instructors: The Miltonist Ernest Sirluck drilled him in linguistic history and rhetoric, Puritan ideologies, and the importance of historical context. The Thomist Richard McKeon taught him to read Aristotle deeply. The poet-critic Allan Tate showed him how to read poetry closely and employed Steiner's Judaism in an eccentric way. Tate had been a member of the jury that awarded the Bollingen Prize for poetry to Ezra Pound. The Jewish poet Karl Shapiro had accused Tate of a protofascist and anti-Semitic bias in this judgment. A courtly southerner, Tate wished to challenge Shapiro to a duel but first inquired of Steiner whether rabbinic law and Jewish practice permitted such swordplay. Steiner assured Tate that it did. Tate issued his challenge; Shapiro laughed it away and instead published his correspondence with Tate. This is the only light episode in Steiner's otherwise somber book.

Steiner's M.A. work at Princeton is never specified. All the reader learns is that he and his wife, "new to marriage," saw much of the brilliant but difficult critic R. P. Blackmur. Blackmur's best work was done in studies of Henry Adams and Henry James, both congenial to his fastidious temperament. Impoverished, lonely, alcoholic, jealous, and vengeful regarding other poets and scholars, Blackmur was a profoundly unhappy person. Steiner generously praises Blackmur's uncompromising commitment to high standards and mourns the injustice of his eclipse in reputation, his work considered "too demanding . . . for a literacy of fast foods"—a dimming that may perhaps also occur to Steiner.

Determined to avoid personal disclosures when possible, Steiner never mentions his Rhodes Scholarship to Oxford and does not clearly explain the university's astounding rejection of his Ph.D. thesis, a first version of his *Death of Tragedy*. Because of the intervention of Humphry House, a Gerard Manley Hopkins and Charles Dickens scholar, he was reexamined and given his doctorate. Only glancingly does

Steiner refer to his stellar academic career thereafter: professorships at the Universities of California at Berkeley, Geneva in Switzerland, Cambridge, and Oxford, as well as invitations to give distinguished lecture series at Harvard, Oxford, and the University of Toronto. Then there has been a good deal of reviewing, of which he mentions only having contributed over 150 review-essays to *The New Yorker*, which asked him to fill the gap left by the death of another great comparativist, Edmund Wilson.

Reviewing his life in literature, Steiner, adhering to his text's title, admits to errors. He has been occasionally careless over details; he has scattered and, thus, wasted his strengths. His intellectual restlessness has made him drop subjects once he had discussed them instead of exhaustively pursuing them. "My belief that cows have fields but that passions in motion are the privilege of the human mind has long been held against me." In his devotion to high culture, he has neglected such popular arts as film, television, and popular music. His errors of commission and omission fill him with sadness. Being a mandarin, Steiner calls his sorrow by the Latin word, *tristitia*.

Love of music has been a *sine qua non* of his life, even though he is unable to hold a melody or play an instrument. He marvels at the connotations of the myth of Orpheus, who played the lyre and sang so beautifully that he charmed savage beasts and caused mountains to move so they could hear him. Orpheus lost his wife Eurydice to the Underworld when his love had him look at her before they could reach home. That love of Eurydice also caused Orpheus's death when jealous maenads tore him apart. Steiner muses on the fable's confrontation between darkness and light, eros and death. Rainer Maria Rilke's *Die Sonette an Orpheus* (1923; *Sonnets to Orpheus*, 1936), he notes, asks whether Eurydice desired rebirth, whether she had not found peace in Hades. In one of Franz Kafka's paradoxes, the finest of songs is that of condemned souls singing in the pit of hell. Music, Steiner concludes, can both madden and heal, be the food of love and trigger feasts of hatred. It functions outside good and evil, is essentially inhuman and mysterious: "Thus, the collaborative interplay as between voice and piano in a *Lied*, or the execution of a string quartet, may well be the most intricate, non-analyzable happening on this planet."

As in a number of his previous essays, Steiner muses on Judaism. Jewish survival contradicts the norms of history, which dictate gradual assimilation, crossbreeding, the effacement of original identity, and sometimes genocide. The disproportionate radiance of the Jewish contribution to civilizations is astonishing: Both Christianity and Islam descend from Jerusalem. One-half of the Nobel winners in science are Jewish. The modern climate stems largely from Karl Marx, Sigmund Freud, Albert Einstein, Marcel Proust, Franz Kafka, Arnold Schoenberg, Ludwig Wittgenstein, and Claude Lévi-Strauss. The ideals of family life are Jewish-inspired. Steiner asks, "Can Western history and culture do without its Jews?"

Why, then, the persistence and ubiquity of anti-Semitism? Steiner rejects the usual explanation that Jews are hated as Christ-killers. Rather, Jews are blamed as begetters of a monotheistic faith. The Mosaic God establishes uncompromising prohibitions on murder, adultery, and greed; a strict discipline of soul and flesh; a counterinstinctual restraint toward all who offend—not only forgiving enemies but also learning to love them. Moreover, Jews have been prominent in preaching utopian socialism, notably in its Marxist version. They are often leaders in movements of social justice and peace. Steiner writes, "Judaism has brought Western civilization face to face with the blackmail of the ideal. . . . Of this pressure, I believe, is loathing bred. . . . Nothing grows more unbearable than to be reminded recurrently . . . of what we ought to be and, so crassly, are not. . . . After that, what forgiveness?" His analysis echoes that of the Grand Inquisitor haranguing Jesus in Fyodor Dostoevski's *Bratya Kamazovy* (1879-1880; *The Brothers Karamazov*, 1912).

Reflecting on modern history, Steiner is appalled. Killing fields have followed killing fields. Between 1914 and the closure of the gulags, at least 75 million people have been killed; even the Holocaust caused by the Germans is not unique in the twentieth century's history. The earth has literally become hell. In such appalling times, how does one justify study of the arts and humanities? The sad fact is that 95 percent of mankind has no interest in them. Moreover, the appalling truth is that, all too often, the arts and humanities fail to elevate or humanize. It is possible to listen to Franz Schubert and Johann Sebastian Bach in the evening then torture victims in a concentration camp the next morning.

George Steiner has no solution to this conundrum. He can only testify to his own passions. All he knows is that for him, literary study, theological and philosophic arguments, classical music, poetry, art—all these are his excuse for living. He cannot breathe without the challenge of these high places, and his works show that he rightfully inhabits them.

Gerhard Brand

Sources for Further Study

The Christian Century. CXV, July 1, 1998, p. 657.
Kirkus Reviews. LXVI, January 1, 1998, p. 44.
Library Journal. CXXIII, February 1, 1998, p. 87.
The New York Times Book Review. CIII, April 12, 1998, p. 18.
Publishers Weekly. CCXLV, January 19, 1998, p. 360.
The Spectator. CCLXXIX, September 6, 1997, p. 39.
The Times Literary Supplement. October 10, 1998, p. 31.
The Washington Post Book World. XXVIII, March 22, 1998, p. 8.
WE Magazine. July, 1998, p. 82.

THE EVOLUTION OF JANE

Author: Cathleen Schine (1953-   )
Published: Houghton Mifflin (Boston). 210 pp. $24.00
Type of work: Novel
Time: 1998
Locale: New England and the Galapagos Islands

A wry and inquisitive look at the theory of natural selection and the human version of it, as seen in the narrator's reflections on a childhood friendship won and lost

> *Principal characters:*
> JANE BARLOW SCHWARTZ, the narrator, a twenty-five-year-old woman
>   on a tour of the Galapagos Islands
> MARTHA BARLOW, a tour guide and former childhood friend of Jane
> ANNA BARLOW, Jane's eccentric late great-aunt
> GRACE BISHOP BARLOW, Jane's mother
> ROBERT BARLOW, Jane's father
> GLORIA STEINHAM, Jane's fellow tourist, a high-school science teacher
> JACK CORNWALL, a fellow tourist

Recently divorced Jane Barlow has been sent by her mother on a tour of the Galapagos Islands to recover her peace of mind. These are the islands to which nineteenth century naturalist Charles Darwin traveled on the famous voyage of H.M.S. *Beagle*, the ship sent by the British navy to map the southernmost coastline of South America. It was on the Galapagos Islands, an area that had not been studied by scientists, that Darwin had the opportunity to study the infinitesimally slow changes in plant and animal life and develop his theory of evolution through natural selection.

Jane, an inquisitive and intellectually curious young woman, finds herself following in Darwin's footsteps in a group tour of those same islands. She gets a shock immediately on arrival when she finds out that the tour leader is Martha Barlow, her old childhood friend and cousin. As children, the two of them spent a series of idyllic summers together in the seaside town of Barlow, New England, named after the founding family fathers. However, they have had no contact for ten years, ever since Martha, without any explanation, broke off their friendship when they were both fifteen years old. Since that time, Jane has racked her brains to figure out what caused the split between them, but after all these years, she is none the wiser.

The central metaphor of the book is the question of how a species is defined. Jane, who has been fascinated by Darwin and his theories since she was a girl, puzzles over this again and again. How is it that mockingbirds, who all look similar, in fact make up several different species? Conversely, why are a greyhound and a Pekinese, who look so dissimilar, members of the same species? Who decides what belongs to one species and not to another, and how? What is the difference between a species and a subspecies?

> Was the wing of one fly slightly bigger than the wings of its cousins? How much bigger did the wing have to be to make the fly a member of a new species? If the wing differed just a smidgen, perhaps the fly was a member of a subspecies. Or could it simply be an individual of the same species which varied slightly from its peers, a fly with a big wing?

The running joke is that no one on the trip takes Jane's questions very seriously. However, Jane herself does, and her inquiry is related to the other question that occupies her: the evolution of friendship, specifically of her friendship with Martha. Originally, she and Martha were not only related but also joined virtually as one in tight friendship. Yet at some point they bifurcated and became two separate, in a sense unrelated, entities, two species rather than one. As Jane tries to understand the nature of the evolution of species, of how one thing becomes another, she also grapples with the equally mysterious question of how a human relationship can change into something very different from what it formerly was.

The story itself, which is told in Schine's finely honed and witty prose, unfolds on two levels. On one level, there are frequent flashbacks to Jane's childhood, showing the two girls meeting for the first time and becoming friends. The relationship as sketched by Schine is charming and thoroughly believable, exactly capturing the way the child sees the world and the people she encounters in it—naïveté held together by a weave of childlike logic.

To sustain the reader's interest, this part of the narrative is kept going by frequent references to a family feud that goes back two generations. Although the feud was part of the landscape of the young girls' lives, young Jane was never able to find out what it was about, although she and Martha would jokingly exchange theories about its origins. As a grown woman, Jane wonders whether the family feud had something to do with the sudden rupture in her childhood friendship.

The second level of the narrative is the exploration of the Galapagos Islands undertaken by Jane and the group of people with whom she finds herself thrown together. Schine enjoys tossing in a wealth of minutiae about Darwin and about plant and animal life on the Galapagos, making it interesting by filtering it through the speculative, questioning mind of her protagonist. Jane cannot read a fact in her guidebook or observe a natural phenomenon without its triggering ideas and questions. Her mind also goes back and forth from natural selection to human relationships. Regarding the family feud, for example, the habit of the blue-footed boobies (large brown birds) she observes is for the oldest chick to push out the younger ones from the nest. Perhaps, Jane speculates, it had been the same with the three Barlow brothers, including the great-grandfathers of Jane and Martha—a kind of inevitable feud that was programmed into the family DNA, in which case she and Martha were genetically incapable of remaining friends.

Thrown into the mix is the unusual collection of tourists that are Jane's companions. Here Schine is at her best; all the characters come across as individuals, even though in this short novel the author does not have much space to elaborate on them. The biggest role is allocated to Gloria Steinham, a middle-aged high-school science teacher, whose appearance is distinctive because her clothing is drawn from so many different cultures that it resembles a kind of ethnic fair or United Nations bazaar. Gloria shares a cabin with Jane and serves as a sounding board for Jane's restless questioning, to which she responds sometimes with common sense, sometimes with flat-out contradiction, sometimes with another theory that has not occurred to Jane.

Schine's description of Gloria reveals her comic technique of applying Darwinian theory to her characters. She comments that once an organism has branched out in one direction, it cannot retrace its steps or leap across to another branch. Gloria however, appears to contradict this:

> She appeared to encompass all the branches of evolution at once. Her earrings were feathers, her necklace was shells, her bracelet was seeds. She was adorned with claws and suede pouches and tiny gourds. Her hat was printed with tropical fish. Wrapped around her, a cloth of a primitive African pattern created an ostentatiously primitive skirt. Her shoes had been woven by an aboriginal Asiatic desert tribe.

The other notables among Jane's companions are the Cornwall family. Widowed Mrs. Cornwall, who carries her husband's ashes around with her, is accompanied by four members of her family. They include her son Jack, who is Jane's age and for whom she forms a brief and vague romantic attachment, until she finds out to her chagrin that Jack, unknown to everyone except his family, is secretly engaged to Martha. Then there is Martha herself, as seen through the eyes of Jane. She is friendly in a detached way, knowledgeable, efficient, confident, as Jane remembers her from her childhood. Martha, though, shows no inclination to respond to Jane's many hints about a past friendship so abruptly sundered.

This leaves Jane to ponder a variety of different possibilities. Could it have been because of an ambiguous note she once left in Martha's room, when Martha was on a trip with her parents? Or was it perhaps because of an essay she wrote that mentioned Martha? Jane sent it to her friend and never heard from her again.

The issue is finally resolved with the help of an entry in Darwin's journal decrying the notion that the length of the day is adapted to the duration of human sleep, rather than the other way round. When Jane reads this, she realizes that she is looking at the issue upside down. It was nothing that she, Jane, had done, that had caused the rupture with Martha. It was simply that Martha had her own life journey to make, involving travels of which Jane had no knowledge and for which she bore no responsibility. Therefore, there was no need of forgiveness. The ending of the friendship was just an accident, like natural selection, that had no meaning other than its unintended outcome.

This realization comes hard on the heels of Jane's resolution of her present feelings about Martha. Sick from sunstroke, Jane vomits violently. When Martha cleans up the mess with quiet compassion, Jane feels only a vast gratitude for her.

As for the feud, it is finally revealed that the cause was a mundane one: money. In a business transaction, one branch of the family deprived the other of its rightful share. Another family secret, which is revealed when Martha lets slip what their great-aunt Anna said on her deathbed, is that Jane's mother and Martha's father were once engaged to be married. The engagement was broken off because, as the result of a complicated (and no doubt random) glitch in family relationships, they turned out to be brother and sister.

In the final page of the novel, Schine suggests a twist to the ideas that she has been exploring throughout her narrative. She has established that, following Darwin, there is no design, no plan, no meaning in evolution. There is only chaos. Yet Jane's mother invests the word "chaos" with positive meaning. When Jane was a child, she would often observe her mother murmuring "chaos" to herself in the mornings, when she was gardening or involved in some other pleasant or mundane activity, and smiling as she said it. Little Jane therefore took "chaos" to be an expression of joy. In the last sentence of the novel, the word recurs, again spoken by Jane's mother, as she looks at a photograph that Jane took on her trip. It is a serene picture of some pigs; the sun is setting in a bright pink sky, amid green grass and the shadows of trees. "Chaos," says Mrs. Barlow, with a smile. It is as if Cathleen Schine is deconstructing the whole edifice that she (and Darwin) have built. Everything may be random, everything may be a chaos, but out of chaos emerges a kind of joy, a kind of beauty that has its own value and its own meaning.

The philosophical subtlety of *The Evolution of Jane*, as well as its delicately comic tone, will undoubtedly enhance Schine's reputation as a novelist of distinction. This, her fourth novel, exhibits the same wit and elegance that Schine displayed in the popular *The Love Letter* (1995), in which she explored the public and private aspects of love. *The Evolution of Jane*, however, has more in common with Schine's second novel, *Rameau's Niece* (1993), a comedy of manners that was also a satire of the philosophy of the Enlightenment. That novel, like *The Evolution of Jane*, possessed a teasing philosophical depth that can only come from solid learning, and reflection on that learning, on the part of the author.

Bryan Aubrey

Sources for Further Study

Booklist. XCIV, July, 1998, p. 1831.
Library Journal. CXXIII, August, 1998, p. 134.
Los Angeles Times Book Review. October 4, 1998, p. 2.
New York. XXXI, October 12, 1998, p. 128.
The New York Times Book Review. CIII, October 11, 1998, p. 13.
Publishers Weekly. CCXLV, July 13, 1998, p. 59.
Seventeen. LVII, October, 1998, p. 116.
The Wall Street Journal. October 2, 1998, p. W14.

EX LIBRIS
Confessions of a Common Reader

Author: Anne Fadiman (1953-　　)
Published: Farrar, Straus & Giroux (New York). 162 pp. $16.00
Type of work: Essays

Personal reflections on a writer's affection for the written word

Bibliophiles come in as many stripes as the books they love. Some are collectors of pristine first editions, while some are literary hedonists whose dog-eared volumes are marked with the splotches of intimate companionship. The specific scent of a new book and the musty redolence of a used one mark addictions to the written word as varied and individual in expression as romantic love. Anne Fadiman is a gifted lyricist whose present collection of eighteen short essays sings the love of words and books in the most concrete and personal terms. These essays were written as regular contributions to the magazine *Civilization*. They are defined as personal rather than scholarly in tone. The collection is arranged in nearly the order of publication. In many of the essays the changing family life of the author may be glimpsed, from early marriage to middle age with two children.

Fadiman's tone is generally light, marked by self-deprecating humor and blithe admissions of literary quirkiness. There is no hint of intellectual pomposity, although the author certainly possesses impressive credentials. She has already published one widely reviewed volume of serious journalism, *The Spirit Catches You and You Fall Down* (1998). Entirely different in subject from *Ex Libris*, this first book documents the often-tragic failures in communications attendant on the intersection of modern science with traditional societies. Her parents, to whom she dedicates *Ex Libris*, are both professional writers, as is her husband, George Howe Colt. So many familiars of the Colt-Fadiman ménage are authors that a section of their home library is devoted specifically to the production of friends and family. Readers of *Ex Libris* are expected to sympathize with a book-centered lifestyle and to come equipped with broad general culture and a large active vocabulary.

"Marrying Libraries," the first essay in this collection, quickly establishes the hallmarks of the volume: humor, personal details, and an abiding passion for the nitty-gritty of books, their classification, and their housing. In Fadiman's world, well-loved books are portable friends, each one redolent of the moment in which it was first read. Her husband, too, is alive to the power of the individual volume to inspire loyalty. When they first set up housekeeping, each brought many beloved books into the same New York City loft, but somehow they avoided the greater commitment of coshelving. In fact, they were married for five years and had shared in producing a child before they could agree on sharing book shelves. Colt's "English-garden" style of cataloguing mingles time period and literary genre according to his own logic. Fadiman arranges her "French-garden" library chronologically and by genre. Once the decision is made to accept one cataloguing style, subsequent negotiations must deal with weeding of unworthy and duplicate volumes. Two outwardly identical volumes are individually precious to their owners, imbued with a fragile and particular essence of the past. Fadiman's light-hearted, self-deprecating explanation of the process reveals a great deal about her marriage and the importance of books in her life.

From earliest childhood, Fadiman has lived and breathed words. Certainly *Ex Libris* celebrates books and reading, but its enthusiasm extends to the smallest units of language. "The Joy of Sesquipedalians" introduces the reader to a childhood friend, Wally the Wordworm, a denizen of bedtime stories told to Fadiman and her older brother Kim by their father. Wally, as an alter ego for the senior Fadiman, seeks out and devours extremely long words, the "sesquipedalians" of the title. With a collector's fervor, the adult Anne Fadiman still pounces on new words, savoring their particular history and poetic ring. Her childhood family relished any kind of competition in information. They spent family evenings in front of the television watching the College Bowl and competing as "Fadiman U." In adult life, when Fadiman discovers an author whose work is replete with unfamiliar vocabulary, her first thought is to test friends and relations with these delicious tidbits. She develops individual word scores keyed to background and profession, as well as her own theory about what kinds of words are current in the late twentieth century. She even provides a key at the end of the essay so that her readers may score themselves, a sort of invitation to matriculate in a branch of Fadiman U.

Picture the family of wordworms gathered together in a restaurant, their heads bent over the menu. Are they seeking novel culinary experiences? No, they are busily acting as copy editors, perusing the menu in search of misspellings and florid misuse of grammar and vocabulary. Fadiman admits to reading everything, from catalogues to car manuals. She views every written text as a chance to savor language, as well as to proofread and emend usage. One essay probes this compulsion to read and correct, and profiles several other individuals equally devoted to correct usage, not only professional copy editors but also zealous amateurs. Another essay, "The His'er Problem," discusses the conundrum created for such wizards of word usage faced with the changing gender politics of the late twentieth century. Fadiman explores the appellation "Ms" and her own realization that she herself is the person for whom this scorned neologism was invented. She carries her reflections further to ponder the inclusiveness of the pronoun "he" and whether it can, indeed, answer the needs of an age when women advocate equal treatment under the laws of language. Although she consults authorities ranging from her sixth-grade grammar book to her father, her decision to read "he" as masculine, not general, reflects her individual parsing of gender, political, and grammatical complexities.

It is no wonder that Fadiman, entranced as she is by words, should have toyed with verse along the way. In "Scorn not the Sonnet," the author reflects on the paradoxical nature of poetry, which can achieve liberation of thought within extreme formal constraints. Her discussion of the sonnet is not a strictly technical one. Its first focus is humorous, with examples of bad sonnets, some drawn from her own youthful production. Its second focus is serious, an account of the consolation drawn from poetry by her elderly father while facing the devastating loss of his eyesight. John Milton's "On His Blindness" reminds the older Fadiman that great works can be accomplished under the weight of adversity. The blind Milton finds consolation in religious faith; the agnostic Clifton Fadiman's consolation is based on the durable literary tradition he shares with his daughter.

There is no mystery about the attraction order holds for Fadiman, whether as a proofreader, versifier, or home librarian. In "The P.M.'s Empire of Books," she peers into an eccentric publication of the great British politician, William Gladstone, four times prime minister to Queen Victoria, a pamphlet that prescribes the optimum arrangement for a home library. As she resumes Gladstone's authoritative reflections on placement of books and engineering of shelving to provide the greatest amount of storage for the smallest investment of room space, Fadiman assumes her readers to share her fascination. Here is a true community, one of people for whom books are precious not only for the thoughts they carry from one mind to another but also for their very physical substance, objects to be manipulated and set in logical spatial order.

Fadiman is also bent on celebrating writing, words, and books as sensual experiences. She incorporates the books she shares with her husband into the fiber of their marriage, folded into the marriage bed itself. She dedicates "Eternal Ink" to the loss of a favorite fountain pen. She celebrates the fact that literature reflects more than literary taste, that it can be as basic an appetite as hunger for food or sex. In "The Literary Gluttons," she asserts that the sensual manner in which John Keats writes about eating a nectarine not only indicates "fireworks" in his love relationship but also affects her enjoyment of his poetry. Why are there so few extant first editions of *Alice in Wonderland*? They were literally devoured by their young owners, as Fadiman's children have occasionally done with their books. Certainly her treatment of bibliophagy is humorous, but it is also literal. Children are expected to develop a taste for books in the most literal sense on their way to becoming "wordworms" and devourers of books in the literary sense. "Sharing the Mayhem" celebrates books as performance, read aloud by parent to child, between lovers, and by an author at a public reading.

As a child, Fadiman used her father's twenty-two-volume set of Anthony Trollope's novels as building blocks. In *Ex Libris* she is still constructing towers and enclosures with her books, each essay providing material for bailey, forecourt, crenellated battlements. The essays were written as distinct blocks, but as they are read together, and reread in varied order, they tell larger stories. One central thread is deeply interwoven with the author's individual identity and bonds with her family. "My Odd Shelf" presents Fadiman's collection of works on polar explorations, books collected in response to a lifelong fascination, and records of her actual Arctic adventures. The "odd shelf" gathers works on a precious area of interest. It is a concrete expression of Fadiman's individual focus, incompletely shared even by her husband. The "odd shelf" takes on new resonance, however, when one reads that Annalee Jacoby Fadiman, mother of the author, also has her own odd shelf, related to her experiences as a correspondent for *Time* magazine during World War II. The books belonging to that adventurous woman seemed exotic and threatening to her young children; her life as a mother replaced the "life of action" she had led before their birth. As Anne Fadiman pauses to contemplate her mother's sacrifice of adventure for family, the implications for her own life and for the changing gender roles of her own time are enormous.

Moreover, the first snippet of Annalee Jacoby Fadiman's story was told in "Nothing New Under the Sun," where her example is cited in a consideration of plagiarism. Initially, this essay is playful, but when the focus shifts to the experience of the author's mother, the tone grows more earnest. Jacoby and her first husband spent three months with General Douglas MacArthur in the Pacific. Her husband was killed in an accident during that time, and her dispatches to *Time* had the "honor" of being plagiarized by John Hersey. The work which most deeply expressed a personal and professional crisis in Jacoby's life was stolen. As Anne Fadiman ponders her mother's life, touching lightly on it from differing angles through the shifting focus of various essays, her deep affection for and identification with the older woman shines through. In all cases, it is the written word that serves as an indication of the bonds and the parallels between these two lives. Even such a problematic inheritance from her mother as the prize book described in "True Womanhood," where women are exhorted to climb onto a pedestal as human sacrifices to the ideals of Christian family life, acts a bond with Fadiman's great-grandmother and a bridge to her daughter's future.

In *Ex Libris*, Anne Fadiman recognizes that she is writing about words on paper and well-bound books in a time when some pundits predict the demise of the conventional book in favor of Internet browsing. However, she persists as an advocate of the word in its concrete and traditional form, a form intimately interwoven with the experiences and affections of her family life. Moreover, the reader is drawn inevitably into the inner circle of that intimacy, invited to share the delights of the wordworm lifestyle, to matriculate in Fadiman U. The subjects broached in the essays of *Ex Libris* vary widely, yet the warm affection for words and the vivacious zest accorded their use by Anne Fadiman gives the volume a transcendent unity. This collection is a potent source of pleasure for other "common readers," a reinforcement of the values of literary tradition, and an optimistic bridge toward the future of written words.

Anne W. Sienkewicz

Sources for Further Study

Biblio. December, 1998, p. 10.
Booklist. XCV, October 1, 1998, p. 303.
Chicago Tribune. October 25, 1998, XIV, p. 4.
The Christian Science Monitor. November 12, 1998, p. B5.
Library Journal. CXXIII, September 15, 1998, p. 78.
The New York Times Book Review. CIII, November 8, 1998, p. 23.
Publishers Weekly. CCXLV, August 24, 1998, p. 34.
The Wall Street Journal. November 27, 1998, p. W5.

EXPLAINING HITLER
The Search for the Origins of His Evil

Author: Ron Rosenbaum
Published: Random House (New York). 447 pp. $30.00
Type of work: History
Time: The twentieth century
Locale: Europe, North America, and Israel

Rosenbaum explores the diverse and conflicting theories that attempt to explain Adolf Hitler's anti-Semitism and his unleashing of the Holocaust

A writer named Milton Himmelfarb plays an important cameo role in Ron Rosenbaum's remarkable book *Explaining Hitler: The Search for the Origins of His Evil.* In March, 1984, Himmelfarb published "No Hitler, No Holocaust," an essay in which he contended that the decision to annihilate European Jewry was Adolf Hitler's alone, a view that has not been shared by every Holocaust scholar. Far from being impelled by historical, political, or cultural forces to murder the European Jews, Himmelfarb continued, Hitler wanted and chose to annihilate them.

More than anything else, links between Hitler (1889-1945) and the Holocaust explain why, as Rosenbaum says, "an enormous amount has been written" about him "but little has been *settled.*" Persuaded by much of Himmelfarb's position, Rosenbaum keeps returning to it but also understands that, while Himmelfarb's position may explain a good deal about the Holocaust, it does not explain Hitler—at least not completely. How badly did Hitler want to destroy the Jews? When did he decide to do so? Even more basically, what made Hitler? Scholars have answered such questions differently, which makes the real Hitler elusive and the puzzles about him persistent.

Those questions and the diverse, even contradictory, responses to them persist partly because a photograph of Hitler was taken when he was probably less than two years old. Years later it was included in a Nazi book called *The Hitler Nobody Knows* (1932). In that context and others, Rosenbaum notes, the baby picture was used to build a wholesome image of Hitler, a tactic that helped to mask Hitler's identity in ways that still haunt us. The same baby picture also appears on the title page of Rosenbaum's book, which thus far is the most comprehensive and provocative account of the dominant attempts to "explain" Hitler. The title page design centers baby Hitler's eyes. Unavoidably drawn to them, the reader can also see the words *Explaining Hitler* and the book's subtitle, *The Search for the Origins of His Evil.*

As Rosenbaum understands, his title and Hitler's baby picture collide. Somehow the infant in the photo became Nazi Germany's führer. That normal-looking child became the leader of a regime that unleashed not only World War II but also an unprecedented genocidal attack on the Jewish people and millions of other defenseless people who were caught in the Holocaust (or *Shoah,* as it is called in Hebrew), which is arguably the quintessential evil of all human history. Hitler's baby picture raises a thousand questions that words must try to answer but perhaps never can. Starting his book with that tension-filled juxtaposition, Rosenbaum ends on a related point more than four hundred pages later. His concluding acknowledgments express special gratitude to the scholars and writers who granted him interviews. Rosenbaum honors their courageous and dedicated pursuit of what he knowingly calls "the impossible challenge of explaining Hitler."

A seasoned scholar-journalist who has turned his disciplined and determined research into grippingly crafted, page-turning prose, Rosenbaum showed his own courage and dedication in writing this book, which was more than ten years in the making. He tracked down people who knew Hitler and got that dwindling number to share what they remembered. He traveled to obscure archives and located long-forgotten files that shed new light on Hitler research. He journeyed to remote Austrian sites in search of details about Hitler's ancestry and youth. All the while, he read voraciously and interviewed dozens of the most influential biographers, historians, philosophers, and theologians who have faced the challenge of bridging the abyss between baby Adolf and Auschwitz Hitler.

Rosenbaum reports the findings of those interpreters, but how he does so makes his book much more than a summary of other people's views. Rosenbaum's meetings with the Hitler scholars are charged with his penetrating questions, his insightful observations that complicate matters for all the writers he encounters, and his skeptical refusal to be overly impressed by the authority of any of the experts he meets. More specifically, Rosenbaum became intrigued by what he identifies as the "wishes and longings, the subtexts and agendas of Hitler explanations." When it comes to explaining Hitler, Rosenbaum asks, what do people want and why? How are the sometimes radical differences in interpretation best understood? What would it mean if Hitler could be explained definitively—or if he cannot? Such questions concentrated Rosenbaum's attention as he met the major Hitler interpreters and then as he reflected deeply about what his investigations revealed. Thus, as the reader travels with him, Rosenbaum shows the strengths and weaknesses in the various Hitler "explanations." He finds the right questions to ask each text he studies, every scholar he meets, and even any insight that more or less persuades him. While learning much about Hitler and the scholarship about him, the reader becomes a partner in Rosenbaum's inquiry, which entails coming to see that the challenge of "explaining" Hitler may be impossible. Even that conclusion, however, is driven home in Rosenbaum's distinctively inquisitive way. His reasons for thinking that it may be impossible to explain Hitler—and the implications that follow—are among the most important findings in this bold and instructive book.

At the outset, Rosenbaum pays tribute to largely forgotten German journalists who reported and opposed Hitler's rise to power. These anti-Hitler journalists—one named Fritz Gerlich gets Rosenbaum's special admiration—wrote for the *Munich Post* and *Der Gerade Weg* ("the right way" or "the straight path"). Before the Nazis brutally shut them down—Gerlich was sent to Dachau and then murdered in June, 1934—these courageous writers sensed Hitler's evil qualities and did their best, even in the early months after Hitler took power on January 30, 1933, to expose the blackmail and murder perpetrated by the Nazis. The German journalists planted seeds of suspicion about Hitler's sexual inclinations to subvert the deceptive wholesomeness of *The Hitler Nobody Knows*. They cast doubt on Hitler's ethnic origins and even his physical appearance to expose the irrationality of his racism and anti-Semitism. As soon as he could, Hitler ruthlessly crushed their dissent.

These anti-Hitler journalists wanted more to stop Hitler than to explain him, but Rosenbaum suggests that they set the stage for post-Holocaust explanations. Probing Hitler's background, they laid the groundwork for a key question in Hitler scholarship: Do Hitler's origins—psychological, familial, sociopolitical—explain him? Disclosing his corrupt and murderous deeds, they began to focus whether Hitler was a cynical political opportunist or an "idealist" who thought that his policies, however deadly, were justified by the "right" and "good" ends they supposedly served. Emphasizing the virulence of his racism and anti-Semitism, the German journalists paved the way for explorations of Hitler's intentionality toward the Jews and, in particular, of whether his intentions were genocidal before he came to power or only afterward. The early anti-Hitler journalists had little doubt that Hitler did evil deeds and even that he was an evil man. Thus, they initiated inquiry about how Hitler's evil ought to be understood: Should Hitler be counted as an "ordinary man" or as an exception, an embodiment of demoniacally destructive power?

Rosenbaum shows that advocates for all of these positions—and many more—can be found among the leading scholars who have tried to explain Hitler. Biographer Hugh Trevor-Roper, for example, thinks that Hitler, thoroughly misguided though he was, sincerely believed in his anti-Semitism and thought that the destruction of the Jews was the right thing to do. Alan Bullock, another biographer, and theologian Emil Fackenheim disagree with Trevor-Roper, finding Hitler to be a cynical political opportunist who used anti-Semitism for his own advancement. Philosopher Berel Lang thinks that neither of those views does justice to the magnitude of Hitler's evil. Lang believes that Hitler was aware of his criminality and even reveled in it. Rosenbaum, who sees Hitler as "a vicious, cold-blooded hater," finds Lang's analysis impressive, if not conclusive. The scope, planning, and sheer brutality of the Holocaust suggest to Lang that Hitler's evil involved what Rosenbaum calls an "art of evil," which required intention, invention, and imagination that relished suffering and destruction. Nevertheless, Rosenbaum stops short of saying that Lang is absolutely right. To say that about any explanation of Hitler would go further than the available evidence permits, for too much time may have passed for anyone to find the key that can unlock the door to Hitler's identity once and for all.

Rosenbaum's conviction is that the yearning to explain Hitler often divulges a need that should be resisted, namely, the desire for closure, comfort, and consolation. Wanting an account that explains everything, we seem to await discovery of what Rosenbaum calls "a long-neglected safe-deposit box" that will grant final, irrefutable answers to the disturbing questions that Hitler raises. Rosenbaum doubts the existence of such a definitive source. His investigations of Hitler explanations—Robert Waite's psychohistorical account, Rudolph Binion's speculation about the importance of the

Jewish doctor who treated Hitler's mother unsuccessfully, or Daniel Goldhagen's emphasis on Hitler's use of a pervasive German "eliminationist anti-Semitism," to name just a few—always leave him skeptical that final and complete answers will be found. This outcome, however, does not mean that Rosenbaum accepts the view of Claude Lanzmann, the filmmaker who produced *Shoah* (1985), an epic Holocaust documentary. Rosenbaum found Lanzmann asserting that it is wrong to seek explanation for Hitler and the Holocaust because answers lead to understanding, understanding leads to legitimation, and legitimation leads to exoneration. According to Lanzmann, one can confront the raw events of the Holocaust, but to "explain" how and why Hitler's power led to Auschwitz would be tantamount to forgiving the unforgivable, an outcome more obscene than rational.

While recognizing that some explanations reduce Hitler's responsibility by making him the pawn of social, political, or psychological determinants—a view that *Explaining Hitler* rejects—Rosenbaum disagrees with Lanzmann's extreme position and concurs instead with historian Yehuda Bauer. Holding that, in principle, Hitler can be explained, Bauer does not think it follows that Hitler has been or ever will be explained. Nevertheless, ongoing effort to explain him remains important. To stop trying would mean that, in principle, Hitler is beyond explanation, an outcome that takes him out of history and thereby promotes problematic mystification.

Rosenbaum thinks that Hitler was certainly human but not ordinary, for ordinary people do not do what Hitler did. Hitler was human, but he was also exceptional in the sense that he can rightly be called an evil man, even an evil genius. Rosenbaum's conclusions on these points—he says he holds them by "default" more than out of "a metaphysical conviction"—are influenced by Lucy Dawidowicz, author of *The War Against the Jews* (1975), who defended the thesis that Hitler formed his intention to destroy European Jewry as early as November, 1918. Coolly obsessed by that goal, Dawidowicz contended, Hitler orchestrated his opportunities until he could do what he wanted. Twenty-five years after Dawidowicz published her views, they are less accepted by scholars than those of Christopher Browning and others who place Hitler's decision to launch the "final solution" in the late summer or early autumn of 1941. Rosenbaum urges that Dawidowicz's position deserves renewed attention. Further inquiry will determine the scholarly status enjoyed by Dawidowicz and every other interpreter of Hitler, including Rosenbaum himself.

Explaining Hitler deserves inclusion among the year's most notable books because it deals so astutely with two of history's most important questions: Who was Adolf Hitler? How and why did the Holocaust happen? Rosenbaum's last word is that inquiry about those questions will be at its best to the extent that it involves resistance. Where Hitler and the Holocaust are concerned, explanatory inquiry should always resist temptations to misplace responsibility. Failure to resist "explanatory excuses" will grant Hitler "the posthumous victory of a last laugh." Not "faceless abstractions, inexorable forces, or irresistible compulsions," but Hitler's choices, Rosenbaum correctly argues, must be at the center of the effort to explain Hitler.

John K. Roth

Sources for Further Study

American Journal of Psychiatry. CLV, December, 1998, p. 1788.
Foreign Affairs. LXXVII, November, 1998, p. 154.
Los Angeles Times Book Review. July 26, 1998, p. 7.
The New York Review of Books. XLV, December 17, 1998, p. 12.
The New York Times Book Review. CIII, July 19, 1998, p. 8.
Newsweek. CXXXII, July 6, 1998, p. 70.
Publishers Weekly. CCXLV, July 13, 1998, p. 57.
Time. CLII, July 20, 1998, p. 64.
The Wall Street Journal. July 9, 1998, p. A16.
The Washington Post Book World. XXVIII, August 23, 1998, p. 7.

THE FACTORY OF FACTS

Author: Luc Sante (1954-   )
Published: Pantheon Books (New York). 306 pp. $24.00
Type of work: Memoirs

An elegantly written, painstaking dissection of what it means to be "Belgian-American" by an American writer who fits that highly specific description, having immigrated at the age of five

In recent years, American society has become accustomed to thinking in terms of "hyphenated" Americans, whether African, Asian, Latino, or other. While "Belgian-American" is not an ethnic category that springs readily to mind, Luc Sante's *The Factory of Facts* is a unique first-person account of the contradictions, subtleties, and nuances of a life lived with exactly that ethnicity. The Brooklyn-based writer is a frequent contributor to *The New York Review of Books* and the author of *Low-Life: Lures and Snares of Old New York* (1990), one of the most fascinating and entertaining histories ever written of the dirty underbelly of New York City. An only child, he emigrated from Verviers, Belgium, with his parents in 1959. After settling briefly in Summit, New Jersey, the family returned to Belgium and then abruptly re-emigrated, resuming their New Jersey life in 1960.

Even Americans well-informed about Europe are likely to overlook Belgium. Brussels especially may be known today as a European political, military, and diplomatic capital and as a major embarkation point for travelers, but little of the country's history and culture is known outside European circles. Even in Europe, "Belgian" is a designation that invites derision. Belgium has been a nation only since 1830, when Belgians gained their independence from the Austrian Hapsburgs. One of the few Western European nations to remain a constitutional monarchy, from its inception it has yoked together two major linguistic communities—Flemish and Walloon—whose relations in recent years have become more and more strained. Brussels persists as a somewhat anomalous Francophonic urban center cut off in Flanders, far removed from the impoverished Walloon (a quasi-Germanic French dialect) areas to the southeast bordering Germany, Luxembourg, and France.

Bearing these constraints in mind, Luc Sante calls the land of his birth an "artificial" country, observing furthermore that "Belgian" jokes circulate in Western Europe and occupy the kind of place that Polish jokes do in American folk culture. The celebrated British comedy troupe Monty Python once suggested as much in a characteristically outrageous skit. In it, Michael Palin presided as the smarmy host of a television game show in which the object of the contest was to think up derogatory terms or phrases for ethnic groups. The chosen target was "Belgians," and the mere utterance of the word occasioned Palin's snide chortling. The winning epithet, Palin exulted, was "bloody fat Belgian bastards!" Thunderous applause in response closed out the brief skit.

Perhaps the heavy Belgian cuisine was behind the joke. As many who have been to

Belgium will, Sante associates the country with fried potatoes—especially twice-fried *frites* served in paper cones with mayonnaise on the side, the omnipresent buttered slices of bread with various toppings called *tartines*, and strong, heavy beer brewed by Trappist monks. Food is also at the center of many of the instances of culture shock Sante describes in his family's first forays into American supermarkets, as they encountered such delights as iceberg lettuce, "Chef Boy-ar-dee" canned spaghetti in sauce, or the salty club soda that was the closest approximation they could locate of *eau gazeuse*, the effervescent bottled water considered a staple by Belgian and French families.

Despite the insults to their palates provided by mass-produced American groceries, the Sante family experienced life in their new world as a rise in class status, even if the riches of the late Eisenhower-era United States did not quite live up to the supercharged fantasies of the Belgian imagination back home. The author conveys the sense that their ancestral home, in the eastern end of the Ardennes region, is something like the West Virginia of Belgium, with a longstanding poverty and bleakness exacerbated by the hardships of the post-World War Two era. Verviers is a small city not far from the German border and due north of Luxembourg. To many Americans, this region is best remembered as the locale of the epic Battle of the Bulge in 1944.

Whatever the hardships of the old country, Sante's parents did not necessarily embrace all aspects of their adopted land. The stereotype applied to earlier generations of immigrants has been that they urged their children to immerse themselves in the new culture. Sante's parents, however, remained skeptical and critical regarding many features of American life. They were appalled by the level of education their son was receiving, which seemed infantile in comparison with what he would have learned at a comparable stage in Belgium. His mother Denise would not even allow him to read books by Dr. Seuss, which she did not differentiate from other childhood influences she saw as insulting to his intelligence. He mentions sneaking away to a friend's house to catch up on his Dr. Seuss reading. Still, as a boy Sante did not completely reject his parents' preference for Belgian influences. He savored his beloved Tintin, the comic-book hero who remains one of the truest Belgian cultural products.

As they took up life in the United States, Sante's parents appear to have been caught up in a number of oppositions besides the obvious ones of language and environment. Having emigrated gained them a certain status back home, yet they experienced tremendous strife with relatives who remained in Belgium. This became acute during the brief period of their return in late 1959. Lucien Sante, the author's father, quarrelled repeatedly with his mother-in-law, in whose home they had taken up residence. Certainly there was also the sense of opposition between persons steeped in European culture they viewed as superior and the philistines they encountered so resentfully once in the United States. Finally, there was the opposition American culture seeks always to deny: that of class conflict.

Issues of class abound in Sante's narrative, and he explores and dissects them with breathtaking sensitivity and skill. He is well aware that painful circumstances of history denied his parents the advanced education and socioeconomic status their own intelligence and resourcefulness merited. As immigrants with an imperfect command of English, they continued to lack opportunities for advancement. Like so many immigrants, they became dependent on their perfectly bilingual child for communication and negotiation with the various agencies and institutions in the new, unfamiliar society around them. The author remembers noticing that his father's employers regarded him as a refined man who could advise them on wines to be ordered with meals in fancy French restaurants, though he was manifestly not a member of their class.

In other important ways, the theme of class is linked to that of language, with often ironic twists. Chief among these is the fact that whereas the French language, to educated Americans, connotes superior cultural sophistication, to young Luc Sante receiving his education in Summit, New Jersey, the language he spoke with his parents was an embarrassing reminder of their humble background. He describes the sense he developed as a child of moving between two radically different worlds, distinct linguistic zones.

All speakers of foreign languages know how dramatically one's behavior alters when switching to another language; the difference may even be experienced physically in the mouth, throat, and nose. Many of Sante's most striking passages explore this feeling of fragmented identity, of becoming quite someone else when moving into a different linguistic register. In his highly personal manner, he dramatizes the fragility of individual identity far more vividly than the many postmodern academic treatises devoted to that theme, as when he writes: "I suppose I am never completely present in any given moment, since different aspects of myself are contained in different rooms of language, and a complicated apparatus of air locks prevents the doors from being flung open all at once."

Concern with proper names is an important part of the author's preoccupation with language. Throughout his life, he has been exasperated equally by mispronunciations by provincial Americans and by persons with knowledge of French who pronounce the monosyllabic "Sante" as if it is the word for "health"—*santé*. Using the impressive resources of the Utah Genealogical Society of the Church of Jesus Christ of Latter-Day Saints at its New York branch near Lincoln Center, Sante learned much about his family's origins and their name in particular. Ultimately, however, he realizes that proper names remain highly arbitrary. Contemplating the profusion of surnames in his family tree, Sante imagines himself trying them on "like hats, imagining each in turn as the sticker pasted across my life. . . ."

The thoroughness with which Sante has pursued his genealogical research is matched by extensive research into Belgian history and culture, as the book's generous bibliography reminds readers. His book *Low-Life: Lures and Snares of Old New York* had already demonstrated this penchant for following often obscure avenues of research. Perhaps it is this very quality that accounts for the one failing of *The Factory of Facts*. The middle chapters dealing with Sante family genealogy and the grim history of their region of Belgium sag somewhat under the weight of all the material the author sees fit to present.

Fortunately, however, the lyrical final chapters on language and identity soar, lifting the book out of that potential morass. The material on the Walloon language is fascinating, and Sante makes readers accept it as a language, not a dialect. As Sante approaches the subject, the reader may view the languages of France and Belgium as merely so many regional dialects. We are accustomed to regarding Breton or Basque as dialects, but what is commonly called "French" can equally be understood histori- cally as the regional dialect of Ile-de-France. The hegemonic triumph of Paris carried with it the ability to define its speech as "French." In present-day Belgium, as Flemish and Walloon communities pull further apart from each other, the former looks to Dutch for some kind of support and vindication, while the latter must cast its lot with French. Yet the French language is presided over by guardians for whom to *parler comme un belge*—to speak like a Belgian—is by definition to speak improperly.

For Luc Sante, the problem of language is most crucially the challenge it poses to his own memoir. In attempting to evoke his childhood experience, he must always work at translation. The young boy's thoughts he would like to describe took place not only long ago but also in another language, that of his parental home. In his attempt at reconstruction, he compares himself to a ventriloquist operating the hinged jaw of a dummy that represents himself as a boy. For even though he can speak French, English has become the language of his interior life. When he travels to Belgium or France, it takes him a while to get up to speed, despite his fluency.

As a book about identity constructed between two cultures and two languages, *The Factory of Facts* is refreshingly different, as its author moves beyond merely advocat- ing his Belgian-ness. Neither does he repudiate it, even if the young boy in New Jersey found many ways to rebel against his parents, most powerfully by becoming as "American" as possible. Throughout, as the book's many eloquent passages attest, Luc Sante's feelings are far too complicated and finely nuanced to fit into an either/or scheme.

James A. Winders

Sources for Further Study

Booklist. XCIV, February 15, 1998, p. 976.
Library Journal. CXXIII, January, 1998, p. 110.
The Nation. CCLXVI, March 30, 1998, p. 29.
The New Republic. CCXVIII, March 30, 1998, p. 33.
The New York Review of Books. XLV, March 26, 1998, p. 34.
The New York Times Book Review. CIII, March 8, 1998, p. 4.
Publishers Weekly. CCXLV, January 26, 1998, p. 82.
The Times Literary Supplement. March 20, 1998, p. 29.
The Village Voice. March 24, 1998, p. 131.
The Virginia Quarterly Review. LXXIV, Summer, 1998, p. 92.

FLANDERS

Author: Patricia Anthony
Published: Ace Books (New York). 354 pp. $23.95
Type of work: Novel
Time: Spring, 1916, to Winter, 1916
Locale: Northern France

A soldier's physical and psychic experience of World War I

> Principal characters:
> TRAVIS LEE STANHOPE, the protagonist, a sharpshooter
> PIERRE LEBLANC, the antagonist, a rapist and murderer
> RICHARD MILLER, the captain of Stanhope and LeBlanc's outfit

Flanders is Patricia Anthony's seventh novel. One of the hallmarks of her work is complex characters, and *Flanders* is no exception. The main character, Travis Lee Stanhope, for example, is from a rural family in Texas, but before he joins the British army in World War I, he becomes a pre-med student on scholarship at Harvard University, where he spends most of his time reading the Romantic poets, especially Percy Bysshe Shelley and John Keats. He admits later that he joined the British Expeditionary Force to avoid becoming a doctor or returning to his family, though in the end he confesses to having no idea why he joined.

The novel is presented in the form of letters and postcards from Travis to his fourteen-year-old brother Bobby in Texas; through these, the reader learns not only what happens to Travis between the spring and early winter of 1916 in Flanders but also what his family background is like. When Travis was a boy, his father beat him and did the same to Travis's half-Cherokee mother. The father also had an affair with a black woman, by whom he had a child. Travis caught his father in bed with this woman and almost shot him, at which point the father deserted the family.

During the novel, Travis's father goes blind and dies, and Travis continually dreams of him sitting humbly on his wife's bed with a wooden horse in his hands. He carved and gave this horse to his son, but Travis would not accept it. His father wants forgiveness, which Travis refuses to give to him, though as the war matures him, he moves toward doing so.

There is no forgiveness in Private Pierre LeBlanc for anyone in his background, and no mercy in him for anyone in general. He comes from Canada and is an orphan, though he has a sister who is a nun. He always projects his memories as a form of hatred. Travis stands up to him, and they become comrades for a while, to the point to which Travis shows him how to ride a horse. LeBlanc may joke about blowing up rats with firecrackers made of spent cartridges, but he displays great gentleness with horses.

He also shares with Travis an abusive Christian background, which has led both men to be disbelievers. Here, however, the similarity ends. Travis is an expert sharpshooter, but he does not enjoy killing. LeBlanc does. He has the battle-courage of a psychotic, and he is much decorated and highly valued by the British Command for all the Germans he has killed. He thus escapes punishment for his other crimes, which include raping and murdering a twelve-year-old girl and raping and mutilating a bakery girl. Travis witnesses the latter when he is drunk, and—much to his abhorrence later—he masturbates while he does so. To atone, he gives the recovering girl a gold cross, but that is all he can do. LeBlanc threatens to reveal what Travis did in witnessing the rape, and as they confront each other with pitchforks—Travis having beaten LeBlanc up earlier—LeBlanc backs down, and all the ties between them are cut.

The paradox of Travis's character includes his ability to empathize with others on the one hand, and his violence when he is drunk on the other. He is capable of hurting a prostitute in bed at one moment and being gentle with her at another. He is capable of killing enemies efficiently and without thought and of trying to save lives as well, even theirs. The demon balances the angel in him, but this is true neither of LeBlanc, in whom the pleasure of maiming and killing predominates, nor of Richard Miller, their captain, in whom the love of justice predominates.

Miller is paradoxical in several ways. As an officer, he has ties to the British upper class, but he is a Jew. He is also gay, and though this is one of the markers he shares with many young men of his social standing, such as Captain Colin Dunston-Smith, his lover, it jeopardizes his relationship to the enlisted men in his command, especially Travis, with whom he falls in love.

Travis shares with Miller a love of horses, an enthusiasm for poetry, and a devotion to fair play. Indeed, Travis comes to love Miller, though not sexually. Miller accepts this, but all along he must treat Travis as a soldier whose insubordination must be controlled, and as a good-hearted and intelligent person who sometimes depends on him for kindness, such as when Travis is falsely arrested for the rape and murder of the twelve-year-old girl.

Like Travis, Miller does not belong. Just as Travis is an American and a rebel, Miller, as a Jewish officer in the British army, is the subject of distrust and contempt from his superiors and the target of betrayal by his peers.

Mediating between the classes, as it were, is Thomas O'Shaughnessy, a Catholic chaplain whose education connects him to the officers and whose understanding of sin connects him to the enlisted men. He has a special tie to Travis because he sees that he, like himself, has the gift of "sight," the ability to see "ghosties," those in transition between their actual death and their acceptance of it. O'Shaughnessy associates Travis's dreams of the dead and soon-to-be-dead to the "brightness of Shelley," thus explaining Travis's attraction to the Romantic poets.

O'Shaughnessy also displays a religious flexibility unusual in a Catholic priest and foreign to Travis's Baptist background. O'Shaughnessy is unself-conscious about his body, stripping in front of Travis to bathe in a canal, and he puts Travis's misconduct in the context of his gift, saying, for example, "When you drink, souls can be lost." Having foreseen his end, he even goes to the extent of asking Travis to remain close by him when he dies, and Travis finds him in a dream.

As for LeBlanc, O'Shaughnessy knows about his misdeeds. Instead of seeing him as damned, though, he views him as lonely and understands the reasons for LeBlanc's behavior: his lack of family, his upbringing by nuns, and his lawless life on the streets of Toronto.

Flanders is about not only carnage and death but also Travis Lee's intricate relationship with characters such as Miller, LeBlanc, and O'Shaughnessy. One of these characters is Lieutenant Blackhall, a former policeman who thinks Travis is guilty of LeBlanc's crimes and who tries to beat the truth out of him. When his investigation leads him to the truth, he relents and tries to protect Travis from trouble. Like Miller, he is pledged to justice. As a working-class person and a policeman, though, he despises Travis for his rebelliousness, his drinking, his education, and his intimacy with Captain Miller. Yet he overcomes these prejudices to the point of making it clear to Travis that if he were to kill LeBlanc, Blackhall would look the other way. Indeed, Blackhall has come to realize that there is as much injustice in the army as in civilian life, for even if LeBlanc were charged for his crimes, he would go free, since the army has profusely decorated him for killing so many of the enemy.

Travis's relationship to his peers in the trenches is touching for its camaraderie, including his feeling for those among them who die. He sees them in his dreams, which always have the same setting—a graveyard with stone angels and flowers, glass-topped graves, a glass-roofed mausoleum, a cypress tree at the far end beyond which a fearsome blackness waits, and a young woman Travis calls the "calico girl" who guides him about the graveyard. Among others, this dream-graveyard contains Travis's comrades Trantham, Marrs, Smoot, and Abner Foy—victims of such horrors as poison gas, flamethrowers, and evisceration. In his visions, Travis tries to soothe them in their passages from death to eternity.

The novel uses the details of carnage as a backdrop to Travis's improvement as a person. The worse these details become, the better he becomes. In the beginning, his talent as a sharpshooter allows him to win bets payable in rum or brandy; he soon becomes a a drunk and often breaks rules. Because of this, he is transferred to a latrine-cleaning detail, which he shares with Private Nye, whose comic philosophizing about defecation foreshadows the humor of the characters Travis meets when, no longer able to shoot the enemy, he is assigned to removing the wounded from the battlefield.

Travis's description of how death saturates his environment becomes more gruesome as he progresses from ending lives to saving them. He writes to his brother, "There must be Boche left in the walls . . . for the smell has settled in all the trenches." Later, he remarks that "the soil is full of stinking bodies and white, knobby bones," and later still, "When the earth falls around us, it vomits out corpses."

At that point, Travis holds nothing back about the wounds he sees. For example, he writes of "a kid whose head had exploded: brains dripping down his chin" and of a soldier with "his heart neatly sliced open and lying on his chest like a medical illustration.'"

That Travis is so objective does not mean that he has become used to destruction but that sanity lies in not taking horror too seriously. The novel provides a sort of low comedy to support this point. Travis's fellow stretcher-bearers—Uncle Tim, Mugs, Turnhill—sound like refugees from a Shakespearean comedy. Their comments and antics reflect this; Uncle Tim, for example, comments, "Trick is, you drown maggots" as he urinates on the boots of two inexperienced soldiers to kill maggots that have fallen there from the sleeve of a corpse. Travis remarks that "We laughed all the way through lunch just thinking about it."

Despite this humor, Travis continues to romanticize the dead. In the end, Captain Miller helps him do this when Miller kills LeBlanc for the latter's crimes. For this, his fellow officers, who have hypocritically failed to court-martial LeBlanc, try Miller and execute him. The bond between Miller and Travis is profoundly tightened by this, and Travis learns from him the Shema Ysrael prayer, which he recites when Miller is led off to death, and the Kaddish, which he recites over him when he is buried. The words that Miller leaves with Travis are these: "What is hateful to you, do not do to your neighbor." This, in short, is the wisdom that the paradox of life defies, and to Miller, it summarizes the Torah.

In one sense, Miller's murder of LeBlanc is revenge by the female on the male which would destroy it. Although Miller is gay, he still treasures his fiancée, and though he is in love with Travis, he does not force himself upon him. As an avenging angel, thereby, he is hard to outdo.

The most important feature of the love that Travis learns to believe in is not sex but care, and Miller has helped him to see this, as have all the dead in Travis's dream. Before his own fate is sealed, he comes close to forgiving his abusive father, and he realizes about death itself, "The black by the cypress looks threatening, but beyond waits a calm and sparkling place. . . . That shimmer . . . is the power of the universe. It runs through me and you, through the dead men in the field and through the rats that eat them. It's love." If this is a distinctly feminine view, and seems somewhat odd in a context as bestial as the one Travis Lee must endure, it is still a powerful and moving moral to the story.

Mark McCloskey

Sources for Further Study

Booklist. XCIV, May 15, 1998, p. 1593.
Kirkus Reviews. LXVI, April 15, 1998, p. 536.
Library Journal. CXXIII, May 15, 1998, p. 118.
Publishers Weekly. CCXLV, April 13, 1998, p. 57.
Starlog. November, 1998, p. 15.

FLAWED GIANT
Lyndon Johnson and His Times, 1961-1973

Author: Robert Dallek (1934-   )
Published: Oxford University Press (New York). Illustrated. 736 pp. $35.00
Type of work: Biography
Time: 1961-1973
Locale: Principally the United States

Dallek concludes his two-volume biography of Lyndon Johnson with an account of the thirty-sixth president's successes and failures in the executive branch of government

Principal personages:
LYNDON BAINES JOHNSON, the thirty-sixth president of the United States
LADY BIRD JOHNSON, his wife
JOHN F. KENNEDY, the thirty-fifth president
RICHARD M. NIXON, the thirty-seventh president
ROBERT KENNEDY, the U.S. attorney general and former senator
RICHARD RUSSELL, a U.S. senator
HUBERT H. HUMPHREY, a U.S. senator and Johnson's vice president
DEAN RUSK, the secretary of state
ROBERT MCNAMARA, the secretary of defense
MARTIN LUTHER KING, Jr., a civil rights leader
EVERETT M. DIRKSEN, the Senate minority leader
BILL MOYERS, a presidential assistant
CLARK CLIFFORD, McNamara's successor as secretary of defense

In *Flawed Giant*, Robert Dallek concludes his two-volume biography of Lyndon B. Johnson, the thirty-sixth U.S. president, whose tenure in office lasted five years and two months, and who, Dallek argues, left a strong if ambiguous legacy. Dallek, who has studied the Johnson presidency for more than a decade, has drawn upon materials recently made public from the LBJ Presidential Library and upon numerous interviews with members of Johnson's staff. Very much a book about Johnson's times, *Flawed Giant* is as much historical narrative as biography. To understand Johnson's character, or at least to view him with sympathy, one should read *Lone Star Rising* (1991), Dallek's first volume, which gives an account of Johnson's family background and formative influences. *Flawed Giant* makes Johnson appear an even larger influence on events than he was, for it recounts events with him at the center.

Chronologically, the biography highlights the following dominant motifs of Johnson's executive career: the vice presidency (1961-1963), an unhappy time for Johnson; the transition to the presidency and consolidation of power (1963-1964); the Great Society domestic programs (1964-1965), when Johnson was firmly in control; Johnson's management of the Vietnam War (1966-1968), a time of frustration and bitter disappointment; and his retirement and death (1969-1973).

Although Dallek's narrative is straightforward for the most part, he occasionally establishes different strands that require alertness from the reader and that may be disconcerting to those not already familiar with the events. For example, he may end a section with a portion of a Johnson speech relevant to that topic, then begin another topic from an earlier time and follow it up to another part of the same speech.

The section on the vice presidency illustrates Dallek's approach effectively. Vice President Johnson devoted himself primarily to three areas: foreign travel as a goodwill ambassador on behalf of American capitalism; the space program, where he shaped policy and dovetailed expansion in accord with his desire for economic growth and integration of the South; and a committee established by President Kennedy to promote equality of opportunity. Dallek narrates Johnson's experiences in all three areas, revealing his varying successes and disappointments. On foreign travel, usually to Asia or Africa, Johnson was often uncomfortable and made his hosts so. He wanted to appear before large crowds and often treated them as if he were a campaigner seeking their votes, even handing out leftover campaign materials he brought along. He did folksy things such as inviting a Pakistani camel driver to visit the United States. Ominously for his later experience, he expressed the view that foreigners were not like the people he knew.

While he was treated with correctness by Kennedy and his staff, he felt like an outsider, removed from really important policy decisions. He was rarely consulted on foreign policy and had little role in the Cuban Missile Crisis of 1962. His earlier conflict with Robert Kennedy, which would last until Kennedy's death, only intensified. As Dallek points out, Johnson reacted to his frustration by indulging in personal excesses.

The personal picture that emerges of Johnson is hardly coherent. He was a physical giant, six feet three-and-a-half inches tall, with an oversized ego, a hypersensitivity to criticism, and an energy level that caused him to be described as a tornado in pants. As president, he usually worked eighteen-hour days, often driven by a sense of urgency about moving legislation forward. Yet Dallek acknowledges that to understand Johnson is almost impossible; even those who were close to him claimed not to have understood him, though some described him as manic depressive. He could be gloomy and withdrawn one day and on the next jovial, regaling his associates with humorous, often earthy, anecdotes and skillfully mimicking opponents.

The desire for power was his dominant trait, but even this desire had many facets. Johnson himself said that he did not seek power for wealth or its perquisites but rather to do good with it, to improve the lot of ordinary people. His life and achievement are testimony to his truth and sincerity, for the use of power to benefit the needy runs like a thread through his public life from its beginning.

Yet this is not the entire story. It is also true that, psychologically, Johnson wanted and probably needed the gratitude, the adulation, of those whom he helped, and he wanted a place in history as the man who outdid Franklin Roosevelt by fulfilling the promises of Roosevelt's New Deal. As for his principal flaw, Dallek's narrative suggests that it was Johnson's tendency toward manipulation and deception, which caused others to lose confidence in him. Yet this may be the negative side of his drive to bend others to his will, an obsession that contributed much to the success of his domestic agenda.

Johnson's most successful period extended from his accession to the presidency following the assassination of John Kennedy in November, 1963, through the end of 1965. In the 1964 election, Johnson's landslide victory over the Republican candidate Barry Goldwater brought a Democratic majority to Congress. There then began a series of unprecedented domestic legislative programs, comparable only to the legislation passed during Franklin Roosevelt's first term. Legislation dealing with civil rights, Medicare, Medicaid, fair housing, the environment, education, and numerous other domestic areas passed with lopsided majorities. Johnson took a direct hand in passage of all the bills, speaking with senators and congressmen—bargaining, convincing, making deals, pressuring if necessary. His background in the House and Senate and his own personal qualities prepared him to master the legislative process better than any president who preceded him. Nor was it only Democratic votes that he obtained; numerous Republicans joined in to vote for the most important bills. Johnson understood that any president's persuasive power with Congress erodes over time, and he made the most of the time he had until Vietnam began to consume his energy.

Although Dallek does not give a full account of the origins of the Vietnam War, the narrative is so extensive that it can almost stand as a history of the conflict during Johnson's years. Clearly Johnson's greatest failure, the war dominates the second half of the biography. When he became president in November, 1963, Vietnam was no more than a minor foreign distraction, one of many that might prove troublesome in the future. At most, a few thousand American troops and advisers had been committed in an effort to defend South Vietnam against a Communist-led revolution.

The greater involvement under Johnson was a failure, not because anyone else could have done better but because Johnson and other government officials had learned the lessons of the twentieth century too well. One lesson had been taught by Nazi Germany: Aggression must not be allowed to succeed, because success only leads to further aggression. Other lessons grew out of the pervasive legacy of the Cold War and the Truman Doctrine, which held that Western interests were served by opposing communist-led takeovers of friendly governments. Not to resist only led to greater losses of territory, since once a nation had been lost, another revolution would break out elsewhere. Moreover, an established American political reality seemed to promote staying the course: the Chinese Revolution had been used as political capital by Republicans against Democrats for many years, as if the United States could or should have intervened on behalf of the Chinese Nationalists. Almost no one questioned whether the conflict in Vietnam actually fit the pattern.

In attempting to set war policy, Johnson saw himself on the horns of a cruel dilemma. He could withdraw, be charged by political opponents with losing the war, and face the real possibility that communist revolutions would break out in other nations. Initially, no one in Congress or the executive branch favored this option. He could continue to aid South Vietnam in an effort to prevail but limit the war so that the Russians and Chinese would not involve their own forces and precipitate World War III. With no one offering better advice, he resigned himself to a long, limited war of attrition. American forces grew from a few thousand to more than five hundred thousand before his term ended. Once he had committed a substantial number of troops to the conflict, he took the position that he did not want to be the first president to lose a war.

He believed successful conduct of the war so important that he accepted its adverse impact on his domestic programs, on the economy, and on his own approval ratings. He scaled back requests to the Congress for funds and for new programs. Yet as the war dragged on, Johnson experienced increasing frustration with the instability and limited efforts of South Vietnam and with the unanticipated staying power of the North. He tried bombing, bombing halts, open and secret diplomacy, and numerous other tactics. He even hinted at American aid for North Vietnam in return for peace. Meanwhile, he received periodical assurances from American military and intelligence officials that the war of attrition was working and that the enemy would soon collapse. All this was cruelly belied by the Communist Tet Offensive of early 1968. As his term drew to its close, he promoted intense but fruitless diplomatic efforts to end the war. Failure to resolve the war problem, more than anything else, led to his decision not to seek a second full term. When Johnson handed over the reins of power to Richard Nixon in 1969, the war was far from over, and Nixon's policies changed little from those of Johnson.

It should not be surprising that Johnson had difficulty adjusting to retirement after wielding power for so many years. Yet Dallek's account does include some surprises. The extent of his bipartisanship is remarkable in a political animal of his nature. Dallek asserts that Johnson really wanted to see Nelson Rockefeller, the New York Republican, succeed him as president. His support of Hubert Humphrey, the Democratic nominee and his own vice president, was muted in the race against Nixon, largely because Johnson did not trust Humphrey on the war issue. He withheld information that would have been damaging to Nixon's chances, although he did throw some support to Humphrey near the end of the campaign.

Dallek finds Johnson, in office and out, a troubled, difficult, well-meaning man. Near the book's end, he quotes from Johnson's last State of the Union Address:

> I hope it may be said a hundred years from now, that by working together we helped to make our country more just, more just for all of its people, as well as to insure and guarantee the blessings of liberty for all of our posterity.
> That is what I hope. But I believe that at least it will be said that we tried.

In light of his leadership in civil rights and the continued acceptance of his domestic programs, Johnson's hope and belief seem well founded. In the area of civil rights, Johnson did more to promote equality than any president since Abraham Lincoln. Despite the overly ambitious and optimistic nature of some of his domestic programs such as federal aid to education and federal housing, the principal programs of the Great Society have endured. Dallek's two volumes represent the only complete scholarly biography of this important president.

Stanley Archer

Sources for Further Study

Campaigns and Elections. XIX, June, 1998, p. 10
The Economist. CCCXLVII, April 18, 1998, p. S8.
Foreign Affairs. LXXVII, July, 1998, p. 118.
Insight on the News. XIV, June 8, 1998, p. 36.
Library Journal. CXXIII, March 15, 1998, p. 74.
Los Angeles Times. March 16, 1998, p. A15.
The New York Times Book Review. CIII, April 12, 1998, p. 5.
Newsweek. CXXXI, April 20, 1998, p. 66.
The Washington Monthly. XXX, May, 1998, p. 41.
The Washington Post Book World. XXVIII, April 26, 1998, p. 1.

FLUTIE

Author: Diane Glancy (1941-   )
Published: Moyer Bell (Wakefield, Rhode Island). 130 pp. Paperback $18.95
Type of work: Novel
Time: 1980's-1990's
Locale: Western Oklahoma

A desperately silent half-American Indian girl struggles to come of age in a small Oklahoma town and to find her voice

Flutie Moses, oppressed by her own silence, has words and images she wants to, but cannot, articulate, not even to provide directions for passing motorists. Her small world is dominated by Hampton's Garage. There her father and brother repair the town's broken and worn-out vehicles, and her father—a Native American whose siblings simply walked away and disappeared, and whose heritage is all but lost—attempts to reclaim something about his personal past by rebuilding an old car like the one he owned in his youth. Flutie's mother careens over the highways of western Oklahoma, collecting traffic tickets, in her pursuit of distance and speed. "As she drove she rushed away from the past so it wouldn't catch up with her."

Anger consumes Flutie's brother Franklin. Six years Flutie's senior, Franklin defiantly refuses to finish high school. He and his leather-clad friends spend their time stealing hood ornaments from cars passing through their small town, fixing old cars, traveling the countryside to salvage yards and car shows, seeking salvation through custom cars. Flutie observes, "Cars were the angels of America. They were full of invisible wings. Chevys. Fords. Plymouths. Buicks. Studebakers. Restored. Rebuilt. Customized. Polished. Worshipped."

Ruther and Luther Rutherford, the old sister and brother who live down the road from Flutie's family, are the only people to whom Flutie can speak freely. Their family claimed Indian land at the turn of the century and stuck it out during the 1930's Dust Bowl. As the two of them wait for their end, with their "Do Not Resuscitate" sign boldly placed above their front door, Ruther hears angels and has visions of the racks of heaven that she imagines to be just like the dark inside of an oven until her prayers turn on the light to reveal the angels and all those who have gone before her. She also feeds bread crumbs to the thousands of buffalo she believes roam the Oklahoma plains; she thinks they would visit her backyard if only her brother would stop his incessant mowing of their dry, dusty yard.

Jess Tessman, Flutie's friend and confidant, lives at the end of a long dirt road with his father on a small, dismal farm. He is a lonely boy whose mother disappeared long ago, leading him to believe that no one who leaves ever returns. He loves Flutie and wants her to marry him and stay in Vini forever.

Swallow Smots, Flutie's best friend, is everything Flutie is not—pretty, flirtatious, and talkative. A waitress at the only restaurant in town, she attracts Franklin's attention as his first marriage fails and becomes his second wife. Once the girl who bails hay in a bikini, she is eventually subdued by the insularity of small town life and by marriage.

The first epigraph of Diane Glancy's novel *Flutie* reads: "There's the sky and the ground with / nothing between them but a landscape / of stories you can hear if you hold / your ear to the air to the land—." That statement, along with the enticing iconic portrait on the book's cover of a saint-like Indian woman, draw us into the world of young Flutie Moses, the novel's confused and lonely protagonist. She dwells in a landscape of not only vast plains of inescapable dust and desolation, but also ancient, eternal geological and cosmological forces, which are available to those able to perceive them. The novel is an engaging—and often depressing—account of Flutie Moses's gradual awakening to this landscape of stories that have the potential to save her.

Flutie is a tale of silence and words, of staying and going, of the immediate place and moment, and eternal space and time. In eighty-seven short chapters, some only a few paragraphs long, as well as in the typographical and imaginative spaces between the chapters the author provides, Glancy presents the moments and events that transform Flutie from a pathologically silent girl to a young woman who finds her voice and in the process recognizes her role as a storyteller.

The girl we meet at the beginning of the novel is trapped in three ways. First, she is imprisoned by the tiny town of Vini, forty miles from the Texas border and a short distance from the Great Salt Plains, both of which might as well be on the other side of the globe for as much access as Flutie has to them. Her world extends only as far as town—including Hampton's Garage, where her father and brother repair cars, the town's only cafe, and Carpter's Drygoods—the Rutherfords' house next door, Jess Tessman's lonely farm down a long dirt road with its small pond, and the two small nearby towns to which her mother flees at breakneck speeds, blurring the occasional road signs and landmarks as she terrifies her daughter-passenger.

Second, Flutie is caught in the isolation, anger, and violence of her family. Her parents seem to stick to each other because they have no one and nothing else. The only vestige of her father's Native American heritage is the sweat lodge he maintains in the backyard. His brother and sisters walked down the road, "falling off into space," never to be heard of again. Flutie longs for connection to her father's past, for stories. She wants to know about grandfather's experience at Indian board school, of being assigned the name Moses, of losing his language and culture. She visits her grandmother's grave hoping to hear something, a story from the old woman's resting place, but nothing comes. The only story from his Indian past that her father will share is a warning: When Flutie spends too much time drinking in the local dance halls as a teenager, he tells her that she, like all Indians, must not drink. Instead, her father connects to old custom cars. The family's excursions to car shows and her father's restoration of Florentine blue 1942 Ford, the car of his youth, are the only links to her father's past Flutie is allowed. Her mother's background, family, and past is just as elusive, available only in her mother's ironic repetition of the one German phrase she seems to have retained, "Ist ja wieder gut," "Everything will be all right." But it isn't.

Flutie's hot attic bedroom—her jeans hanging from nails driven into the walls, and her box of rocks wrapped in string, an ancient bone, and a piece of deer hide her only comforts—provides her with some refuge from her father's and Franklin's arguments and from her parents' physical violence toward one another, evidenced occasionally in her mother's marked face. Some nights, the oppressive heat from the weather and her parents' temperaments drive her from her room to the porch, to the seat of the pickup truck, or as far as the Rutherfords' sofa. Franklin's frequent midnight escapes in the family pickup lead to sheriff's visits, eventual arrests and jail terms, and his own unhappy marriages.

These forces ultimately reinforce the suffocating silence overwhelming Flutie, the third factor trapping her. She cannot find words, though she wants to say so much. Always fascinated by rocks, water, and sky, she realizes through her study of geology in school that she resembles an underwater volcano. The quiet enveloping her is like an underground ocean—traces of which are glimpsed in Jess's pond and the nearby Salt Flats—the lava exploding, the water boiling. But she cannot spit out words, only hot tears. "And under the tears was her anger in knowing that she couldn't talk when it counted."

Finding a voice means finding the stories that the landscape has to tell. Since her parents won't tell her their stories and since she seems to have no stories of her own, Flutie must learn to listen in order to repeat the stories the land, the air, and the animal and human ancestors reveal. For most of her life, however, Flutie's immediate circumstances seem to suffocate her. She cannot breathe. The narrowness of the world, the closeness of the sky choke her words before she can speak them. "Release. . . . Flutie wanted space. She wanted flight. She wanted something more than she had." But what? Ruther expands her world through her visions of the racks of heaven. Flutie is visited by a spirit—part Christian saint, part Indian girl—who is just enough encouragement for Flutie to reject Jess Tessman's marriage proposal and her future with him consisting of kids, living with Jess's father at the end of a dirt road, car shows, and no one asking her to speak. Staying means more silence. Leaving to return to college—after her short and dismal first attempt—might mean liberation.

Flutie's journey to find the voice to articulate the stories held by the landscape, her people, and she herself is not the stuff of high drama. It consists of the subtleties of everyday life—some steps so modest that they are hardly remarkable but that lead cumulatively to real progress and to a life that matters.

Since the publication of M. Scott Momaday's 1969 novel *The House Made of Dawn* initiated the Native American Renaissance in literature, Native American writers have added a richness and texture to the American literary canon that cannot and should not be ignored. Diane Glancy's contribution to this tradition is undeniable. She demonstrates that there is no single Native American voice, identity, or experience. In fact, Flutie Moses—half-Indian and half German, growing up in rural America rather than on a reservation—reflects the author's own experience. Glancy and her characters add to the colorful and diverse tapestry that is Native America. When one converses with Diane Glancy, one hears a voice of quiet intensity. The same is true of her prose. With a few well-crafted words, she is able to create a world, populate it with very distinctive people, and provide them with lives that are as memorable as they are meaningful. *Flutie* may not be a major novel, but it is an important one, providing a reader with a literary experience worth having.

Laura Weiss Zlogar

Sources for Further Study

Booklist. XCIV, March 15, 1998, p. 1201.
Kirkus Reviews. LXVI, February 15, 1998, p. 212.
Library Journal. CXXIII, March 1, 1998, p. 127.
The New York Times Book Review. CIII, May 17, 1998, p. 40.
Publishers Weekly. CCXLV, March 16, 1998, p. 55.

THE FOLDING CLIFFS
A Narrative

Author: William Stanley Merwin (1927-   )
Published: Alfred A. Knopf (New York). 331 pp. $25.00
Type of work: Poetry

A book-length poem recounting the Hawaiian legend of two native outcasts who rebel against the world imposed on their people by the invasion of Western values and economic constraints

> *Principal characters:*
> PI'ILANI, the narrator, a nineteenth century Hawaiian woman
> KO'OLAU, her husband, who leads a rebellion against European
>   domination of Hawaii

W. S. Merwin's new book-length story of the impact of Western civilization on the indigenous peoples of Hawaii is an epic narrative told simply but powerfully. While focusing on the extraordinary lives of two characters, the rebel outcast Ko'olau and his loyal, stoic widow Pi'ilani, Merwin's three-hundred-pages-plus poem includes legend and history, legends of the past and legends in the making. The heroism of an oppressed, nonliterate people reacting against a culture that steals their land, suppresses their religion, and ultimately attempts to determine the lives of natives with the cold heart of Christian certainty is unfolded with both impressive technique and credible historical authority. Set in the latter decades of the nineteenth century, Merwin's narrative captures a people and place in rapid transition, moving from the primitive past of magic to a world of Westernized values and conceits. Yet the story is also both personal and striking, with the imagery drawn from places and events both undeniably and tragically all too familiar and harshly unique in the American past.

On many levels, *The Folding Cliffs* is an achievement for both the Hawaiian people and Merwin personally, as the Pulitzer Prize-winning author draws from many wells to shape this epic. From the beginning of his poetic career, Merwin established himself as a student of international mythology, cultures, and traditions, beginning with *A Mask for Janus* (1952), *The Dancing Bears* (1954), and *Green with Beasts* (1956). His lifelong theme of humanity's separation from nature and its consequences, again predominant in *The Folding Cliffs*, made *The Lice* (1969) Merwin's most noted book to date. On several levels, *The Folding Cliffs*, while not as technically difficult as his earlier verse, is a return to the political and ecological concerns of *The Lice*, including the motifs of generational change, historical sweep, and the betrayal of nature. *The Folding Cliffs* also reiterates themes of Merwin's *The Vixen* (1996), which was built on descriptive details of country life and examples of human stupidity and inhumanity.

The Folding Cliffs brings together these characteristics of Merwin's previous verse and drama, along with lessons learned from his translations of French and Spanish literature as well as the understanding of Hawaiian history and culture he has gained from his living in Haiku, Hawaii, since the mid-1970's. In the decades since, he has worked on rebuilding an old pineapple plantation and collected native oral histories for his respectful essays on the island of Kaho'olawe. While exploring the conflicts between modern natives and the U.S. military, Merwin began interviewing contemporary lepers, and the poetic outgrowth of these multiple interests helped shape the content of *The Folding Cliffs*, an important story in its own right but perhaps even more significant for the way it is told in Merwin's broken-back line structure.

The story is framed in the mind of Pi'ilani, a woman born in 1864 looking back over her own past as well as that of her people. As widow of the rebellious Ko'olau, who championed the cause of lepers after he contracted the disease on the island of Kauai, she seeks to determine the sanctity of his grave, which opens the door to her memoirs. Pi'ilani's youthful, premarital setting is framed by stars and water as well as the cliffs, which will serve as both shelter and metaphor for her adventure. She begins her tale surrounded by the words of women, each seemingly separate from the world of men apart from her betrothed, the singer of stories, in the pristine, beautiful world.

The past is first opened with the retelling of the origins of the gods, notably Pele, the fire goddess, who is quickly juxtaposed with the fire and thunder of white men on ships surrounding the islands. The pace of history is first evident with the coming of Captain James Cook to the islands and the natives' quick understanding that the English are not gods. After the first encounter, trade is established, with the islanders offering fruit, fresh water, and sandalwood while the men on the floating black islands, the ships from an unknown world, offer guns, venereal disease, and the missionaries of the one true God.

The perspectives of the narrative open as the speaking voices expand to include other natives, various Europeans, and Merwin himself as omniscient narrator. These points of view dramatize the rapid change of events, as violence begins to intrude on the islands with the massacre of competing rival tribes and the usurpation of the monarchy by a Western-dominated legislature. The arrival of the Christian Church has less to do with spirituality than it does with commerce, with the islanders becoming workers for the enterprises of foreigners who bring cattle, molasses, rice, and sugar. Commerce, as described by the early missionaries, is the Lord's work. The land of the islands moves under the control of the outsiders, who preach the better world is the next world, supplanting the earthly paradise with promises of another after death.

A generation passes, and a church becomes the center of the community, while youngsters think they are subversively preserving the old ways. In fact, the new generation is misinterpreting ruins as the old religions are being lost in the mix of cultures. The central characters become the humane Judge Kauai, who sympathizes with the natives but is powerless to be an effective advocate for them, and the Norwegians Vladldemar and Sinclair Knudsen, who attempt to learn the language of the people but can never sound natural speaking the words. This image develops in several subplots, as Westerners demonstrate their hypocrisy by ineffectively practicing the local language while not letting their children play with the natives. This section is a powerful merging of linguistics with morals in a poignant example of cultural suppression that is achieved without using force. The new message is clear: The islanders must learn they need to want.

The narrative's tone intensifies with the introduction of leprosy, which the natives call "the separating sickness." The new government begins taking infected natives away by force, with no regard for family feelings, treating the infected as criminals, and separating loved ones without allowing communication between the diseased and those left behind. Both the white doctor and the pastor, the Reverend Rowell, become figures of distrust, unwilling to assist attempts to send items to inflicted friends quarantined in a remote settlement. Absence transforms lepers into central figures in the community when the inability to get answers about their loved ones begins to arouse resentment. A leper house is moved nearby for easier communication, ironically marked with the Christmas sign proclaiming "Good will to men." While the disease primarily affects the workers, the sympathetic judge and legislator also becomes infected, and in his isolation he becomes a symbol of those who would dare take up the cause of the natives.

An insurrection led by Ko'olau ensues, but the rebellion is short lived, as he and his wife and young son, Kaleimanu, are relentlessly pursued by gunboats and soldiers seeking to make an example of him. The family takes to the cliffs for hiding, successfully outwitting and evading their potential captors. Linking the present with the past, Pi'ilani realizes her husband is reliving the quest of a mythological hero from her people's stories set on the cliffs. In the section most likely to be excerpted in literary anthologies, the couple hides for three years, keeping away from both whites and family members. After the death of their son and Ko'olau, Pi'ilani returns to her home and becomes a legendary character in the lives of the community, the one who lived the life of a hero and who guards the secrets of her husband. While outsiders continue to pursue Ko'olau after his death by repeatedly claiming to find his grave, Pi'ilani quietly submerges herself into the new world of her people, a dignified symbol of a past now buried in the usurper's civilization.

In an overlong denouement, Merwin describes the waning years of Pi'ilani's life, connecting her fame with the new world of the twentieth century as she dictates her story to unreliable Christian missionaries, notably the anthropologically oriented John Shelton. While the conclusion lacks the drama of the previous passages, Merwin is clearly attempting to tell the story from beginning to end, and the final, resigned tones do reflect the transformation of a generation from unspoiled islanders into historical curiosities in their own homeland. Merwin's rendering of Hawaii's most beloved local legend, first drawn in long, flowing cadences without punctuation, capitalization, or traditional quotation marks, is followed by terse lines emphasizing the increasingly dark subject matter. The narrative, broken into seven sections of 281 short stanzas, is a synthesis of Hawaiian chant with Western prosody, a form both ironically appropriate and equally ironic in its fresh use of language and poetic structure, including several types of line enjambment and Whitmanesque detail that neither slow the pace nor complicate the complex tale of plot and subplots. Attempting to keep as much of the local diction as possible, Merwin provides helpful notes and a glossary of terms that will assist readers willing to delve into the flavor of the tale beyond the poignant and powerful plot.

Based on Frances Frazier's 1973 translation of the soliloquy, "Pi'ilani's Lament" (published in 1987), Merwin's epic is not only a major contribution to English verse but also is likely to give a wider audience to the lore and history of the conquering of Hawaii. Thus *The Folding Cliffs* should prove to be an important social document elevating the characters within the tale to national prominence. While critics have determined Merwin's career has been in decline since *The Lice*, his new book should rapidly reverse such claims, and it may well serve as a poetic watershed for Merwin, Hawaii, and American verse in general. Merwin's innovative epic should also bring new interest to the form of the long poem, challenging other crafters of verse to expand their horizons in contemporary subject matter and structure.

Wesley Britton

Sources for Further Study

Booklist. XCV, September 15, 1998, p. 188.
Esquire. CXXX, November, 1998, p. 43.
Library Journal. CXXIII, October 15, 1998, 74.
Publishers Weekly. CCXLV, September 14, 1998, p. 47.

FOR KINGS AND PLANETS

Author: Ethan Canin (1960-   )
Published: Random House (New York). 335 pp. $24.95
Type of work: Novel
Time: The 1970's to the 1980's
Locale: New York City, Cape Cod, Missouri, and Maine

A Bildungsroman developing the lives and relationships of two young men

Principal characters:
ORNO TARCHER, a Columbia University student who becomes a dentist
MARSHALL EMERSON, also a Columbia student, who becomes a film and
  television writer and producer
SIMONE EMERSON, Marshall's sister, who marries Orno
PROFESSOR EMERSON, Marshall's father
MRS. PELHAM, Marshall's mother, who keeps her maiden name
  professionally
DRAKE TARCHER, Orno's father
SOFIA, a Columbia student who dates Orno, then Marshall

Ethan Canin has had an impressive start as a writer of stories, some of which are long enough to qualify as novellas. His first collection, *Emperor of the Air* (1988), won praise from reviewers for the maturity of his intelligence, the sensitivity of his perceptions, and the grace of his prose. His second, *The Palace Thief* (1994), was even more widely acclaimed for its steady moral compass, confident voice, acuteness of detail, and, above all, for the extraordinarily sensitive way in which it dealt with the consequences of feelings when people's dreams tremble and then dissolve. He has already been proclaimed as a master of short narratives comparable to Peter Taylor, Lorrie Moore, Alice Munro, and even John Cheever.

Not so with his novels. His first, *Blue River* (1991), was a disappointment: too much background, not enough narrative drive. *For Kings and Planets* proves a flat-out failure. The plot is all too familiar: A friendship between a Midwestern hayseed and a Manhattan sophisticate turns increasingly problematic. Orno is an insecure, wide-eyed, not particularly bright grind from small-town Missouri; Marshall is a brilliant son of brilliant professors from Morningside Heights. It's all too predictable: the tortoise with and then against the hare, the provincial against the slickster and trickster, innocence opposed to decadence. Not only have readers been here before, but usually in better company: many of Honoré de Balzac's novels, some of Charles Dickens's, F. Scott Fitzgerald's *The Great Gatsby*, and Thomas Wolfe's autobiographical opus, for examples.

In September, 1974, Orno is driven to New York by his parents from Cook's Grange, Missouri, the first in his family to go east for higher education. He is dressed in corduroy pants and tie, reads Wolfe's 1929 novel *Look Homeward, Angel*, rises early and, his second day at Columbia, meets Marshall Emerson, returning at dawn from sybaritic revels. They share a history class on Ancient Greece and Rome. Orno works every evening in the library; Marshall never studies. Orno tells Marshall of his farming background, recounting simple memories of Missouri winters; Marshall quotes the mystic G. I. Gurdjieff and charms Orno with stories of extravagant adventures when he lived in Istanbul as a child with an Irish nanny, while his mother, an anthropologist, did her field work in the Turkish countryside. Then Marshall tells of evenings in his parents' apartment when Margaret Mead, Francis Crick, Ralph Ellison, and other distinguished company visited; in return, Orno can only identify Steve McQueen on Columbus Avenue. Orno gets B to B- grades; Marshall's are A+. Blessed with an eidetic memory, Marshall scores the highest grades in all of his classes while not even bothering to attend lectures. Orno has to struggle.

His first spring in New York, Orno makes the acquaintance in one of his classes of Sofia, a Russian, the daughter of a physicist who had defected. Canin flatly describes what happens next: "He was a virgin but she was not, and soon he wasn't either." His grades decline as they have sex daily. Marshall withdraws from Orno to date a girl descended from J. P. Morgan, but then phones him for help. Orno finds him overdosed on drugs, gets him home, and there meets Marshall's family. Professor Emerson, an authority on vertebrate biology, cruelly informs Orno that his history professor, Winthrop Scott, has changed his name from Irving Greenstein. Later in the novel, Marshall's sister, Simone, will reveal to Orno that her father's real name was Mendelsohn, that he is descended from a Lithuanian Jewish barrel salesman, and that he had made up a false genealogy that he traced back to Ralph Waldo Emerson.

Manipulated by the charismatic Marshall, Orno joins a clique of heavy-drinking would-be poets, with Marshall cruelly mocking whatever targets he can find among them. He also takes Sofia from Orno; neither can resist him. The next stage in this predictable narrative finds Marshall leaving Columbia for Los Angeles, ostensibly to write a novel, actually to write film and television scripts. Orno plods on at Columbia. With his grades too low for admission to medical school, he settles for dental school and is admitted to Stony Brook's. The summer after his first, difficult year there, Orno visits Marshall in his Venice Beach townhouse. Yes, Marshall gives the stereotypical show-business party. Yes, the guests lie about their careers and sniff cocaine, while Marshall introduces Orno as a surgeon and comforts himself with starlets. And yes, Orno is repelled by this kind of existence.

Meanwhile, Orno and Marshall's sister, Simone, have fallen in love. In contrast to her mercurial brother, she is modest, candid, unpretentious, and stable. She settles in with him during his later dental studies and reveals not only her father's mendacity but his need to impress people with a Cape Cod cottage and expensive boat, neither of which he can afford. Orno is repelled yet also fascinated by the Emersons, father and son. As Marshall takes Orno for a drive down Los Angeles's Sunset Boulevard to the Pacific Ocean, Marshall's moral resolution is delivered in clunky prose:

> He tapped the brake. He'd never wanted a life like this. Hard work and an honest standing in the world—that's what he'd been after. A wife and children. A house and neighbors. He'd wanted to be able to look his father in the eye.
> "It's nice," Marshall said. "Isn't it?"
> Orno was startled. "It's not for me," he answered. He wanted to be home.

Graduated from dental school, Orno joins a small practice in Preston, Maine. He and Simone buy a modest house and plan their wedding. However, Professor Emerson takes over its preparations, insisting it be at the Cape and promising "a Kennedy or two at the ceremony." The two sets of contrasting parents meet, with Canin illustrating the gulf between them by having Orno's mother misunderstand the professor's field of taxonomy for taxidermy. Marshall, in a confessional moment, tells Orno that both he and his father are hollow at their center. As if to illustrate the point, he has brought Sofia for the wedding and attempts to "return" her to Orno; she and he are appalled. Marshall's destructive drive then kicks into high gear: He maligns his sister to Orno as perfidious and promiscuous, tells Orno his parents are opposed to the wedding, and disappears. Simone and Orno spend days hunting for him. When he is still missing on the dawn of their wedding day, they decide to leave the Cape and elope; they are married by a judge in Portland, Maine. Simone tries to explain Marshall's erratic behavior. His mother was too preoccupied with anthropological field work to care for him, his father was too busy making his academic mark; inadequate love from either parent has streaked Marshall with self-centered cruelty. As for the Emersons' elaborate wedding plans, the Kennedys had never been asked.

Both male Emersons break down: Marshall shows up at Simone and Orno's house but has to be rushed to the hospital with an acute case of alcoholism and bleeding ulcers. Professor Emerson takes the terminal step of drowning himself at sea. Mrs. Pelham asks her children to forgive her for not having taken them, when young, away from their father.

Marshall then concludes a long anecdote he has related to Orno on several occasions. When the young Marshall and his mother were in Istanbul, her purse was stolen their first day. Luckily (or so it then seemed) an older man caught the thief, returned the purse, and became their protector. His name was Selim Aziz. A retired ferry captain, he knew both the local countryside and the islands, was intelligent, interesting, and courteous, and spent much time with Marshall while his mother did her field research. However, the day they were to leave Turkey, all of their money and valuables were stolen. They figured out that the purse's first theft and return had been arranged between Aziz and his confederate so that Aziz could gain their trust, only to betray it to his fullest advantage. After his father's death, Marshall confides to Orno that he would occasionally steal his father's cash and send a money order to Selim. Granted, he was a thief, but he had played the role of father admirably and had shown Marshall much grace. "And to this day," he concludes, "it's the greatest thing I've ever done." However, Simone later reveals to Orno that Marshall has never been to Turkey, with or without his mother. At the novel's end, Orno has written off Marshall's treacherous friendship and has decided that "he had come a great distance in his life"; he and Simone become the joyous parents of a son.

The only artistic grace note of this deeply flawed novel is the tale of Selim Aziz. Up to this point in his career, Ethan Canin has shown himself a masterful story writer but, unfortunately, a failure in the longer fictive form. *For Kings and Planets* flounders with sentences that are carelessly and flatly written, such as "Spring peaked early and inside him expectancy opened," or "all kinds of buildings seemed to have been joined together to make the hospital," or "and then soon afterward he understood that this meant that from then on he was going to cast his lot elsewhere."

Ethan Canin's characters ring largely false: Both pairs of parents as well as Simone are too sketchily drawn. What do convince the reader are Marshall's deviousness and Orno's dullness. As for the central theme, we have read too many times before about the simple, honest hick from the sticks who is dazzled by the glamour of the worldly denizen of the metropolis. Canin's command of elegant prose and mellow irony has here deserted him; instead, banality and sentimentality infest his text. Gifted as he has shown himself to be, Ethan Canin should file this mishap under "Mistakes Made" and move on to better things.

Gerhard Brand

Sources for Further Study

Booklist. XCIV, August, 1998, p. 1920.
The Christian Science Monitor. September 17, 1998, p. B6.
The Economist. CCCXLIX, October 17, 1998, p. 16.
Library Journal. CXXIII, September 1, 1998, p. 212.
Los Angeles Times. November 18, 1998, p. E1.
The New York Times Book Review. CIII, September 13, 1998, p. 12.
Publishers Weekly. CCXLV, July 6, 1998, p. 49.
The Spectator. CCLXXXI, October 31, 1998, p. 46.
The Wall Street Journal. September 17, 1998, p. A20.
The Washington Post Book World. XXVIII, September 13, 1998, p. 11.

FRANCIS BACON

Author: Perez Zagorin (1920-   )
Published: Princeton University Press (Princeton, New Jersey). 286 pp. $29.95
Type of work: Biography and philosophy
Time: 1561-1626
Locale: England

A study of the development of Francis Bacon's intellectual life, with attention to his thought in the areas of science, morals, politics, language, law, and history

As was no doubt inevitable in the case of a thinker and gifted writer who saw his work as a major initiative toward a fresh orientation of human knowledge, Francis Bacon has engaged the attention of many scholars in various fields, particularly historians of science. Whereas the proliferation of studies focusing on this intriguing early seventeenth century thinker has made possible a more discriminating understanding of his contribution, the increasing specialization of these studies has served other specialists better than nonspecialist readers, and Bacon is both interesting and important enough to deserve the attention of the latter group.

Professor Perez Zagorin has not undertaken a detailed life of his subject but rather a study of his philosophical writings in the context of an active and ambitious life strewn with evidences of the follies and frailties that as a thinker he recognized and, in his famous essays, analyzed dispassionately. In his essay "Of Ambition," Bacon recommends that princes select ministers more motivated by sense of duty than determination to rise; yet to rise in the service of the two monarchs of his time, Queen Elizabeth I and her successor King James I, Bacon was capable of betraying friends and neglecting an intellectual project that he must have realized required all of his powers and constituted his best chance at an enduring achievement. As Zagorin points out in his introductory chapter, Bacon could not resist the attractions and challenges of the political life. Although James I eventually appointed him lord chancellor, he was convicted of corruption (to a considerable extent, to be sure, through the efforts of the political enemies he had no trouble in making) and banished from that office and the hope of any future one. Even then, with his magnum opus unfinished, Bacon in his seventh decade kept soliciting the king for further public responsibilities. Zagorin hardly exaggerates in attributing to Bacon "two lives."

Bacon's energy was ferocious, however, and his works constitute fourteen substantial volumes in the still definitive nineteenth century edition of his works, to which an edition currently in progress will add other materials more recently discovered. From the early 1590's on, Bacon committed his intellectual life to a reform and reordering of human knowledge. He saw early that this project required a new philosophy that would jettison the assumptions and attitudes of the ancient and medieval world as well as many characteristic of the more promising Renaissance worldview. Aside from his *Essays* (1597), which most scholars do not regard as part of this scheme, his first important work, *The Advancement of Learning*, appeared in 1605, while he was still fruitlessly attempting to obtain a position of some consequence from James, who had succeeded to the throne at Elizabeth's death two years earlier. In Book I, nominally a defense of learning against its detractors, Bacon, a tireless classifier, distinguishes three chief varieties of "vain learning." The first, which he disposes of briefly, consists of meaningless words, ones which do not pertain to "matter." To exemplify the second vanity, matter that is itself vain, he cites the "cobwebs of learning" of the medieval Scholastic philosophers, contentious but insubstantial and unprofitable. The third distemper of learning, outright deceitfulness, he finds well illustrated in such pseudo-sciences as astrology, natural magic, and alchemy. These and other errors have given learning itself a bad name. In Book II, Bacon proceeds to divide true learning into three branches: history, poetry, and philosophy, corresponding to the faculties of memory, imagination, and reason, respectively. The most important of these for Bacon is philosophy, encompassing, among other things, all that is now thought of as science. One of the most interesting parts of Book II is the discussion of the various ways learning is presented, or, as Bacon usually puts it, "delivered." He favors the aphorism, a spare kind of presentation that, eschewing examples in favor of the writer's pith, readily reveals the quality of his thought. Bacon always suspects a style he calls "magistral," wherein the reader is offered a finished product that encourages belief and easy satisfaction, whereas a "probational" delivery engages the reader to inquire actively into the soundness of what is being presented.

Bacon's *Instauratio Magna* ("The Great Instauration") appeared fifteen years later, in 1620. Composed in Latin to ensure its availability to the educated readers of Western Europe, it consists of a *proemium* (a kind of preliminary announcement), a dedication to King James, an eloquent preface, and the plan of the work, which was to be in six parts, beginning with Bacon's inevitable "Divisions of the Sciences" and proceeding to "The New Philosophy, or Active Science." The *Instauratio* was accompanied by his justly famous *Novum Organum* ("The New Organon"), in effect the second part of the scheme, and the only one completed at that point. This well-known work, in two books, comprises a series of aphorisms, some of them the terse statements that the term suggests, others several pages long, the best known being his identification and discussion of the four "idols" of the mind. The Idols of the Tribe are impediments to understanding indigenous to human nature itself. The Idols of the Cave are the errors attributable to the individual owing to constitution and upbringing. The Idols of the Marketplace derive from words that pertain to nonexistent things or to faulty abstractions from existing ones. The Idols of the Theater, the most serious of all, derive from false philosophies and demonstrations. Only if purged of these idols could human knowledge advance through experimentation and rigorously applied inductive logic.

Bacon's main purpose in Book II of the *Novum Organum* was to develop his theory of induction, the logical approach by which natural philosophy (or natural science) could be put on a sound footing and facilitate true intellectual progress. Zagorin takes issue with unhistorical critics who fail to realize the limited understanding of inductive logic in Bacon's time and unjustly condemn his contribution to the subject. Bacon's reform of induction was a solitary attempt to make straight a way through a scientific wilderness. Zagorin also absolves Bacon of the frequently made charge of an undirected, naïvely empirical approach that reduced his method to ungoverned fact-collecting. Bacon indeed recognized the importance of hypothesis in the process, although Zagorin concedes that Bacon's main deficiency as an investigator of nature—his failure to appreciate the value of mathematics—vitiated his conception of induction.

The third part of the *Instauratio*, a compilation of natural histories, would in itself have kept him busy for a lifetime. He expected to have help in this endeavor, but he did later compose a few of these works, intended as raw material for subsequent inductive reasoning. It is easy today to see the futility of this laborious approach, but as Zagorin makes clear, it is consistent with Bacon's dissatisfaction with the tainted available knowledge and with his conviction that the evidentiary basis for the envisioned new philosophy had to be made good as it proceeded. The fourth and fifth parts would furnish "anticipations" of the new philosophy, or "active science," that would finally be set forth in the sixth part. As has been noted, only the second part of this scheme, *Novum Organum*, is in anything approaching complete form, but his *De Dignitate et Augmentis Scientiarum* (1623; Of the Dignity and Advancement of Learning), a Latin reworking of his 1605 treatise, serves as the part one preliminary.

Bacon saw himself as a precursor. By virtue of selective examples and enthusiastic advocacy, he would provide the momentum for this coming era of "active science" that would replace the current hopeless mélange of ancient, medieval, and post-medieval thought. The plan did not recommend itself to those whom Bacon envisioned his disciples, but his urgency and eloquence made him an extremely influential man. The part he played in dismantling an old worldview and arguing a new one into existence has been exaggerated both by partisans and opponents. He has been excoriated for undermining religion and, more recently, for serving as patron of the pillagers of nature so odious to modern environmentalists. Zagorin has some especially trenchant comments for those who have deplored these aspects of Bacon's influence. He cites plentiful evidence that Bacon was a sincerely religious man of his time and reminds critics that Bacon's world was a precarious one in which disease, harvest failure, famine, and chronic poverty prevailed. Bacon's heavy emphasis on control over nature reflected his sincere hope of lightening human burdens intolerable by modern standards. Zagorin reprimands those twentieth century writers who hold Bacon accountable for antienvironmental developments he could not possibly have envisioned and would doubtless have considered perversions of his philosophy.

The extent of Bacon's contribution to the seventeenth century scientific revolution is a controversy of long standing. To the criticisms that Bacon did not make any significant scientific discoveries and devised an unfruitful scientific method can be opposed his influence on the philosophy of science. Not only did his withering criticisms of the inadequacy of prevailing knowledge contribute to the scientific awakening of his time, but his vision of scientific possibilities also inspired his followers. His posthumous Utopian fiction *New Atlantis* (1627), though fragmentary, is generally seen as inspiring the scientific societies that arose in the decades after his death, particularly the Royal Society of London.

The author devotes about 40 percent of his text to Bacon's writings in the areas of moral and political philosophy and to his interest in law, history, and language. The *Essays*, as well as his works devoted to his philosophy of science, are peppered with shrewd observations on negotiation, empire, counsel, ambition, and many other topics in the Machiavellian tradition of moral realism, while his *New Atlantis* is strikingly original in its depiction of an ideal society that values and promotes systematic inquiry into the secrets of nature. His writings on the law are characteristically practical, mainly efforts toward the recompilation of English common law. His *History of the Reign of King Henry the Seventh* (1622), while inaccurate in many of its details, is notable for its artistry and keen analysis of the policies of the first Tudor king. Finally, Bacon was a brilliant stylist who, understanding the seductiveness of style, insisted that the pursuit of learning required language that provoked inquiry rather than encouraged belief.

A book such as Zagorin's could only be written by someone who has digested the considerable mass of scholarly books and monographs on Bacon from recent decades. Perusal of the more than fifty pages of Zagorin's endnotes confirms his mastery of secondary sources as well as of the Bacon canon. Except where they are essential to his own critique of Bacon's thought, this thirty-year student of Bacon has wisely confined his critiques of other studies to these notes and resisted the temptation to produce the long book that such a well-qualified scholar might have written. He has thus succeeded in his aim to produce a history of Bacon's mind, the need for which many specialized studies have made apparent, without repeating detail inessential for such a purpose and without discouraging readers unfamiliar with the burgeoning Baconian scholarship. The restriction of this book, after its introductory chapter, to the genesis and development of Bacon's mental life will undoubtedly make it essential reading for Baconian experts, but its readership should extend to all who are interested in the seventeenth century climate of thought and in Bacon's role in forming the modern worldview. In short, it is that too-rare phenomenon: a book for both the scholar and the serious nonprofessional reader.

Robert P. Ellis

Sources for Further Study

Kirkus Reviews. LXVI, April 15, 1998, p. 572.
New Scientist. CLVIII, May 2, 1998, p. 45.
Publishers Weekly. CCXLV, April 6, 1998, p. 70.
The Times Literary Supplement. June 19, 1998, p. 12.
The Wall Street Journal. July 23, 1998, p. A14.
The Washington Post Book World. XXVIII, May 31, 1998, p. 13.

FREEDOMLAND

Author: Richard Price (1949-   )
Published: Broadway Books (New York). 546 pp. $25.00
Type of work: Novel
Time: The present
Locale: Two neighboring but uneasy inner-city towns in northern New Jersey

A single mother tells police that her young son has been kidnapped during a carjacking; the truth slowly emerges, conveyed in alternating chapters by a black detective and a white newspaperwoman

> *Principal characters:*
> LORENZO (BIG DADDY) COUNCIL, a compassionate, religious, tough-talking policeman
> JESSE HAUS, a newswoman who rises above a predatory job to pursue a crime's elusive truth
> BRENDA MARTIN, a thirty-two-year-old unwed mother and addict who tells a violent story of a carjacker and a lost son
> CODY MARTIN, Brenda's son, on whose fate the novel turns
> DANNY MARTIN, Brenda's volatile but loyal brother, a policeman
> BEN HAUS, Jesse's brother, a "freelance expediter"
> THE REVEREND LONGWAY, a black preacher suggestive of Al Sharpton
> KAREN COLLUCCI, the head of a cultish volunteer group devoted to finding abducted and missing children
> ANIL CHATTERJEE, a physician
> ULYSSES MALDONADO, Cody's father
> JOSÉ, Jesse's city editor

As a novelist, forty-nine-year-old Richard Price speaks for the nonspeaking. In *Clockers* (1992), he rendered the drug trade in a midsize city in New Jersey—Dempsy—and did so from the viewpoints of both the disenchanted police and the down-but-not-quite-out crack dealers. In his acclaimed first novel, *The Wanderers* (1974), he gave voice to working-class Bronx teenagers locked into dead-end lives. "I want to create an awareness that certain people exist," he told an interviewer. "Let me just put them on paper so the reader can see who they are." In *Freedomland*, his sixth and most ambitious novel, Price goes to extraordinary lengths to make good on his imperative to let readers see. What the reader sees—what Price shows—are lives lived at nerve-end torpor.

Drawing on a common practice of such contemporaries as Don DeLillo and Tom Wolfe, the author finds his basic scenario in recent headlines. In 1994, Susan Smith told police in a South Carolina town that an African American carjacker had abducted her two sons. Later, she confessed that she had drowned the boys by pushing her car, with them in it, into a lake. The deep human interest that is inherent in the Susan Smith story—its catalog of horrors, including child murder, domestic abuse, and racism—could not help but have given Richard Price a catalyst. However, what he extracts from this tabloid material he elaborates into a fictive world that he claims as his alone. In a prologue that is suggestive but in no way derivative of the opening of Stephen Crane's

Maggie: A Girl of the Streets (1893), a thin figure (later to be entered formally on a police blotter as "female, 32, Caucasian, disoriented") makes her way to the butt end of Hurley, the main street of a Dempsy, New Jersey, housing project. As she approaches, then passes, two young men, frozen "in postures of alert curiosity," taunt her ("bitch on a mission") but in no way impede her progress to the emergency room of Dempsy Medical Center.

For all but the final hundred of *Freedomland*'s 546 pages, it is indeed Brenda Martin's skewed "mission" that the reader follows. She tells the attending doctor, a project-assimilated East Indian, and, later, Lorenzo "Big Daddy" Council, a black detective who is the novel's hero, that she was the victim of a carjacking by a black man and that her four-year-old son, Cody, was in the back seat when her car was stolen.

The reader does not require the tedious tracking-down of clues by the novel's two "reflector" characters to doubt Brenda's story. As Francine Prose noted in an otherwise glowing review in *The New York Times*, Price leaves his readers morally adrift as he provides Brenda with monotonous replies to vital inquiries about her son and the putative kidnapper. For long stretches, Brenda resides in a heartland of ambiguity where the reader might expect at least once to hear her rail against the carjacker. Brenda, though, seems to prefer that the phantom abductor the cops call the "actor" remain in limbo.

So does Lorenzo. Assigned to watch Brenda, he senses her relief whenever the news on Cody and the mystery carjacker amounts to no news. "Nonetheless, he recommitted himself to breaking her down, to maintaining a one-prong mind-set on this." What really attracts him to Brenda, fifteen years his junior, is not sexual but something more complex: empathy and the belief that no one escapes his or her history. Lorenzo and Brenda are both products of the area; he is an eight-years-sober alcoholic, she is a drug addict. Her son is missing, his in jail.

The other sensibility, on which Brenda's agony plays like the tuning of a fine instrument, belongs to Jesse Haus, a white female reporter for the *Dempsy Register* who had grown up in Dempsy, where her family, among the project's last white residents, still lives.

Jesse, in fact, is so taken by Brenda that José, her editor, wonders whether his reporter is in love.

There may be more truth to José's ribbing than he imagines. Jesse finds herself beguiled at being in the now-haunted house where Brenda was reared:

> Then it came to Jesse why she was really here—because this house had known Brenda . . . [I]f Jesse couldn't have Brenda in the flesh anymore, then she would settle, would have to settle for her haunts. . . . [I]t was all she could do not to ask to be shown Brenda's childhood bedroom.

The novel is a triangle, with Lorenzo and Jesse occupying the legs and Brenda the base. Early on, the religious, compassionate, tough-talking cop and the tabloid journalist become symbiotic caretakers in a vain attempt to save Brenda from herself and the lie that has been coaxed out of her. Until the finale, when he combines their voices in elegiac remembrance of Brenda, Price alternates chapters between Lorenzo's voice, which is knowing and sad for knowing, and Jesse's, whose dissonance eventually finds unexpected harmony.

In a social milieu in which the wily art of quid-pro-quo is the rule (police pry information from youths—"jugglers"—in exchange for favors and beat up colleagues, including Brenda's brother Danny, for violently expressed loyalty), the contracts between the three principals, unwritten, mostly tacit, are the ties that bind the novel.

Brenda Martin, who lives in white Gannon but teaches black youngsters in Dempsy, is a tarnished romantic who dreams of heaven but lives in hell. She is a character who can neither be judged nor enjoyed. Not all readers will accept Price's efforts to redeem her from the mother who may have committed an unspeakable crime to someone like Joseph Conrad's Lord Jim, who was credited as being "one of us." Members of the Friends of Kent, a group devoted to the finding of missing children, eventually bully Brenda into full disclosure. There was no abductor, no carjacker; Brenda, with the help of a former boyfriend, had buried Cody in a shallow grave in Freedomland, an abandoned New Jersey theme park that was modeled after an earlier theme park in New York carrying the same—the book's—name. Her story, subject again to revision, is that Cody died after swallowing a bottle of Benadryl. However, the reader soon learns that Cody deliberately swallowed the drug because he was upset at his mother for leaving him home alone so she could be with her boyfriend. The final chapters cover the novel's culminating events with unexpected concision: Cody's wake, Brenda's arraignment, a protest march by hordes of Dempsyites in the mistaken assumption that the mother and accomplice murdered the child, Brenda's suicide in her cell.

Richard Price is a skilled screenwriter who has scripted Martin Scorcese's *The Color of Money* (1986), Harold Becker's *Sea of Love* (1989), Irwin Winkler's *Night and the City* (1992), among other films. His ear for street dialogue and his eye for the telling visual detail no doubt contributed to the sale of the film rights to *Freedomland* for $2 million. If he writes the screen adaptation and follows his novel, the resulting movie will not be one of those staples that program audiences to a single viewpoint. As reviewer Earl L. Dachslager has commented, Price has skillfully but cynically composed the final chapters to allow Brenda to rest in a moral neutral zone: "We may blame Brenda for being a careless and irresponsible mom, but we are also asked to understand her, even forgive her, because of the dire consequences of her selfishness."

Price is at his best when he vivifies tensions along the Dempsy-Gannon border in a series of jolting scenes, including a session in which Brenda collaborates with a police sketch artist—and produces a sketch of the artist himself. Perhaps the novel's most surreal moments involve a palpably useless search for Cody through the grounds of a ruined mental institution.

Describing the impact of reading as a teenager Hubert Selby, Jr.'s harrowing *Last Exit to Brooklyn* (1964), Price told an interviewer that he "heard the voice of the housing projects, and there was music in it, and it was 'literature.'" In *Freedomland*, Richard Price has orchestrated that music.

Richard Hauer Costa

Sources for Further Study

Library Journal. CXXIII, May 1, 1998, p. 140.
Los Angeles Times Book Review. May 31, 1998, p. 10.
The Nation. CCLXVII, July 20, 1998, p. 25.
National Review. L, July 6, 1998, p. 50.
The New York Review of Books. XLV, June 11, 1998, p. 30.
The New York Times Book Review. CIII, June 7, 1998, p. 14.
Publishers Weekly. CCXLV, April 6, 1998, p. 56.
Time. CLI, May 18, 1998, p. 93.
The Times Literary Supplement. July 10, 1998, p. 25.
The Washington Post. May 12, 1998, p. D3.

FREUD
Culture and Conflict

Edited by Michael S. Roth (1957-   )
Published: Alfred A. Knopf (New York). Illustrated. 273 pp. $26.00
Type of work: Biography and psychology

Scholars from a number of disciplines assess the impact of Freud's writings and practices on the twentieth century, particularly in the areas of psychoanalysis, literary criticism, and women's studies

Principal personage:
SIGMUND FREUD, the author and founder of modern psychoanalysis

"Others abide our question," the poet Matthew Arnold wrote of William Shakespeare, "Thou art free." Indeed, Shakespeare may be one of the few giants in any field to have escaped the vicissitudes of public opinion—and even he has come under fire in the twentieth century. Therefore, it should be no surprise to see that Sigmund Freud, the man whose discoveries about the human psyche had made him a household name even before his death, is now as often vilified as vindicated by scholars. What may be surprising, however, is the rapidity with which Freud's star has fallen after its meteoric rise. Less than a century has passed since he published *The Interpretation of Dreams* (1900), his seminal work on the way the mind functions. Once the most revered practitioner of the art of psychology, Freud is now viewed with skepticism and even disdain by many who consider him not only misguided in his scientific method but also misogynous and myopic in his assessment of the human condition.

Of course, there are still some in the scholarly community who hold Freud in high esteem, and many in the general public who still assume he is responsible for much of the good that has come from the practice of psychology. For anyone who has spent time on an analyst's couch, the debt to Freud and his methods is felt most keenly. The assumption among those not practicing in the field is that Freud is truly the father of modern analysis. Moreover, students of literature trained between 1930 and 1970 would probably claim to be as familiar with Freud as they are with the tenets of the New Critics. Psychological critiques of the writings of figures as diverse as Edgar Allan Poe and Shakespeare were commonplace among the works of scholars in Europe and especially in America during those decades.

The tide has certainly ebbed, however, since the zenith of Freud's influence was reached in the years immediately following World War II. Psychological research during the latter half of the century, coupled with the criticisms of feminist scholars who take strong exception to Freud's dismissive portrait of women, has done much to discredit the value of his work. In academic circles, he has suffered the fate of Christopher Columbus, George Washington, Thomas Jefferson, and others; his faults seem to outweigh any contribution he may have made to the advancement of knowledge. Nevertheless, even feminist critic E. Ann Kaplan is forced to conclude that "Freud's long shadow still lingers over the twentieth century as it nears its end," and

Magill's Literary Annual 1999

despite feminism and post-modernism, his "powerful influence" will undoubtedly
extend into the twenty-first.

For that reason, and because the Library of Congress has for many years held a large
collection of Freud's papers, curators there decided in 1996 to mount an exhibit
honoring him. That, too, met with controversy, and the opening was delayed two years.
Plans to provide as a part of this exhibit a catalog which would also serve as a
retrospective examination of Freud's work went forward, though, and the result is
Freud: Culture and Conflict.

Edited by Michael S. Roth, the book collects eighteen essays by Freudians and
anti-Freudians whose professional disciplines range from psychology and psychiatry
to literature and history. *Freud: Culture and Conflict* is an anthology about Freud and
his impact on modern society. Medical doctors and museum directors offer their
opinions side by side with editors and journalists. Roth, who also curated the Library
of Congress exhibit, has divided the volume into major sections that focus attention
on Freud's methods and talents as a writer; his work as a practicing psychoanalyst; his
influence on disciplines such as history, literature, and popular culture; and his
checkered reputation. Roth's introduction summarizes these themes and offers a brief
biographical sketch focusing on Freud's career. James Billington, the Librarian of
Congress, provides a brief foreword outlining the history of the library's acquisition
of its collection of Freud's papers. The intent of this collective effort is, in Billington's
words, "to motivate a new generation of researchers to mine the Library's Freud
Collection for the continuing study of the impact psychoanalysis and Freud's thinking
more generally have had on our society."

Though both acknowledge that there is no consensus about the value of Freud's
contributions, neither Roth nor Billington admit the seriousness of the disagreement
that exists among their contemporaries about Freud's real merits. Furthermore, almost
all the contributors to *Freud: Culture and Conflict* are in Freud's camp. Ilse Grubrich-
Simitis, an editor of Freud and author of several studies about him, writes almost
lovingly about his method of composing from notes that reflect his remarkable insight
into the human psyche. Patrick Mahony, emeritus professor of the University of
Montreal, discusses Freud's insatiable need to write as if he were driven with the
conviction of a religious zealot. Mahony even goes so far as to suggest that Freud knew
his work would be misunderstood and that only those readers who "focus on both the
content and the communicative strategy" will be able to appreciate fully the lessons
laid out before them. In essays on the famous (or infamous) Oedipus complex,
historians John Toews and José Brunner are more analytic and less fulsome in their
praise for Freud; nevertheless, they also are emphatic in pronouncing the lasting
significance of Freud's discoveries about the primal urges that drive all human beings
to act out or repress tendencies that shape both their personal lives and the collective
behavior of their culture.

Roth includes several essays about Freud's impact on America, where his ideas were
in vogue as early as 1909, when he visited Clark University in Massachusetts. Robert
Coles, a Harvard University professor and perhaps the most distinguished child

psychiatrist in the country, contributes a personal memoir of his encounters with famous Freudians, including his colleague Erik Erikson, a disciple of Freud and patient of Freud's daughter Anna. Edith Kurzweil, the editor of the prestigious *Partisan Review*, examines the growth of psychoanalytic studies in the United States. Like so many writers for the volume, she too concludes that "Freud has irrevocably altered the Western tradition."

This is not to suggest that those contributors who admire Freud are blind to his failures. Several essayists note his penchant for jumping to sweeping conclusions on the basis of scanty evidence and his tendency to mine others' works to support his own theories, sometimes ignoring the context of the originals. Hannah Decker writes candidly about Freud's inability to cure Ida Bauer, the "Dora" of whom he writes in his famous case study "A Fragment of an Analysis of a Case of Hysteria." She acknowledges that Freud's own review of his dealings with this confused teenager has provided evidence for feminists' accusations that he was guilty of "an overweening masculine bias, grossly unsympathetic treatment, and significant errors of technique." Decker, however, uses this case to show how Freud developed his theory of transference, whereby patients confuse their analysts with others in their lives who have caused pain or suffering. She excuses Freud by pointing out that Dora came to him early in his career and that what he learned from his treatment of her assisted him in curing many others who followed her to his couch.

A few anti-Freudians offer counterarguments to the panegyrics that dominate the volume. The harshest of these are by Adolf Grünbaum and Muriel Dimen. Grünbaum, chair of the Center for Philosophy of Science at the University of Pittsburgh, delivers his own retrospective on the growth of psychoanalysis and the impact of Freud's theories during the twentieth century. He begins by pointing out the derivative nature of much of Freud's early work. He then offers a critique of many of Freud's most prominent and popular theories about the unconscious, disputing findings and illuminating inconsistencies in both methodology and conclusions. Believing that Freud was himself fixated on the notion that infantile wish-fulfillment was the cause of all human neuroses, Grünbaum searches among Freud's writings to point out places where a priori reasoning and willful dismissal of contradictory evidence abound.

Dimen's remarks, while less analytic than Grünbaum's, are both more accessible for the general reader and less dogmatic in assessing Freud's limitations. Her essay, "Strange Hearts: On the Paradoxical Liaison Between Psychoanalysis and Feminism," focuses on the consequences of what she calls Freud's "failure of nerve": his unwillingness to deal honestly with femininity. She recounts Freud's arguments that paint women as malformed men and then explains the obvious anger such a position has evoked in women since pioneer feminist Karen Horney began writing about the inadequacy of Freud's theory. Dimen's essay ends up being as much a critique of feminism as it is of Freud, highlighting the paradoxical nature of a movement that contains at its center a "tension between two main goals, one ameliorative, the other revolutionary." Like Freud, she ends up asking what it is that women really want, and she does not provide a clear answer.

Why then, asks British philosopher Frank Cioffi, "after almost a century of debate, has no consensus emerged as to the authenticity of Freud's achievement?" In a balanced assessment that responds to critics such as Dimen and Grünbaum, Cioffi points out that the grounds for acceptance of Freud's principal theories does not lie ultimately in the realm of science. Too frequently, he observes, the zeal of Freud's disciples to prove his theories in the same way physical scientists set out to prove the laws of gravity or entropy results only in confusion. Nevertheless, those who dispute Freud's achievement have similar problems denying the efficacy of his observations about the human psyche; after all, too many people have found psychoanalysis effective to deny its usefulness. Therein lies the dilemma, Cioffi concludes: For some, Freud will always be a charlatan, while to others he will remain a savior.

One cannot help but wonder what Freud himself would say if he were to see what scholars and practitioners have made of his discoveries. No doubt Freud the dogmatic, egocentric misogynist, the obsessed and obsessive propagandist for a theory of sexual repression, would not be satisfied with the representation of his ideas by some of the contributors to *Freud: Culture and Conflict*. On the other hand, Freud the scientist, who argued persuasively for a theory of the mind to rival Charles Darwin's theory of natural selection, would be most pleased.

Laurence W. Mazzeno

Sources for Further Study

Library Journal. CXXIII, November 1, 1998, p. 115.
Mirabella. September, 1998, p. 96.
The New York Times Book Review. CIII, November 22, 1998, p. 12.
Publishers Weekly. CCXLV, September 28, 1998, p. 88.
US News and World Report. CXXV, October 19, 1998, p. 60.
The Washington Post Book World. XXVIII, November 15, 1998, p. 11.

FROM WEALTH TO POWER
The Unusual Origins of America's World Role

Author: Fareed Zakaria
Published: Princeton University Press (Princeton, New Jersey). 199 pp. $29.95
Type of work: History
Time: The nineteenth century
Locale: The United States

Zakaria uses the emergence of the United States as a world power during the later decades of the nineteenth century to validate the political theory of state-centered realism as a means of explaining and predicting a nation's decision to expand its influence on the world stage

What makes a nation great? What causes its leaders to channel national resources and direct the sentiments of the populace toward a position of prominence in the international arena? Why do some countries build large armies and navies and become entangled in political matters far beyond their borders? Can a theory be developed that accounts for such actions, and will the theory be strong enough to be used as a means of predicting future actions? These matters are ones political scientists mull over routinely, and the writings that fill journals such as *Foreign Affairs* and *International Affairs* provide what seem to be endless answers to these and similar questions. Library shelves are filled with monographs that purport to explain the causes for any nation's entry into and behavior on the world stage. Consequently, any scholar adventurous enough to produce a new work on the subject must be grounded on a considerable body of scholarship, in both political theory and history.

Fortunately, Fareed Zakaria is particularly well qualified for the task. An editor for years with *Foreign Affairs*, he brings to his analysis a command of previous scholarship that few others might claim. In *From Wealth to Power*, he takes as his starting point the fact that the United States rose dramatically from a minor trading partner with Europe and Latin America to a world power—perhaps the predominant world power—in less than half a century. He then looks to both political theory and history to determine if the example provided by the United States can be used as the basis for a theory that would account for any nation's decision to make a mark in global affairs.

As a consequence, for the educated general reader, *From Wealth to Power* may well seem to be two books: a theoretical analysis of the causes for a country's leaders to enter the world arena and exert their will on other nations, and a historical review of the U.S. rise to international prominence near the turn of the twentieth century. The introductory chapters on political theory seem to be directed at specialists in the field. Zakaria reviews the work of dozens of noted scholars who have sought to develop explanations for the motivations behind individual countries' attempts to exert their will beyond their traditional national borders, and to construct predictive models allowing scholars to forecast the behavior of nations and their leaders. He offers insights into the limitations of the two traditional theories used to describe the conditions under which a state determines to expand its political interests: classical realism and defensive realism. These he finds fundamentally different: "classical realism supposes that a nation's interests are determined by its power," while defensive realism "posits that states seek security rather than influence." Both theories have had strong proponents among academic critics and politicians. In fact, attributing the growth of a country's international influence to its increase in production of goods and harvesting of natural resources has long been a commonplace among both political theorists and historians. The United States has been a kind of poster child for classical realists who claim economic growth demands international expansion. At almost the same time, another group of scholars has long posited the more benign theory that a nation's decision to increase its military capabilities and annex territories is largely a response to perceived threats to its sovereignty and security.

Even before he examines the case of the United States in the late nineteenth century, however, Zakaria argues that neither theory is sufficient to explain fully the peculiar situation that, in his view, has driven many countries toward expansion, either in territory or influence. Instead, Zakaria proposes his own theory, a modified version of ideas espoused by early theorists Otto Hintze and Leopold von Ranke: state-centered realism. Proponents of this theory argue that there is a distinction between the nation and the state: The former describes the people and the resources available within a given geographic area, while the latter more accurately represents the political infrastructure set up to govern within that region. Hence, Zakaria believes it is not sufficient to focus simply on the total wealth of a nation and its growing demand to obtain more resources to continue economic expansion, as the classical realists might argue. Neither is he willing to follow the line of argument put forth by defensive realists, who would claim that a country's sudden desire to gain territory or insinuate itself in the affairs of other nations arises because there is a general fear among a populace that its way of life is threatened. Rather, Zakaria contends that the underlying element determining the willingness of a nation to enter the international arena is the structure of its governing apparatus. He chooses as his test case the United States during the period 1860 through 1910 because during those decades there occurred a radical transformation in the relative power of the branches of government that permitted the country's leaders to engage in international affairs on a scale much greater than had been permitted in previous years. While he acknowledges that the growth in resources, especially manufacturing, was important because the leaders had at their disposal the means to work as equals with other world powers, his principal line of argument is that the most significant factor determining the U.S. ability to become a world leader was the emergence of the presidency as the most powerful branch of government.

The central section of Zakaria's study reviews the political history of the United States during the administrations of presidents Andrew Johnson, Ulysses S. Grant, Rutherford B. Hayes, James Garfield, Chester Arthur, Grover Cleveland, Benjamin Harrison, William McKinley, and Theodore Roosevelt. In three brilliantly conceived and tightly constructed chapters, Zakaria describes the slow shift in power from the Congress, especially the Senate, to the executive branch. The first of these, aptly titled "Imperial Understretch," outlines the struggles that post-Civil War presidents such as

Johnson, Grant, and Hayes had in convincing members of the Senate to approve even the most benign treaties with foreign powers. Each suffered reversals at the hands of a legislative body reluctant to grant anything to the chief executive lest it be seen as ceding its precedence within the federal structure of governance. "The Rise of the American State," the second historical chapter, describes how the balance began to shift, not simply because presidents were more forceful and congressional leaders less so, but because growth and complexity in the economic sector demanded more centralized government with a professional bureaucracy managing national affairs. That phenomenon, coupled with a gradual demise of legislative power caused by internal squabbling and political corruption, permitted presidents such as Cleveland, McKinley, and Roosevelt to exercise significant influence in promoting policies that permitted the United States to take its place beside powers such as Great Britain, France, and Germany in determining international affairs.

In the course of his historical review, Zakaria is especially harsh in denouncing proponents of defensive realism, constantly pointing out the absence of real threats that would have given the United States government adequate justification for building up its military strength or rushing into alliances with other nations to fend off the aggressive actions of another country. Instead, Zakaria finds numerous instances in which politicians—especially American presidents and their cabinet members—took pains to orchestrate crises or to maneuver public opinion in such a way that the United States seemed to have no choice but to extend its influence outside its continental boundaries. The most famous example is the country's behavior toward Spain at the end of the century, when every action taken by the Spanish government in Cuba or as far away as the Philippines was painted as horrific and in need of redress. Zakaria finds numerous other examples as well, however, including the decades-long attempt by a series of American presidents to bring the Hawaiian Islands under U.S. control.

Not surprisingly, the central figure in Zakaria's study is Theodore Roosevelt. Committed to expanding U.S. presence and influence wherever and whenever he could, Roosevelt became the symbol of American imperialism both to his countrymen and to other nations. Roosevelt's use of the bully pulpit, and his desire to have the United States surpass Britain as the world's leading nation, is given prominence of place among the author's analysis of key figures in the country's drive toward international prominence. Zakaria is not wholly taken in, however, by Roosevelt's aggressive stance on his country's manifest destiny; his portrait of the president-diplomat is balanced, revealing some of the more mundane, egotistical motivations for the actions Roosevelt took both as assistant secretary of the Navy and later as president. Zakaria is also exceptionally astute in his assessment of figures such as Arthur and Cleveland, who are seen by other historians as being less prone to expansion than Zakaria finds them. In fact, as Zakaria demonstrates, considerable efforts toward expanding American influence in Latin America were made during Cleveland's second administration, when the country found itself embroiled in disputes with Chile, Nicaragua, and Brazil. The analysis of early American theorists such as Alfred Thayer Mahan helps explain how the intellectual climate of the day gave

McKinley and Roosevelt the arguments they needed to convince the country's citizens that their future lay in achieving prominence among the nations of the world.

What is especially useful in Zakaria's study is the author's ability to sift from the historical record some general principles that undergirded American foreign policy during this unusual and turbulent period. His careful review of virtually every major and minor foray by the United States into international affairs during this half-century allows him to construct a series of charts that display graphically the opportunities the country had to expand its territory and influence, as well as the outcomes of those efforts. As he demonstrates conclusively, the majority of the successful efforts occurred when the country's presidents made decisive efforts to exert themselves in favor of imperialist goals. When more chauvinist elements were in power, the United States remained aloof from the affairs of other nations. In Zakaria's view, the amazing growth in the country's economic base provided a necessary but not sufficient condition for the U.S. emergence as a great power. Instead, he concludes, the root of expansion and the rise to greatness rests within the political sphere: Politicians, especially presidents, make the crucial difference.

Zakaria is cautious in extending his theory to cover all cases of expansion. He claims, though, that a study of the role of state government should be a complement to any analysis of a nation's economic growth as a predictor of its rise to prominence internationally. Nevertheless, one lesson to be drawn from his study is both enlightening and sobering: It suggests that those whom the public elects to power in America will shape the country's destiny—but not always in accordance with the wishes of those who elected them.

Laurence W. Mazzeno

Sources for Further Study

Foreign Affairs. LXXVII, July, 1998, p. 120.
International Affairs. LXXIV, July, 1998, p. 719.
International Security. XXIII, Fall, 1998, p. 157.
National Interest. Fall, 1998, p. 113.
The New York Times Book Review. CIII, May 3, 1998, p. 25.
ORBIS. XLII, Fall, 1998, p. 631.
The Wall Street Journal. May 13, 1998, p. A20.

FROM WEST TO EAST
California and the Making of the American Mind

Author: Steven Schwartz (1948-   )
Published: The Free Press (New York). 566 pp. $30.00
Type of work: History
Time: 1500-1965
Locale: California

A critical examination of the development of California's social and political ideas, with an emphasis on liberalism and radicalism

Stephen Schwartz is a staff writer for the *San Francisco Chronicle*. He is an engaging, skilled writer given to subtly wry observations and ironic wordplay. His previous history books include *A Strange Silence: The Emergency of Democracy in Nicaragua* (1992) and *Brotherhood of the Sea: A History of the Sailors' Union of the Pacific, 1885-1985* (1986).

California has long been celebrated and, just as often, vilified as a unique and bounteous land populated by a diverse collection of trendsetting visionaries, fad-following dilettantes, self-indulgent hedonists, solipsistic hermits, iconoclasts, environmentalists, and moguls. Originally appearing on fifteenth century maps as a separate landmass surrounded by the Pacific Ocean, California continues to be depicted as a figurative island, removed from the conventions, mores, and even the economic and political environments that putatively characterize the rest of the lower forty-eight states. The reality of California's land and people is much less exotic than the myth that enshrouds it, but the persistence and acceptance of this notion provides the state with an unusually powerful influence in the realm of ideas.

It is this influence, this psychological power, that Schwartz examines in *From West to East: California and the Making of the American Mind*. As suggested by the title, Schwartz seeks to explain how major facets of American culture and politics—the American psyche, in effect—have been shaped by California. Not merely notable individual Californians, but rather the entire entity, or organism, that is California has worked upon the nation that annexed and admitted it during the mid-nineteenth century. Such, at least, is the author's argument, attributing to California a liberalizing and, at times, radicalizing influence on "the American mind." As the author writes, "This volume is intended as a counterargument to conventional histories of American expansion, in which California is described as a mere pawn of such."

The book develops as a historical narrative, uncluttered by footnotes or other references to sources. (At the end of the book there is a bibliography and a set of acknowledgments.) At the same time, the text carries considerable authority, reflecting care and craftsmanship in its writing and making extensive use of historical detail. If the book lacks the quantitative data, precise dates, and tables of academic history texts, it excels in its ability to convey the emotions and ideas that helped drive California's social and political development during the nineteenth and twentieth centuries.

The book is divided into six parts (following a brief prologue), proceeding in a chronological order. Part 1 concerns the arrival of European explorers during the sixteenth century and the subsequent events leading up to the admission of California into the Union. Part 2 examines the effects of California's early economic and demographic growth, owing, in large part, to the railroads. Part 3 opens with the dawn of the twentieth century and traces the rise of communism as a force in state and global politics. Part 4 examines communism's eventual dominance of radical politics in the late 1920's and 1930's—the Red Years. Part 5 concerns events coincident with World War II and its immediate aftermath, an era that involved various societal revolutions and initiated a new Red Scare. Part 6 examines the postwar transformation of California radicalism from an elite-based intellectual movement to a mass social movement in the 1950's and early 1960's. A short epilogue briefly assesses the subsequent three decades and offers some striking and powerful conclusions.

Schwartz begins by examining the arrival in California of a Portuguese explorer, Juan Rodrígues Cabrillo, who claimed the land for Spain. Cabrillo's landing presaged an influx of explorers and settlers from various countries, including Great Britain, Russia, and China. The competition among the different powers for control of California, including missionary settlements and sundry wars and rebellions, is traced in sequence, though in no particular depth. This is by design. Schwartz presents California's preadmission history not for its own sake but rather to trace the origins of the state's multiethnic society and its activist, at times rebellious, political environment.

Even when examining the history of California as the Union's thirty-first state (which is the book's focus after the first seventy-five pages), the author treats major historical events only superficially, as guideposts and reference points. His narrative emphasizes the emergence and interplay of left-wing political, social, and cultural forces. While many of the figures (such as Jack London, Upton Sinclair, and Henry George) are well known, many other fascinating figures have been lost in history. In any event, the narrative recounts relatively unknown facts and events from even the most famous figures' lives—what the author calls "hidden" or "secret" history. The result is a colorful pastiche of people, events, and ideas that illustrates the evolution of radicalism in California.

Schwartz tends to associate the ideology and ideas of political radicals with the provocative behavior and alternative lifestyles of cultural radicals. Drug use, for example, is a recurring theme in the book. From the use of psychedelic drugs by California's indigenous American Indians to the growing use of lysergic acid diethylamide (LSD) among hippies in the 1960's, Schwartz refers to drugs and their hallucinogenic effects as metaphors for various aspects of California's culture. He even seizes on an innocent sixteenth century description of sailors encountering seas "so high they became crazed" and notes with intentional irony that the description was "a portent of California's history."

Schwartz notes some of the social and political progress that has been fostered by California's left-wing movements. The improvement of working conditions that accompanied various trade union movements is one obvious benefit, as are the protection of civil rights and the expansion of free expression. However, this book is not meant as a celebration of West Coast enlightenment or a hagiography of California radicals. Indeed, although the author harbors evident sympathy for many aspects of radicalism, his book does not gloss over the darker aspects of California's radical movements and standard-bearers. He plainly describes the manipulation of socialist and communist organizations by Soviet agents, the infiltration of union apparatus by organized crime, the cynical appropriation of liberal and socialist themes by opportunistic politicians, the totalitarian tendencies of some left-wing ideologues, and the myriad examples of radicalism's failure in the transition from ideas to actions—such as the preference of the Black Panthers to "spend most of their time parading with weapons for the TV cameras and skirmishing with police" rather than working toward their presumed goal of "organizing the ghetto masses."

The book also illustrates some of the inevitable internal conflicts that have occurred within the state's radical Left, and in so doing helps to explain some of the disarray in which the modern inheritors of that legacy find themselves. For example, the incomplete overlap between the state's racial minorities and its lower socioeconomic classes has repeatedly been the sources of rifts within left-wing coalitions. Schwartz illustrates, for example, how racism caused some trade unions to exclude African Americans and how economic self-interest caused some labor advocates to oppose Chinese immigration. Similarly, Schwartz observes that the liberal principles of personal freedom and self-expression embodied in the "free love" movement in the 1960's were assaulted by the exploitive and dangerous pornography industry that followed from it: "[T]he sudden freedom of young people to wander hitchhiking around the country became the freedom of perverts to murder hitchhiking girls and boys with impunity."

Along the way, Schwartz attempts to reconcile some of the disputes between traditional historians and radical revisionists concerning California's history. His conclusions frequently take a justifiable, though frustratingly vague, middle ground. In his assessment of the Franciscan missionary Junípero Serra, Schwartz rejects both the "sentimental civic myth" that Serra and the other missionaries benevolently "introduced civilization to their Indian converts" and the revisionist description of Serra "as a tool of pure Spanish imperialism and a brutal enslaver of the Indians." Instead, Schwartz describes Serra as a much more complex man of contradictions and mixed motives.

Still, although he does not hesitate to debunk various myths about California and Californians, he continues to accept the central myth that California is somehow qualitatively different than all other states and perhaps all other societies. He embraces the self-indulgent idea, shared by many other native Californians, that there is something mystical or unnaturally powerful about the state. As Schwartz writes, "It may simply be that there have always been some people who find contact with California deranging, as they still do."

In the end, Schwartz concludes that, by the 1960's, "California [had] swept the world with its radical culture." What was the meaning and purpose of this radicalism? What did it amount to? Schwartz is unmercifully critical: "Revolutionary parties that organized nobody, riot and rebellion for the benefit of television news, and liberation armies that fought no wars, [California's radical culture] had produced no new idea, no new movement; rather it evinced an innovation that was radical, but on a wholly different level: the transformation of *social revolt* into *aesthetic style*." By the 1960's, in other words, California's radicalism had blossomed (if one can use that word) into a mass phenomenon: a watered-down, superficial, anti-intellectual fashion in the thrall of mass media and, to a large extent, the "Establishment." Radicalism not only withered as an intellectual force but also turned against its original ideals. As Schwartz writes, "radical protest was eventually transformed into 'political correctness,' or Stalinism *redux*."

Such critiques of the radical Left were commonly made by academics on the conservative Right in the 1990's. However, coming from a wild-bearded journalist from the *San Francisco Chronicle*—a student of radicalism and a thoughtful liberal himself—these conclusions cut especially deep. Schwartz's prognosis for California's radicalism emerges in part from his observation that the great reforming tool of the ballot initiative, the legacy of Governor Hiram Johnson, was being successfully used in the 1990's to reverse "establishment radicalism" such as affirmative action.

These are compelling conclusions and critiques, but what of the task explained in the prologue? Although Schwartz chronicles critical and overlooked aspects of California's cultural and political development with wit and skill, he never convincingly demonstrates his thesis that California's radicalism has indelibly altered the American psyche, that California "[took] over the world." He includes as many examples of California being affected by outside events—the French Revolution, World War II, and the Red Scare, for example—as examples of California's influence beyond its borders. Further, although he plausibly notes the linkage in the 1960's between California's fads—many abetted by Hollywood—and the emergence of a worldwide mass culture, it is not clear that California is the primary source of that mass culture. Still, these are hardly serious failures. At the very least, Schwartz has written a thought-provoking, engaging analysis of the sociopolitical evolution of one of the world's most diverse and powerful societies.

Steve D. Boilard

Sources for Further Study

Booklist. XCIV, March 1, 1998, p. 1090.
Choice. XXXV, July, 1998, p. 1916.
Kirkus Reviews. LXVI, February 1, 1998, p. 182.
Los Angeles Times Book Review. March 15, 1998, p. 9.
National Review. L, April 20, 1998, p. 50.

The New York Times Book Review. CIII, March 15, 1998, p. 41.
Publishers Weekly. CCXLV, February 2, 1998, p. 75.
Reason. XXX, December, 1998, p. 58.
The Wall Street Journal. March 3, 1998, p. A16.

GAIN

Author: Richard Powers (1957-   )
Published: Farrar, Straus & Giroux (New York). 355 pp. $25.00
Type of work: Novel
Time: The early 1800's to the 1990's
Locale: Massachusetts, Ohio, and central Illinois

This multiplot novel traces the 170-year history of the Clare Company and presents the plight of Laura Bodey, who contracts cancer from exposure to the company's contaminants

> *Principal characters:*
> JEPHTHAH CLARE, immigrant from England and patriarch of the Clare family
> SARAH CLARE, Jephthah's wife
> SAMUEL, RESOLVE, and BENJAMIN CLARE, Jephthah and Sarah Clare's sons
> ROBERT EMMET ENNIS, Irish immigrant and chandler
> ANTHONY HEWITT, equipment designer for Clare
> PETER, DOUGLAS, and WILLIAM CLARE, third-generation Clares
> HIRAM NAGEL, Clare's advertising manager
> LAURA BODEY, a real-estate broker in her forties
> TIM AND ELLEN BODEY, Laura's son and daughter
> DON BODEY, Laura's ex-husband, and Tim and Ellen's father

Richard Powers's multiplot novel *Gain* is another volume in which the author seeks to understand and trace some major currents that have shaped postmodern American society. In his five previous novels, Powers has focused on the automobile industry, the brokerage business, the computer revolution, immigration problems, genetics, medicine, and a host of crosscurrents that have formed the character of contemporary America. In each of these novels—*Three Farmers on Their Way to a Dance* (1985), *Prisoner's Dilemma* (1989), *The Gold Bug Variations* (1992), *Operation Wandering Soul* (1994), and *Galatea 2.2* (1996)—Powers has posed searching questions about the modern world, always focusing upon one or more salient aspects of modernism, interspersing the chapters that deal with the roots of postmodernism with other chapters or sections that present individualized portraits of characters involved in creating revolutionary technologies or upon whom such technologies have significant effects.

Powers uses a similar format in *Gain.* A major story line presents, in considerable detail, the development of the Clare Soap and Chemical Company from a small soap and candle manufacturing operation begun in 1831 to a huge industrial conglomerate that, by 1900, has spread from its original site in Massachusetts to Ohio and subsequently as far west as central Illinois, in which much of the novel is set. The family-run business is eventually incorporated and then goes public, expanding its base and product line meteorically as it becomes transnational.

The generations of the Clare family, depicted in a genealogical chart, are matched by the expansive growth of the Clare Soap and Chemical Company, whose organizational chart resembles a branching genealogical tree. Each member of the Clare family, three generations of which have been intimately involved in the company, contributes to new blocks on the corporation's organizational tree.

Running parallel to the story of Clare's development and expansion is the more personal story of Laura Bodey, a middle-aged real estate broker in Lacewood, Illinois. The town was rescued from its agricultural prairie existence when Clare, ardently pursued by visionaries in Lacewood who realized that the town needed an industry in order to prosper, said "yes" to Lacewood's proposal that the company establish a large industrial and manufacturing complex there. For decades the marriage between the town and the company was propitious for both parties. Clare brought employment and prosperity to a region that much needed the economic base Clare provided. Clare was a model of civic responsibility, treating its employees decently, helping to support the cultural life of the community, sponsoring the annual corn boil, contributing to the local college, and generally observing the protocols of good citizenship.

Clare was founded by the family of Jephthah and Sarah Clare, ethical New Englanders to whom success came accidentally. Robert Emmet Ennis, an Irish immigrant who had recently lost his wife, came to the door of the Clare's fledgling import business peddling tallow candles he had made. Samuel Clare bought a few candles from him and thought little more of the transaction until he began to burn the candles and found that they were of such high quality that they burned longer and offered more illumination than any candles the family had previously used.

The Clares now needed to find Ennis with the hope of getting him to make candles for their company. Their search seemed futile until the day when Resolve Clare saw the chandler near the Boston fish market. Resolve employed him to work in the small import business and soap factory that the family had recently launched. It was efficient to make soap and candles in the same factory using by-products from one to manufacture the other.

Soon the Clares had hired a fifty-year-old self-styled engineer, Anthony Hewitt, on the brink of retiring, to develop the equipment they needed to mass-produce soap and candles with the utmost frugality, wasting none of the runoff from one product if it could be reprocessed for use in making another. Hewitt's equipment also permitted heightened production through the economy of scale that such an increase permitted. Clare lowered the price of its products and made them competitive with those imported from England. Before long, Clare was not only selling its soap to a ready market in the United States but was also exporting fine soap to England rather than importing British soap to the United States for the American market. Yankee ingenuity, ironically based on the efforts of immigrants, enabled Clare to grow exponentially.

The company's most enduring and profitable product, Native Balm, came about accidentally. Benjamin Clare, the youngest of Jephthah's sons, also became the only son to be a college graduate. Upon his graduation from Harvard, Ben spurned the business and set out on a research expedition to Antarctica and the South Seas, during which he purchased a native herbal substance from which he eventually created Native Balm. Floating soap also came about accidentally when too much air was put into a

Clare kettle in which soap was being made. (The pragmatic Harvard philosopher C. S. Peirce espoused a philosophy called "tychism," which posits that much of what happens in life is the result of chance. The Clare Company, as Powers presents it, illustrates quite fully the likelihood that such a philosophy has validity.)

Clare Soap and Chemical survives because it grows and changes: "The days of people working for other people were over. The company was no longer a band joined together for a common purpose. The company was a structure whose purpose was to make more of the same." Those who directed the company, including Douglas, a third-generation Clare, realized this as early as 1900 and shaped the company accordingly.

Interspersed with the story of the Clare Soap and Chemical Company is the personal story of Laura Bodey. Powers first introduces her at the funeral of one of her daughter Ellen's teenage friends, who has succumbed to a mysterious wasting disease. Before long, Laura is found to have an ovarian cyst that, upon removal, is revealed to be malignant. The rest of the Laura story relates her unsuccessful struggle against ovarian cancer, but it also depicts many of the struggles that women must face to survive in the workplace, particularly when they must balance work against family responsibilities. In Laura's case, the situation is intensified because she has divorced her husband, Don Bodey. Powers's understanding of the dynamics of Laura's relationship with her ex-husband, especially in light of her health problems, is penetrating and sensitive.

Don, a decent man, is still devoted to Laura and their children. Realizing that the source of Laura's hopeless illness may well be contaminants from Clare Soap and Chemicals, he presses Laura, who is in no way litigious, to join in a class-action suit against the company to protect the futures of their two children. Before she dies, she receives an out-of-court settlement, which helps to assure the children's futures. Ellen, however, will not touch her windfall. Tim, Laura's son, touches little of his until it has compounded into a huge sum. Then he uses it, ironically, to launch a business that one day may grow into a transnational corporate enterprise not unlike Clare.

Powers demonstrates a prodigious grasp of history in relating his story and in associating it with the various social and political currents of the 170 years during which it takes place. He also has a remarkably good grasp of both the philosophy and psychology of modern merchandizing and of corporate management. He understands, in detail, the complex history of the labor movement in the United States, which he uses effectively as a backdrop to Clare's corporate development. The details of manufacturing processes presented in the novel are also extensive and accurate. Equally accurate are Powers's references to the business side of Clare Soap and Chemical. The power struggle that leads to the replacement of Douglas Clare with Hiram Nagel as head of the enterprise is presented convincingly, as is the change in business philosophy that overtakes a corporation as it grows. With expansion, corporations build and fill more executive suites. As companies expand, their main goal often veers away from improving existing products and developing new ones toward spawning more corporate bureaucracies.

Powers's descriptive abilities are remarkable. Observing a garden in springtime, for example, he writes, "Tight, hard globes of Christmas ornament relax into peonies. Daisies already droop their tutus like sad, also-ran, Degas dancers. Bleeding hearts hang in group contrition." The similes and metaphors he uses here are uniquely visual and highly successful. Powers also revels in writing about fairs and expositions, as he did in *Prisoner's Dilemma*, in which detailed references to the New York World's Fair of the late 1930's are a central part of the novel. In *Gain*, he writes kaleidoscopically of the Chicago Exposition of 1893, using Whitmanesque catalogues to capture the sense of what the exposition was about:

> A model of St. Peter's, a monster peristyle, an "Electric Scenic Theater," an ice railway, the halls of Electricity, Machinery, Agriculture, and Transportation, paint shops and log cabins, stables for private motor vehicles, a loggers' camp, grain silos, sawmills, windmills, stills, mines, Izaak Walton's house, the transplanted ruins of Yucatán—all came together in an ordered and stately frenzy, celebrating every ability known to collective man and predicting those countless skills yet to be learned.

If such a catalogue suggests Walt Whitman, readers will find suggestions of other authors sequestered arcanely in many of *Gain*'s sentences—a shadow of Robert Emmet Sherwood, a hint of W. H. Auden, a slant suggestion of Emily Dickinson. Although *Gain* contains fewer of the puns for which Powers is well known, they are replaced by sly references to various literary luminaries.

Gain achieves much of its substantial impact by appearing, at times, to be a novel that suggests Nietzschean recurrence. When Laura dies, Don sells his house and returns with the children to Laura's house, with all its memories and Laura's legacy of adhesive notes to help the family perform its mundane household chores of cooking and doing laundry. Tim ultimately uses his part of Clare's settlement with his mother to create a fledgling enterprise that may conceivably grow into another Clare Soap and Chemical Company, although its chief product will probably be computerized information about folding proteins and other molecules rather than soap and candles. Ellen leaves home to study nursing but returns to Lacewood, where she presumably will live out her days with Sporty Tom, her doting husband. Clare, meanwhile, closes and eventually sells off its parts, including the Lacewood plant, returning Lacewood to the slow agricultural community it once was. Perhaps Powers is saying, "You *can* go home—or at least back—again." He may even be suggesting that one has no choice.

R. Baird Shuman

Sources for Further Study

Business Week. July 27, 1998, p. 12.
Library Journal. CXXIII, May 1, 1998, p. 140.
Los Angeles Times Book Review. June 21, 1998, p. 2.
The Nation. CCLXVII, July 27, 1998, p. 33.

The New Leader. LXXIV, June 29, 1998, p. 26.
The New York Review of Books. XLV, December 17, 1998, p. 38.
The New York Times Book Review. CIII, June 21, 1998, p. 11.
The New Yorker. LXXIV, July 27, 1998, p. 76.
Publishers Weekly. CCXLV, April 13, 1998, p. 50.
The Wall Street Journal. July 1, 1998, p. A16.

GENUINE REALITY
A Life of William James

Author: Linda Simon (1946-   )
Published: Harcourt, Brace (New York). 467 pp. $35.00
Type of work: Biography
Time: 1800-1910
Locale: New York, Massachusetts, England, and Western Europe

Simon chronicles the life and accomplishments of America's first great philosopher, the proponent of Pragmatism and one of the founding fathers of the academic study of psychology in the United States

Principal personages:
WILLIAM JAMES, an American writer and teacher who influenced the
    study of philosophy and psychology in the United States
HENRY JAMES, SR., William's father, an iconoclastic moral philosopher
MARY WALSH JAMES, William's mother
HENRY JAMES, JR., an American novelist, William's brother
ALICE GIBBENS JAMES, William's wife

The popularity of the James family as subjects for biography has held steady throughout the twentieth century. A number of factors account for this phenomenon. First, it is one of the few nuclear families to produce two giants of American letters, William James in philosophy and psychology and Henry James, Jr., in fiction. Second, its members wrote to one another frequently and at length not only about their everyday affairs but also about their feelings regarding family conflicts. Hence, the plethora of source materials, coupled with the stature of the two brothers, has led a number of distinguished scholars to explore the lives of these enigmatic figures whose love-hate relationships lie at the base of some of the most important literary works produced in America in the decades on either side of the turn of the twentieth century.

William James, eldest son of Henry James, Sr., and Mary Walsh James, comes alive for readers in Linda Simon's *Genuine Reality*. An accomplished biographer whose life study of twentieth century literary figure Alice B. Toklas received highly favorable reviews, Simon focuses her attention on the man behind the public persona. Known for nearly a century as the chief proponent of the philosophy of Pragmatism in America and one of the founding fathers of the study of psychology, James emerges from the pages of Simon's book as a neurotic, confused, but caring son, sibling, husband, father, and colleague. As Simon carefully demonstrates, his cheerful public presence and his captivating lecture style masked a personality torn by doubts about the reality of life beyond death and concerns about his ability to achieve the high standards set for him by a father who, for nearly four decades, dominated every aspect of his life.

Consequently, Simon devotes more than a quarter of the book to an examination of the career of Henry James, Sr., a self-made intellectual whose pursuit of religious truths drove him to a mental breakdown and whose mania for finding a place where he would be appreciated drove the family hither and yon in New York, New England, and across England and the European continent. The elder James was a domineering presence in the lives of all of his children; psychologists and biographers of the James family have had a field day exploring the impact that the father had on everyone living under his roof. William's desperate pleas for acceptance and acclaim are chronicled in letters to his family members; those of Henry, a more fluent and accomplished writer, appear not only in private missives but also in a number of books that give insight into the strange lifestyle Henry, Sr., forced upon his precocious and sensitive children and his long-suffering wife. These documents, and scores of others in collections at New England's major research universities, provide Simon valuable insight into the growth of William's mind and character as he struggled to define for himself who he was and what he was to accomplish in his life.

In Simon's view, William suffered more than any of the other children because he was the eldest, and his father was most anxious that he make something of himself. Henry, Sr., never realized that it might be necessary to establish roots for the family in order for William, or any of the others, to grow and blossom into an intellectual giant. Disdaining traditional forms of schooling (although he had attended Union College in New York), Henry, Sr., moved his sons and daughter from school to school, hired a string of private tutors, and insisted all along that the children would be great thinkers and sound moral citizens only if they learned directly from him. Simon's unflattering portrait of Henry, Sr., is not drawn in order to elicit malice toward this misguided and distraught intellectual; rather, it is intended to explain why William turned to the studies that would occupy his adult life, moral philosophy and psychology.

As Simon demonstrates, young William James was nothing like the self-confident and popular teacher who was the darling of Harvard undergraduates during the first decade of the twentieth century. More badgered than his siblings, William struggled to make his father proud of him. He tried to become an artist when he heard his father glorify that life, only to find that what his father praised in theory he despised in practice. He went into medicine for similar reasons, but he discovered that he did not have the aptitude to take up a practice. The stress to please his demanding and somewhat unbalanced parent drove him to fits of fatigue, nervous anxiety, and physical distress. Like his father before him, he flitted from city to city in America and on the Continent, looking for an appropriate profession and a sense of inner peace. Not until he was offered the chance to teach a seminar at Harvard in 1872 did he find an environment conducive to his talents. Starting with a temporary appointment to deliver lectures in one class, James moved steadily upward in the Harvard faculty hierarchy, retiring more than four decades later as a figure internationally known for his lectures and publications.

As both a philosopher and psychologist, William James was essentially a self-taught scholar, never attending school regularly; his only sustained formal education was in medicine. This lack of systematic training may well have been an advantage, since it did not cause him to specialize in one or another academic discipline, a trend just starting to take hold at the end of the nineteenth century in America. Consequently,

James had colleagues in medicine, psychology, and philosophy, all of whom were exploring the functioning of the human mind from differing perspectives. He was fortunate, too, to have a brother who was writing novels that explored the subtleties of human thought and conduct; although William constantly encouraged Henry to write more simply, no doubt he distilled from works such as *The Ambassadors* (1903), *The American* (1877), *The Wings of the Dove* (1902), and *The Golden Bowl* (1904) something of human character in a social setting that helped him to form his own ideas about the psyche.

Because he was interested in defining the boundaries of disciplines that were still in flux, James found himself keeping up with the latest theories and discoveries in medicine, philosophy, and psychology. Although he recognized the value of experimentation as a basis for psychological research, James was never comfortable with the notion that psychology should be pushed too far away from its mother discipline, philosophy. Simon devotes considerable attention to her subject's ongoing debates about the nature of reality and the function of the human mind with men such as Charles Peirce, Henry Bowditch, Hugo Münsterberg, and Josiah Royce. She notes his discomfort with the theories of the Vienna School, particularly those of Sigmund Freud; reflecting his Victorian upbringing, perhaps, James thought Freud placed too much emphasis on the role sexual fantasy played in shaping human character. Simon chronicles James's lifelong fascination with psychic phenomenon, including his dogged belief that at least some of the mediums he supported and observed could really communicate with the dead. In this pursuit he was certainly not alone; the list of members of the American Society for Psychical Research contains a number of famous doctors, professors, and scientists who, like James, desperately wanted to establish the certainty that the soul lived on after the body died.

Simon portrays James as a careful writer who developed his lectures and books with great caution, always looking to anticipate objections to his theories and always sensitive to the reception his works received from professional colleagues and the public at large. While she gives appropriate space to summaries of James's works, she is more concerned about his associations with family, friends, and professional acquaintances. The pages of *Genuine Reality* are filled with anecdotes about James's relationships with family members, including conspiratorial efforts with Henry, to whom he was closest, in the management of family affairs; attempts to assist Alice, who suffered from depression throughout her adult life; and schemes to prop up the continually sagging fortunes of younger brothers Robertson and Garth, who never managed to rise to the level of acclaim reached by both of their elder siblings. She represents Alice Gibbens, whom James married in 1878, as a strong, sensitive, and self-confident woman who was able to give her husband the love he required and the physical space he needed to accomplish his role as a teacher and public person. Simon does not shy away from what might be perceived as two unusual relationships James had with women other than his wife. Boston socialite Sarah Wyman Whitman, James's contemporary in age, was the center of a circle of intellectuals that included William James on numerous occasions. Although Simon offers no suggestion that there was more than conversation taking place at the frequent meetings between these two, she does note James's strong emotional attachment to this *femme savant*, with whom he shared an intimate correspondence until her death in 1904. Similarly, Simon offers without much speculation an account of James's continuing liaison with Pauline Goldmark, a woman thirty years younger than he who was a regular correspondent and with whom James was in close contact on numerous occasions during the last fifteen years of his life. If nothing else, these encounters show that the stuffy philosopher had a human side and that he responded to human urges and emotions in a decidedly normal way.

The chief value of Simon's study lies in her ability to bring out the private side of a man whose reputation has all but obscured his personal struggles. The William James whom readers encounter in volumes such as *The Principles of Psychology* (1890), *The Will to Believe and Other Essays* (1897), *The Varieties of Religious Experience* (1902), and *Pragmatism* (1907) emerges as the confident teacher offering practical suggestions for confronting problems of human experience. Simon's biography shows readers the price James had to pay to achieve that level of confidence in print. She displays an ability to sift through the extensive correspondence left behind by the James family and a genuine sympathy for her subject as he struggled to achieve certainty about his self-worth and assurance of life after death. Never too judgmental, she is nevertheless willing to acknowledge James's personal shortcomings and take him to task for treating his family as inconsiderately as his father had done to the five siblings who grew up under the immense shadow of Henry James, Sr. If she leaves readers feeling deprived of detailed analyses of James's works, she makes up for this shortcoming by illuminating the complexities of the man behind the writing.

Laurence W. Mazzeno

Sources for Further Study

The Atlantic. CCLXXXI, March, 1998, p. 116.
Booklist. XCIV, February 1, 1998, p. 878.
Library Journal. CXXIII, January, 1998, p. 110.
The New York Review of Books. XLV, December 17, 1998, p. 81.
The New York Times Book Review. CIII, March 15, 1998, p. 11.
Publishers Weekly. CCXLIV, December 8, 1997, p. 61.
The Wall Street Journal. February 6, 1998, p. A20.
The Washington Post Book World. XXVIII, February 2, 1998, p. 1.
The Wilson Quarterly. XXII, Summer, 1998, p. 109.

THE GIFTS OF THE JEWS
How a Tribe of Desert Nomads Changed the Way
Everyone Thinks and Feels

Author: Thomas Cahill (1940-   )
Published: Doubleday (New York). 291 pp. $23.50
Type of work: History and philosophy
Time: 3200-450 B.C.
Locale: Israel and the Middle East

*A selective reading of the Hebrew scriptures in an effort to determine the nature of the Jews'
contributions to western thought*

This volume is the second in what Thomas Cahill intends to be a seven-volume
series that will consider what he calls the "hinges of history"—critical moments at
which civilization has received special gifts from whatever culture is under consideration. In the introduction, Cahill is careful to distinguish this sort of history from the
series of military, political, or economic events that constitute history in the minds of
many readers. The first volume in the series, *How the Irish Saved Civilization* (1995),
considered the role of Irish monasticism of the early Middle Ages in preserving crucial
texts (and the ideas they contained) in the face of the disintegration of civilization after
the fall of Rome. *The Gifts of the Jews* considers the Jews' special contributions of
monotheism and their increasingly sophisticated perceptions of God that are recorded
in the Hebrew scriptures.

Cahill's background fits him for his task in several ways. His undergraduate degree
from Fordham University was in classics and philosophy; his M.F.A. from Columbia
University was in film and dramatic literature; and he has done additional study at
Fordham, Union Theological Seminary, and the Jewish Theological Seminary. For six
years, he directed religious publishing at Doubleday (he was responsible for publishing the six-volume *Anchor Bible Dictionary*, a basic tool of Bible scholarship).
Moreover (suggesting his sense of marketing as one source of his popular success),
he and his wife spent a decade as Cahill & Company producing the *Reader's
Catalogue*, a book catalog characterized by the literate but unstuffy tastes of its
creators. Perhaps the range of his studies and interests suggests why he might wish to
produce a history in which scholarship is clothed in a breezy, conversational style
intended to engage readers who are thoughtful and interested but not necessarily
academic.

Most of Cahill's history consists of retelling some of the central narratives of the
Hebrew scriptures in order to focus on the Jews' growing understanding of their God;
yet because, he says, most people find the Bible "a confusing hodgepodge" and few
people ever read all of it, he begins his history before the Bible's writers ever were
called to their tasks, in ancient Sumer, where writing first developed. Cahill describes
the glamour of Sumerian cities as they must have appeared to the wandering Semitic
nomads, and he follows that description with a list of the barbaric qualities that the

Sumerians saw in their nomadic neighbors—people who ate raw meat, had no houses, knew no religion, and died unburied. Cahill notes that the tone of this list reflects "the prejudice of imperialists throughout history," but he goes on to look at the Sumerians' worldview as it is reflected in their mythology, giving particular attention to the implications of the epic of *Gilgamesh*, the best-known literary relic of this ancient world. In *Gilgamesh* Cahill sees a world where human beings exist purely to serve the gods, the source of all real power and innovation. Cahill notes that some elements of *Gilgamesh*, particularly the flood theme, will surface again in the Hebrew Bible (Cahill is no biblical literalist), but he is especially interested in the differences that he finds between the world of this epic, a world in which human individuality counts for little, in which fertility is the cardinal virtue, in which "human life, seen as a pale reen- actment of the life of the eternal heavens, [is] ruled by a fate beyond the pitifully limited powers of human beings."

This is the world in which Semitic Avraham (Abraham, in the usual translation) and his family lived as longtime residents, the land from which old Avram was called to go forth by a god whose interests in human welfare seemed quite different from the attitudes of the Sumerian gods. Cahill sees Avraham's departure with his wife and household (but without children; his wife Sara was barren) as a bold step into a future that will be governed by an understanding of God that has nothing to do with the tyrannical fatalism represented by the Sumerian deities. Cahill's retelling of Avram's calling and Sara's geriatric pregnancy focuses on this boldness and, as in the story of the sacrifice of Yitzhak (Isaac, as the name is usually anglicized), it also dramatizes their willingness to put their trust in this god who seems so different from the Sumerians' Ishtar.

Throughout the book, Cahill's user-friendly notes identify his sources, suggest additional readings, and defend his editorial decisions, such as his unfamiliar but more accurate spellings of familiar names or, contradictorily, his decision to use the term B.C. (before Christ) rather than B.C.E. (before the common era) on the grounds that it is more familiar to most readers (a claim that non-Christian readers may well dispute). Cahill's text draws from a selection of translations ranging from Everett Fox's *The Five Books of Moses* (1995) to the New Jerusalem Bible, even to including a few passages from the King James version. Accompanying the notes is an appendix listing the books of the Hebrew scriptures along with their names in transliterated Hebrew and a brief summary of their content. Another appendix offers a chronology of the main events and periods of the scriptures.

Cahill's narrative goes on to include the stories of Sodom and Gomorrah, of Joseph in Egypt, of the calling of Moses, of the exodus from Egypt and the wandering in the wilderness, of the development of the monarchy under Saul, of Saul, David, and Jonathan, and a rather compressed retelling of the prophets leading to the Babylonian exile. A final narrative chapter summarizes the Book of Ruth.

Cahill sees each of these steps in Israel's history as an important contribution to Western thought. In the story of Moses' confrontation with Pharaoh over the fate of the Israelites in Egypt, for instance, Cahill identifies several significant themes. One concerns the identity of YHWH, the god whose name is too holy to be said aloud (early translators' misunderstandings of the workings of ancient Hebrew reproduced this name as "Jehovah"); again and again, Pharaoh questions the identity of the god who demands freedom for his people. In response, YHWH makes clear that he understands Pharaoh completely, an understanding that is implicit in the powers of the creator of the universe. Pharaoh imagines that he controls things that are far beyond his rule: "The comedy of the narrative lies in ironic juxtaposition: Pharaoh, supposedly all-powerful, understands nothing. It would not be too much to say that this narrative asserts that power . . . makes you stupid, blinding you to your true situation. . . ." Cahill argues that the lessons implied by this confrontation "were radical in their time, since there was no political edifice that did not claim to be founded by a god." Pharaoh's defeat in the face of God's power undermines all political claims of divinely ordained human institutions. The god of creation will have his own way.

Perhaps the most significant of these insights is the understanding of God that Cahill sees emerging from the Jews' captivity in Babylon. The old ideas of God as a receiver of sacrifices and a ruler whose permanent throne was Jerusalem—that is, of God as like the local gods of the area, except for his supreme power—those ideas have crumbled under the scornful attacks of prophets such as Jeremiah, whose message is that "God's people will no longer be the proud nobles of Israel and Judah but the marginalized and powerless—the blind, the lame, and the pregnant. . . ." Moreover, the prophets asserted, God is interested not in tribute and ritual but in justice for the oppressed. This concept led to another level of understanding: What God wants is the human heart. Cahill identifies this idea as God's means of making the Jews into a sort of spiritual nation, one that existed beyond the ark and the tablets of the commandments and the temple in Jerusalem, beyond the map of Israel, because it existed in the hearts of its people.

All the insights of these narratives are offered in Cahill's breezy style, which ranges from informal to downright flippant, at some points interweaving contemporary references with scriptural events: "Fade-in: Sodom's main square, where Lot, encountering the angels, invites them to stay at his house. . . . But the men of the city surround the house like the ghouls in *Night of the Living Dead*. . . ." The many sexual escapades of the Scriptures' characters offer Cahill special opportunities for exercising his gifts for this sort of humor in a way that a few readers may find offensive. When he discusses the heart of the Scriptures' themes, however, Cahill is dead serious and very respectful.

These are, after all, the "hinges of history," the moments in which Western thought turned in new and important directions. In the case of the Jews, the direction was away from the limited understanding that their ancient neighbors held of their gods into a concept of spirituality that feels fresh today, away from stone altars to an awareness of the still, small voice that Elijah heard, away from generalities and the status quo to a reverence for risk, adventure, individuality, and surprise. For these "gifts of the Jews," Cahill feels nothing but reverent gratitude.

Cahill's book appears at the end of a decade that has seen a number of well-received books about religion. Cahill himself notes Jack Miles's popular work *God: A Biogra-*

phy (1995) as demonstrating the underlying thematic unity of the Hebrew scriptures, a theme that also interests Cahill. The conclusions Cahill draws, however, seem more predictable, less surprising, than those of some other religious popularizers. Although he makes some effort to address the completely secular reader (noting that some of his readers will doubt the existence of God, not to mention the accuracy of the ancient stories of a book such as Genesis), and although he makes plentiful reference to the scholarship both of the Bible and of the mythologies of others, finally Cahill proposes that the gifts of the Jews are those same gifts that are commonly described in Religion 101—a growing understanding of monotheism and of a personal god whose desire is for justice rather than ceremony. To say this is not to disparage *The Gifts of the Jews*; Cahill's obvious delight in his subject and his highly readable style make the book extremely accessible without making it merely trivial. Readers who enjoyed his best-selling *How the Irish Saved Civilization* will find much to enjoy in this work as well. Cahill is not writing for biblical literalists, nor is he writing New Age theology; his rather orthodox promise is to remind us that much of our worldview originated in Judaism. He keeps that promise with humor and grace.

Ann D. Garbett

Sources for Further Study

America. CLXXIX, September 26, 1998, p. 22.
Booklist. XCIV, March 15, 1998, p. 1197.
Commentary. CVI, November, 1998, p. 63.
Commonweal. CXXIII, May 8, 1998, p. 22.
Crisis. XVI, September, 1998, p. 46.
Los Angeles Times. June 23, 1998, p. E2.
Maclean's. CXI, June 1, 1998, p. A6.
National Catholic Reporter. XXXIV, May 8, 1998, p. 16.
The New York Times Book Review. CIII, May 24, 1998, p. 16.
Publishers Weekly. CCXLV, March 16, 1998, p. 39.

GIRL IN LANDSCAPE

Author: Jonathan Lethem (1964-   )
Published: Doubleday (New York). 280 pp. $22.95
Type of work: Novel
Time: The near future
Locale: Brooklyn, New York, and the fictional Planet of the Archbuilders

*A motherless thirteen-year-old girl discovers the complexity of adult life after she, her father,
and her brothers emigrate to a distant planet*

> *Principal characters:*
> PELLA MARSH, a thirteen-year-old girl
> CLEMENT MARSH, her father, a failed politician
> CAITLIN MARSH, her mother
> RAYMOND MARSH and
> DAVID MARSH, her brothers
> EFRAM NUGENT, the self-proclaimed leader of the settlers on the Planet
>   of the Archbuilders
> HUGH MERROW, an artist
> DIANA EASTLING, an anthropologist, Clement's lover
> HIDING KNELL and
> TRUTH RENOWNED, Archbuilders

Jonathan Lethem's fourth novel could easily be mistaken for a feminist tract, for a parable about racism, for a satirical view of childhood and family relations, or for a genre spoof. Unsympathetic readers might see it as a mishmash of conflicting influences. Yet *Girl in Landscape* is much more than any of this. It is a highly original treatment of several traditional themes in American literature and popular culture. Though it recalls several other works, it is finally a distinctive achievement on its own that unifies all of its themes with a brilliant, disturbing conclusion.

The Marsh family leaves Earth after some ecological disaster that Lethem leaves suggestively vague, but their main motive is the disgraced father, Clement, a New York politician who has failed in his efforts to create a more livable city. Caitlin Marsh is enthusiastic about the new adventure, reading to Pella, thirteen, Raymond, ten, and David, seven, about the Planet of the Archbuilders. Her positive approach to their trip continues even after she collapses and is hospitalized, but she soon dies of brain cancer.

Lethem has acknowledged the influence of writers such as Carson McCullers and Flannery O'Connor in his portrayal of Pella as a tomboy outsider. Not only is she taken away at an impressionable age from everything familiar to her, but she also loses the one person she truly loves and trusts, the one most likely to help her understand the enormous changes her life is undergoing. Pella constantly resents that Caitlin is the parent who had to die, seeing Clement as a compulsive do-gooder who cares more about strangers than about his family.

Pella's alienation is increased by the desolate landscape of the Planet of the Archbuilders, a place much like a desert in the western United States. Then there are the potatoes that taste like different types of food, even fish; the household deer, the rat-sized creatures that are always present both outside and indoors and are constantly staring at the humans; and the Archbuilders themselves, furry human-sized creatures with tendrils who love the English language and use it more sophisticatedly than the settlers. In creating the Planet of the Archbuilders, Lethem is careful to keep a balance between the unusual and those qualities that recall life on Earth. His model, as he has noted in interviews, is Ray Bradbury's *The Martian Chronicles* (1950).

Pella discovers more than she expects on the Planet of the Archbuilders. Clement decides that his family will not take the pills the others use to protect them against the unspecified effects of an Archbuilder virus. Pella is the first of the Marshes to be affected, and her mind enters the body of a household deer, allowing her to travel about quickly and to spy on her neighbors without their knowledge. In this way, she learns about Diana Eastling, an anthropologist whom she hopes might become a replacement for Caitlin; Hugh Merrow, an artist who paints portraits of the Archbuilders; and Efram Nugent, the first settler, who has been there for seven years and sees himself as the moral force on the planet. Pella, experiencing a sexual awakening, finds herself strangely drawn to the severe, masculine Efram, who hints at a reciprocal interest in her.

Pella becomes friends with the Archbuilders, especially with a particularly talkative and philosophical one who calls himself Hiding Knell. (Other Archbuilder names, growing out of their love of English, include Truth Renowned, Lonely Dumptruck, Gelatinous Stand, Unimportant Lust, Grinning Contrivance, and Specious Axiomatic.) She considers the natives harmless eccentrics, but Efram, the only settler to speak the Archbuilders' original language, claims otherwise because the superior Archbuilders have abandoned their planet to explore other worlds, leaving only the dregs behind.

Diana disappoints Pella by having an affair with Clement only to become disenchanted with him and leave. Efram, who overshadows Clement's weak efforts at leadership, chases Merrow away with charges of having sex with Truth Renowned and then accuses Hiding Knell of molesting the children. Without understanding that Efram may be motivated by guilt over his feelings for her, Pella enlists the other children to strike back at him.

Girl in Landscape is a coming-of-age novel with feminist overtones, but it is much more. While all of Lethem's novels have science-fiction elements, he, much like Bradbury, uses the genre to examine the everyday American life of the past. His first novel, *Gun, with Occasional Music* (1994), explores not only science-fiction conventions but those of hard-boiled private-detective fiction as well. With its frontier setting, *Girl in Landscape* is a space-age Western.

With his arrogance, muddy motivations, and insistence that he understands the Archbuilders better than anyone, that they cannot be trusted, Efram Nugent recalls Ethan Edwards, the tormented hero played by John Wayne in John Ford's classic Western *The Searchers* (1956), from a screenplay by Frank S. Nugent. (Efram is introduced standing at a distance with one arm crossing his middle and the other at his side, a posture Wayne assumes during key moments in *The Searchers*.) With his insistence that his moral code is superior to that of anyone else, even if it means killing his niece because she has been soiled by living with Comanches, Edwards isolates himself from everyone around him. In Lethem's version, Pella ends up the most isolated because she knows more, partly from her spying, about the settlement's complicated morality than anyone else. In this context, wisdom only increases her alienation.

In each of his novels, Lethem makes direct and indirect allusions to popular culture, not only because of its profound influence on American values, on how Americans conduct themselves in their daily lives, but also because of the essential playfulness of his approach to fiction. Hugh Merrow's name, for example, recalls actor Hugh Marlowe, who appears in the classic science-fiction film *The Day the Earth Stood Still* (1951) as well as the less-than-classic *Earth Versus the Flying Saucers* (1956). Pella, the observer, may be named for a prominent manufacturer of windows.

Efram is an ironic figure: a spokesman for moral authority intent upon instigating discord. Pella is drawn to him at their first meeting but also sees him as an antagonist: "Efram Nugent could seem too big, out here. She wanted him adjusted, made smaller." Far from a stereotypical villain, Efram is a complex character about whom Pella learns something surprising at almost every meeting. He even seems to be a frustrated artist; his house is a more elaborate, imaginative structure than those of the other settlers.

Clement is seen as ridiculous by Pella for contributing to chaotic conditions on Earth only to begin laying the groundwork to make the new planet more like Earth. Yet Efram is also guilty of an irrational need to impose his concept of civilization upon what he interprets as the disorder of the Planet of the Archbuilders: "I think we ought to draw a line around this town we're starting here, Marsh. Make it a *human* settlement, a place where kids are safe." His first step would be to run off the Archbuilders. The danger of people such as Efram, Lethem suggests, is that they do not want merely to impose order on chaos but also to impose their concept of order on all those around them.

As Pella grows in her understanding of her new environment, she also understands more about adult behavior. She suspects that Efram is not really interested in persecuting Hugh Merrow but somehow is making accusations "for her sake." Exactly why takes her longer to figure out: "With Efram, talk was all interruptions. He was like the Archbuilder landscape, a series of things broken off." She is confused when he says of the Archbuilders that "if they touch the children I'll kill them" while his leg is touching hers. He also makes threats against Clement. "This isn't the place for him to practice his politics," he says to Pella, asserting that his idea of order is superior to her father's. "He should go home. Maybe he'll leave you here, though. I wouldn't mind that." Efram is John Wayne as Humbert Humbert, the nymphet-obsessed hero of Vladimir Nabokov's *Lolita* (1955). Unlike Ethan Edwards and Humbert, however, Efram is unaware of any defects in his character and is all the more dangerous.

Pella is an equally complex character. Forced by the death of her mother and the move to a new planet to be stronger than a thirteen-year-old normally has to be, she does not always comprehend why she acts as she does, often feeling she is guided by a stubbornness inherited from Caitlin. She realizes that she must discover the truth about things for herself and cannot trust anyone else's versions of the truth. This realization leads to a "burden . . . of lonely knowledge." One of Lethem's themes is how individuals can trust only their interpretations of events rather than interpretations imposed by those who want to control them. Pella wishes to escape this burden of knowledge and her growing awareness of herself as a woman by becoming "lost in childishness, in her own ebbing childhood," but her moral responsibilities will not allow this escape. She thinks briefly that she can cope with life only by becoming like Efram, but she finally realizes that she must destroy him to survive.

Lethem takes one of his epigraphs from John Wayne himself: "Screw ambiguity. Perversion and corruption masquerade as ambiguity. I don't trust ambiguity." Lethem portrays those who—like Efram—want to see life in clear-cut, black-and-white terms to be dangerous but somehow essential. *Girl in Landscape* ends ambiguously, with Pella, who has grown to see complexity and conflict as inescapable, hoping to see Efram's spirit reborn. There must be a balance between the unimaginative conformity represented by Clement and the rugged individuality of Efram. Neither, finally, can prevail alone. In its imaginative examination of the archetypal war between the frontier and civilization, of the tension between trying to fit in society and asserting one's individuality—the duality at the center of the American character—*Girl in Landscape* is in the great American tradition established by novelists such as James Fenimore Cooper, Herman Melville, Mark Twain, and William Faulkner. It offers further evidence that Lethem, with his playful but insightful reinterpretations of American myths, is a distinctive voice in American fiction.

Michael Adams

Sources for Further Study

Atlanta Journal-Constitution. April 12, 1998, p. K10.
Booklist. XCIV, March 15, 1998, p. 1207.
Kirkus Reviews. LXVI, February 1, 1998, p. 139.
Library Journal. CXXIII, April 1, 1998, p. 123.
Los Angeles Times. April 8, 1998, p. E6.
The New York Times Book Review. CIII, May 24, 1998, p. 21.
The New Yorker. LXXIV, April 20, 1998, p. 22.
Publishers Weekly. CCXLV, March 30, 1998, p. 50.
Science Fiction Studies. XXV, July, 1998, p. 225.
USA Today. June 25, 1998, p. D6.

THE GREATEST BENEFIT TO MANKIND
A Medical History of Humanity

Author: Roy Porter (1946-   )
Published: W. W. Norton (New York). 831 pp. $35.00
Type of work: History
Time: Prehistory to the present

An exhaustive and compelling history of medicine

> *Principal personages:*
> HIPPOCRATES, an ancient Greek physician
> GALEN, a Roman physician of the second century
> ANDREAS VESALIUS, a sixteenth century anatomist
> WILLIAM HARVEY, a seventeenth century English physician
> LOUIS PASTEUR, a nineteenth century French researcher
> ROBERT KOCH, a nineteenth century German researcher

With *The Greatest Benefit to Mankind: A Medical History of Humanity*, Roy Porter has produced a monumental history of medicine, both as an institution and as an aspiration. It can be read as an encyclopedia of medical development through the ages. It is also an extended meditation on the purposes and limits of medicine. On both levels, it is a highly impressive work. Porter's history will likely live as a standard work for years to come.

Porter writes with authority. He holds a chair in the social history of science at the Wellcome Institute for the History of Science in Great Britain, and he is the editor of the Norton History of Science Series. He has published extensively on the history of medicine. Even so, the ambition of his undertaking is breathtaking. He had to master a voluminous and complicated literature, ranging over thousands of years of medical activity. Although his work is chiefly concerned with the evolution of medicine in the Western world, Porter does not ignore medical traditions in other parts of the world, and he pays attention to the medical practices of Africa, India, and China. Such a prodigious exercise in erudition could easily become an unreadable litany of doctors, diseases, and drugs, but Porter manages to keep his book fluid and engaging, leavening his facts with witty observations and fascinating anecdotes. Readers of this work will lay in a rich store of medical information, ranging from the ancient Egyptian recipe for curing baldness to the surgical techniques of heart-transplant pioneer Christiaan Barnard.

The organization of Porter's book is straightforward. He begins his narrative with the Near-Eastern precursors to Western civilization in Mesopotamia and along the Nile. He then moves to ancient Greece and Rome before settling comfortably in the familiar Western European heartland. Aside from forays to India and China, Porter moves forward chronologically through the great Western epochs, Middle Ages, Renaissance, and Enlightenment, before reaching the more modern times of the nineteenth century. There, because of the accelerating expansion of medical knowledge, Porter's treatment becomes more topical. His chapters reflect the growth of medical specialization, and he addresses such subjects as the new discipline of psychiatry and the institutionalization of medical research.

One reason that Porter's story is so absorbing is because medicine, and the questions that it raises, touches us all. Human beings have always wrestled with their nagging physical frailty. All human societies have possessed ideas about life and death, disease and health. Most have linked the individual's well-being to forces immanent in the wider world, attributing bodily distempers to such powers as divine will or malevolent spirits. In such societies, the way of health lay in one sustaining the proper relationship with the cosmos.

The Western medical perspective took a distinctive turn in antiquity, when Greek healers began to treat illness as simply a derangement of the body itself. The Greeks shifted medical explanation from the realm of the transcendental and began looking for purely natural causes of diseases and their cures. The Greeks thus laid the foundations of medicine as a science. In addition, Greek writers would shape the parameters of Western medical discourse for millennia. The library of medical works associated with the legendary Greek physician Hippocrates stressed the importance of maintaining the bodily equilibrium of the four humours, or "fluids" (blood, phlegm, choler, and black bile), the balance of which regulated a person's health. Disturbances in the humoral order led to illness; restoration of the natural state of the humours in a person was the task of medicine. The humoral vision of the human constitution would persist for almost two thousand years, into the eighteenth century. It encouraged physicians to emphasize the importance of what would today be called "lifestyle," urging their patients to monitor their diet, exercise, and cleanliness, striving always for the classical idea of moderation. Ancient medical men devoted themselves to preventing health problems in part because there was little that they could do to assist ailing patients. Such trusted remedies as bleeding probably did more harm than good. Physicians lacked accurate anatomical and physiological knowledge. The Greeks refused to dissect human beings, relying on animal studies and the practical insight gleaned from battlefield medicine. Only later, in Hellenistic Alexandria, and beyond that, during the period of the Roman Empire, did medical men begin to speculate openly about the working of the human body. The most notable example was the Roman physician Galen, who took great pride in his anatomical expertise. Yet even Galen confined himself to dissecting apes and other animals. The stigma attached to the cutting open of human subjects remained a powerful impediment to further learning.

Medicine in the Middle Ages continued on the path laid down in antiquity. The disruption of the barbarian invasions only increased the status of Hippocrates and Galen, as their texts became rare and more precious. Islamic writers played a key role in preserving ancient medical works as the West descended into chaos. The intellectual legatees of the Greeks and Romans, many Arab physicians became revered medical authorities in the West when their writings were translated during the high Middle Ages. In this period, medicine remained much more an art than a science. Physicians cultivated skill in diagnosing ailments and were judged on the accuracy of their prognoses. A close doctor-patient relationship was highly valued. Only if physicians knew their patients well could they provide useful advice, in sickness and in health. Unable to cure most of the diseases of their day, medieval physicians aspired to the humbler, but necessary, role of soothing the pains of the afflicted and helping their patients cope with the frightening and inevitable consequences of mortality.

A profound revolution in medical thinking started during the Renaissance. At the heart of this transformation was a renewed dedication to anatomical and physiological study. The celebration of the human body, so central to the painting and sculpture of the Renaissance, found its medical expression in a systematic investigation of the natural man. Dissection of human corpses became the foundation of a medical education. Pioneers such as Andreas Vesalius, who published an influential anatomical atlas that challenged many traditional beliefs about the body, and William Harvey, who explained the functions of the heart and blood in the circulatory system, helped make medicine a more rigorously scientific profession.

As the Renaissance gave way to the Enlightenment, the Age of Science, great advances were made in understanding the human body as an organism. Beautifully illustrated volumes from these centuries stand as eloquent testaments to the surgical skill and enthusiasm of early modern investigators, men enraptured by their own powers as they gradually unveiled the physical secrets of life. Yet the growth of medical knowledge did not lead directly to greater medical effectiveness in treating sickness. Most diseases remained beyond cure, or even relief. The only significant therapeutic success of the period, the practice of inoculating against smallpox, was based on folk knowledge rather than scientific research. Indeed, by the early nineteenth century, many leading physicians were arguing that the true mission of medicine was not to cure disease but to explain it.

Then came an era of stunning breakthroughs in knowledge and practice that began to transform the expectations of both doctors and their patients. The discovery of the existence and effects of bacteria by researchers such as Louis Pasteur and Robert Koch resulted in a series of treatments for previously uncontrollable conditions. The practice of antisepsis in hospitals led to a spectacular reduction in the death rates from childbirth and surgery. Systematic medical research became a fixture at universities and at private and public laboratories. This made possible an exciting acceleration of knowledge in fields as varied as genetics, organic chemistry, and nutrition. By the twentieth century, medicine and physicians had come to enjoy unprecedented public esteem. For the first time in history, it seemed possible that humanity could control the ravages of disease.

Yet success brought challenges as well. In a democratic age, the prospect of increased health and extended longevity raised questions about access to the new medicine. Once, rich and poor had shared a common physical misery. Would the poor now be able to partake of the newfound medical advantages of the rich? Governments had acted on advances in medical knowledge, taking steps to promote public health; it was but a short step to begin providing various forms of national health insurance. This extension of the modern regulatory state was often ardently resisted by physicians, who feared that their ancient professional autonomy was threatened. During the course of the twentieth century, doctors and the state reached a degree of accommodation, but the relationship was an uneasy one.

Porter has not written a triumphalist history of medicine. While he acknowledges modern achievements, he is always sensitive to the ambiguities of progress and the limits of human understanding. Porter points out that some of the great advances in human evolution came at a steep medical price. The domestication of animals, and the resulting proximity of man and beast, led to the jumping of diseases across species. Tuberculosis, smallpox, influenza, and measles all originated with domesticated animals. The presence of high concentrations of animals also attracted parasites, which soon took up residence in human beings. The development of agriculture made possible the growth of population, but overreliance on staple grains often led to a deterioration in nutrition and resulted in deficiency diseases such as pellagra and scurvy. Civilization also encouraged the spread of malaria, thought by some to be the most devastating and enduring scourge in history. The leveling of forests and spread of farmlands created splendid breeding grounds for disease-bearing mosquitoes. This tragedy of unintended consequences did not end in prehistory. Migration and trade have often been the agencies through which plagues are spread. The opening of the New World to European settlement had disastrous consequences for the indigenous peoples, who were decimated by unfamiliar diseases. European colonizers in the nineteenth century justified their conquests in Africa and elsewhere by arguing that the introduction of Western medicine would be a blessing to the native peoples. In fact, the diseases wrought by the social disruptions attendant on colonization far outweighed the benefits bestowed by a handful of missionary doctors. Recent development of hitherto inaccessible jungles is probably responsible for the emergence of diseases such as Ebola. Modern medicine must grapple with the price of prosperity. Many contagious diseases have disappeared or been brought under control, but they have been replaced in popular fears by chronic conditions such as cancer, heart disease, and diabetes, which are in part caused by modern lifestyles. Medicine can ameliorate these conditions, but cures have proven maddeningly elusive.

Porter reminds readers that various distempers have proved remarkably resilient. Humanity is locked in an evolutionary battle with the diseases that prey on it. Malaria remains a threat to millions of people around the globe. Tuberculosis was thought to be in a decisive retreat earlier in the twentieth century, but toward the century's end it returned with terrible force in the Third World and even reappeared in American inner cities. AIDS has revived concerns about plagues and has so far defied a definitive treatment because the AIDS virus mutates too rapidly for researchers to create an effective vaccine.

Porter thus ends his work with the stoic injunction that we must recognize medicine's limits. It has accomplished much, fulfilling many of the dreams of its founders. In the end, though, medicine can only alleviate our state; it cannot liberate us from the human condition.

Daniel P. Murphy

Sources for Further Study

Booklist. XCIV, March 1, 1998, p. 1081.
The Economist. CCCXLVI, February 14, 1998, p. R4.
History Today. XLVIII, June, 1998, p. 60.
The Lancet. CCCLII, September 19, 1998, p. 993.
Library Journal. CXXIII, February 15, 1998, p. 166.
Nature. CCCXCI, January 15, 1998, p. 241.
The New England Journal of Medicine. CCCXXXIX, July 2, 1998, p. 54.
The New York Times Book Review. CIII, May 3, 1998, p. 11.
Publishers Weekly. CCXLV, February 9, 1998, p. 82.
The Times Literary Supplement. January 30, 1998, p. 8.

HAPPY ALCHEMY
On the Pleasures of Music and the Theatre

Author: Robertson Davies (1913-1995)
Edited by Jennifer Surridge and Brenda Davies
Published: Viking (New York). 384 pp. $27.95
Type of work: Essays, theater, and music
Time: 1939 through 1995
Locale: Canada, the United States, and Sweden

A collection of speeches, essays, and miscellaneous pieces focusing on theater and music, by Canada's most eminent novelist and playwright

In a 1993 lecture at Niagara-on-the-Lake's Shaw Festival, Robertson Davies provided a lively introduction to the nineteenth century drama *The Silver King*, then in production at the Festival. Describing the personalities that first brought *The Silver King* to the stage, Davies regaled his audience with stories about the play's original star, the strikingly handsome actor William Barrett; about the playwright, Henry Jones, and the manner in which Jones's political and religious views were brought to bear on his plays; and about Henry Herman, Jones's probable collaborator and a man given to practical jokes involving the unexpected removal of his glass eye.

Davies explained that he was telling these stories "to counteract a tendency in modern theater historians to make the nineteenth century too solemn, too loaded with deep artistic significance." He continued, "Of course it was artistic—splendidly so—but artistry is not a solemn, dead thing . . . art is alive, or it is nothing, and the people who create it are highly coloured." This lecture is one of many collected in *Happy Alchemy* to illustrate Davies's ability to bring to life the "highly colored" people, times, and circumstances that combine to produce that "happy alchemy" that makes theatrical and musical performances more than simply displays of talent.

At his death in 1995 at the age of eighty-two, Davies left a number of such speeches, articles, book reviews, and other matter, largely unpublished and uncollected, from which Brenda Davies and Jennifer Surridge (respectively, Davies's widow and daughter) selected material for two posthumous volumes. The first, *The Merry Heart: Reflections on Reading, Writing, and the World of Books* (1996) offered a selection of Davies's writings on literature; *Happy Alchemy* focuses on his passion for the worlds of theater and music.

An inveterate playgoer, Davies began keeping a "Theatre Diary" in the late 1950's, writing a mini-critique of every musical and theatrical performance he saw. Excerpts from this diary and from his personal diaries are used to introduce each chapter. Many offer insight into Davies's views of himself as a performer; Davies often noted concerns about his delivery and how successful he felt he had been with a lecture, as well as noting any compliments he might have received afterwards. These brief introductions provide context and may hearten the weary playgoer: "Have I ever seen a really good *Macbeth*? Not in my eighty years. . . ." Davies's dry humor is frequently in evidence: "The star of the [Gothenburg Book] Fair, I gather, is to be a writer called

Jackie Collins, of whom I have never heard. . . . Several children present me with scraps of paper for autographs: obviously don't know who I am and don't care. I sign 'Jackie Collins' and they go away quite content."

The pieces collected in *Happy Alchemy* encompass several of Davies's recurring interests and favorite themes, among them language in dramatic performance, Jungian archetypes in the theater, Canadian literature and culture, and sketches of personalities important to nineteenth and twentieth century theater.

Several pieces in *Happy Alchemy* touch on the playwright's necessary artistry with language, using as examples lesser-known writers such as Henry Jones as well as larger lights such as George Bernard Shaw and, of course, William Shakespeare. Davies's remarks on language and speaking touch not only on the written word but also on the musical qualities of the lines when spoken, and on the physical condition of the actor who successfully conveys the meaning of the finest poetry and prose.

As often as Davies reminded audiences that the language they heard spoken on the stage was not really everyday speech, he also frequently pointed out that successful drama is not necessarily that which comes closest to showing people and events as they really are. "Realism" in Davies's view was a misnomer for dramatic prose and speech that was truly theatrical and that only seemed natural on the stage: "painting, as opposed to photography." Davies often argued that drama should not simply re-create events but should remind the audience of some deeply felt truth. Davies referred to sex scenes in modern movies and theater as examples of writers' failure to give the audience a collective "memory, or ideal vision, of love." As Davies explained in a 1990 lecture, "Opera makes us feel and believe in passion through music. Great theater makes us feel and believe in passion through poetry, or great prose, which is much the same thing. . . . We want something that awakens deep and powerful feeling in ourselves. We want art, not nature, in fact."

Davies attributed this "deep and powerful feeling" to the dramatic expression of archetypes, such as the ideas of true love, lost love, or wartime heroism. Many of the pieces collected here discuss examples of such archetypes in particular works. *Happy Alchemy* includes Davies's 1989 lecture "Jung and the Writer," in which Davies offers a personal account of how he became interested in the philosophies of Carl Jung and why he responded to Jung's point of view more warmly than to that of Sigmund Freud. Typically assuring his audience that he does not speak as an expert, Davies offers an accessible discussion of the Jungian collective unconscious wherein the archetypes reside, and of the connection between the writer's unconscious and the creative process. Davies touches on other authors but speaks especially of his own novels *Fifth Business* and *The Manticore*, discussing the creative evolution of the works and the vision that crystallized for Davies his characterization of the hero in the latter book.

The second half of *Happy Alchemy* is chiefly devoted to pieces on opera and musical performances, including pieces on Scottish folk songs, popular music in the works of Charles Dickens, and a humorous sketch of Davies's own unsuccessful attempt to become a musician. Davies's libretto for a children's operetta (never produced) called *Children of the Moon* also appears here, as does the script for a ghost story set to music,

Harper of the Stones, which was performed in 1987 at the Young People's Theatre in Toronto. Also included are several lectures written to precede operatic performances, in which Davies gave his audiences not only background information and synopses of specific works but philosophical thoughts on humor in opera and what makes an opera "grand." Davies often argued that opera is technically melodrama, although audiences conventionally view melodrama as an emotionally exaggerated dramatic form. In Davies's view, opera reflects an audience's true character more closely than comedic or tragic drama because melodramatic characters' emotions and situations are closer to those of everyday people.

Davies, who had been instrumental in founding Ontario's Stratford Festival (now the premier North American home for classical theater) in the 1950's, frequently wrote and lectured on Canada's struggle to develop and maintain its own intellectual and artistic culture apart from any European or American influence. His introduction to the Stratford Festival's fortieth anniversary program evokes the pioneering spirit of the handful of visionaries who launched the first festival. Introductions written for collections of Canadian plays and for his own plays are included here to offer a further sense of how Canadian theater has grown and of Davies's personal experience as a playwright in Canada's early theatrical history. The collection also offers a blistering 1992 speech wherein Davies asserts that Canadian politicians' disregard for formal education is having a decaying effect on Canadian culture.

Happy Alchemy include several otherwise unclassifiable pieces that show the range of Davies's interests and talents and emphasize his sometimes elaborate sense of humor. "Look at the Clock! (A Suggestion for a Film Scenario)" is a humorous update of the Oedipus myth in which Queen Jocasta tires of the tragedy's perpetual reenactment and proposes that she and Oedipus simply remain happily married. There are two prologues to plays written by Davies in verse, one for a production of Richard Sheridan's *The Critic* and one for a 1939 production of Oliver Goldsmith's *The Good Natur'd Man*. The latter is offered as an example of Davies's talent for parody; the prologue imitated Goldsmith's style so well that it was received without question as part of the original play. In an address written for a symposium at Johns Hopkins University on "An Allegory of the Physician," Davies offered a brief history of doctors in the plays of Shakespeare, Henrik Ibsen, and Molière, as well as in television drama (apparently circa the early 1960's). Davies's "Letter From Friar Bacon and Friar Bungay" is a rather elaborate hoax sent as a practical joke to theatrical designer Tanya Moiseiwitsch during a production of *Macbeth* that had entirely omitted the weird sisters and their infamous "eye of newt and toe of frog" speech. The fictional Bacon and Bungay assume that Moiseiwitsch cut the scene because she could not obtain ingredients for the witches' brew, and they offer to supply her with the necessary reptilian eyes and toes: "Pleasing minor items, shipped dry."

Happy Alchemy also collects profiles and sketches of personalities including Sir Laurence Olivier, Lewis Carroll, George Bernard Shaw, Tanya Moiseiwitsch, and Stratford Festival founder Tyrone Guthrie. Davies's scholarship, in the case of historical personalities, and his eloquent personal recollections of contemporaries brings these "highly colored" artists to life and lends new depth to the audience's appreciation of their work. *Happy Alchemy* serves the same function for Davies himself, bringing to life before a new audience one of the great personalities of modern arts and letters and preserving many of his most important and memorable observations and thoughts on the state of the arts.

Davies frequently assured his audiences that he would not speak to them as an expert or scholar but intended simply to share his thoughts in "friendly talk." Typical is his disclaimer prior to an extended lecture on Scottish folklore that he is "an enthusiastic but not wholly reliable guide." Davies in fact possessed a remarkable range of knowledge and scholarship, but he was able to distill these into quite accessible lectures designed to enhance an average audience's appreciation of whatever subject was at hand. An amiable and friendly tone persists throughout the collection, which reveals a number of Davies's techniques as a lecturer. Davies's speeches are informative but accessible, true to his oft-stated goal not to deliver scholarly lectures but to invite his audience along on an enjoyable discussion of his thoughts. Davies assures audiences that he knows how knowledgeable and intelligent they are, and he will often pursue some happy tangential topic only to stop and assure his audience that he is still aware of the subject at hand.

During his lifetime, Robertson Davies made important contributions to the ongoing life of theater and music, not only through his own works and material support but through his argument that present-day drama and performers were as good as those of the past. Davies demonstrated that "artistry is not a solemn, dead thing," and *Happy Alchemy* conveys this message to a wider audience, showing the works and artists discussed throughout to be "highly coloured" while confirming Davies's place as a powerful spokesman and advocate for the performing arts. Davies successfully personified Canadian intellect and high culture, the life of the mind that his country had struggled to establish and then to acknowledge as its own. While Davies's insights made the live performances he discussed the more enjoyable, *Happy Alchemy* serves to keep alive the ideas of one of Canada's most eminent literary lions.

Maureen J. Puffer-Rothenberg

Sources for Further Study

Booklist. XCIV, July, 1998, p. 1849.
Library Journal. CXXIII, July, 1998, p. 92.
The New York Times Book Review. CIII, July 26, 1998, p. 18.
Publishers Weekly. CCXLV, June 8, 1998, p. 55.

HAY

Author: Paul Muldoon (1951-   )
Published: Farrar, Straus & Giroux (New York). 131 pp. $22.00
Type of work: Poetry

The eighth collection of Paul Muldoon's poetry further confirms his position as one of the most versatile, inventive, and technically adept of trans-Atlantic poets

While it is an understandable matter of critical convenience to place poets in groups determined by geographical proximity (the Black Mountain poets; the New York School) or by perceived peculiarities of behavior (the Beats), these simplistic categorizations are often as deceptive as they are illuminating. The proliferation of powerful poetry from Ireland—by poets born both in the North and in the Republic—and the publicity attendant to Seamus Heaney's well-deserved Nobel Prize has resulted in an amorphous mass called "Irish poetry" that assumes a commonality of interests and styles that, not surprisingly, is a simplistic reduction of the individual concerns and voices of the poets themselves. Still, as is historically evident, the possibilty of maintaining the "conversation of other poets" that Donald Hall posits is what poets "need," since "the history of poetry is a history of friendship and rivalries," has encouraged and sustained some of the most prominent of contemporary Irish poets. Ciaran Carson, Paul Muldoon, and Medbh McGuckian were students at Queen's University in Belfast in the 1960's, several years after Heaney's graduation; McGuckian has recalled that Heaney was "the first person who didn't make me feel that poetry was a closed shop. . . . There was this openness and friendliness that I trusted." How these poets, among others born in Ireland, have dealt with the weight of Irish history and politics, as well as the specific experiences of their own lives, is one of the most useful means of approaching their work.

Paul Muldoon was born in Belfast in 1951. A professor at Princeton University, living in New Jersey, married to an American woman, he has been a citizen of the United States for several years. In his poem/diary "The Prince of the Quotidian" (1994), he directly addressed Seamus Deane, who has written a critical essay that, the poet complains, "has me 'in exile' in Princeton." Muldoon's irritation with this judgment is expressed with characteristic dry wit:

> To Deane I say, I'm not in exile,
> though I can't deny
> I've been twice in Fintona.

The fact that Muldoon chooses to mention Fintona, a small town in County Tyrone near Moy where he grew up, is a reaffirmation of the importance of the local in the face of Deane's accusation that he is a kind of cultural traitor, as well as a pointed query about the influence of any one among the complex of occasions of a writer's life. It is both a resistance to the narrowly parochial, the pressure of the parish, and a declaration of personal autonomy—his claim for the artist's right to determine where he belongs and what he will choose to say. It recalls Heaney's well-known response in "The Flight Path" when he, home from America, is challenged by a "grimfaced" republican to "write something for us." Heaney's defiant "'If I do write some-thing...It'll be for me, not you or anybody/ About to tell me what I should be writing" is close to the first principle of artistic independence, and one of the most striking aspects of Muldoon's writing is his pursuit of subjects and styles that are distinctly personal, somewhat idiosyncratic, and expertly rendered in terms of the requirements of the particular poem.

The extensive range of the poems in *Hay* is similar to that of previous collections. The placement of individual poems and groups is designed to reveal a subtle interplay among them, but this is not apparent until the entire book has been scrutinized. Even then, the relationship of the poems is fluid, depending on an order of reading that does not depend on going straight through. Muldoon begins with "The Mudroom," a dream vision addressed to his wife ("my love") that joins moments of their life together with Hebrew myth, culinary delicacies, pop-culture features, and other ephemera in a kind of journey that merges inner landscape with a trek through space and time. The mixture of erudition and evocative sensual imagery is one of the characteristics of Muldoon's work, as is the offhand juxtaposition of esoteric items from a transnational amalgam of cross-cultural references with the most mundane circumstances of a man's life. The last "poem" in the book is a numbered sequence that the publisher describes as "thirty sonnets," set initially in a restaurant in Paris, where a waiter locates a "muldoon"—a stolen credit card—belonging to the poet. An exuberant chain of associations launches another excursion involving the play of the poet's mind upon details of the dinner, an incident with his father in the past, the *Aeneid*, a sea voyage, and more. Muldoon has worked with the sonnet before, notably in *Quoof* (1983) and *Meeting the British* (1987), and his efforts are a strong refutation of the opinion that the form is a relic of another time. Muldoon stirs the sonnet into new shapes, permitting shifts in place and time that are rapid and often closely interior and incorporating plays on words much beyond the obvious puns that sometimes pass for verbal virtuousity. The elaborate cultural matrix of the poem is jagged and fluid, casually indifferent to boundaries between languages and nations. Even if some of the components of the assemblage will be elusive for almost any reader, the sense of a removal of limits and the determination to find modes of coherence (often linking rhyme) make his longer poems continuously engrossing.

Muldoon seems especially fond of these extended sequences, as if he cannot resist linking an image or word with a tangentially connected one drawn from a dynamic, densely assembled, vast store of interesting material. In the poem "Errata" specifically, but in other places as well, he permits this impulse to reach its ultimate expression by making a poem out of a tendency to list associative word-patterns:

> For "Antrim" read "Armagh."
> For "mother" read "other."
> For "harm" read "farm."
> For "feather" read "father."

The poem continues thus for eight stanzas. Because he is aware of the perils to a particular poem of these endlessly unfolding thought-patterns, Muldoon uses numerical divisions to provide points of pause within the sequential gatherings, so that individual entries can often stand by themselves as relatively complete poems. The two other sequences in *Hay* are "Sleeve Notes," in which he writes a series of personal responses and evocations directed toward albums by Jimi Hendrix, the Beatles, Eric Clapton, and U2—the rock musical pantheon of his era; and ninety numbered haiku ("Hopewell Haiku" for their New Jersey point of location or inspiration), which are another example of his interest in the permutations of traditional form. These haiku rhyme the first and third lines, as "While the goldfinch nest/ in the peach tree's eye level/ with a stallion's crest," which could also be called a stretched couplet, but any English version of haiku is so radically different from the original Japanese form that the use of rhyme is not a distortion that makes much difference. A more important consideration is the way in which Muldoon uses haiku to flash moments onto the page, creating an instantaneous mood, conveying a palpable feel for a setting, delineating a facet of the natural world with indelible strokes, thus capturing with deft, concise language the piercing perception that is at the source of a haiku's origin.

As interesting as the structural connections of these longer poems may be, and as appealing as it is to consider what George O'Brien has accurately identified as the "elliptical, poker-faced, riddling, and somewhat surreal perspective of his verse," Muldoon's very solid grasp of the traditional demands of his craft accounts for the success of many of the shorter poems in the collection. Perhaps protected by his obvious erudition, Muldoon seems completely at ease with an open expression of immediate emotion, so that a poem in celebration of his wife's heritage ("The Throwback") is written as a love sonnet; an account of their travels ("A Journey to Cracow") is composed as a ballad in stanzas of quatrains; a loving tribute to the Russian Nobel laureate Joseph Brodsky ("The Hug") also uses quatrains, although with some dazzling rhyme-inventions; and a poem in recollection of an earlier affair ("Longbones") is arranged in densely related triads continuing an *a-b-a* rhyme throughout while building in intensity through the use of incremental repetition in the manner of an old ballad. In an open confession of admiration, Muldoon in the "Sleeve Notes" sequence pays tribute to the Canadian poet and songwriter Leonard Cohen by saying, "his songs have meant far more to me/ than most of the so-called poems I've read." The spirit of song, a centuries-old component of the Irish literary tradition, is evident throughout Muldoon's work, in multiple references to single pieces, in echoes of familiar tunes, in word/sound collages akin to songs, and in the snatches of song that are often the signature feature of people in the poems.

The long continuum where song meets speech, a blurring of boundaries common to Muldoon's work, is another indication of his inclination to approach matters of importance from more than one angle. Deane's accusation of exile is an expression of the uneasiness that surrounds the issue of heritage for an Irish poet, particularly pertinent in terms of the number of writers who have lived or are living outside of Ireland. Muldoon's earlier work was clearly Irish-centered, to the degree that Edna

Longley observed that Muldoon's "native Moy" is a "locality translated by his early poetry into a mobile and metaphoric 'parish.'" The circumstances of living in the United States have not, however, removed him from either his past or his homeland. The title poem considers an encounter with "another beat-up Volvo/ carrying a load/ of Hay" on a road in New Jersey, but there are references to hay in many other poems, including the "Third Epistle to Timothy," which reaches back to his father's boyhood in Killeeshill, then to his own youth when he helped with a hay-gathering gang and heard his destiny proclaimed. He is told, "Though you speak, young Muldoon,/ though you speak with the tongue/ of an angel, I see you for what you are . . . Malevolent.

Three centuries of the Troubles are encapsulated by a man who tells him that he is "a member of the church malignant" (that is, the wrong religion), but also a "*malevolent* spirit (that is, a potential troublemaking artist). Amid the narration of the hay-gathering, section 7 sketches a tale of political murder and revenge, suggesting something of the danger that a man who speaks dangerous truth faces from a local community committed to the old ways. Similarly, "Wired" deals with some interesting items that the author notices when hiking in Connecticut, linking them to inescapable fragments of memory that recall typical incidents of violence in Ireland. Image and thought lead to related image and thought throughout the collection, as its title is touched again and again—a haycock, the phrase "Paul./ Make hay while you can . . . , " a boot tamped with hay, the river "Hay's meanderings." Disinclined to reduce the range of his vision, it is as if Muldoon has taken as a working principle Robert Frost's comment that "there is always something more to everything."

Paul Muldoon was recognized as a poet of exceptional promise at the time of the publication of his first volumes of poetry in the 1970's, and his reputation has grown steadily since then. His *The Annals of Chile* (1994) won the prestigious T. S. Eliot Prize, Seamus Heaney has called him "one of the era's true originals," and *The Times* has summarized his writing career by saying that he "began as a prodigy and has gone on to become a virtuoso." *Hay* supports Richard Tillinghast's contention that he is "one of the two or three most accomplished rhymers now writing in English"; Tim Kendall's remark that the "sheer ambition" of *The Annals of Chile* "reminds us that there are few contemporary poets, if any, who can match his achievement" is reinforced by the poetry in *Hay*. As Muldoon has moved further into the experience of living in America, his verbal facility has been undiminished, while his range and depth—already impressive—have continued to expand. Although there is a degree of gentle self-mockery in his account of his intentions in the poem "Anonymous: Myself and Pangur," his real aspirations as a poet are revealed when he declares that "I, sharp-witted, swift and sure,/ shed light on what had seemed obscure."

Leon Lewis

Sources for Further Study

The Guardian. October 17, 1998, p. SAT10.
The New Republic. CCXIX, November 30, 1998, p. 56.
Publishers Weekly. CCXLV, June 29, 1998, p. 52.
The Village Voice. September 8, 1998, p. 133.

THE HEALING

Author: Gayl Jones (1949-   )
Published: Beacon Press (Boston). 283 pp. $23.00
Type of work: Novel
Time: The late 1990's
Locale: The eastern United States

Gayl Jones's first novel in twenty years tells how a beautician-turned-rock-star-manager discovers powers that transform her into a travelling healer

> *Principal characters:*
> HARLAN JANE EAGLETON, the novel's narrator, who discovers healing
>   powers when she herself is attacked with a knife
> JOAN SAVAGE, a black rock star whose career begins to meet
>   international success when Harlan becomes her manager
> JOSEF EHELICH VON FREMD, a wealthy German of African ancestry
>   whom Harlan meets at the races
> NAUGHTON JIM "JAMEY" SAVAGE, Joan's former husband, a scientist
> NICHOLAS J. LOVE, Josef's bodyguard, who travels with Harlan as a
>   witness to her healing ability
> NICODEMUS SANDOVAR, a Haitian revolutionary and poet
> GRANDMOTHER JABOTI, Harlan's grandmother, who was once featured in
>   a travelling carnival as a Turtle Woman
> NORVELLE, Harlan's former husband, an anthropologist studying healing
>   practices in Africa

In 1975, the brilliant young black writer Gayl Jones published a beautiful and powerful blues novel, *Corregidora*, about a blues singer, Ursa Corregidora, and her hatred of the slave owner who had fathered both her grandmother and her mother. A year later, her somewhat less successful but no less grim novel *Eva's Man* appeared, about a woman caught in the grips of a bleak sexual obsession that turns deadly; the next year, she published a book of short stories, *White Rat*. Although she would in 1981 publish a novel in verse, *Song for Anninho*, about two lovers who flee to Brazil, and a scholarly work, *Liberating Voices: Oral Tradition in African American Literature* (1991), the author herself largely disappeared from public view, and she left her professorship at the University of Michigan. She thus became something of a mystery woman, rumored at times to have fled to Brazil, like the characters in her verse novel, to be living in Paris, and to be at home in Lexington, Kentucky. In February, 1998, her third prose novel, *The Healing*, appeared, and the attention it garnered led the police in Lexington, Kentucky, to make the connection between the Bob Jones who was threatening local officials over the death of Lucille Jones, Gayl's mother, and the Bob Higginson with whom Gayl Jones had fled in 1983 after he had been arrested on a weapons charge. The police department's attempt to arrest Higginson on this charge led to a police standoff that ended with his suicide and Jones's hospitalization.

This harsh story is the one that will serve as an implied introduction to most readers of *The Healing*, and that is a shame. Though *The Healing* is a worthy equal, at least, to *Corregidora*, the more successful of her earlier novels, it is a far more mature work, at least as daring in its stylistic innovations but far more generous in its characterizations. Most surprising, in *The Healing*, the streak of irony that cuts through all of Jones's novels occasionally crosses over into humor.

When readers meet Harlan Jane Eagleton, she is a faith healer who travels from small town to small town, mainly peddling her services to small Southern black churches. Jones immerses the reader into this world in what amounts to a dizzying introduction, as she reports not only on the people she sees and meets but also about the skeptical gossip they are probably sharing behind her back. Jones writes all dialogue without the benefit of quotation marks (or even the James Joycean introductory dash) and a minimum of "he said" and "she said" attributions. This formal technique demands an absolutely perfect pitch from the writer to prevent the dialogue from running together into unintelligibility. Jones succeeds admirably, and if the technique demands precise attention from the reader, the payoff is that the reader is made to inhabit the main character's skin more thoroughly.

The novelistically promising prospect of following a faith healer in her travels is detoured when a man from her past shows up with a message that Nicodemus has been freed from his prison. The rest of the novel is devoted to telling readers who this mysterious man is, who Nicodemus is, and how Harlan became a healer. Before her first healing (which she performed on herself after she was attacked with a knife), she was the manager of a rock star, Joan Savage, who emerges as one of the novel's most commanding characters.

A brilliant woman with a hyperkinetic intelligence, Joan is presented as an artistically ambitious but only moderately successful musician before Harlan assumes management of her career. Harlan and Joan meet at a party, and when Joan learns that Harlan is a beautician, she impulsively asks for a beauty makeover right there at the party. Harlan becomes first her travelling make-up artist and later Joan's business manager, in an unlikely transition that is never explored but that makes sense in the world of small-time travelling shows. Harlan's management is presented as successful not so much because of her brilliance as a manager but simply because she devotes herself to the business at hand. Seeing opportunities for money to be made abroad, she gets Joan several international bookings, with the result that Joan's career takes off in exciting new directions. The interplay between the direct Harlan and the unpredictable Joan makes for the novel's central relationship, and its dynamic is implied by Harlan's middle name, Jane: Not only is Jane Joan's other half, but her straightforward plainness is also contrasted with Joan's persona, as real in her personal life as on stage, as "Savage Joan, the Bitch Darling." (In fact, it is hard not to suspect that both Joan and Jane are ego projections of the author—one the quiet, businesslike professional that those who know Jones personally report her to be, the other the savage, intuitive intellect that can produce novels of vicious sexuality such as *Eva's Man*.) Inevitably, the lives of these two characters intermingle, but it takes on a decidedly acid edge after Harlan seduces Joan's former husband and close friend, James Savage.

The dialogues between Joan and Harlan contain pages of some of Jones's most virtuoso writing. Joan is presented as a self-important, brilliant rambler, someone used to speaking from a position of power, enamored of her considerable intelligence and knowledge, and unaccustomed to being upstaged intellectually, socially, or (as the reader increasingly suspects, watching the undercurrent of antagonism between the two women grow) sexually. Her talks with Harlan are full of allusions, lists, pronouncements, and implications. The reader may be tempted to keep a pen and paper handy; one suspects that Joan would expect no less. The dialogues in *The Healing* dart crazily from topic to topic, returning to the original topic in odd, unexpected ways. This may indeed be the way that dialogue in the real world develops, but one is unaccustomed to seeing it portrayed so in fiction. In the hands of a lesser writer, this could make for tedious material indeed, but Jones pulls it off and makes it interesting because it pulls the reader into Joan's energetic intellect.

Open a novel to the middle and, if the novel is well constructed, there is a good chance that one will find what lies at the heart of it—a central encounter, insight, revelation, or plot development from which everything else in the novel flows. Open *The Healing* to the middle and one finds two central riddles in the form of Harlan's grandmother, the "Turtle Woman" whose shoulders were Harlan's second healing, and Josef Ehelich von Fremd, a mysterious African German whose brief liaison with Harlan is told in small bursts throughout the novel. The story about Harlan's grandmother, Japoti, that comes up in the middle of the novel tells of her travels around the country with a fake turtle shell that she would slip over herself to become the Turtle Woman. She travelled with a woman whose genuine deformity made her the "Unicorn Woman," a woman whose popularity grew so that she was able to create her own carnival, featuring herself as a headliner. The grandmother understands that if she wanted to go back to being the Turtle Woman, she could rejoin the carnival, but she has become too accustomed to life as human being to go back. This tale of rejecting an exceptional life for the ordinariness of everyday life, a story Harlan heard when she was five, foreshadows the dynamic between Harlan's apparent ordinariness and Joan's extreme nature. While the extreme might be attractive, the everyday is where most people will choose to live.

The relationship with Josef is less fully integrated into the novel, but it offers a different message than do the memories of Grandmother Japoti. A wealthy, secretive German émigré and horse dealer whom Harlan meets at the Kentucky Downs racetrack, Josef is a businessman who may or may not be paranoid and may or may not have a conspiracy of forces aligned against him. His talk is filled with references to the Central Intelligence Agency, and after he has accused Harlan of being a spy, she finds that a mysterious man is following her around, who may or may not be an employee of Josef's.

Much of the life of the novel deals with careful and precise observations of those encounters with the edges of personality where people are almost but not quite revealed. Thus it is almost a surprise in the latter part of the story to find a plot emerging that ties together several strands introduced throughout the novel. Sandovar, who has earlier been depicted as a gambling friend of Harlan, turns up again as a revolutionary and a friend of Joan seeking political refuge in the United States. Joan provides him with refuge and later backs him and a small group of revolutionaries in their attempt to return to Haiti to spearhead a revolution. It is clear that in Joan's mind, this constitutes a sort of payback: In retribution for Harlan's having seduced her former husband, she befriends and supports a man Harlan had befriended. The pure petulance implied by Joan's act is suggested by the disastrous results of Sandovar's return. His compatriots are killed, and he is arrested. The only person to whom Harlan and Joan can think to turn for help is Harlan's onetime lover, Josef—a suggestion that Harlan dismisses but that Joan acts on, though not until she and Harlan have gone their separate ways. Thus, when they meet again at Josef's, the stage is set for the violence that will trigger the healing that sets Harlan on her new career as a healer. Is this violence between them in a sense a reconciliation, a healing, of the wounds in each other's life? Jones's story suggests this possibility but most certainly does not provide an answer. She is more interested in leaving readers with the dilemma.

The brief ending, which takes Harlan back to her contemporary career as a healer, manages more or less to resolve the darkness that surrounds the characters of Josef, Sandovar, and even Nicodemus without in any way removing it. If this is somewhat unsettling, it also epitomizes the novel's great strength, which is its portrayal of healing and reconciliation as a natural extension of the forces that draw people apart and tear them up, inseparable from those painful forces. It is a lesson with a power that will outlive the bare facts of the life surrounding the novel's appearance and that a reader can only hope will have profound truth as the author herself begins the process of healing from the shocking tragedy of her own life.

The Healing is without a doubt the most accomplished work of Gayl Jones's career. The firestorm surrounding the author's personal life may have done much to give it a wider audience than it would otherwise have received, but such attention has probably hindered the book from finding the literarily sensitive and thoughtful response the author deserved. *The Healing* is a fully human work of art that will be finding new readers long after the details of the author's life have been forgotten.

Thomas Cassidy

Sources for Further Study

Artforum. XXXVI, March, 1998, p. S24.
Booklist. XCIV, February 1, 1998, p. 899.
Essence. XXVIII, February, 1998, p. 76.
Library Journal. CXXII, December, 1997, p. 152.
The Nation. CCLXVI, May 25, 1998, p. 30.
The New York Times Book Review. CIII, May 10, 1998, p. 28.
The New York Times Magazine. July 19, 1988, p. 32.
Newsweek. CXXXI, February 16, 1998, p. 68.

People Weekly. IL, March 16, 1998, p. 81.
Publishers Weekly. CCXLV, January 19, 1998, p. 372.
Time. CLI, March 9, 1998, p. 80.
The Washington Post Book World. XXVIII, March 1, 1998, p. 9.

HERE BUT NOT HERE
A Love Story

Author: Lillian Ross (1927-   )
Published: Random House (New York). 240 pp. $25.00
Type of work: Memoirs
Time: 1945-1992
Locale: New York City

An account of the forty-year love affair between the author, a staff writer for The New Yorker, *and William Shawn, the magazine's legendary editor*

Principal personages:
WILLIAM SHAWN, the editor of *The New Yorker* from 1952 to 1987
LILLIAN ROSS, a staff writer for the magazine from 1945 to 1987, and again starting in 1993

In its heyday, the 1960's and 1970's, *The New Yorker* was arguably the most influential magazine in America, and the man who made it so, William Shawn, was arguably the most influential magazine editor the country has ever known. In 1933, Shawn joined the staff of what Harold Ross, *The New Yorker*'s founder, originally conceived of as a humor magazine for the upper crust. By 1939, when he became managing director, Shawn had already begun to transform the magazine into a highly sophisticated, highly serious weekly devoted to the kind of literary journalism that reflected his own interests and personality. Upon Ross's death in 1952, Shawn became only the second editor-in-chief the magazine had ever known, and the transformation was complete.

The other principal player in *Here but Not Here*, Lillian Ross (who is not related to Harold Ross), was one of four women who were hired in 1945 as replacements for male reporters who were serving in World War II. Shawn interviewed her, hired her, and acted as her editor for the next forty-two years. He also fell in love with her. In 1952, Ross and Shawn became lovers, a few years later setting up a household together that would last until Shawn died in 1992. Theirs was a remarkable love affair, not merely because it endured for forty years, and not merely because they also worked together until 1987 as editor and writer, but mainly because it constituted virtually an alternative life for Shawn.

Throughout their years together, Shawn, the father of three children, was married to another woman. Ever the gentleman, Shawn not only told his wife about his relationship with Ross but also permitted her to make the choice about whether or not they should divorce. Cecille Shawn chose to remain in the marriage, and so did William Shawn. He thus began his bifurcated life, dividing his time between his legitimate home—where he was, as he told Ross "there, but not there"—and an apartment he shared with Ross from 1958 onward. The two locations were ten blocks apart.

It was an odd and complicated arrangement that seemed to suit this odd and complicated man. As Ross says of him, "Bill had the ability to draw an uncrossable line between his secret self and most other people while simultaneously responding to people in a close, mindful, and sympathetic way." He seems to have managed his dual existence with remarkable agility, aided by an uncommon charm that provoked everlasting allegiance in most of the people who crossed his path. Most evenings, after dropping Ross off at one apartment, he would return to his family for dinner, only to walk the half mile back to Ross's in time to watch the 11 P.M. news with her. Before the night was out, he invariably returned to his family to spend the rest of the night, but he would swing by in a taxi to pick up Ross on the way to work the next morning. At *The New Yorker*, most of the couple's coworkers knew about the relationship, but—at least in Ross's account—they did not seem to find it remarkable.

Yet it was remarkable, especially in the early years of the relationship. It became more so in 1966, when Ross, unable to have biological offspring with Shawn, went to Norway to adopt a child. She returned with a son, Erik, whom Shawn seems to have nurtured as much as she did, teaching Erik how to play baseball, playing the piano for him, buying him a puppy. Thereafter, when Shawn went to the office in the morning, his retinue would often include not only Ross but also Erik and the dog.

One can only speculate about the jealousies this cozy arrangement must have inspired. Shawn was a gifted and much beloved editor who was able to give his writers the kind of respect and attention they craved. "Nobody else can do what you can do," he would tell them, and they would invariably respond, "I write for you." Yet while they might have envied what was clearly a very special relationship between Ross and Shawn, it seems possible that their devotion to him could have damped many resentments. They loved Shawn and wanted him to be happy. What is more, Shawn's attention to Ross did not seem to diminish his regard for them. Cecille Shawn may have felt something like this herself. One of Shawn's greatest achievements was his being able to be all things to all people.

Yet *Here but Not Here* makes it clear that Shawn paid an enormous price for his generosity of spirit. He was famously phobic, frightened of travel and tight places, unable to ride in elevators without discomfort. Over the years, he would frequently ask Ross odd questions: "Why am I more ghost than man?" and "Do you know who I am?"; he also asked her, "Please do not let me forget my own life." He gave so much of himself to others that it seemed he had nothing left for himself. His relationship with Ross must have taxed his resources further—but it also seems to have been his salvation.

Here but Not Here also makes it clear that with Ross, Shawn was able to be his secret self, to live out many of his fantasies. Because of her, he was able regularly to ride the elevator up to their twelfth-floor apartment. With her, he was able to buy a sports car and race around the countryside. While others only saw him eat cornflakes for lunch, with Ross he was eager to indulge in fine food. In many senses, his life with her was a life apart from his everyday world. Had it been otherwise, it is doubtful that Ross would have enjoyed such a long and happy alliance with him, and although she does not say so, Ross seems to know this.

Ross also seems to know that the relationship was not without its cost to her.

Struggling to escape Shawn and the suffocating passive-aggressiveness that characterized his early attachment to her, she left New York for Hollywood, where she wrote about the making of the John Houston film version of Stephen Crane's classic novel *The Red Badge of Courage* (1895). Her pieces, which first appeared in *The New Yorker*, would later be published together in the book *Picture* (1952), confirming her reputation as a top-flight journalist and pioneer of the nonfiction novel. Finding she could not stay away from Shawn, she returned to New York and *The New Yorker*, where she kept on turning out superior journalism. Once she was committed to the relationship with Shawn, however, her attitude toward her work began to change. In her customary noncommittal fashion, she writes:

> Bill as my editor seemed to want me to write more and more, but I was in ferment and was losing energy for writing. I've always resisted the intellectualizing with which some people try to diagram their lives. Now I found myself intellectualizing. I would ask myself what I was doing with my life. Why did I seem to be losing my energy for the work I so deeply loved? I tried to stand back from the path I was taking. I tried to figure it out, but I didn't know *how* to figure it out. I wasn't writing enough. I wanted to do more.

Ross is a gifted individual, but not as gifted as was William Shawn—and unlike Shawn, she had no other life apart from the one they shared. Having accommodated herself gracefully to Shawn's needs, she seems not to have been able to juggle her personal and professional lives as adroitly as he did his. Although Ross repeatedly claims that she was perfectly happy with her lot and would not have had it otherwise, her memoir nonetheless betrays her. The first half of the book, which recounts many of her accomplishments as a writer, is vivid and fast paced. In contrast, the second half, which lovingly, even obsessively, details her life with Shawn, bogs down in repetition.

Nonetheless, *Here but Not Here* is a good book, an honest and heartfelt book. Its opening, which re-creates a scene in Ross and Shawn's apartment in 1987, is wonderfully reported. Moreover, Ross's habit of saying less rather than more in most instances results in just the right tone. One morning in 1992, Ross as usual dialed the number of the telephone Shawn had installed in his bedroom so that he could receive calls from her at home. For the first time, Cecille picked up the phone. Thus it was that Ross learned that the man the two women had shared was dead. Ross then raced over to the Shawn apartment, where she embraced Cecille, who responded by stating, "He died in my arms." Ross says little more about this encounter, merely reporting what happened, but the scene could hardly be more resonant or affecting.

The story of the reception of *Here but Not Here* is as important as the story it contains. Lillian Ross has been roundly denounced by most of her reviewers, many of whom have their own connection to Mr. Shawn and *The New Yorker*. Effie Taylor-Parkes "reviewed" *Here but Not Here* by writing a parody of the memoir published in *The New York Review of Books*. *The New Yorker*'s former science correspondent, Jeremy Bernstein, published a diatribe in the *Los Angeles Times*, taking Ross to task for having gone back to work at *The New Yorker* after Shawn's death (she and some others had left the magazine when Shawn was fired in 1982). Still others, such as former *New Yorker* deputy editor Charles McGraith and staff writer James Wolcott, expressed anger with Ross for having published her account of her love affair with Shawn while his wife is still alive.

For her part, Ross professed to be untouched by such responses. In her view, William Shawn spoiled his writers, many of whom became overly dependent on him. "These people," she said, "were like children who simply didn't want to think of their parents having sex." To be sure, many of them have behaved in a juvenile fashion, using the excuse of Ross's memoir to settle an old score. She was the favored one, the one who commanded the most attention and affection from Shawn, and one of the only defectors who was allowed to come back to the magazine, even as other Shawn acolytes were being squeezed out.

Here but Not Here owes much of the attention it received not to the revelations it contains but to the fact that *The New Yorker* has played such a central role in the intellectual life of the country—and particularly of New York City. Many consider Tina Brown, one of Shawn's successors, to be the person responsible for undermining much of Shawn's work, and some consider her to be the person responsible for putting Ross up to the job of writing her memoir. When Brown resigned in July, 1998, the news made the front page of *The New York Times*, the country's newspaper of record, further evidence of the central role of this small community of writers and editors in the nation's intellectual life.

Lisa Paddock

Sources for Further Study

Atlanta Journal and Constitution. July 5, 1998, p. K10.
Booklist. XCIV, May 15, 1998, p. 1563.
Library Journal. CXXIII, June 15, 1998, p. 80.
Los Angeles Times. May 17, 1998, p. 3.
Mirabella. August, 1998, p. 116.
New England Review. XIX, Fall, 1998, p. 167.
The New York Review of Books. June 25, 1998, p. 19.
The New York Times. May 29, 1998.
The New York Times Book Review. CIII, June 7, 1998, p. 9.
Newsday. June 7, 1998, p. B09.
Newsweek. CXXXI, May 4, 1998, p. 71.
Publishers Weekly. CCXLV, May 4, 1998, p. 194.
Time. CLI, June 1, 1998, p. 86.
The Wall Street Journal. May 22, 1998, p. W10.
The Washington Post Book World. XXVIII, June 21, 1998, p. 11.

THE HIDDEN WORDSWORTH
Poet, Lover, Rebel, Spy

Author: Kenneth R. Johnston (1938-   )
Published: W. W. Norton (New York). Illustrated. 965 pp. $45.00
Type of work: Literary biography
Time: 1770-1850
Locale: England and France

A thoroughgoing re-examination of the poet's life that places him far more firmly in the tradition of liberal Romanticism than previous twentieth century critics or even his own contemporaries might have thought

> *Principal personages:*
> WILLIAM WORDSWORTH, the Romantic poet; subject of the study
> JOHN WORDSWORTH, his father; a Westmorland land agent
> ANN COOKSON WORDSWORTH, his mother
> DOROTHY WORDSWORTH, his sister, who figures prominently in many of his poems
> SIR JAMES LOWTHER, a wealthy landowner, his father's employer
> ANNETTE VALLON, Wordsworth's French wife
> CAROLINE VALLON "WILLIAMS," their daughter
> MARY HUTCHINSON WORDSWORTH, Wordsworth's British wife
> SAMUEL TAYLOR COLERIDGE, Wordsworth's friend and collaborator

Romanticism conjures up the notion of unconventional behavior, though collegiality was often strained even among those who accepted its general principles. Percy Bysshe Shelley could willingly accept the political views of his friend George Gordon, Lord Byron, and even tolerate Byron's sexual excesses. Indeed, the exoticism of Byron made him a far more important figure in his own day than either the passing of time or the quality of much of his poetry have justified. What captured Shelley's imagination about Byron, the willingness to risk everything for an ideal or an experience, likewise caused him to shun John Keats, a dying poet whose obsession with death allowed him to equate poetry with sleep and immortality with an imagined Greek vase.

Shelley reserved special excoriation for William Wordsworth, even committing his thoughts on Wordsworth to paper. This was a rarity, since Shelley frequently thought but rarely wrote negatively about his colleagues. Shelley's sonnet "To Wordsworth" (1816) is in effect an epitaph (written thirty-four years before Wordsworth's death!) on what Shelley considered the poet's squandered promise.

> Thou wert as a lone star, whose light did shine
> On some frail bark in winter's midnight roar:
> Thou hast like to a rock-built refuge stood
> Above the blind and battling multitude:
> In honored poverty thy voice did weave
> Songs consecrate to truth and liberty,—
> Deserting these, thou leavest me to grieve,
> Thus having been, that thou shouldst cease to be.

Shelley's poem effectively turns the beetle-crag of Wordsworth's *The Prelude* (1798-1839) on its end and directly attacks Wordsworth where he lives, in Grasmere, the Lake District, as its poet-hermit. Samuel Taylor Coleridge, Wordsworth's friend and collaborator, must have seen Shelley's poem. His "To William Wordsworth: Composed on the Night After His Recitation of a Poem on the Growth of an Individual Mind" is actually an affirmation of Wordsworthian romanticism directly aimed at Shelley's attack on *The Prelude*.

Reading Kenneth R. Johnston's *The Hidden Wordsworth: Poet, Lover, Rebel, Spy* probably would not have changed Shelley's mind about *The Prelude*, a poem that he loathed, but it might have caused him to reassess Wordsworth as a man. It is surely the case that Johnston's book will provoke debate among contemporary scholars. Some of these will at least reconsider their long-held preconceptions about Wordsworth as a reclusive self-exile and evader of scenes political.

In essence, Johnston's book presents a long series of small surprises about its subject. Johnston describes Wordsworth's conservative family standards and essentially rootless adolescence following his mother's death. He considers Wordsworth's diffident behavior as a student at Cambridge University, surely uncharacteristic for a boy of moderate means at the time. Then there are Wordsworth's political and amorous involvements in France, his abrupt return to England at the start of the Reign of Terror, and his possible connections with the British secret service at precisely the time at which he was self-consciously creating his poet-hermit persona.

The first of these surprises concerns Wordsworth's childhood years. His father, John Wordsworth, was not only a dependent of Sir James Lowther, the most feared, powerful, and hated aristocrat in all of Cumberland and Westmorland, but also his agent. In addition to collecting Lowther's rents, the elder Wordsworth served his master as political agent and kept his ear to the ground to keep Lowther's estates compliant and politically safe. To work for "Jimmy Grasp-all," as Lowther's tenants called him, ensured a comfortable home and suitable income along with the distrust and disdain of the Westmorland populace.

The poet Wordsworth may have indeed been the "child of nature" he idealizes in his poetry, but he may also have been solitary as a child by necessity. This withdrawn existence evidently became even worse after his seventh year, when his mother, Ann Cookson Wordsworth, died. After her death, the elder Wordsworth separated the poet and his three brothers, each of whom was reared by families of strangers who boarded children near the schools the boys attended. Their sister Dorothy remained at home. The fact that the Cooksons, Wordsworth's mother's family, were enemies of Lowther made any close relationship with the Wordsworth children awkward. In the years following their mother's death, Wordsworth and his brothers, John, Christopher, and Richard, saw their father and sister relatively rarely, mostly during school holidays. Their guardians were the women of the families that boarded them. Their father turned increasingly inward, becoming more distant and cold toward his children; his position with Lowther evidently kindled his general misanthropy.

Despite an adequate income, Wordsworth's father had serious economic problems.

Mostly, this was the consequence of having to board and educate his sons separately. One might imagine that as a result Wordsworth would have felt enormous pressure to succeed brilliantly when he entered St. John's College, Cambridge. It is a well-known fact that he did not, and his failure to pursue an honors degree has always puzzled Wordsworth scholars.

Johnston supplies another of his small surprises at this point by patently examining the academic topography of St. John's for the years of Wordsworth's attendance, which started in 1787. He argues convincingly, citing specific cases, that honors and prizes often came to those with powerful connections or to those whose finances allowed them to hire influential tutors. Though the academic curriculum appears formidable when assessed as printed, Johnston shows that it was possible to avoid whole areas of supposedly required study and still leave Cambridge with an honors degree, which would assure political and social preferment after graduation.

Clearly, Wordsworth did not waste his time at college. He read classical literature extensively, far beyond Greek and Latin requirements at St. John's, and he did indeed achieve academic prizes in these areas. He was weakest in mathematics, essentially because he refused to sit for the university examinations. The irony is that had Wordsworth been able to play the game in other ways, by hiring the proper tutors or by currying favor with college authorities, he might still have obtained university recognition. Even so, he refused to submit to rigorous studies that did not interest him, even if it cost him the prospect of a comfortable, conservative future in politics, civil service, or holy orders. It was to the last of these options that Wordsworth was supposedly moving, ostensibly on the promise of Lowther and family support. His experience in France would effectively put an end to any hope for a future in the ministry.

It was a typical act of Wordsworthian disobedience—a walking tour of Europe that he began in the summer of 1790, when he should have been reading for his examinations—that changed the course of his life irrevocably. This is the tour that Wordsworth portrays in his verse recollection known as *Descriptive Sketches* (1793). He undertook the trip with Robert Jones, a friend from St. John's, but the actual experience was more political than the early verse indicates.

Wordsworth was present in Paris on July 14, 1790, to observe the first anniversary of the fall of the Bastille. He watched Louis XVI submit to an oath of loyalty to the new constitution, an event staged in the Champs de Mars in the manner of a wedding ceremony, with Louis as bridegroom. Even many of Wordsworth's liberal contemporaries at Cambridge would have cringed at the thought of such a diminution of monarchy, but Wordsworth was thrilled at the prospect of a new kind of civil state. It was the same kind of enthusiasm that impelled Thomas Paine, and for that matter Annette Vallon, the young woman with whom Wordsworth would share his love.

It was also on this tour that Wordsworth first saw Mont Blanc, which would become a symbol for romantic poets generally. Modern readers think of Mont Blanc and Shelley simultaneously, since for him it became a symbol of intellectual power, the beauty that remains latent before bursting forth unexpectedly, like the Arve that flows from the mountain. For Wordsworth, who was filled with insight though less inclined to personal symbol, Mont Blanc seemed the Alpha and Omega, at once primal chaos and ultimate ruin.

It was this walking tour that paved the way for Wordsworth's year of residence in France, 1791-1792. The Revolution still captivated him, but only because the Reign of Terror had not yet come. He was, in essence, a Girondist, a liberal but not a radical. He avidly read the interventionist journals of the period, following in the political wake of Helen Maria Williams, another British resident. He was one of the many British intellectuals filled with idealism and hoping to participate in the shaping of a new world order. It is at this time that the most enigmatic period of Wordsworth's life begins, centering on the figure of Annette Vallon, an underground fighter against the Revolution's excesses. She ultimately won the epithet "the valiant Chouanne of Blois" and was pensioned as a heroine of royalist resistance to Napoleon.

Johnston reveals another of his small surprises in the course of discussing the relationship of Wordsworth and Vallon, though in this case his conclusions seem less definitive. Certain facts are beyond question. Vallon was four years older than Wordsworth. There was a marriage of some kind, despite the commonly held view that none occurred. The proceeding, though, may have been of dubious legality; there are no fewer than three misspellings of Wordsworth's name on the registry document. In contrast, again, with generally accepted opinion, Johnston argues that Wordsworth and Vallon continued to see each other even after marriage no longer seemed to be a viable option. Johnston also contends that both Vallon and her daughter continued to feel real affection for Wordsworth and that Wordsworth's English wife, Mary Hutchinson, encouraged their occasional visits.

It was upon the death of Raisley Calvert, a friend and contemporary who lived in Westmorland, that Wordsworth received a small annuity that allowed him the security of a continuing income. He grew closer to his sister, and she assumed the duties of his secretary, a task she would continue to fulfill even after Wordsworth's death. The friendship that would again redirect Wordsworth's life, that with Samuel Taylor Coleridge, began at this time, 1797. Wordsworth was twenty-seven years old; their joint publication of *Lyrical Ballads* (1798) would bring both poets to national attention.

After 1799, the pattern of Wordsworth's existence was firmly fixed in Grasmere and Dove Cottage, where he lived with his sister Dorothy and his wife Mary Hutchinson; Coleridge was only thirteen miles away, at Greta Hall in Keswick. Wordsworth would find himself becoming part of the literary establishment and, by 1843, poet laureate. There would be tragedies, such as the drowning of his brother John, a sea captain, in 1805, but on the whole Wordsworth's career would trace a long, steady, upward trajectory. It is this conspicuous acclaim that Shelley found so hard to appreciate.

Robert J. Forman

Sources for Further Study

Choice. XXXVI, October, 1998, p. 316.
Contemporary Review. CCLXXIII, November, 1998, p. 277.
The Economist. CCCXLVI, August 29, 1998, p. 75.
Library Journal. CXXIII, July, 1998, p. 91.
Los Angeles Times Book Review. June 28, 1998, p. 8.
The New Leader. LXXXI, June 29, 1998, p. 10.
Publishers Weekly. CCXLV, May 11, 1998, p. 58.
The Spectator. CCLXXXI, August 8, 1998, p. 28.
The Times Literary Supplement. September 18, 1998, p. 3.
The Wall Street Journal. June 23, 1998, p. A18.

A HISTORY OF GAY LITERATURE
The Male Tradition

Author: Gregory Woods (1953-   )
Published: Yale University Press (New Haven, Connecticut). Illustrated. 456 pp. $39.95
Type of work: Literary history
Time: The fifth century B.C. to the present

An encyclopedic critical study that proposes a provocative new definition for gay literature and traces the contours of the homoerotic tradition from classical Greece to contemporary America

Gregory Woods has undertaken a positively herculean task in writing this history of the gay male tradition in literature. Although he is not the first to attempt such an encompassing study, in the sheer breadth of his coverage and the persuasive force of his critical commentary, he succeeds in a much more comprehensive way than any of his predecessors.

The Gay and Lesbian Literary Heritage: A Reader's Companion to the Writers and Their Works, from Antiquity to the Present (1995), one of several volumes edited by Claude J. Summers in the early 1990's, is certainly a valuable guide, as are the various dictionaries on gay men's literature available from Greenwood Press and St. James Press; but Woods has produced something much more monumental than an exhaustively annotated bibliography of gay figures and texts. He has effectively identified a new canon, or rather given a penetrating re-reading of the established canon from a gay perspective, and in a series of magisterial essays has created a sense of a usable literary past for gay readers.

Gay readers, in fact, are essential to Woods's construction of this canon, since it is his contention that gay literature is not simply limited to the productions of gay authors nor confined to literary works containing recognizable gay characters or themes. Although gay literature may begin with an openly gay author writing explicitly about the experience of being gay, Woods proposes that it must finally expand to comprise any literary material that is "amenable to gay readings." The question then becomes: Can these poems or novels be read as if they were gay poems or novels? This makes the gay reader the locus for determining the canon—a tactful and savvy reader, it should be said, but a gay reader nevertheless. The power to authorize inclusion or exclusion no longer lies solely with the heterosexual critic, hiding behind a mask of disinterestedness and claiming to speak for universal standards and unbiased views, nor with the bookish homosexual critic, wary of pushing beyond the already agreed-upon cadre of "queer" writers (the Christopher Marlowes, Oscar Wildes, and Thom Gunns) and not wishing to appropriate any more than appears seemly. Here Woods borrows from Roland Barthes the notion that a critic's job is not so much to reveal a work of art's secret meaning for all time but to construct a way of understanding the work in the critic's own time. This is what he does, arguing that in the absence of stable definitions and in the presence of destabilizing homophobic prejudices, gay literature is always something in the process of being identified in the critic's (or the critical reader's) own time. It exists, he suggests, in the spaces between texts, in the constant readings and rereadings, in the ongoing conversations about what constitutes literature and what constitutes sexuality.

The texts themselves, of course, are there, a matter of record—from ancient Greek pastorals to medieval Arabic elegies, Renaissance dramas to Victorian pornography, modern European novels to African friendship verses and contemporary AIDS journalism. By 1998 it is not difficult to make extensive lists of potential gay texts. Indeed, the first fruits of a new wave of gay publishing in the late 1970's were the numerous anthologies of gay fiction and collections of gay verse that Woods views as a continuation of the late nineteenth century practice of listing, of gathering into one place, one anthology, the defining texts of homosexuality. It was at that time—when homosexuality was being reconceived as an identity category, a distinct human type—that gay readers needed a tradition, a past that would bring legitimacy and a sustaining mythic dimension to lives that had hitherto been seen largely in sinful, criminal, or pathological terms. Thus a canon began to take shape, beginning, not surprisingly, with Greek classical literature, where myth and history could easily provide a Ganymede or Apollo, a Socrates or Achilles as the foundation of a gay pantheon.

Woods handles these opening chapters on classic Greece and Rome, part of what he calls the "pre-homosexual world," very carefully, alert to any anachronistic assumptions that might result in distorted analysis. He is, for example, acutely aware that for all of the exuberant pederastic verse in every Greek writer from Theocritus to Pindar, the insistently exalted notions of love between men and boys must be seen in the light of the accompanying gender system that assigns clear active and passive roles to each. Only within that context does the sexual relationship have meaning. The same applies to Latin writers: While it can seem in reading Roman literature that the culture took for granted what is now known as bisexuality—judging beauty by age rather than gender—the celebratory same-sex poetry of Catullus or Martial or even Vergil must be located within the prevailing gender order and its authorized scripts for amorous male conduct. Nevertheless, these works do make clear that same-sex desire is a persistent phenomenon; classic literature is suffused with the homoerotic imagination. For a gay male, there is much here that is "amenable" to a gay reading.

It is Woods's practice in writing these essays not only to offer his own succinct but thoroughly keen-eyed readings of the literature in question but also to provide a gloss on other significant critical interpretations that have clustered around these texts. Nowhere has this yielded such rich results as in his chapters on the Middle Ages and on William Shakespeare. His survey of medieval literature relies heavily on John Boswell's pioneering reassessment of the period—in particular, on Boswell's finding that it was only in the late twelfth century that a condemnatory view of homosexuality came into play, as popular and theological writers began to focus on the body as a site of pleasure to be policed, enlisting the myth of Sodom as an authority for enforcement. Earlier, there had been an uncontroversial and fairly robust tradition of same-sex literature that showed real variety and scope. Woods gives these medieval works inspired readings, none more so than Dante Alighieri's *Inferno*, in which sodomites are—to the consternation of Dante scholars over the centuries—regarded leniently, their behavior seen not as unnatural but rather as a category of excessive love (love always, in Dante, being a potential good).

In the chapter on Shakespeare, Woods makes insightful comments on both the plays and on some provocative late twentieth century stagings of the plays, but he understandably makes the sonnets the focus of his attention, as these are the crucial texts in the battle over who "owns" this national and cultural icon. The sonnets raise explicitly the question of whether profoundly canonical texts can ever be allowed to be seen as gay texts. Woods quickly rehearses the history of the ongoing controversy, how the first one hundred twenty-six poems addressed to a young man have been read either as private expressions of love for the mysterious "Mr. W. H." or as extravagant public performances in a fashionable literary genre.

Woods neatly compiles the critical record on this debate, showing how research into the identity of "W. H." has produced intense acrimony, since if Shakespeare's dedicatee is a real man, and these are not simply literary exercises, then Shakespeare must have been gay or (given that the other half of the sonnets are addressed to the "Dark Lady") at least bisexual. Eric Partridge, for one, in *Shakespeare's Bawdy* (1968), will not have that. He denounces gay readings as a waste of time and simply asserts the "normality" of Shakespeare, claiming that while gay readers have vested interests and are therefore blinded by personal biases, he and his "normal" readers, clearly without vested interests, are providing "impersonal" readings of the sonnets and giving a thoroughly straight Bard. Partridge's blindness to his own need to see the poet and the poems as exclusively heterosexual is self-indicting, but still the controversy continues.

Surviving all of this critical warfare, however, are the sonnets themselves. No amount of blustering assertion or special pleading can make them any less available to gay readers or any less open to gay readings, and this is the point Woods most tellingly makes.

As the chronology unfolds, Woods produces revelatory chapters on the love/death theme of pastoral friendship elegies and on the indiscriminate sexual voraciousness of libertine drama and gothic fiction. There is also a wonderfully wry reading of the great American Renaissance writers, from Walt Whitman to Herman Melville, which makes use of Leslie Fiedler's classic formulation about male-male bonds and the desire to escape the entrapment of the female. Woods exits the nineteenth century with a fine summing up of the *fin de siécle* aesthetic movement, showing how a curious marriage of hellenic paganism and devotional Christianity produced at first a transgressive sense of style and then, in the work of Edward Carpenter, for one, a transgressive sense of politics, a commitment to living in the world as fully aware and fully enfranchised homosexual persons: men loving other men. When Woods arrives at this point, the literature he has available for examination undergoes a clear change, one which accompanies a shift in genre as well, from poetry to fiction. The novel, the principal medium for investigating and representing individual characters and their social environments, now looms as the principal site for the realistic portrayal of gay lives.

With the ascendance of the novel and with more writers writing out of a clearer understanding of what constitutes a gay identity, a new stage in the gay literary tradition begins, and the last half of Woods's history is concerned with this more recent material. At this point, Woods must become somewhat more selective, choosing representative texts for discussion. Although this is the only tractable way to proceed, given the proliferation of gay writing, it does mean that some figures, such as Allen Ginsberg and other Beat writers of the 1950's or the Violet Quill writers of the 1970's, get less than their due. However, Woods's choices do finally seem unimpeachable. The deft, well-wrought essays on C. P. Cavafy and Angus Wilson, for example, make the Alexandrian poet and the English novelist emerge as much bolder and much more important voices than might have been previously imagined. In addition, Woods's traversal of popular literature, from the fiercely heterosexual romances of Barbara Cartland to the dark gay fantasies of Clive Barker, makes clear just how the ideologies of sexuality and gender play out in the powerful culture of entertainment.

It should be said that Woods is largely concerned with the Western literary tradition, though he does include chapters on Japanese and Chinese writers and on some of the literatures of black Africa and the Middle East. Yet within his parameters, he covers enormous territory, with clear-sighted essays on gays under Nazism, gays in the Harlem Renaissance, gays in (and out of) families, the exhilarating changes in gay art and culture in the years of post-Stonewall liberation, and the traumatic changes in the age of the AIDS epidemic. This last part of the narrative, though sobering to read, is nevertheless illuminating for the way Woods shows how AIDS shaped both the subject and the form of art. Traditional genres such as the elegy were reconceived in the 1980's to create a different expression of remembrance; while still a literature that would bear witness to the tragedy as well as sustain the gay community in the face of its losses, many of these unconventional laments were now inescapably reflexive documents, poems in which the lover grieves over a beloved's death while anticipating the imminent arrival of his own. A new awareness of personal vulnerability becomes enmeshed in the very nature of gay desire. As Andrew Holleran has said, in such times of crisis a simple naming of names (those who lived, those who loved, those who behaved well or badly) has frequently been the only possible response.

This is a landmark history of the gay male literary tradition, a riveting yet judiciously weighted and persuasively argued study that in spite of its obvious scholarship is easily accessible and hugely engaging. The field of gay studies has been notably advanced with the publication of this important, if understandably controversial, book.

Thomas J. Campbell

Sources for Further Study

The Advocate. December 22, 1998, p. 63.
Kirkus Reviews. LXVI, January 15, 1998, p. 102.

Lambda Book Report. VI, June, 1998, p. 12.
Library Journal. CXXIII, April 1, 1998, p. 90.
The New Republic. CCXVIII, April 6, 1998, p. 36.
Publishers Weekly. CCXLV, February 9, 1998, p. 88.
The Times Literary Supplement. May 8, 1998, p. 25.
The Washington Post Book World. XXVIII, March 22, 1998, p. 9.

A HISTORY OF THE AMERICAN PEOPLE

Author: Paul Johnson (1929-   )
Published: HarperCollins (New York). 1088 pp. $35.00
Type of work: History
Time: 1580-1997
Locale: The United States

A British Tory's survey of America's past, with particular emphasis on the nation's political and economic elite and on the effect its religious impulses had on determining its development

Near the beginning of *A History of the American People*, Paul Johnson defines the "proto-American":

> He had certain strongly marked characteristics which were to be associated with the American archetype. He was energetic, brash, hugely ambitious, money-conscious, none too scrupulous, far-sighted and ahead of his time, with a passion for the new and, not least, a streak of idealism which clashed violently with his overweening desire to get on and make a fortune.

The man thus referred to is Sir Walter Ralegh, Elizabethan planner of the ill-fated seventeenth century Roanoke colonization venture to the New World. The laudatory description, however, could well have applied to most of the individuals whose exploits are recounted in a series of what might be called mini-biographies. Among the more colorful of these: Captain John Smith, Nathaniel Bacon, Benjamin Franklin, Eli Whitney, Henry Clay, John C. Calhoun, Edward H. Harriman, and Andrew Carnegie. During America's formative years, the author believes, a free-market economy allowed a meritocracy to develop and thrive. Noting the central role of religion in fomenting freedom—in contrast to European practices, where prelates generally were on the side of autocracy—Johnson distinguishes between separation of church and state and manifestations of civic religion. At the outset, he announces his intent to grapple with three fundamental questions: First, has America atoned for dispossessing an indigenous people and employing slave labor? Second, has the nation successfully blended its altruistic ideals with its acquisitive economic system? Finally, does the United States deserve to be a model for the entire planet? His answer to these questions appears to be an unqualified, though unstated, yes. On the title page, he endorses the United States' acting upon its "Jupiter complex" as the world's lone remaining superpower by quoting from William Shakespeare's *Twelfth Night*: "Be not afraid of greatness." Johnson credits fellow countrymen Winston Churchill and Margaret Thatcher with helping Great Britain's former colony live up to its twentieth century mission, the former during World War II and at the outset of the Cold War (with his "Iron Curtain" speech in Fulton, Missouri), the latter during the 1990 Gulf War (the author credits Thatcher with persuading President George Bush to resist the Iraqi invasion of Kuwait and claims that had she not fallen from power, the war might have been prosecuted until Saddam Hussein was ousted).

In 1994, a national debate arose on how to teach American history after a panel of historians commissioned by the National Endowment for the Humanities (NEH) put out *National Standards for United States History*, which stressed a multicultural approach. The recommendations caused a furor among conservatives led by NEH director Lynne Cheney, who called the tone of the guidelines "grim and gloomy" and recommended a more celebratory approach. Right-wingers are no doubt pleased with *A History of the American People*. Johnson, the author of *Modern Times* (1985) and *A History of the Jews* (1987), a columnist for *The Spectator*, and a frequent contributor to *The Wall Street Journal*, is a throwback to the Victorian Age, when amateurs wrote grand, nationalistic histories. Anecdotal, unanalytical, opinionated, lucidly written, with provocative interpretations and meant for general readership, *A History of the American People* essentially is a succession of colorful sagas, history as pageant. The heroes, almost without exception, are bold men of action who served the interests of the country's business class (a typical judgment on George Washington's secretary of the treasury, Alexander Hamilton, is to rank him "alongside Washington himself, Franklin, Jefferson, Madison, and Adams as a member of the tiny elite who created the country") and who did not allow constitutional scruples to stand in their way, whether establishing the principle of judicial review (John Marshall), destroying the Cherokee Republic (Andrew Jackson), obtaining California and Texas (James K. Polk), preserving the Union (Abraham Lincoln), seizing the Panama Canal (Theodore Roosevelt), ending World War II (Harry S Truman), or opposing Nicaraguan revolutionaries (Ronald Reagan).

Johnson's story is divided into eight parts: "'A City on a Hill' (Colonial America, 1580-1750)"; "'That the Free Constitution Be Sacredly Maintained' (Revolutionary America, 1750-1815)"; "'A General Happy Mediocrity Prevails' (Democratic America, 1815-1850)"; "'The Almost Chosen People' (Civil War America, 1850-1870)"; "'Huddled Masses and Crosses of Gold' (Industrial America, 1870-1912)"; "'The First International Nation' (Melting-Pot America, 1912-1929)"; "'Nothing to Fear but Fear Itself' (Superpower America, 1929-1960)"; and "'We Will Pay Any Price, Bear Any Burden' (Problem-Solving, Problem-Creating America, 1960-1997)." While there is coherence to the first sections, the last chapters lose all semblance of objectivity, and the optimistic tone turns sour. In Johnson's opinion, the nightmarish 1960's produced a rancid effect on public policy and higher education felt to this day. A liberally biased media is blamed for allowing Fidel Castro to assume power in Cuba, for creating the "Myth of Camelot," for making protest fashionable, for preventing the successful prosecution of the Vietnam War, for creating the Watergate "hysteria," for abetting the collapse of family values, and for creating a therapeutic society devoid of ethical values.

> Normally circumspect men and women, who had once made a virtue of prudence, and were to resume responsible behavior in due course, did foolish things in those years. Such waves of folly recur periodically in history. The wise historian does not seek too assiduously to explain them. He merely notes that they occur, and have baleful consequences.

Not by accident are the likes of Frederick Douglass, Jane Addams, and César Chávez left out of *A History of the American People* (not to mention Elvis Presley,

Willie Mays, or Selena). Johnson basically thumbs his nose at contemporary American historical scholarship, claiming that it has been crippled by postmodernist theories and political correctness (on which his asides are incessant). He studiously avoids social history with the quip that students of popular culture would elevate comic books to a level with literary classics. One exception: Johnson passes along more information about the soft drink "cola wars" than about the labor-management strife of the 1870's or 1930's.

A History of the American People thus suffers from a strain of anti-intellectualism and reverse snobbery. For example, of poet Henry Wadsworth Longfellow, Johnson writes, "There were no sexual hang-ups in his life, no mysteries, no hidden, smoldering pits to be explored. So he has been largely ignored by 20th-century literary academics." Johnson bemoans the influence on U.S. public policy of two European leftists, English economist John Maynard Keynes, author of *The General Theory of Employment, Interest, and Money*(1936), and Swedish sociologist Gunnar Myrdal, author of *An American Dilemma* (1944). Thanks to them, deficit spending and intrusive social engineering became liberal orthodoxies. Myrdal's reasoning became part of the intellectual underpinning for the Supreme Court's landmark 1954 *Brown v. Board of Education* decision, which Johnson sees as a major step backward in race relations because it led, in his words, to "an enormous race-quota compliance bureaucracy." He repeats approvingly the following diary entry from Harry S Truman as he was about to start his Senate career:

> Some day we'll awake, have a reformation of the heart, teach our kids honor and kill a few sex psychologists, put boys in high school with *men* teachers (not cissies), close all the girls' finishing schools, shoot all the efficiency experts and become a nation of God's people once more.

There is apparently no room for pluralism in Johnson's lexicon of American virtues. Declaring his opposition to the concept of hyphenated Americans, he champions the myth of the American melting pot and offers virtually no information about ethnic identity, never mind those immigrants who sought to preserve their cultural roots. Native Americans (whom Johnson calls "Indians") are described as "improvident, unreliable, sometimes treacherous, vacillating, [and] above all lazy" because elderly women customarily did the farm chores. African American culture receives short shrift (in a discussion of ragtime music, he betrays his ignorance of its tempo), and the modern Civil Rights movement is seen as an unfortunate by-product of the crisis of authority so prevalent in the 1960's. Malcolm X is dismissed as a black racist, and Howard University is ridiculed for starting an ambitious African Studies program. Johnson includes no discussion of people of Mexican ancestry, and he virtually ignores American women except to rail against supposedly overbearing First Ladies and women's rights advocates. The only female leader afforded the mini-biography treatment is Anne Hutchinson, the Puritan lay preacher who, according to Johnson, deserved to be banished from Massachusetts Bay Colony for her antinomian heresies and whose husband is described as long-suffering (Hutchinson's nemesis, Governor John Winthrop, whom Johnson praises, was so convinced that she was a witch that he ordered exhumed a stillborn baby she had delivered). Concerning the Salem hysteria, Johnson concludes that residents recovered remarkably quickly, and the affair to his mind resembled the rash of false charges of Satanic practices leveled against child care professionals by sex psychologists in the 1980's.

Overrated as presidents, Johnson argues, are Thomas Jefferson, Woodrow Wilson, Franklin D. Roosevelt, John F. Kennedy, Lyndon B. Johnson, and Bill Clinton. He accepts controversial claims that Thomas Jefferson had a long liaison with mulatto servant Sally Hemmings, concludes on stronger evidence that Wilson had an affair in Bermuda with a "frisky widow," believes rumors of Roosevelt's dalliances with staffers, claims that Eleanor Roosevelt was bisexual, and believes that Arkansas state troopers acted as sexual procurers for then-governor Clinton. Richard M. Nixon is praised as an intelligent, farsighted family man whose use of the Watergate-era "plumbers" and obstruction of justice were offenses too trivial to warrant impeachment; Johnson also accuses Congress of having attempted to run the country in the aftermath of the "Putsch" that removed Nixon. He also attempts to salvage the reputation of President Calvin Coolidge, allegedly one of Ronald Reagan's favorites. While governor, both solidified their popularity with Republican faithful by condemning radicalism, Coolidge during the 1919 Boston Police Strike, Reagan during the 1960's campus unrest at the University of California at Berkeley. In Johnson's sunny synopsis of the Reagan years, there is no mention of the savings-and-loan scandal, and Reagan's colossal budget deficits are attributed to the president's intellectual denseness in understanding the reports of aide David Stockman rather than to political timidity.

Factual errors also intrude into Johnson's work. Consumption of alcohol did not rise during Prohibition; it declined. Herbert Hoover did not order the military to move against the Bonus Marchers at Anacostia Flats; General Douglas MacArthur did that on his own. Johnson confuses the Columbia and Colorado rivers and stumbles over such American organizations as the Joint (not Combined) Chiefs of Staff and the National Association (not Federation) of Manufacturers. More egregious are his obsolete *Gone with the Wind* interpretation of Reconstruction and his characterization of the Gilded Age as a time of upward mobility. Johnson is often sloppy on causation: Regarding the Spanish American War, he declares, "America drifted, or blundered—or perhaps strode—into its one imperialist adventure." Which was it? He ignores the war's bloody aftermath, the Filipino insurrection led by Emilio Aquinaldo, and the severe criticism U.S. tactics in suppressing the revolt engendered from such observers as Grover Cleveland, Mark Twain, Andrew Carnegie, and William Jennings Bryan.

One of the most controversial books of 1998, *A History of the American People* is must reading for those seeking to understand the conservative point of view in academia's culture wars. It is more opinionated but less insightful than *The Americans: The National Experience* (1965), Daniel Boorstin's sophisticated celebration of American inventiveness. Johnson, no stranger to controversy, seems to have gone out of his way to outrage leftist critics both by his omissions and by his parenthetical broadsides at feminists, multiculturalists, and postmodernists. Politically like-minded readers, though, will no doubt appreciate his felicitous style and chuckle at his asides.

James B. Lane

Sources for Further Study

Commentary. CV, April, 1998, p. 31.
Commonweal. CXXV, March 27, 1998, p. 22.
Forbes. CLXI, April 6, 1998, p. 28.
Foreign Affairs. LXXVII, July, 1998, p. 118.
Library Journal. CXXIII, February 15, 1998, p. 156.
National Review. L, March 9, 1998, p. 59.
The New York Times Book Review. CIII, March 1, 1998, p. 12.
Newsweek. CXXXI, March 2, 1998, p. 78.
Publishers Weekly. CCXLIV, December 22, 1997, p. 45.
The Times Literary Supplement. November 21, 1997, p. 3.

HONOR'S VOICE
The Transformation of Abraham Lincoln

Author: Douglas L. Wilson (1935-   )
Published: Alfred A. Knopf (New York). 303 pp. $30.00
Type of work: Biography
Time: 1831-1842
Locale: Illinois

An investigation of the formative years and rise to greatness of Abraham Lincoln

> *Principal personages:*
> ABRAHAM LINCOLN, the sixteenth president of the United States
> WILLIAM H. HERNDON, Lincoln's law partner and early biographer
> ANN RUTLEDGE, Lincoln's first love, who died in 1835
> JOSHUA SPEED, Lincoln's closest friend in Springfield, Illinois
> MARY TODD, Lincoln's wife

As Abraham Lincoln is by far the most-written about president in American history, there hardly seems room for yet another book about his life. Douglas Wilson's *Honor's Voice: The Transformation of Abraham Lincoln*, however, sheds new light on the relatively unknown period during which Lincoln made the remarkable transformation from backwoods surveyor and country lawyer to a national political figure.

The author reminds readers that the work is not a complete account Lincoln's life during the eleven years between the time he left home and his marriage to Mary Todd. Wilson has chosen instead to focus upon what he considers to be important themes and episodes of Lincoln's life that contributed to his success as a politician and a lawyer. Wilson explores Lincoln's attempts at self-education, his problems with women, and his transition from "country" to "town" as he moved into more sophisticated and cosmopolitan social circles. He is shown working as a storekeeper and mill operator, a skilled surveyor, a competent postmaster, and finally a self-taught country lawyer—vocations that served to enlarge his circle of acquaintances and hone his skills as he endeavored to become a successful local, and eventually national, political figure. Throughout the book, one can see, as the title states, the remarkable transformation of Lincoln's character during these critical years. Also visible is another side of the man—times when he loses his nerve and self-confidence, when he becomes despondent almost to the point of suicide. In addition, there is a rarely seen private side to Lincoln: his fondness for telling off-color stories, his explorations into sex, and his uncanny ability to "skin" an opponent as a stump speaker or in the newspapers.

Most of the popular traditional historical accounts of this period in Lincoln's life are plagued by evidence that is either missing, sketchy, or contradictory, making it difficult to reconstruct what really took place. Many are recollections recorded years after his death by those who knew Lincoln personally, long after he became a legendary figure. Historians are always suspicious of such evidence, subject to the fading of memory over time. Because of this, little Lincoln scholarship in the last fifty years has dealt with his early life. By a careful sifting of what he considered to be the most reliable evidence—the letters and interviews collected by Lincoln's law partner, William H. Herndon—Wilson reexamines this period in Lincoln's life. Herndon was nine years Lincoln's senior when the two became law partners in Springfield, Illinois, in 1844. From then until the time that Lincoln went to Washington as president in 1861, Herndon was his trusted confidant and closest friend. After Lincoln's assassination, Herndon was determined to preserve Lincoln's place in history, but instead of trying to elevate him to martyred sainthood as did many other biographers, Herndon sought to portray Lincoln as he really was. Part of the problem, however, was that information on Lincoln's first thirty years of life was exceedingly sparse; even in later years as president, he would give few details of his youth. All Herndon could do was to track down people still living after 1865 who knew Lincoln during his formative years. Herndon's collection of interviews and recollections remains the only remotely reliable source on this period of Lincoln's life.

Wilson's story begins in 1831, when Lincoln was in Decatur, Illinois, with his father. He signed on to build a flatboat and sail a cargo of goods down the Mississippi to New Orleans. Upon his return, he took a job in a general store in New Salem, Illinois.

The portrait that emerges of Lincoln at this stage of his life is one of a young man who is at times quite unsure of himself, who broods about his own death and frequently suffers from terrible bouts of depression, and who yet is determined to find a place for himself in the world, to leave his mark, to prove himself a great man. He was determined to test and prepare himself, both mentally and physically, to make something of his life.

One of the most interesting incidents in this regard was his encounter with Jack Armstrong, supposedly the toughest and strongest man in the area. Like all newcomers, Lincoln was challenged to a fight. Lincoln would not fight Armstrong, but he would wrestle; at least wrestling had rules. The encounter was really a test of strength more than anything else. Many biographers have considered the wrestling match to be a turning point in Lincoln's life. Wilson does not share this view, pointing out that the story came to light during the 1860 presidential campaign to help create part of the Lincoln "legend" of his humble beginnings and physical toughness. Wilson uses this incident to point out the pitfalls in making historical judgments based on incomplete or biased evidence. Although Wilson regards the incident as an effective story for the purposes of campaign rhetoric, he does not believe it deserves the significance bestowed upon it by other historians. In any case, Armstrong won the match (probably by using an illegal move); what made the incident important was that Lincoln had established his masculine credentials of physical strength, courage, and self-assurance.

One of the most intriguing aspects of Lincoln's personality emerged in his encounters with women. Although his skills as a speaker, businessman, and politician continued to improve, he seemed utterly incapable of forming comfortable relationships with those of the opposite sex. Although admired by many women for his intelligence, honesty, and wit as well as for his growing public reputation, as a suitor he was nervous and awkward. His first love was Ann Rutledge, the most eligible young woman in New Salem when Lincoln arrived there. By the time Lincoln came to know her, she was already engaged to another man. When her fiancé went East and did not return for two years, Lincoln courted her, and they became engaged in 1835. In August of that year, she became ill with what was probably typhus, and she died shortly thereafter. Lincoln took her death very hard. Some thought that he was on the verge of insanity or suicide. He was cared for by friends until, after a few weeks, he began to recover from the shock of her loss. Many believe that he never fully recovered, that because of Ann's death Lincoln became a generally sad and melancholy figure for the rest of his life.

Another of the most interesting sections of the book is Wilson's reconstruction of Lincoln's courtship of Mary Todd, which has often been characterized as a classic American love story but which in reality was far more complex. Lincoln first met Mary in Springfield in 1839 and was fascinated by her; she was intelligent and well spoken, and it was reported that he could sit and listen to her talk for hours. He found that they had much in common, and by 1840 they had become an "item" in Springfield. Most historians state that they were engaged in that year, but her own letters reveal that Lincoln had been charmed by an eighteen-year-old girl named Matilda Edwards and wanted to get out of their relationship. Mary told him that this was "dishonorable" and that he would be breaking a solemn vow if he did not marry her as he had promised. Lincoln sank into despondency, unable even to fulfill his duty as a state legislator for a week in January of 1841. Herndon claimed that the wedding was planned for New Year's Day of 1841 and that Lincoln failed to show up, but this story has long been discredited. Mary was willing to release him from his vows, she but wanted to win him back. Lincoln felt guilty that he had betrayed her trust and made her unhappy by breaking up the relationship. For the next two years, they maintained an uneasy friendship until suddenly, to the amazement of everyone, they reconciled and announced that they would quickly marry. It seems that Lincoln's conscience and sense of honor would not permit him to renege on his promise to marry Mary Todd.

Another revealing aspect of Lincoln's personality during this time involved his religious beliefs. As a young man, he was not religious, but those who knew him well said that he considered himself to be a freethinker on religious matters, and he eventually portrayed himself as being "unfortunate in his unbelief." It seems, Wilson says, that Lincoln was not an unbeliever in God but had serious doubts about many aspects of Christian doctrine, such as the resurrection.

The last part of the book deals with the "Honest Abe" myth. Although it is true that he was indeed an enormously honest man, Lincoln also did do some things that were not so honorable. Especially in the political arena, he was not above the use of ridicule, satire, and personal attacks on his opponents, and he was very much the crafty politician and opportunist when the situation required it. One of his favorite tactics was to write anonymous or pseudonymous letters to the local newspapers attacking his political opponents. In 1842, for example, Lincoln, who was by then a prominent member of the Whig Party, wrote a series of letters, purporting to have come from a place called the "Lost Township" and from the pen of a farm woman named "Rebecca," which satirized James Shields, the Democratic state auditor. Shields was furious at the personal attacks, and when it was revealed that Lincoln was the author of the letters, Shields challenged him to a duel. To retain his honor, Lincoln could not refuse, but before it was to take place, friends of both men intervened and persuaded Shields to accept a written apology from Lincoln. The incident taught Lincoln much about the art of politics. Although such written, anonymous newspaper attacks were a common political tactic of the time, Lincoln came to realize that it was not an honorable way to engage a political opponent. Interestingly, Mary Todd probably had a hand in writing at least one of the letters, an event that brought her and Lincoln closer together. More important, however, it taught Lincoln an important lesson about honor and fair play, traits he would rely upon when he ascended to the presidency.

Working largely from the thousands of pages of almost illegible manuscript pages and interview notes left behind by Herndon, Wilson and his colleagues have performed an invaluable service to the history profession. In addition, Wilson gives the reader a real feel for the problems encountered by the historian when compiling a biography, especially the weighing and evaluating of often contradictory evidence. This volume is part of a projected trilogy on Lincoln's formative years. Wilson has done a remarkable job in an area of Lincoln scholarship that was largely neglected by historians, and while not all may agree with his conclusions and historical judgments, he has set a high standard with this well-written and highly entertaining book.

Raymond Frey

Sources for Further Study

America's Civil War. XI, September, 1998, p. 90.
Booklist. XCIV, January 1, 1998, p. 773.
Library Journal. CXXIII, February 15, 1998, p. 158.
The New York Review of Books. XLV, March 26, 1998, p. 6.
The New York Times Book Review. CIII, February 15, 1998, p. 13.
The New Yorker. LXXIV, June 8, 1998, p. 89.
Publishers Weekly. CCXLIV, December 22, 1997, p. 48.
The Wall Street Journal. February 12, 1998, p. A20.

HOURMASTER

Author: Christophe Bataille (1972-   )
First published: Maître des heures, 1997, in France
Translated from the French by Richard Howard
Published: New Directions (New York). 108 pp. $17.95
Type of work: Novel
Time: The seventeenth century
Locale: An unnamed duchy in France

The story of an unlikely friendship between the bored duke of a decaying French port and his hourmaster, whom the duke employs to keep the clocks in his palace running

> *Principal characters:*
> DUKE GONZAGA, the ruler of the Realm, a single-city French duchy
>   located on the North Sea
> ARTURO, or GOG, the Polish hourmaster employed by Duke Gonzaga
> HELEN, Arturo's wife
> LODVOISKA, daughter of Arturo and Helen
> JERDAN AND GUISEPPE TASSINARI, hourmasters who are predecessors to
>   Arturo

When French novelist Christophe Bataille was twenty-one, he published his first novel, *Annam* (1993; English translation, 1996). Winner of the prestigious 1993 Prix du Premier Roman, *Annam* is a slim volume about the adventures of early French missionaries in late eighteenth century Vietnam. Bataille again turns back the clock in *Hourmaster*, an evocative, fablelike work that takes place in seventeenth century France. It is a fanciful story about the insidious encroachment of evil, the inexorable passage of time, and the disintegration of society.

Set in a North Sea port simply called the Realm, the story is told by an unnamed first-person narrator who had been the ambassador to the tiny duchy. A string of stark, bleak images mirrors the decay eating away at life in the Realm—the black, wind-eroded stone of the buildings; the dark alleyways; the overgrown paths; and the empty, slime-coated quays. The nightmarish, almost surreal atmosphere created by Bataille is reminiscent of Edgar Allan Poe's poem "City in the Sea." Neither the Realm nor Poe's city are centers of bustling commerce. Rather, they exist on the outer edges of civilization, liminal places wrapped in gloom. The narrator's brief description of the Realm captures the essence of its deterioration:

> To foreigners, the City seemed immense, dangerous. Since no ship inscribed its masts upon the sea, it was easy to get lost in the lower town. The sopping plain that encircled the Realm betokened the deceptive waters. Names of the alleyways had been lost or erased, and no one knew them. For essentials, people trusted to luck. Long since, the horizon had imposed its wavering rhythm, straight into the infinite. There was no point in trying.

The feeling of futility evoked by the city's landscape is reflected in the attitudes and activities of its citizens. Selfish, cruel, and decadent, the people are unconcerned about the garbage littering their streets, prostitutes openly soliciting customers, or smugglers offering illegal wares "under the benevolent gaze of the guards." Everybody is on the take, and no one cares.

At the heart of the city lies the ducal palace, the ancestral home of Duke Gonzaga. Although the furnishings and hangings are opulent, they are remnants of a faded glory. Cinnamon leaves are burned throughout the palace to cover the pervading odor of musty fabric and decaying woodwork. Amid this general entropy, Duke Gonzaga indifferently administers the affairs of his contentious people. Sick with boredom, he finds fleeting pleasure in deflowering prepubescent daughters of noble families. He seems more comfortable in the darkness than the light of day. Vampirelike, he feeds his senses with the sexual favors of his young mistresses. In the morning, "only their throats revealed the kisses they had received, the cries they had uttered."

Yet even Gonzaga's nocturnal adventures are not enough to hold his boredom at bay. The only events that seem to rouse him out of his lethargy are the mysterious disappearances of two hourmasters, caretakers of the palace's 218 clocks. The first is an old man named Jerdan. He performs his job for so long that he comes to regard the clocks as living things. He compiles a secret list, later discovered by Gonzaga, that records a name for each clock—names such as Dawn, Zoroaster, and Foritudo. Jerdan's successor, Guiseppe Tassinari, a young, foppish man, proves to be inept at his job. One night he is beaten by two attackers, and he disappears soon after he recovers. Because there is no one to wind the clocks, time itself seems to stop. The narrator notes that "the palace could not live without hours." The ticking of the clocks at least provides the Realm with the illusion of forward momentum and rhythm to life. When the clocks fall silent, the duke feels the insignificance of his life threatening to engulf him.

With the arrival of the new hourmaster, Arturo—also derisively called Gog—a change takes place in the duke. At first Arturo's lumbering form, coarse dress, and uncouth ways amuse Gonzaga. Stiff, regular, and mechanical, Arturo's personality and habits mirror the timepieces he tends. Yet the duke is impressed by something deeper driving his hourmaster: Arturo's unwavering sense of purpose and commitment to his duties. Lacking focus in his own life, Gonzaga is drawn to this mysterious man and begins to accompany him on his evening rounds. As he shares the all-night ritual of tending the clocks with Arturo, the duke feels the power of bringing order out of chaos through the simple action of winding the mechanical devices.

Attempting to control the uncontrollable proves to be a heady antidote to the disease of ennui affecting the duke. Ironically, Gonzaga is not bored but invigorated by the nightly routine, and a strange friendship develops between him and his hourmaster. Arturo brings an odd type of joy to Gonzaga's life—joy that is rooted in purpose and camaraderie. Arturo plays a bumbling Polish Percival to Gonzaga's dark Fisher King. Gonzaga's boredom and loneliness are intimately linked to the disintegration of his kingdom and the decadence of his people. When Gonzaga joins Arturo on his nightly rounds, Arturo's simple friendship begins to close the wound of Gonzaga's loneliness. The duke also stops sleeping with his young mistresses, a sordid practice that hurts the people he rules.

Gonzaga and Arturo become so close that when they wind the clocks, they act as one person: "Gog thrust a hollow key into the orifice and stepped aside. Then Gonzaga turned the key to the right, until the hourmaster made a gesture with his hand." Class distinctions, which govern the society of the Realm, are overturned in the master-disciple, teacher-student relationship that the duke and Arturo share. It is inconceivable to the noble families that a servant could become a friend. The friendship between Arturo and the duke is considered a minor scandal that becomes the subject of gossip among the courtiers and provides a diversion from the humdrum existence of their purposeless lives.

The bond between the duke and his hourmaster is severed when Arturo announces his impending marriage to Helen, a linen maid. The duke reacts to the news at first with pleasure and then with melancholy:

Do princes ever have friends? It is doubtful. Now that Gonzaga was in the habit of following his hourmaster, enjoying him in his idiot task, now that he had divined the secret order of the hours, his friend had denied him his time; he was marrying. What was the use of such entertainment, since everything vanishes? How was he to love those dawn hours, silent and shared, when another man's happiness would be celebrated? Arturo was happy; Gonzaga was alone.

Although Gonzaga feels abandoned by his friend, he gives Arturo and Helen a magnificent wedding reception. The duke's subjects remember the event as unusual since "no encounter was of note, no crime was committed." Because everyone is caught up in the gaiety, including Arturo and Helen, the clocks stop, and no one notices. It is a timeless moment of light and joy in the dark history of the city.

In succeeding years, Arturo and Helen live happily together, while the duke falls into his old habits. He sporadically accompanies Arturo as he carries out his duties but no longer finds joy in performing the repetitive tasks. With Gonzaga's growing hopelessness, the Realm continues on its downward spiral as it becomes more of a wasteland:

It grew ever colder. Fogs crept in from the ocean and rose into the interior. Certain plants vanished, such as the Bohemian onion. What the mind noted as absurd, nature seemed to prefer. Water took hold of everything and, contrary to the flood which bears alluvion, this inundation, wasted by the heavens, withdrew from earth its very strength, its essence.

In contrast to the further decay of the Realm, the rooms of Helen and Arturo are the brightest in the kingdom, and Arturo no longer lives in darkness:

Gog's existence changed. He had always lived shut in, sleeping by day in a cavern almost impossible to imagine, visiting by night the blue halls of the palace. With a certain grace, Helen transformed their apartments. . . . To enter these apartments was to be astonished by their brightness. Arturo came home to them filled with desires.

Although they remain friends, the duke envies his hourmaster's happiness. Helen and Arturo become parents of a daughter, Lodvoiska, who grows into a beautiful child. When Lodvoiska begins to enter puberty, however, she attracts the wandering eye of the duke. Without regard for his friendship with Arturo, he savagely rapes her. The next day, Lodvoiska's dead body is found on the beach. Consumed by grief, Arturo goes the way of the previous two hourmasters. He disappears, never to be heard from again.

Well received by the critics, *Hourmaster* has been described as a fable without a moral. Postmodernists would probably agree because the novel does not seem to emphasize any objective truth. However, the themes of *Hourmaster* mirror a modern rather than a postmodern sensibility. Bataille's work reflects the nothingness and emptiness of a dissolute society on the edge of extinction. The stark setting of the Realm and blighted images Bataille uses to underscore the corruption of life in the city are reminiscent of T. S. Eliot's poem "The Waste Land." Such images paint a profoundly pessimistic portrait of a culture in disarray. The despair stemming from the breakdown of a society often results in apathy and moral relativism. This is certainly the case with the duke. His disinterest in life and the purposelessness of his existence drive him to embrace decadence and evil. Arturo's simplicity and love almost save him—almost. However, Gonzaga cannot lift himself entirely out of the hopelessness that increasingly claims him.

The book invites comparison between late twentieth century culture and seventeenth century European society. Is it really a fable without a moral? That depends on one's point of view. It certainly seems as if Bataille is attempting to offer a grim moral lesson: that stagnation in society breeds evil, which in turn has a detrimental effect on individuals. There is hope, however. Sometimes good can overcome depravity, even temporarily. That moment in time is worth celebrating and remembering.

Pegge Bochynski

Sources for Further Study

Booklist. XCIV, March 15, 1998, p. 1200.
Kirkus Reviews. LXVI, March 15, 1998, p. 1200.
The New York Times Book Review. CIII, May 10, 1998, p. 18.
Publishers Weekly. CCXLV, March 2, 1998, p. 60.

THE HOUSE GUN

Author: Nadine Gordimer (1923-   )
Published: Farrar, Straus & Giroux (New York). 256 pp. $24.00
Type of work: Novel
Time: The present
Locale: South Africa

After their son kills a man, apparently in cold blood, Harald and Claudia Lingard are forced to re-examine their lives, their presuppositions and beliefs, and the manner in which they brought up their son

Principal characters:
CLAUDIA LINGARD, Duncan's mother, a socially conscious physician
HARALD LINGARD, Duncan's father, an insurance executive and devout Christian
DUNCAN LINGARD, a promising young architect
HAMILTON MOTSAMAI, a prominent black lawyer chosen to defend Duncan
CARL JESPERSEN, a Norwegian immigrant, the victim of the murder
NATALIE JAMES, Duncan's girlfriend

"This is not a detective story" says the narrator of Nadine Gordimer's latest novel. If by that she means that *The House Gun* is not a conventional "whodunit," she is correct, but in a deeper sense, the book is indeed a detective novel. The question, however, is not who committed the crime; readers know almost from the first page of the novel that Duncan Lingard shot and killed his roommate and former lover, Carl Jespersen. What readers do not know, and what Duncan's parents cannot comprehend, is how a young man of Duncan's upbringing and constitution could possibly have committed such a crime. Deepening the mystery is that Duncan did not act in a fit of rage when he found his girlfriend Natalie having sex with Carl, with whom he had once had a brief homosexual affair; rather, he waited twenty-four hours and then, apparently cooly, shot his friend through the head.

What unravels as the novel progresses is the circumstances that led Duncan to commit this terrible crime. As any parents would, the Lingards search their memories for any incidents or clues that could possibly explain how Duncan could commit the crime he has confessed. The only incident they can point to, and it seems of no help at all, is the suicide of one of Duncan's boarding-school classmates. Yet this leads nowhere. Rather, like sidekicks of Perry Mason, the Lingards can only watch as Hamilton Motsamai slowly uncovers aspects of Duncan's life that even they did not know. Also in good Perry Mason fashion, the most significant clues come out during the lawyer's cross-examination of Duncan's friends, especially Natalie.

What the Lingards learn is not that there is some monstrously dark side to their son's character. Natalie claims that Duncan was almost pathologically controlling, that after saving her from a suicide attempt, he tried to direct her life, as if by saving her he had made it his own. Natalie's charges, though, are exposed by Motsamai as essentially untrue: Duncan cared about her and, in spite of her infidelities, continued to love her.

The greatest shock they receive is to learn that Duncan had a brief homosexual affair with Jespersen. When he came upon the two of them, therefore, he discovered his former homosexual lover with his current heterosexual one. The shock and strain, Motsamai argues, tipped an otherwise decent, nonviolent young man over the edge. The problem with this explanation is that Duncan waited almost a full day before killing Jespersen. Does this not make his crime, as the prosecutor claims, one of cold premeditation?

Such revelations and conundrums are indeed the stuff of conventional detective novels, and Gordimer exploits these devices brilliantly, especially in taut scenes of courtroom drama. Yet ultimately, as she claims, this is not a detective novel because the central mystery is never really solved. Like the Lingards, and indeed like Motsamai himself, readers never fully understand what drove Duncan to murder Jespersen. In part, this is a function of the novel's point of view, which, while technically omniscient, seldom takes readers inside Duncan's mind. The brief periods during which Duncan does speak in his own voice are too brief or ambiguous to supply anything like an answer. The words of explanation he utters while on the witness stand—that he shot Jespersen in order to silence his babble—have only the ring of partial truth about them.

For much of the novel, readers see events through the eyes of the perplexed Lingards. Claudia, the atheistic humanist who works part-time in a clinic for the poor, can find nothing in her medical training to explain her son's behavior. Perhaps Gordimer made her a physician to emphasize that probing within the body, knowing the human being as a biological mechanism, leads to no wisdom about an individual's character and motives. That Claudia is also his mother only deepens the helplessness of her art in the face of this inexplicable act.

Duncan's father, by contrast, is an avid and serious reader as well as a devout Christian—yet he, too, is helpless to explain his son's action. Perhaps better than anyone else, he knows that one human being can never understand another; he also comprehends "original sin," or whatever one wants to call it, the dark side that allows even the most decent people to commit horrible crimes. Moreover, in his search of Duncan's room, he discovers a quotation from Fyodor Dostoevski that bears directly on Duncan's situation, yet he shares his discovery with no one, as if the special knowledge his reading has afforded him cannot be conveyed. There is another curious and perhaps telling literary allusion: "There was good sport at his making." The reference is to Gloucester in William Shakespeare's *King Lear*, who uses these words to explain his fondness for Edmund, his bastard son. Duncan, too, was conceived out of wedlock. Interestingly, Harald never pursues this literary angle, but he is similar to Gloucester in at least this one aspect—that he, too, was blind to his son's evil capabilities.

Yet another of the novel's compelling qualities is its consideration of society itself as the "cause" of Duncan's crime. Gordimer being the artist she is, she does not reduce this possibility to the simplicities of journalism or pop psychology, but without suggesting that Duncan is an automaton or innocent by reason of insanity, she does confront the influence a violent, racist society can have on anyone. The Lingards, however, are not like many of her other protagonists, active in antiapartheid movements, deeply political. They are politically informed but uninvolved—until Duncan's crime changes even the way they listen to the news and follow the deliberations of the court that hears arguments over whether South Africa's new constitution outlaws the death penalty. Legally, at least, this line of reasoning leads them nowhere. As a privileged white with an excellent education, a good job, and only a brief time of service in military training, Duncan can hardly be considered a victim of society's inequities. His act of murder cannot be construed as a product of social pressures, however defined.

Yet if "society" cannot be blamed for Duncan's inexplicable action, the question of race is never far from the surface in postapartheid South Africa. Hamilton Motsamai is the Lingard's best choice for a lawyer in part because he is black. Ironically, the whites are now dependent upon the blacks; roles are reversed, and the black man speaks for the white man. The whole complicated calculus of racial bias and antibias, including the new values assigned to skin color, provide an undercurrent of collective guilt and the consciousness of that guilt, throughout the novel and in the Lingards. This is not a novel about race—except that in modern South Africa, as in modern America, everything is about race.

A final possibility to the reason behind Duncan's act is suggested by the novel's title. The "house gun" refers to the pistol bought by the household of which Duncan is somewhat a part. (Duncan lives not in the house shared by Jespersen and the others but slightly apart, in a cottage in the garden.) The gun was purchased to provide protection against the ever-present possibility of crime. Usually, it was kept out of harm's way in a drawer, but for reasons no one can explain, it found its way to the table beside the couch on which Natalie and Carl were lying when Duncan found them there. It remained there the next day when Duncan, revisiting the house, again saw Jespersen on the couch. Thus it happened that Duncan was able to use the weapon to silence Jespersen.

Clearly, this gun is a symbol for the omnipresence of guns in South Africa. As in America, the gun has been used as the means of oppression as well as the means by which to fight oppression. With apartheid officially ended, however, the gun has not lost its appeal as the weapon of choice both for criminals and those who want to defend themselves against crime. Having a gun in the house is "normal." As so often happens, however, the gun ends up being used not to prevent a crime but to commit one. It literally backfires on its owners. Motsamai and others in the novel make the point repeatedly that Duncan would not or could not have committed the murder without the gun's being within easy reach. Does this, then, make the easy availability of the gun the "cause" of Duncan's crime?

Fortunately for the reader and for the artistic success of the novel, Gordimer does not use this easy answer to solve the mystery she has set. Yet the reader is left with the nagging feeling that the gun is somehow a necessary, if not a sufficient, cause. Yet what other factors were also necessary? How much a part does each play in the drama as a whole?

The fact that all these questions are not answered will frustrate some readers and satisfy others. One of the weaknesses of the conventional detective novel is that all such ambiguities are eventually resolved. Readers typically know the motive: revenge, greed, lust, anger—whatever. Yet no one in this novel and no reader confronting it can finally know why Duncan killed Jespersen. Readers are left with the deep mystery of human behavior, the inexplicability—the banality—of evil.

Dean Baldwin

Sources for Further Study

Artforum. XXXVI, March, 1998, p. S21.
Booklist. XCIV, October 15, 1997, p. 362.
Library Journal. CXXII, November 1, 1997, p. 115.
Los Angeles Times Book Review. January 18, 1998, p. 2.
The Nation. CCLXVI, March 2, 1998, p. 25.
The New York Review of Books. XLV, May 14, 1998, p. 42.
The New York Times Book Review. CIII, February 1, 1998, p. 10.
Partisan Review. LXV, Spring, 1998, p. 259.
Publishers Weekly. CCXLIV, October 20, 1997, p. 52.
The Washington Post Book World. XXVIII, February 8, 1998, p. 15.

HOW IT ALL BEGAN
The Prison Novel

Author: Nikolai Bukharin (1888-1938)
Published: Columbia University Press (New York). 345 pp. $27.50
First published: Vremenà, 1994, in Russia
Translated from the Russian, with a preface, by George Shriver
Edited, with introduction, notes, and a letter from Bukharin to his wife, Anna Larina, by Stephen
 F. Cohen; photographs from the Anna Larina Collection
Type of work: Novel
Time: The late nineteenth century
Locale: Russia

This closely autobiographical novel covers Nikolai Bukharin's first fifteen years and was written while he was in prison knowing he was to be executed

> *Principal characters:*
> NIKOLAI IVANOVICH PETROV (NIKOLAI BUKHARIN), commonly called
> KOLYA
> IVAN ANTONOVICH PETROV (IVAN GAVRILOVICH BUKHARIN), Kolya's
> father
> LYUBA IVANOVNA PETROVA (LYUBOV IVANOVNA BUKHARIN), Kolya's
> mother
> VLADIMIR IVANOVICH PETROV (VLADIMIR IVANOVICH BUKHARIN),
> Kolya's oldest brother, known as VOLODYA
> NIKOLAI MIKHAILOVICH YABLOCHKIN (NIKOLAI MIKHAILOVICH LUKIN),
> the son of Nikolai Bukharin's mother's sister; he became a leading
> Soviet historian
> MARYA MIKHAILOVNA YABLOCHKIN (MARYA MIKHAILOVNA LUKIN),
> Nikolai Lukin's sister, known as MANYA, who became Nikolai
> Bukharin's first wife

This beautifully evocative novel has an extraordinary genesis. Nikolai Bukharin was a leading Bolshevik with close ties to Vladimir Lenin; he fell into disfavor with Joseph Stalin and, after a notorious show trial, was executed in 1938. *How It All Began* was written along with three other manuscripts in Moscow's Lubyanka prison on odd scraps of paper and miraculously saved from oblivion. Bukharin wrote the following plea to Stalin from prison in 1937: "I wrote [the prison manuscripts] mostly at night, literally wrenching them from my heart. I fervently beg you not to let this work disappear. . . . Don't let this work perish. I repeat and emphasize: *This is completely apart from my personal fate.* Don't let it be lost! . . . *Have pity*! Not on me, *on the work!*"

Thanks to Mikhail Gorbachev, Bukharin was officially "rehabilitated" in 1988; in 1992, with the cooperation of Anna Larina, Bukharin's widow, the Princeton University historian Stephen F. Cohen procured photocopies of Bukharin's four prison manuscripts from the top-secret presidential archive. This superbly readable translation by George Shriver is one of the results of Cohen's efforts.

Bukharin provides no precise dates in his third-person narrative, but it clearly takes him from early childhood through about his fifteenth year, when it ends abruptly. Several themes emerge vividly: Bukharin's close relationship with his family; his lifelong passion for natural history, art, and literature (his favorite novel was *Huckleberry Finn*); his early contempt for the Church; his deep sympathy for the poor; and the awful depression and spiritual desolation he experienced at the deaths of his younger brother Andryusha and his brilliant but frail young friend Tosya (Anton Antonovich Slavyansky).

Kolya Petrov was born in the Zamoskvorechye district of Moscow in an "Academy" belonging to the Aleksandro-Mariinsky Zamoskvorechye Merchants Association. This was a quiet neighborhood where the churches were filled with merchants and self-important government officials (*chinovniks*) accompanied by their wives. Kolya's father, Ivan Antonovich (Vanya) Petrov, was a *raznochinets*—a member of the intelligentsia but not of noble birth—who taught mathematics at the Academy. His mother, Lyubov Ivanovna, was descended from Polish gentry on her mother's side and also taught at the Academy.

Kolya, the oldest of three brothers, was a precocious child who at the age of four could read, draw, and recite poetry from memory. The family were close and merry and spent their summers in a rented peasant hut in the country, an idyllic setting for Kolya to pursue his obsession with capturing everything that crawled or flew. Their lives changed drastically when Kolya's father lost his job after a petty dispute with his boss and neighbor, the irascible Mikhail Vasilyevich Yablochkin, husband of Kolya's mother's sister, and had to relocate to Byeltsy, Bessarabia (now Moldavia), as a tax assessor. Although life around Byeltsy was exciting for Kolya because of its wealth of animal life to investigate, the *chinovniks* and petty officials were viciously anti-Semitic, a prejudice that Kolya's generous father did not share; after a short tenure, he was fired for nothing more than his fair-mindedness.

With the loss of the tax assessor's position, the Petrovs began a difficult period of job searching and living with Ivan Antonovich's brothers, two of whom were doctors and the third an accountant. Living in the little village of Tesovo with his Uncle Misha, Kolya got to know the misery in his uncle's hospital. At the same time, he was shocked by the poverty of the peasants, one of whom sneered at him one day, "Agh, you fancy lords! Prob'ly eat meat every day." Kolya became very close to the blacksmith Stepan and his young son, Vasya, and first encountered real peasant squalor in their miserable hut, making him aware of the great gulf between the rich and the poor. This new social consciousness was strengthened by the grim conditions he and his family experienced when forced to live in the dingy apartment of his accountant uncle.

When his period of living with his Uncle Misha ended and the family had to lodge elsewhere, Kolya traveled with his father through small villages, where they came upon beggars and pilgrims of all sorts: "They moved along with slow, measured steps, lost in their thoughts, sunk in their cares and worries. There is something elemental in those monotonous movements, that steady step. As though they weren't walking but being drawn along, the way birds are drawn by some powerful ancient instincts, the secret call of nature, to fly across continents and oceans, taking their great long routes, and no one can hold them back. . . ." Occasionally, on their way they see the great estates set back from the road, "the grand old nests of the gentry," and Kolya thinks of how the parquet floors, the crystal and silver, were "soaked through with [the] blood and tears" of peasants such as his blacksmith friend Stepan and his son Vasya.

Not long after this journey with his father, Kolya is walking with his Uncle George, a warmhearted and worldly man, when they meet an elegant woman with whom George obviously enjoys considerable intimacy. The woman—Antonina Nikitichna—cajoles George into bringing Kolya with him to her house for supper. The evening is cultivated, with jokes about the young atheist Kolya being a "Voltairean" and with Frédéric Chopin nocturnes played on a Beckstein concert piano. Yet Kolya realizes that Antonina Nikitichna, "a typical landowner of bourgeois-progressive persuasion," owes her gracious life to the sweat of many workers—capital derived from labor—and not to her clever management; he knows that if ever the workers had "encroached" upon her possessions, she would have brought the law down fiercely upon them as an "unenlightened mob."

Other factors contributed to the growth of Kolya's democratic sympathies. The Boers' struggle against the British in South Africa became a popular cause in Russia because of the Tsar's desire to create as evil an image of the British as possible. Moreover, many of the Russian common people identified with the Boers as small farmers like themselves, and the press played up to this perception. Although the black people of South Africa seemed quite overlooked in the rush of warm feeling for the Boers, Kolya was not indifferent to racial injustice. When his school class went to the Zoological Garden to gawk at some blacks who had just arrived from Dahomey, Kolya became angry with his fellow pupils, calling them "a bunch of idiots" for their racist remarks. Although he had never seen black people before, he remembered Heinrich Heine's "Slave Ship," Harriet Beecher Stowe's *Uncle Tom's Cabin* (1851-1852), and the noble Jim who rafted down the Mississippi with Kolya's beloved Huck Finn. In all of the thoughtful child's musings upon social inequities, it is easy to see not only the youthful conscience of the Bolshevik revolutionary that Bukharin became but also the sympathy for the peasantry that led Bukharin to clash with Stalin over his policy of squeezing the peasants to finance the proletarian industrial effort.

When he entered the *gimnaziya*, Kolya was for the first time at school with bourgeois children of means, and Bukharin's account of these years provides amusing glimpses of high-spirited boys and their teachers. It was during this period of adolescence that Kolya's friend Tosya died suddenly of meningitis, and the youngest of the three brothers, Andryusha, died from a fall on the ice. In his depression, Kolya tried to hang himself, but his amateurish knot came undone and he survived. Yet there were good times as well in this period, especially a trip to the country with his art class and their eccentric teacher, who fed them rotten sturgeon and moldy pork rind.

Several digressions on politics and ideology create a different tone toward the end. Many students were inevitably drawn to participation in campus political organizations, and chapter 20 describes a "decisive confrontation" between Social Democrats and Socialist Revolutionaries. Although the arguments of these student activists are not always rigorous, it is easy to see in their intense debates a hotbed of future rebels against the status quo. In another chapter, Bukharin muses on the exhausted polemic between the Slavophiles and the Westernizers, as well as on the Narodniks' (Populists') romantic hopes for prosperity through cooperatives and communal land ownership among the peasants. Yet in the new century, the "factory whistles and industrial smokestacks" have changed everything. The aristocrats' cherry orchards are falling everywhere, the industrialists are growing fat, "black masses of factory workers" are looming up in the background, and "the new ideologists of the proletariat were mastering the gleaming weapons of Marxism, that highest product of the revolutionary side of Western European development." Meanwhile, "The feeble-minded tsar did not understand that he resembled, more than anything, a mouse crawling into a skillfully contrived mousetrap."

Bukharin's astonishing prison accomplishment is summarized by Cohen. The first of the manuscripts, completed in four weeks, was *Socialism and Its Culture*, a companion volume to *The Degradation of Culture and Fascism*, the manuscript of which was confiscated from Bukharin's apartment and never found. Cohen explains that *Socialism and Its Culture* "argued effusively for the 'humanist' potential of the Soviet system while pleading with the despot [Stalin] for its humanization, even a 'transition to democracy,' so that the nation could play its essential antifascist role." The second and third volumes were a collection of poems, *The Transformation of the World*, and a dialectical attack on Stalinism entitled *Philosophical Arabesques*.

Whatever value scholars eventually assign to these other volumes, *How It All Began* is indubitably a masterpiece in the old literary genre of the *Bildungsroman*. It has been enthusiastically received in Russia and universally praised for its vivid depiction of Russian society on the edge of great changes. Cohen identifies the novel's importance as an "authoritative firsthand account" of the state of mind of Russia's brightest young people, stressing that Bukharin wanted future readers to understand how they began to see the world "from the bottom up": "Bukharin's own story was to stand for all his boyhood contemporaries who soon would be swept into power by a revolution they so wanted and who, twenty years later, would be destroyed in its aftermath."

In the whole affecting account of Nikolai Bukharin and his story of Kolya Petrov, no detail is more piercing than Cohen's account of the old Bolshevik's last two days:

Immediately after sentencing Bukharin to death, Stalin demanded another humiliating ritual, a formal plea for mercy. Bukharin wrote two, on March 13 and 14, 1938, the first perfunctory but the second an elaborate profession of complete political and psychological repentance: "The former Bukharin has already died; he no longer lives on this earth. . . . Let a new, second Bukharin grow—let him even be called Petrov." Whether or not Stalin already knew the ruse, they were, of course, one and the same Kolya. He was shot the next night.

Frank Day

Sources for Further Study

Booklist. XCIV, May 15, 1998, p. 1587.
Choice. XXV, November, 1998, p. 529.
Library Journal. CXXIII, June 1, 1998, p. 132.
Los Angeles Times Book Review. June 7, 1998, p. 12.
The New York Times Book Review. CIII, June 14, 1998, p. 7.
Publishers Weekly. CCXLV, May 11, 1998, p. 58.
The Washington Post Book World. XXVIII, July 5, 1998, p. 9.

HULLABALOO IN THE GUAVA ORCHARD

Author: Kiran Desai (1971-   )
First published: 1998, in Great Britain
Published: Atlantic Monthly Press (New York). 209 pp. $22.00
Type of work: Novel
Time: Vaguely contemporary
Locale: Northern India

A fanciful and entertaining story of Indian life from first-time novelist Kiran Desai

> *Principal characters:*
> SAMPATH, a simple young man who yearns for peace and freedom
> KULFI, his mother
> MR. CHAWLA, his father

Once upon a time, in the West, Indian literature was represented by, or reduced to, a handful of sacred texts that exerted a profound influence on a rather select group of readers, most notably Henry David Thoreau. Thoreau's writings in turn influenced Mohandas K. Gandhi more than half a century later. In 1913 Rabindranath Tagore won the Nobel Prize for Literature, thanks in large part to the efforts of the Irish poet William Butler Yeats, who was drawn to Tagore's mysticism and his situation under British colonial rule.

Although India after independence was politically important to the West, literarily it was pretty much off the map. Its biggest names seemed its only names: the South Indian N. K. Narayan and the Trinidad-born, England-educated V. S. Naipaul. For all practical purposes, Indian literature was still represented in the West by the West, by Rudyard Kipling's *Kim* and E. M. Forster's *Passage to India*, by Paul Scott's *Raj Quartet* and the novels of Ruth Prawer Jhabala, and by Anita Desai and J. G. Farrell, whose *The Siege of Krishnapur* (1973) dealt with British colonialism in decidedly deprecating fashion. Then in 1980 came the publication of Salman Rushdie's award-winning novel *Midnight's Children*, which in a single stroke appeared to save British fiction from creeping provincialism and opened the way for a new generation of Indian writers, just as Rushdie's way had been prepared by Edward Said's highly influential, if controversial, study *Orientalism*, which treated the "East" as a Western textual and ideological construct.

After Rushdie came the deluge not only of Indian writers but also of Western interest in their work: Bharati Mukherjee (some of whose best fiction antedates Rushdie's success), Rohinton Mistry (twice nominated for the Booker), Vikram Seth (author of the enormously long novel *A Suitable Boy*), Amit Chaudhuri, and Chitra Banerjee Divakaruni. As the fiftieth anniversary of India's independence approached, Indian writing was showcased in special issues of *Granta* and *The New Yorker*, where works by Arundhati Roy and Kiran Desai debuted. The enormous critical and commercial success of Roy's *The God of Small Things* (1997), which beat out Seamus Deane's extraordinary *Reading in the Dark* for the Booker Prize and has had long runs on both hardcover and paperback best-seller lists, attests not only the novel's strengths but also its marketability. It cashed in, so to speak, on interest in India during the country's fiftieth year of independence and on its author's mediagenic sex appeal. On the heels of Roy's success comes Kiran Desai's *Hullabaloo in the Guava Orchard* and an advertising campaign that capitalizes on its author's exotic attractiveness in ways that Rushdie's and Mistry's publishers never have and never could.

The novel's dust jacket sports a suitably Indian-style "painting" on its front by John Martinez and, along with the familiar author photo, snippets of "advance praise" on the back. "Lush and intensely imagined," gushes Rushdie, "Welcome proof that India's encounter with the English language continues to give birth to new children, endowed with lavish gifts." "With this radiant novel," Divakaruni adds, "Kiran Desai parts the waters. *Hullabaloo in the Guava Orchard* evokes a bright, brilliant world, and the warmth and generosity of her writing makes for a joyous debut." And from Gita Mehta, the author of *River Sutra* (1993) and *Snakes and Ladders* (1997): "A hullabaloo of a debut from a vibrant, creative imagination." How well does Desai's novel live up to so much advance praise? Not well, although the failure may tell us less about this talented young author than it does about the hyperinflated cash value of Indian literature in English at a particular point in time.

Unlike Rushdie, whose fantastic narratives are rooted in real locales, Desai, trying to stake out a space (and style) for herself, creates a version of Narayan's Malgudi. Shahkot is a hazily defined yet perfectly realized town, or city, not far from the Himalayan foothills. It is bustling yet sleepy, orderly yet labyrinthine, filled with self-important people yet overlooked even by the relief planes dropping supplies during a drought so severe that the butcher becomes a vegetarian and daughters turn too dark to marry. In the midst of this drought is Kulfi, newly married and pregnant, with her enormous belly, expansive imagination, and insatiable hunger. Offered parathas, she expresses a preference for pheasants and pomegranates. (Her improbable name, incidentally, refers to an Indian ice cream—a joke presumably lost on most of Desai's non-Indian readers.) Because her son is born with a birthmark on his face and because his birth coincides with the arrival of the long overdue monsoon (and of a crate of supplies accidentally dropped from a plane that has become lost in the storm), he is given the name Sampath, "good fortune," and is said to be "destined for great things."

From the celebration of his birth—by candlelight, of course, because there has been a power failure—the novel leaps ahead twenty years. Now the age that Kulfi was when she married, Sampath embodies his mother's hunger for something more than traditional Indian life with middle-class respectability, but he does so in accordance with Karl Marx's well-known addition to the words of the philosopher Georg Wilhelm Friedrich Hegel that history indeed occurs twice, the first time as tragedy, the second as farce.

Sampath is farcical in part because he lacks his mother's manic imagination and energy, which is to say that he is also his father's son. Mr. Chawla, his father, is the head clerk in a local bank, an officious little man, "the head of a family and he liked it that way," or he would have liked it that way had it not been for his crazy wife and the shame of having a son like Sampath. Unlike his father, who takes pride in his drab existence in provincial Shahkot, Sampath is drawn to vivid colors and the faraway places he learns about at the post office, where he steams open and reads his neighbors' mail. At the wedding of his supervisor's daughter, he wanders into a bedroom, dresses up in women's clothing, and returns to the celebration to perform an impromptu striptease before the startled guests, which he ends by thrusting "his brown behind up into the air and wriggl[ing] it wildly in an ecstatic appreciation of the evening entertainment he had just provided."

At once pariah and prisoner, Sampath escapes Shahkot and ends up in a tree in a guava orchard where he hopes to "exchange his life for this luxury of stillness." Instead of stillness, this Chaplinesque little fellow, or Siddhartha as played by Buster Keaton, finds his father ordering him down while a mob of pilgrims mistake the knowledge of their private lives which he gained from perusing their mail for evidence of spiritual powers. Suddenly, the young man who was always too timid to speak becomes renowned for his sermons in the Guava Tree to an attentive, absurdly adoring audience. Unable to beat them (or his stubborn son), Mr. Chawla joins them, devoting himself to what Rushdie has called India's other religion, business.

Worthless before, Sampath now proves a highly marketable (though no more marriageable) commodity. Business booms—souvenirs are sold, kickbacks from transportation wallahs taken, improvements planned, and donation schemes arranged. Even the monkeys play their part. Leaving Shahkot, they take up residence alongside Sampath, where, because of their association with the Hindu monkey god Hanuman, seem to authenticate his supposedly spiritual nature. (Never mind that what draws the monkeys is the abundance of free food laid at his feet by his followers.) Unfortunately for all—all but author and reader, that is—the monkeys soon develop a taste for alcohol and begin to create a hullabaloo in the guava orchard. A debate on the best way to rid the orchard-turned-shrine of the monkeys ensues, creating a hullabaloo of its own that quickly spreads across the district and the entire nation.

Not surprisingly, Sampath yearns for something quite different. Longing to escape the orchard that has become for him just another Shahkot, he seeks what amounts to a comic variation on the Hindu theme of release from the endless cycle of death and rebirth. His sister Pinky, meanwhile, wonders how she and the ice cream vendor with whom she has fallen in love can live as happily ever after as the lovers do in the formulaic Hindi film she has recently seen. Then there is the novice spy from the Atheist Society who longs to make his mark by exposing Sampath as a fraud. Desai weaves these and a number of other plots together in the novel's hilariously complicated, obstacle-strewn conclusion, in which Sampath at least gets what he wants. Transformed into his favorite fruit, he is carried out of the guava orchard into the Himalayas by the faithful, hungry monkeys.

In this tale of the man who became a guava, Kiran Desai, daughter of the novelist Anita Desai, adopts the *faux-naïve* style of the literary folktale to create a novel in the form of a comic strip that for all the broad strokes bears a surprising resemblance to the amazingly detailed Indian paintings of the Mughal period. Desai combines studied naïveté, lighthearted satire, excess of a strangely abstract kind, cartoon-like distortion, deadpan delivery, numerous lists (both long and short), endless similes, and characters who are by design caricatures, walking eccentricities. Their two-dimensionality contributes significantly not only to the novel's cartoonishness but to the flatness of perspective that is characteristic of so much Indian art.

Desai's lengthy list of all that a prospective Hindu bride should and should not be is one of the novel's high points. Another is the grand finale, in which her juggling act grows steadily wilder and funnier. Overall, however, the novel unfolds a bit too leisurely—at times even tediously—so much so that the reader begins to wonder whether Desai really has enough material here for a novel, even a relatively short one. Worse, when the narrative momentum slackens, the reader, confronting Desai's writing head-on, begins to question whether her considerable talent amounts to anything more than a number of slightly annoying stylistic tics (those lists and similes in particular).

There is the question of "tradition and individual talent." Like it or not, *Hullabaloo in the Guava Orchard* exists in the shadow of the very work that made its publication possible. Part of the achievement of *Midnight's Children* is the way Rushdie was able to deal so successfully with what Harold Bloom has called the anxiety of influence, drawing extensively on the work of his predecessors—from the Indian epic the *Mahabharata* to Laurence Sterne's *Tristram Shandy*, Günter Grass's *The Tin Drum*, and Gabriel García Márquez's *One Hundred Years of Solitude*. However, Rushdie made the appropriated works seem entirely his own.

Desai is up to something similar, as her bow to Narayan's 1949 novel *Mr. Sampath* demonstrates, but the effect is rather different, less playfully parodistic, more youthfully derivative. Desai's magic realism makes the reader think wistfully of Garcia Marquez's; her monkeys remind one of Rushdie's; Sampath's specialness evokes memories of *Midnight's Children*, his situation Italo Calvino's *The Baron in the Trees*, and his sage advice the deadlier humor of Jerzy Kosinski's *Being There*.

In a sense, comparisons such as these, although certainly merited, are nonetheless unfair. They merely try to compensate for the overblown "advance praise" that is sure to arouse in prospective readers false expections about a novel that is, to use one of Desai's own lines, nothing less than "endearing in [its] naughtiness." Not just endearing; important too. *Hullabaloo in the Guava Orchard* is sure to help keep Western interest focused on the growing body of Indian writing and to offer, as a bonus, to an audience used to the far blander fare of Anglo-American realism, a spicy bit of fabulation from a young writer well worth watching.

Robert A. Morace

Sources for Further Study

The Atlantic. CCLXXXI, June, 1998, p. 113.
Booklist. XCIV, April 15, 1998, p. 1427.

Far Eastern Economic Review. CLXI, April 30, 1998, p. 56.
Library Journal. CXXIII, May 1, 1998, p. 136.
The New York Times Book Review. CIII, July 19, 1998, p. 12.
Publishers Weekly. CCXLV, January 12, 1998, p. 32.
The Spectator. CCLXXX, May 30, 1998, p. 34.
The Times Literary Supplement. May 15, 1998, p. 21.
The Wall Street Journal. May 1, 1998, p. W4.

I KNOW THIS MUCH IS TRUE

Author: Wally Lamb (1950-   )
Published: HarperCollins (New York). 901 pp. $27.50
Type of work: Novel
Time: The twentieth century
Locale: Three Rivers, Connecticut

Lamb's bulky second novel explores the troubled history of identical twin brothers, one a paranoid schizophrenic, the other emotionally shattered

Principal characters:
> DOMINICK BIRDSEY, a forty-year-old divorced housepainter
> THOMAS BIRDSEY, his schizophrenic twin
> CONNIE TEMPESTA BIRDSEY, their gentle, harelipped mother
> RAY BIRDSEY, Connie's husband and the twins' stepfather
> DESSA CONSTANTINE, Dominick's former wife
> JOY HANKS, Dominick's current girlfriend
> DR. RUBINA PATEL, the psychologist who counsels both Dominick and Thomas
> DOMENICO TEMPESTA, the twin brothers' Sicilian grandfather
> LEO BLOOD, Dominick's best friend and former brother-in-law
> RALPH DRINKWATER, the twin brothers' former classmate

Wally Lamb's first novel, *She's Come Undone* (1992), achieved popular success five years after its publication when television talk-show host Oprah Winfrey selected it for Oprah's Book Club. *I Know This Much Is True*, also a Winfrey choice, is more ambitious than its predecessor, although they share similarities. Both books are narrated by a protagonist who struggles with rage and rejection. Both feature psychotherapy as a significant plot device, and both are studded with references to television, popular culture, and current events.

Thomas and Dominick Birdsey are identical twins, but Thomas, always a timid child, has been schizophrenic, with accompanying paranoid delusions, since the age of twenty. On October 12, 1990, upset by the Gulf War that threatens to break out between the United States and Iraq, Thomas cuts off his right hand in the public library, believing God requires a sacrifice to avert further bloodshed. His sacrifice is interpreted as violence, and he is immediately sent to the state hospital for observation.

Dominick, the younger twin, is a former high school history teacher who, after the death of his baby daughter and a failed marriage, now paints houses. His urgent concern is to have Thomas transferred from a maximum-security building to a less threatening environment, and to this end he is aided by his brother's new social worker, a British-educated psychologist from India named Dr. Rubina Patel. In addition, Dominick's troubled boyhood, unresolved grief over the loss of his wife and child, and continued problems with his irresponsible girlfriend, Joy Hanks, complicate his life.

Through flashbacks, the reader learns that Thomas and Dominick were born to harelipped and unmarried Connie Tempesta a few months after the death of her autocratic father, Domenico Tempesta. Her father, a Sicilian immigrant for whom Dominick was named, once described his harelipped daughter as "that red-haired girl with the rabbit's face" too homely for any man to marry, but he is content enough to have her keep house and cook for him. Only Connie knows who fathered her twins, and she will not tell. She struggles as a single mother until she meets and marries Navy veteran Ray Birdsey, a pipefitter at the local shipyard. All of them soon learn to fear Ray, a short, violent man, although Connie tries to make peace even after he breaks her arm. Dominick quickly masters Ray's most important lesson: Never show weakness. Thomas, on the other hand, is bullied more often because he is hypersensitive, cries, and will not stand up for himself. While Connie remains a mild and loving presence in her sons' lives, she is essentially passive. She calls Thomas her bunny rabbit—fearful, soft, and affectionate like her; Dominick is her inquisitive little monkey.

When Connie develops breast cancer in 1986, she accepts "what God wants," but her husband and sons cannot. She shows Dominick the autobiography penned by his grandfather in his native Sicilian just before his death. Because she has never been able to read the manuscript, Dominick determines to have it translated for her before it is too late. Unfortunately, the translator he has hired disappears with the document, and Dominick can only give his mother his deathbed promise always to take care of Thomas.

At first the twins' relationship appears to be central, but the story actually belongs to Dominick. The real strength of the book lies in Lamb's complex portrait of this private man. He has been scarred by his stepfather's physical and emotional brutality, responsibility for his mother and increasingly erratic brother, and the divorce from Dessa Constantine, the woman he still loves. From Connie, who has absorbed the Sicilian code of silence (*omerta*) from her stern father, Dominick has learned to withdraw, to hold himself in check. Under rigid control except for his anger, Dominick nearly self-destructs. Emotionally, he is as frozen as his Italian grandmother, who drowned herself under the ice of a winter pond.

Still, Dominick does his best to extricate Thomas from the apparent indifference of the hospital administration. When Dr. Patel asks for his assistance with some personal background on Thomas, Dominick begins to meet with her regularly, describing his brother as "this abandoned building. No one's been home at Thomas's for years." Patel gently points out that "If no one is home, then someone is missing." She convinces Dominick that his intimate knowledge of Thomas will be the key to her ability to help him. In addition, she encourages Dominick to look back at 1969 and the first signs of his brother's illness, memories he has avoided. After he confesses that Thomas has been a weight on him all his life, Patel realizes that "there are *two* young men lost in the woods" and begins to counsel him as well.

In 1969 Thomas, Dominick, their friend Leo Blood, and Ralph Drinkwater, a former classmate and surviving twin, held summer jobs together on a city work crew. Dominick, who had roomed with Thomas at college the previous year, now regrets that he pushed Thomas away in favor of the others and that he decided to room with

Leo during the next term. He admits to Patel that he feels guilty that his brother is the one who is ill. His guilt continues to manifest itself in uneasy dreams. In one, he saves Ralph's life in Vietnam but allows Thomas to die; in another, he becomes a monkey in a tree and strangles his brother, then begs for forgiveness.

During that same summer Dominick met Dessa, a college student working as a waitress, and married her three years later. Dessa, who loved children, started a day-care center to aid women working at the shipyard. Both Dessa and Dominick desperately wanted children, but after several miscarriages they were forced to seek the aid of fertility specialists. Their only child died at three months of age; Dominick found her body stiff in the crib. Distraught, the parents could not talk about their grief. On what would have been his daughter's first birthday, Dominick underwent a vasectomy so that he could not be hurt again, but he neglected to discuss his decision with his wife, who wanted another child. Heartbroken, she decided to leave him. At present Dessa works in a hospital, where she comforts dying children.

The author takes a major risk with Dominick, who is initially an unsympathetic character with very limited insights. A nasty sarcasm has become both his weapon and his shield; otherwise he has shut down emotionally. His narrative voice is flat and mostly devoid of imagery until it becomes enriched by his increasing self-awareness.

Lamb's second risk is connected with plot structure. The present action takes place largely between 1990 and 1991, but flashbacks to the twins' early life occur in most alternate chapters. More than five hundred pages into the book, Domenico's missing personal history surfaces and is reprinted in full, introducing an almost entirely new set of characters. The resulting triple plot line slows the novel and is often confusing.

This is a book about secrets and silence, about questions that should be asked but are not. Grandfather Domenico, proud of his Sicilian traditions, cannot perceive the damaging effects of his family secrets until they ultimately spill out in his story. Connie's refusal to name the man who fathered her children becomes Dominick's destructive obsession. Even the twins keep important secrets from each other, and the explanation for Ray's cruelty to his family is withheld until the final chapters.

Three sets of twins and a number of parallels are featured here. The twins appear as mirror images: Patel tells Dominick he is his brother's mirror, his healthy self. Domenico's autobiography is "another hall of mirrors." Its dramatic function is to set up the parallels between grandfather and namesake so that Dominick can recognize this negative part of himself and reject his grandfather's behavior. Domenico is selfish, arrogant, and often brutal; his grandson Dominick is likewise proud and arrogant. A key difference between them is that Domenico is a man who *cannot* feel anything but rage and pride, while his grandson is a man who *chooses* not to feel. After forcing himself to read the translated manuscript, Dominick tears it up, warning himself not to repeat his ancestor's mistakes. He is able to change and become wiser than his grandfather.

Dominick's young lover Joy forms an interesting mirror image of his ex-wife Dessa. Joy, already twice divorced at twenty-three, works at a health club called Hardbodies with her best friend, a homosexual massage therapist, and refuses to deal with Thomas.

Unlike Dessa, Joy is devious and immature, with a propensity for shoplifting. When Dominick finds the remnants of her home pregnancy test, Joy admits that she is pregnant. She is not aware of his vasectomy, but he knows he cannot be the father. Joy too has her sick secrets.

The dual imagery is repeated as Dominick, who views himself and his brother as fatherless, discovers not one but two fathers. He recognizes that Ray, whom he has always seen as a harsh man, has softened after Connie's death. In fact, Ray has been planting flowers on the family graves for years. Dominick learns that his stepfather was devastated by the illness and subsequent death of Thomas, but most important, that Ray has always loved them both and is still trying to help him. Ray finally reveals the identity of the twins' biological father, the secret that Connie would never tell Dominick in order to protect him from himself.

An obvious symbol of the dualism that pervades this book is Patel's statue of the Hindu god Shiva the Destroyer and Reviver. Shiva destroys in order to make room for new creation; he both annihilates and heals. Another relevant symbol is the family home, a duplex that Domenico built eighty years ago to isolate himself and his wife. Ultimately the interior wall that separates the two apartments is demolished in order to form a shelter for battered women and their families. The reader who is so disposed can also have a fine time with a number of symbolic names. One of the most obvious is a priest named Father LaVie (Father Life), a survivor of cancer who presides at Connie's funeral service.

I Know This Much Is True belongs to the everything-but-the-kitchen-sink school of literature, containing a mixture of Hindu and Native American philosophy with an overlay of myth and fable. Lamb succumbs to the siren call of melodrama as he touches upon betrayal, distorted love, child pornography, homosexuality, rape, incest, bestiality, murder, and dismemberment. The list reminds one of William Faulkner's infamous list that formed the basis of his novel *Sanctuary* (1931).

The book sustains the reader's interest despite its nine hundred pages, even though Domenico's story is filled with unrelenting cruelty and could profit from judicious pruning. Regrettably, several characters seem to exist merely to reinforce a theme or symbol, and in the final pages all loose plot ends are perhaps too neatly tied. Yet even though the novel is flawed, its heart is in the right place.

This novel of recognition and reconciliation quickly gained a national audience when it was selected by Oprah Winfrey and the Book-of-the-Month Club, but its popularity may be explained in large part by its compassionate treatment of its subject matter: the close relationship of twins, survival of the death of a twin, and the heartache of living with a schizophrenic loved one. Lamb handles this material in a way that is accessible to most readers, adding a short bibliography of his sources. By bringing this discussion to light, he has certainly increased public awareness. He also adds insight into the overriding human hunger to communicate, to belong, to be loved.

Joanne McCarthy

Sources for Further Study

Booklist. XCIV, May 15, 1998, p. 1564.

Christianity Today. XLII, December 7, 1998, p. 70.

Library Journal. CXXIII, June 1, 1998, p. 152.

Los Angeles Times Book Review. July 12, 1998, p. 14.

The New York Times Book Review. CIII, June 14, 1998, p. 15.

Publishers Weekly. CCXLV, May 4, 1998, p. 204.

Time. CLI, June 15, 1998, p. 81.

The Writer. CXI, October, 1998, p. 15.

The Washington Post Book World. XXVIII, July 5, 1998, p. 1.

I MARRIED A COMMUNIST

Author: Philip Roth (1933-   )
Published: Houghton Mifflin (Boston). 323 pp. $26.00
Type of work: Novel
Time: The 1920's to the 1950's.
Locale: Newark, New Jersey; New York City; Chicago; and Connecticut

Zuckerman's ninety-year-old former English teacher narrates the tragic story of his brother, Ira, Nathan's boyhood idol, an idealistic Communist betrayed by his wife

> *Principal personages:*
> NATHAN ZUCKERMAN, a famous author
> MURRAY RINGOLD, his former high school English teacher
> IRA "IRON RINN" RINGOLD, Murray's tormented brother, a Communist
> EVE FRAME, Ira's wife, a fading actress
> SYLPHID, her daughter by her second marriage
> JOHNNY O'DAY, Ira's Communist mentor

Running into Murray Ringold, a ninety-year-old former high school teacher who first taught Nathan Zuckerman the importance of critical thinking and whose own vigorous style of classroom presentation was legendary, Zuckerman invites Ringold to visit at his secluded Connecticut home. Over the course of six nights, Murray narrates the story of his brother, Ira, to whom he had once introduced Nathan and who, as the famous radio personality "Iron Rinn," had become Nathan's early hero and mentor. Now long dead, Ira had led a colorful if tortured life from childhood on, often comforted and helped by his brother but often to no avail, for Ira's impetuous, "wild man" personality carried him into ever more troublesome relationships that he was by nature unable to resolve.

As G.I.s who worked as stevedores on the docks in Iran during World War II, Johnny O'Day first met Ira and introduced him to Communism, making him a lifelong adherent to the cause of helping the proletariat—the working class poor and down-trodden. After the war Ira lived with O'Day for a time in the Midwest, where he worked as a factory hand. During this time, his impersonation of Abraham Lincoln, whose tall build and large physique he resembled, gained him popularity. He was brought to New York, where he became a radio personality and starred in the radio show *The Free and the Brave.* Through his performances he more or less successfully attempted to promote his left-wing ideals. He then met and fell in love with Eve Frame, now also a radio star, although formerly she had been a Hollywood actress who had been famous during the heyday of silent films.

Eve had been married three times previously. Her first marriage, to a childhood sweetheart with whom she eloped from Brooklyn to go to Hollywood, ended when the studio arranged for her to marry Carlton Pennington, her leading man, notwith-standing that he was a closet homosexual. With him she had a daughter, Sylphid, and acquired her anti-Semitic attitudes and gentile characteristics, despite the fact that she herself, as Chava Fromkin, was born Jewish. After living essentially like a nun for twelve years, she divorced Pennington and married Jumbo Freedman, a Jewish entrepreneur who promised to make her rich, but did not. After that marriage ended, she found and married Ira. During all that time, she and her daughter spent summers in France so that Sylphid could be near her father.

Eve's slavish devotion to her daughter is largely responsible for the breakup up of her fourth marriage. The pivotal crisis arrives when, pregnant with Ira's child, which he badly wants her to have, she lets Sylphid browbeat her into getting an abortion. Serious problems trouble the marriage, including Ira's political ideals, which he loudly and forcefully proclaims no matter what the social occasion. For a brief period these ideals deeply influence Nathan Zuckerman who, when he meets O'Day during his freshman year at the University of Chicago, is almost ready to abandon his studies and follow O'Day's propagandizing and proselytizing.

Ira's marriage to Eve protects him, some believe, from the Red-baiting of the early 1950's engaged in by Senator Joseph McCarthy and some of Eve's friends, such as Katrina Van Tassell and her husband, Bryden Grant, a notorious gossip columnist. When Ira finally leaves Eve for good, she betrays him by writing *I Married a Communist*, which was actually ghostwritten by the Grants, thus ruining his career. After a terrible breakdown, he ends his days in Zinc Town, New Jersey, where he had once worked as a miner in the quarry, living an idyllic and secluded life with one of the few friends remaining loyal to him, the old miner Tommy Minarek. The mine long since abandoned, Tommy sells rocks to tourists who visit the quarry. He teaches Ira all about minerals so that when Tommy dies Ira takes over the small-time operation in his place and lives there until his own death.

Ira's Communism affects those around him. During the Communist witch-hunt of the 1950's, Ira's brother Murray is fired from his teaching position and only later restored to it (with back pay) after he wins a lawsuit against the school board. Because of his association with Ira, Nathan loses a Fulbright scholarship to England, although Ira only learns of this many years later after a conversation with Murray. Ira eventually has his revenge against Eve when he gets his liberal journalism friends to go after her. As a result of the ensuing scandal, she dies a lonely, impoverished drunk in 1962, two years before Ira's death. She is even abandoned by Sylphid, now married and living in France, having inherited wealth from her father.

Throughout *I Married a Communist* the theme of betrayal plays a central role. Eve's betrayals of Ira—not only her exposé of his Communist activities, but also her abortion and her failures as a spouse—are only the most obvious ones the novel depicts. Through Zuckerman, Roth also questions Ira's betrayal of his ideals by being a famous radio celebrity, marrying Eve, and otherwise compromising what he believes in—certainly much as Johnny O'Day finally views his own career. By staying in Newark after the riots of the 1960's and the evident danger for whites living in the nearly all-black city, Murray believes he has betrayed his wife, Doris, who is killed in a mugging while returning from the hospital where she worked across the street from where they lived. Murray suggests that by his reclusiveness Nathan, too, may be betraying something important—his natural propensity for life, the liveliness that first made him attractive and interesting as a student. Self-betrayal is thus also brought into the matrix of ideas in the novel.

By reviving so vividly the professional and psychological holocaust brought about by the anti-Communist scare while showing the foolish and futile sacrifices committed by idealists like Ira Ringold, Philip Roth provides readers with another searching, at times profound, analysis of the American psyche, such as he did in his previous novel *American Pastoral*. His political satire, both amusing and biting, also serves as a warning against the extremes to which even the most well-motivated individuals may be led. In his portraits of Eve Frame and her daughter and of the effect of that relationship on Ira, Roth may also be responding to Claire Bloom's account of her marriage to Roth in her autobiography *Leaving a Doll's House*. Besides her own failed marriages and the many ups and downs of her career, Bloom recounts the friction that developed almost immediately between Roth and her daughter Anna who, like Sylphid, is a musician. However, as always in Roth's fiction it is advisable not to press the parallels too far.

Although Zuckerman insists that this is Ira's story, not his, much about Zuckerman's own life appears in the novel: his early years growing up in Newark as the older son of a middle-class Jewish family, his boyhood enthusiasms, his matriculation at the University of Chicago. While a freshman student at the university he meets Leo Glucksman, his composition teacher, who advocates the theory of art in the service of art and not as a weapon in the service of "the people" or anything else that smacks of propaganda or ulterior motives. Glucksman also introduces Nathan to classical music and philosophy—Ludwig van Beethoven and Søren Kierkegaard, for example. Although a homosexual, Glucksman makes no advances to Nathan. Once, however, after his meeting with Johnny O'Day, Nathan comes to Glucksman's room in the middle of the night to announce that he is leaving college to work with Johnny. Mistaking his motives and outraged when he discovers what they really are, Glucksman throws Nathan out even before the young man has a chance to consult him about his decision.

Whether writing about Ira Ringold, his surrogate Nathan Zuckerman, or Nathan's relationship with Murray Ringold, Roth is mainly doing what he says Zuckerman does: working to gain possession of history—that is, when he is not alternatively moved to lose contact with it altogether, sitting alone on his mountain-top retreat looking up at the night sky. That is how the novel ends—with Zuckerman contemplating all the characters in this narrative, now dead, turned figuratively into stars in the firmament, where error does not intrude and antagonism does not exist, entirely unlike their earthly existence.

Jay Halio

Sources for Further Study

Los Angeles Times Book Review. October 11, 1998, p. 2.
The Nation. CCLXVI, November 16, 1998, p. 26.

The New Republic. CCXIX, October 12, 1998, p. 38.
The New York Review of Books. XLV, November 5, 1998, p. 38.
The New York Times Book Review. CIII, October 11, 1998, p. 6.
Publishers Weekly. CCXLV, July 20, 1998, p. 204.
Time. CLII, October 12, 1998, p. 114.
The Times Literary Supplement. October 23, 1998, p. 23.
The Wall Street Journal. October 9, 1998, p. W8.
The Washington Post Book World. XXVIII, October 25, 1998, p. 5.

IDENTITY

Author: Milan Kundera (1929-   )
First published: L'Identité, 1997, in France
Translated from the French by Linda Asher
Published: HarperFlamingo (New York). 168 pp. $23.00
Type of work: Novel
Time: The present
Locale: Northern France, Paris, and London

A fablelike story that traces the inner solitude, anxiety, and self-doubt of a middle-aged French couple's love affair

Principal characters:
CHANTAL, a French advertising agent
JEAN-MARC, Chantal's live-in lover

Born in Brno, Czechoslovakia, but having lived and written since the 1970's in France, Milan Kundera is considered by many literary critics one of the finest modern practitioners of the art of the novel. Besides his two most recent novels, *Slowness* (1996) and *Identity* (1998), both written originally in French, Kundera is the author of several other works of fiction and nonfiction, including *The Unbearable Lightness of Being* (1984), the novel which won for him international acclaim and has since been translated (from his native Czech) into fifteen languages. Kundera's novels are often touted for their nontraditional narrative forms and their philosophical investigations into the public and private histories of the human character.

In *Identity* Kundera again concerns himself with the puzzle of the self and the imminent threat of its loss, a major theme throughout many of his previous fictions. The mystery of personality, or the ability to reconcile one's outer and inner "selves" into a coherent whole, becomes the central conflict for the novel's two main characters: Chantal, a middle-aged divorcée now working for a Paris advertising agency, and Jean-Marc, her slightly younger and less socially ambitious lover. These characters, who are given no surnames and few distinguishing or detailed physiological features by the author, serve as Kundera's medium for exploring the enigma of human "identity" in all its stripes: personal, psychological, social, professional.

Such contrasting versions of selfhood and its perplexities are first introduced in the context of the couple's brief absence from each another. Chantal, waiting for Jean-Marc to join her at a "hotel in a small town on the Normandy coast," is disturbed when she overhears two waitresses at an adjoining restaurant discuss the disappearance of people documented on a local television program called *Lost to Sight.* "She imagines losing Jean-Marc that way someday," in spite of the fact that she nurtures the obsessive, even paranoid, belief that we live in a society in which our every move is monitored, recorded, watched. This opposition between the individual's being and nothingness, it turns out, obsesses Jean-Marc as well. Arriving at the resort the next day and looking for Chantal on the beach, Jean-Marc mistakes her for another woman who is "old, ugly, pathetically other." Such instances of mistaken identity stand as recurring motifs for both characters and for the novelist's musings through them. Jean-Marc thinks, "does that mean that the difference between her [Chantal] and other women is so minute? How is it possible that he cannot distinguish the form of the being he loves most . . . ?"

Distinguishing past from present selves becomes as much a dilemma for Jean-Marc as it is for Chantal. For example, when he goes to visit "F.," a dying friend, he fails to recognize the earlier version of himself that his friend nostalgically recalls. Jean-Marc concludes (and again, such statements seem more the pithy epigrams of the author than the psychological turmoil of a full-fledged character), "this is the real and only reason for friendship: to provide a mirror so the other person can contemplate his image from the past, which . . . would long ago have disappeared."

Even Chantal's dead son from her previous marriage becomes merely the premise for her philosophical ruminations on selfhood. Now, because her child has died, she feels free to despise the world, whereas when he was alive, she felt apathetically joined to a collectivity—the family structure—that she could at least tolerate. Chantal's belief that she has "two faces," or two separate selves often warring against each other, is not unlike Jean-Marc's conviction that he possesses an "alter ego"—that of a marginal person that clashes with his role as lover/part of a couple.

This alter ego takes concrete form when he begins sending anonymous love letters to Chantal, who has come to believe that "men don't turn to look at me anymore." However, if Jean-Marc in his role as "Cyrano" is only trying to flatter his lover and convince her of her continuing desirability to other men, Chantal interprets his action in a quite different and opposite manner. After two wrong guesses as to the letter writer's identity, Chantal finally deduces the source but then only sees Jean-Marc's subterfuge as a cruel hoax meant to "trap her" and reduce her life to a "single possibility": the life and love of Jean-Marc alone. Again, the issue of misunderstanding, misinterpretation, or miscommunication surfaces as the fixed idea of their relationship and of the novel in general. As Jean-Marc finally admits, "[H]e does not understand her . . . she hasn't understood anything either. Their ideas have gone in different directions, and it seems to him they will never converge again."

Another binary opposition Kundera employs in *Identity* to chart his characters' fear of their dissolution of self-identity is that of dream versus reality. Early on, Chantal has a disturbing dream about her former husband and sister-in-law making erotic passes at her; she wakes and is troubled by "the dream's effect of nullifying the present," the way in which "it has obliterated a whole chunk of her life." Likewise, a few chapters later Jean-Marc has a dream of chasing after Chantal, but when he catches up with her, he "is transfixed by the different face before him, an alien and disagreeable face." Still, he recognizes that "it is Chantal . . . but his Chantal with a stranger's face," a "transformed face" that has lost its original features. For Jean-Marc, then, the previous "real" instance of mistaking his lover's identity on the Normandy beach is being played out or repeated again in his subconscious state. Even for Chantal, the fine line between the real and the hallucinatory, her consciously acting versus dreaming selves, begins to become horribly blurred. Neither state provides Chantal and

Jean-Marc with answers to the endemic uncertainties of their personalities; for Chantal, the more lush her imaginative or fantasy states become, the less secure she seems about possessing any traditional markings of self-identity.

The novel's concluding chapters, following the couple's misunderstanding over the love letters, suggest that we have entered a realm of complete fantasy or hallucination. Chantal has left Jean-Marc and gone to London, but once there she gets trapped in a bizarre orgy, thinks she may in fact be dead, and then confronts a nameless, septuagenarian sensualist who addresses her as "Anne" and seems to be attempting to seal her in his mansion. Jean-Marc has trailed after her and, after being denied entry to the house of orgies, finds himself alone in the streets of London and finally in possession of "his true self": "I really am who I am, a marginal person, homeless, a bum." Sitting naked before the inquisitive old man, Chantal too, called by a name not her own, feels that the "they" of her paranoid imagination "keep on stripping her! Stripping her of her self! Stripping her of her destiny!" as if she has been transformed, ultimately, into one of those "disappeared" or "lost to sight" of the waitresses' conversation at the start of the novel.

Both characters' sense of the self cast completely adrift is somewhat undercut, in the penultimate chapter, by Kundera's suggestion that some, if not all, of the preceding narrative was a dream. Jean-Marc calls out his lover's name, tells her to "Wake up! It's not real," which leads into the novelist's self-reflexive commentary on the nature of fact versus fiction:

> And I ask myself: who was dreaming? Who dreamed this story? Who imagined it? She? He? Both of them? Each one for the other? And starting when did their real life change into this treacherous fantasy? . . . At what exact moment did the real turn into the unreal, reality into reverie? Where was the border? Where is the border?

The end of the novel has the two lovers thus back together again, gazing at each other, reassuring themselves about their mutual presence. Following the recurrent metaphors for sight and vision throughout the rest of the story, Kundera concludes *Identity* with the (by now) rather glib notion that when one's "gaze" is lost, the "other"—lover or friend—ceases to exist, that only by keeping the other in constant sight can that person's "identity," in any sense of the word, be ascertained.

Given Chantal's psychological complex of problems—her obsessions, phobias, insecurities, and anxieties—which muddle her perceptions of self and others, Kundera's ending confuses more than resolves the questions of his characters' identity or sense of well-being. Both Chantal and Jean-Marc's contradictory feelings and repeated miscommunications leave them in a condition of inner solitude, in which they cannot reveal their humanity, much less any true expression of love, to each other. Perhaps, finally, this edgy "novel of ideas" turns on this notion of the characters' lack of depth or dearth of emotions.

Caught in the conundrum of trying to decipher their separate, individual personalities, Chantal and Jean-Marc lose, ironically, both their sense of self-identity and their connection to any larger communality or community. Their relationship fails, or at best only tenuously holds together, because they have shaped themselves into a purely subjective "identity" that is unrecognizable to the other and unmanageable to the self. Paradoxically, however, it is each character's shameful objectification of the other that also strains the relationship and threatens it with dissolution. Hence, the lovers' perceptions of each other seem at constant cross-purposes, their differing and warring ideas of subjective and objective "identity" arresting them in a state of psychic unrest or limbo.

Identity trades in many of the philosophical and stylistic traits that typified Kundera's earlier, major works, such as *Life Is Elsewhere* (1974), *The Book of Laughter and Forgetting* (1980), and *The Unbearable Lightness of Being* (1984). The self-consciously pared-down narrative technique, the subordination of traditional novelistic devices such as plot and characterization to issues of form and structure, and the detailing of metaphysical oppositions whose connotations keep changing and collapsing in on themselves all mark *Identity* as a quintessential example of this postmodern storyteller's art. Moreover, the novel raises those existential questions about love and death, being and nothingness, that have become the thematic calling cards of Kundera's work. Upon its publication *Identity* received rather mixed reviews. Some praised it for its technical virtuosity and self-reflexive commentary, while others criticized its somewhat cliché-ridden, epigrammatic style and lack of discernable fictional devices, such as "round" characters, plot, and denouement. (Some of these latter critics believe that Kundera's use of French for this novel, instead of his native Czech, may be the cause of such gaffes.) Despite this reception, *Identity* is notable for the author's insight into the interplay between the individual's preoccupations and the social, public self, and for his continuing uncanny ability to employ foreground elements of form and theory as a means of addressing some of the universal dilemmas of the contemporary human condition.

David Buehrer

Sources for Further Study

Library Journal. CXXIII, March 15, 1998, p. 93.
Los Angeles Times Book Review. June 28, 1998, p. 4.
The Nation. CLXVI, May 11, 1998, p. 54.
The New Leader. LXXXI, June 29, 1998, p. 29.
The New York Review of Books. XLV, July 16, 1998, p. 31.
The New York Times Book Review. CIII, May 17, 1998, p. 11.
Newsweek. CXXXI, May 4, 1998, p. 82.
Publishers Weekly. CCXLV, February 16, 1998, p. 200.
Review of Contemporary Fiction. XVIII, Fall, 1998, p. 239.
The Washington Post Book World. XXVIII, May 31, 1998, p. 1.

INFORMATION AGES
Literacy, Numeracy, and the Computer Revolution

Authors: Michael E. Hobart (1944-   ) and Zachary S. Schiffman
Published: Johns Hopkins University Press (Baltimore). 301 pp. $29.95
Type of work: History of science; technology
Time: 3000 B.C. to the present
Locale: Western Europe, the Middle East, and Asia

The current information age is seen as only the latest in a series of such ages that have been evolving since ancient times

Because of the growing impact of computers in general and the Internet in particular on all aspects of daily life, ours has been termed the "Information Age" by many. Was this an overnight development or the result of a series of stages that grew out of one another? In *Information Ages: Literacy, Numeracy, and the Computer Revolution*, Michael E. Hobart and Zachary S. Schiffman, professors of history at Bryant College and Northeastern Illinois University, respectively, argue that civilization has experienced a series of interrelated information ages from the birth of the alphabet to the present, with the development of writing, literacy, printing, mathematics, and science all leading to the creation of the computer.

What they call "our historical essay" is a blending of analyses of history, science, mathematics, anthropology, literature, philosophy, and technology. Their multidisciplinary approach works reasonably well, since the concept of information is central to so many fields. Exactly what information consists of, however, is another matter. Hobart and Schiffman cheat a bit by claiming information, "the dominant metaphor of our age," is too elusive and mercurial a concept to define. Their goal is to place the term in a historical context.

In tracing the evolution of information, Hobart and Schiffman expand beyond developments in Europe but admit they have omitted such key topics as how writing came to exist in China. Their justification is their need to keep the scope of their investigation manageable, but this admission that they "have left important topics unexplored" may lead the general educated reader they have identified as their audience to question the final validity of this history. Is this approach perhaps too scattershot? Is it possible to prove definite links between all the information ages they outline?

Hobart and Schiffman begin with *The Iliad* and *The Odyssey* to demonstrate how the oral literary tradition has been seen as a means of transmitting information. According to classicist Eric A. Havelock, Homer's epic poems preserve such essential information as how to launch and land a ship. Without writing, these encyclopedic poems formed the basis of education in pre-Socratic Greece. Hobart and Schiffman disagree with Havelock, however, by arguing that Homer's works are more abstract than Havelock acknowledges, that they are acts of commemoration rather than vessels of information storage. They even deny that information existed in the oral world.

While the intention of Homer and those who passed down his work may have been to commemorate the glorious past, his epics still contain information as a by-product, even if it is not as stable as that communicated in literate cultures. Hobart and Schiffman trace the evolution of pictographic, syllabic, and alphabetic writing in several cultures and times, designating the development of writing in ancient Mesopotamia as "the birth of information." Writing creates information by "giving mental objects a sustained existence apart from the flux of the oral world—apart from evanescent speech, apart from practice, apart from ritualized communication and its maps—writing gives these objects a stability they cannot otherwise have."

Other key contributions of writing are the concepts of record-keeping and classification. Hobart and Schiffman explore how the pressure of accounting needs in Mesopotamia caused tokens and emblems to be superseded by an alphabet, since matters such as sixty sheep were more easily expressed in words than in symbols. Writing made it easier to keep track of a wider range and growing number of goods in an economy centered around trade. Using language to classify thus translated physical objects into mental objects and created information storage. Mesopotamians carried the urge to classify further by making extensive lists of these new mental objects: "Beginning as a pedagogical device for teaching Akkadian scribes how to write and pronounce Sumerian words, the activity of list making transformed itself into a topical compendium of all received knowledge."

Such developments as accounting, classifying, and list making were significant steps toward the computer age because they served similar functions as today's personal computer. In addition to making communication easier, they had the liberating effects of encouraging intellectual activity and of imposing order on an increasingly complex world. In classifying and making lists, the Mesopotamians were forced to develop critical skills unnecessary in the oral world. *Information Ages* itself is a list of intellectual breakthroughs, but Hobart and Schiffman do not always make clear if the developments in different cultures directly affected one another. If their goal is to demonstrate how these matters resulted in the computer revolution of their subtitle, they should have drawn many more parallels between contemporary and earlier concepts of information. They do not always show the links between the items in their list. The section about the Mesopotamians is followed by one about the invention of the Greek alphabet, with no mention of any connection beyond similarities of Hesiod's genealogies to the earlier list making.

Information Ages is notable for going beyond the obvious in exploring the earlier information ages. For example, Hobart and Schiffman devote considerable space to philosophers, arguing that philosophy grew out of classifying. They explain how "Aristotle's philosophy stands as the culmination of the first information age, for it seeks to define and systematize the mental objects that had been wrought by literacy." According to Hobart and Schiffman, information is created when "intuitive extracts" are transformed into concepts, the very procedure with which Aristotle was concerned.

The invention of printing in the fifteenth century created the information age most comparable to the current one because of its revolutionary effect on all aspects of life, overloading the literate public with information of a diverse and contradictory nature previously unknown; the authors assert that "modernity itself began to take shape as recent scientific theories, religious doctrines, and geographical discoveries quickly found their way into print." The account of medieval book production that preceded printing and the subsequent changes in book formats in the sixteenth century (and the creation of such features as tables of contents, indexes, and bibliographies) is a highlight of *Information Ages*, one of the best instances of how developments in one age led to further developments in another. Hobart and Schiffman are good at outlining the specific effects of the printing explosion such as the renewed interest in list making, "a symptom of intellectual dislocation" caused by the sixteenth century citizens' having too much on their minds.

One of the underlying themes of *Information Ages* is how the humanities and sciences come together to create information. At the center of this theme is the portrait of René Descartes: "Although his philosophy was not specifically mathematical, Descartes would lay the foundation for an analytical vision of knowledge based upon mathematics, in which symbolic language would supplant natural language as the most effective means for organizing and managing information." Hobart and Schiffman praise Descartes for his insight in seeing the need "to create a core of knowledge more useful than that of the humanists." They explain how Descartes's ideas and other mathematical theories of the seventeenth century "made it possible to articulate, store, manipulate, and transmit exact information about phenomena by means of completely abstract symbols," paving the way for modern mathematics and the computer.

Mathematics is central to the long evolution toward the computer, and Hobart and Schiffman argue that universal mathematics is the foundation of all knowledge. By breaking things down into their constituent parts, translating these parts into abstract symbols, and plugging these symbols into formulas, mathematics enabled "humankind to identify new sorts of information, to discern true from false information, and to manage information in ever-increasing quantities." Among the significant steps in this process was the *Encyclopedia* (1751-1772) edited by Denis Diderot and Jean le Rond d'Alembert, which was "the first major attempt to create an entire compilation and organization of knowledge based on the abstractions of modern numeracy" and "the culminating moment in the rise of the modern information age."

The most interesting sections of *Information Ages* are not the theoretical ones but the accounts of the ideas of such thinkers as Descartes, Diderot, and d'Alembert. These portraits become even more vivid with the mathematicians whose ideas had a more direct bearing on the movement toward the computer: Charles Babbage, Sir William Rowan Hamilton, Joseph Louis Lagrange, Pierre-Simon Laplace, Augustus de Morgan, George Boole, John von Neumann, and Alan Turing. Babbage envisioned the first modern computer and devised a punch-card system. Hamilton, Lagrange, and Laplace extended d'Alembert's concept of mathematical mapping, which permits storage of massive amounts of information. De Morgan assigned symbols to mathematical relations. Von Neumann and Turing linked logical operations to electronic circuitry.

If *Information Ages* can be said to have a hero, however, it is Boole, the main transitional figure between the earlier information ages and the contemporary one. With *An Investigation of the Laws of Thought* (1854), Boole created a new logic expressed in symbols. Boolean logic begins not with words or things but with abstract symbols, and it "launched the transformation of natural language syntax into a flexible, rule-governed instrument for describing the world with precision." Boole's ideas led to more sophisticated techniques of quantification, becoming "the driving conceptual force behind the modern computer."

Hobart and Schiffman praise Turing's idea of a general-purpose computer because the latest information age centers around easy access to all types of information for anyone, not merely for mathematicians, scientists, or other intellectuals. That both Turing and von Neumann insisted upon computer hardware that was reasonably simple helped lead to this democratic revolution. Hobart and Schiffman end their history with an analysis of theories of play, since the idea of play is crucial to the diverse ways computer users seek and manipulate information.

Nothing in *Information Ages* will be new to specialists in any of the fields the book encompasses, but its point is to bring together diverse ideas from numerous disciplines so that its readers will be able to see how the concept of information has changed over the centuries and how seemingly unrelated developments have resulted in a revolution that has had a profound influence on their lives. While Hobart and Schiffman do not always make the connections between all the stages in their history as clear as possible, they have avoided most of the pitfalls of such a far-ranging study, being neither too general nor too technical, though some of their explanations of mathematical principles might have been simplified a bit further for readers with backgrounds in the humanities. They bring everything effectively together at the end by showing clearly how these centuries of developments have created this handy information device. They are particularly good at explaining how digital computers are superior to their analog ancestors and how information is transferred within the components of a computer. Never condescending, this history is almost a model for interdisciplinary studies attempting to unite the sciences and humanities. The sixteen-page bibliographical essay provides guidance for further explorations of this fascinating subject.

Michael Adams

Source for Further Study

Publishers Weekly. CCXLV, September 28, 1998, p. 945.

AN INSTANCE OF THE FINGERPOST

Author: Iain Pears (1955-   )
Published: Riverhead Books (New York). 694 pp. $27.00
Type of work: Novel
Time: The 1660's
Locale: England

A murder mystery set amid the complex political machinations of England's Restoration period and featuring several historical figures among its characters

> *Principal characters:*
> MARCO DA COLA, a Venetian scholar and traveler
> SARAH BLUNDY, a young servant girl, daughter of political radicals
> JACK PRESCOTT, an Oxford University student whose father was accused of treason
> JOHN WALLIS, an Oxford mathematician, a founder of the Royal Society, and cryptographer to both Oliver Cromwell and Charles II
> ANTHONY WOOD, a historian and diarist
> RICHARD LOWER, a physician, a founder of the Royal Society
> ROBERT GROVE, an Oxford Fellow and theologian

With *An Instance of the Fingerpost*, author Iain Pears enters literary territory previously explored by writers as diverse as Umberto Eco, Don DeLillo, and E. L. Doctorow: the historical novel that weaves actual events and individuals into its fictional story. It is in Eco's footsteps that Pears follows most closely. Like the acclaimed Italian author of *Il nomo della rosa* (*The Name of the Rose*, 1980), he has chosen the murder mystery as his genre and then used it as a means of examining subjects far beyond the ordinary mystery's scope. Pears's ostensible focus is the death of a garrulous Oxford Fellow, Robert Grove, but his true subject is England during the tumultuous period known as the Restoration.

After years of bloody civil war, the beheading of Charles I, and the strife-ridden Protectorate of Oliver Cromwell, the restoration of the monarchy under Charles II saw a flourishing of art, science, and philosophy. The strains of discord within English society ran deep, however, and long-held religious enmity continued to shape political policy. It is in this climate of change, unrest, and religious intolerance that Pears has set his story, and its conflicts and complexities provide the book with its dramatic substance.

At the center of Pears's story is the death by poisoning of Robert Grove. The person suspected of the crime is Sarah Blundy, a servant girl Grove had recently dismissed after rumors of suspected intimacy between the two began to circulate within the university. Grove had also refused to assist Sarah's badly injured mother, Anne, who is herself a religious reformer and the wife of a political radical. As information about Grove's final hours becomes known, a web of gossip and possible evidence begins to ensnare Sarah, and she is imprisoned. What emerges as layer upon layer is added to the complex tale is the young girl's extraordinary position as a touchstone for a number of sensitive political issues of the day.

In a technique used perhaps most famously by Japanese director Akira Kurosawa in his 1950 film *Rashomon*, Pears makes use of multiple narrators to tell his story. The book is divided into four sections, each of which relates the events surrounding Grove's murder from a different point of view. As each section unfolds, a new layer of information—and at times misinformation—is added, often throwing what has gone before into doubt. The first section, entitled "A Question of Precedence," introduces the Venetian scholar Marco da Cola, who informs the reader that in 1663 he traveled to England to investigate problems threatening his merchant father's business interests. It is through the outsider da Cola's eyes that readers first encounter the world of seventeenth century England and meet the individuals who will play a role in the novel. Written many years after the events he is describing, da Cola's manuscript serves as the catalyst for the sections that follow, as three of the story's key characters read his accounting and respond with versions of their own.

Da Cola is thrust into the center of the events in Oxford when he offers to treat Sarah Blundy's injured mother. A student of medicine with an interest in theories of blood circulation, he is soon befriended by Richard Lower, an Oxford doctor and actual historical figure who would later become the best-known physician of his day. Through Lower, da Cola also meets philosopher John Locke, architect Christopher Wren, and chemist Robert Boyle, three men whose ideas and discoveries helped shape the age in which they lived. In Lower's company, da Cola attends a performance of William Shakespeare's *King Lear*—which he dislikes—and takes part in several medical and scientific experiments, often performed on live animals, that seem barbaric by modern standards. His most notable experiment, however, is performed on Anne Blundy when he and Lower attempt to cure her with a transfusion of her daughter's blood.

One of the strengths of Pears's storytelling is his ability to capture not only the physical details of seventeenth century life but also the ideas and attitudes of the period as well. Through da Cola's discussions with Lower and his friends, the reader receives a picture of the exact state of medical knowledge in 1663—and the gaps in that knowledge that could be supplied today by anyone with even a rudimentary grasp of human physiology. As the men speak with assurance of the dangerous vapors that fresh air will bring to a sickroom or the vital spirits that blood transports to the mind, the reader is presented with a portrait of another time that feels accurate in far more than merely its surface details.

Da Cola's manuscript also introduces the book's other narrators: Jack Prescott, an Oxford student and the son of a lord disgraced by accusations of treason; John Wallis, a skilled mathematician and cryptographer who worked for both Cromwell and Charles II and who sees political conspiracies in everyday events; and Anthony Wood, a scholar and historian. Like Lower and his friends, both Wallis and Wood are historical figures, while Prescott is a fictional character based loosely on fact.

In Prescott's section, "The Great Trust," the reader learns of Jack's passionate belief in his father's innocence, and how this conviction and his efforts to clear his father's name lead him to actions that will influence Sarah Blundy's fate. While da Cola believes Sarah to be immoral and lacking in proper respect for her social betters,

Prescott believes her to be a witch bent on his destruction, only one of several factors pointing to the workings of an increasingly unbalanced mind. Jack's casual brutality to Sarah and the utter lack of a true moral center that his actions and comments unwittingly reveal make his narrative perhaps the novel's most disturbing section.

In John Wallis's account of events, entitled "The Character of Compliance," the reader begins to gain a fuller picture of the political intrigue that is in fact driving much of the story's action. Wallis casts doubt on da Cola's manuscript, insisting that the Catholic Venetian's visit to England was in reality part of a dangerous political plot against the newly restored Protestant monarchy. Sarah Blundy, he believes, also played a role in the plot, and the question of the girl's actual guilt or innocence in the matter of Grove's murder is of little interest to Wallis; it is her removal as a political threat that drives his actions. As Wallis's story adds yet another layer to the book's intricate plot, Jack Prescott's tale is placed in perspective, and inexplicable omissions in da Cola's account come to light. Yet Wallis himself is so consumed by conspiracy theories that his own version of "the truth" becomes suspect even as he is relating it. It is in Wallis's section that Pears makes clear to the reader that all of his narrators thus far are to be regarded with varying degrees of suspicion.

The title of the novel, and of its final section, is a phrase that refers to evidence that can be trusted absolutely; in Anthony Wood, Pears presents the reader with as trustworthy a narrator as he has on offer. Wood's account is the testimony of a man for whom historical accuracy is of overriding importance, and any misrepresentations in his version of events are the result of vagaries of personal perception rather than deliberate deception. A quiet scholar and antiquary whom the other characters often dismiss, Wood is in fact the possessor of key pieces of information on which the solution to the mystery of Grove's death rests. Through his eyes, the reader comes to see the flaws at the heart of Wallis's conspiracy theories as well as the true nature of the intrigue unfolding at the highest levels of political power.

Wood's view of Sarah Blundy is also radically different from that of the first three narrators. Prior to her implication in Grove's murder, Sarah had worked for Wood and his mother, and Wood had fallen in love with her. His perception of her undergoes a startling change, however, when he witnesses her spiritual revelations before a secret congregation of worshippers and comes to believe she is a modern-day messiah. Sarah's eventual fate brings together the themes of science and religion that have dominated the book, as Pears presents his readers with the very rare literary device of a female Christ figure. Wood's belief in Sarah's divinity is clear; the reader, however, is allowed to draw his or her own conclusions.

At the heart of *An Instance of the Fingerpost* is the question of how we ascertain the truth, and the problems inherent in trusting any individual account of events one has not witnessed. Pears draws on the writings of Francis Bacon for his chapter introductions, examining in each of the book's sections a different way in which those seeking the truth may be misled. Indeed, Pears's titles offer the reader a hint as to the nature of the deception or misdirection that is about to unfold, a fact that becomes apparent only when a fuller picture of each narrator has emerged. With the book's final section, Pears offers for the first time a full and accurate recounting of the physical events of the story, then adds an ultimately unknowable spiritual dimension that each reader must either take on faith or reject. It is a daringly open-ended and enigmatic conclusion to an engrossing, thought-provoking novel.

An Instance of the Fingerpost is a literary mystery in the tradition of Eco's *The Name of the Rose*, making use of historical figures and events to frame its fictional story. Like Eco's acclaimed novel, the book uses the form of the murder mystery to approach larger issues. The mystery of Robert Grove's death provides Iain Pears with a device for exploring the events surrounding the return of the monarchy to power following the fall of Oliver Cromwell's Protectorate and the byzantine structure of political life during the Restoration. The story's skillful intermingling of fictional and historical characters and events gives the book a striking verisimilitude, even as its use of multiple narrators examines the subjective nature of personal histories and the difficulty in ascertaining an objective historical truth. Pears's vivid re-creation of the complex world of England under Charles II shows painstaking research into not only the physical details of seventeenth century life but its ideas and attitudes as well. The Restoration was a period of upheaval both politically and scientifically, and Pears's choice of widely differing narrators allows him to present a broad spectrum of subjects and experiences. In so doing, he captures the inherent drama of a period in which extraordinary changes were altering the lives of ordinary people caught up in the sweep of history.

Janet Lorenz

Sources for Further Study

The Atlantic. CCLXXXI, April, 1998, p. 117.
Booklist. XCIV, December 1, 1997, p. 587.
The Christian Century. CXV, November 18, 1998, p. 1119.
Library Journal. CXXIII, January, 1998, p. 143.
Los Angeles Times Book Review. March 8, 1998, p. 6.
New Statesman. CXXVI, September 19, 1997, p. 47.
The New York Times Book Review. CIII, March 22, 1998, p. 12.
Newsweek. CXXXI, April 27, 1998, p. 75.
Publishers Weekly. CCXLIV, December 1, 1997, p. 43.
The Times Literary Supplement. August 29, 1997, p. 24.
The Washington Post Book World. XXVIII, March 8, 1998, p. 1.

THE IRON TRACKS

Author: Aharon Appelfeld (1932-   )
Translated from the Hebrew by Jeffrey M. Green
Published: Schocken (New York). 196 pp. $21.00
Type of work: Novel
Time: The 1980's
Locale: Central Europe

In a novel about the continuing burdens of a traumatic past, a Holocaust survivor spends each year making a railway circuit of Central Europe in search of Jewish artifacts and of revenge against the Nazi officer who murdered his parents

> *Principal personages:*
> ERWIN SIEGELBAUM, the narrator, an itinerant dealer in Judaica
> COLONEL NACHTIGEL, a seventy-two-year-old Nazi war criminal
> MAX RAUCH, a successful Jewish merchant
> BERTHA KRANZ, a Holocaust survivor whom Siegelbaum loved and lost
> RABBI ZIMMEL, an ailing clergyman who clings to his sacred books in a
>   village left without Jews
> LOTTE, Zimmel's laconic cousin
> STARK, a Jewish Communist activist
> GIZI, a converted Jew who runs the buffet in the train station at Salzstein
> MRS. GROTON, an innkeeper at Pracht
> MRS. BRAUN, the half-Jewish manager of a buffet in Gruendorf
> AUGUST, a quarter-Jewish peasant who lives in Zwiren
> BELLA, a nineteen-year-old with whom Siegelbaum had a romantic
>   relationship immediately after the war
> ROSA TAG, a deaf woman the narrator meets on a train

Though he did not begin to learn the language until 1946, when, at age fourteen, he left Europe for Palestine, Aharon Appelfeld is, along with Amos Oz and A. B. Yehoshua, one of the preeminent figures in contemporary Hebrew fiction. Born in Czernowitz, Bukovina (then Romania, but now part of Ukraine), to an assimilated, German-speaking Jewish family, Appelfeld was deprived of childhood by the Nazis' genocidal schemes. Both of his parents were murdered in the labor camp to which they were sent, but the eight-year-old Appelfeld managed to escape from captivity and survive on his own in the woods for two years. It is understandable that the Israeli author, described by American Jewish novelist Philip Roth as "a displaced writer of displaced fiction, who has made of displacement and disorientation a subject uniquely his own," would return again and again in his fiction to the scene of the century's most horrific crime.

First published in Hebrew as *Mesilat barzel* in 1991, *The Iron Tracks* is the eleventh novel by Appelfeld to be translated into English. Like most of the others, it is set in Central Europe, site of the monstrous endeavor to eradicate the Jews. Its narrator, Erwin Siegelbaum, whose first name is the German version of the author's Aharon, is a fifty-five-year-old Holocaust survivor who, four decades after liberation from a forced labor camp, continues to be obsessed with the Nazi atrocity. He spends most of each year revisiting towns in Austria that, though now virtually devoid of living Jews, remain rife with anti-Semitism. Every March 27, Siegelbaum boards the train in Wirblbahn, the location of the camp where both his parents died, and makes his way through twenty-one more stations, eventually completing his circular journey a few weeks before it is time to start the cycle all over again. His ostensible purpose is to seek out and then sell the vestiges of vanished Jewish culture—menorahs, kiddush cups, and, especially, sacred texts. His secret aim, though, is to track down and exact vengeance against the Nazi officer who ran the camp at Wirblbahn.

"The trains make me free," proclaims Siegelbaum, extolling his rootless, itinerant life. Though trains were the principal means of transporting hundreds of thousands of Jews to their destruction during the Holocaust, Appelfeld's Jewish narrator perversely celebrates the iron tracks of Central Europe; he also bribes railroad employees to play classical music, which is what the Nazis arranged to be performed in the death camps in order to distract the inmates from the slaughter. *"Arbeit macht frei"* ("work makes you free") proclaimed a sign on the gate to Auschwitz, and Siegelbaum seems to submit to this perverse logic, savoring his own enslavement to the undeviating railway route and to the horrors of the past. Siegelbaum embraces his fate as a contemporary version of the Wandering Jew—the legend, promulgated by anti-Semites, of a miscreant who, for denying Jesus Christ, was condemned to eternal restlessness. He pretends to find pleasure in his agony, liberty in his ironclad compulsions.

Siegelbaum finds fleeting relief from the burdens of the past in an occasional glass of cognac or in brief erotic encounters. However, nothing can divert him from his route along the iron tracks. "My memory is my downfall," he explains. "It is a sealed well that doesn't lose a drop, to use an old expression. Nothing can deplete it." Yet for someone so obviously and thoroughly dominated by the past, Siegelbaum is remarkably frugal in sharing recollections.

During the course of recounting one year's journey north from Wirblbahn, the narrator provides fragmentary details about his earlier life. Readers slowly learn that, though his grandfather was a rabbi, his parents abandoned Jewish tradition. Refusing to allow Yiddish to be spoken in their house, they reared their son to speak Ruthenian and German. Ardent Communists, they dedicated themselves to organizing the Ruthenian peasants and workers, often in opposition to Jewish entrepreneurs. After taking part in the assassination of the head of the secret police, Siegelbaum's mother withdrew from political activity and from her marriage to his father. The young Siegelbaum spent much of his childhood out of school on the road with his father, moving among hostile Ruthenians who never accepted his Marxist faith or regarded the missionary as anything but an alien Jew. It is both ironic and appropriate that Siegelbaum now replicates the rootless wandering of his childhood and that he makes his living by trading in Jewish artifacts. He seeks out and sells ritual paraphernalia from a culture that was largely expunged from Austria; he acquires tattered books in Hebrew, Yiddish, and Aramaic, languages that he never learned (his parents, internalizing the ambient anti-Semitism, thought Yiddish "exuded the odor of grocery stores and sounded like the rustle of money"). When Mrs. Groton, an aging innkeeper in Pracht, insists on bequeathing to Siegelbaum the mezuza that her Jewish grandmother, who had converted to Christianity, passed on, he is reluctant to accept the amulet and unsure what to do with it. When August, the old quarter-Jewish peasant who lives in Zwiren, tries to give him a family kiddush cup, Siegelbaum is embarrassed by the trust. Appelfeld's own painstakingly acquired Hebrew gives voice to a Jew who has been trapped in a cycle of self-loathing.

During the railway journey that he undertakes forty years after first departing Wirblbahn, Siegelbaum encounters numerous innkeepers, buffet managers, and merchants. Among them is a successful businessman named Max Rauch, a Jew married to an anti-Semite, who encourages Siegelbaum in his work and purchases his wares. Also notable is Rabbi Zimmel, who, despite failing health, insists on remaining in the village of Sandberg, the last surviving Jew, devoted to his sacred books. In Upper Salzstein, he greets old Comrade Stark, an unreconstructed Communist still active in the cause. A paternal figure to the orphaned Siegelbaum, who abandons him to an isolated death, Stark is writing a book with a title, *The War Against Melancholy*, that points to what the narrator has lost. "Man is an insect," contends Siegelbaum, for whom his father's irrepressible optimism is no longer tenable. "Not even in hell will I deny my faith in man," proclaimed the father, from the hell of a Nazi concentration camp.

Contributing to the narrator's melancholy and even despair is the loss of Bertha Kranz, the beautiful Jewish woman he met at the train station in Sternberg twenty years ago. She rejected his proposal of marriage and, a year ago, perversely returned to live in her home town of Zelishtshik, amid Poles and Ukrainians but no other Jews. Siegelbaum's relations with other women are curt and carnal.

Though many characters are given names and are old acquaintances from earlier excursions, they remain spectral presences in the novel, not much more substantial than the "rivals" the narrator occasionally alludes to—a half-dozen or so unnamed, and perhaps unreal, travelers who he believes work the same route. Theirs, he is sure, is the identical objective of stalking the remnants of Jewish culture in a land from which, aside from a few pathetic converts and hybrids, Jews themselves have been removed.

Yet another mission beckons, one that, either because Siegelbaum lacks self-awareness or because it is an operation that requires discretion, emerges only gradually during the course of the narrative. Readers eventually surmise that Siegelbaum, who carries a pistol with him in his travels, is intent on tracking down Nachtigel, the Nazi colonel who ran the camp in Wirblbahn. Throughout his expeditions, Siegelbaum cultivates informants who provide him with news about his prey. After the war, Nachtigel had escaped to Uruguay, but he is now back in Austria, brazenly inhabiting a new house in Weinberg. *The Iron Tracks* culminates in Siegelbaum's confrontation with the seventy-two-year-old mass murderer.

In the dining car of the train that carries him to Weinberg, Siegelbaum meets an amputee veteran who still boasts of his military service ridding the world of Jews. Siegelbaum beats the legless old bigot, but Nachtigel is another matter. What sort of tardy vengeance, if any, would be appropriate against the unrepentant, unregenerate demon who killed his parents and so many others? When he finally does catch up to Nachtigel, Siegelbaum's banal actions lack moral grandeur or even dramatic power. They are as unsatisfying as everything else in the traveler's blighted life. In the final sentences of his narrative, Siegelbaum recognizes that: "As in all my clear and drawn-out nightmares, I saw the sea of darkness, and I knew that my deeds had neither dedication nor beauty. I had done everything out of compulsion, clumsily, and always too late."

Yet Appelfeld manages to endow this wretched, benighted existence with forceful aesthetic form. In *Beyond Despair: Three Lectures and a Conversation with Philip Roth*, a nonfiction book that he published in English in 1994, the novelist reflects on how meager the literary imagination is in its efforts to convey the enormity of the Holocaust. After Auschwitz, German philosopher Theodor Adorno famously pronounced, all poetry is barbaric. Appelfeld, though, has made bracing poetry out of the very inadequacy of the human response to atrocity. He has done so by returning again and again to the Holocaust, but by treating it obliquely. Wary of trivializing the Nazi horrors, Appelfeld almost always situates his stories at the margins of slaughter; they are placed either in the prologue to the conflagration, among characters too complacent to credit what is soon to occur—as in *Badenheim 1939* (1980) or *To the Land of the Cattails* (1986)—or else, as in *The Iron Tracks*, among survivors coping with the aftermath of devastation.

The novel's spare, laconic style reinforces its author's respect for the limitations of art. Silence, whether in the mute depression to which Siegelbaum's mother lapses or the terse remarks of Rabbi Zimmel's cousin Lotte, is a persistent theme in *The Iron Tracks*. Recalling his romance with nineteen-year-old Bella immediately after the war, Siegelbaum is most wistful about her aversion to speech; he reamrks that "only with Bella did I know true silence. Today I know there is much pretense in talk. Only a quiet person earns my faith." Amid the din of voices on the Holocaust, Appelfeld's reticent narrator affirms: "Silence. That is what I need. And that is just what you can't have on trains." The silence toward which Siegelbaum aspires eludes him not simply because of the din of railroad engines but also because of the clamor of agonizing memories from which iron tracks offer no escape. "I hate rhetoric," insists Siegelbaum, and in *The Iron Tracks*, as in ten other novels, Appelfeld fashions an elliptical rhetoric that does not betray the magnitude of his disturbing subject.

Steven G. Kellman

Sources for Further Study

Booklist. XCIV, January 1, 1998, p. 773.
The Boston Globe. February 15, 1998, p. E1.
Chicago Tribune. March 8, 1998, p. 5.

Kirkus Reviews. LXV, December 1, 1997, p. 1720.
Library Journal. CXXIII, January, 1998, p. 137.
Los Angeles Times. February 25, 1998, p. E2.
The New York Review of Books. XLV, March, 1998, p. 18.
The New York Times Book Review. CIII, February 15, 1998, p. 8.
Publishers Weekly. CCXLIV, December 1, 1997, p. 46.
The Washington Post Book World. XXVIII, February 15, 1998, p. 3.
World Literature Today. LXXII, Summer, 1998, p. 493.

ISRAEL
A History

Author: Martin Gilbert (1936-   )
Published: William Morrow (New York). Illustrated. 750 pp. $30.00
Type of work: History
Time: 1860-1997
Locale: Israel

> *Gilbert surveys the rise of modern Israel from its origins in the mid-nineteenth century to the end of the twentieth century*

Principal personages:
YASSER ARAFAT, a Palestinian leader
DAVID BEN-GURION, Israel's first prime minister
MOSHE DAYAN, an Israeli general and defense minister
THEODOR HERZL, the founder of the World Zionist Organization
VLADIMIR JABOTINSKY, a militant Zionist
GOLDA MEIR, an Israeli ambassador to the Soviet Union and prime
    minister of Israel
YITZHAK RABIN, an Israeli chief of staff and later prime minister
YIGAEL YADIN, an archaeologist and Israel's chief of staff in 1948

Although the state of Israel celebrated its fiftieth anniversary in 1998, the story of the country's establishment dates back to the nineteenth century, when immigrants, mainly Russian, began acquiring land and creating settlements in what was then Turkish Palestine. In 1896, Hungarian-born Theodor Herzl took the significant step of founding the World Zionist Organization and calling for massive Jewish immigration to Israel. The first Zionist Congress met at Basel in September of the next year; at the end of that gathering, Herzl prophetically wrote in his diary: "At Basle I founded the Jewish State. If I said this out loud today, I would be answered by universal laughter. Perhaps in five years, and certainly in fifty, everyone will know it." In 1947, exactly fifty years after the First Zionist Congress, the United Nations would vote to make Herzl's dream a reality.

Even in the Jewish community, not everyone shared Herzl's optimism or his dream. Baron Edmond de Rothschild willingly financed settlements in Israel, but he feared that the rapid growth of the Jewish population that Herzl envisioned there would anger the Turks. Many nonreligious Jews throughout the Diaspora believed that the key to Jewish success lay in assimilation. Orthodox Jews disliked Herzl's secular vision. These early conflicts persisted as fault lines in late twentieth century Israel. The ultra-Orthodox, for example, do not serve in the Israeli armed forces, and the religious student Yigal Amin assassinated Prime Minister Yitzhak Rabin on November 4, 1995, because of Rabin's willingness to trade what Amin considered sacred land for peace.

Despite such opposition, Herzl persevered, but the creation of the Jewish state did not come easily. Gilbert might have adopted as the epigraph for his book Vergil's statement in Book I of the *Aeneid*: "So hard it was to found the race of Rome." The fifty years between the First Zionist Congress and the creation of Israel witnessed difficult times for Jews in Israel and the Diaspora, culminating in the Holocaust. Gilbert notes that the impulse behind Zionism lay as much in contemporary political reality as in the two-thousand-year-old dream of return to the land of Israel. In 1893, the anti-Semitic Karl Lueger was elected mayor of Vienna; in December, 1894, Captain Alfred Dreyfus of France was falsely convicted of treason; in Russia, pogroms were routine. So precarious was the situation of Jews in Europe that in 1903 Herzl accepted British colonial secretary Joseph Chamberlain's offer of a Jewish homeland in Uganda. Herzl was able to force the Sixth Zionist Congress (held in Basel in 1903) to agree to this proposal, but with Herzl's death in 1904, the idea died, too. In 1903 in Paris, a Russian-born Jewish student fired on Max Nordau for supporting Herzl, though in fact Nordau had concurred only reluctantly. Such violent extremism is a theme that pervades Gilbert's narrative.

As more Jews moved to Israel, Arab opposition increased, as did attacks on Jewish settlements. In November, 1917, in the midst of World War I, British foreign secretary Arthur James Balfour persuaded the cabinet to state that "His Majesty's Government view with favour the establishment in Palestine of a national Home for the Jewish People, and will use their best endeavours to facilitate the achievement of this object." The Balfour Declaration, as it is known, rested on an idealistic recognition of the Jewish right to a refuge, but it was prompted by Great Britain's desire to curry favor with the large Jewish population of Russia, a country that was growing increasingly disenchanted with the war and that would indeed shortly conclude peace with Germany. England also hoped that the declaration would bolster its postwar claims to Turkish territory in the Middle East. While Balfour remained highly respected among Jews for the rest of his life, secret agreements that Britain concluded with France and the Arabs at the same time as it was promising a Jewish homeland rendered the Balfour Declaration meaningless from its inception.

Throughout the 1920's and 1930's, Britain increasingly opposed Jewish settlement in Israel, precisely as the extinction of European Jewry grew ever more imminent. Gilbert, though himself British, does not mask the hostility to Jewish immigration that Britain showed during this period. On March 10, 1938, Britain limited to 3,000 the number of Jews it would allow into Palestine over the next six months. Five days later, Adolf Hitler entered Vienna, adding Austria with its more than 200,000 Jews to the German Reich. Even after World War II began, Britain did not relax its opposition to the entrance of Jews into its mandate. Not until 1943 did Winston Churchill reverse this policy.

Gilbert shows that in the interwar years, Jewish factionalism also hampered settlement efforts. In 1933, for example, Chaim Arlosoroff, a leading Zionist, was killed, perhaps by Jewish militants. These militants certainly had opposed Arlosoroff's negotiations with the Nazis, even though his aim was to rescue Jews from the Reich and bring them to Israel.

After the Conservatives lost in the 1945 British elections, the new Labour government returned to the prewar policy of restricting Jewish immigration. The most egregious example of this attitude was its handling of the *Exodus*, a ship that reached the coast of Palestine in July, 1947, with 4,500 Jewish survivors of the Holocaust. The British Royal Navy fired on the vessel, killing three passengers. The others were sent back to Germany.

Once the United Nations voted in favor of the establishment of the state of Israel, war broke out between Jews and Arabs, not merely in Palestine but throughout the Arab world. Jewish refugees fled from their homes in Asia and Africa to Israel, where, at great expense, they were integrated into the life of the country. Gilbert, who has written about both world wars, paints a vivid picture of Israel's battle for its life in 1947-1948 and provides many accounts of individual heroism. Pinhas Ben-Porat, using a Piper Cub airplane equipped with a machine gun operated by a man strapped to his seat, virtually single-handedly raised the siege of the Jewish settlement of Nevatim in the Negev (southern Israel) in February, 1948. Not all such efforts ended so successfully. All forty-six members of a relief column attempting to reach the besieged kibbutz of Yehiam were killed.

Israel declared its independence on May 14, 1948, but sovereignty remained to be won on the battlefield and preserved in three subsequent wars in 1956, 1967, and 1973. As Abba Eban has remarked, every such test was for Israel a final exam, since its enemies were committed to the nation's destruction. Israel passed each of these tests with what appears to outsiders to have been remarkable proficiency. Yet even the dramatic victory in the Six Day War of 1967, in which Israel destroyed the Egyptian Air Force in the first two hours of fighting and went on to triple the size of its territory, cost 777 lives. Gilbert rightly describes these deaths as "a heavy blow to a small, tight-knit community of less that three million people."

These wars, which might have been expected to unite the Jewish community within Israel, instead exacerbated old divisions and created new ones. During the period of the British mandate, Jewish moderates under David Ben-Gurion and hardliners such as Menachem Begin both created military organizations that proved essential to the survival of the country in 1947-1948. The Haganah under Ben-Gurion and the more militant Irgun and Stern Gang generally operated independently. During the war of independence, they temporarily joined forces, but in June, 1948, the Irgun refused to surrender to Ben-Gurion, now leader of Israel, the weapons it had imported from France aboard the ship *Altalena*. Ben-Gurion thereupon ordered the Israeli Defense Force to fire on the ship. Forty passengers were killed and the ship sunk.

The 1967 victory undermined the Labor government that achieved it because the religious parties, for whom Gilbert has little sympathy, grew increasingly determined to retain the territories occupied as a result of the fighting, while the Labor Party wanted to return most of the land in exchange for peace with Israel's neighbors. The 1973 war left Israel with still more land, but the cost in lives—more than 2,500—and in money—the equivalent of an entire year's gross national product—raised questions about Labor's competence. In 1977, Menachem Begin, whom Gilbert portrays unflatteringly, and his right-wing coalition took power.

The history of Israel since 1967 has centered on its struggle to achieve peace both with its Arab neighbors and within its borders. Gilbert's sentiments lie with Labor's efforts to make concessions to surrounding countries and on the subject of a Palestinian state, and he devotes much attention to organizations within Israel that have opposed harsh government treatment of Arabs and the invasion and continued occupation of Lebanese territory. Gilbert's heroes are Yitzhak Rabin and Shimon Peres, without whose efforts the conclusion of a peace treaty with Jordan and the ending of the intifada (the Arab uprising within Israel) would have been unlikely.

Yet Rabin and Peres proved unable to convince a majority of Israelis that accommodation with the Arabs would promote safety, and in 1996 Peres lost the premiership to Benjamin Netanyahu, who promised peace with security. Netanyahu's election slowed the peace process without markedly affecting terrorism. Fifty years after its creation, though, Israel is less threatened from enemies outside its borders than from internal divisions over how best to preserve the country and make it prosper. Perhaps such arguments are themselves a sign of strength, of healthy democracy and national dynamism.

Gilbert recounts an epic struggle, and his book is of epic proportions, with more than six hundred pages of text. He includes seventy-two photographs that in themselves serve as a pictorial history of Israel, from a portrait of Theodor Herzl and the construction of Jewish settlements in the 1930's to the concluding of peace between Egypt and Israel at Camp David in 1978, the funeral of Rabin in 1995, and Benjamin Netanyahu's meeting with Yasser Arafat. The volume also contains more than forty pages of maps showing, for example, Jewish settlements in Palestine in 1914 and Jewish immigration from Europe between 1948 and 1955. One of the most fascinating of these maps compares the size of Israel with that of California, Florida, Sri Lanka, Britain, and Egypt, into any of which the country could fit easily.

Gilbert tells his story in serviceable prose. The chronological approach allows the reader to experience diverse events as they happen. Thus, succeeding paragraphs discuss the establishment of Kibbutz Shomrat and the first use of Messerschmitts by the Israeli Air Force, both of which occurred on May 29, 1948. The creation of separate chapters focusing on military and domestic matters would nevertheless provide clearer focus and smoother transitions.

Typographical errors are inevitable in publications, but given the length of this book, the text is remarkably clean. Still, Jimmy Carter rather than Richard Nixon is named as the U.S. president in 1972 (page 418), and on page 598, "1988" appears for "1998."

Despite these lapses, Gilbert has produced an important book that will long serve as a valuable reference, perhaps even as the standard text for the period covered. This work gains added significance because it treats a story intimately connected with all facets of the twentieth century. To take but one example, the collapse of the Soviet Union in 1989 deprived the Arab states of support, thus shifting the military balance in the Middle East. The demise of the Soviet Union also allowed hundreds of thousands of Jews to leave for Israel, greatly increasing its population and accompanying problems of integrating these immigrants into the country. Gilbert's history is important, too, because the problems that Israel faces confront many other countries around the world: terrorism, nationalism, religious fundamentalism, racism. The prophets of the Old Testament imagined that from Zion would come wisdom and justice. If Israel can cope successfully with the challenges before it, it may again serve as a light unto the nations.

Joseph Rosenblum

Sources for Further Study

Booklist. XCIV, February 1, 1998, p. 875.
The Economist. CCCXLVII, April 18, 1998, p. S3.
Foreign Affairs. LXXVII, July, 1998, p. 90.
Kirkus Reviews. LXVI, March 1, 1998, p. 329.
Library Journal. CXXIII, March 15, 1998, p. 81.
Publishers Weekly. CCXLV, February 2, 1998, p. 71.
San Francisco Chronicle. April 26, 1998, p. REV1.
The Times Literary Supplement. May 22, 1998, p. 26.
The Washington Post Book World. XXVIII, May 3, 1998, p. 1.

JACK MAGGS

Author: Peter Carey (1943-   )
Published: Alfred A. Knopf (New York). 306 pp. $24.00
Type of work: Novel
Time: The 1800's
Locale: England and Australia

A fast-paced tale that draws from Charles Dickens to recount the life and times of a convict banished to Australia who returns to England to visit his surrogate son, then finds himself entangled in an improbable chain of events

> *Principal characters:*
> JACK MAGGS, a British convict transported to Australia for the term of his natural life
> TOBIAS OATES, a rising young fiction writer interested in hypnotism and mesmerism
> PERCY BUCKLE, a former tradesman who has assumed the trappings of a gentleman
> MERCY LARKIN, Buckle's maid and secret mistress
> HENRY PHIPPS, an orphan who has become a gentleman through the patronage of his benefactor, Maggs

Peter Carey, an Australian who has lived in New York for several years, continues to write fiction that engages directly or indirectly with his homeland, whatever its subject. He first gained notice in 1974 with a book of experimental short stories, *The Fat Man in History*, then again in 1979 with another volume of equally fantastic short fiction, *War Crimes*. These two striking collections, widely acclaimed in Australia and overseas, previewed the breadth and inventive structure of his work once he turned to full-length fiction.

His first major novel, *Illywhacker* (1986), covers the history of 150 or so years of European settlement in Australia through a whimsical revision of fact and myth, told through the eyes of an "illywhacker" (Australian slang for a con artist or carnival spieler). In 1988, Carey received the Booker Prize for *Oscar and Lucinda*, which follows the misadventures of a nineteenth century Australian couple who attempt to defy colonial reality by moving a glass church into the outback, where so fragile a symbol of civilization shatters. His next novel, *The Tax Inspector* (1991), centers on contemporary Sydney to depict private and public corruption. In *The Unusual Life of Tristan Smith* (1994), Carey invents a postcolonial nation called Efica and its powerful ally, Voorstand; through this contrivance, he subtly handles the perceived neocolonialism that Australia undergoes at the hands of the United States.

Thus it is no surprise to Carey's readers that his 1998 novel, *Jack Maggs*, embraces the nineteenth century as its period but at the same time focuses on modern Australia's relationship with the larger world—in particular, the Australian search for national identity. While this quest has occupied Carey throughout his career, he has managed to masquerade the recurrent theme in varied guises.

Widely reviewed in English-speaking countries, *Jack Maggs* received undue notice from critics for its debt to Charles Dickens's *Great Expectations* (1860-1861). Granted, the newly minted Maggs owes his origins to the beleaguered convict Magwitch in the Dickens novel, just as Phipps represents another version of Magwitch's surrogate son Pip; parallels with other characters in the earlier book have also been drawn, but highlighting such likenesses is not especially useful. Carey's creation of the rising young writer Tobias Oates also led reviewers to speculate on how extensively Oates in both his professional and personal life resembles Dickens. Yet, once all these similarities have been pointed out, Carey's expansion of the classic novel stands on its own, first as a lively and rousing story, then as a narrative with a strong subtext that examines not only the nature of fiction writing but also the uncertain identity and precarious condition of a postcolonial nation such as Australia.

Although a product of the late twentieth century, *Jack Maggs* resembles a work from earlier times with its mannered prose, its vivid details that re-create nineteenth century England, its meticulous development of character, and its old-fashioned narrative force. The story begins as Maggs returns to London after spending twenty-four years in Australia, first as a convict, then as a free man once he had completed his sentence. It was the practice in the early 1800's to transport criminals to the farflung British colony in the antipodes. Once the convicts had completed their sentences, they were required to remain in Australia; if they dared return to England, they would be hanged. Some of the former convicts wasted away the rest of their lives as free men or women, carousing, drinking, and longing to go "home"—that is, to the England that had rejected them. Others adjusted and prospered in the developing colony. Maggs belongs to the latter company; he set up a brick-making factory in rapidly growing Sydney and accumulated a fortune. Like the first group, though, he still dreams of "home . . . the long mellow light of English summer" and would "build London in his mind . . . brick by brick." Rebelling against the harsh life on the world's underside, Maggs declares: "I am not of that race. . . . The race of Australians." His passion is to see the orphan, now a grown man living in London, who had befriended him on his way to deportation those many years ago. With his newfound prosperity, he has secretly supported Phipps and financed his transformation into a gentleman. Maggs has long imagined the two of them living a genteel life together in his beloved London.

Thus Maggs, in spite of the threat of death, returns to the much-changed city, fully rendered in Carey's descriptive prose:

> The city had become a fairground, and as the coach crossed the river at Westminster the stranger saw that even the bridges of the Thames were illuminated.
> The entire Haymarket was like a grand ball. Not just the gas, the music, the dense, tight crowds. . . . Dram shops had become gin palaces with their great plate-glass windows. . . . This one here—it was like a temple, damned if it was not, the door surrounded by stained panes of rich dye: rosettes, bunches of grapes.

Before long, however, Maggs's enthusiasm is dampened when he finds the house he purchased for Phipps deserted. The ungrateful recipient of the ex-convict's generosity has learned of his benefactor's identity and imminent visit and has gone into hiding to avoid him.

Ever resourceful, Maggs takes a job in the house next door as a footman so that he can keep an eye on Phipps's residence. His employer, Percy Buckle, is a former shopkeeper who inherited money and set himself up as a gentleman. Maggs soon learns that the household staff shows little respect for its upstart master. Fancying himself a man of letters, Buckle is delighted when the well-known writer Tobias Oates accepts an invitation to dinner, and Buckle does not object when Oates takes undue interest in his host's new footman.

This meeting initiates a strange and often stormy relationship between Maggs and Oates, who eventually learns the bad-tempered footman's secret past as a convict. By promising to help Maggs find the vanished Phipps, the writer convinces the suspicious Maggs to act as his subject in his amateur ventures into hypnotism and mesmerism. This agreement sets the narrative on its course when the unlikely pair intermittently delve into Maggs's past and search in vain for the missing Phipps. Their personal explorations and wider hunt provide the basis for a series of adventures that lead the two men into varied avenues of nineteenth century English life. To augment the immediate narrative, Maggs writes long letters to Phipps. Through this one-sided correspondence, the neglected benefactor discloses how he grew up in London and trained as a thief who specialized in stealing silver from fine houses, for which he was eventually tried and exiled; here the first-person voice replaces the detached third-person narrator. Interwoven into these assorted strands are scenes revealing Oates's turbulent household, his unfortunate romantic entanglement, and his financial problems, along with incidents picturing the disorderly ménage headed by Buckle.

At the novel's end, Maggs discovers his true identity as an Australian. The romanticized picture of England he once carried dissolves when he finally grasps that his much-anticipated return "home" has brought him only suffering, humiliation, ingratitude, and disillusionment. Maggs, unrefined and given to violence though he is, and Mercy Larkin, albeit a former prostitute still plying her trade with Buckle, emerge as the two most admirable characters in the story. The rest of the British personages Maggs encounters, that "race" with whom he had once identified so fervently, display only selfish, grasping, pretentious, and perfidious streaks. Even a character who loosely suggests "Mother England" turns out to be an abortionist.

In addition to being an engaging narrative, *Jack Maggs* offers insights into the creative process itself through the alliance between Oates and Maggs. Fascinated by his subject, the ambitious writer attempts to enter deeply into Maggs's experience, past and present, to gather material for a proposed novel about the former convict's life. How stories originate and accumulate, how they unfold and grow, has always intrigued Carey, who has investigated the act of storytelling in his previous novels. Here the parallel between the imaginary Oates and the actual Dickens is legitimized, as Carey imagines the way Dickens may have set *Great Expectations* into creative motion. Further, the contemporary author has helped out his nineteenth century counterpart by providing the missing details from the life and times of Magwitch/Maggs. In an interview, Carey admitted that he had always been curious about the mysterious benefactor in the earlier novel.

The ending, which should not be revealed in its entirety, makes a strong statement about national identity. Maggs discovers that he does indeed belong to "the race of Australians," an identity he had earlier rejected. Mercy Larkin, who had been turned into the London streets by her mother to work as a prostitute, then rescued by Buckle, who took advantage of her weakness, finds salvation and happiness in Australia. The all-important concluding sequence, although clearly enough defined, turns out to be the book's weakest part. The narrator seems to be in a hurry to tie the loose strands together, and too much happens too fast. Earlier scenes that are less essential get fuller treatment. The reader, in the final pages, tends to feel cheated and wishes that Jack Maggs and Mercy Larkin had been granted more extended treatment as they discover themselves, that their redemption and their awareness of their rightful identity had been more thoroughly developed.

Carey's work is popular in his homeland, and no doubt this novel's emphatic conclusion, which stresses Australia's superiority over England, will please Australian readers. Although the country itself still pledges allegiance to the British monarchy, a strong movement has developed to sever these traditional ties and form an independent republic. While the current political maneuverings may have accounted in large part for the novel's enthusiastic reception in Australia, readers overseas would not likely be aware of such parochial matters. The novel's success outside Australia undoubtedly rests to some degree on its solid story, intriguing characters, and remarkable style. In addition, the book's connection with *Great Expectations* surely accounts for part of its appeal. Although enlargement, revision, or updating of literary classics fails more often than it succeeds, *Jack Maggs* does full justice to the original work.

Robert Ross

Sources for Further Study

The Christian Science Monitor. April 8, 1998, p. 14.
Los Angeles Times Book Review. February 1, 1998, p. 2.
The Nation. CCLXVI, March 2, 1998, p. 27.
The New York Review of Books. XLV, February 19, 1998, p. 26.
The New York Times Book Review. CIII, February 8, 1998, p. 10.
Publishers Weekly. CCXLIV, December 1, 1997, p. 45.
Time. CLI, February 23, 1998, p. 84.
The Times Literary Supplement. September 12, 1997, p. 8.
The Wall Street Journal. February 4, 1998, p. A20.
The Washington Post Book World. XXVIII, March 15, 1998, p. 1.

JEWS
The Essence and Character of a People

Authors: Arthur Hertzberg (1921-   ) and Aron Hirt-Manheimer (1948-   )
Published: HarperSanFrancisco (San Francisco). 294 pp. $25.00
Type of work: History and religion

A history of the Jewish people that examines Jewish cultural uniqueness and perseverance despite the pressures of assimilation and persecution

Arthur Hertzberg is Bronfman Visiting Professor of the Humanities at New York University and Professor Emeritus of Religion at Dartmouth. He has also been president of the American Jewish Policy Foundation and the American Jewish Congress. He has written seven other books on Judaism, including *The Zionist Idea* (1959) and *Being Jewish in America* (1987). Aron Hirt-Manheimer is the editor of *Reform Judaism* magazine and the 1988 recipient of the Anne Frank Medal. In the preface to *Jews: The Essence and Character of a People*, Hirt-Manheimer explains that Hertzberg dictated the entire first draft of the manuscript to him, which Hirt-Manheimer then "rendered into a workable text." Further revision and editing was accomplished together. Therefore, it is Hertzberg's "viewpoint and scholarship" that defines the book.

Hertzberg has attempted a difficult task, even a provocative one, in his search for the defining characteristics of the Jewish people. His stated aim is to provide a means to embrace all types of Jews, rather than taking a position that narrowly defines Jewishness. Hertzberg himself is descended from Hasidic scholars and rabbis, yet he considers himself to have grown up in the mainstream of Jewish experience. His father, the rabbi of the Hasidic community in Baltimore, Maryland, hosted Jews from varied sects and viewpoints in his home, and the young Hertzberg experienced firsthand the endless discussion and debate of Jewish scholars. He believes that this experience has allowed him to be more accepting of all brands of Judaism.

Hertzberg poses the question: What is a Jew? The simplest answer would be a religious one: that a Jew is someone who believes in the one God of Abraham, the God of the Hebrews. Yet this is too simple. In the first chapter, "The Chosen," Hertzberg proposes the psychological consequences of being a chosen people. He does not believe that Jews invented the concept of chosenness but that they have clung to it in their fierce determination to remain distinct from other peoples. They are different because they believe that God has required them to be different, to stand apart from other peoples and at the same time to serve as a moral beacon to the world. In chapter 3, "The Outsider," Hertzberg examines a second characteristic, that of "otherness." The insistence of Jews in maintaining their culture and beliefs throughout the history of the Diaspora, or Jewish exile from the Holy Land, has caused them to remain outside the dominant cultures of their geographic homes. In chapter 4, "The Wild Streak," Hertzberg identifies a facet of the Jewish character, most often expressed as martyrdom, which causes them to rise up in the face of persecution. Jews fought back in

Masada in 73 B.C., slaughtering themselves and their families rather than submit to the Romans, and fought back in the Warsaw Ghetto uprising in 1943, when the Nazis were exterminating Jews. Hertzberg mentions many other examples of this "wild streak" in this chapter and throughout the book.

Having stated these three major points in his analysis of Jewish character, Hertzberg goes on to provide a detailed history of Judaism and the Jewish people. He uses the biographies of individual scholars and influential Jews to illustrate how these characteristics influenced the experience of all Jews as they left Israel and spread throughout the world.

In chapter 5, "The Synagogue of Satan," Hertzberg examines the relationship of the Catholic Church and Protestantism to the Jews. He finds in the writings of Jules Isaac an answer to the anti-Semitism expressed so violently in the Holocaust, or *Shoah*. Isaac revealed that the Church had taught contempt for the Jews from its beginnings, and the Church's subsequent influence in Europe rooted this hatred in all European Christian cultures. Hertzberg acknowledges the role that Isaac's writings have played in moving the Catholic Church toward a reconciliation of this prejudice, beginning with the reforms of the mid-1960's.

The history of the Jews in Spain is discussed in chapter 6, "The Terrible Choice." A large and prosperous community of Jews had existed in Spain during the Middle Ages and had prospered under Muslim rule. They "had achieved prominence in every sphere of society, from the affairs of state and commerce to art and science." It was a complete shock, then, when in 1492 the Jews were given an ultimatum. They had four months to convert to Christianity, or they were to leave the country forever, leaving all of their property and possessions behind. Certainly, Jews had been persecuted since the return of Spain to Christian rule between the thirteenth and fifteenth centuries. There had been other choices to make between conversion and death, but this complete exile proved that Jews were not safe anywhere. The population was evenly divided, with half choosing exile, half converting. Among the converts, however, were many who converted in name only and sought to continue their unique worship in secret; these were known as crypto-Jews. Hertzberg examines the nature of Jewish worship, study of the Torah and the Talmud, as being the ultimate goal of Jewish life. Examination of the Word is a never-ceasing task that Jews will perform until the "end of days." Following the period of the Spanish expulsion, a new study began of the Kabbalah, an apocalyptic message that taught that the end of the world was near, when Jews would return to Zion (Israel). The focus of the new kabbalists was to use supernatural means to bring about the end times and the redemption of the world.

The phenomenon of messianic leaders is examined in "Messianic Mania." Hertzberg recounts the story from the 1660's of Shabbetai Zvi, who was touted as the Messiah returned to lead his people to freedom and usher in the last days. Half the Jewish world chose to believe in Shabbetai Zvi, but when the would-be Messiah announced a specific date of redemption, he was arrested by the Turks and forced to convert to Islam or die. Shabbetai chose conversion. Hertzberg speaks of other Messianic pretenders arising in nearly every generation, finding ready followers eager to believe that the redemption of the Jews is at hand.

In "The Age of Dissent," Hertzberg discusses the rise of Protestantism and the renewed attempts, by these new sects of Christianity, to convert the Jews. Martin Luther, especially, reacted viciously when his overtures were rejected. Hertzberg believes that Luther's condemnation of the Jews had a lasting effect, both in Protestant Christianity and in German culture. The subject of money is also discussed, and the jealousies invoked by the majority culture at the financial success of the Jews. This effect of Jewish success can be traced back to the Spanish experience and forward to Germany of the 1930's. Hertzberg looks at many reformers, including Baruch Spinoza, who is excommunicated by the Jewish community in Amsterdam for his heresies. Skeptical Spinoza identified all religious texts as having human origin and, therefore, human error; he chose to identify reason as superior to faith. Spinoza himself redefined the concept of chosenness as reserved for those who led virtuous lives.

During this time, many Jews were assimilating, but Jewish culture, tradition, and worship continued. Hertzberg does not abandon his examination of character in these historical snapshots; he relates the lives of these influential Jews and shows how chosenness, otherness, and the wild streak play a part. Even Jews who assimilated found that they were not accepted fully into the majority society; despite all of their efforts at renouncing their Jewishness, they were still perceived as "other." Spinoza wrongly asserted, according to Hertzberg, that Jews "continued to exist by a defiant act of will." Hertzberg claims that it was not the doctrine of chosenness that influenced Abraham but the act of defiance in breaking the idols of his father, and thus choosing God, that continues to operate even in Spinoza, who criticized Western society.

Chapter 10 contains a history of the Hasidic movement. Although Hertzberg was reared in this tradition, he is uncomfortable with the "partisan and usually polemical usurpation" of the Hasidim. Hertzberg relates a personal anecdote of his meeting, at the age of twenty-eight, with Martin Buber, an important and culturally celebrated Jewish philosopher. Buber's stories about the Hasidim, including some of Hertzberg's ancestors, did not strike Hertzberg as accurate portrayals of the descriptions handed down to him. Hertzberg challenged Buber's claim to be a Hasid, which affronted the philosopher. Hertzberg believes that Buber failed to notice the "profound and absolute obedience of the Hasidim to the religious practices and laws in the Talmud." Hertzberg goes on to link the Hasidic movement with an increased interest in returning to Zion and leaving the life of the Diaspora behind.

"Unrequited Love" deals with the yearning of some Jews to assimilate into the dominant culture, mainly through conversion to the majority faith. He roots this desire in self-contempt brought on by widespread and persistent anti-Semitism in the age of Enlightenment in the eighteenth century. Jewish educational reform often meant an abandonment of Torah and Talmud for study of the language and literature of the dominant European cultures. A call to universal morality, which meant for Jews a conversion to Christianity, gained adherents but failed to destroy the community of Jewish believers. Karl Marx, son of a German rabbi who had become a Deist (a believer in reason over faith), attacked the Jews as parasites, as representatives of the bourgeois merchant class who lived off the labor of the workers.

In chapter 12, "Reinventing Jewishness," Hertzberg examines the experience of Jews in the United States. Jews found a more open society than they ever had, without the exclusionary laws that Jews had been forced to live under in European societies. Although anti-Semitism was still present, Jews were able to prosper and to live as Jews freely. This led to a lessening of the messianic message and even to a loss of interest in the return to Zion. Hertzberg traces the rise of the three main branches of Judaism today: Orthodox, Reform, and Conservative. He seeks to show how, even in their differences, these movements retain the essential identification of Jews as a unique people.

Hertzberg examines Jews who do not believe in God and decides that the character traits of the Jews still operate within them and move them to act as moral examples to the world. He examines the crisis of faith brought on by the Holocaust. He explains that to the Orthodox, the Holocaust was no surprise, because they "had never doubted that Jews were other." It did not matter to the Nazis that these Jews had converted; the Nazis were bent on exterminating anyone who could be identified as Jewish by blood. Hertzberg calls for a full self-examination of all nations that were complicit in the slaughter and plunder of the Jews before these nations can be at peace. Hertzberg shows how, paradoxically, the Holocaust served as a means to renewed pride in Jewish identity and a beginning to Jewish studies programs in colleges and universities.

Hertzberg concludes with a look at the future, specifically, the future of the state of Israel. He decries the actions of the religious right, who have impeded the peace efforts, and cautions against the "wild streak" that has brought destruction on the Jews before. He admonishes the Israelis to continue to be examples of morality by learning to live with and to accept their Palestinian Arab neighbors. He provides a "Chronology of Jewish History," along with notes to the text.

As the Jews and the Palestinians in Israel continue to move toward a peaceful solution to their decades-long conflict, this book provides insight into the fierce Jewish will to continue as a people and the historical experiences that have shaped the desire for a Jewish homeland. As Hertzberg shows, historically Jews have not been safe anywhere in the world from persecution or expulsion. He longingly speaks of the "port of Haifa and Ben-Gurion airport near Tel Aviv" as places where "the young women and men in uniform who are inspecting passports will never say that Israel already has too many Jews." Through centuries of exile from their homeland, Jews have looked forward to the day when they did not have to live under the rule of an alien culture. Hertzberg's assertion that Jews exist to provide a moral guide to the rest of the world is a worthy goal of an admirable people. Not everyone, however, will agree that there is a definable Jewish character.

Patricia Masserman

Sources for Further Study

Commentary. CVI, July, 1998, p. 63.
Kirkus Reviews. LXVI, April 15, 1998, p. 552.
The New York Review of Books. XLV, August 13, 1998, p. 34.
The New York Times Book Review. CIII, May 17, 1998, p. 36.
Publishers Weekly. CCXLV, April 27, 1998, p. 52.
The Washington Post Book World. XXVIII, September 13, 1998, p. 8.

JUST AS I THOUGHT

Author: Grace Paley (1922-   )
Published: Farrar, Straus & Giroux (New York). 332 pp. $24.00
Type of work: Miscellaneous
Time: 1950-1998
Locale: United States, Vietnam, Russia

A collection of Paley's previously written articles, letters, introductions, and other writings about her antiwar activities, environmental protests, and feminist and literary ponderings

Grace Paley is perhaps best known as a poet and short-story writer. She has published one volume of poetry, *New and Collected Poems* (1994), and three volumes of short stories, including her *Collected Stories* (1994), which was nominated for the National Book Award in 1994. A keen political presence in the United States, Paley has been vocal in her opposition to war, most specifically the Vietnam and Gulf Wars, as well as to nuclear testing. Furthermore, she has been a strong advocate of women's rights, and she speaks frankly about the average citizen's need to speak out about political concerns. She has published extensively on these issues in *The New Yorker*, *Ms.*, *TriQuarterly Review*, and other feminist and antiwar periodicals.

The writings collected in *Just As I Thought* (1998) represent Paley's ruminations, observations, and frequent indictments of cultural, political, and personal events from the early 1950's into the late 1990's. Paley's leftist political leanings show clearly in all the pieces in the volume, which include introductions to books, graduation addresses, scholarly articles, and interviews with herself. Those unfamiliar with Paley's life and political agenda will learn quickly about her Russian Jewish parents, who reared her as a socialist, and her involvement with many causes, including world peace, nuclear protest, and women's rights. The book includes Paley's insights about the Seabrook nuclear protest organized by the Clamshell Alliance in 1977 and about a women's rights march from Seneca, New York, in 1983. Paley's use of first-person anecdotes, however, puts these larger protests and movements into clearer perspective. By including texts that were previously written during the political moment, Paley can also capture the feel of the period, as well as her personal frustrations and triumphs. Yet, despite the positive effects of individual pieces in this volume, *Just As I Thought* suffers from Paley's having to organize and make sense of a wide variety of often disparate material. Weakly organized and poorly edited materials create problems with redundancy and clarity, problems the book ultimately has difficulty overcoming.

The reader benefits in some degree from Paley's decision to include original texts previously published. In her introduction to the volume, Paley rationalizes some of the inconsistencies and overlapping of texts she chooses to incorporate into the volume, noting that she has "left the articles, reports, and prefaces pretty much as they were originally written." With the exception of very brief contextualizing remarks at the beginning of each of the book's six chapters, Paley does not comment on the validity of these original texts. By not second-guessing or elaborating on her original text, Paley lets the reader glimpse her (and often an event) without the various lenses of time, creating an immediacy that quickly engages the reader.

Paley's pieces concerning the Vietnam War offer some of the best examples of how this immediacy works to the reader's advantage. In "Report from Vietnam," for example, Paley takes the reader with her to Hanoi, then onward through the Demilitarized Zone, where she journeyed in 1969 as a member of a peace coalition sent to pick up prisoners of war from North Vietnam. Her pro-North Vietnam sentiments are far from the anticommunist rhetoric she believes the U.S. government wants her to recognize. She feels no affinity for the South Vietnamese and uses examples of returning POWs who praise the North Vietnamese for their humane treatment. When she mentions South Vietnam, she describes that country's ill treatment of political prisoners and the corruption in the U.S.-supported South Vietnamese regime. Because Paley does not add a rejoinder to this anecdotal coverage by including information learned about POWs since the end of the Vietnam War, she preserves a sense of the overall antiwar climate, as well as the rhetoric, beliefs, and concerns of those involved in the peace movement.

This immediacy also causes problems, however, when Paley's dogmatic rhetoric seems to resist any factual certainties. Paley makes no pretense of being evenhanded in her discussions because, as she states in the introduction, "I am not a journalist." In her persuasive illustrations about what she characterizes as the positive treatment of POWs in North Vietnam and her conviction that Vietnamese children should not have been shipped to the United States for adoption, Paley provides little data for support of her ideas. In some cases, her leftist rhetoric without documentation makes her sound a bit naïve, or at least uninformed. Though a more comprehensive introduction to each chapter might have destroyed some of the immediacy of the articles or reports included, when Paley speaks without using factual information as background, the reader wishes for more even coverage of the issues.

The book's inclusiveness also creates some real problems with organization and cohesion. The individual chapters follow a loose chronological order, and individual chapters force topics that are only moderately appropriate together. In "Beginnings," she addresses family and upbringing. In "Continuing," Paley discusses her involvement in the peace-related projects. Nuclear protests and feminist protests, as well as personal anecdotes from these movements, dominate the chapter entitled "More." In "A Few Reflections on Teaching and Writing," Paley includes her writing lectures, reviews of books, and memories of writers. In "Later," Paley looks at various subjects from the 1980's and 1990's. "Postscript," the last chapter, includes poems about and a story by Paley's father.

Within each chapter, Paley pays little attention to relationships between individual texts. In "Continuing," for example, where texts generally relate to Vietnam or its aftermath, she also includes the rather lengthy "Conversations in Moscow"; this article, which focuses on her trip to Moscow and her discussions with Russian dissident Andrei Sakharov, relate only tangentially to the situation in Vietnam. Paley makes little effort to explain her choices for the chapter; thus, any particular relationship between the articles is lost to the reader. Ultimately, forcing texts into chapters without benefit of a clear introduction makes for the lack of clarity that pervades the book.

The lack of cohesion between and within chapters suggests that Paley had trouble finding an overall purpose for the book other than its pastiche appeal. Another problem with such inclusiveness occurs when she includes several articles about the same issue or topic. Though this structural choice for the book allows her to include different types of writing on the same subject, this effect adds little to the book other than to suggest that Paley wants to reveal herself in many different ways, under many different guises, creating a compendium of experience for the reader to uncover. On issues such as the Vietnam War, for example, Paley often includes speeches and antiwar articles about the same topic in order to underscore its importance in many areas of her life.

In this attempt to give different perspectives on the same events, however, Paley repeats herself frequently, a quality she recognizes in the introduction to "Continuing": "I should say that there are certain problems of what I'd call overlapping in the following reports—that is, repeated information, since I spoke these stories to different audiences." Unfortunately this repetitiveness remains consistent throughout the course of the book, even in chapters on subjects that would not seem to lend themselves to this problem. At least five times during the course of the book, for example, she mentions that her uncle was killed for carrying a flag during a protest in Russia. Eventually, the reader comes to know that she will add this particular detail when she mentions her uncle in any context.

This redundancy occurs most frequently in the section concerning the Vietnam War. In most of the Vietnam section, for example, Paley alludes to her 1969 peace trip. She often uses the same phrases or descriptions whenever she discusses this trip. She refers to the "green of Hanoi," for example, in three of the pieces in this chapter, in almost the same context. Twice when she discusses Donghoi, she references its placement as seen from the helicopter: "like my city, New York, it lay with its nose in the water." In later chapters, she refers again to the Vietnam trip, often coming back to the same details from earlier texts. In the process, Paley loses the freshness of the language, creating the sense that she should have been more circumspect in her choice of texts.

Despite these flaws, however, many of the individual pieces included, particularly ones that allow Paley to use her short-story skills, make the book memorable. In the section concerning her early life, Paley uses clear personal experiences to illustrate more pervasive issues. In "The Illegal Days," Paley describes the mood of the country in the early 1950's toward sexuality, birth control, and abortion. When Paley finds herself facing an unwanted pregnancy, she describes the unofficial women's advice network: "I talked the situation over with the women in the park where I used to hang out with the kids. None of them thought having an abortion was a terrible thing to do." Using these women as mentors, Paley chooses to have an illegal abortion, a decision that she does not regret. In her descriptions of this illegal activity and the helpful networking of all women for this "common cause," Paley illustrates some of the situations that women faced in the 1950's. By using her own experience and that of her friends, Paley does not force these issues on her reader. Rather, she allows the stories to speak for themselves.

Another of the most insightful anecdotes from the collection occurs later in the book as part of an oration Paley presents at Harvard University's 1991 graduation. She spends the bulk of the address discussing her hot topics—the Vietnam War and environmentalism—but concludes with a thought-provoking story about the problems of prejudice in the world as shown in three arms she has seen: one inscribed with a concentration camp number, one with AIDS lesions, and one a Haitian black. Again in this episode, Paley draws back from making a conclusion for her readers as she describes her three meetings. When she allows what she has actually seen and observed to predominate, she is much more effective in conveying her message.

Grace Paley's collection of work offers a look into political and cultural movements from the 1950's through the 1990's. As a recorder of leftist sentiment of the period, Paley's work functions as a cultural record. Furthermore, since many of the texts were originally written for mainstream audiences, one gets an overview of the protest movement and the life of a political protester—the nights spent in jail, the insults hurled from the opposition, and the painful realizations of thwarted efforts. The attention to detail and language that make Paley a gifted poet and short-story writer also bring to these more political subjects a poetic grace that contributes to the overall immediacy and readability of the collection.

Rebecca Hendrick Flannagan

Sources for Further Study

Booklist. XCIV, March 1, 1998, p. 1086.
Library Journal. CXXIII, February 15, 1998, p. 143.
Los Angeles Times. May 27, 1998, p. E6.
The Nation. CCLXVI, May 11, 1998, p. 38.
The New Republic. CCXVIII, June 29, 1998, p. 35.
New York. XXXI, May 18, 1998, p. 100.
The New York Times Book Review. CIII, April 19, 1998, p. 42.
The Progressive. LXII, December, 1998, p. 41.
Publishers Weekly. CCXLV, February 2, 1998, p. 72.
Vanity Fair. March, 1998, p. 220.

KADDISH

Author: Leon Wieseltier (1952-   )
Published: Alfred A. Knopf (New York). 588 pp. $27.50
Type of work: Religion and history
Time: The Middle Ages to the present
Locale: Europe, the Middle East, and Brooklyn

The literary editor of The New Republic *and a son of Holocaust survivors ponders the origin and meaning of the Kaddish prayer—the cornerstone of the mourning ritual in Judaism*

Mourning is a highly prescribed ritual in Judaism. For a year after the death of a parent or other family member, the mourner must attend morning and evening prayers faithfully and, in the company of at least ten worshippers, recite the kaddish prayer, which glorifies the Deity and pleads for the "coming" of his "Kingdom." Its poetic center consists of six parallel phrases that rise with incantatory power as they seem to grope for the best words to praise the power of the "Holy One (He is Blessed!)." Although the mourner's kaddish is only slightly different from the kaddish said at other points of the Jewish service or sometimes after study (in which contexts it is known as the "rabbis' kaddish"), it is universally associated with mourning in the Jewish mind. Many Jews who know little of the Hebrew liturgy find themselves uttering this prayer with relative ease when it is recited in unison by the congregation in both Reform and Conservative services or chanted at a gravesite. Despite its profound association with death, nowhere in any version of the prayer is there an allusion to death, the dying, or the individual mourner's grief.

With the death of his father on March 24, 1966, Leon Wieseltier elected to recite the kaddish three times daily at an Orthodox synagogue, and when away from his home in synagogues wherever he might be. For a modern person caught up in the busy lifestyle of a literary editor, this was no idle commitment. Immediately, he felt that his compulsion to do this, fed by grief and respect for his father, was somewhat embarrassed by the fact that he did not really know much about the ritual, the prayer, or its traditional and theological history. The intellectual in him seemed to be calling the devout and grief-stricken son to account. How would it be possible to carry out such a demanding ritual without knowing more about it? He had no choice but to begin a careful study of its background. Emotionally, he would have despised himself if he had not assumed the responsibility of the year's demanding ritual, but he had the foresight to know that unless he accompanied his feelings of filial obligation with intellectual curiosity, he would not have been able to follow through.

In his initial researches, Wieseltier discovered that in the early Middle Ages the kaddish had little to do with mourning; gradually, the prayer was connected to mourning because of the difficulties arising from the clash between funerals and holidays. Mourning was not allowed, traditionally, on feast days, but the forces of compassion eventually prevailed under the leadership of such sages as Rashi. The deciding factor, however, was the Crusades. In 1084, the Jews of Mainz and Worms were subjected to a terrible presecution by the army of Crusaders making their way down the Rhine:

In the years before the Crusades, there was no mourner's kaddish. In the years after the Crusades, the mourner's kaddish makes its appearance. This cannot have been a coincidence. The Crusades provoked the first major attempt to exterminate an entire Jewry in Europe. It failed, but it left many, many mourners in its wake.

Wieseltier is intrigued to discover that after the Crusades veneration for men of learning reached a new peak. Having to mourn its own in such great numbers, the Jewish community was more grateful than ever for its sages and rabbis, who continued to support faith in the sustaining power of Torah and the law. The "charisma of learning," as Wieseltier puts it, trumped the festivals, and it became customary to say the mourner's kaddish for dead scholars at the most important religious holidays and services.

Linking scholarship with the catastrophe of the Crusades and the mourner's kaddish, Wieseltier weaves into his narrative one of its essential strands: the joining of study with survival. His curiosity over the origins of the mourner's kaddish is driven by the same will to preserve the community that has sustained Jewish life for more than three thousand years. The obligation of the learned person is to study for more than merely his personal growth in piety and intellect. The great martyr Rabbi Akiva, who submitted to the Roman sword rather than deny the law, went out of his way to convey the Torah to the son of a "condemned" man who had failed to pass on his religious heritage to his family. Even if the son chose to ignore the rabbi's instruction, Wieseltier remarks,

Somebody else needed that the son should know these things. Somebody else was counting on it. This motive for study is often overlooked. Knowledge is not only for oneself . . . but also for the fulfillment of one's obligations to others, whose occasions require the interventions of tradition. The great unlettered Jewish community of America could use a couple of million encounters with Akiva. Or do they expect their children to save them? Their children, who will inherit an ignorance of Jewish tradition unprecedented in Jewish history?

In many ways, *Kaddish* represents the author's attempt to provide a substitute for the traditional training in Torah study that today is limited to the Orthodox community. The Orthodox Jew begins his schooling in Torah at a very early age and soon moves intuitively from commentary to commentary in a dialogic analysis of scriptural passages with his teacher or peers. In *Kaddish*, the reader is moved from commentaries and response to the kaddish prayer to reflections by the author on his own life and thoughts. The effect is somewhat similar to the alternating rhythms of law and parable that characterize Talmudic study. Instead of parables, however, Wieseltier shares the daily routine of his day. He stares out of the window of the teahouse where he goes daily to read arcane books dealing with changing attitudes toward the mourner's kaddish; his thoughts turn to the ordinary, but he is disciplined by his vow to say the prayer in the synagogue three times a day. Eventually, this ritual becomes a great burden; there are many mornings when he would prefer to stay in bed. At the same time, his consciousness becomes increasingly dependent on the demands of the routine. When the year is finally over, he finds it painful to stop, and he manages to get the rabbi of his synagogue to wean him gradually from the passion of his commitment.

The reader is gradually drawn into the ritualistic structure of Wieseltier's quest. In the process, something of the strategies of Jewish hermeneutics (or scriptural interpretation) is evoked—even though the actual texts under study do not constitute the traditional subject matter of Talmudic study. This is a tour de force, and Wieseltier deserves high marks for finding a way to introduce traditionally "ignorant" Jews to the habits of mind and study they must cultivate before they can go on to the real thing. The gentile reader also gets more than merely a feel for the way Jewish study, in its broadest sense, works.

Just as the Akiva parable stresses the importance of studying for others, many of the discoveries Wieseltier makes in his scrutiny of the many different ideas on how, why, where, and when the mourner's kaddish should be said support his growing contention that his own imagination is no better than its incorporation of the way others have used theirs: "The mind cannot do without the imagination, but the imagination can do without the mind. Is this proof of the superiority of the imagination? Not at all. This is proof of its inferiority. . . . One's pictures must be tested. Beauty must be examined for truth."

The "truth" turns out to be different from the personal when it comes to a full grasp of the mourner's kaddish. Many readers will puzzle at the absence of any display of significant personal grief in the book. Wieseltier certainly conveys the pain, traumatic confusion, and loss he felt when his father died, but he refrains from dramatizing or personalizing that grief for the reader. The father remains in the background of a book about the prayers said to honor his passing. Why is this so? For one thing, Wieseltier does not identify with psychologically therapeutic ideas about mourning that encourage letting out emotions and feeding on real memories of the dead. "The real lacks the power to heal. For therapy to be effective, it must be impractical. It must refer to the ideal." What he means is that the ritual of the mourner's kaddish generalizes the grief so that it becomes a communal responsibility and is idealized. The mourner must share his grief with nine other men in a ritual service two or three times a day. In the process, grief is shared and profoundly interwoven with the entire community's sense of its own integrity and loss, life and death. This transcends the personal and provides a form of elegiac closure by the time the year of mourning ends.

The deeper Wieseltier goes into the traditions surrounding the mourner's kaddish, the more he becomes persuaded that he is strengthening his religious ties, his religious life. There is a gain in felt affiliation with his religion that seems to grow in proportion to his embrace of his filial obligation to say the kaddish prayer for his father. There is more here than the obvious truth that piety is its own reward. After all, the kaddish prayer is for the dead, and yet it is also for the living; but it can only be for the living if they do it for the dead. This paradox brackets the gap between the living and the dead. It fuels a trust in those rituals, such as the kaddish, which must be constantly reacquired: "Or it is not being acquired; the world is full of Jews who are not Jewish, Christians who are not Christian, Muslims who are not Muslim."

If the author is patient with readers in the beginning of his dual quest (the meaning of the kaddish and the return of his readers to tradition), by the middle and end of this long meditation, he becomes almost relentless: "If something happens to the tradition in your time, on your watch, if the tradition is corrupted or lost, it is still your fault. The terms of this bargain are severe." Bereft of a proper religious education in childhood, the majority of the present generation of Jews are hopelessly separated from the traditions they are obligated to maintain. "A wise old liberal once said to me . . . that the only people who have freedom of choice in matters of religion are people who were indoctrinated in a religion as children."

From the Crusades of the eleventh century to the Holocaust of the twentieth, Jews have kept a terrible company with death. "The more death, the more kaddish," the author notes. The prayer has extolled "The Holy One" in a rising incantation of compounded tradition. It asserts the Jews' identification with transcendence in the very face of extinction. Very near the end of study, the author tells readers of "the most terrible kaddish there ever was." Three days after the liberation of the concentration camp at Buchenwald, two survivors hear a "bestial moan" coming from a mound of corpses. One of the men whispered, "It's the prayer for the dead. . . . Two minutes later we have extracted from a heap of corpses the dying man through whose mouth death is singing to us."

Peter Brier

Sources for Further Study

Booklist. XCV, September 1, 1998, p. 35.
Commentary. CVI, December, 1998, p. 74.
The Economist. CCCXLVII, September 12, 1998, p. S3.
Library Journal. CXXIII, September 1, 1998, p. 190.
National Review. L, September 28, 1998, p. 56.
The New York Times Book Review. CIII, October 4, 1998, p. 10.
The New Yorker. LXXIV, September 28, 1998, p. 100.
Publishers Weekly. CCXLV, August 31, 1998, p. 67.
The Washington Post Book World. XXVIII, September 13, 1998, p. 8.

KEATS

Author: Andrew Motion (1952-   )
First published: 1997, in Great Britain
Published: Farrar, Straus & Giroux (New York). Illustrated. 636 pp. $35.00
Type of work: Literary biography
Time: 1795-1821
Locale: Great Britain and Italy

A biography that emphasizes the social and political context in which Keats's outlook was formed and the continuing role played by these factors in the development of his poetry

> *Principal personages:*
> JOHN KEATS, the English Romantic poet
> GEORGE KEATS and
> THOMAS KEATS, brothers of John Keats
> FANNY BRAWNE, Keats's fiancée
> BENJAMIN HAYDON, a painter and friend of Keats
> LEIGH HUNT, a poet, journalist, editor, and friend of Keats
> JOHN HAMILTON REYNOLDS, a poet and friend of Keats
> JOSEPH SEVERN, a painter and friend of Keats
> BENJAMIN BAILEY,
> CHARLES BROWN,
> CHARLES COWDEN CLARKE, and
> CHARLES WENTWORTH DILKE, friends of Keats

Any biographer approaching a life as well documented as that of John Keats has to answer the question, why another biography? Andrew Motion argues that although earlier biographers have adequately laid out the details of Keats's day-to-day life and explored his psychology and his aesthetics, too little attention has been paid to the social and political context that shaped his attitudes throughout his short life, which ended in death from tuberculosis in Rome in 1821, at the age of twenty-five. In this respect, Motion is building on a recent trend in Keats criticism. Critics such as Jerome J. McGann and John Barnard in the 1970's and 1980's, Stephen Coote in his 1995 biography *Keats*, and Nicholas Roe in his 1997 *John Keats and the Culture of Dissent* (which appears to have been published too late for Motion to have made use of), are among the scholars who have recently drawn attention to this dimension of Keats's life and work.

This new emphasis on Keats's continuing engagement with the important social issues of the day presents a welcome righting of the balance, a process that has taken a good 150 years to accomplish. When interest in Keats first began to awaken in the mid-nineteenth century, Keats was seen not only as a physical weakling whose demise was hastened by hostile reviews but also as a dreamer, a man who immersed himself in Greek mythology and was content to celebrate beauty in lush, sensual poetry, ignoring wider concerns. A century later, the publication of Hyder E. Rollins's *The Keats Circle: Letters and Papers 1816-1878* (1948) and of several biographies, including Walter Jackson Bate's magisterial *John Keats* (1963), put paid to the idea that Keats was a sickly, delicate young man, unsuited for the rough-and-tumble of life. A picture emerged of a robust, energetic, manly Keats who was capable of great enjoyment of life and who commanded the loyalty of a wide circle of friends. At the same time, more respect was being given to Keats's ideas, but the emphasis remained firmly on his aesthetics.

Motion's position, one that seems eminently balanced and reasonable, is that Keats's radicalism and his liberalism, his engagement with history and with the political process, vitally inform his work throughout his brief career. Even Keats's later works, which lack the overt political references that some of the earlier poems contain, are nevertheless marked by this quest to "combine a political purpose with a poetic ambition, a social search with an aesthetic ideal."

Given Keats's social background, it is not surprising that he became a radical sympathizer. Born into the lower-middle classes at a time of great social change, Keats was never secure in his position. Orphaned at an early age, he spent his whole life poor, and his financial worries were often acute. Part of the reason for Keats's poverty (other than the fact that he never knew of the existence of one of the two trust funds in his name) was that after passing his qualifying exams to become an apothecary at the age of twenty, he abandoned the medical profession in order to make his living from poetry. There is something magnificent about the absolute determination that Keats showed in the vocation to which he felt certain he had been called, in spite of the ridicule to which the literary establishment subjected him and in spite of his failure to find a public. It is also pertinent, as Motion points out, that renouncing medicine did not mean that Keats withdrew from his goal of bettering humanity; he believed that poetry might accomplish a similar end, that the poet was "a sage,/ A humanist, physician to all men."

Keats's first volume of poems, published in 1817, shows ample evidence of his radical liberalism. Again, given that Keats had since his schooldays been an avid reader of the *Examiner*, the liberal periodical edited by Leigh Hunt, and that he met Hunt in 1816 and quickly became part of his circle, this political stance was to be expected. Keats inherited Hunt's credo that the political and the literary were two sides of the same sword; he believed that poetry should advance a politically liberal argument and also be subversive of the old order in its diction and idiom. Keats saw this as part of the task he had set himself to reconcile "thought" and "sensation."

To the Tory critics who wrote for literary periodicals such as *Blackwood's Magazine* and *The Quarterly Review*, such a credo was like a red rag to a bull. Their famous attacks on Keats's long poem *Endymion* (1818) were merciless examples of politically motivated criticism and also of sheer snobbery. In the view of these critics, poetry should be reserved for those who had received a classical education and should certainly not be practiced by the "Cockney" school—as they christened it—which included Hunt and Keats; these Cockney upstarts used "effeminate" diction (so described because it broke traditional constraints) and employed subversive themes (a love of liberty).

Although it is true that the reviews of *Endymion* were savage, even Keats's friends realized that, many fine passages notwithstanding, it was far from being a perfect poem. Charges of incoherence have been made against it ever since. Andrew Motion makes a brave attempt to boost its reputation by arguing that the poem's lack of linear development, far from marking it as a failure, is itself an example of the very freedom that lies at the heart of Keats's liberal philosophy. In this "socially conscious" reading, the poem becomes a testimony to Keats's search for the principles of a democratic, free human community, one that rejected the social and political order of the age in which he lived.

Apart from the blow Keats suffered as a result of the bad reviews, during 1818 he endured more traumatic events: His brother George, to whom he had always been close, emigrated to America, and his youngest brother, Tom, died of tuberculosis in December. Keats's own health was often poor, his finances were unstable, and he was forced into the bitter realization that his attempts to forge a reputation as a poet were unlikely to succeed. And yet, paradoxically, he was entering a twelve-month period, which lasted from September, 1818, to September, 1819, in which he would produce the works for which he is best known: the unfinished epic "Hyperion"; "The Eve of St. Agnes"; the six odes, including the "Ode to a Nightingale," "Ode on a Grecian Urn," and "To Autumn"; and "The Fall of Hyperion." It was a dazzling rush of creativity expressing itself in a variety of poetic forms. Keats was still only twenty-three years old.

These poems, published in Keats's third and last book, *Poems* (1820), have sometimes been interpreted as his retreat from earlier political engagement into a desire to meditate on transcendental questions of art and beauty. Once more, Motion argues that this is too simple a view. Although Keats no longer makes overt references to contemporary events, he nevertheless subtly incorporates political and social issues into the meditation—in the great odes, for example, he acknowledges the full weight of history rather than trying to escape from it.

In October, 1819, Keats became ill with tuberculosis, which he had probably caught while nursing his brother Tom the previous year. By the following January, his condition had worsened, and he was to write virtually no more poetry before his death. In what Keats probably knew would be a vain attempt to restore his health, he agreed to travel to Italy, leaving England in September, accompanied by his friend, the painter Joseph Severn. In Rome, Keats lingered for four more months, bitterly distressed by his enforced separation from his fiancée, Fanny Brawne, and contemplating the ruin of all of his hopes. He died without any awareness that he had in fact fulfilled his ambition to "be among the English poets after my death."

Most people who have studied Keats have probably wondered about what he might have produced had he lived. After all, at the time of his death, Keats had achieved more than William Shakespeare (the poet to whom he is most often compared) had at a comparable age. The question is of course unanswerable, but Motion suggests that the last major poem Keats wrote, "To Autumn," shows that he was on the point of entering a new creative phase in which he could have achieved the "disinterestedness" for which he had been aiming, and which would indeed, had he been granted the time to develop it, have placed him even closer to the Shakespearean pedestal.

Since each generation must reinterpret the lives of great historical figures in the light of its own beliefs and concerns, Motion's biography is a welcome addition to the large number of studies about Keats. Apart from his attempt to anchor Keats's work more firmly in the political and social circumstances in which it was written, Motion also offers a lively and engrossing picture of the day-to-day life of the man. He includes informative sketches of Keats's many friends (Keats was extremely fortunate in his choice of friends, who showed him great loyalty and devotion); Keats's opinions of and interactions with other poets and writers, such as William Wordsworth, Percy Bysshe Shelley, Samuel Taylor Coleridge, and William Hazlitt; and insightful analysis of Keats's complex and difficult feelings about women, which were shaped by the early loss of his mother.

However, although Motion does take issue with a couple of interpretations advanced influentially by Robert Gittings in *John Keats: The Living Year* (1954), his narrative of the poet's life does not substantially change any of the details that have been unearthed by previous biographers. Primarily, *Keats* is important because it shows Keats's aesthetic and his political beliefs to be of a piece; his work is embedded in his response to the life of the times. In this way, Motion's biography complements the approach of Walter Jackson Bate in *John Keats* (1963), which also offered critical analysis of the poems but from a New Critical perspective. Motion's historicist approach yields many new insights, often in surprising places—even, for example, in the epitaph that Keats composed for his gravestone: "Here lies one whose name was writ in water." This has always been seen as an indication of Keats's sense of failure, but in Motion's analysis it becomes ambiguous. Being written "in" water, his name has "made itself permanent. His poetry had come to him as naturally as leaves to a tree; now it was part of nature—part of the current of history"—a viewpoint that recalls the words of Lord Byron in *Childe Harold's Pilgrimage*: "I live not in myself, but I become/ Portion of that around me. . . ."

Bryan Aubrey

Sources for Further Study

America. CLXXIX, September 12, 1998, p. 21.
Choice. XXXV, July, 1998, p. 1856.
The Economist. CCCXLV, November 15, 1997, p. 13.
Essays in Criticism. XLVIII, July, 1998, p. 269.
Library Journal. CXXIII, December, 1997, p. 106.
The New Leader. LXXX, December 29, 1998, p. 20.
The New York Review of Books. XLV, May 14, 1998, p. 39.
The New York Times Book Review. CIII, February 1, 1998, p. 13.
Publishers Weekly. CCXLIV, November 10, 1997, p. 60.
The Times Literary Supplement. October 24, 1997, p. 3.

KING OF THE WORLD
Muhammad Ali and the Rise of an American Hero

Author: David Remnick (1959-   )
Published: Random House (New York). Illustrated. 326 pp. $25.00
Type of work: Biography
Time: 1942-1996
Locale: The United States

Pulitzer Prize winner David Remnick presents the chronicle of boxing legend Muhammad Ali as perhaps the quintessential story of the 1960's

> *Principal personages:*
> MUHAMMAD ALI, who as twenty-two-year-old CASSIUS CLAY defeated Sonny Liston for the heavyweight boxing title
> SONNY LISTON, the "bad" heavyweight champion
> FLOYD PATTERSON, the "good" heavyweight champion
> ARCHIE MOORE, a seemingly ageless boxer who recognized in the young Ali the intelligence and guile that were his own trademarks
> DREW "BUNDINI" BROWN, Ali's cornerman, a motivator and jester
> ANGELO DUNDEE, Ali's faithful trainer
> FERDIE PACHECO, Ali's discarded physician, who advised his retirement when he found evidence of brain damage
> MALCOLM X, the Nation of Islam crusader whom Ali first lionized, then denounced, and later respected
> ELIJAH MUHAMMAD, the leader of the Nation of Islam
> JAMES BALDWIN and
> NORMAN MAILER, novelist-reporters who wrote powerfully on Ali
> LONNIE, Ali's fourth wife and his devoted caretaker

"It never occurred to me that you couldn't like both Walt Whitman and the New York Knicks," wrote thirty-nine-year-old David Remnick in reference to his first full-time job in journalism as a sportswriter for *The Washington Post*. "That kind of false dichotomy has always seemed ridiculous to me." Remnick's "false dichotomy" is inseparable from the misperceptions of him and of *The New Yorker* magazine, whose editor he became in mid-1998, succeeding Tina Brown. Covering the infamous ear-biting Evander Holyfield-Mike Tyson heavyweight title fight in Las Vegas last year, his sixth as staff writer for the magazine, Remnick was approached by a middle-aged couple who saw his reporter's ID. "*The New Yorker*?" he was asked. "Do they cover boxing?"

Remnick early cherished *The New Yorker* essays on boxing by the late A. J. Liebling. He also recognized that literature's touchstone is dramatic conflict, whether found in large in the death agony of the century's most formidable totalitarian system or, in smaller but no less galvanic terms, the legend of Ali, a transcendent sports hero. The transition from his 1995 Pulitzer Prize-winning *Lenin's Tomb* to *King of the World*, which will be among the essential books for students of the American 1960's, was easy.

The quintessential locus for naked conflict in sports is the boxing ring, according to Remnick. It pits two men, without any protective apparatus other than padded gloves, whose mutual intent is to destroy. Yet professional boxers have always been sport's walking wounded—kept alive by mobsters and media.

Neither support group took seriously an eighteen-year-old 1960 Olympic gold-medal winner from Louisville, Kentucky, who boasted to a young sportswriter named Dick Schaap that "I'll be the greatest of all time." Big men were supposed to wade in and flatten their foes—not, like the young Cassius Clay, to "float like a butterfly, sting like a bee" and have the brass to write self-celebrating doggerel about it.

To Liebling, "Clay had a skittering style, like a pebble scaled over water . . . good to watch but making only glancing contact." To the midcentury's dean of boxing columnists, Jimmy Cannon, Clay was the "fifth Beatle. . . . He was all pretense and gas." Only apprentice sportswriters such as Schaap and, especially, the socially conscious Robert Lipsyte recognized in the young contender a figure outside the heroic image of the mechanical destroyer Joe Louis, a man whose bold charisma might end the grip of organized crime, save the sport, and help break society's color line.

However, as Remnick reveals in this riveting account, the Cassius Clay/Muhammad Ali phenomenon benefited from interacting forces. The usual mob suspects were in disarray when Clay emerged in the early 1960's. For him, the Frankie Carbos were benevolently supplanted by the Black Muslims, to whom he pledged undying loyalty even as he rose to boxing's pinnacle.

The usual patronizing tribute accorded a book like this is that it reads like a novel. *King of the World* reads like higher journalism in the best mold of a David Halberstam, to whom Remnick acknowledges a "real debt." Its kinship with strong fiction, of which Remnick is a tireless reader, lies in its seamlessness. From a splendid prologue set in the 1990's—Remnick and the Parkinson's-afflicted Ali watch in the latter's rural southern Michigan retreat films of his first fight with the fearsome Sonny Liston—the narrative flashes back to the pre-Ali days of boxing and its two archetypes, Floyd Patterson (the "good black" heavyweight) and Liston (the "bad" one).

Remnick devotes part 1's four chapters to Patterson ("the most doubt-addled of titleholders," a man who wore a disguise to escape notice after being dismantled by Liston in 126 seconds in 1962) and to the new champion Liston, an ex-convict with a withering stare and deadly punch whose gangster sponsors supplied him with prosti-tutes during training. The book is a triangle, with Liston and Patterson occupying the contrasting legs and Ali the base. Remnick's portrait of Liston as one whose end bore the inevitability of the boxer rather than the comeuppance of the bully, contains some of his most nuanced prose. When Liston's wife, away visiting her mother, returned to Las Vegas, she found his body in their hotel room. Liston, thirty-eight, had been dead six days. His was a drug addict's death, although the report listed the causes as lung congestion and heart failure. Remnick quotes a publicist who knew him well as believing that "Liston died the day he was born."

Part 2—also four chapters—places at center stage Ali, "a man of independence and American originality who would transcend the worlds of Sonny Liston and Floyd Patterson." A son of the black middle class, the irrepressible Cassius Clay, named for a nineteenth century abolitionist who inherited a plantation and forty slaves, was conceded a diploma by a principal who recognized his boxing skills early. (The principal is quoted as having remarked, "Do you think I'm going to be the principal of a school that Cassius Clay didn't finish? Why, in one night, he'll make more money than the principal and all you teachers make in a year.")

The principal proved a prophet. At fifteen, Clay sparred with Willie Pastrano, a highly regarded light heavyweight, while the famous handler Angelo Dundee watched. Dundee, who would become Ali's trainer, stopped the sparring, pleading that Pastrano was stale. Pastrano is supposed to have retorted that "the kid beat the hell out of me."

The comet never veered in its path upward. Remnick covers his man's two-year taunting of Liston in a few deftly selected set pieces. Although admitting afterward that he feared the menacing champion with the intimidating stare, the then-challenger, as he would do years later against such formidable opponents as George Foreman and Joe Frazier, always mounted a strategy. He never forgot that Sonny Liston had learned during years in prison to fear the "crazies"—so Clay would act crazy. Liston, to an extent not even realized by his young foe, never had a chance.

Other parts of Muhammad Ali's worldwide appeal make *King of the World* an essential book for students of America in the 1960's: Ali's resistance to stereotyping, leading to his conversion to the Nation of Islam; and his open defiance of his draft board during the Vietnam War, for which he was sentenced to five years in prison and a heavy fine, a decision reversed by the Supreme Court. Despite vindication, Ali was unable to fight during the three-year-long appeal process, at a cost of millions of dollars in gate receipts and endorsements.

Despite his book's subtitle—"The Rise of an American Hero"—Remnick allows the warts to show. As D. Keith Mano points out, Ali put Elijah Muhammad's Nation of Islam on the American spiritual map. However, loyalty to one spiritual leader led to a rending disloyalty to another. Malcolm X became personal apostle to Cassius Clay, and Clay converted to Islam. When, after his tour to Mecca, Malcolm began thinking in universal terms that no longer included hating whites, Elijah Muhammad repudiated him and persuaded Ali to follow suit. Although Ali, perhaps more than anyone, should have understood an apostasy such as Malcolm's, only his onetime friend's martyrdom restored Ali's deep regard.

Perhaps the book's major contribution is to demonstrate that while much of Ali's appeal derived from boxing, his is a story that reaches far beyond. Ring physician Ferdie Pacheco, who left Ali's entourage when his warnings about brain damage were ignored, put it best when referring to Ali's crippling Parkinson's syndrome: "Ali and boxing are two different subjects. The only thing that Ali did that was pure boxing was the tragic end, which all boxers have if they've been too good and won't quit."

Among "old-school" sports aficionados, boxing's have been the most fervent. From the tainted 1927 "slow-count" victory of Gene Tunney over Jack Dempsey to the 1998 restoration of Mike Tyson's license after he had been banned for biting off a piece of Evander Holyfield's ear, boxing fans have always had to face up to scandals and controversy. For almost two decades, Ali made wonderment a component of violence, for he, like Rafael Sabatini's Scaramouche, "was born with a gift of laughter and a sense that the world was mad."

Richard Hauer Costa

Sources for Further Study

Booklist. XCV, September 15, 1998, p. 172.
Library Journal. CXXIII, October 1, 1998, p. 104.
Money. XXVII, November, 1998, p. 207.
National Review. L, November 9, 1998, p. 59.
The New York Times. November 17, 1998, B1, p. 8.
The New York Times Book Review. CIII, October 25, 1998, p. 11.
Publishers Weekly. CCXLV, October 5, 1998, p. 68.
Sports Illustrated. LXXXIX, October 19, 1998, p. R16.
Time. CLI, November 2, 1998, p. 97.
The Wall Street Journal. October 21, 1998, p. A20.
The Washington Post Book World. XXVIII, October 18, 1998, p. 1.

KINGSLEY AMIS
A Biography

Author: Eric Jacobs
First published: 1995, in Great Britain
Published: St. Martin's Press (New York). 392 pp. $26.95
Type of work: Biography
Time: The twentieth century
Locale: England and Wales

The authorized biography of a famous, prolific, but progressively controversial British writer best known for his comic first novel, Lucky Jim

Principal personages:
KINGSLEY AMIS, a prolific British writer and an often acerbic literary
  personality
PHILIP LARKIN, a noted British poet and Amis's close friend from their
  years at Oxford University
ROBERT CONQUEST, an Anglo-American historian and Amis's close
  friend from the 1950's
HILARY (BARDWELL) AMIS, Amis's first wife
ELIZABETH JANE HOWARD, a noted British novelist and Amis's second
  wife

When he died on October 22, 1995, Sir Kingsley Amis had been an important and highly visible fixture on the British literary scene for more than forty years. Although he had already published two volumes of poetry, it was his phenomenally successful novel, *Lucky Jim* (1954), that catapulted him to fame. Amis went on to write another two dozen novels (including the award-winning *The Old Devils*, 1986), several collections of short stories, and further volumes of verse. He published a quantity of journalism, much of it of high quality, and edited popular and influential collections of light verse and science fiction.

Amis also remained in the public eye thanks to his provocative views on politics, the arts, and society, many of which seemed to grow increasingly belligerent. One late novel, *Stanley and the Women* (1984), reportedly was rejected by many American publishers because of its aggressively unsympathetic portrayal of women.

Jacobs opens his biography with a kind of overture, an introduction entitled "Portrait of the Artist in Age," that candidly—perhaps too candidly for some readers—describes Amis in his early seventies. The figure Jacobs portrays rises from his solitary bed, goes to the toilet, shaves, showers, and dresses—in what are now oversize clothes, as Amis has put on considerable weight in the last few years. A healthful and thus fairly unappetizing breakfast has been prepared by his former wife Hilary ("Hilly"), and while Amis forces down his food and reads the papers, Hilary's current husband Alastair Boyd, Lord Kilmarnock, makes Amis's bed. At last Amis approaches his study and his typewriter, where, despite his considerable anxieties about writing, he finishes his minimum of five hundred precisely chosen and usually very funny words.

There follows a taxi ride to a pub, club, or restaurant, where Amis can finally relax and—most important—talk with friends and drink. He eats moderately and without great enthusiasm, talks more and drinks more, then finally navigates the stairs for a taxi ride home, where he will nap, write more, drink more, watch television, and eat a dinner cooked by Hilary or by their daughter Sally, who lives nearby. Amis concludes his day with more television, more alcohol, and light reading. Although his current domestic arrangements allay a lifelong anxiety—sleeping alone in an otherwise empty house—he downs several pills to assure uninterrupted sleep. The rest of Jacobs's biography describes the route Amis followed from his birth to this destination (a pretty much ultimate one, it turns out), with its bizarre domestic arrangements and its carefully balanced elements of domesticity, conviviality, and all-important solitude.

Kingsley Amis was born in Clapham, south London, on April 16, 1922, the only child of a lower-middle-class family in which he was both spoiled and regimented. He attended the City of London School and St. John's College, Oxford, thanks to scholarships. It was at Oxford that he met Philip Larkin, later a noted poet and, until his death in 1985, a close friend and reliable sounding board for Amis's evolving public and private views.

Amis served in the British Army as a signal master during World War II, returning to Oxford in 1945. He met Hilary Bardwell the following year and married her in 1948. The next year, he accepted a position as lecturer at the University College of Swansea, an arm of the University of Wales. He would remain a member of the academic world until 1963.

Jacobs admits that he and Amis disagreed on only one major point, the extent to which Amis incorporated himself and the people around him into his fiction. Jacobs opted for "more," Amis for "less," with the resulting biography approaching a reasonable and livable compromise. Jacobs thus finds much of Amis in his first and still most popular novel, *Lucky Jim*.

The protagonist of that novel, Jim Dixon, is a lower-middle-class lecturer in history at a provincial university, living in a boarding house and finding himself perennially short of the money he needs for alcohol and tobacco. His position at the university is precarious, and he must toady up to the cunning but notably witless head of the department, one Professor Welch. (According to Jacobs, this figure is modeled closely upon Amis's new father-in-law.) To deal with boors and buffoons such as Welch, Jim resorts to a kind of coping mechanism hilariously familiar to those who knew Amis—face-making. Thus, Jim's "Sex Life in Ancient Rome" face is one Amis used to share with friends, and the admittedly boring paper that the hapless Jim is trying to get published—"The Economic Influence of the Developments in Shipbuilding Techniques, 1450 to 1485"—turns out to be on a "suitably dim and dreary topic" suggested by one of Amis's colleagues at Swansea.

Many of Amis's subsequent works would explore variations on the themes Amis announced in his first published novel and, according to Jacobs, would reveal further aspects of their author's personality. Probably the most important after *Lucky Jim* was *The Green Man* (1969), a ghost story lauded by many as one of the best modern novels of the supernatural. Although its protagonist Maurice Allington is an innkeeper—a role the impractical author himself had never attempted—Allington and Amis share many less than attractive characteristics: hypochondria, an extreme fondness for alcohol, and a selfish and predatory attitude toward women and sex.

In fact, Amis's affair with fellow writer Elizabeth Jane Howard led to his divorce from Hilary in 1965. He and Howard were married the same year, but the marriage ultimately soured, and the two were divorced on far from amicable terms in 1983. At one point, Howard had apparently given as a condition for her returning to the marriage that Amis give up alcohol completely—a step Amis refused as unreasonable, as he suspected Howard knew he would. The increasingly dark and misogynistic tone of Amis's fiction from *Girl, Twenty* (1971) through *Jake's Thing* (1978) and *Stanley and the Women* (1984) thus coincides with the deterioration in Amis's relationship with Howard. As Jacobs notes, "For Amis, love wore off, then liking, then sex." Significantly enough, *Jake's Thing* deals with a subject that seems to have been uppermost on Amis's mind—impotence—although few men would have been able to treat it as comically as Amis managed. More significantly still, when informed by his doctor at novel's end that there is a simple cure for his impotence, Jake refuses the treatment.

The end of Amis's second marriage and his apparent loss of interest in women as sexual partners led to an unlikely but undeniably golden autumn. Thanks to efforts by Amis's sons Philip and Martin, Amis came to share a household with Hilary and her third husband Alastair in 1981.

The relatively mellow tone of Amis's last novels seems to reflect his new domestic arrangements. *The Old Devils* is set in Wales—a favored locale of Amis's in both personal and fictional terms since his years at Swansea—and deals at some length with the latter years of a large cast of friends and acquaintances. The novel, a logical capstone to Amis's long career, deservedly won him the Booker Prize, Britain's most prestigious literary award. Yet more revealing are *The Folks That Live on the Hill* (1990) and *You Can't Do Both* (1994). The former profiles a household much like Amis's (although the relationships are strategically disguised), while the latter follows the first four decades of a feckless protagonist very much like the younger Amis himself. Here Amis comes to fictional terms with a man whose persona and values he rejected at one time—his father—and casts a cold eye on the young man he was. In Jacobs's sober words, the novel is "an apology, a message of love and regret. And it is addressed to Hilly."

Biographer Jacobs and his subject met over a period of two and a half years at the London club they shared (the Garrick), at the nearby Queen's Pub, and at Amis's home. The resulting biography reflects the informality and somewhat boozy bonhomie of such locales; like Amis's own work, it is never less than highly readable and is often incisive and provocative. However, because Jacobs has intentionally avoided writing a literary biography, the question of Amis's ultimate achievement looms unanswered throughout his work. Even the award of the Booker Prize to *The Old Devils* receives less than a sentence.

Of the several elements that Amis's final domestic arrangements assured him, solitude was clearly the most important in terms of his accomplishments as a writer.

As recounted by Jacobs, Amis's life has its high and low points and its comic moments, but it was not remarkably busy or involved. It was in his hours alone that Amis achieved what was in many ways a complex body of work, and yet these are the hours that Jacobs—for all his access to the myriad (and sometimes uncomplimentary) details of the writer's life—never quite penetrates.

Jacobs's biography was originally published in Great Britain in 1995. In an epilogue to subsequent editions, he explains that he wrote the work's opening chapter, "Portrait of the Artist in Age," first, some eighteen months before he finished the work. During that period, he explained, Amis had grown noticeably older. The original portrait now "seemed slightly out of focus." By the time of the publication of the British paperback edition, Amis had died at University College Hospital, London.

Jacobs concludes his biography with the obituary he had written (several months before the event) for *The Guardian* and the brief tribute he subsequently wrote for *The Spectator*. The former pays tribute to the writer whose works defined his place and times better than those of any of his colleagues, while the latter bids farewell to the man. Neither these nor his epilogue, however, mentions the diaries Jacobs attempted to publish detailing Amis's final months. His plans to sell these within a few days of Amis's death were attacked by the writer's family, who found their content insensitive. Perhaps not coincidentally, the Amis family had just chosen another editor over Jacobs to prepare a collection of Amis's caustic letters. At the very least, the timing of Jacobs' efforts suggests a predatory aspect to his relationship with Amis.

In authorizing an acquaintance such as Jacobs to write his biography and in choosing to correct him for the most part on "small points of fact or punctuation" only, Amis may have been thumbing his nose one last time at the literary establishment. Was he daring critics to judge him on the often uncomplimentary facts of his life, as opposed to the very real and wide-ranging accomplishments of his stories, novels, and poems? Future biographers will be in debt to Jacobs for the firsthand information he has gathered from Amis and his friends, but they may find that his yeoman efforts have obscured the value of a complex and significant writer.

Grove Koger

Sources for Further Study

American Scholar. LXV, Autumn, 1996, p. 624.
Booklist. XCIV, May 15, 1998, p. 1588.
Boston Globe. June 21, 1998, p. C3.
Library Journal. CXXIII, May 15, 1998, p. 84.
National Review. L, September 14, 1998, p. 66.
New Statesman & Society. VIII, June 30, 1995, p. 37.
San Francisco Chronicle Book Review. July 19-25, 1998, p. 3.
Sewanee Review. CIV, Summer, 1996, p. 452.

Spectator. CCLIV, June 10, 1995, p. 36.
TLS: Times Literary Supplement. June 16, 1995, p. 26.
The Washington Post Book World. XXVIII, August 23, 1998, p. 5.
World Literature Today. LXX, Spring, 1996, p. 413.

LAMBS OF GOD

Author: Marele Day
Published: Penguin Putnam (New York). 330 pp. $23.95
Type of work: Novel
Time: The present
Locale: An imaginary island

An atmospheric tale involving three mysterious nuns and a priest on an isolated island

> *Principal characters:*
> SISTER IPHIGENIA, an aging nun
> SISTER MARGARITA, a middle-aged nun
> SISTER CARLA, the youngest of the three nuns
> FATHER IGNATIUS, a young priest, secretary to the bishop of the diocese

The bizarre events described in *Lambs of God* take place in a decaying monastery on an imaginary island in an unspecified part of the world. The author is so careful about avoiding dropping any clues that the reader can only surmise that the island is located off one of the coasts of Australia or else is somewhere near Great Britain. It is clear, at least, that the island is in an area where the people speak English and where their principal occupations are fishing and raising sheep. (The author herself is a native Australian, which makes that country seem like a slightly better bet than Great Britain.) Although sheep-raising is big business in Australia, in a published interview Marele Day has revealed that she had known nothing about sheep before she started her novel and was in fact a little afraid of real sheep. Day was a fairly successful writer, best known for her Claudia Valentine mystery novels, before the inspiration for the purely escapist fantasy that became *Lambs of God* impelled her to follow her muse in an entirely new direction.

The sheep in her novel all have names and are all thought to be reincarnations of the many nuns who have died over the years. Since they are regarded as fellow nuns with names inherited from those who have died, the sheep have free run of the monastery and even appear in the chapel, where the survivors hold a whole round of daily devotions. Only three nuns, the island's only human inhabitants, remain alive. They grow much of their own food and earn a little money by spinning and knitting the wool from their flock of sheep. They entertain one another by making up stories that are loosely based on memories of old fairy tales, stories from the Old Testament, and parables from the New Testament. They have become unkempt and more than a little eccentric in their isolation. They have knitted themselves strange new garments that bear no resemblance to their original habits, which have long since worn out. They still read the Bible, but—not unlike the marooned schoolboys in William Golding's novel *Lord of the Flies* (1954)—they seem to be gradually losing the veneer of civilization and reverting to primitive behavior and superstition.

The bishop of the local diocese has not heard from any of the sequestered nuns in years, and he assumes that the monastery and the island are now deserted. His bright, ambitious young secretary Father Ignatius has conceived a plan to restore the decaying buildings as historical curiosities and to create a luxury tourist resort around them. He thinks the isolation and silence will appeal to wealthy businessmen who want to get away from it all, and he thinks that the island could also serve as an expensive, tax-deductible setting to hold secret, high-level conferences. It is implied, though not stated, that the new resort might be an ideal location for conventions at which notables could romp with playmates without attracting attention.

The island is connected to the mainland by a strand that is underwater most of the time. Father Ignatius drives across at low tide in a rented car but gets stuck in a rut on the disintegrating dirt road while trying to make it up the steep hill. He has to travel the rest of the way on foot. He has a terrible time, because nobody remembers exactly where the monastery was located and because the hills are overgrown with thickets of thorns (as was the castle in the story of "Sleeping Beauty"). In fact, Father Ignatius is destined to reawaken not one but three "sleeping beauties" from their separate dream lives. Many of the events in *Lambs of God* resemble those in fairy tales, including "The Three Bears" and "Beauty and the Beast." The nuns spend much of their time telling one another their own modified versions of these and other stories. The island seems almost as mysterious and enchanted as the one in William Shakespeare's *The Tempest*, and when Father Ignatius first encounters the women, he is reminded of the Weird Sisters in Shakespeare's *Macbeth*.

Father Ignatius, all tattered and torn, is first discovered by Sister Carla, the youngest of the three nuns. Like Shakespeare's Miranda, Carla has never seen a man before and thinks this must be a brave new world that has such handsome strangers in it. She is a true child of nature. She was discovered as a squalling newborn infant on the doorstep and reared by the nuns, who were much more numerous at the time, on diluted ewe's milk. No one has ever explained anything about sexual development or sexual attraction to Carla, who is now approaching middle age, although it turns out that Sister Margarita and Sister Iphigenia know far more about the subject than they have ever acknowledged. As a mystery writer, Marele Day could not resist the temptation to add an element of mystery to her fantasy; the greatest mystery in the book is the identity of Carla's mother and the way in which she managed to bring her newborn baby to the spot in the middle of the night and escape undetected. The mystery is not cleared up until the very last pages of this unusual novel.

By this point, Day's effective, often poetic prose has likely beguiled readers into the sense that the tide has come in to cover up the strand and cut them off from the real world, with all its demands and frustrations. Readers will be fully in sympathy with the three sisters when they realize that their handsome, sophisticated, well-educated visitor intends to exile them to some urban asylum for superfluous nuns, slaughter their beloved sheep, and desecrate their home by turning it into a playground for the jet set.

All three former Mother Superiors have died and, in the minds of the three surviving sisters, have been reborn as lambs of God. Sister Iphigenia, the eldest of the trio, has become the de facto Mother Superior. She is a strong-willed woman who possesses an unusually keen sense of smell. This gift proves to be an insurmountable obstacle to Ignatius when he tries to escape from the island. He wakes from a deep sleep to find that the nuns have taken away all his clothes, supposedly to mend them; after several days confinement, he realizes that they have no intention of giving them back. He fashions a crude garment out of a couple of sheepskins and tries to slip away barefoot in the dead of night, but the sisters pursue him, with Iphigenia leading with the tenacity and assurance of a bloodhound. The frightened, disoriented, torn, and bleeding priest falls into a deep ditch and loses consciousness.

When he wakes, Ignatius finds himself a real prisoner. Under the pretext that his legs are broken, the nuns have wrapped them together in a plaster cast that extends all the way up to his hips. They have taken the added precaution of binding his wrists together. Here the novel takes on a resemblance to Stephen King's novel *Misery* (1987), in which Paul Sheldon, a famous writer with two broken legs in full plaster casts, is being held captive by Annie Wilkes, "his biggest fan ever," and must use his wits to try to escape. Like Sheldon, Ignatius is forced to make up stories to entertain his captors. He has tried to keep his intentions about their island home a secret, but they have gone through his belongings and found his maps, sketches, and written proposals. They have also used their combined strengths to push his rented car over the cliff into the ocean. Ignatius concludes that his best ploy is to use his masculine sex appeal to charm one of the sisters into helping him escape. There can be no doubt that all three are affected by the presence of a man whom they have seen completely naked on more than one occasion.

The only woman who makes no attempt to conceal her interest is Carla, who visits the immobilized priest in secret and causes him to experience a whirlwind of conflicting emotions by exploring the most intimate parts of his body with her hands. Iphigenia pretends to be totally indifferent to him, and Margarita is overtly hostile. Instead of arousing sexual interest in himself, the handsome young priest's effect on these older women is to revive their memories of the past. Margarita's memories have been repressed since childhood. She was sold by her own father to a perverted scoundrel who took her to a seedy hotel and brutally raped her. When Ignatius's nudity reminds her of that traumatic event, she decides to repeat the revenge she took against the rapist: She had set his bed on fire while he was in a drunken stupor and let him burn to death. She begins to think of doing the same thing to the helpless priest when the opportunity presents itself.

Iphigenia's memories are not unpleasant and have never been repressed. However, they contain a dark secret that she has never shared: When she was a young initiate, she had been sent to find the bone-setter to set the broken leg of an elderly nun. On that memorable night, the strand was covered by the tide, and a handsome young fisherman volunteered to row her across. Young Iphigenia never did find the bone-setter, and the nun remained crippled for the rest of her life, but Iphigenia enjoyed one memorable night of lovemaking with the fisherman. The baby who appeared at the convent's doorway nine months later and became Sister Carla was Iphigenia's own daughter.

By the time Ignatius is freed from his cast and permitted to leave the island, the conflict has resolved itself as if by magic. The nuns not only will be allowed to remain in their home but also will actually own the island. When Carla, passionately in love with Ignatius, breaks her vow of sequestration and follows the young priest across the strand, Iphigenia understands her daughter's feelings and does nothing to try to stop her. It seems unlikely, however, that Ignatius will break his vows and sacrifice his privileged position for this infatuated woman. It seems far more likely that a rejected and disillusioned Carla will eventually recross the strand and remain with Iphigenia and Margarita until the not-too-distant time when they have all died and the island has been inherited by a flock of wild sheep.

Marele Day's novel has received enthusiastic reviews. Almost overnight, she was transformed from a category fiction writer into an international celebrity. Under the headline "Fox Grabs Lambs," *Variety* reported that Winona Ryder (twice nominated for Academy Awards as Best Actress) had a film deal to produce and star in a screen adaptation of *Lambs of God*. Such interest is understandable. The novel has a highly unusual love story and obvious cinematic potential. It somewhat resembles the beautifully photographed 1947 British film *Black Narcissus*, based on the 1939 Rumer Godden novel about a group of Anglican nuns isolated in the Himalayas. In Godden's story, young Sister Ruth falls madly in love with a handsome man and, like Carla, breaks her vow of chastity to follow him into the outside world. *Black Narcissus* won two Academy Awards, and its star, Deborah Kerr, received the New York Film Critics Award as Best Actress. The fact that *Lambs of God* also a strong resemblance to Stephen King's novel *Misery*, made into a highly profitable 1990 motion picture that won Kathy Bates an Academy Award and a Golden Globe Award as Best Actress, could hardly have escaped the attention of filmmakers. *Lambs of God* was a best-seller in the author's native Australia and may become a best-seller internationally because of the media attention her sincere, well-written novel has received.

Bill Delaney

Sources for Further Study

Booklist. XCIV, March 1, 1998, p. 1091.
The Christian Century. CXV, July 15, 1998, p. 693.
Library Journal. CXXIII, February 15, 1998, p. 169.
The New York Times Book Review. CIII, July 19, 1998, p. 18.
Publishers Weekly. CCXLV, February 2, 1998, p. 79.
The Times Literary Supplement. September 5, 1998, p. 21.

THE LAST RESORT

Author: Alison Lurie (1926-   )
Published: Henry Holt (New York). 321 pp. $24.95
Type of work: Novel
Time: The late 1990's
Locale: Key West, Florida

Against the backdrop of tropical Key West, novelist Alison Lurie's characters face illness and death and explore the joys of living in the present

> *Principal characters:*
> WILKIE WALKER, a seventy-year-old environmentalist suddenly facing
>   physical and intellectual infirmity
> JENNY WALKER, Wilkie's much younger wife
> LEE WEISS, the lesbian owner and manager of Artemis Lodge, Jenny
>   Walker's lover
> MOLLY HOPKINS, a retired artist who lives in Key West
> PERRY JACKSON, an HIV-positive Key West gardener and property owner
> BARBIE MUMPSON, a Key West visitor who changes her life for a cause
> MYRA MUMPSON, Barbie's mother

Alison Lurie, the Pulitzer Prize-winning author of *Foreign Affairs* (1985), typically addresses social as well as interpersonal issues in her novels, often as they relate to the rarefied world of the academic. In *The Last Resort* (1998), however, Lurie's emphasis shifts away from the confines of the university into the vacation paradise of Key West, Florida. Though most of the characters in *The Last Resort* arrive in Key West to escape the "cold climate" of their other lives, they also use the otherworldliness of the island to contemplate more serious concerns about aging and death, concerns that Lurie does not typically address in such an extended fashion. Because of this shift in emphasis, *The Last Resort* is a darker Lurie effort—and, because of her reliance on quick character change in the Key West setting, a not altogether successful one.

Lurie's use of Key West as a fecund paradise, a place for characters to retreat to and marshal their strengths to change, serves the novel in an obvious way. Confused and crisis-stricken characters arrive seeking answers, then either leave having made a positive change or stay when they learn how to live with the despairing issue at hand. Characters roam the palm-lined streets, marvel at the bright orchids and thick, green undergrowth, and swim in pools and the ocean as methods of contemplating their problems. Though useful as a dramatic metaphor for the action of the novel, Lurie's dependence on the island for this purpose seems contrived, particularly in how quickly some characters must change because of the average length of a vacation.

Lurie does, however, create memorable characters whose actions keep the narrative engaging. The novel opens in the fictional New England town of Convers as Wilkie Walker, famed naturalist and environmentalist, contemplates what he perceives as his imminent death. Recently retired from Convers College, Wilkie believes he is finished professionally as well as physically; he thinks he has colon cancer. Rather than waste away as a failure, Wilkie considers elaborate strategies for killing himself, contemplations that alter his usual demeanor, making him morose, despondent, and angry. Because he believes his much younger wife could not accept his sudden loss of power and vigor, he keeps his fears from her. As a result, he grows more distant and aloof, and she fears he has stopped loving her or has found some sort of fault with her intellectual powers. As Jenny searches for answers to Wilkie's dark mood, she decides that a holiday to Key West might be one way to get him to open up and share his problems with her. He agrees to go with Jenny only because he thinks he will be able to commit suicide more effectively in this new environment.

Lurie systematically makes Wilkie an unlikable and pompous character. His homophobic and sexist attitudes grate on modern temperaments. Yet she also manages to keep him sympathetic because of his large yet increasingly pitiful ego, which convinces him to kill himself but finds excuses not to at every turn. Through Wilkie's self-questioning character, Lurie forces readers to find remnants of their own frailties. Because of his brush with death, Wilkie changes from a man in control of everything and everyone to someone who recognizes how much in common he has with the many animals he has fought to keep from extinction.

Yet Wilkie's ego keeps him from noticing the distancing of his wife, whose entire life has revolved around serving his physical, emotional, and intellectual needs. Other characters in the novel frequently describe Jenny as a "Victorian wife," and until she arrives in Key West, she has few interests outside serving her husband. There, Jenny's pain and anguish over her perceived failures as a wife open her eyes to possibilities outside her rather rigid marriage. Because of Wilkie's preoccupation with himself, Jenny can step out of the marriage and find some element of happiness in the arms of Lee Weiss, the lesbian owner of a local bed-and-breakfast. Lurie, however, fails to make Jenny's sudden change believable. Constantly referred to as ethereal and pale, Jenny threatens to drift out of the text. Even when passionate, she seems inclined to do whatever someone else tells her to do. This type of women seems unlikely to suddenly realize she has always liked women. Furthermore, Lurie does little to prepare for Jenny's sudden decision to become Lee's lover. Considering her lifelong relationship and adoration of her homophobic husband, one feels that she might have been more troubled by such a decision, or that she might have realized this inclination earlier in the text. As is, the relationship makes a convenient and positive change for Jenny that does not seem plausible. Though Jenny has changed in major ways in the novel, by the end of the text, she seems just as lost and cowed by her husband as she did at the beginning.

Jenny's lover, Lee Weiss, personifies a woman who could create such change in Jenny. A former Brooklyn therapist, Lee has bought and transformed Artemis Lodge into a bed-and-breakfast for women only. As the sole proprietor, she observes and comments on the rest of the island. Lurie constantly uses images of bright and beautiful flowers to augment Lee's physical presence, suggesting a fecund and ripe rebirth that Lee makes possible for those who listen to her. She hears Jenny's tirades against her husband, as well as Barbie's against hers. She advises Myra Mumpson to run for Congress. Yet her exoticism, more so than that of the island, refreshes and intoxicates those with whom she speaks. In a more vivid and realistic way than the island, Lee becomes a final recourse for others who cannot make decisions on their own. In essence, Lee teaches others to live in the moment as she does. As she says, ". . . as you grow older and the future shrinks, you have only two choices: you can live in the fading past, or, like children, in the bright, full present."

Perry Jackson would rather not think about death, either. In fact, he wishes he did not know he was HIV-positive, although he tells Lee he has been a kind of murderer, perhaps for years, because he did not know. Unlike Wilkie, who uses his fears of death to drive him to bitterness and thoughts of suicide, Perry does not reveal his sealed fate. Instead, he chooses to "live in the moment" as Lee does. Though he carries no health-insurance policies and has little prospect of long-term care, he refuses to let his sentence of death affect his future. He calls his mother to Key West to help him in his gardening and to observe the tropical growth. (She is most impressed with how the ordinary houseplants from the North get wild and huge in the climate of Key West.) Perry thinks of viral death as a purple-splotched figure coming to get him, but he does not isolate or limit his interactions with others because of the "specter" that lurks within his own body. Instead, he attempts to hold onto the joy of the present, tending his gardens and visiting with his friends. As in his relationships with men, Perry feels that learning too much about someone (or, by extension, some thing) ruins the moment, the pure joy of living in the present. Consequently, *carpe diem* becomes his creed. He plans trips to Europe with his mother, despite the fact that the illness already seems to be working on his immune system. For Perry, Key West is, both literally and figuratively, his last resort.

Members of Perry's family, the Mumpsons, also visit Key West as a way to sort through their problems. Barbie, the wife of a prominent Oklahoma congressman, is sent to Key West by her domineering mother to decide about her marriage. Destroyed by evidence of his philandering, Barbie feels worthless, with no place in anyone's life. Yet, though weak and annoying, Barbie exerts more force of will than the more attractive Jenny Walker. Barbie does not want to sacrifice her life for an emotionless marriage, even though her mother feels she should. Rather, Barbie learns in Key West that she has value when she becomes a key defender of the nearly extinct manatee, an aquatic mammal that Wilkie Walker nastily says she resembles. Furthermore, her decision allows her to live with ailing painter Mollie Hopkins, whose arthritis threatens to limit her life. No longer interested in suicide, Barbie becomes surer of her choices in the course of her short stay on the island. Even Barbie's horrible mother Myra leaves the island with some promise for the future; rather than spend time and money finding a man to support for Congress, Myra has decided to run for Congress herself.

Unfortunately, many of Lurie's characterizations in *The Last Resort* seem a bit heavy-handed and predictable. Though Perry Jackson and a much older Molly Hopkins face ongoing, deteriorating lifestyles caused by illness, most of the characters in the novel resolve their issues fairly easily, as if the climate and the distancing from more realistic circumstances "outside paradise" creates new understanding almost immediately. Barbie and Myra Mumpson stay less than a week and seem to have their lives completely in order. Jenny discovers new love with Lee in less than a month. Despite these problems, however, *The Last Resort* does handle the darker themes of death and aging in Lurie's characteristic detailed and imaginative manner. She adeptly juxtaposes the horrors that living with death can impose to one who does not care to enjoy the present. For Lurie and the characters who "learn" in this novel, the solutions to such quandaries seem to involve giving up on all but the present, and the hope that the moment can offer.

The Last Resort, like many of Lurie's other novels, explores the complexities of human relationships set against the backdrop of conflict and crisis. Lurie examines lives that seem to be ending, either by disease or by circumstance, and in this examination, she attempts to isolate appropriate responses to these situations. Her themes are darker than in earlier novels, particularly in her preoccupation with death and dying. Yet, her message of rejuvenation, her "carpe diem" attitude, provides a rejoinder of positivism that typifies her work.

Rebecca Hendrick Flannagan

Sources for Further Study

Booklist. XCIV, June 1, 1998, p. 1725.
Library Journal. CXXIII, May 1, 1998, p. 138.
New Statesman. CXXVII, May 22, 1998, p. 56.
The New York Review of Books. XLV, November 5, 1998, p. 23.
The New York Times Book Review. CIII, July 12, 1998, p. 7.
Publishers Weekly. CCXLV, April 27, 1998, p. 41.
The Spectator. CCLXXX, June 13, 1998, p. 40.
The Times Literary Supplement. May 22, 1998, p. 8.
The Wall Street Journal. June 26, 1998, p. W9.
The Washington Post Book World. XXVIII, July 19, 1998, p. 3.

LEARNING A TRADE
A Craftsman's Notebooks, 1955-1997

Author: Reynolds Price (1933-   )
Published: Duke University Press (Durham, North Carolina). 603 pp. $34.95
Type of work: Diaries
Locale: Oxford, England; Durham, North Carolina

Reynolds Price's working journals reveal the writing process in both mundane detail and mystical depth and, along the way, show an apprentice writer growing into a mature novelist and poet

Reynolds Price began these notebooks soon after his graduation from college; he continued them during his graduate study at Oxford University, and he kept them up after he returned to a teaching position at Duke University, which he still holds. Increasingly, they have become the foundation for the dozens of books he has written, including plays, poetry, and fiction. These notebooks are one writer's laboratory, the quiet place he goes to try out his ideas, characters, and plots. In minute detail, they show a writer practicing his profession and learning his craft.

Price writes in his preface to the volume that the value of the notebooks is twofold: For nonwriting readers, the notes give some notion of the origins of books, how they "are made, not found." For the apprentice writer, however, they also provide some sense of the strategies writers employ, information that could prove useful to anyone learning the trade. Familiarity with Price's books will make these notebooks doubly useful, but even the general reader may find some value in watching a writer work out his ideas on paper, then leave them to "marinate" in the notebooks themselves. The creative process for the professional writer is laid out on the pages here, and it is a passionate, lifelong occupation.

Price is a writer's writer. Elected to the prestigious American Academy and Institute of Arts and Letters in 1988, he has found real popularity with only a few of his works: his first novel, *A Long and Happy Life* in 1962, certainly, and perhaps *Kate Vaiden* in 1986. Yet he has produced at least thirty other volumes in his long and fruitful career, including novels, collections of poems and short stories, and printed versions of his plays. All of his work is marked by the same exacting concern with language, an almost poetic quality that is his trademark. He is, in the truest sense, the "craftsman" of his subtitle. Price is also an amazingly visual writer; he had early training as an artist, and paintings and photographs have been very influential on his work. It is not difficult to understand how Price renders human life as vividly and precisely as he does.

The chronology of these notebooks reveals Price's evolution as a writer and the development of his own particular creative process. The early journals are choppy and fragmentary, filled with story ideas, possible book titles, lists of characters' names, and fragments of poems. He tries out lines, beginnings, whole paragraphs, and scraps of dialogue. The first half of the journal (through the late 1970's) is also "antiphonal" in structure: In his first two decades as a writer, Price used a double-paged journal, commenting on the left page about earlier notes on the right. Early entries show him reading in order to learn to write and commenting on other authors, including Virginia Woolf, William Faulkner, Mark Twain. There is a certain literary self-consciousness to these early journals, but there is also a strong strain of self-criticism and self-education. In the notebooks, readers can witness a writer teaching himself to write by doing it. In April, 1957, he writes, almost prophetically:

> Perhaps—if I ever get good enough for anybody to care, so good that it won't just seem pompous foolishness—I might publish these notes with a long essay on the evolution of this story [*A Long and Happy Life*], and it might help to reproduce all the pictures—everything—that bore directly or indirectly on the story at any stage.

He has not produced that essay here, but the notes are invaluable without it. Increasingly, the notebooks begin to map whole works, from early conception through to final manuscript, and the fullest sections here (such as the fifty pages on the 1981 *The Source of Light*, or the thirty-five pages on the 1992 *Blue Calhoun*) carry readers through the entire writing process. In those sections readers can watch Price struggling with the whole work, from beginning to end. He creates characters, plans their lives, listens to their voices, imagines their next moves, and then watches as they begin to carry the story for him. He plots a character's life carefully—and the figure turns out to be vastly different from the detailed conception. He gets stuck and cannot figure how to go forward. He writes, reads what he has written, and realizes he has made a wrong turn ninety pages back. What should he do now? Scrap the last ninety pages, or plow on? He plots and plans, from the smallest matters (opening lines, the names of minor characters) to the largest issues (themes, meanings). At times, scenes come to him almost as revelations; at other times, he spends months working on them. He worries about repeating what he has written years before; he changes a character's first name because another writer has just used it.

Readers who are looking for revelatory diaries here will be disappointed. These are not personal journals, and for long stretches of time, the only characters are in Price's mind and on the pages of his notebooks. The world intrudes very little, especially in the early years of these notes, and the few personal comments generally involve the writer's trade: counting up the pages of a day's or a week's work, cleaning off his desk, answering mail and filing away manuscripts, struggling to learn a new word processor.

Increasingly in later years, however, readers share more of Price's life. The reason is part of Price's personal tragedy: from 1984 through 1986, he battled spinal cancer; although he won, he was left a paraplegic. (Price wrote a memoir of his medical experiences, *A Whole New Life*, in 1994.) Price notes how his drugs affected his life, and therefore his writing, after 1986; he talks about the series of companions who have helped him in his daily life in a wheelchair; and he discusses friends who come to share meals and company.

The second half of the notebooks introduces a much more human world. Price talks about his teaching, especially the reactions of his students when he shares drafts of his fiction with his writing classes at Duke. Friends carry him back to Camp Sequoyah, where he was a counselor decades before, so that he can revisit the scene before writing about it. The singer James Taylor stays for several days at Price's house so that the two artists can work on song lyrics. A companion accompanies him to the opening of a play, to a joint reading with Eudora Welty, to New York to meet with editors and publishers.

Still, the notebooks are most valuable when they show Price's creative process at work. He speaks of "a good deal of unconscious work going on," and readers can witness it. He writes out ideas, sketches out characters, wakes up and jots down his thoughts and dreams. Weeks later, characters and situations reemerge in the notebooks, but changed, altered. The notebooks become, Price learns, a "means for persuading my unconscious mind to concern itself all day and night with a project I couldn't attend to constantly"—and it does. Price hears a family story about someone with a rich boyfriend who flies her home; a hundred pages and three years later, the story emerges as a scene in his first novel. Price wrestles with an awkward chronology in a character's life, and weeks or months later, the matter resolves itself.

More and more, Price trusts that process. He spends less and less time working out plots and characters, and more and more time thinking about atmosphere and arguing with himself about themes and ideas. In 1988, he realizes something about his ability as a short-story writer: "When I began my serious writing with stories in 1954, they were hard as hell. Now I just need to remember their secret, *Permit mystery. Don't work to explain.*" He writes here in 1990 "that a well-tended unconscious mind will invent one's work and deliver it." The writing process thus becomes, in part, a process of letting go: "Summon a true hypnotic voice and let it *tell.* . . . Prepare your life and mind to write." The "yeast is working already," he writes in 1995, as he is preparing *Roxanna Slade.*

Of course, there is a price that the writer pays. He is compulsive about his work, giving himself daily, weekly, monthly, even yearly deadlines, and only later in his career does he begin to relax this rigorous, sometimes obsessive routine. It is not until 1988 that he can write, "A good feeling, after all, to remind myself—for the first time since the summer of 1985—that I *can* survive, sane, without writing." Perhaps it is his battle with cancer and his multiple surgeries that have helped to soften and humanize Price; his commentaries on National Public Radio's "All Things Considered" since 1995 certainly reveal a rounder, more human figure than the rigid writer who begins these notebooks. In July, 1995, he records the idea for a new novel about a family reunion in North Carolina, but in the very next paragraph, he notes the passing of his friend, the British poet Stephen Spender. "A piece of my life, very nearly as large as my parents', has slipped away—this suddenly. I never knew a more alive human being, a vitality he sustained right on to age eighty-six. . . . I feel a great sadness." Readers will treasure these moments of self-discovery.

Finally, Price is a poet, not only in his own very accomplished poetry but in his prose as well. Few writers have the deft touch and complex texture of Price's writing, and the notebooks reveal that evolving as well, in fragments, in dialogue, in drafts of letters that Price plans his characters to write. The pleasures of Price's prose are immeasurable, and certainly one is his meticulous concern for language that readers will find everywhere in these notebooks.

This is not the year's most important book, not even the most significant work that Price himself will write. The fact that a university press has published the volume, and not Price's regular commercial publisher (Atheneum), is an indication of where the publishing world ranks this kind of collection. Yet the book has several intrinsic values unmatched by other works. For one thing, in these notes to all the different words and works that he has created, Reynolds Price reveals his evolution as a writer. Reading these notes to forty years of creativity is almost like standing in a gallery and looking at the retrospective show of an important painter; it is an experience readers only rarely get to share. Moreover, this is one of those rare instances where the writer's creative process itself is revealed, particularly the way that it functions as a dialogue between conscious planning and unconscious work. The creative artist, *Learning a Trade* shows, is someone who allows the "yeast" to rise while the "craftsman" of the subtitle sleeps. Finally, the notebooks reveal the active working life of one important American writer, a contemporary Southern novelist and poet who has created memorable scenes and characters, has deepened appreciation for literary language, and who, in his own life, has struggled with the most crippling crises and emerged a stronger, more vital human being. Few volumes this year will give readers as much on as many different levels.

David Peck

Sources for Further Study

Atlanta Journal-Constitution. July 19, 1998, p. L1.
Booklist. XCV, November 15, 1998, p. 561.
Publishers Weekly. CCXLV, November 16, 1998, p. 64.
The Wall Street Journal. November 27, 1998, p. W5.
The Washington Post. December 18, 1998, p. D10.

LETTERS

Author: Kenneth Tynan (1927-1980)
Edited by Kathleen Tynan (1937-1995)
Published: Random House (New York). 665 pp. $30.00
Type of work: Letters
Time: 1938-1980
Locale: England, New York, and California

A carefully crafted collection that reveals the colorful life and fierce professionalism of one of the modern period's best theater critics and cultural impresarios

The first letter in this collection, dated February 12, 1938, written when Kenneth Tynan was only ten years old, already shows a distinctive personality, one that would concern itself with the making of great work in the performing arts. He writes to the editor of *Film Weekly* to protest the report that Warner Bros. intends to cast Humphrey Bogart in a series of "B" (that is, second-rate or modest) movies. He confidently points out that the studio is making a great mistake. Bogart had shown his great talent as a character actor in films such as *Dead End* (1937), *Marked Woman* (1937), and *Stand-In* (1937). He deserved "real recognition." The letter is only two sentences long, but it assumes an air of authority surely unusual for one so young. It is almost as if this youth thinks his opinion will carry some weight. At any rate, he will not let such a travesty occur without putting in his oar.

Kenneth Tynan made his reputation as a postwar critic and theatrical impresario with just this kind of sound judgment, which sometimes—as in the case of Bogart—had the air of prophecy. In 1938, Bogart had not yet made *Casablanca* or *The African Queen*. He was not a screen icon. Even the precocious Tynan could not forecast Bogart's development not merely as a great character actor but as a romantic lead as well, but it was his way of drawing attention to the important figure, work, or phenomenon that made him a bellwether.

Yet why should even such a shrewd observer merit first a long recent biography and now a large collection of letters? One answer is simple. Both were written and edited by his last wife, the late Kathleen Tynan, who championed her husband's significance as a cultural figure larger than the term "critic" encompasses. Her judgment seems correct. For Tynan did not merely review what came his way; he looked for and established trends and styles. He argued in eloquent terms for what art should be. Most revealing is that he had so many friendships with first-rate creative people—with novelists such as William Styron and the actor/director Laurence Olivier, for example. For Tynan, the act of criticism took him right to the center of the arts. He conveyed the impression of not writing simply from an audience seat but as someone deeply immersed in the process of creating art.

It is something of a mystery as to why Tynan did not do more than write about the theater. Early on, he tried his hand at directing and was humiliated when a distinguished actress had him removed from a production. Did he lose his nerve? Did writing serve as a more satisfying form of participation in the arts—one over which he had total control? Perhaps, but Tynan did get his hands dirty, so to speak, in his collaboration with Olivier on Great Britain's National Theatre. As literary manager, Tynan urged the famous actor, then head of the new institution, to do daring plays and to battle censorship. In this context, Tynan showed no fear of failure or controversy. Quite the contrary; he thrived on it, even to the point of annoying Olivier. In fact, Olivier only half-jokingly remarked that he chose Tynan as his collaborator because he could then at least silence Tynan's more vitriolic reviews of his performances.

Perhaps Tynan saw at the start of his career that as a director he would have to do all kinds of plays—popular and avant-garde, good and bad—and disliked the prospect of submitting to that kind of grind. He enjoyed the good life, travel, many affairs with women, and the exercise of wit, little of which would have been his lot as a director in a Britain taking a long time to recover from World War II. Tynan was a man of expansive moods and ambitions; he did not want to harness himself to productions. He simply wanted to go where the action was. He saw himself as pushing the envelope of what it was possible to do in the theater.

A good example is his 1969 production of *Oh! Calcutta!*, essentially a confection of pornographic skits that he solicited from many prominent writers. Tynan wanted the shock value of bringing a show (it can hardly be called a play) with full frontal nudity to the Broadway stage in New York and to the fabled West End theaters in London. He promised his collaborators that though their names would be listed in the credits, no one would know which author wrote which sketch. That he succeeded in mounting these productions was a kind of triumph in itself, if hardly a major contribution to dramaturgy. Yet Tynan seems to have realized that it was not the nudity per se that was important, but rather his insistence that neither sex nor any other subject matter should be segregated or declared, by definition, out of bounds for art and artists.

Oh! Calcutta! did contribute to the image of Tynan as one of the swingers of the 1960's and 1970's, but in fact he thought that full frontal nudity was not appropriate for most drama. He was not a sexual voluptuary in the sense of searching for new kinds of sexual expression. He was quite conventional in that respect; in one of his letters, he confessed that he did not take to the idea of group sex and had never tried it.

Tynan wrote for the best publications in both Britain and America. He had a long association with *The New Yorker*. He is perhaps best remembered for his brilliantly evocative profile of the silent film star Louise Brooks, who was living in obscurity in Rochester, New York when Tynan rediscovered her. This was pure Tynan: remembering and resurrecting an important figure and a lost art. Part of the story consisted of Tynan's wooing of Brooks—not in the sexual sense but in the literary/biographical one, in which he had to coax her to tell her story and to make herself available once again to the public. Tynan made art of the artist, showing why people should still care about someone who had had a relatively brief career but who had established a type and an inimitable style. In a society marked by commercials for "the real thing," Tynan sought out people, events, and works that were a kind of antidote to hype.

The Brooks profile and others established Tynan not merely as a critic or cultural commentator but also as, in some indefinable way, a writer's writer. What he produced, at his best, were not simply magazine assignments or reviews, but also primers on how to look at art, and explanations of why people should care about it as deeply as he did. He never lost the spirit of that ten-year-old writing to say that "attention must be paid," that a great artist or art is getting short shrift.

Tynan wrote, in other words, with an obligation to art itself, to what art should be able to accomplish. Like any critic, he produced a welter of judgments—some fair, some unworthy of the art he criticized, and most of them passionate and frequently amusing. His letters and collections of criticism and commentary, such as *Tynan Right and Left* (1968), *A View of the English Stage 1944-63* (1975), *The Sound of Two Hands Clapping* (1975), and *Show People* (1980), demonstrate clearly that he felt a great sense of responsibility to the art he loved.

What is not so often emphasized about Tynan, and what comes through clearly in these letters, is his ethical thrust. Although he seemed so stylish, so much an open, permissive 1960's figure, he had standards and requirements that brought him into conflict not merely with censors or other critics but also with fellow writers. A case in point is Truman Capote's celebrated *In Cold Blood* (1966). Capote had touted himself as having invented the "nonfiction novel," a work of journalism reporting on real events but told with the elegance and the full resources of fiction, including scene setting, dialogue, and character development. Capote swore it was all true and all literary. Many lauded him for traveling to Kansas to cover a murder trial and for investing in his story such insight and humanity.

A skeptical Tynan began asking pointed questions. What was Capote's relationship with the criminals, especially with Perry, who became, in many ways, the most sympathetic character in the book? Tynan deplored what he saw as Capote's exploitation of the story and self-aggrandizing tactics. Tynan doubted that Capote had exerted himself enough to appeal Perry's conviction (he was eventually hanged). Tynan believed that if Capote was going to tie literature that closely to life, the author had an obligation to his real-life characters that transcended merely his attachment to the story he was writing. At bottom, Capote had shown not great compassion and insight, but rather a callous disregard for human life. To be sure, Tynan was not the only writer to criticize Capote or to take issue with some of his more extravagant claims for *In Cold Blood*, but it was Tynan who demonstrated the most persistence and thoughtfulness about the process that yielded a "nonfiction novel."

There is a sadness that creeps into the letters and activities of Tynan's last days. An inveterate smoker, he had been warned by doctors that he was irretrievably damaging his lungs. He was given not only the typical warning about the dangers of cigarettes but also a specific diagnosis about his lungs, which doctors found particularly susceptible to damage. Yet even as his health began to fail and he sought refuge in Southern California, Tynan continued to smoke. It was of a piece with his obsessive, compulsive personality. He could no more give up cigarettes than he could give up love affairs with women.

Living with such a man was hard on Kathleen Tynan, although she seems to have been able to give as good as she got. She obviously believed in her husband's greatness and in his legacy. There is an affecting preface to the letters, in which Leon Wieseltier reveals that she worked on this edition of the letters even as she herself was dying. She did a splendid job, making available the voice of a great personality and a superb letter writer. She divides the book into eight parts covering Tynan's school days, his period at Oxford University, his reputation as "boy wonder," his growing accomplishment in the 1950's, his exuberant embrace of the 1960's, the controversies surrounding his productions of *Oh! Calcutta!* and *Soldiers* (1968), his rather fitful efforts to find the right subjects and activities in the 1970's, and finally what she deems his "exile" in Los Angeles, where he seemed to hold on, hoping for the best yet knowing that he was destroying his own health.

The book's eight sections are carefully buttressed with italicized sections, largely culled from Tynan's biography of her husband, which give a running biographical commentary and summary of the activities referred to in the letters. Individual letters are also judiciously footnoted with identifications of persons, titles of works, and other data needed to appreciate the context of Tynan's correspondence. These annotations, plus the index and photographs, provide a well-rounded and almost palpable picture of the man and the writer. The index also reveals just how steeped Tynan was in the culture of his time and how many first-rate minds came to be stimulated by his own.

Tynan's place as theater historian, critic, and visionary seems secure. These letters document his superb judgment and engagement in vital issues that merit his high place in cultural discussions of the postwar period.

Carl Rollyson

Sources for Further Study

American Theatre. XV, July, 1998, p. 58.
Library Journal. CXXIII, May 1, 1998, p. 102.
National Review. L, May 18, 1998, p. 57.
The New Republic. CCXIX, August 31, 1998, p. 29.
The New York Times Book Review. CIII, May 10, 1998, p. 9.
Publishers Weekly. CCXLV, March 9, 1998, p. 54.
The Washington Post Book World. XXXVIII, May 17, 1998, p. 5.

LINDBERGH

Author: A. Scott Berg (1949-   )
Published: G.P. Putnam's Sons (New York). Illustrated. 628 pages. $30.00
Type of work: Biography
Time: 1902-1974

An excellent account of the life of the great aviator Charles Lindbergh, one of the most famous, and most tragic, heroes of the twentieth century

> *Principal personages:*
> CHARLES AUGUSTUS LINDBERGH, an American aviator and hero
> CHARLES AUGUST LINDBERGH, Lindbergh's father
> EVANGELINE LODGE LAND, Lindbergh's mother
> ANNE MORROW LINDBERGH, Lindbergh's wife
> ALEXIS CARREL, a French medical researcher

Charles Lindbergh exploded onto the world scene in 1927, flying his single-engined monoplane *The Spirit of St. Louis* nonstop from New York to Paris. To a postwar world mired in cynicism and hungry for heroes, the modest young flyer from Minnesota seemed the answer to a prayer. Lindbergh was immediately lionized as no man of modern times had been before. His appeal transcended celebrity. He became an icon, a shining beacon of human enterprise and courage in an age of machines. For Lindbergh himself, however, fame would prove to be as much a curse as a blessing, and he would struggle with the smothering effects of his own legend for the rest of his life.

A. Scott Berg's *Lindbergh* is an ambitious attempt to understand the man behind the myth. This is no easy task, for even those closest to Lindbergh found him something of an enigma. Berg, moreover, is no literary magician, able to achieve the impossible. At the end of his book, the great flyer still remains something of a mystery. Yet Berg comes closer than any previous biographer to explaining his elusive subject. His book is especially valuable because he was the first scholar allowed unrestricted access to the Lindbergh papers. As a result, he is able to add much new detail and nuance to a familiar story, and his work will likely be the standard biography of Charles Lindbergh for years to come.

Charles Augustus Lindbergh was born on February 4, 1902. His father, Charles August Lindbergh, was the son of Swedish immigrants and a prosperous lawyer in Little Falls, Minnesota. His mother, Evangeline Lodge Land, was the daughter of the man who had pioneered porcelain dentistry; she met her husband while teaching school in Little Falls. Unfortunately, Lindbergh's early years were not happy. His parents' marriage proved to be a failure. Charles August Lindbergh allowed friends to persuade him to run for Congress in 1906. At least part of the attraction of the race was the prospect of escaping his home. He won the election, and the first of five consecutive terms. The ensuing years would be a blur of homes and schools for his son, who was shuffled between his father and mother, between Washington, D.C., and Minnesota. Lindbergh grew up intensely shy, more comfortable in the company of his pets than that of other people. He also learned to be extremely self-sufficient and self-reliant, qualities that would later undergird his greatest successes but that would also frustrate those closest to him.

Lindbergh early demonstrated an affinity for machines, especially automobiles. For this reason, his father tapped him to be his driver as he ran for the Republican nomination for U.S. Senate in 1916. In his years in Congress, the elder Lindbergh had been a fiery champion of the Progressive wing of the Republican Party. As a candidate for the Senate, he ran as an opponent of American intervention in World War I. His message proved unpopular in a country already girding itself for war, and he was heavily defeated. Even more disastrous was a 1918 campaign for the governorship of Minnesota. Charles August Lindbergh's antiwar sentiments now seemed treasonous to many, and he was regularly harassed and even, on occasion, threatened with lynching. Lindbergh watched the destruction of his father's career, and he imbibed long-lasting lessons about politics, politicians, and the passions unleashed by war.

A more traditional education continued in a somewhat haphazard fashion. In the fall of 1920, Lindbergh entered the University of Wisconsin. Less than two years later, he flunked out. His parents' marriage was now irretrievably broken, and neither possessed the means to support him. Lindbergh thus had to strike out on his own. He chose to indulge a dream that had been growing within him: He decided to learn to fly. He took some commercial lessons, then honed his skills working with pilots barnstorming across the Midwest. Lindbergh became an aerial stuntman, walking wings and testing parachutes. Eager to fly more modern machines than the war-surplus planes available to him, Lindbergh enrolled in the Army's Air Service Advanced Flying School in 1924; the next year, he graduated first in his class. The Army did not need many pilots, so Lindbergh found himself in the Reserves and in need of employment. He barnstormed for a period, then settled in St. Louis and accepted an offer to become a pioneer of the fledgling air-mail service. His route to Chicago was considered one of the most dangerous in the country because of the tempestuous weather. Lindbergh survived two crashes, becoming known as "Lucky Lindy" in flying circles.

In St. Louis, Lindbergh began pondering the possibility of flying nonstop from New York to Paris, a common dream for airmen of his day. In 1919, Raymond Orteig had further spurred interest by offering a prize of $25,000 for the first men who accomplished the feat. Until the mid-1920's, such a flight had seemed a technical impossibility. Yet as the decade wore on, new planes were being designed that seemed capable of sustaining such a test of endurance. In 1926, a famous French flyer made an attempt in an experimental multiengined plane that crashed on takeoff, killing two of the crew. Soon, several other world-famous aviators were planning transatlantic flights. Lindbergh, tired of flying the mail, wanted to measure himself against the greatest challenge in his profession, but he was virtually unknown and had no money of his own. Working diligently, he found backers in St. Louis and a manufacturer, the Ryan Aeronautical Company of San Diego, California, to build his plane. Lindbergh bet his life, and his backers' money, that he could fly the Atlantic alone in a single-engined monoplane, a sharp contrast to the large and expensive machines being tested by his competitors.

The race to win the Orteig Prize captured the imagination of the press. Suddenly, the quest to surmount this aeronautical hurdle became a drama engrossing millions of readers. A pair of French aviators took off from Paris' Le Bourget aerodrome, passed observers on the French coast, and then disappeared. Technical and legal problems delayed the leading American teams. The glare of publicity descended on Lindbergh. Though few newspapermen thought much of his chances, they began to lionize him as a solitary hero, the "Flyin' Fool." From this point, Lindbergh would never be able to disentangle his life from the demands of the mass media. When he took off in *The Spirit of St. Louis* on May 20, 1927, his departure was a headline story on both sides of the Atlantic, and millions followed his progress as he was sighted over land and sea. By the time he approached Paris, he already was an international sensation. Upon landing, he reaped the whirlwind. He was the most famous man in the world. An age that needed a hero embraced Lindbergh; he soon realized that it would not let go.

Lindbergh proved an attractive hero. He demonstrated grace and dignity in public, and he resisted crass attempts to exploit his fame. He devoted himself to promoting the cause of commercial aviation. In the midst of this activity, he met Anne Morrow, the daughter of Dwight Morrow, a distinguished Wall Street banker who was serving as ambassador to Mexico. Anne was quiet, sensitive, and a gifted writer. She and Lindbergh were married in 1929, and they entered into a highly public life together. The photogenic pair became a team, exploring remote parts of the world by airplane. A son born to them in 1930 was named after his father. They seemed America's golden couple.

Tragedy scarred the Lindberghs's lives with searing abruptness in 1932, when their young son was killed in a kidnapping. The crime shocked the nation, and it became one of the most sensational news stories of the century as police searched first for the baby, then for his killer. Lindbergh blamed his son's death on the incessant publicity that surrounded his family. To escape the press, the Lindberghs moved to Europe in 1935. During these bleak years, Lindbergh assuaged his grief through work. He and Anne continued their explorations. Lindbergh found funds to support the research of Robert Goddard, the father of American rocketry, and, working with the medical theorist Alexis Carrel, designed a precursor to the artificial heart.

As the decade wore on, Lindbergh became increasingly disturbed by the threat of war. At the behest of the U.S. War Department, he accepted invitations to inspect Nazi Germany's developing air force. He was highly impressed by what he saw, and he was haunted by the conviction that a war would be a catastrophe for Western civilization. In 1939, he returned to the United States and began a campaign to persuade Americans to stay out of the coming conflict with Germany. This pitted him against President Franklin Roosevelt, who was committed to aligning the United States with the nations struggling to contain German aggression. Lindbergh quickly emerged as the leading spokesman of the America First movement, arguing that the United States should look to its own defenses and avoid foreign entanglements. His father's son, he refused to compromise his principles, despite their high price. For the first time in his life, Lindbergh became a controversial figure. Because he would not condemn Germany,

many Americans began to believe that he was a Nazi.

Pearl Harbor found Lindbergh isolated and under a cloud of suspicion. The Roosevelt Administration blacklisted him, and he was refused permission to enter the military. Lindbergh was forced to spend the war as a test pilot, though he did manage to fly fifty "unofficial" combat missions in the Pacific. Attitudes toward Lindbergh began to thaw with the death of Franklin Roosevelt in 1945. He was sent on an official mission to occupied Germany to inspect the wreckage of the Nazi jet and rocket programs; he also became a consultant to the Air Force and helped reorganize the Strategic Air Command. President Dwight Eisenhower honored him for his service by awarding him the rank of brigadier general.

Lindbergh furthered the cause of his own rehabilitation by writing a memoir of his 1927 transatlantic flight. *The Spirit of St. Louis* was published in 1953, and it became a best-seller. The book reminded Americans of the seemingly more innocent era when Lindbergh first burst onto the scene, and the film rights were quickly sold. Lindbergh's success was crowned when he received the Pulitzer Prize in 1954. The next year, Anne Morrow Lindbergh had a literary triumph of her own, publishing *A Gift from the Sea*, a meditation on modern womanhood. The book became a publishing phenomenon, and the Lindberghs were re-established in Americans' minds as a model couple. The reality of their marriage, however, was not as rosy as the image. Lindbergh's lifelong restlessness became almost compulsive in the 1950's. He was constantly on the move and rarely home. When he was about, his perfectionism worked like acid on his more emotionally vulnerable wife. It is one of the revelations of Berg's biography that Anne in these years engaged in a long-standing affair with a family friend. The Lindberghs eventually reached a tacit accommodation with each other, spending long periods apart.

Almost to the end of his life, Charles Lindbergh remained active. His last great cause was environmentalism, and his projects ranged from saving whales from commercial fishermen to protecting the aboriginal Tasaday people of the Philippines. He was struck down by cancer in 1974. He died in Hawaii, calmly supervising the digging of his grave.

A. Scott Berg contents himself with telling the tumultuous story of Charles Lindbergh. He does not place Lindbergh's life in a larger cultural context, but his book does provide the raw material for a powerful study of fame in the age of the modern mass media. Few men have achieved the heights of celebrity enjoyed by Charles Lindbergh, or suffered as much for that gilt privilege.

Daniel P. Murphy

Sources for Further Study

Business Week. November 9, 1998, p. 38.
The Christian Science Monitor. November 12, 1998, p. B5.

The Economist. CCCXLVII, November 14, 1998, p. NA.
Los Angeles Times Book Review. September 20, 1998, p. 3.
National Review. L, October 26, 1998, p. 50.
The New York Times Book Review. CIII, September 27, 1998, p. 14.
Publishers Weekly. CCXLV, August 24, 1998, p. 38.
Time. CLII, September 21, 1998, p. 103.
The Times Literary Supplement. October 30, 1998, p. 3.
The Washington Post Book World. XXVIII, September 20, 1998, p. 1.

LIVING WITH OUR GENES
Why They Matter More Than You Think

Authors: Dean Hamer (1951-   ) and Peter Copeland
Published: Doubleday (New York). 368 pp. $24.95
Type of work: Science, psychology, and technology
Time: The twentieth century
Locale: The United States and Western Europe

A survey of the most important discoveries about how genes contribute to such personality traits as novelty-seeking, aggression, sexual orientation, and intelligence

Many people were first introduced to the core issues of this book through the 1978 film *The Boys from Brazil*, based on a popular Ira Levin novel. In that story, the infamous Nazi doctor Josef Mengele tried, using genetic techniques and controlled childhood environments, to breed ninety-four clones of Adolf Hitler (the "boys" of the title). The hope was that these young men who had the Führer's genes and were reared in conditions similar to the young Adolf's would mature into creators of a Fourth Reich. Most critics found the film farfetched, but cloning is now a reality for certain animals, and the fears raised by the novel and film have returned. In the concluding chapter of *Living with Our Genes*, Dean Hamer and Peter Copeland tell a mini-tale of a clone they call Andrew who, as an adult, campaigns to stop those scientists who see no difference between cloning sheep and mass-producing humans. These cautionary tales center on the question of how much human behavior is determined by genes and how much this behavior can be manipulated by modifying the environment.

The scientist and journalist who wrote *Living with Our Genes* stress the evidence for the genetic control of human behavior. Hamer, who received his doctorate in biological chemistry from Harvard University, heads the Section on Gene Structure and Regulation at the National Cancer Institute in Bethesda, Maryland. He gained wide attention (and notoriety) through his discovery of the heritability of male homosexuality. In fact, the authors of *Living with Our Genes* previously wrote *The Science of Desire: The Search for the Gay Gene and the Biology of Behavior* (1994), which dealt with how Hamer discovered the genetic basis of male homosexuality and how he dealt with the controversy this discovery provoked. *The Science of Desire* was a successful book (*The New York Times* named it one of the "Notable Books" of 1994), and in *Living with Our Genes*, Hamer and Copeland have continued their collaboration. Hamer handled the explanations of scientific research, and Copeland used his journalistic skills to make Hamer's ideas understandable to nonscientists.

According to Hamer and Copeland, nonscientists need to know why humans behave the way they do. In the past, religious explanations were satisfactory, but in the twentieth century, scientists have attempted to explain human behavior in terms of genetics (nature) and the environment (nurture). Geneticists use the term "nature" to refer to what people generally think of as biological inheritance and what scientists see as the differences in the deoxyribonucleic acid (DNA) molecule transmitted from generation to generation. For many scientists, a person's inherited biological nature is not sufficient to explain his or her behavior; these scientists emphasize that humans behave the way they do because of their social conditioning (nurture). Hamer, a molecular geneticist, tends to emphasize that human behavior is heavily influenced by genes, which he sees as "the single most important factor" determining an individual's uniqueness. This does not mean that genes make people into molecular robots, since human genes program them to respond creatively to complex and changing environments.

The theme of *Living with Our Genes* is that genes control many core personality traits such as how we eat, drink, feel, think, and interact with others. Each chapter begins with a specific human situation, for example the meeting of two people with strongly contrasting personalities at a class reunion. The authors then discuss the scientific research that has been done to illuminate the behavioral issues that they have raised, for example a twin study that shows that a trait such as shyness is influenced by genes. Sometimes the authors play the role of reductionists, insisting that a woman has as much choice in her personality as she does in the size of her feet, but they also point out that the genes controlling personality are very flexible, allowing humans to adapt in various ways to life's complexities.

Hamer and Copeland use the distinction between temperament and character to bolster their position as moderates in the nature-nurture controversy. Unlike other psychologists, they use temperament to refer both to how people feel about the world and to how they act. Indeed, temperament is the focus of their book: "what it is, how to recognize it, and where it comes from." They attack those social scientists who deny that inborn temperament exists and who believe instead that human beings are solely products of their environment. On the other hand, they avoid the excesses of those reductionists who claim that humans are nothing but molecular machines by qualifying their enthusiasm about genetic explanations. Genes do not program people to behave only in certain ways. Human beings are born with particular temperaments, but these are not created fully formed—they evolve in response to the environment. The authors are ideological liberals; they want to see the knowledge they convey used by their readers as a tool for liberation.

The genetics of behavior can help humans in their quest for liberation. For example, scientists have discovered a temperamental difference called novelty seeking. Novelty seekers find pleasure in intense and unfamiliar experiences, and a study of identical and fraternal twins revealed that this behavioral trait had genetic roots. Some scientists wondered whether dopamine, the "pleasure chemical," is related to novelty seeking. One study found that the gene making a particular dopamine receptor called D4DR was very important, and in his laboratory, Hamer confirmed that the D4DR gene was affecting novelty-seeking behavior.

Despite their emphasis on genes predisposing people to particular behaviors, the authors also stress that human character can control genetic predispositions. For example, the human brain is genetically programmed to be capable of anger, since hostile feelings are advantageous when a person is threatened by an enemy, but most people learn to manage their aggressive feelings in ordinary life. On the other hand, many twentieth century societies have experienced a dramatic increase in violent behavior. The authors believe that this increase in violence is not biological but social; it is not caused by "crime genes" but by family breakdown and urban decay. They may not believe that genes make criminals, but they also do not believe that ghettoes make them either. What causes crime is the combination of genes and a bad environment. Most important in determining whether a person is violent is the Y chromosome, which designates gender. The statistical evidence is persuasive that men are responsible for many more violent crimes than women, but predisposition is not predestination. Having a Y chromosome is certainly a strong genetic predisposition to violence, but this does not mean that judges should excuse a murderer simply because he is a male.

Many genes, in addition to the Y chromosome, are needed to distinguish a man from a woman. The authors view the sex drive as one of the most deeply rooted and genetically programmed of all human behaviors. However, many feminists will be appalled by the authors' insistence that biology is destiny. They claim that men behave like sperm, for which the best strategy is to find an egg, fertilize it, and then forget it, whereas women behave like eggs which, once fertilized, require a substantial investment of time and energy. The scientific basis for their analysis of the genetic roots of sex differences is the pivotal role that the master gene TDF (for testis-determining factor) plays in differentiating male and female embryos. This emphasis on the genetic basis of sex differentiation is to be expected, since Hamer achieved fame through his discovery of what news reports called "the gay gene." Although he did find that male sexual orientation had many of the characteristics of a genetically influenced trait, he believes that his discovery was important not because of what it revealed about the hereditability of male homosexuality but because of what it revealed about sexual differences in general. What he discovered was that sexual orientation in men was similar to being right-handed or left-handed (degrees of ambidexterity are rare), but for women, sexual orientation was more like height (a wide range of values is common). Furthermore, Hamer does not believe that a single gene exists in every male homosexual that is responsible for his sexual orientation. Multifarious genetic and environmental factors are involved in making homosexuals and heterosexuals.

The twin themes of complexity and environmental influences characterize the final chapters of the book, on thinking, hunger, and aging. Indeed, the authors see the thinking brain as the place where nature and nurture are inseparable. Genes certainly play a role in how the brain is made, but human contact is essential for its healthy development. In the debate over genes and intelligence, the authors believe that no single factor is more important in determining intelligence than genes. However, they admit that it is difficult to define human intelligence and quantify it. Intelligence tests have also been contaminated by ideologues who have used them to identify what they viewed as the incurably (because genetically) defective whose breeding posed a menace to the welfare of the state. Despite this controversial background, Hamer and Copeland still uphold the value of intelligence tests as the single best predictor of academic success. On the other hand, they admit that such tests cannot measure the full range of human intelligence. Environmental factors such as prenatal care, good nutrition, and stimulating schooling do influence the development of human intelligence, but various twin studies have also shown that none of these environmental factors has a greater impact than genes.

On the controversial issue of race and intelligence, the authors criticize the approach of Charles Murray and Richard Herrnstein in *The Bell Curve* (1994). Hamer and Copeland accuse Murray and Herrnstein of confusing individual intelligence differences (what twin studies measure) and group differences (which cannot be studied by these methods). Indeed, studies of blacks raised in relatively privileged environments showed an average increase of about sixteen intelligence points, about the size of the difference in intelligence scores between whites and blacks in America. Genes do play a role in the formation of brains, but a person's genes are not all "switched on" at conception. Humans have been designed to develop gradually, with some genes brightening while others dim, in response to a changing environment.

For the brain to develop and function properly, nourishment is needed, and humans have evolved genes that encourage them to eat. However, genes that encouraged humans to store fat when food was scarce are much less essential now, when food is plentiful (at least in the developed world). Twin studies have shown that body weight is about 70 percent inherited, and experiments on obese mice have revealed that a hormone, leptin, is involved in controlling body weight. Besides obesity, Hamer believes that such conditions as anorexia nervosa and bulimia are biological diseases that represent distortions of genetic mechanisms that developed in the course of evolution to help people survive famines.

The authors conclude their treatment appropriately with a discussion of the genetics of aging. Nurture (better diets and health care) has been largely responsible for humans living longer in the twentieth century, and nature (genetics) has only a minor influence on longevity. On the other hand, genes certainly play a role in various diseases such as Werner's syndrome, which causes a person to live a lifetime in several years (sometimes called premature aging), and Alzheimer's disease, the fourth-leading cause of death in America. Studies of early-onset Alzheimer's have uncovered some information about its genetic origin, but since some people with the bad form of the gene never get the disease, and since some people who get the disease do not have the gene, many of the mysteries of Alzheimer's remain unsolved.

In the book's conclusion, the authors speculate on what the genetics of human behavior will look like in the twenty-first century. They predict that the three billion nucleotides of the human genome (with its hundred thousand genes) will be completely mapped, and the meaning and function of these genes will begin to be deciphered. This new knowledge, along with gene-therapy technologies, will enable human beings to change and manipulate human behavior. This knowledge and these technologies raise immense moral issues. Which human traits will be valued and which will be eliminated, and who will decide? Politicians, military leaders, insurance companies, and employers will all want this information, but will it be used to help or to discriminate against people? The authors realize that human gene manipulation is a very serious business. Further complicating the picture is the realization that the genes for personality are so complicated that it is impossible to know for certain what might happen if one were altered. The dividing line between madness and genius, between a cure and a tragedy, is thin, and the correction of one problem might well mean the creation of worse ones.

The scientific research discussed in *Living with Our Genes*—the "gay gene," the "crime gene," the "obesity gene," as well as the genes involved with addiction and Alzheimer's disease—has been in the news for the past several years. Because of the relevance of this research to human health and happiness, it has stimulated significant public debate, and this book, which summarizes this research in a way that general readers will find attractive, will contribute to this important discussion. Even though the authors take a balanced approach to the nature-nurture controversy, they do tend to view nurture from the perspective of nature. Thus it might be helpful to supplement their treatment with a book such as *Not in Our Genes: Biology, Ideology, and Human Nature* (1984), by R. C. Lewontin, Steven Rose, and Leon J. Kamin, which raises serious questions about the ideological neutrality of those scientists emphasizing the genetic roots of human behavior.

Behavior geneticists will continue to discover new knowledge which, if used wisely, may help to improve the physical and mental health of many suffering human beings. Critics of Hamer and other behavior geneticists argue that their science makes human beings slaves of their genes, but Hamer considers this a mistaken evaluation. Genetic knowledge has the power of expanding the capacities of human beings by revealing the full range of human potential. Much human greatness is lost to the world because of lack of knowledge and love. In sum, human beings are creatures who, in a profound way, transcend their genetic origins, since they are beings whose freedom can only be enhanced when they truly understand who they are.

Robert J. Paradowski

Sources for Further Study

The Advocate. February 17, 1998, p. 32.
Booklist. XCIV, February 15, 1998, p. 946.
Chemical and Engineering News. LXXVI, June 1, 1998, p. 49.
Journal of Sex Research. XXXV, November, 1998, p. 408.
Kirkus Reviews. LXVI, February 1, 1998, p. 171.
Publishers Weekly. CCXLV, February 2, 1998, p. 76.
Time. CLI, April 27, 1998, p. 60.
The Times Higher Education Supplement. July 31, 1998, p. 14.

THE LOVE OF A GOOD WOMAN

Author: Alice Munro (1931-   )
Published: Alfred A. Knopf (New York). 340 pp. $24.00
Type of work: Short fiction
Time: The mid-to-late twentieth century
Locale: Ontario and British Columbia, Canada

The modern Canadian master of the short story continues to explore the secret lives of girls and women in eight new stories

Readers still dazzled by Alice Munro's *Selected Stories* (1996)—an abundant harvest of fictions from her previous eight collections—will find these eight new stories a delightful bonus. The title story, the longest and most elaborate, begins in Wally, Ontario, a familiar Munro location, with three boys finding the body of the town's optometrist in his car submerged in the river. Although one might expect the plot immediately to focus on the mystery of the drowned man, Munro is in absolutely no hurry to satisfy the reader's curiosity. She follows the three boys into their individual homes and leisurely explores their ordinary secrets. However, the drowned man is one secret they are in no hurry to divulge; even when they go to the police station, at the last minute they make a joke and run away without telling. Finally, almost incidentally, one of the boys tells a parent, who calls the authorities. The body is retrieved from the river, and the case is ruled an accident or suicide.

At the beginning of the next section of the story, Munro leaves the body and the boys altogether and focuses on a cranky dying woman, Mrs. Quinn, cared for by a lonely home nurse named Enid. Then, just as the reader becomes involved in the empty life of Enid, having given up on the story of the drowned optometrist, Mrs. Quinn tells Enid that Rupert, her husband, killed the optometrist when he saw him trying to fondle her. However, because Mrs. Quinn is neurotic and quite ill, Enid is not sure that she is telling the truth. When Mrs. Quinn dies, Enid decides she must tell Rupert, for whom she has feelings, the story she has heard and urge him to give himself up. The way she decides to do this, however, creates the open-ended ambiguity of the story: She asks him to row her out on the river, where she will tell him what she knows, also informing him that she cannot swim. At the last minute, she changes her mind, but cannot get out of the situation. The story ends just before they leave the shore, so the reader does not know whether she confronts him or not, and if she does, whether he pushes her in the river or rows them both back to the shore.

"The Love of a Good Woman" begins like a novel, but instead of continuing to broaden out as it introduces new characters and seemingly new stories, it tightens up, slowly connecting what at first seemed disparate and unrelated. It is a classic example of Munro's characteristic technique of creating a world that has all the illusion of external reality while all the time pulling the reader deeper into what becomes a hallucinatory inner world of mystery, secrecy, and deception. Unlike a novel, which would be bound to develop some sort of satisfying closure, Munro's story reaches a moral impasse, an ambiguous open end in which the reader suddenly realizes that instead of living in the world of apparent reality, he or she has been whirled, as if by a centrifugal force, to an almost unbearable central point of intensity.

Munro also returns to other favorite themes: infidelity, separation, divorce. "The Children Stay," the third-prize winner in the 1998 O. Henry Awards competition seems, on the one hand, a conventional eternal triangle story, with the central female character leaving her husband and family for another man. However, Munro complicates this predictable story line by making the woman an amateur actress and the man she runs away with the director of a local theater company's production of the play *Eurydice*. Munro has said that the story is about the way people make choices and how those choices are not usually about the things people think they are. The story explores the young woman's irrational decision to leave a husband and family for whom she cares, not for love or sex but for some romantic and compulsive obsession that she cannot quite control. Classical allusions to Orpheus, whose seductive music is not to be resisted, underlie the story's structure. "The Children Stay" is a variation of the romance story, practiced so well by Edna O'Brien, in which a woman cannot resist following a romantic image, even as she knows that it bears little relationship to reality.

"Jakarta" also centers on this theme. Focusing on two couples during the 1960's, when wife-swapping and open marriages were in fashion, the story ponders the disappearance of one of the husbands, Cottar, on a trip to Jakarta. However, thirty years later, when the other husband, Kent, along with his new wife, goes to visit the wife of the missing man, they both articulate their suspicion that Cottar ran away with Kath, Kent's first wife. Like "The Children Stay," the story is about how people try to find a way to snap themselves apart from a life decision to which they refuse to reconcile themselves. However, as is typical with Munro, this story never suggests that either path taken is the one that will assure happiness.

The most curious story in the collection is "My Mother's Dream," which is ostensibly told by a baby who is born just after her father has been killed in World War II. Although the story is told by the woman the baby becomes, the point of view is presented as if the baby were making conscious decisions, the main one of which is to reject the mother and prefer instead the father's mentally unstable sister, Iona. Particularly difficult for the mother is the fact that the baby cannot tolerate her playing the violin, one of the activities that gives her life some meaning. On one crucial day, when the mother must care for the inconsolable baby alone, she gives it a few grains of a sedative and takes the rest herself and falls asleep. When Iona comes home, she is terrified that the mother has smothered the baby. After this climactic day, in an almost allegorical way, the baby becomes more receptive to the mother, Iona's mental illness lessens, and the mother returns to her violin as a professional musician.

"Before the Change" is the closest thing to a social message story in the collection. The title refers to, among other things, a change in Canadian abortion law. Presented as a long letter from a young woman to a theology professor who has gotten her pregnant, the story focuses on the woman's relationship with her doctor father, who performs illegal abortions in his home office with the help of an older woman. The most important single event in the story occurs when the old woman cannot be present and the daughter must help her father with an abortion. When she tells him about her own pregnancy and how her lover would not marry her while she was pregnant for fear of losing his job and his reputation in the community, the father has a stroke. The story ends with the girl's realization that, in spite of a thriving regular practice, her father has left her very little; she suspects the old woman has been blackmailing him. Although the story, like many other Munro fictions, focuses on some ambiguous secret, its emphasis on the abortion issue makes it more polemical and less mysterious than the best of Munro's short fictions. As leisurely as Munro's stories are, the short-story form cannot easily bear the weight of polemical rhetoric and social lesson without seeming awkwardly and obviously rigged.

"Rich as Stink" centers on Karen, an eleven-year-old, whose divorced mother is helping a self-important historian do research on a book on the explorer Sieur de La Salle. The conflict of the story is based on the mother's affair with the man and the effect this has on the young girl, particularly because of his paternalistic control over the child. The story comes to a frightening climax when Karen, wearing the man's wife's wedding dress as a joke, drags the lace train through a candle and is badly burned. The burn, like the young girl's realization of her father's secret blackmail in "After the Change," is not a source of anger and resentment, however, but rather a sign of liberation from old ghosts and male control.

"Cortes Island" centers on a young woman nicknamed "Little Bride," who lives with her new husband in the basement apartment of Mrs. Gorrie and her invalid husband. At the request of Mrs. Gorrie, the young woman cares for the husband, until one day he tells her, by means of his scrapbook, a story about Cortes Island in which a man dies in a fire and leaves his seven-year-old son an orphan. The story somehow liberates the young woman, and she gets a job in a library and begins to devote time to her own writing. However, at the end of the story, when she and her husband move to a new place, she dreams erotic dreams of Mr. Gorrie and is obsessed with images of the burned house.

The central event of "Save the Reaper," another mother/daughter story, focuses on a woman who is taking her two grandchildren on a drive in the country. While playing a game called "Aliens," in which the children pretend that the driver of another car is from another planet, the grandmother, seeming to recognize some scene from her childhood, follows a car to a rural house in which a group of half-dressed men are playing cards and drinking. If the men are reminiscent of William Faulkner's Snopes family, the grandmother's mistake is an obvious borrowing from the famous story "A Good Man Is Hard to Find," by Munro's acknowledged mentor, Flannery O'Connor. After a few tense minutes in the house, the grandmother leaves, only to be flagged down by a young girl who has been living there and who wants a ride away from the place. Again there are tense moments, then a second escape when the girl gets out, but not before the grandmother tells her that she can come and stay with her if she finds no other place that night. The final lingering fear that something dangerous may be waiting is a typical theme of modern American short fiction from Flannery O'Connor to Raymond Carver.

Although in the last thirty years the short story has been characterized first by experimentation and then by attenuation, Alice Munro has continued to go her own way, so confident of the nature of the short story and her control of the form that she needs to observe no trends nor imitate any precursors. Certainly she does not write in a vacuum—she is clearly aware of short-story masters who have preceded her, including O'Connor and Anton Chekhov—but Munro has found her own unique rhythm and controls it consummately. Although there is always something mysterious and unspeakable in her stories, there is never the cryptic compression of much late twentieth century short fiction. In an almost novelistic fashion, as if she had all the time in the world, Munro lovingly lingers on her characters and seldom misses the opportunity to register an arresting image. Yet a Munro story is deceptive; it lulls the reader into a false sense of security in which time seems to stretch comfortably out like everyday reality, only to suddenly turn and tighten so intensely that the reader is left breathless.

Charles E. May

Sources for Further Study

Booklist. XCV, September 1, 1998, p. 6.
The Canadian Forum. LXXVII, October, 1998, p. 49.
Library Journal. CXXIII, September 15, 1998, p. 115.
Maclean's. CXI, November 16, 1998, p. 82.
The New York Times Book Review. CIII, November 1, 1998, p. 6.
Publishers Weekly. CCXLV, September 7, 1998, p. 81.
Time. CLII, November 30, 1998, p. 119.
The Times Literary Supplement. December 4, 1998, p. 22.
The Wall Street Journal. October 30, 1998, p. W4.
The Washington Post Book World. XXVIII, November 15, 1998, p. 5.

LOVE UNDETECTABLE
Notes on Friendship, Sex, and Survival

Author: Andrew Sullivan (1963-   )
Published: Alfred A. Knopf (New York). 256 pp. $23.00
Type of work: Essays

The three extended essays in this volume explore the dimensions of gay love and many of its attendant health and social implications

When Andrew Sullivan first gained national attention, he was twenty-eight years old and had been named editor of *The New Republic*, a position he held for the next five years. Sullivan, occupying a position of considerable visibility, was not secretive about his own homosexual orientation.

The author of *Virtually Normal: An Argument About Homosexuality* (1995) and the editor of *Same-Sex Marriage: Pro and Con* (1997), Sullivan has served as a remarkably talented role model for many gays. He has been particularly effective in writing objectively and with unique insights about gay issues.

Love Undetectable, which consists of three long essays, deals with three issues relating to gay life: the effect of AIDS upon gay communities, the origins of homosexuality and the religious and moral conflicts that being gay arouses in many people who are so oriented, and, in the book's most touching essay, "If Love Were All," the history of gay love relationships and close same-sex friendships through the ages.

Although each essay can stand alone, taken together, the three provide one of the most intelligent and well-reasoned statements about homosexuality thus far in print. Sullivan offers some startlingly fresh insights as well as vast stores of background information. His understanding of Sigmund Freud's stand on homosexuality is especially perceptive. Sullivan demonstrates how latter-day Freudians have distorted and misinterpreted many of Freud's observations about human sexuality.

Sullivan points out that Freud was "aware of the problem of psychoanalysts generalizing from their patient populations, a group who naturally tend to be disturbed, psychologically troubled, and likely to be in conflict with their sexual identity, whatever it is." Most psychiatrists or psychologists base their writing about homosexuality on their exposure to their patients. Sullivan questions whether their samples are valid and representative. He suggests that many well-adjusted gays do not seek psychiatric help; thus, they are excluded from the population from which many writers in the field draw their examples.

Typical of common conceptions regarding the origins of male homosexuality, a subject that Sullivan treats in depth in the second of his three essays, is the stereotypical son with a dominant, overly protective mother and a weak, indifferent, or abusive father. In other words, dysfunctional family situations are widely thought to underlie much male homosexuality.

Sullivan observes that in such families, one son may turn out to be homosexual whereas other sons do not, which casts doubts upon the psychological explanations given for homosexuality. Sullivan contends that some people are destined to be homosexual from infancy. In their earliest life, as they begin to display overt behaviors widely associated with homosexuality, their parents react in such ways that the dysfunction that typifies the families from which many gays come begins to take hold.

In such instances, the father, who is a role model for the very young child, may distance himself from the son or may be abusive to him, demeaning him for not being more typically male and demanding more masculine behavior from him, such as involvement in sports or in other activities usually associated with virile males. The mother may then enter into the situation as the overly protective champion of the persecuted child.

The role of the father in the child's upbringing is therefore diminished, while the role of the mother is enhanced. The family situation is dysfunctional, but the origins of the dysfunction lie not with the parents so much as with the homosexual child who evokes parental reactions of the sort noted.

Gays come in many varieties, but Sullivan focuses at one point on two general groups, closeted gays and gays who do not mask their homosexuality. Among closeted gays may be people who pass for straight, perhaps married men who carry on clandestine gay lives or who long to adopt the forbidden lifestyle. Many of them cannot maintain an erection with a woman unless they fantasize about men during the sex act. Writing insightfully about closeted gays and gays who are out, Sullivan characterizes them succinctly and accurately: "Shame forces you prematurely to run away from yourself; pride forces you prematurely to expose yourself."

The essays in this book are peppered with personal anecdotes, many of them relating to Sullivan's discovery that he is HIV-positive. He writes poignantly of his friend Dennis, who was diagnosed at about the same time Sullivan was and whose refusal of many of the treatments that might have saved his life led to his early death. In a sense, when Sullivan receives his diagnosis, as grim as the revelation is, it makes him feel one with a vast brotherhood of fellow sufferers.

Walt Odets's *In the Shadow of the Epidemic: Being HIV-Negative in the Age of AIDS* (1995) suggests that some gay HIV-negative men feel guilty for being among the healthy minority in areas with high concentrations of gay people such as California's Bay Area, where Odets, a gay psychologist, practices. People who live while those about them die suffer a survivor guilt akin to that experienced by European Jews who survived the Holocaust. Although Sullivan does not cite Odets directly, he credits him in his bibliography and echoes a number of Odets' conclusions in *Love Undetectable*.

Pervading much of this book is the feeling of sadness, discomfort, and frustration Sullivan harbors because of the silence that accompanies gay life. As they grow up, gays usually have few role models and almost no one with whom they can talk about their sexuality. Parents who detect their tendencies often tolerate them, but they do so silently, perhaps waiting for their offspring to outgrow their homosexuality, considering it a developmental phase, which in some people it clearly is.

A staunch, church-going Roman Catholic, Sullivan discusses the attitude of his church toward homosexuality: "In my adolescence and young adulthood, the teaching of the Church was merely a silence, an increasingly hollow denial even of the existence of homosexuals, let alone a credible ethical guide to how they should lead their lives."

He relates how he went to see the AIDS quilt displayed at the Mall in Washington, where he lives. Afterward, he attended Mass in his parish church, located in Washington's gay ghetto. The priest that day spoke about the biblical account of Jesus Christ's curing the lepers, and went on to remark how fortunate it is that such plagues do not exist today. After the service, Sullivan confronted the priest and asked him if he knew about AIDS, telling him sarcastically that news of it is everywhere. The priest admitted knowing about AIDS but said that he doubted talking about it would be relevant to his parishioners.

Sullivan's first essay, "When Plagues End," focuses on the effect AIDS has had on the gay community, on how it has forced sexual responsibility upon a group that theretofore had not been publicly viewed as particularly sexually responsible. He makes the distinction between a plague and a manageable disease, the former being "something that cannot be controlled, something with a capacity to spread exponentially out of its borders, something that kills and devastates with democratic impunity." A disease, which Sullivan contends AIDS can now be designated, is manageable and, although possibly incurable, as diabetes is incurable, can be successfully controlled for long spans of time in those who are afflicted.

The essay on AIDS ties in directly to the book's final essay, "If Love Were All," in which Sullivan explores the matter of friendship, its meaning and manifestations through the ages. He writes about close same-sex relationships between people of note, always clearly differentiating between friendship and sexual relationships. He points out that in friendship, there is equality of status and that at the heart of friendship is acceptance.

In writing about his friend Patrick, he notes that their relationship was a love relationship but not a sexual one. Their closeness was both an ideal and an idealized friendship. At one point early in their relationship, Sullivan was in love with Patrick and wanted a physical relationship with him, but Patrick, then involved with two other people, demurred. As a result, their closeness deepened and endured.

In Sullivan's eyes, the problems posed by AIDS united the gay community as nothing else previously had. It demonstrated the extent to which friendship can extend the boundaries of true loyalty that a crisis can help to define. It also winnowed out the shallow friendships that characterized some sectors of the gay community.

In discussing the sixteenth century French essayist Michel de Eyquem Montaigne, who wrote about his intense relationship, presumably platonic, with another man, Sullivan addresses the question of the kinds of love one can feel. In Montaigne's eyes, familial love, essentially an accident of birth, should occupy a much lower position in the hierarchy of affection than close friendship. Still, as Sullivan points out, the highest compliment one can pay a friend is to say that he or she is like family.

Sullivan discusses with insight, restraint, and equanimity the recent reparative theories current in some psychological circles that are appealing to members of the religious right and other conservative groups. He notes that if people who are by nature gay can be transformed into heterosexuals, then it should be equally possible to transform heterosexuals into gays.

Of course, those who stand foursquare against homosexuality might counter that this precisely is the greatest fear they have: Gays may indeed be able to proselytize, particularly among the young and innocent. The point of Sullivan's argument, however, is that one's sexual orientation is a fundamental part of one's being and that it cannot be altered.

Sullivan views heterosexuality as the norm within which questions of homosexuality are characteristically considered. He acknowledges that some people are by nature bisexual and that others, whose nature it is to be heterosexual, are forced by circumstances to practice homosexuality in some situations, such as confinement in prison. Such people revert to their innate heterosexuality when circumstances permit. On the other hand, the success rate among reparative psychologists is, by their own admission, quite low.

Sullivan focuses closely upon Charles W. Socarides' reparative theories as expounded in *Homosexuality: A Freedom Too Far* (1995), a highly controversial work in the field. Socarides denies that there can be any truly deep, committed relationships among homosexuals. Socarides contends that homosexual development takes place before the age of three and that it results more from a child's having a distant relationship with the father than from having an extraordinarily close attachment to the mother. Sullivan considers this a perversion of Freudian psychology and does much to debunk the contentions of Socarides (who, ironically, has a gay son who serves as President Clinton's chief political liaison with the gay and lesbian community).

Love Undetectable is a timely book, being published as the AIDS epidemic in the United States has been somewhat contained in the gay community, although it is spreading in the straight community. The final chapter, "If Love Were All," has particular relevance to the question of gay marriage, which is being discussed, often hysterically, in many circles and will likely become a possibility in at least a few states within the next decade.

Through the use of cogent anecdotal material, Sullivan has humanized gays, has portrayed them as people who contribute positively to society, who face everyday problems, and who have much in common with heterosexuals. His encounter with AIDS, both through the loss of friends to the disease and through his own seroconversion, adds authority and credibility to Sullivan's writing, which is clear and direct throughout.

R. Baird Shuman

Sources for Further Study

The Advocate. October 13, 1998, p. 94.
Booklist. XCV, September 1, 1998, p. 41.

Lambda Book Report. VII, November, 1998, p. 25.
Library Journal. CXXIII, October 15, 1998, p. 87.
National Review. L, December 7, 1998, p. 64.
New Statesman. CXXVII, November 6, 1998, p. 56.
The New York Times Book Review. CIII, October 11, 1998, p. 10.
Publishers Weekly. CCXLV, August 24, 1998, p. 37.
The Washington Post. November 12, 1998, p. C2.

LUCKY BASTARD

Author: Charles McCarry (1930-   )
Published: Random House (New York). 385 pp. $24.95
Type of work: Novel
Time: The late twentieth century
Locale: The United States

> Soviet agents blackmail a young American man who shows political promise with the intention of electing him to the presidency, thereby clearing the way for the Sovietization of the United States

Principal characters:
> JOHN FITZGERALD ("JACK") ADAMS, a charming young man who believes that he is the illegitimate son of President John F. Kennedy and who rises in politics with the backing of Soviet agents
> DMITRI ALEXEYIVITCH, the narrator, an officer in the KGB who chooses Adams as a target for subversion and becomes his controller
> PETER, a maverick high-ranking officer in the KGB who is Dmitri's superior and the originator of the plot
> MORGAN WEATHERBY ADAMS, a Soviet agent, Jack's wife
> DANNY MILLER, Jack's best friend from infancy, later a wounded veteran of the Vietnam War and Jack's law partner
> CINDY MILLER, Danny's wife and Jack's enemy
> GRETA, Jack's lover, a young German woman who is a Soviet agent

The premise of this thriller is that during the Cold War, a high-ranking officer in the Soviet intelligence agency KGB conceives and carries out a plan to subvert a young American destined for high political office. If the plan succeeds, the young man will ascend to the presidency and will pave the way for a communist takeover of the U.S. government. Peter, the officer who conceives the plot, acts without the knowledge or approval of his superiors in the KGB.

Peter's agent in the United States is known as Dmitri; he is the narrator of the novel. His orders are to identify a young man who has demonstrated the qualities necessary for political success in the United States: charm, sex appeal, ruthlessness, the ability to take up and abandon positions on important issues without appearing to be weak or unprincipled, and a quality or a pattern of behavior that will make him vulnerable to blackmail. One of Dmitri's American agents, a professor at Columbia University named Alan, comes up with a candidate in one of his students, Jack Adams.

Jack's mother was a nurse in the naval hospital where John F. Kennedy was treated during World War II, and she has led her son to believe that Kennedy was his real father. Jack is amoral and without principles, sexually attractive and highly sexually active (although he never bothers to engage in intercourse with a woman more than once), and blessed with a quick but shallow intelligence. Peter tests and observes the young man and gives his approval to the choice, giving Dmitri the job of controlling Jack Adams. As a reward for discovering Adams, Alan is later sent to Cuba, where he is executed at Peter's orders.

Before he is dispatched, Alan is ordered by Dmitri to arrange a fellowship of some kind that will send Jack to Europe, preferably to West Germany. The arrangement is made, and Jack travels to Heidelberg, where he is welcomed by Manfred, a German who is a Soviet agent controlled by Peter through Dmitri. Manfred introduces Jack to Greta, a member of the terrorist group known as the Baader-Meinhof Gang. Greta had become a communist in rebellion against her parents, members of Germany's wealthy upper-middle class. After seeming to despise Jack, Greta seduces him on a public street, and thereafter introduces him to a wild sexuality that enchants him. Eventually, after a final sexual adventure, Greta joins other members of her gang in an attempted bank robbery in which she and her accomplices are gunned down by police. It is implied that the police have been tipped off by Manfred, acting on Dmitri's orders. After arranging for Jack to go for a visit to the Soviet Union, Manfred himself is killed.

Jack is taken to meet Peter, who shows him photographs and videotapes of Jack's sexual activities with Greta, which also implicate him in the attempted bank robbery. He then lays out Jack's role in the plot that is to develop. If Jack declines to participate, the damning material will be made public, and Jack will be disgraced and sent to prison. Jack does not hesitate to accept.

The program set forth by Peter includes law school and a law practice, leading to a career in politics. Jack will be supported by funds funneled through Dmitri, but he will not receive any money directly; an agent he does not know as yet will manage the funds and will pass on to him orders from Dmitri, orders Jack must obey. In addition, the KGB will assist Jack in a variety of ways, sometimes without his knowledge. There is one ironclad rule for Jack: In his political career, he is not to attack or threaten the business of trafficking drugs into the United States. Jack does not know that this prohibition results from the fact that Peter's principal source of income, which enables him to operate outside the control of the KGB, is the drug trade.

Jack returns to the United States and enters Harvard University Law School, where he excels less because of any intellectual superiority than because of his charm and his unusually sharp memory. While at Harvard, he meets, apparently by accident, a student at the Harvard Business School named Morgan Weatherby, who epitomizes the radical hippie of the 1970's. She wears thick eyeglasses and unattractive clothes, she belongs to every radical political and feminist group, and she seems to have no interest in the opposite sex. She participates in every possible rally and protest. Jack, despite his usual busy sexual life, finds her intriguing.

Predictably, Morgan turns out to be deliberately masking her true attractiveness, as Jack discovers when she finally becomes the major partner in his sex life. Predictably also, she is the agent of the KGB whose approach to Jack has been directed by Dmitri. There is, however, an unexpected element in Jack's relationship with Morgan. She has been the most inventive and passionate sexual partner Jack has had since Greta's death, but Peter decrees that while they are to marry, they are to have no further sexual relations. Their twin sons, which eventually complete the politically perfect family, are conceived by Morgan with Jack's sperm in a new and sexless clinical procedure. Both Jack and Morgan proceed to find other, secret, sexual outlets.

Morgan serves one other important function. Jack is under orders not to appear too radical in his political statements, so that his appeal to the mass of voters will not be threatened. Morgan, on the other hand, is to continue in her radical activities and to resume her unattractive clothing, keeping liberal voters safely in Jack's camp and assuring a strong base for his campaigns.

Once married to Morgan, Jack returns to Ohio, where he had grown up, and enters a law practice with Danny Miller. Danny, his only real friend, has followed a different path. Where Jack is sexually hyperactive and promiscuous, Danny has a single girlfriend and is permanently attached to her. While Jack is a physical coward and does everything he can to avoid combat, Danny is a genuine patriot who willingly fights in Vietnam, where he is seriously wounded and left with terrible burns. His scars put an end to any possibility of his likely success as a professional athlete. His longtime girlfriend, Cindy, enters law school with Danny, supports him while both get their degrees, marries him, and joins a large law firm in Columbus. Because of her aversion to Jack, the two couples have no social interaction.

Cindy is the only character in the book, aside from Soviet agents, who is not taken in by Jack's charm. Even in high school, she had found Danny's protective friendship with Jack an annoyance, but this turns to outright hatred because of an incident following Danny's departure for Vietnam. She and Jack had driven Danny to the airport and said separate goodbyes to him. On the way back to town, Cindy had wept inconsolably and Jack, with no predatory intentions, had stopped the car in a secluded place to try to stop her tears. She cried on his shoulder; before long, Jack did what he had learned to do with unhappy women and had made love to her. Cindy, paying little attention to what was happening, had made no resistance and in the event had responded sexually to Jack's lovemaking. She never forgives Jack for leading her to her only betrayal of Danny.

Jack's career proceeds according to plan. He makes a reputation as a defense attorney by gaining an acquittal for a popular police lieutenant who had been framed by crooked officers. He uses this triumph as a springboard to the nomination for state attorney general. He proceeds from that office to lieutenant governor of the state, always assisted by funds and other kinds of support from Peter's agents. When his courage is called into question, thugs hired at Peter's orders without Jack's knowledge invade his home in the dead of night and shoot up the place. Jack is terrified, but he emerges in the press as a brave man and a hero.

A successful plot engineered at Peter's orders compromises the governor, a man who had hated Jack. Ironically, the plan makes use of the governor's sexual predilections, while Jack's sexual activities never harm him politically. When the governor is forced to resign, Jack succeeds to the office, which he uses to capture national attention. Most of his advisers, including Morgan, now less a plain-looking frump and more a wholesome politician's wife, believe that Jack leaps too soon into presidential politics, but Jack is determined, and he demands increasing amounts of cash from his sponsors to support his campaign.

When the Soviet Union collapses, Peter manages to survive. With a duplicity that is second nature to him, Peter makes a deal with the Central Intelligence Agency (CIA) and at the same time arranges for the funds needed by Jack's campaign to be supplied by newly rich Chinese. Communism will still benefit from Jack's election, but the beneficiary will be China rather than the defunct Soviet Union. Coming from far behind, Jack manages a narrow victory in the race for the presidency and prepares to take office. Cindy, surprisingly, is the agent of Jack's destruction.

Lucky Bastard is the ninth work of fiction by Charles McCarry, who specializes in suspenseful novels dealing with espionage and subversion. The dedication of the novel to the memory of the late novelist Richard Condon is an acknowledgment that *Lucky Bastard* owes its central premise of a Soviet attempt to put its man in the White House to Condon's popular novel *The Manchurian Candidate* (1959). McCarry's book has a less violent conclusion, but McCarry lacks Condon's sense of humor and the biting, satiric edge of Condon's prose. *Lucky Bastard* does have suspense, a plot with interesting twists and reversals, lots of sex, and a convincingly cold and dispassionate narrator in Dmitri. McCarry's experience with the CIA lends a note of authenticity to his depiction of espionage.

McCarry's political message is clear. The American electorate's preference for charm in its candidates rather than principle or character makes the United States vulnerable to subversion. He believes that liberals are soft on communism and that even the disintegration of the Soviet Union does not remove the possibility of a communist takeover; China, he thinks, is still a serious threat.

Despite disclaimers at the beginning and end of the book providing assurances that no real persons are represented, it is evident that McCarry is not an admirer of John F. Kennedy or Bill Clinton. Reviewers have noted the timeliness of the similarities to the latter at a time when he is under attack from many quarters. The message, however, is less important in *Lucky Bastard* than the element of suspense and the machinations of the subverters.

John M. Muste

Sources for Further Study

Booklist. XCIV, May 15, 1998, p. 1565.
Business Week. August 24, 1998, p. 14F.
The Economist. CCCXLVII, September 19, 1998, p. 99.
Library Journal. CXXIII, June 15, 1998, p. 107.
National Review. L, August 17, 1998, p. 43.
The New York Times Book Review. CIII, August 16, 1998, p. 7.
Newsweek. CXXXII, July 20, 1998, p. 69.
Publishers Weekly. CCXLV, May 25, 1998, p. 61.
The Wall Street Journal. July 24, 1998, p. W10.
The Washington Post Book World. XXVIII, July 12, 1998, p. 3.

M. F. K. FISHER: A LIFE IN LETTERS
Correspondence 1929-1991

Editors and compilers: Norah K. Barr, Marsha Moran, and Patrick Moran
Published: Counterpoint (Washington, D.C.). 500 pp. $35.00
Type of work: Letters
Time: 1929-1992
Locale: California, France, and Switzerland

This wide-ranging selection of M. F. K. Fisher's personal correspondence, much of it previously unpublished, illuminates Fisher's life

> *Principal personages:*
> MARY FRANCES KENNEDY FISHER, a renowned food and travel writer
> NORAH KENNEDY BARR,
> LAWRENCE CLARK POWELL,
> ELEANOR FRIEDE,
> JULIA CHILD, and
> PAUL CHILD, friends and correspondents

M. F. K. Fisher was a beloved writer of books, articles, and essays on food, eating, and travel, in which she shared with her audience her personal perspectives and experiences, beginning with her life in Dijon, France, as the young wife of academic Al Fisher. This book, published posthumously, consists of a selection of letters kept by correspondents, particularly her youngest sister, Norah, and Lawrence Clark Powell, Mary Frances's friend since the 1920's.

The letters are presented chronologically and divided into five sections: Dijon, France: 1929-1932; Le Paquis, Switzerland, and Bareacres, California: 1935-1949; Kennedy Ranch, Whittier, California: 1950-1953; St. Helena, California, and Aix-en-Provence, France: 1954-1970; and Last House, Glen Helen, California, 1970-1992. At the beginning of each section, there is a brief overview of the events in Mary Frances's life during that period. Some letters have brief footnotes, primarily identifying unfamiliar correspondents.

The book's first section is small—ten letters to her parents and siblings, and her first letter to Lawrence Clark Powell. These are the letters of a wide-eyed, exuberant innocent abroad, describing the people, customs, and culture of Dijon, France, with the sharp eye for detail and witty but elegant style that infused her later writings.

The second section reveals a time of great turbulence and tragedy in Mary Frances's life. She and Al Fisher had returned from France to California, where they met Dillwyn and Gigi Parrish. The Parrishes soon divorced, and in 1937, Dillwyn and the Fishers moved together to Switzerland. The Fishers quickly separated, and Al Fisher returned to the United States and accepted a job as a college professor; Mary Frances and Dillwyn eventually married. Dillwyn was Mary Frances's great love and her artistic and intellectual partner; however, he developed an embolism and suffered constant, agonizing pain after having a leg amputated. He and Mary Frances returned to California and settled on a ranch near Hemet, which they named Bareacres. There,

Dillwyn painted and Mary Frances wrote. In 1941, however, pain and depression drove Dillwyn to suicide; the next year, Mary Frances' only brother, David, also committed suicide. In 1945, Mary Frances married Donald Friede, a publisher, three weeks after they met. As that marriage collapsed, Mary Frances and her two daughters returned to Whittier, where she had been reared, to care for her father, Rex, after the death of her mother.

The book's middle section consists of only eighteen letters. Some of these were unsent, and many vented her frustrations and anger at the time. Both her father and the family ranch were dying, and Mary Frances's creative energies were diverted to caring for Rex and her two daughters; feeding and accommodating visiting family and friends; managing the ranch and the family business, the *Whittier News*; and dealing with the end of her third marriage. Her writing career was reduced to magazine articles, one novella, and helping her father write his daily column. The time with her father, however, deepened her understanding of old age and crystalized her feelings on death and dying, subjects that came up often in her later letters.

The fourth section chronicles a time of renewed productivity and adventure in Mary Frances's life. She first moved to St. Helena, in California's Napa Valley, after her father's death. She and her daughters had two lengthy stays in Europe, celebrated in various writings, especially *Map of Another Town*, first published in 1964 and reprinted along with *A Considerable Town* (1978) as *Two Towns in Provence* (1983). Donald Friede and his last wife, Eleanor, were instrumental in the publication of *The Art of Eating* (1954), a one-volume publication of Mary Frances' first five books. Mary Frances also met and became close friends with the well-known chef Julia Child and her husband, Paul, as a result of her writing *The Cooking of Provincial France* (1968) for Time-Life's cooking series. Also in this period, Mary Frances responded to the Civil Rights movement by going to Mississippi to teach at Piney Woods, a school for disadvantaged African American students.

The final section of *A Life in Letters* covers the last two decades of Fisher's life, which she spent in a two-room house built for her by a friend on his ranch in California's Sonoma Valley. Although declining health diminished her literary output—she had long suffered from arthritis and later developed Parkinson's disease—she still maintained a constant correspondence with relatives and old friends, as well as an increasing series of letters to fans. The book's final letter is a few lines written to her oldest friend, Lawrence Powell, a year before her death.

Although the letters are at times quotidian, a thorough reading uncovers fascinating nuggets that add new dimensions to the self-portrait Mary Frances painted in her books and articles. Still, one of the frustrations of a book such as this is the questions that are left unanswered. Longtime fans familiar with the story of her travels in Europe with daughters Anna and Kennedy may have envied Fisher's daughters' apparently privileged, idyllic childhoods. *A Life in Letters* discloses many of the girls' problems and leaves its readers with many questions about their lives. Daughter Anna Parrish was born two years after Dillwyn's suicide. Letters written prior to Anna's birth refer to Fisher's plans to adopt one or two daughters, then report her joy at successfully completing the adoption of her first child. The introduction to that section, however, reveals that Mary Frances actually was Anna's birth mother, a fact that she apparently was able to conceal from even her closest friends by spending the later months of her pregnancy at the isolated Bareacres while claiming to be working in Washington, D.C., on a classified job for the war effort. Her second daughter, Mary Kennedy Friede (known as Mary as a child and Kennedy as an adult) was the child of Mary Frances and Donald Friede. A letter written late in her life attributes the failure of her third marriage, in large part, to Friede's lack of ease with and interest in children, and her letters confirm the feeling evident in her books that Mary Frances was a concerned and loving mother.

Stray sentences in later letters hint at Fisher's concerns about both girls, Anna in particular. Anna had serious mental problems, apparently diagnosed as manic depression, and after the birth of her son, Chris, Anna alternated long stays with Fisher with periods of total estrangement from her mother. Daughter Kennedy, on the other hand, had a less tempestuous life, marrying a professor and rearing two children. A late letter, however, mentions serious problems between Kennedy and her husband.

Similarly, there are several mentions in letters of a passionate affair with an unnamed, and presumably married, man. It seems from her glowing letters about this affair that its end would have been painful to Fisher, but there is no mention of when or how it ended, nor of the emotional effect of its ending on her. In the same vein, there is little discussion of her reaction to either Dillwyn's or her brother's suicide. Whether such letters were not available or were excluded from the book is not explained.

An additional frustration with the book is its limited referencing. The index is scant: a two-page index of the recipients of the included letters, but no index to subjects covered in the letters. This makes it quite challenging to revisit an earlier discussion of a topic of interest.

Despite these negatives, *A Life in Letters* is a valuable addition to the Fisher library. Dozens of pictures, many previously unpublished, complement the text. They range from a childhood picture of Mary Frances with her two younger sisters, Anne and Norah, and their brother, David, to a picture of Mary Frances, still writing, in the last decade of her life. Other photographs show her two daughters, her parents, her three husbands, and several of the friends whose letters are included in the book, including pictures of Lawrence Powell over six decades.

In addition to providing new information on Fisher's love affairs and deep friendships with men, *A Life in Letters* reveals a woman deeply devoted to her women friends. Mary Frances's relationship with Eleanor Friede was warm on both sides and continued long after Donald's death in the mid-1960's. It is particularly interesting to see the progression of Mary Frances's relationship with her youngest sister, Norah: from indulgent older sister, to irritated sibling, to a loving and accepting woman genuinely glad to have her sister as a friend.

Fisher's experiences teaching in the African American school in Mississippi in 1964 and 1965 were not covered in her well-known books. Several lengthy letters on this subject provide a different portrait of Mary Frances than the conventional one of a sparkling intellectual, glamorous traveler, and gourmand. In fact, her time there was one of early rising, mediocre food, and a lack of intellectually stimulating peers. However, the hardships she endured in order to teach in the civil rights school can be seen as further evidence of her strong and deep need to nurture, a continuation of the devotion she showed to Dillwyn Parrish before his suicide, her caring for her father in his dying years, and her commitment to Anna and Kennedy as a single mother. She had a deep concern for and interest in the students; in fact, she brought one of them back to Northern California to stay with her for a time and helped her to prepare for a career in nursing.

In a letter to Norah in January, 1976, Mary Frances says, "It always shocks me to think that anything I've written to a *person* would be kept. . . . Until lately I haven't kept any correspondence at all." Where and how most of the letters were collected is not explained. It does say that Lawrence Powell kept every letter Mary Frances Fisher ever wrote him—perhaps not surprising, since Powell was not only her oldest and dearest friend but also the librarian at the University of California, Los Angeles. Her mother and Norah also saved her letters, and some few letters were noted in the book as not having been ever sent; apparently, these were kept by Mary Frances.

M. F. K. Fisher's audience spans decades and generations. Her literary output over almost six decades includes memoirs and essays, numerous articles for such magazines as *The New Yorker*, *The Atlantic Monthly*, and *Gourmet*, a children's book, a novel, and a scholarly translation and annotation of J. A. Brillat-Savarin's *The Physiology of Taste, or Meditations on Transcendental Gastronomy* (1949). She has been credited with inventing the genre of food writing, as opposed to creating recipes and cookbooks. Much of her writing was drawn from her personal life, which was one of its attractions to many of her readers.

These letters, selected by her sister Norah, her secretary and friend Marsha Moran, and Marsha's husband, Patrick, offer additional details of her life and a presumably unguarded glimpse at many aspects of her personality: passionate woman, disillusioned wife, dutiful but stressed daughter, delighted mother of curious young girls, concerned mother of a troubled and alienated adult child, writer fretting over deadlines and lack of inspiration, senior citizen dealing with limitations and disabilities and facing impending death. *A Life in Letters* offers readers familiar with Fisher through her books insights as well as new questions, and it introduces readers unfamiliar with the works published during her lifetime to a fascinating woman and delightful writer.

Irene Struthers Rush

Sources for Further Study

American Scholar. LXVII, Spring, 1998, p. 154.
Booklist. XCIV, February 15, 1998, p. 962.
Kirkus Reviews. LXV, December 1, 1997, p. 1750.

Library Journal. CXXIII, February 1, 1998, p. 95.
The New York Times Book Review. CIII, January 18, 1998, p. 8.
Publishers Weekly. CCXLIV, November 24, 1997, p. 60.
The Virginia Quarterly Review. LXXIV, Summer, 1998, p. 90.
The Washington Post Book World. XXVIII, March 8, 1998, p. 4.

THE MAGICIAN'S WIFE

Author: Brian Moore (1921-   )
Published: E. P. Dutton (New York). 231 pp. $23.95
Type of work: Novel
Time: 1856-1857
Locale: Tours and Compiègne, France; Algeria

> *France's foremost magician is persuaded by Emperor Napoléon III to travel to Algeria to perform for the local Muslim marabouts and dissuade them from opposing France's imperialistic schemes*

Principal characters:
EMMELINE LAMBERT, the narrator, the magician's wife
HENRI LAMBERT, her husband, a celebrated illusionist
COLONEL DENIAU, the chief of the Arab Bureau and architect of the plan to manipulate Lambert
NAPOLÉON III, the emperor of France
JULES, Lambert's assistant
BOU-AZIZ, the leader of the Algerian marabouts

In October, 1856, after he has retired to his estate in Tours, Henri Lambert is invited to Compiègne, Emperor Napoléon III's winter palace, for one of his highness's celebrated *séries*, weeklong rounds of hunting, shooting, and parties. Such invitations are highly coveted and a sign of royal favor, and while Lambert is delighted, his wife disapproves, complaining that the expense will be prohibitive and that her husband will be only a minor diversion for aristocratic entertainment.

Once at Compiègne, Emmeline feels utterly ill at ease, deserted by her husband while he heads off for male-only meetings and embarrassed that she is a bourgeois pretender among the aristocracy. The isolation provokes a reassessment of her marriage, which has grown stale, and she fears that she has been hoodwinked, just as all her husband's audiences have. She is more than flattered by Colonel Deniau's attention and contemplates an affair with him. At a shooting outing, she is horrified by the spectacle and grows ill.

She and her husband eventually have an audience with the emperor, and they learn that he has grand plans for her husband to visit Algeria, where he must perform and dazzle the crowds. Within weeks, the couple arrives in Algiers and must prepare for the first of Lambert's performances, in which he must convince the local sheiks that his powers surpass those of any of their leaders. One of those leaders, Bou-Aziz, is on the verge of declaring himself Mahdi (chosen one) and thus inaugurating a jihad, or holy war, to rid the desert of the European intruders. If Lambert can overwhelm the audience with his conjuring powers, he may undercut the marabout's authority and divide his followers.

The performance is a resounding success, except that Bou-Aziz is not in attendance, and they must journey across the desert to his home at Milianah. During the trip, Jules falls seriously ill, and Emmeline is forced to assume his role as her husband's assistant. While performing her duties, she cannot take her eyes off the charismatic Bou-Aziz, and she feels overpowered by his presence. By means of an extraordinarily clever charade, Lambert escapes certain death and startles the crowd.

As Lambert revels in triumph, his loyal attendant, Jules, dies of cholera, and Emmeline gradually realizes the futility of her and her husband's lives. In a moment of courage and utter self-determination, she travels out to the marabout's quarters and reveals the deception that has duped his followers. Bou-Aziz delays the announcement of jihad, and just when Lambert appears victorious, he is shot by a disgruntled Arab and paralyzed, his career and future rendered dubious.

At the heart of the novel's concerns is the notion of magic and its effects on audiences. The most obvious source of magic is, of course, Henri Lambert, whose prestidigitation is fairly pallid fare once its secrets have been revealed. Lambert is a fraud, especially in the grandiose terms with which he presents himself to Muslims: as someone appointed by God to demonstrate supernatural powers. His role as national hero is also a matter of deception and an empty performance, for Bou-Aziz simply capitulates, not because he fears Lambert's gifts but because he is convinced of his own spiritual superiority.

Emmeline comes to the conclusion that her marriage is the result of a sleight of hand and coincidence. She mistook her husband for a gentleman but was in fact simply enchanted by a false air of command and enchantment. "Looking back now, I believe that on some occasions he does have a sort of magical power, or at least a summoning of his will so strong that he can make people do things they would never dream of doing."

The trickery, however, goes much further, and soon it fairly surrounds Emmeline. The attendants at Compiègne are the grand and powerful, but she quickly sees another side to them. They are lecherous, predatory, and shallow. Their leader, Louis-Napoléon, imagines himself an ally to all social groups, though his progressiveness is simply self-serving. The man who imagines himself a restorer of the Napoleonic Empire is a hapless imperialist, most of whose schemes for international glory are repeatedly thwarted.

The concern with trickery allows Moore to explore once again a favorite theme—spiritual belief. In novel after novel, Moore examines characters who wrestle with the subtleties of faith, often left either with delusions or a yearning to fill some inner emptiness. Emmeline is one of these yearners; she feels divorced from a life of meaning, and when she thinks, "Compiègne has changed me," she has no idea how portentous her words will prove.

The novel abounds in contrasts between Christianity and Islam, and a morning at Mass proves instructive to the impressionable Emmeline:

> This morning the Mass was not, as might have been expected in these surroundings, a High Mass, sung, with a choir. Instead it was a Low Mass, as it might be celebrated in any provincial chapel, the priest seeming to hurry through it, as though, as with most events in the *série*, Their Majesties would permit no dawdling. . . . Soon they would all file out of the chapel, this ceremony completed, a ceremony which, to Emmeline this morning, seemed only that: a ritual of society, a service which, in the court of Napoléon III, had no more meaning than a military parade.

However, the vast implacability of the Sahara and Bou-Aziz's serene demeanor provide her another view of faith:

> Behind those voices was a world of silence, as though their praise of God rose into heavens in total submission to divine will. Never in France, in cathedral, convent, or cloister, had she felt the intensity of belief everywhere present in the towns, villages, farms, and deserts of this land. It was a force at once inspiring and terrible, a faith with no resemblance to the Christian belief in Mass and sacraments, hellfire and damnation, sin and redemption, penance and forgiveness.
>
> *Everything comes from God.*

Where the provincial woman from the suburbs once wanted only to return to her quotidian world, she now sees Moorish culture as a true home.

In the largest sense, Emmeline's journey is an uneasy odyssey to the self. Like many nineteenth century women, Emmeline is a creature of the projections of others. She is first her father's daughter, child of a physician who is appalled at her choice in a mate whom he feels is her social inferior. Once married, she is simply the magician's wife, a man she barely knows, with whom she rarely sleeps, and whose professional life is a mystery. Emmeline has always bent to the will of others, accepting their opinions as her own, forever reaching for satisfaction somewhere outside herself.

Part of Moore's artistry is his refusal to write a hortatory tract about female oppression and gender inequities; those points are made far more subtly and convincingly through the words of the protagonist herself. Emmeline's gradual awakening and transformation spring from a sense of genuine realization rather than from authorial machinations forced upon the character acting as his marionette. Emmeline's awakening hinges on moral outrage—her presumed social superiors are frauds, her marriage is an empty charade, her country's foreign policy is imperialism pure and simple, and her religion is hollow formalism. Her decision to reveal her husband's deception to Bou-Aziz has nothing to do with marital revenge and everything to do with a desperate reach for the truth. For one moment, she seeks a release from hypocrisy, deceit, and illusion and places her faith in the power of honesty. Like the honest writer that he is, Moore offers no facile solution to the dilemmas proposed in the novel. The French, of course, were successful in the colonization of Algeria, and one woman's intervention could do little to alter the future.

Moore returns once more to the writing of an historical fiction, and he is now among modern literature's foremost practitioners of this subgenre of the novel. His concern is never with history for its own sake nor with the use of actual incidents as local color or a curious backdrop for pedestrian fiction; instead, Moore sees in the actual all the suspense and intrigue of drama itself. In *Black Robe* (1985), he investigated the Catholic Church's missionary zeal in North America; in *No Other Life* (1993), he examined the election of a priest to the presidency of a small Caribbean island; in *The Color of Blood* (1987), he considered the role of the Catholic Church in the stability of an East European country; and in *The Statement* (1996), he turned his attention to the Church's complacency during the Holocaust.

The outlines of this story Moore is said to have obtained from a collection of letters between George Sand and Gustave Flaubert in which a nineteenth century magician, Jean-Eugène Robert-Houdin (the namesake of Harry Houdini), was sent to North Africa by the French government to undermine the faith the Arabs placed in their spiritual leaders. Robert-Houdin was evidently successful, as Lambert is, and the fictional character's tricks are closely modeled on Robert-Houdin's. Both employ the emerging technology of the day, such as electricity, and both are fascinated by intricate machines that each invents. In this minor footnote to history, Moore finds a parable for the modern age, where cultural dominance is achieved through technological sophistication and downright chicanery rather than through the attractions or persuasiveness of a culture and its representatives.

The Magician's Wife is further proof of Moore's subtle powers as a storyteller. Historical novels are often baggy creatures, filled with unrefined observations and bloated documentation. Moore is, on the other hand, a master of understatement. His spare prose captures perfectly the meretricious elegance of the emperor's court and the tortured psychology of an initially unprepossessing woman. His descriptions of Compiègne and Algeria are exotic and deliciously atmospheric. Moore is a writer of remarkable control who can do more in a single page than most writers do in an entire chapter.

The Magician's Wife is a remarkably timely novel, dealing with significant incidents in the West's disruption of African culture and its suspicion of and antipathy toward Islamic religion. Since 1992, more than 65,000 people in Algeria have been killed as a result of violence stemming from the cancellation of a general election that an Islamic party was expected to win. Moore's novel does as much as any news report or historical treatise could to reveal the disastrous legacy of Western intervention that seems everywhere evident in Africa. The novel's sparse conclusion gives an air of utter finality to those events and presages the late twentieth century situation there:

> *The following summer, the summer of 1857, French armies under the command of Maréchal Randon and General MacMahon subdued the tribes of Kabylia, thus completing the conquest of Algeria by France.*
> *In the summer of 1962, Algeria officially declared its independence, ending the French presence in that country.*

David W. Madden

Sources for Further Study

America. CLXXVIII, May 2, 1998, p. 23.
Booklist. XCIV, November 15, 1997, p. 546.
Commonweal. CXXV, February 27, 1998, p. 22.
Forbes. CLXI, March 9, 1998, p. 28.
Library Journal. CXXIII, November 1, 1997, p. 117.
Los Angeles Times Book Review. January 25, 1998, p. 8.

The New York Times Book Review. CIII, February 1, 1998, p. 14.
Publishers Weekly. CCXLV, January 5, 1998, p. 44.
The Times Literary Supplement. September 12, 1998, p. 7.
The Washington Post Book World. XXVIII, January 11, 1998, p. 9.

A MAN IN FULL

Author: Tom Wolfe (1931-   )
Published: Farrar, Straus & Giroux (New York). 742 pp. $28.95
Type of work: Novel
Time: The 1990's
Locale: Atlanta, Georgia; Oakland, California

An acidly etched survey of the influences of race and wealth, caste and class on life in the New South

Principal characters:
    CHARLIE CROKER, an Atlanta real-estate developer
    SERENA CROKER, Charlie's young and beautiful second wife
    MARTHA CROKER, Charlie's older first wife
    RAYMOND PEEPGAS, an official with PlannersBanc
    INMAN ARMHOLSTER, an Atlanta businessman and friend of Charlie
    ELIZABETH ARMHOLSTER, Inman's daughter
    ROGER WHITE II, an African American attorney
    WES JORDAN, the African American Mayor of Atlanta
    ANDRE FLEET, a former basketball star, Jordan's opponent
    FAREEK FANON, Georgia Tech's star football player
    CONRAD HENSLEY, an employee of Croker Global Foods

In 1988, Tom Wolfe's sprawling novel *The Bonfire of the Vanities* examined in unrelenting and often scathing detail the varied worlds of New York City, ranging from the conspicuous consumption of all sorts in the city's glittering penthouses to the burned-out, blasted landscapes of the decaying Bronx. It was a work worthy of Honoré de Balzac, the definitive portrait of a greedy decade in the nation's trading center.

With *A Man in Full*, Wolfe returns to fiction. Again, his sweep is broad and inclusive, and his cast of characters ranges from the elite to the underclass. This time his setting is the New South, specifically its unofficial capital, Atlanta, Georgia, the city that symbolizes the dynamism, growth, and wealth of the nation's fastest-growing region. Atlanta, home of champion sports teams, jeweled setting for the 1996 Olympics, international hub of finance, proclaims itself "too busy to hate."

Until just before the beginning of *A Man in Full*, this had been the world in which Charlie Croker lived—or believed he lived. Charlie, who came roaring out of southwestern Georgia to become famous playing both offense and defense for Georgia Tech's football team, earning the nickname the "Sixty Minute Man," is one of Atlanta's most successful and best-known real-estate developers. His latest creation, Croker Concourse, gleams proudly northeast of the central city, a symbol of his triumph.

It is a hollow triumph, almost literally a facade, for office space at Croker Concourse remains largely unleased as hundreds of millions of dollars in bank debt remain unpaid. Soon, the loan officers at PlannersBanc are threatening Charlie and demanding that he restructure his company and sell off executive toys such as his jets. They even cast coldly calculating eyes on his beloved plantation, Turpmtine. While Charlie's attention is fixed on his financial problem, his nemesis stalks him from an entirely different direction and through a highly unlikely messenger.

It was at Morehouse College, Atlanta's prestigious school for the African American elite, that Roger White II was first dubbed "Roger Too White" by his fraternity brother Wes Jordan, now Atlanta's mayor. Now, Roger Too White is tapped to perform a delicate mission: to enlist Charlie Croker's public support of Fareek Fanon, "The Cannon," a star football player at Georgia Tech accused (although not officially nor publicly) of date rape by the daughter of one of Atlanta's most influential businessmen. Roger White's means of persuasion is his ability to ease Charlie Croker's financial problems by having PlannersBanc ease up on its repayment demands. Yet for Charlie to support Fanon will mean deserting his circle of friends, including his oldest, Inman Armholster—father of the young woman Fanon is supposed to have raped. It is a cruel dilemma, the full extent of which Charlie only slowly comprehends.

While Charlie cannot initially fathom his potential destruction, he is not even aware that he has set into motion his eventual salvation. In Oakland, California, Conrad Hensley, a warehouse worker for Croker Global Foods, is laid off as part of a drive to cut costs for Charlie's far-flung companies. Before long, in a series of misadventures, Conrad sits in a prison cell, his only diversion a volume of Epictetus, the Stoic philosopher, sent to him by mistake. He begins to read and then to understand.

Delivered from his California prison by a providential earthquake, Conrad goes through a series of equally implausible (but, in Wolfe's handling, utterly believable) events that bring him to Atlanta and Charlie Croker himself, for whom Conrad (known as Connie) serves as a male nurse following Charlie's knee replacement. Gradually, Conrad imparts to the invalid the teachings of Epictetus, which will allow him to redeem himself at the conclusion of the novel. At the news conference during which he is expected to support Fanon, Charlie turns away from both the banks and the white power structure to reclaim his own integrity.

Once he has set the main plot in motion, Wolfe allows it to unfold gradually, letting it develop its power and momentum through the reader's growing understanding and appreciation of the large cast of characters and their environment. The reader comes to learn that their vision of their lives and their city is essentially flawed.

Hell, someone once observed, is the truth discovered too late, and Atlanta's truth can be sufficiently diabolical in *A Man in Full*. The city's vaunted economic strength, like Charlie Croker's real-estate empire, is built largely on credit lines and credulousness. The splendid new towers of downtown are deserted at the end of the day as their inhabitants begin the longest and worst commute in the United States, leaving the inner city three-quarters African American. The rift between that population and the suburb-dwelling whites, especially in the fabled enclave of Buckhead, continues to grow, even while officially it is ignored. Within the African American community, there is a further split between the Morehouse elite and the general population—a split that Andre Fleet, a former professional basketball star, seeks to exploit in his campaign for mayor against Wes Jordan. Nor is the white community uniform, as Charlie Croker is reminded when his foundation of wealth is threatened. Without that money (or illusion of money), he is just another cracker from south Georgia.

Wolfe captures the nuances and subtleties of these divisions of class and caste with his typical skill and verve. Physical descriptions that go beyond the surface to reveal the inner nature of his characters have long been a Wolfe forte; *A Man in Full* shows his descriptive powers at their highest, and the fact that his tone is often sardonic only emphasizes the vividness of his portraits. No reader will come away from this book with a vague image of Charlie Croker, Wes Jordan, or even the generally pallid banker Raymond Peepgas. Even Fareek Fanon, whose appearance is a brief one, is rendered with impressive fullness.

Wolfe observes and reproduces the language of his characters with impressive ability. He deftly captures Charlie Croker's south Georgia accent and inflections, where a "court of law" becomes a "coat a law," and a "very easy favor" is rendered "veh easy favuh." In a similar fashion, with selective quotations at appropriate moments, Wolfe both presents Mayor Wes Jordan's own personal linguistic style and captures something of the individual. Jordan's tendency is to repeat the same observation, slightly altered, in triplets: "I have no firsthand knowledge of what, if anything, if anything, if *any*thing did or didn't happen on the night in question. . . ." Out of such touches are Wolfe's characters created and his contemporary American social settings observed.

It is as a social observer that Wolfe is at his best in *A Man in Full*. The American South is one of the few places in the nation where both class and caste remain truly important in the way human beings relate to one another, and Wolfe makes full use of the various signals that its citizens can produce, from the choice of their clothes to the location of their homes. His discussion on the "hard wood" homesites of Buckhead versus the "soft wood" homesites of the newer developments is a minor dissertation on the sociology of Atlanta and, by extension, the entire region. A whole series of cultures are captured by *A Man in Full*.

There are the cultures of Atlanta, white and African American, of the rich and powerful and the less affluent, whose potential power becomes actual only when directed, even manipulated, by leaders such as Wes Jordan. Money and politics are the obsessions of this culture, and both are valued not so much for what they can actually achieve but for themselves—as expressions of pure power. As Wes Jordan admits, the most addictive aspect of politics is the pleasure in watching others jump at your beck and call, even your mere presence.

Charlie Croker exists partially in this culture of power and money, but largely by its sufferance. His rise, due in large if unacknowledged part to his first wife, Martha, has brought him into the circle of rich businessmen and the banks that fuel their ever more grandiose projects. He has become one of those automatically invited to major cultural events, such as the gala opening of recently rediscovered paintings by Atlanta artist Wilson Lapeth. In this gathering, though, Charlie has flown beyond his orbit, and his supposedly humorous barbs at Lapeth's homoerotic works mark him as an outsider. In a sense, the scene is another foreshadowing of Charlie's approaching torments as a scorned outsider, first by the relentless loan officers of PlannersBanc avid for their interest, then by the hectoring presence of Roger White insistent for Charlie's endorsement of Fareek Fanon.

Charlie at first seems more at home at Turpmtine, his enormous plantation in rural Georgia, where he delights in quail hunts and in shocking his city visitors with a visit to the mating barn to watch the powerful, brutal coupling of bloodlined stallions and mares. In his meticulously restored antebellum house, surrounded by loyal retainers who call him "Cap'm Charlie," he can believe himself master of his fate. Yet Turpmtine is no longer a working plantation; it is a rich man's fancy that ultimately has no greater reality than the rest of Charlie's illusory riches: his real-estate empire, his beautiful trophy wife, his standing in Atlanta society, and his own physical strength and vitality, once so great but now taken from him by time, age, and a bad knee. It is only when Charlie Croker accepts the fact that none of these are his, that Epictetus was right and that all one truly possesses (if one maintains it) is one's individual integrity, that he does in fact become "a man in full."

In 1965, Tom Wolfe published *The Kandy-Kolored Tangerine-Flake Streamline Baby*, an early example of the "New Journalism" of writers such as Wolfe, Truman Capote, Norman Mailer, Joan Didion, and Hunter S. Thompson. The New Journalism and its view of reality was supposed to supplant the novel with its old-fashioned insistence on fiction as the central feature of literature. In 1988, Wolfe published *The Bonfire of the Vanities*, his first novel, which received favorable reviews. With *A Man in Full*, Wolfe returns to the novel and makes a significant contribution. When reviewing Wolfe's earlier pronouncements compared to his later productions, one might be mindful to echo his contemporary, Jerry Brown, once governor of California and serious presidential contender: "That was then. This is now."

A decade after *The Bonfire of the Vanities*, Wolfe has shifted his target, but not his focus: to a society in transition from a sense of what it has been and what it has long expected to one in which the rules are being rewritten by forces that do not fully understand the culture of a special region. *A Man in Full* makes as much sense of the shifting shape of the American South as one can expect while still providing an outstanding narrative of characters in pursuit of the American Dream.

Michael Witkoski

Sources for Further Study

American Banker. CLXIII, December 8, 1998, p. 1.
The Christian Science Monitor. November 12, 1998, p. B5.
Los Angeles Times Book Review. November 8, 1998, p. 2.
The New York Review of Books. XLV, December 17, 1998, p. 18.
The New York Times Book Review. CIII, November 8, 1998, p. 17.
Newsweek. CXXXII, July 6, 1998, p. 76.
Publishers Weekly. CCXLV, November 9, 1998, p. 58.
The Times Literary Supplement. November 27, 1998, p. 21.
The Wall Street Journal. September 23, 1998, p. B1.
The Washington Post Book World. XXVIII, November 1, 1998, p. 3.